MARK CRILLEY

FLIGHTS of FANCY

The High~Flying
Expanded Edition

SIRIUS ENTERTAINMENT
UNADILLA, NY

In memory of Al Shippey
1959 ~ 2007

AKIKO: FLIGHTS OF FANCY - THE HIGH FLYING EXPANDED EDITION. September 2007.
Published by SIRIUS Entertainment, Inc. Lawrence Salamone, President. Robb Horan,
Publisher. Keith Davidsen, Editor & Production. Correspondence: P.O. Box X, Unadilla,
NY 13849. AKIKO and all related characters are TM & © 2007 Mark Crilley. SIRIUS and
the DogStar logo are TM & © 2007 SIRIUS Entertainment, Inc. All rights reserved. Any
similarity to persons living or dead is purely coincidental. Printed in the USA.

Table of Contents

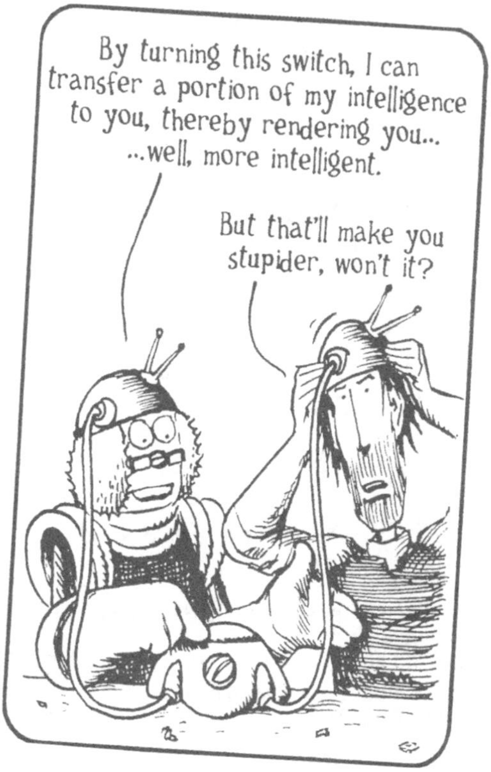

By turning this switch, I can transfer a portion of my intelligence to you, thereby rendering you... ...well, more intelligent.
But that'll make you stupider, won't it?

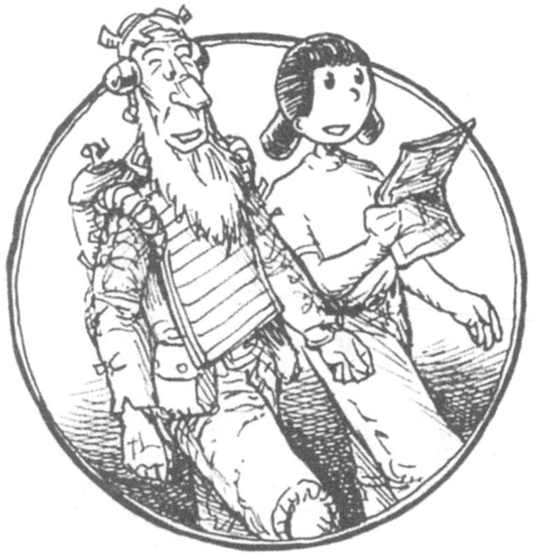

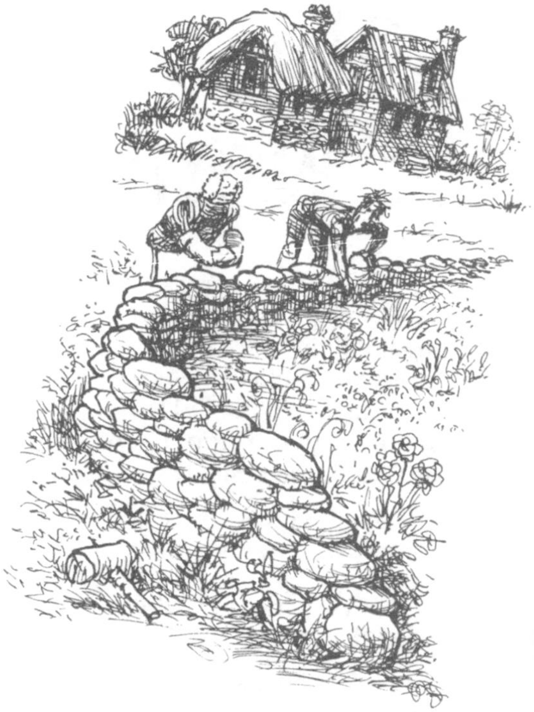

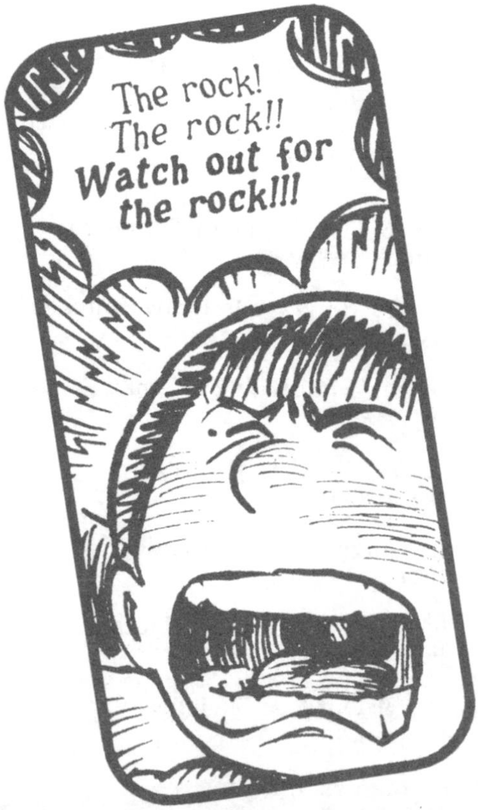
The rock!
The rock!!
Watch out for the rock!!!

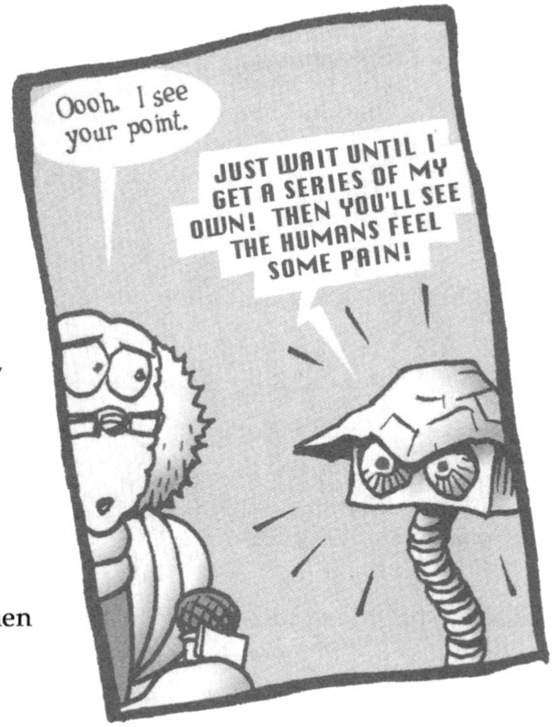
Oooh. I see your point.
JUST WAIT UNTIL I GET A SERIES OF MY OWN! THEN YOU'LL SEE THE HUMANS FEEL SOME PAIN!

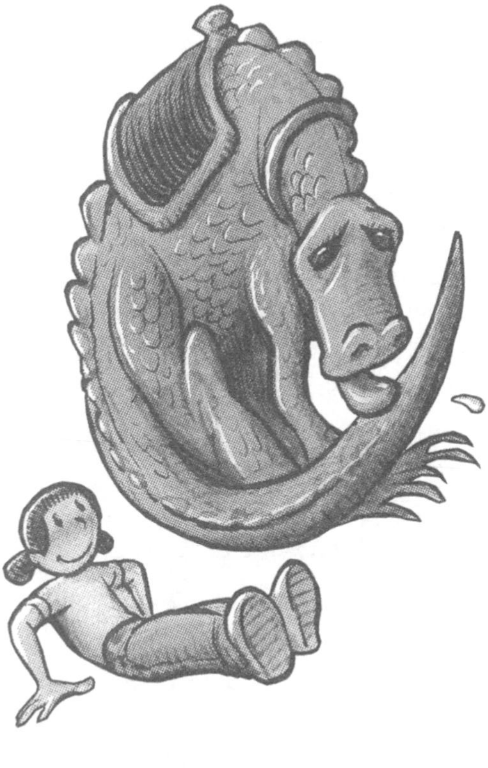

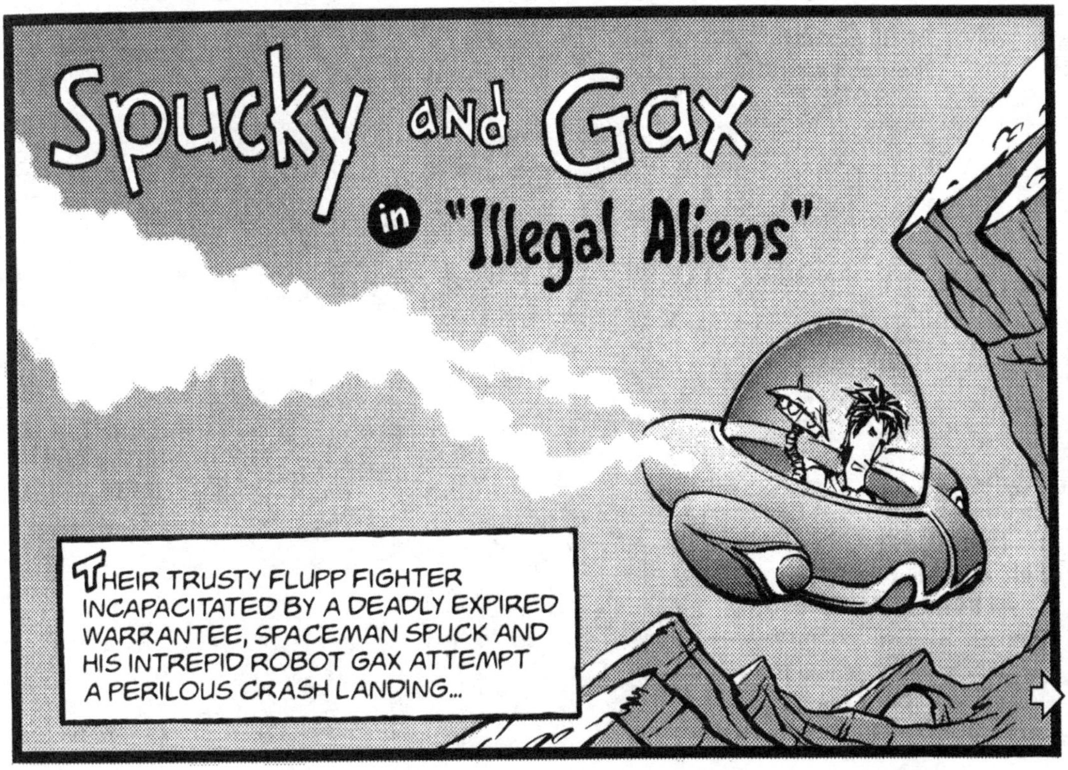
Spucky and Gax
in "Illegal Aliens"
THEIR TRUSTY FLUPP FIGHTER INCAPACITATED BY A DEADLY EXPIRED WARRANTEE, SPACEMAN SPUCK AND HIS INTREPID ROBOT GAX ATTEMPT A PERILOUS CRASH LANDING...

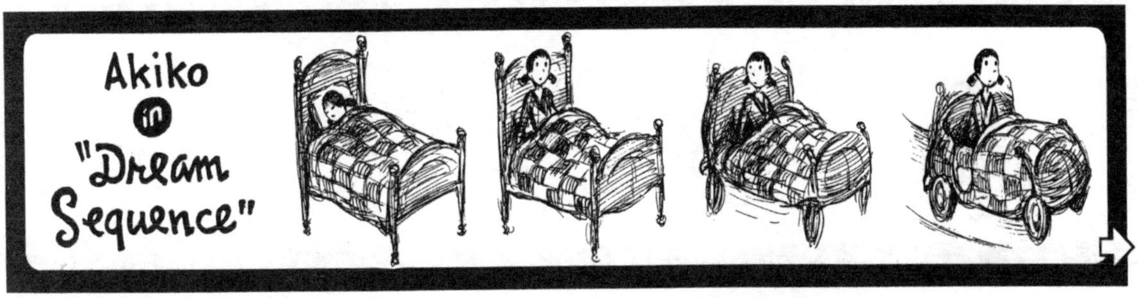
Akiko in "Dream Sequence"

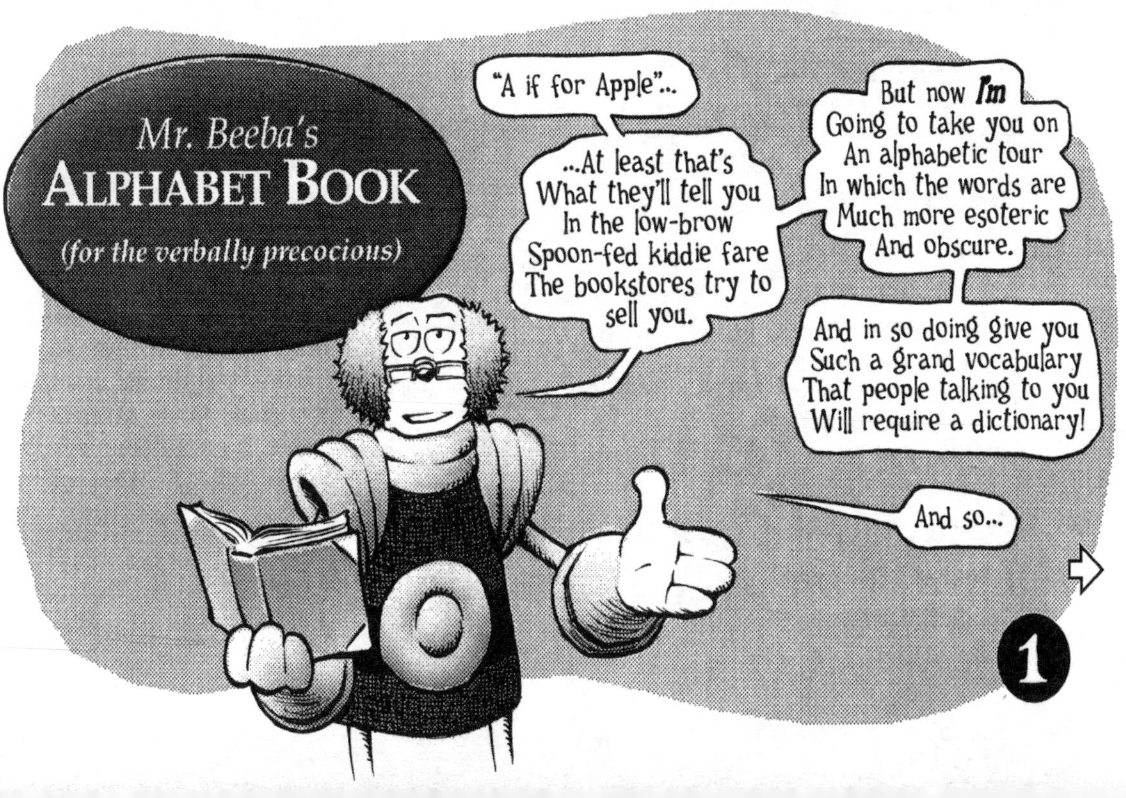
Mr. Beeba's ALPHABET BOOK
(for the verbally precocious)
"A if for Apple"..
...At least that's What they'll tell you In the low-brow Spoon-fed kiddie fare The bookstores try to sell you.
But now I'm Going to take you on An alphabetic tour In which the words are Much more esoteric And obscure.
And in so doing give you Such a grand vocabulary That people talking to you Will require a dictionary!
And so...

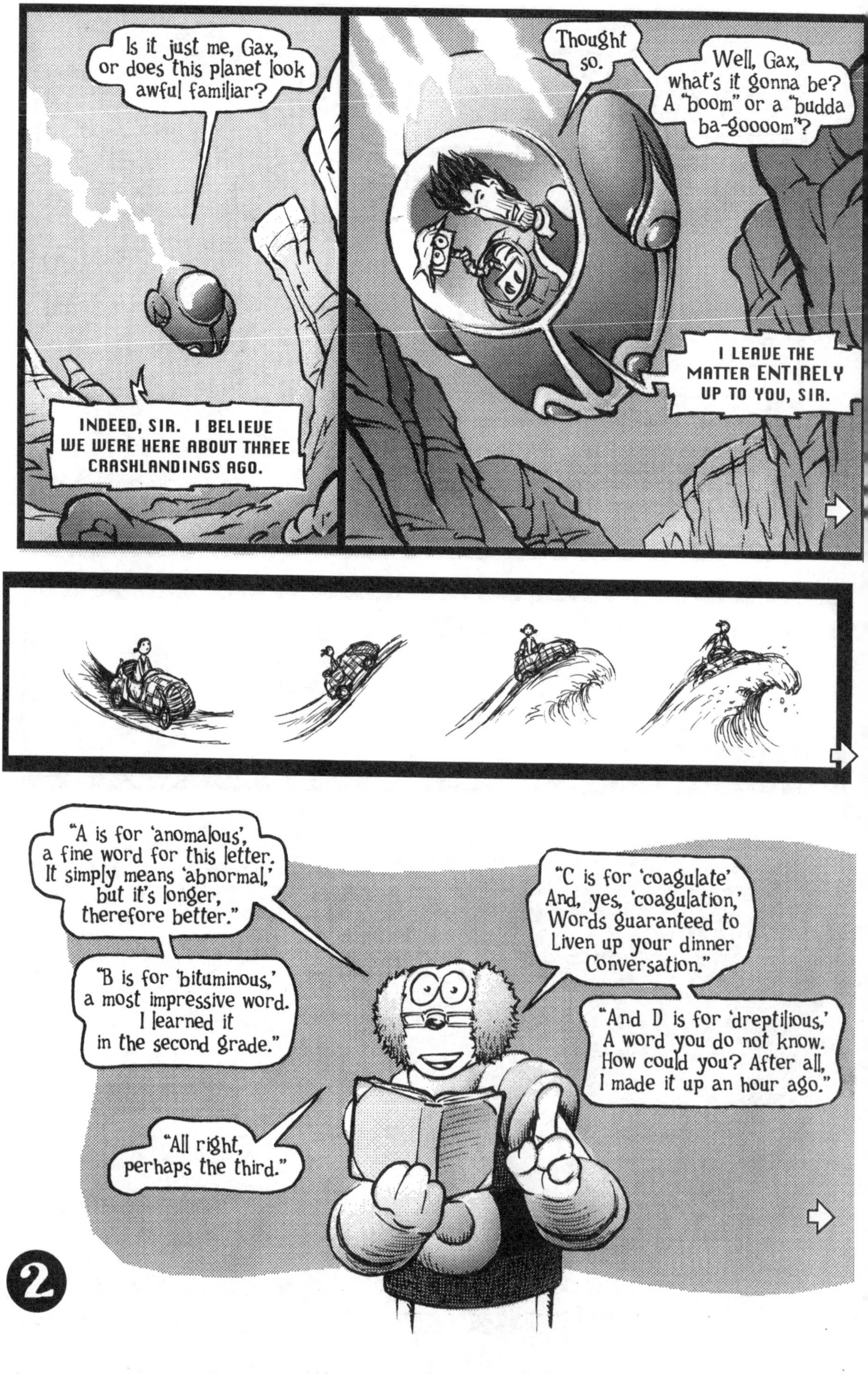
Is it just me, Gax, or does this planet look awful familiar?
INDEED, SIR. I BELIEVE WE WERE HERE ABOUT THREE CRASHLANDINGS AGO.
Thought so.
Well, Gax, what's it gonna be? A "boom" or a "budda ba-goooom"?
I LEAVE THE MATTER ENTIRELY UP TO YOU, SIR.
"A is for 'anomalous', a fine word for this letter. It simply means 'abnormal,' but it's longer, therefore better."
"B is for 'bituminous,' a most impressive word. I learned it in the second grade."
"All right, perhaps the third."
"C is for 'coagulate' And, yes, 'coagulation,' Words guaranteed to Liven up your dinner Conversation."
"And D is for 'dreptilious,' A word you do not know. How could you? After all, I made it up an hour ago."

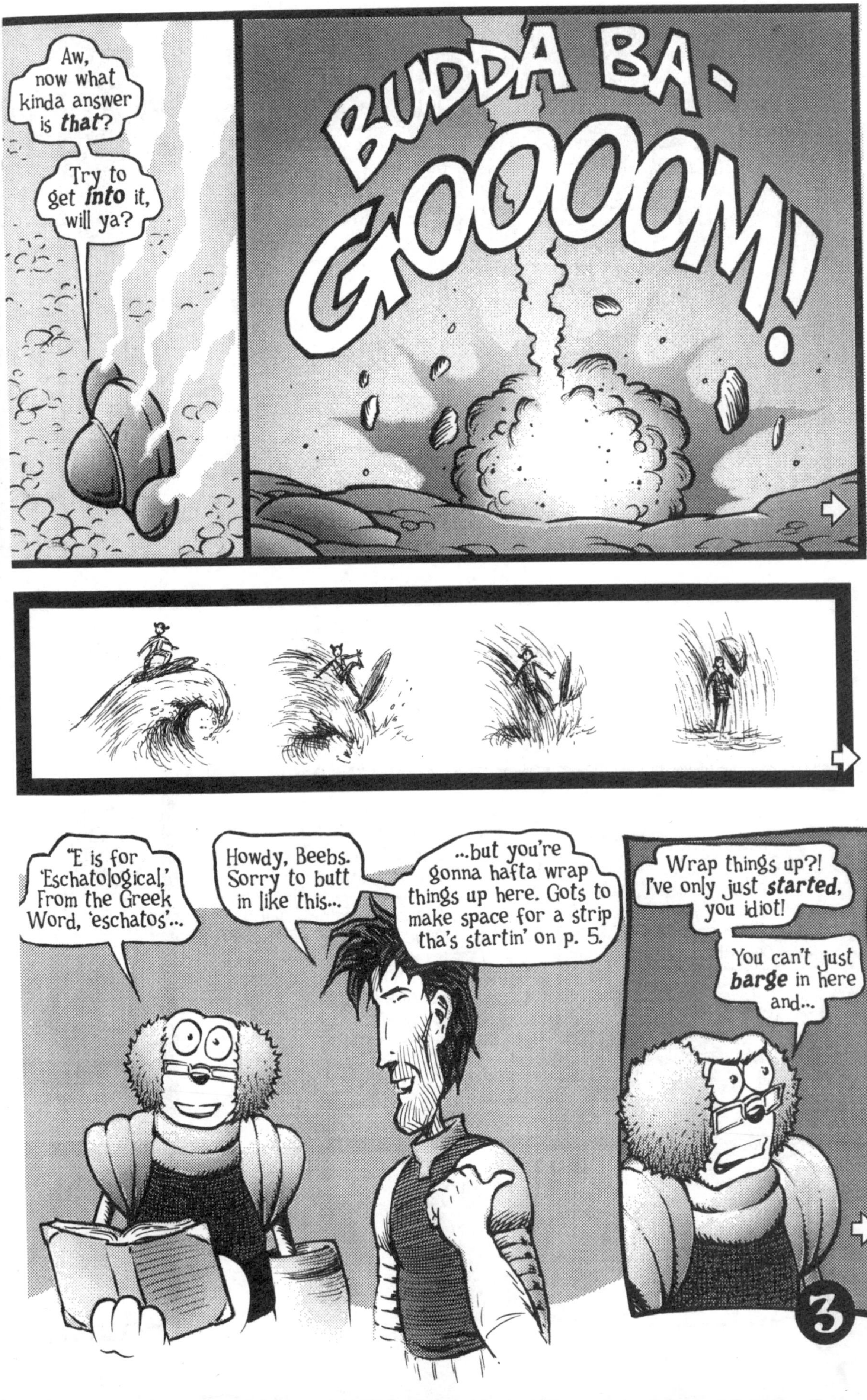
Aw, now what kinda answer is *that*?
Try to get *into* it, will ya?
BUDDA BA-GOOOOM!
"E is for 'Eschatological,' From the Greek Word, 'eschatos'...
Howdy, Beebs. Sorry to butt in like this...
...but you're gonna hafta wrap things up here. Gots to make space for a strip tha's startin' on p. 5.
Wrap things up?! I've only just *started*, you idiot!
You can't just *barge* in here and...
3

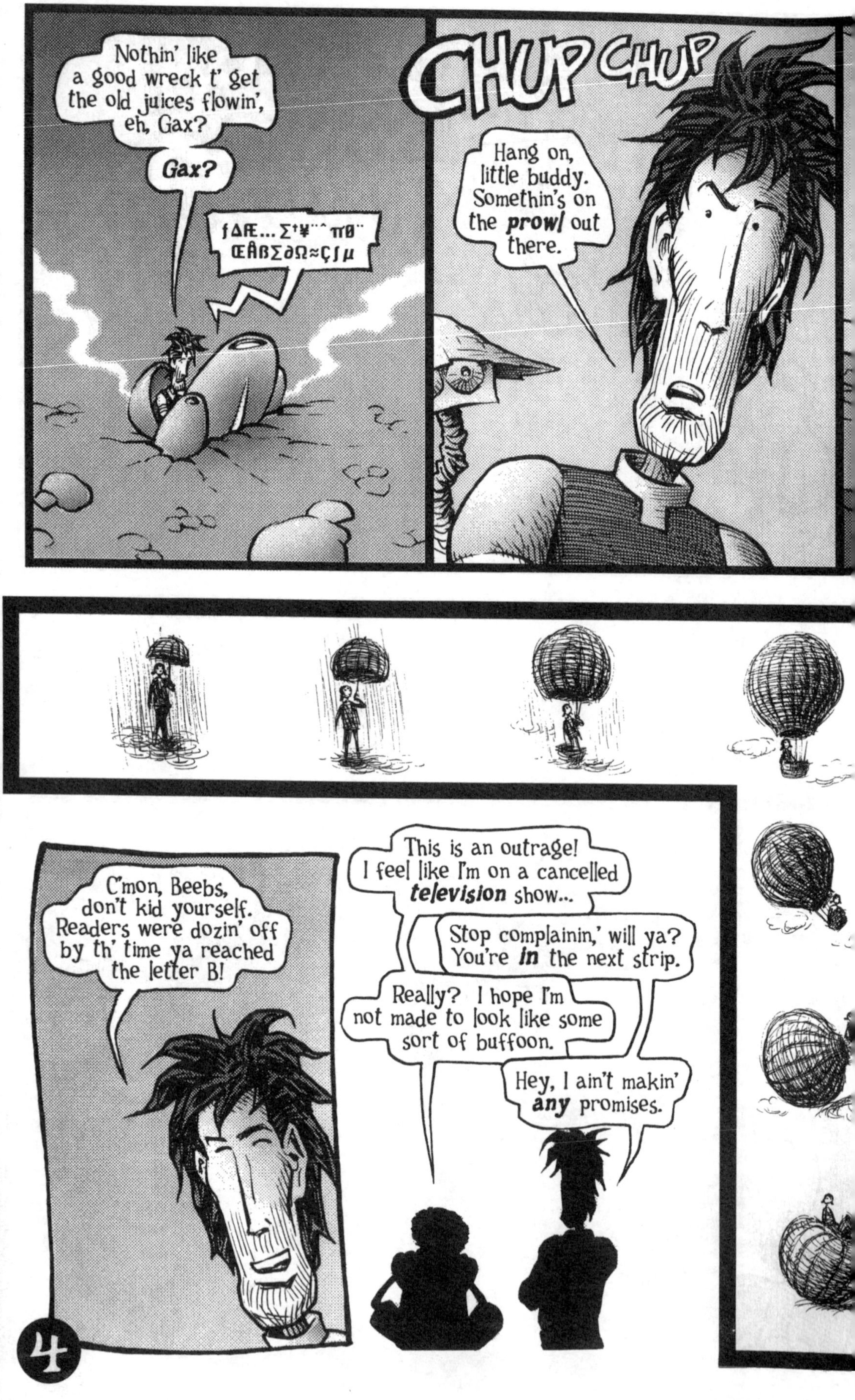
Nothin' like a good wreck t' get the old juices flowin', eh, Gax?
Gax?
ƒΔÆ... Σ†¥¨ˆ π∅¨ ŒÅßΣ∂Ω≈Ç∫µ
CHUP CHUP
Hang on, little buddy. Somethin's on the prowl out there.
C'mon, Beebs, don't kid yourself. Readers were dozin' off by th' time ya reached the letter B!
This is an outrage! I feel like I'm on a cancelled television show...
Stop complainin,' will ya? You're in the next strip.
Really? I hope I'm not made to look like some sort of buffoon.
Hey, I ain't makin' any promises.

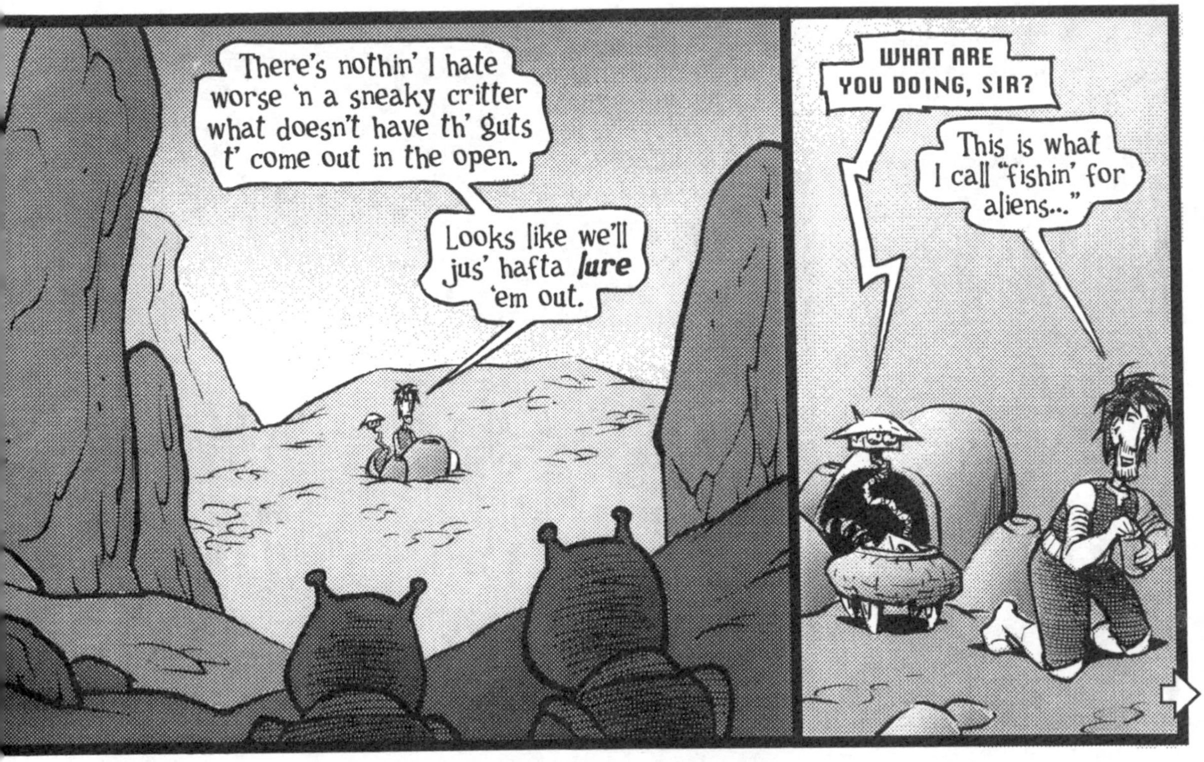
There's nothin' I hate worse 'n a sneaky critter what doesn't have th' guts t' come out in the open.
Looks like we'll jus' hafta *lure* 'em out.
WHAT ARE YOU DOING, SIR?
This is what I call "fishin' for aliens..."

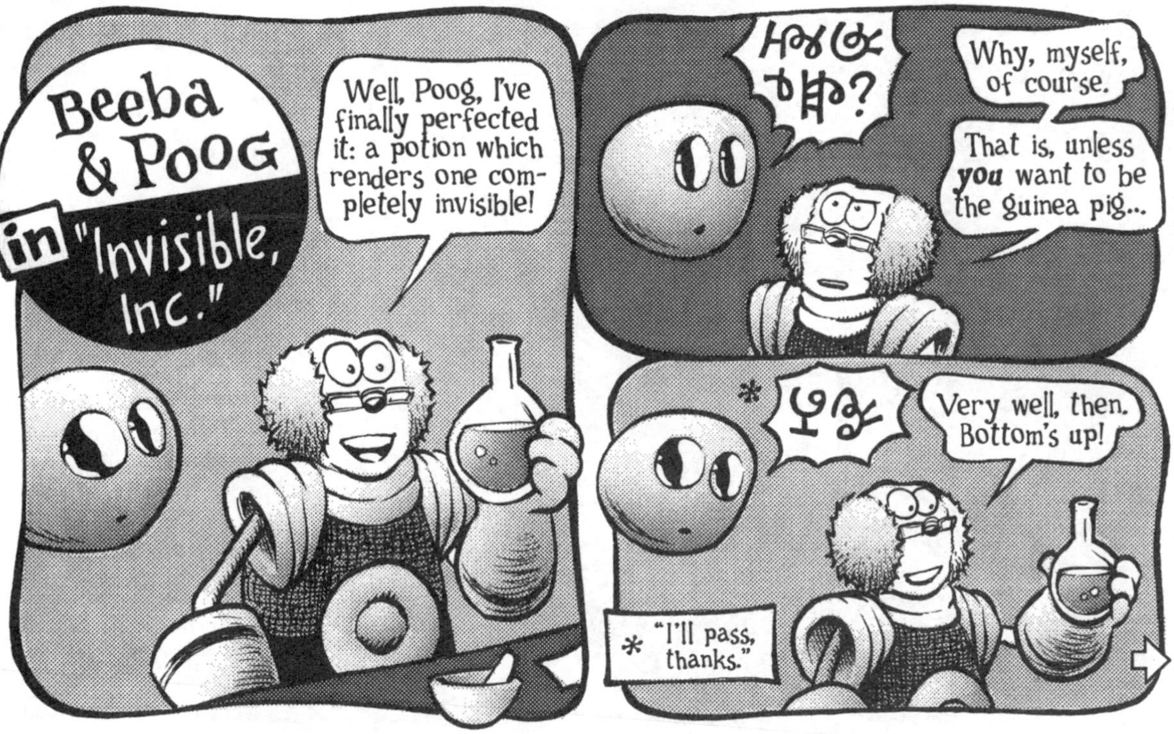
Beeba & Poog in "Invisible, Inc."
Well, Poog, I've finally perfected it: a potion which renders one completely invisible!
Why, myself, of course.
That is, unless *you* want to be the guinea pig...
Very well, then. Bottom's up!
* "I'll pass, thanks."

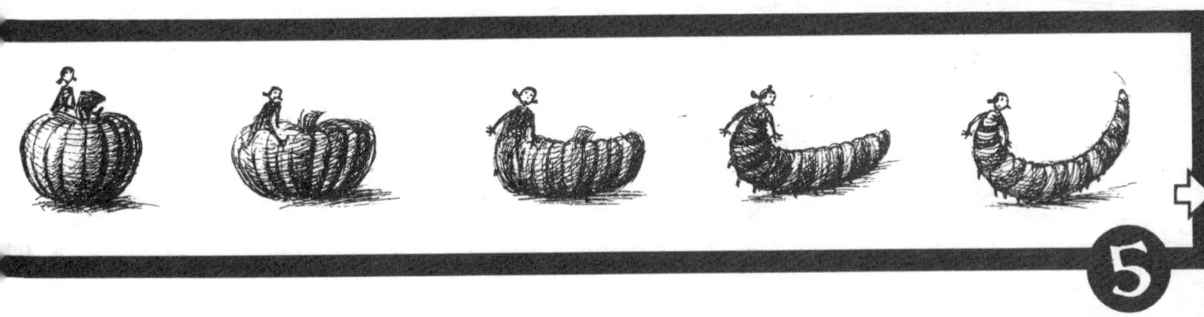

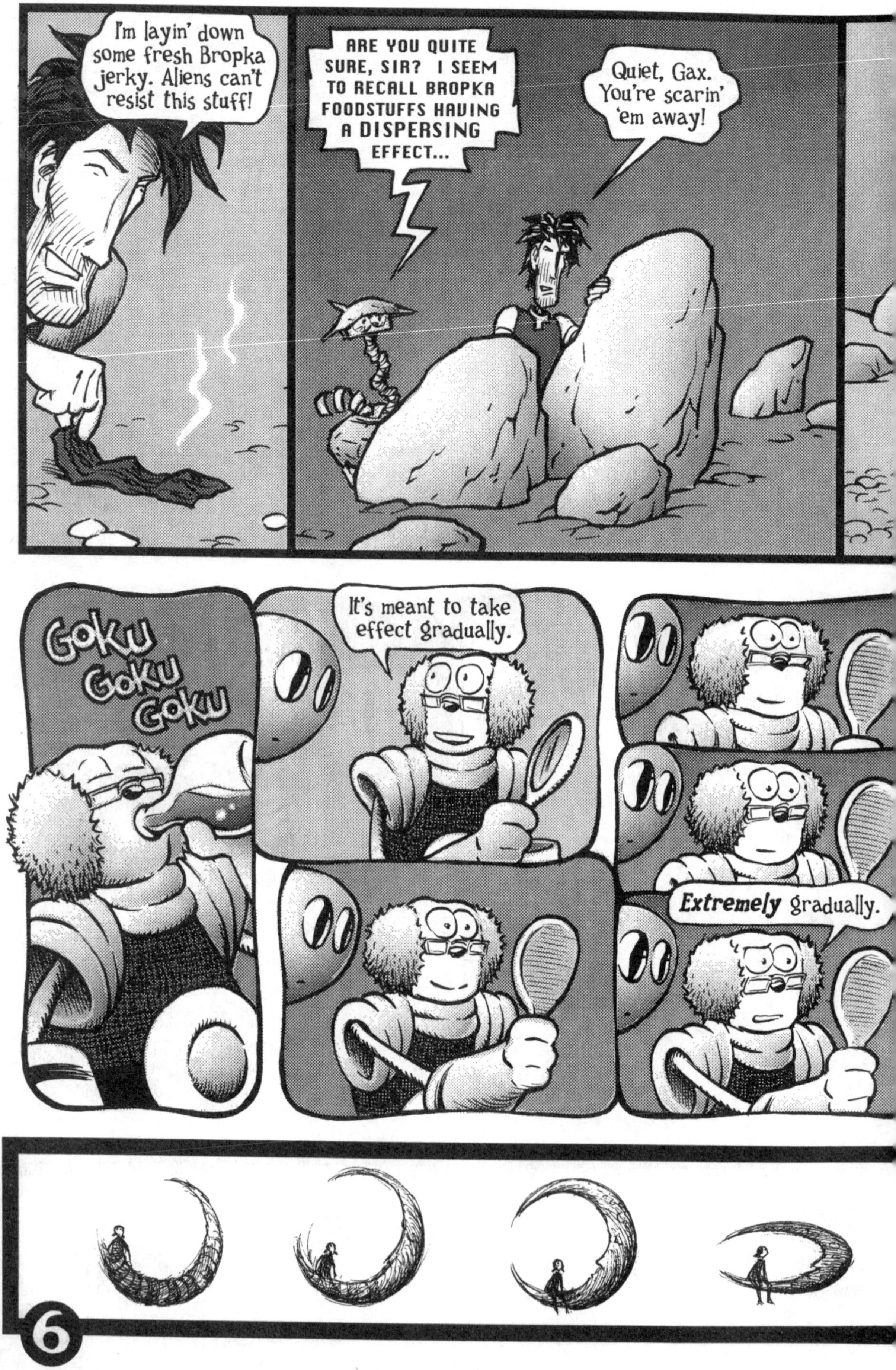

I'm layin' down some fresh Bropka jerky. Aliens can't resist this stuff!
ARE YOU QUITE SURE, SIR? I SEEM TO RECALL BROPKA FOODSTUFFS HAVING A DISPERSING EFFECT...
Quiet, Gax. You're scarin' 'em away!
GOKU GOKU GOKU
It's meant to take effect gradually.
Extremely gradually.

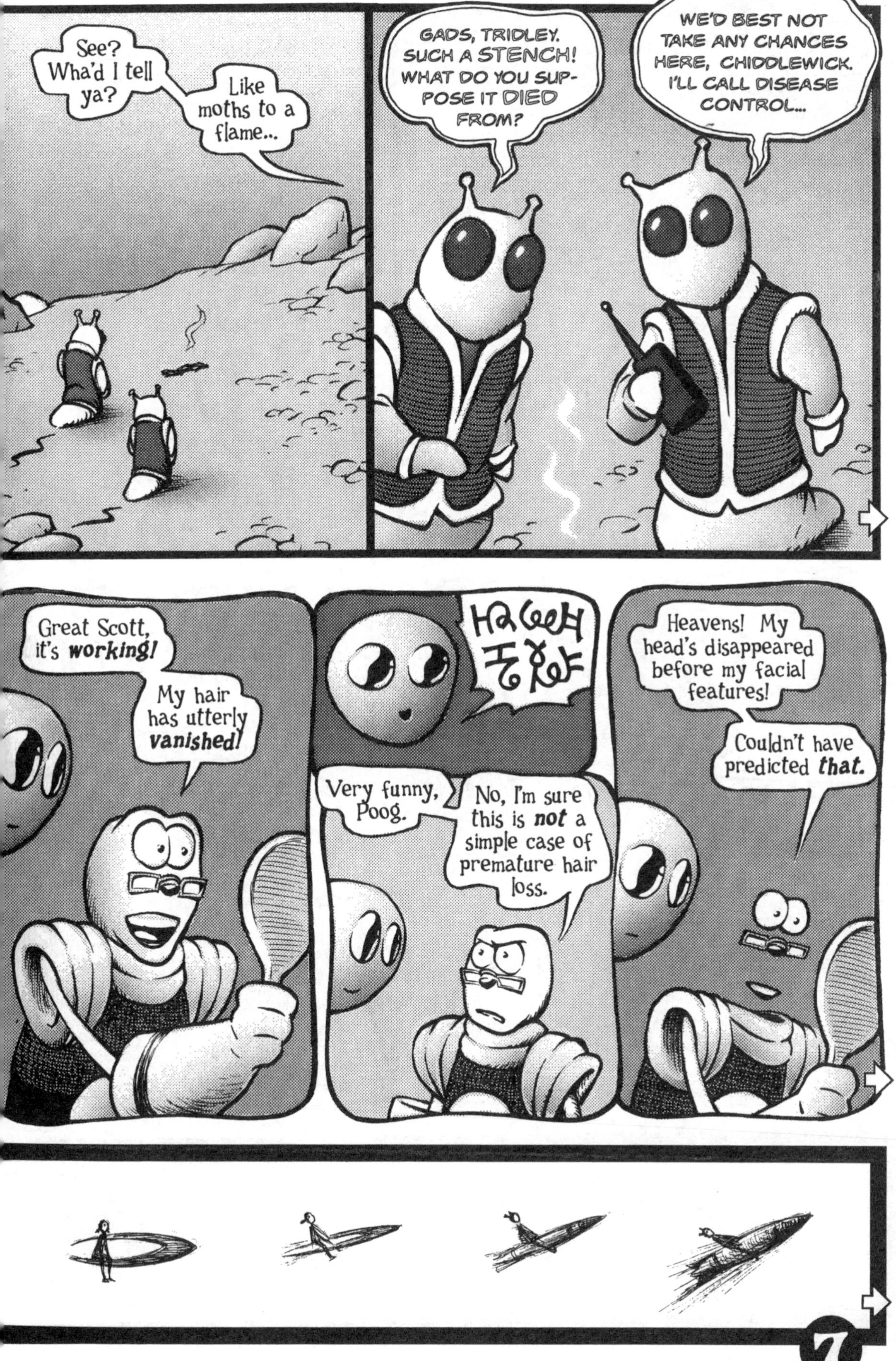
See? Wha'd I tell ya?
Like moths to a flame...
GADS, TRIDLEY. SUCH A STENCH! WHAT DO YOU SUPPOSE IT DIED FROM?
WE'D BEST NOT TAKE ANY CHANCES HERE, CHIDDLEWICK. I'LL CALL DISEASE CONTROL...
Great Scott, it's **working!**
My hair has utterly **vanished!**
Very funny, Poog.
No, I'm sure this is **not** a simple case of premature hair loss.
Heavens! My head's disappeared before my facial features!
Couldn't have predicted **that.**

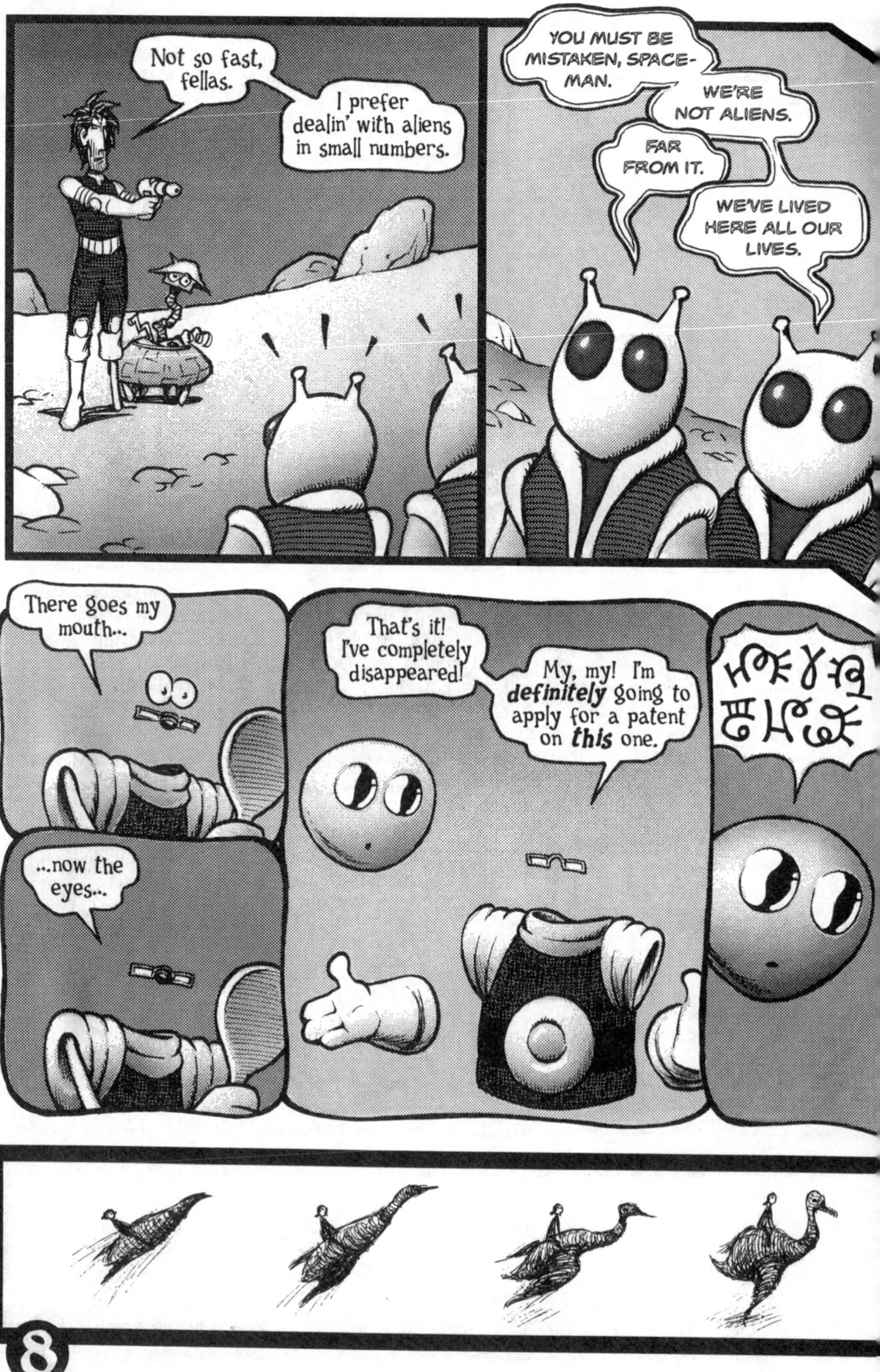

Not so fast, fellas.
I prefer dealin' with aliens in small numbers.
YOU MUST BE MISTAKEN, SPACE-MAN.
WE'RE NOT ALIENS.
FAR FROM IT.
WE'VE LIVED HERE ALL OUR LIVES.
There goes my mouth...
...now the eyes...
That's it! I've completely disappeared!
My, my! I'm *definitely* going to apply for a patent on *this* one.

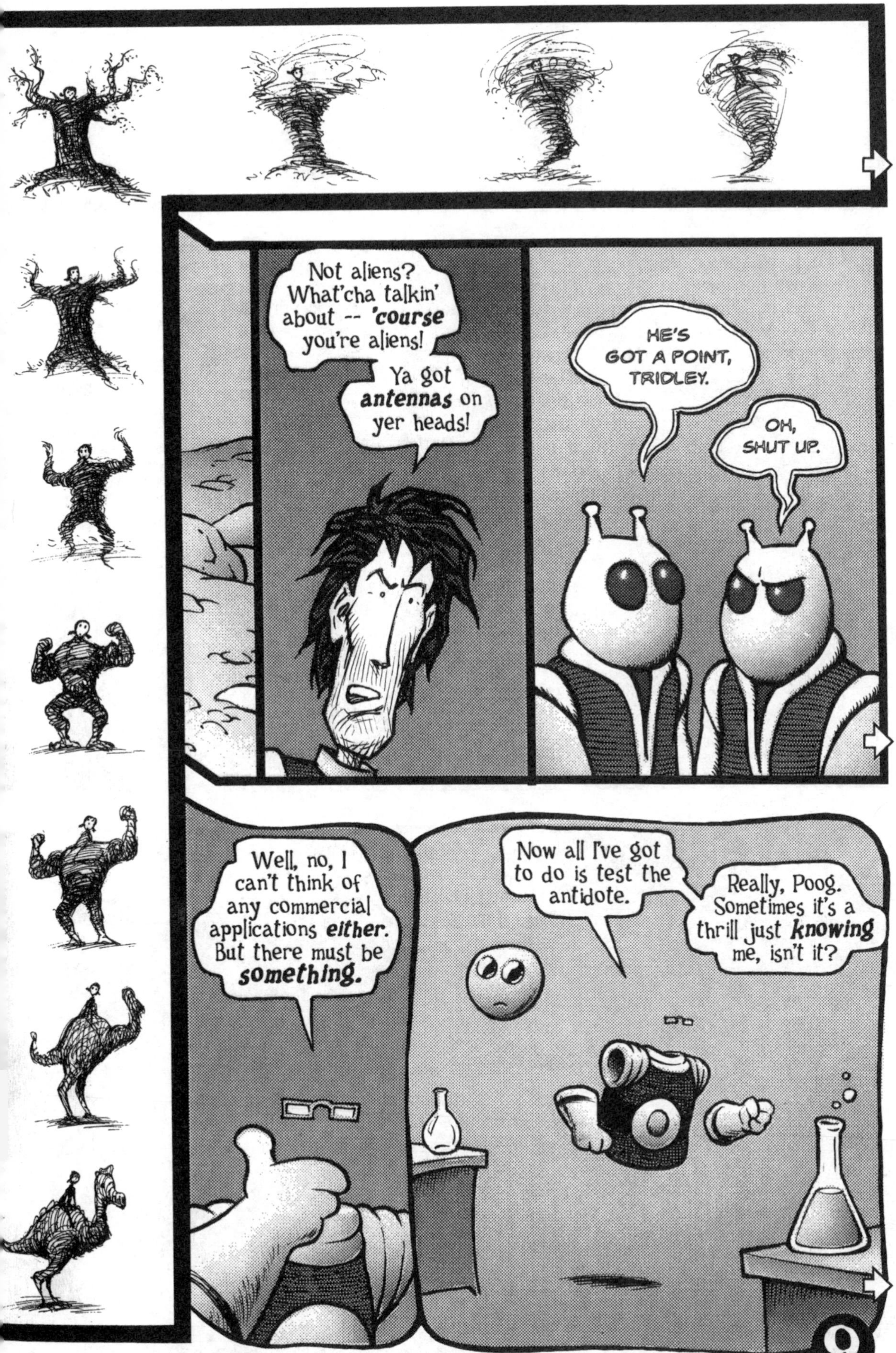

Not aliens? What'cha talkin' about -- 'course you're aliens!
Ya got antennas on yer heads!
HE'S GOT A POINT, TRIDLEY.
OH, SHUT UP.
Well, no, I can't think of any commercial applications either. But there must be something.
Now all I've got to do is test the antidote.
Really, Poog. Sometimes it's a thrill just knowing me, isn't it?

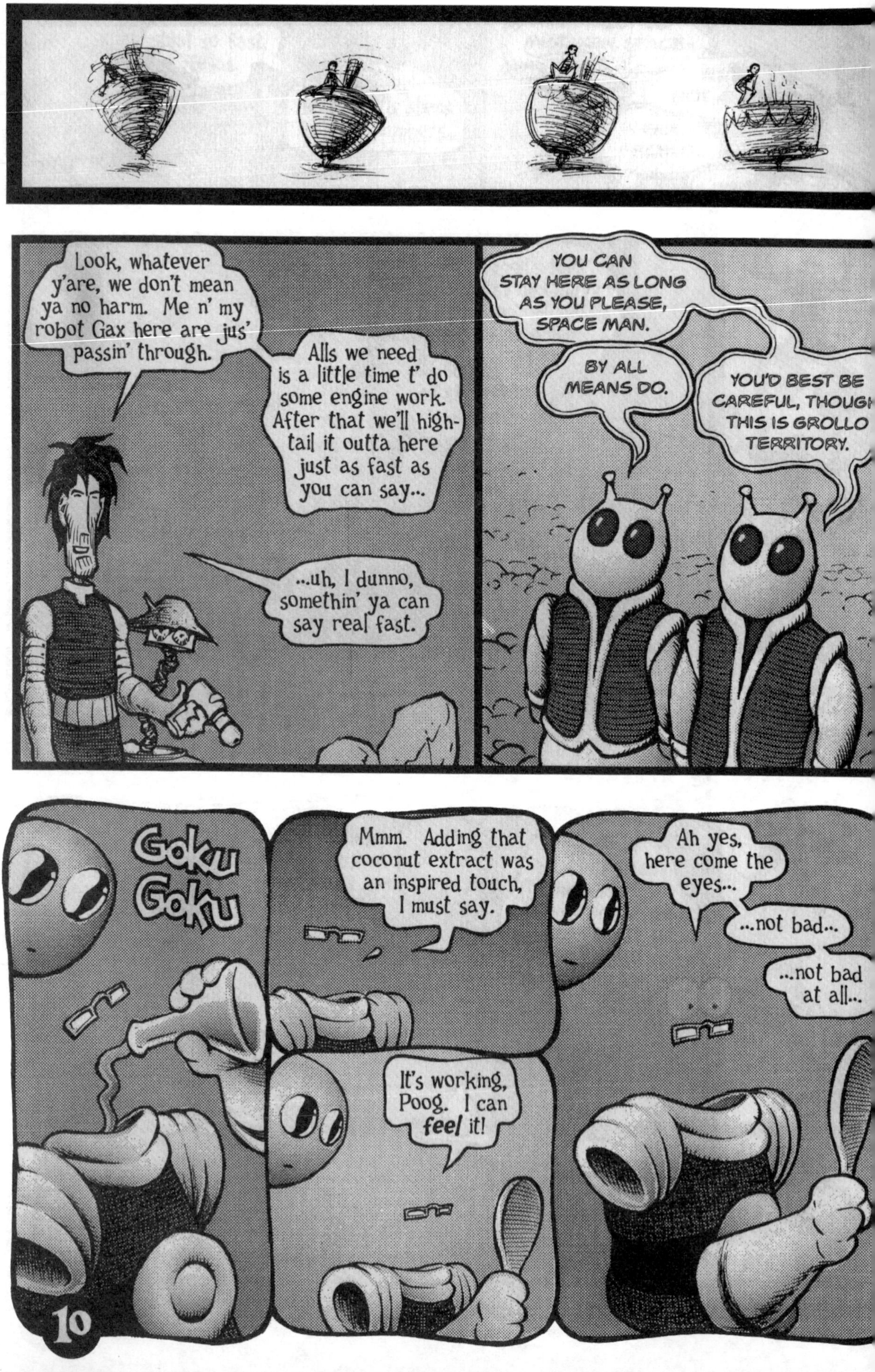
Look, whatever y'are, we don't mean ya no harm. Me n' my robot Gax here are jus' passin' through.
Alls we need is a little time t' do some engine work. After that we'll high-tail it outta here just as fast as you can say...
...uh, I dunno, somethin' ya can say real fast.
YOU CAN STAY HERE AS LONG AS YOU PLEASE, SPACE MAN.
BY ALL MEANS DO.
YOU'D BEST BE CAREFUL, THOUGH THIS IS GROLLO TERRITORY.
Goku Goku
Mmm. Adding that coconut extract was an inspired touch, I must say.
It's working, Poog. I can *feel* it!
Ah yes, here come the eyes...
...not bad...
...not bad at all...

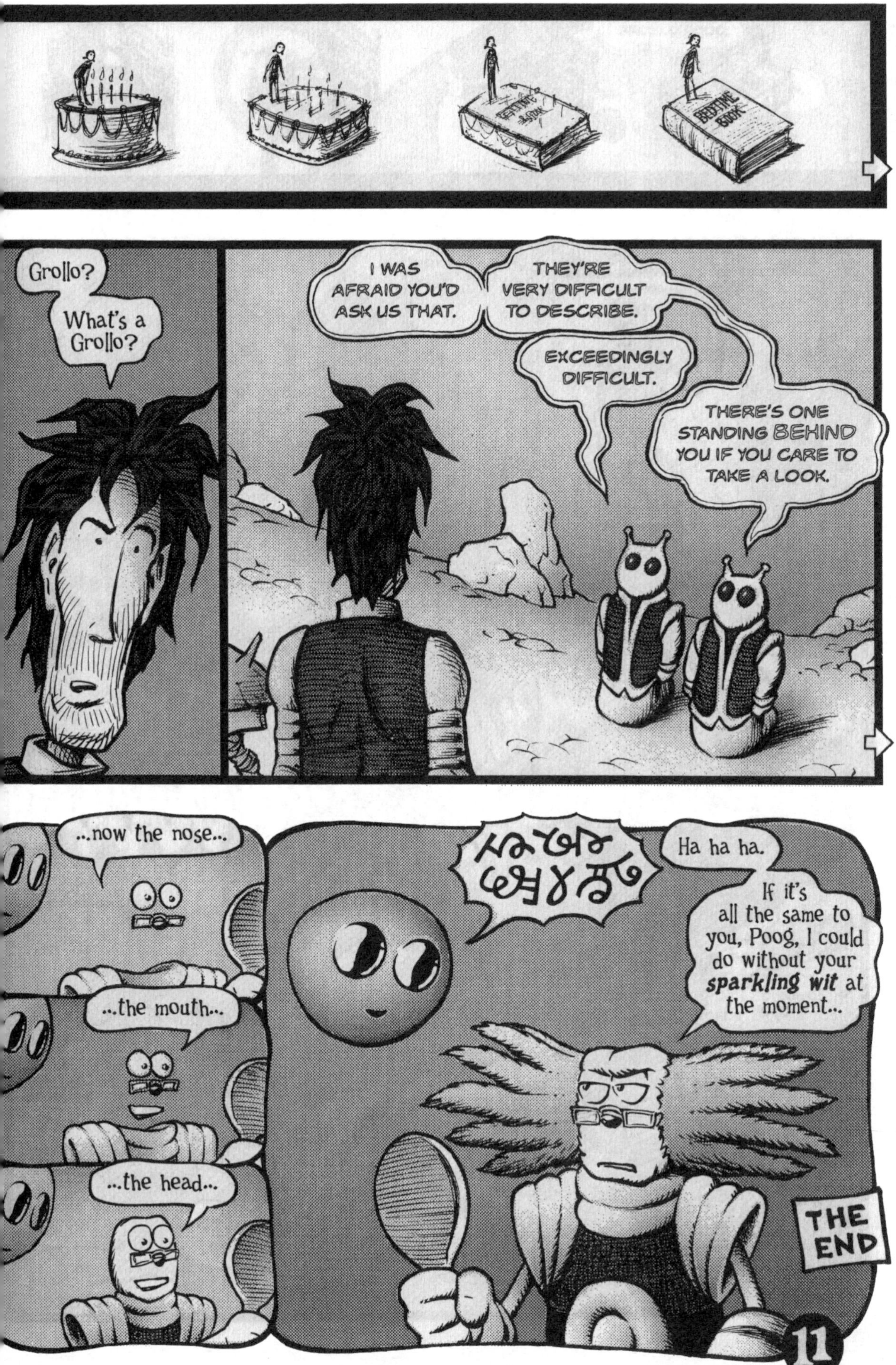
BEDTIME BOOK
Grollo?
What's a Grollo?
I WAS AFRAID YOU'D ASK US THAT.
THEY'RE VERY DIFFICULT TO DESCRIBE.
EXCEEDINGLY DIFFICULT.
THERE'S ONE STANDING BEHIND YOU IF YOU CARE TO TAKE A LOOK.
...now the nose...
...the mouth...
...the head...
Ha ha ha.
If it's all the same to you, Poog, I could do without your *sparkling wit* at the moment...
THE END

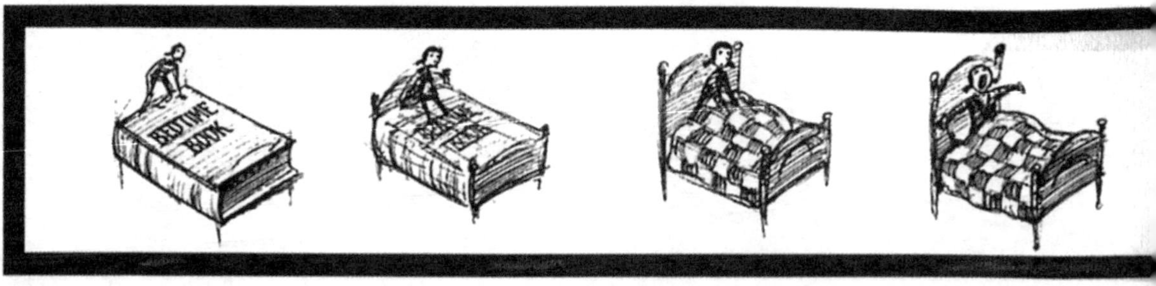
BEDTIME BOOK

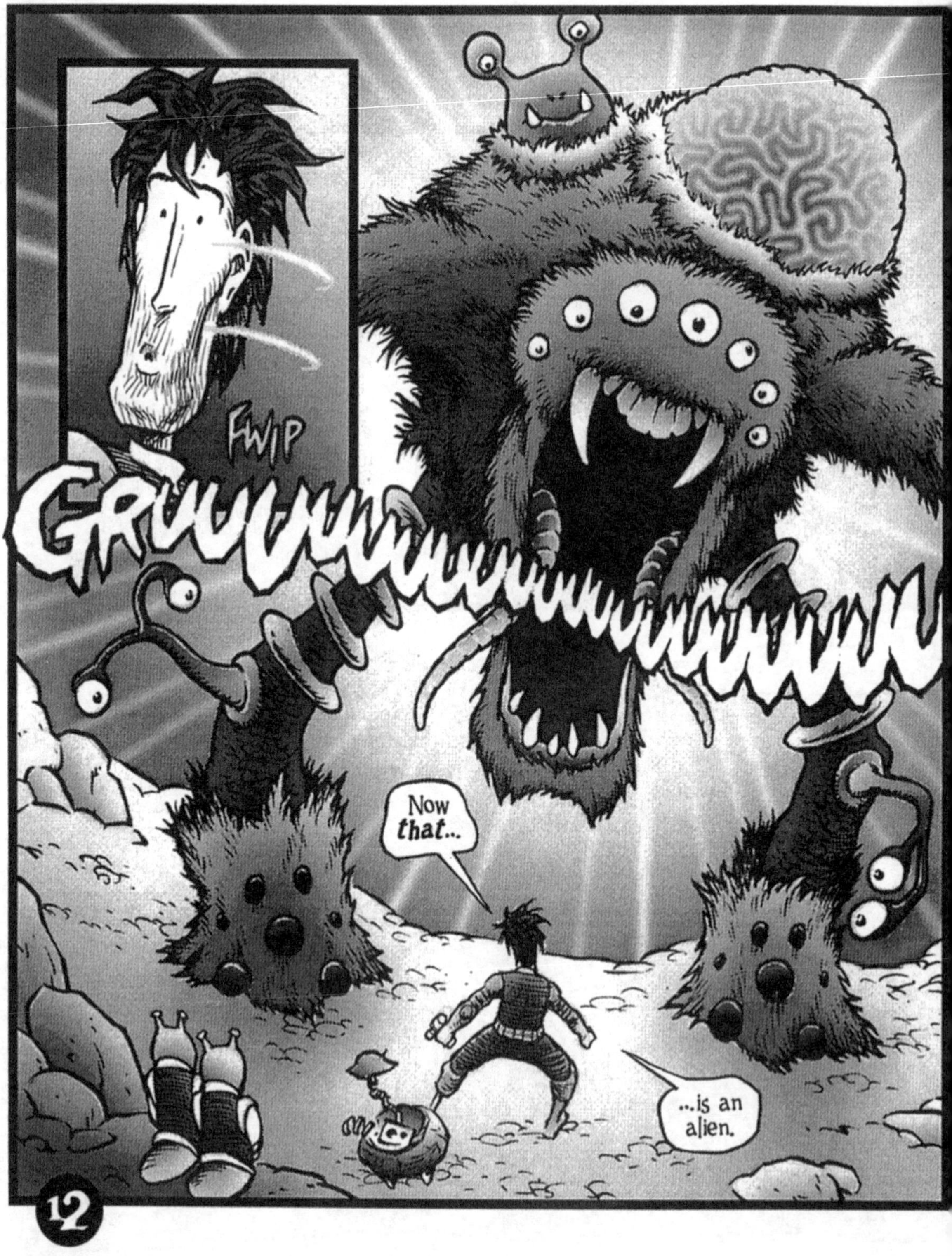
FWIP
GRUUUUUUUUUUUUUUUU
Now *that*...
...is an alien.

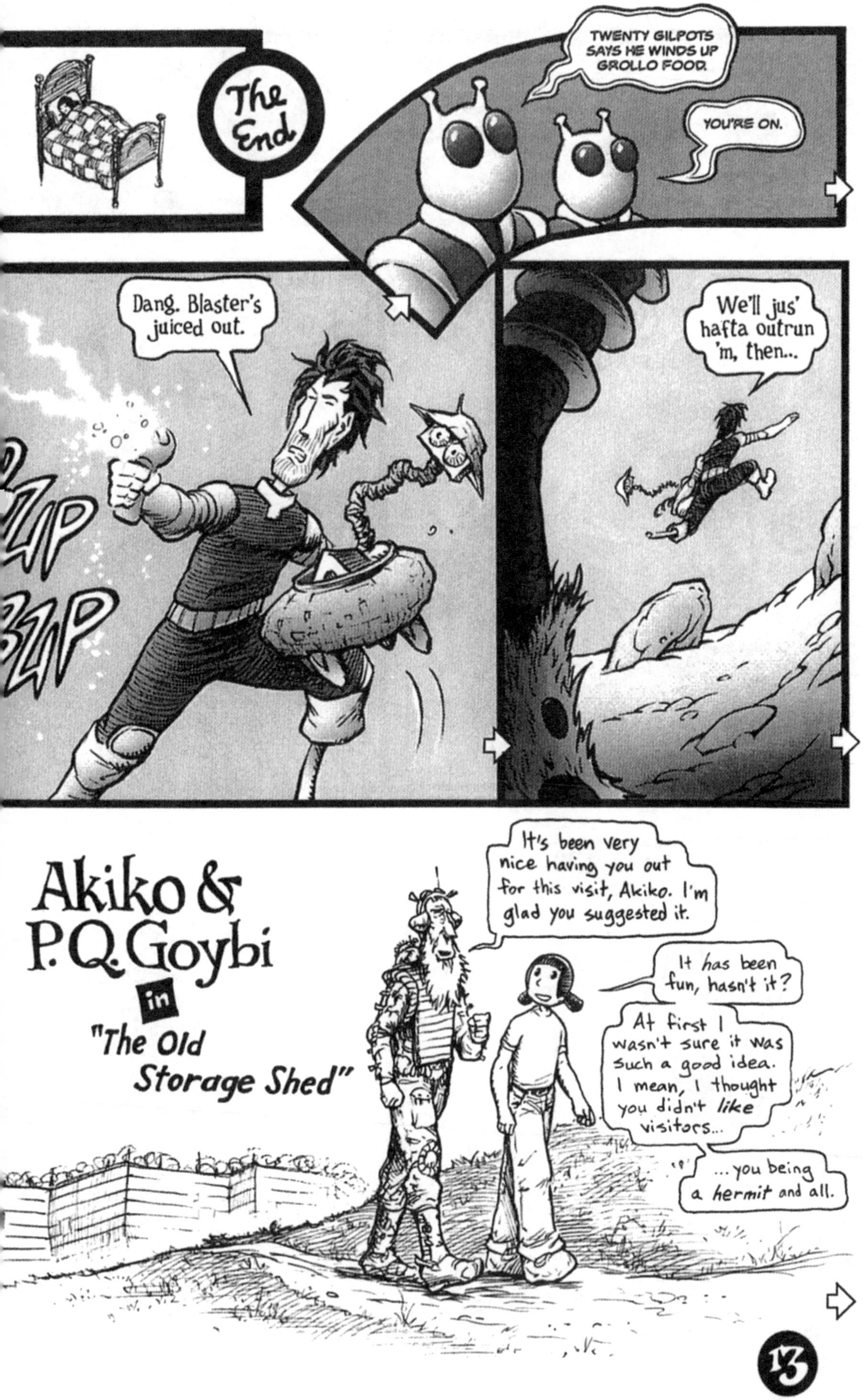
The End
TWENTY GILPOTS SAYS HE WINDS UP GROLLO FOOD.
YOU'RE ON.
Dang. Blaster's juiced out.
ZZUP
ZZUP
We'll jus' hafta outrun 'm, then...
Akiko & P.Q. Goybi in "The Old Storage Shed"
It's been very nice having you out for this visit, Akiko. I'm glad you suggested it.
It *has* been fun, hasn't it?
At first I wasn't sure it was such a good idea. I mean, I thought you didn't *like* visitors...
...you being a *hermit* and all.

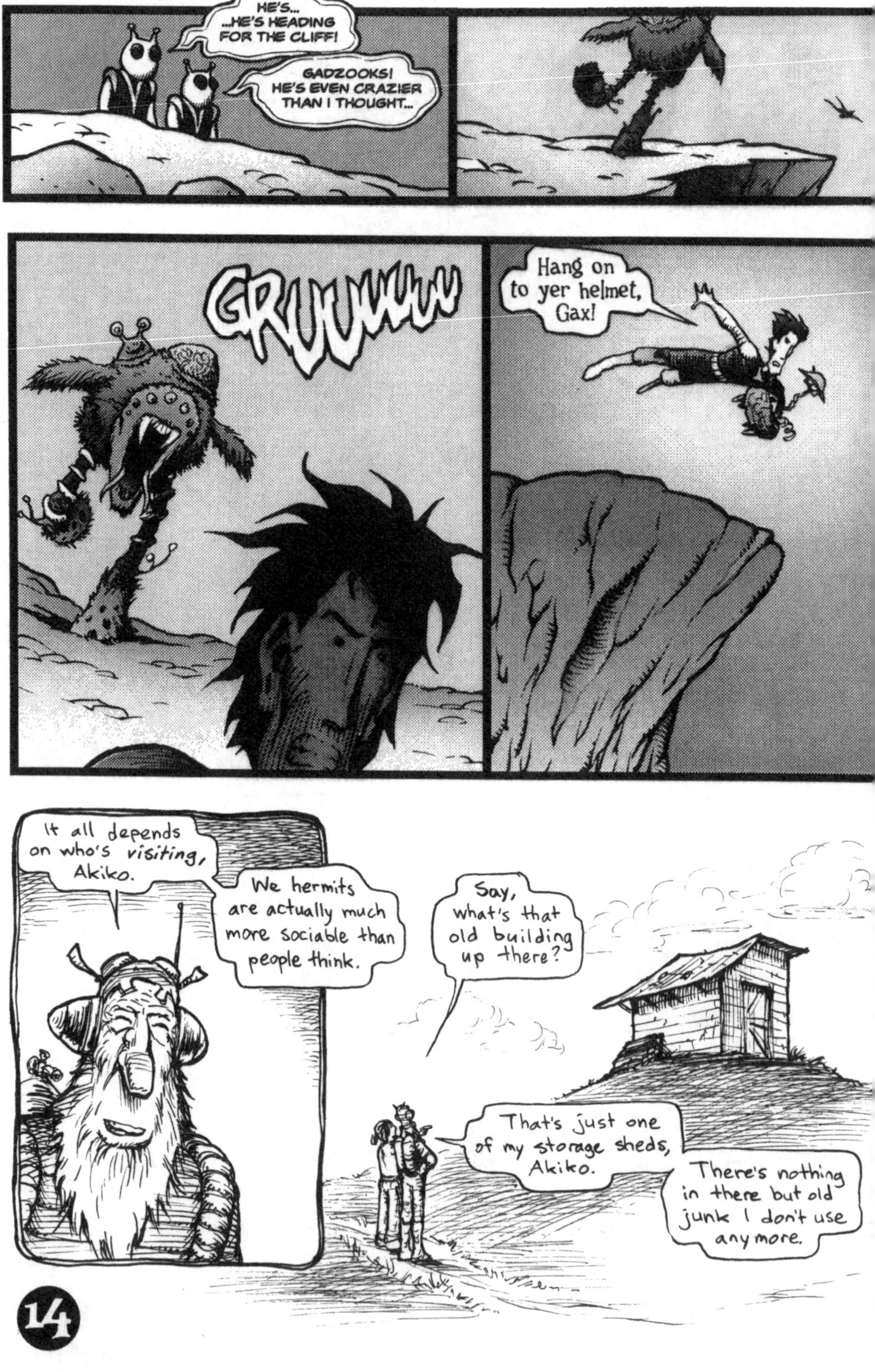
HE'S... ...HE'S HEADING FOR THE CLIFF!
GADZOOKS! HE'S EVEN CRAZIER THAN I THOUGHT...
GRUUUUU
Hang on to yer helmet, Gax!
It all depends on who's visiting, Akiko.
We hermits are actually much more sociable than people think.
Say, what's that old building up there?
That's just one of my storage sheds, Akiko.
There's nothing in there but old junk I don't use anymore.

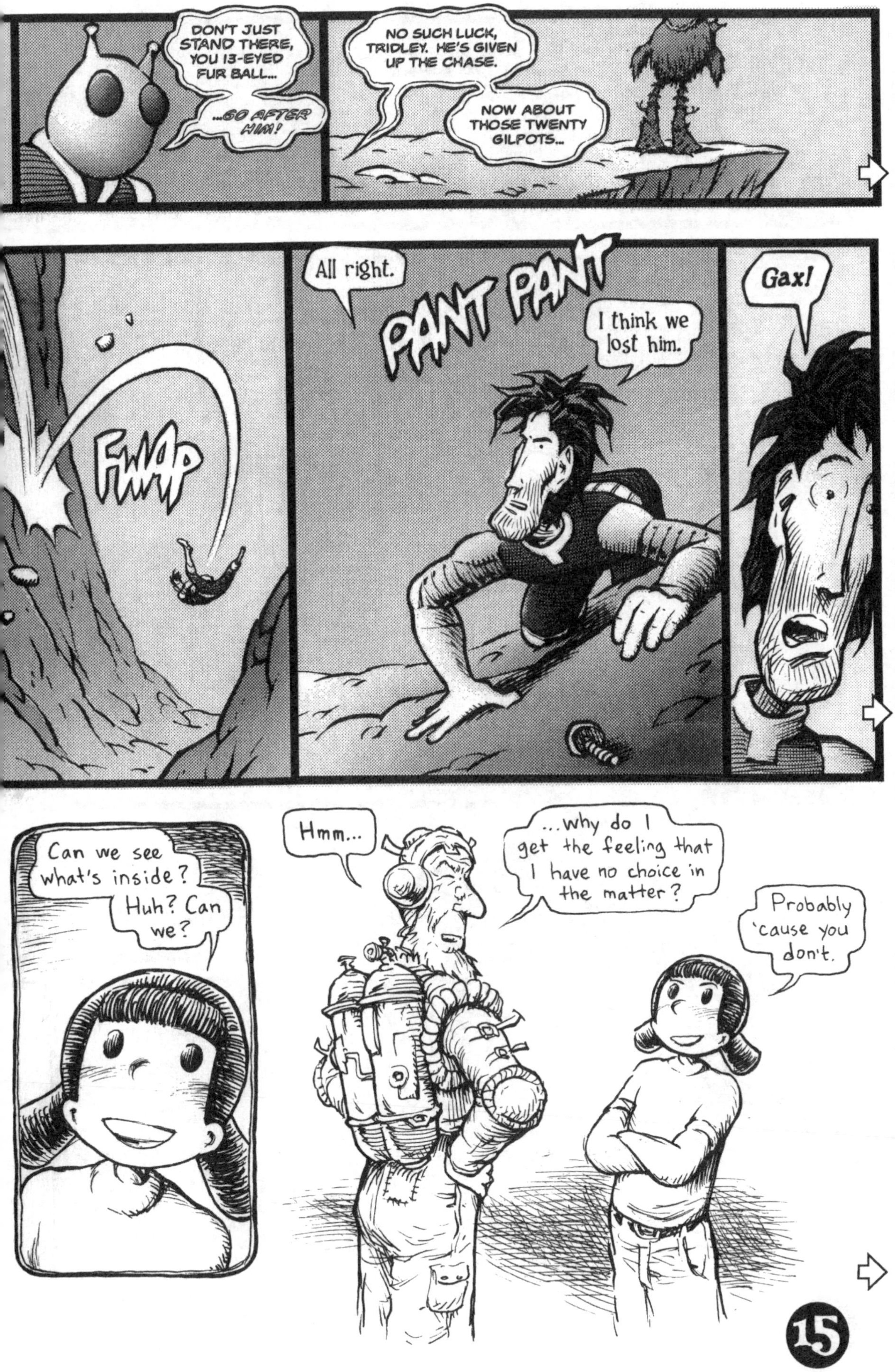
DON'T JUST STAND THERE, YOU 13-EYED FUR BALL...
...GO AFTER HIM!
NO SUCH LUCK, TRIDLEY. HE'S GIVEN UP THE CHASE.
NOW ABOUT THOSE TWENTY GILPOTS...
FWAP
All right.
PANT PANT
I think we lost him.
Gax!
Can we see what's inside?
Huh? Can we?
Hmm...
...why do I get the feeling that I have no choice in the matter?
Probably 'cause you don't.

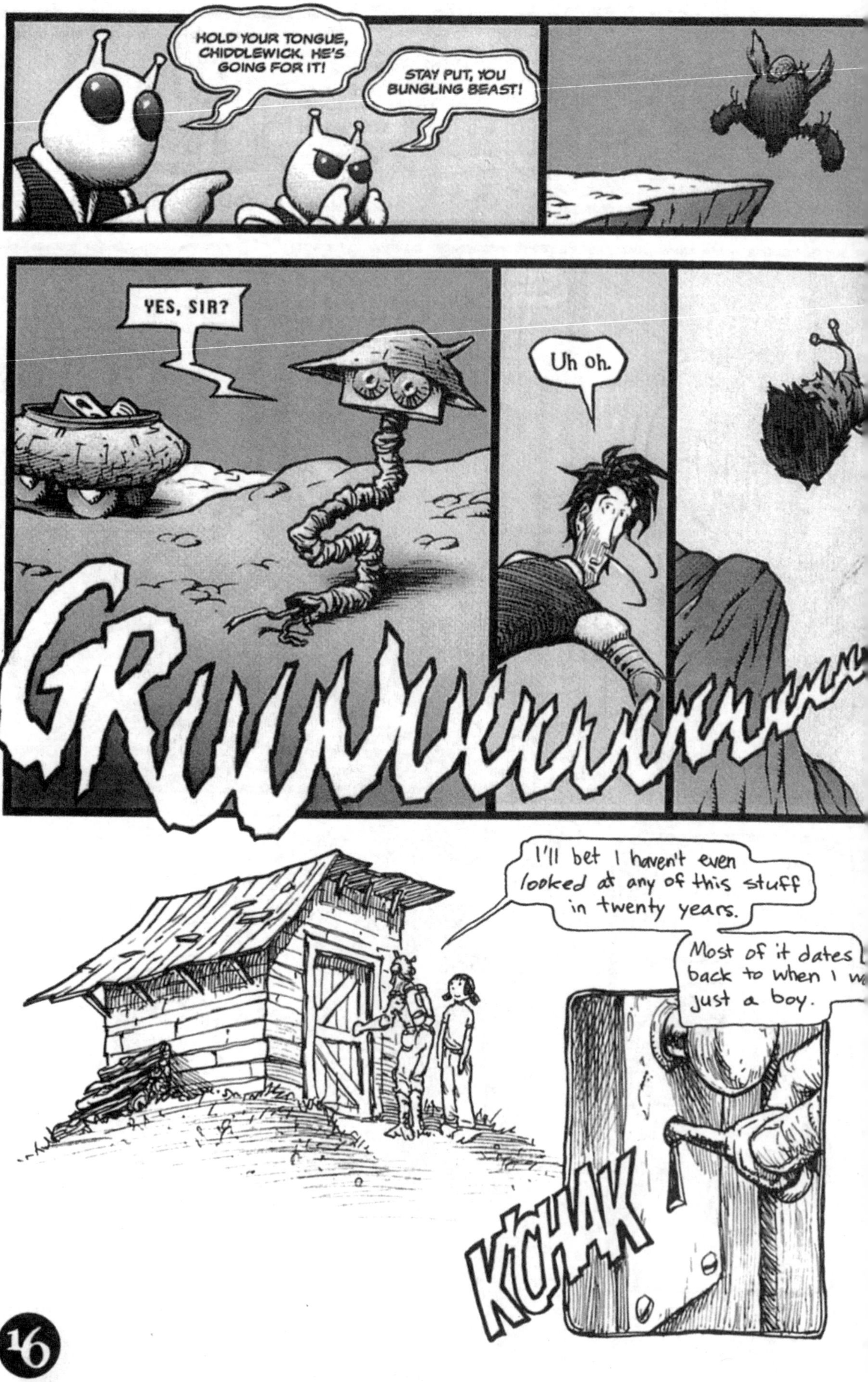
HOLD YOUR TONGUE, CHIDDLEWICK. HE'S GOING FOR IT!
STAY PUT, YOU BUNGLING BEAST!
YES, SIR?
Uh oh.
GRUUUUUUUUN
I'll bet I haven't even looked at any of this stuff in twenty years.
Most of it dates back to when I w just a boy.
K'CHAK

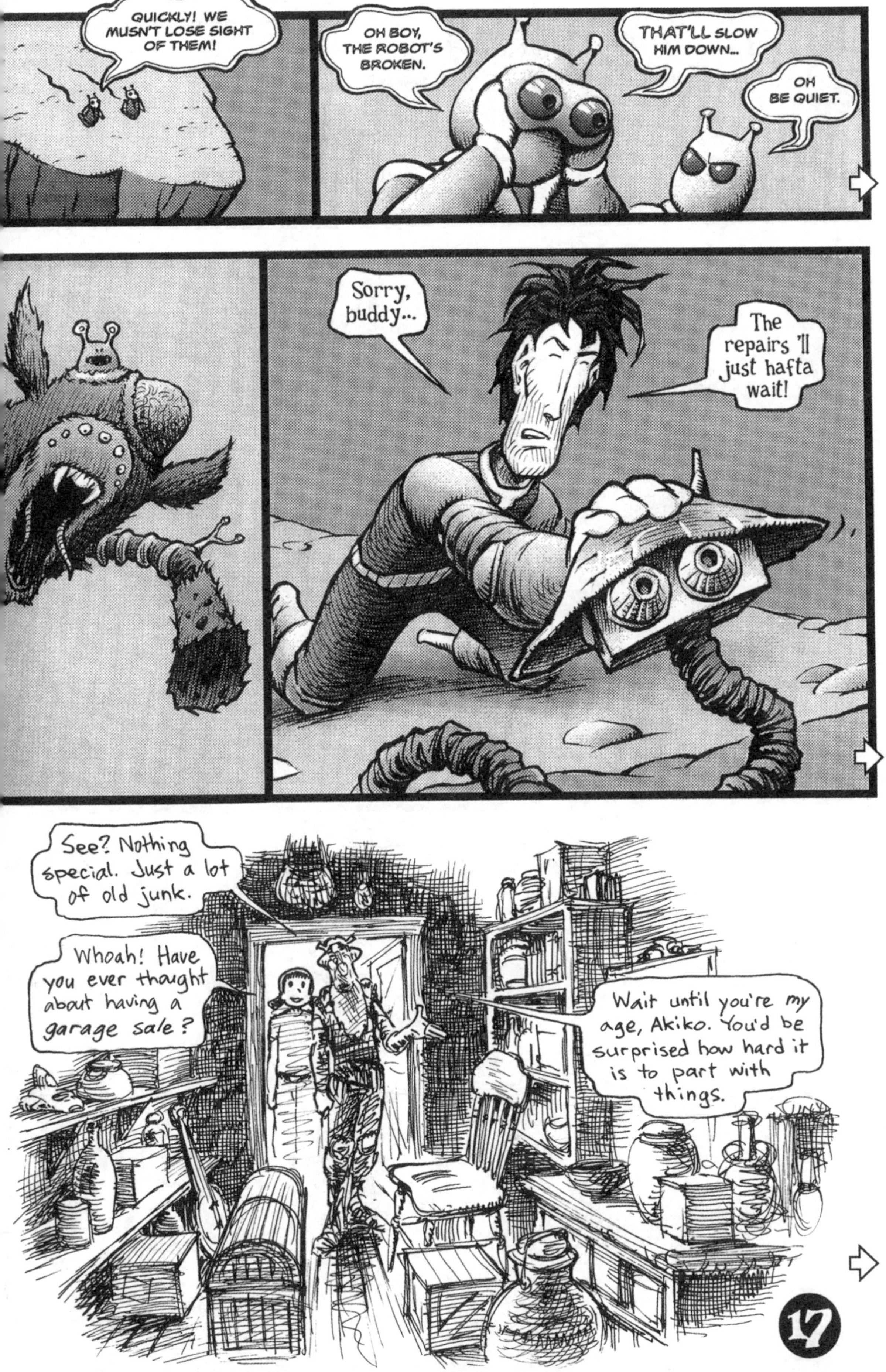

QUICKLY! WE MUSN'T LOSE SIGHT OF THEM!
OH BOY, THE ROBOT'S BROKEN.
THAT'LL SLOW HIM DOWN...
OH BE QUIET.
Sorry, buddy...
The repairs 'll just hafta wait!
See? Nothing special. Just a lot of old junk.
Whoah! Have you ever thought about having a garage sale?
Wait until you're my age, Akiko. You'd be surprised how hard it is to part with things.

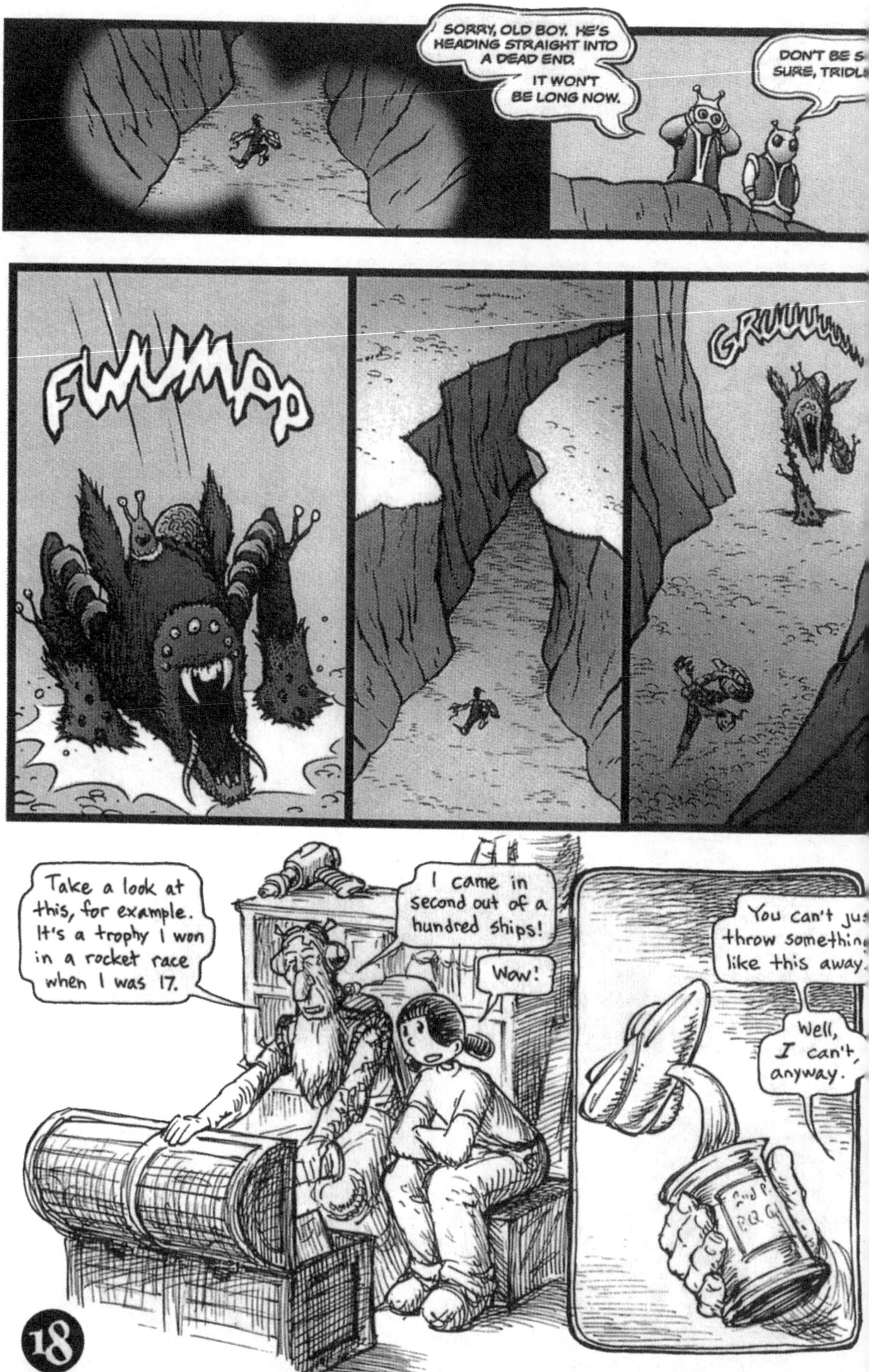
SORRY, OLD BOY. HE'S HEADING STRAIGHT INTO A DEAD END.
IT WON'T BE LONG NOW.
DON'T BE S SURE, TRIDL
FWUMPP
GRUUUU
Take a look at this, for example. It's a trophy I won in a rocket race when I was 17.
I came in second out of a hundred ships!
Wow!
You can't ju throw somethin like this away.
Well, I can't, anyway.

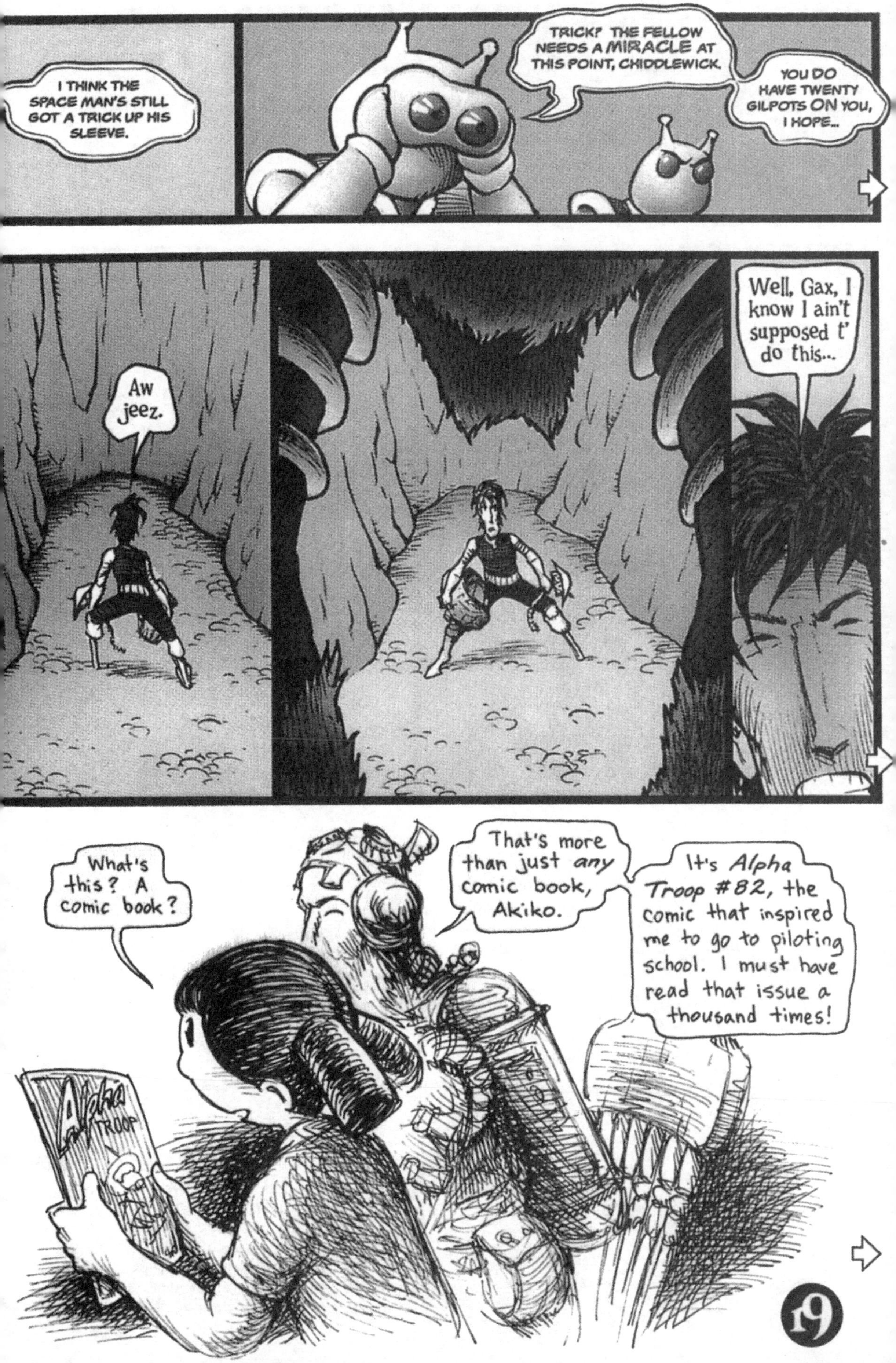
I THINK THE SPACE MAN'S STILL GOT A TRICK UP HIS SLEEVE.
TRICK? THE FELLOW NEEDS A MIRACLE AT THIS POINT, CHIDDLEWICK.
YOU DO HAVE TWENTY GILPOTS ON YOU, I HOPE...
Aw jeez.
Well, Gax, I know I ain't supposed t' do this...
What's this? A comic book?
That's more than just any comic book, Akiko.
It's Alpha Troop #82, the comic that inspired me to go to piloting school. I must have read that issue a thousand times!
Alpha TROOP

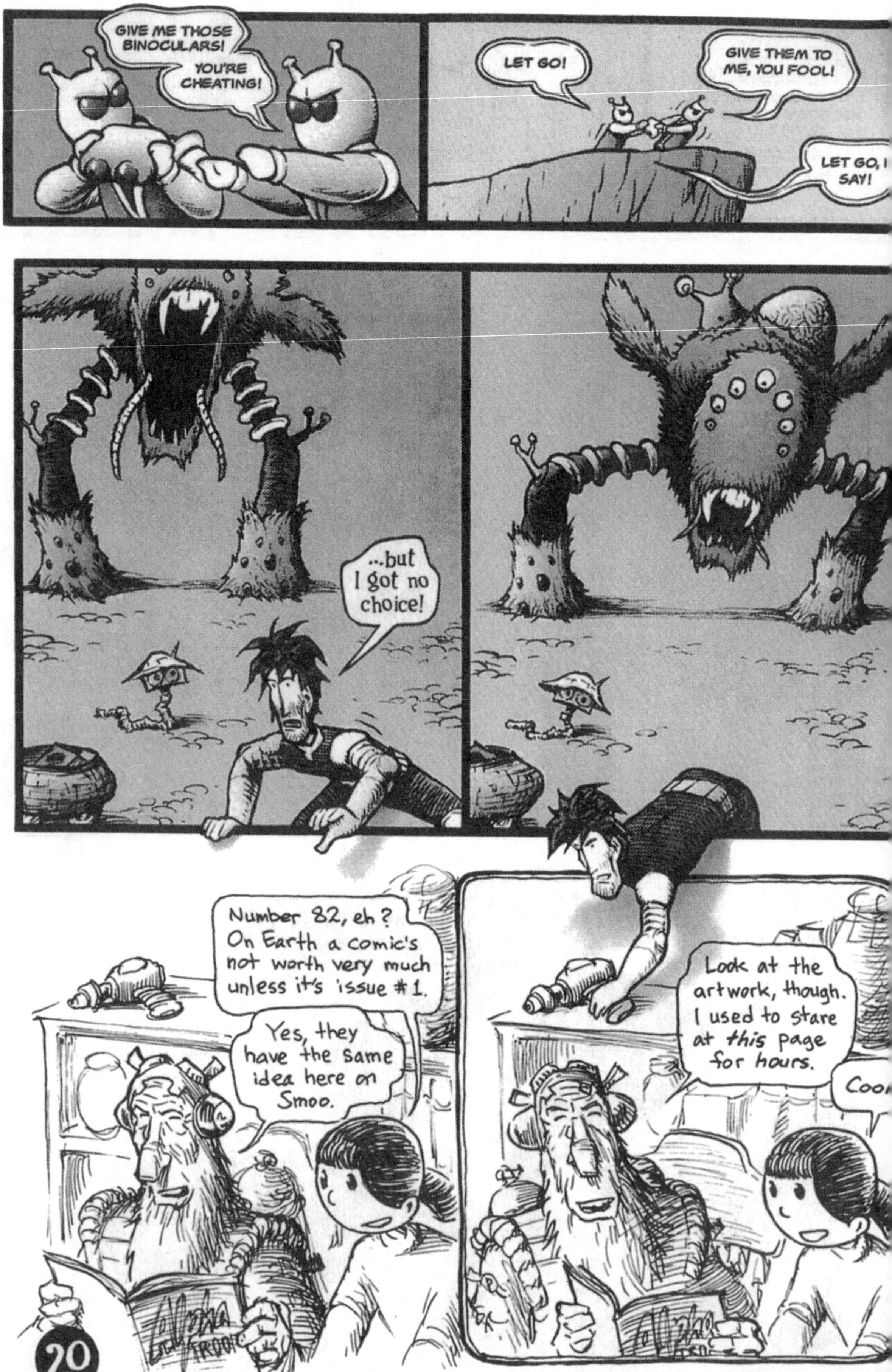
GIVE ME THOSE BINOCULARS!
YOU'RE CHEATING!
LET GO!
GIVE THEM TO ME, YOU FOOL!
LET GO, I SAY!
...but I got no choice!
Number 82, eh? On Earth a comic's not worth very much unless it's issue #1.
Yes, they have the same idea here on Smoo.
Look at the artwork, though. I used to stare at *this* page for hours.

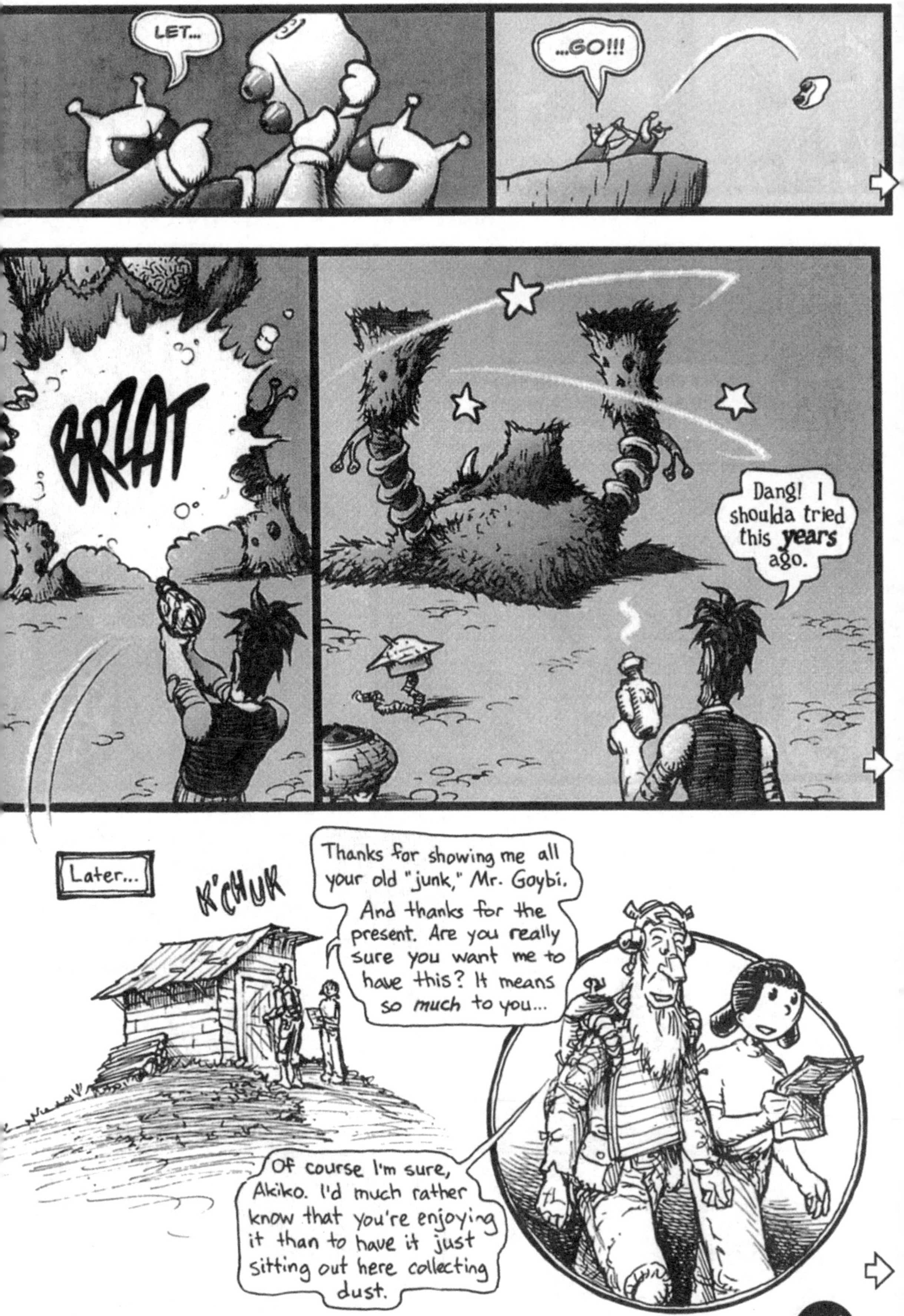
LET...
...GO!!!
BRZAT
Dang! I shoulda tried this **years** ago.
Later...
K'CHUK
Thanks for showing me all your old "junk," Mr. Goybi.
And thanks for the present. Are you really sure you want me to have this? It means so *much* to you...
Of course I'm sure, Akiko. I'd much rather know that you're enjoying it than to have it just sitting out here collecting dust.

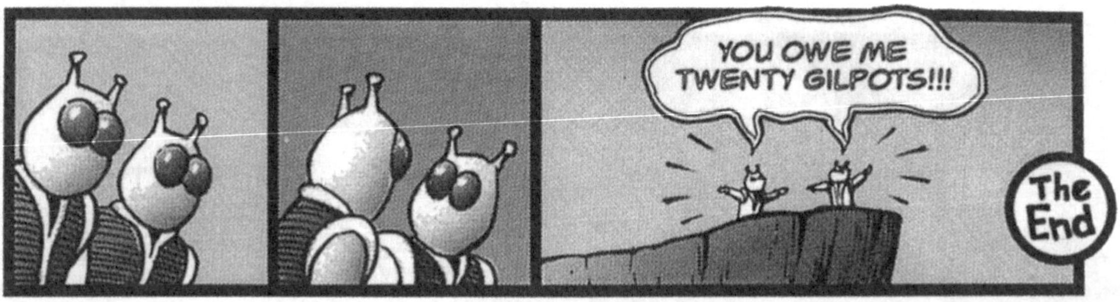
YOU OWE ME TWENTY GILPOTS!!!
The End

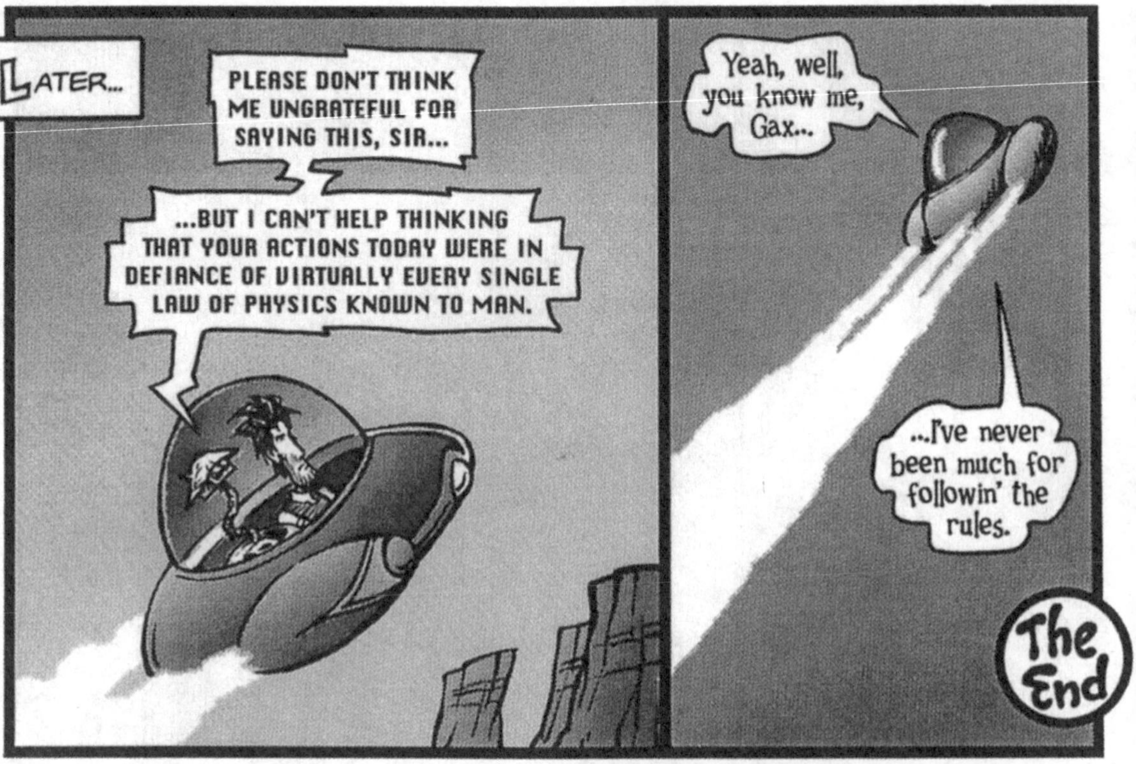
LATER...
PLEASE DON'T THINK ME UNGRATEFUL FOR SAYING THIS, SIR...
...BUT I CAN'T HELP THINKING THAT YOUR ACTIONS TODAY WERE IN DEFIANCE OF VIRTUALLY EVERY SINGLE LAW OF PHYSICS KNOWN TO MAN.
Yeah, well, you know me, Gax...
...I've never been much for followin' the rules.
The End

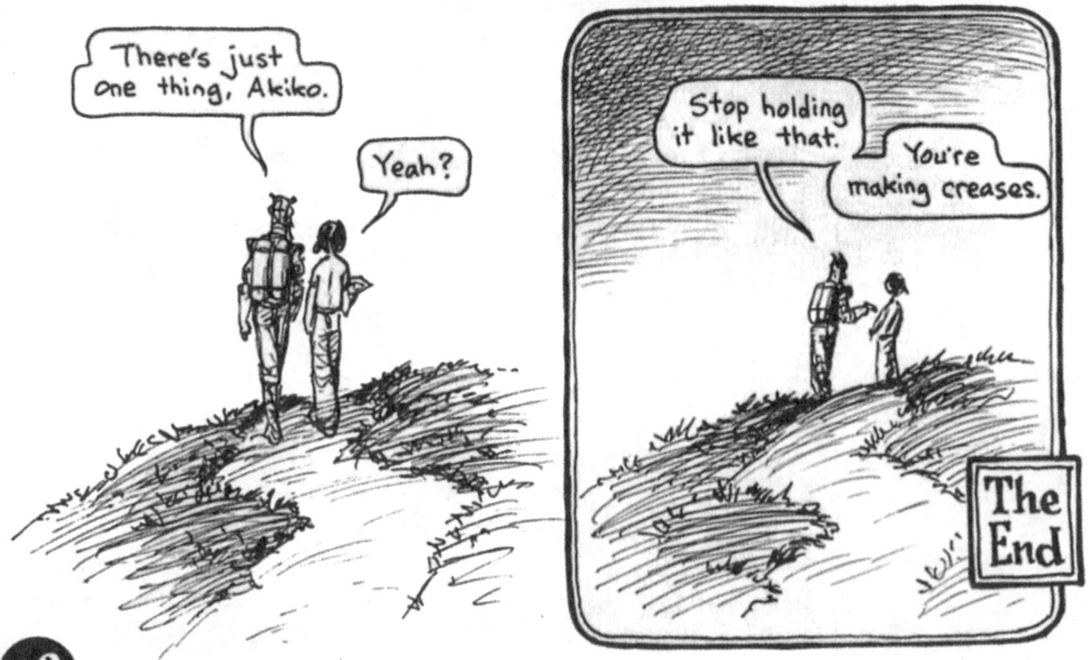
There's just one thing, Akiko.
Yeah?
Stop holding it like that.
You're making creases.
The End

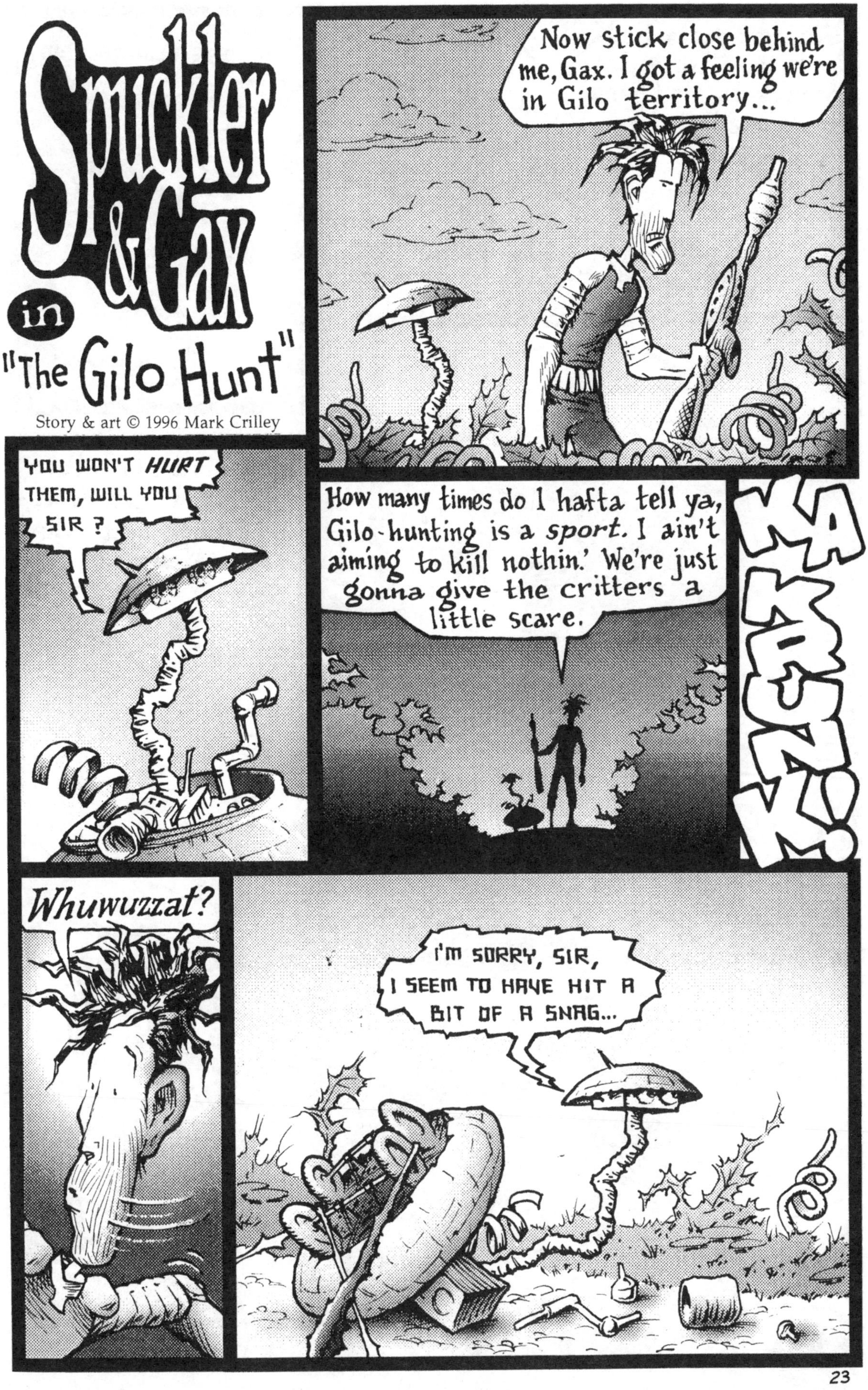

Spuckler & Gax
in
"The Gilo Hunt"
Story & art © 1996 Mark Crilley
Now stick close behind me, Gax. I got a feeling we're in Gilo territory...
YOU WON'T *HURT* THEM, WILL YOU SIR ?
How many times do I hafta tell ya, Gilo-hunting is a *sport*. I ain't aiming to kill nothin.' We're just gonna give the critters a little scare.
KAKRUNK!
Whuwuzzat?
I'M SORRY, SIR, I SEEM TO HAVE HIT A BIT OF A SNAG...

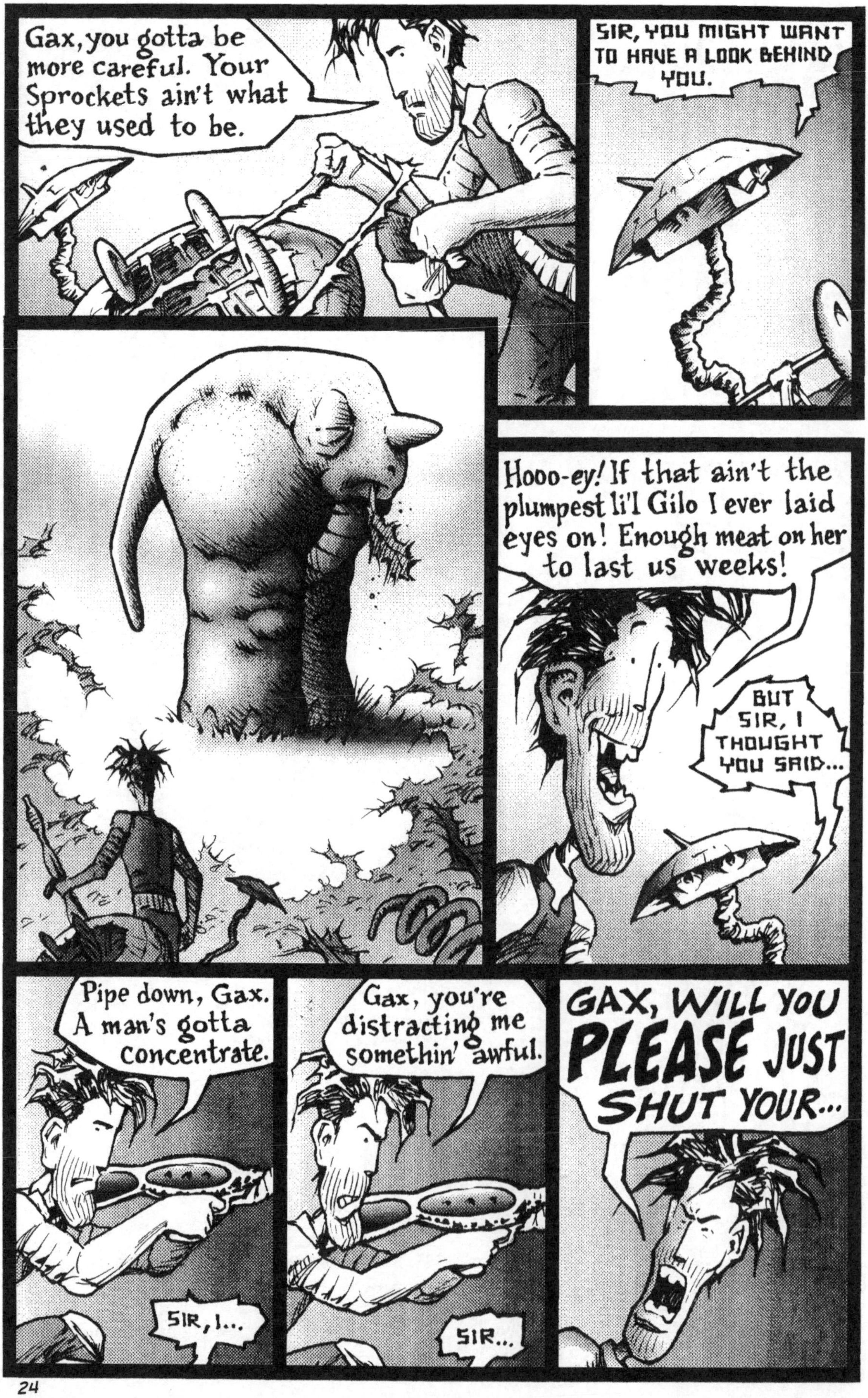
Gax, you gotta be more careful. Your Sprockets ain't what they used to be.
SIR, YOU MIGHT WANT TO HAVE A LOOK BEHIND YOU.
Hooo-ey! If that ain't the plumpest li'l Gilo I ever laid eyes on! Enough meat on her to last us weeks!
BUT SIR, I THOUGHT YOU SAID...
Pipe down, Gax. A man's gotta concentrate.
SIR, I...
Gax, you're distracting me somethin' awful.
SIR...
GAX, WILL YOU PLEASE JUST SHUT YOUR...

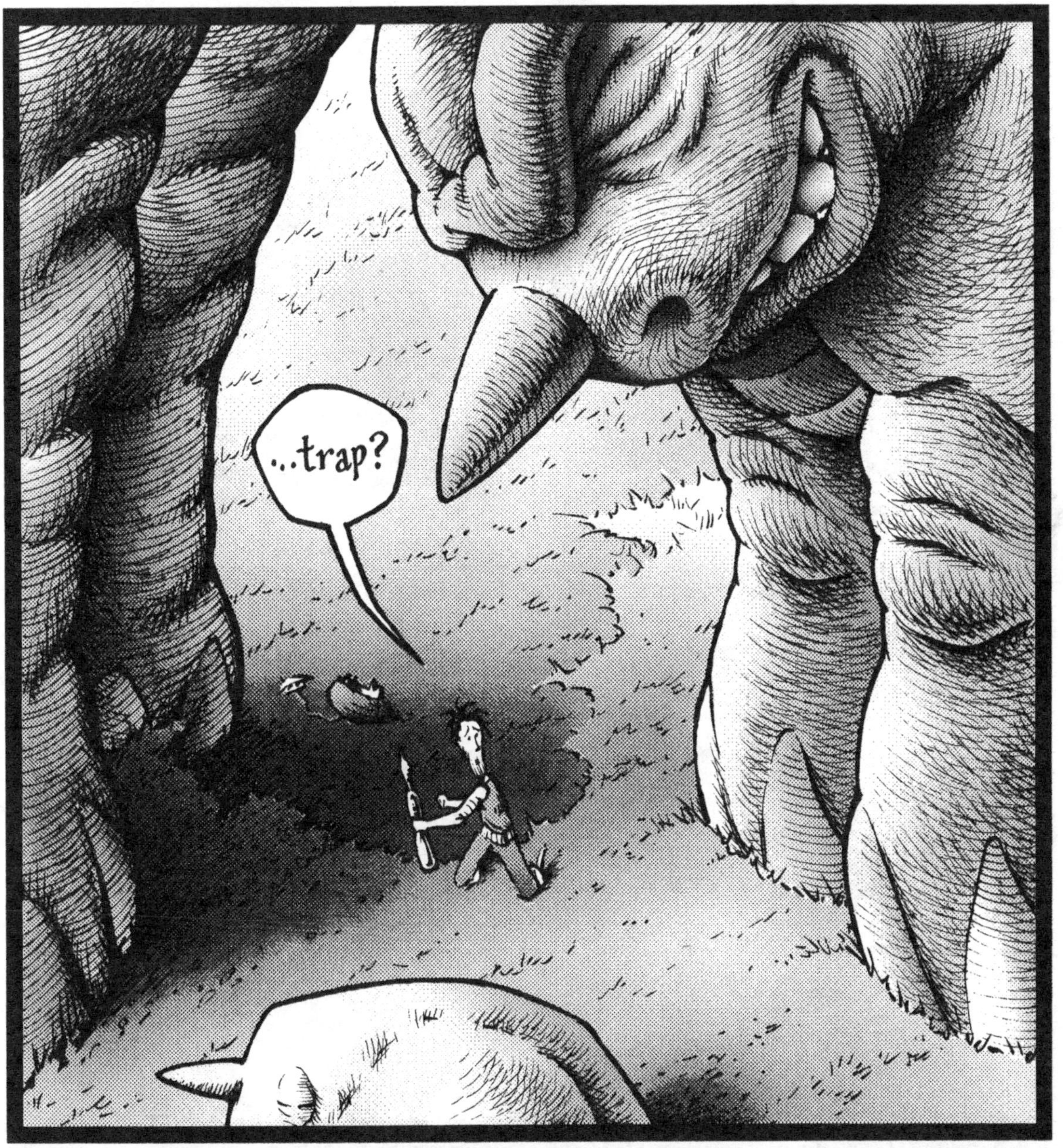
..trap?

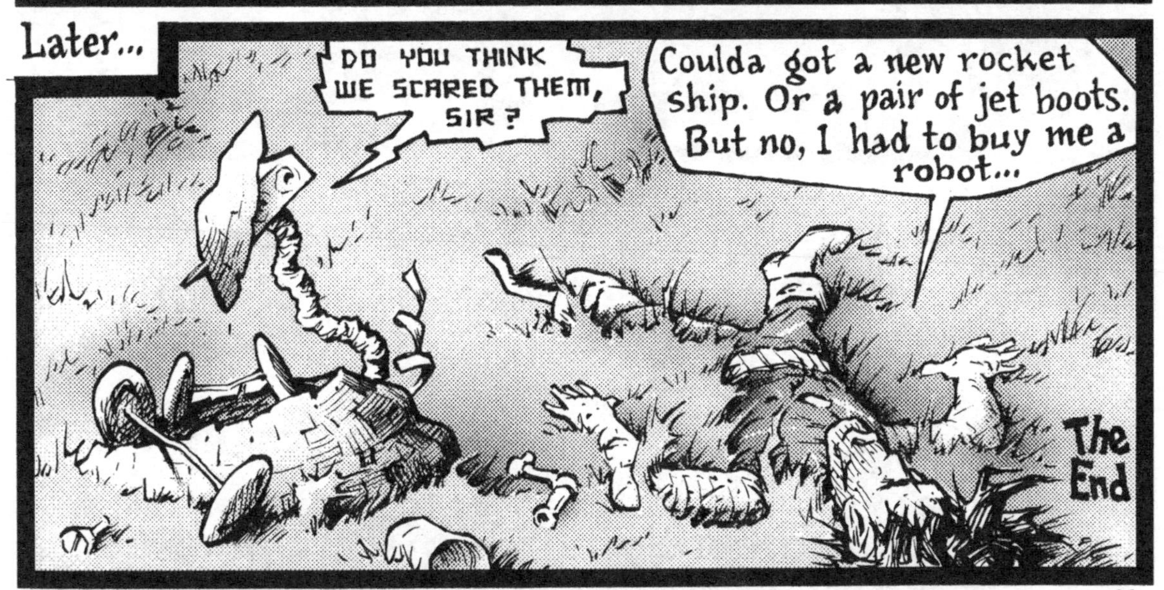
Later...
DO YOU THINK WE SCARED THEM, SIR?
Coulda got a new rocket ship. Or a pair of jet boots. But no, I had to buy me a robot...
The End

Akiko in "Everyone's a Critic"

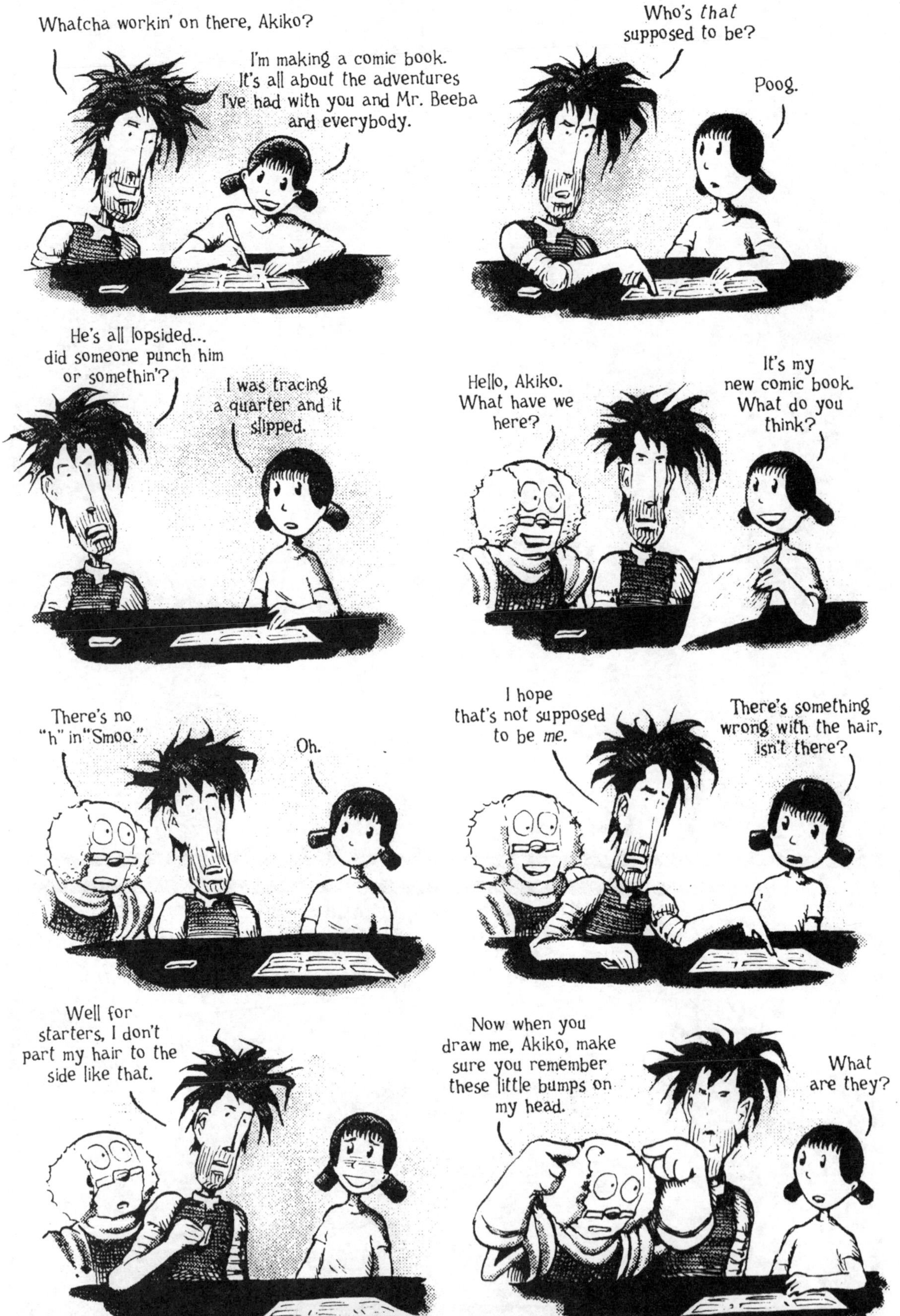

Whatcha workin' on there, Akiko?
I'm making a comic book. It's all about the adventures I've had with you and Mr. Beeba and everybody.
Who's *that* supposed to be?
Poog.
He's all lopsided... did someone punch him or somethin'?
I was tracing a quarter and it slipped.
Hello, Akiko. What have we here?
It's my new comic book. What do you think?
There's no "h" in "Smoo."
Oh.
I hope that's not supposed to be *me*.
There's something wrong with the hair, isn't there?
Well for starters, I don't part my hair to the side like that.
Now when you draw me, Akiko, make sure you remember these little bumps on my head.
What are they?

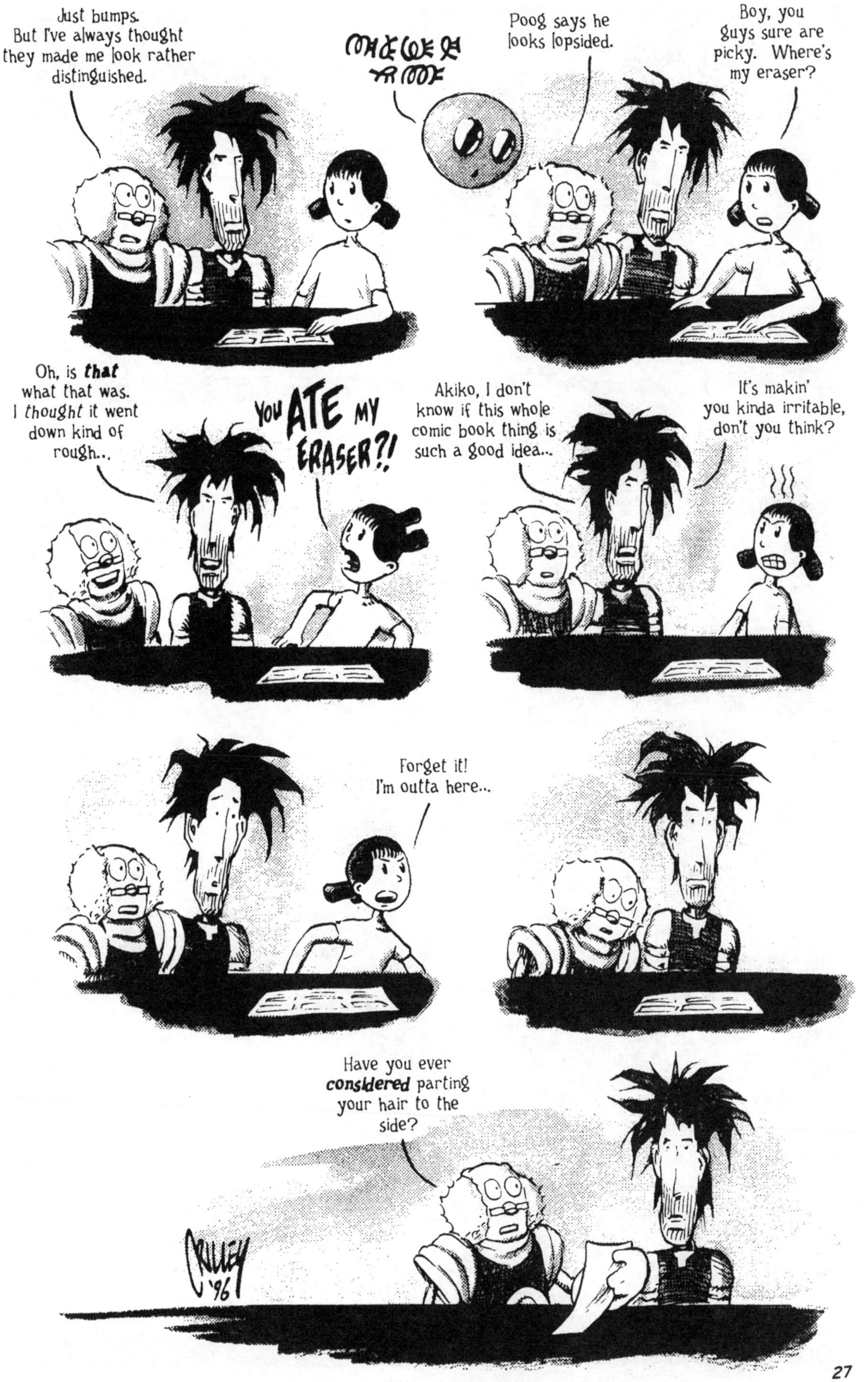
Just bumps. But I've always thought they made me look rather distinguished.
Poog says he looks lopsided.
Boy, you guys sure are picky. Where's my eraser?
Oh, is **that** what that was. I *thought* it went down kind of rough...
YOU ATE MY ERASER?!
Akiko, I don't know if this whole comic book thing is such a good idea...
It's makin' you kinda irritable, don't you think?
Forget it! I'm outta here...
Have you ever **considered** parting your hair to the side?
CRILLEY '96

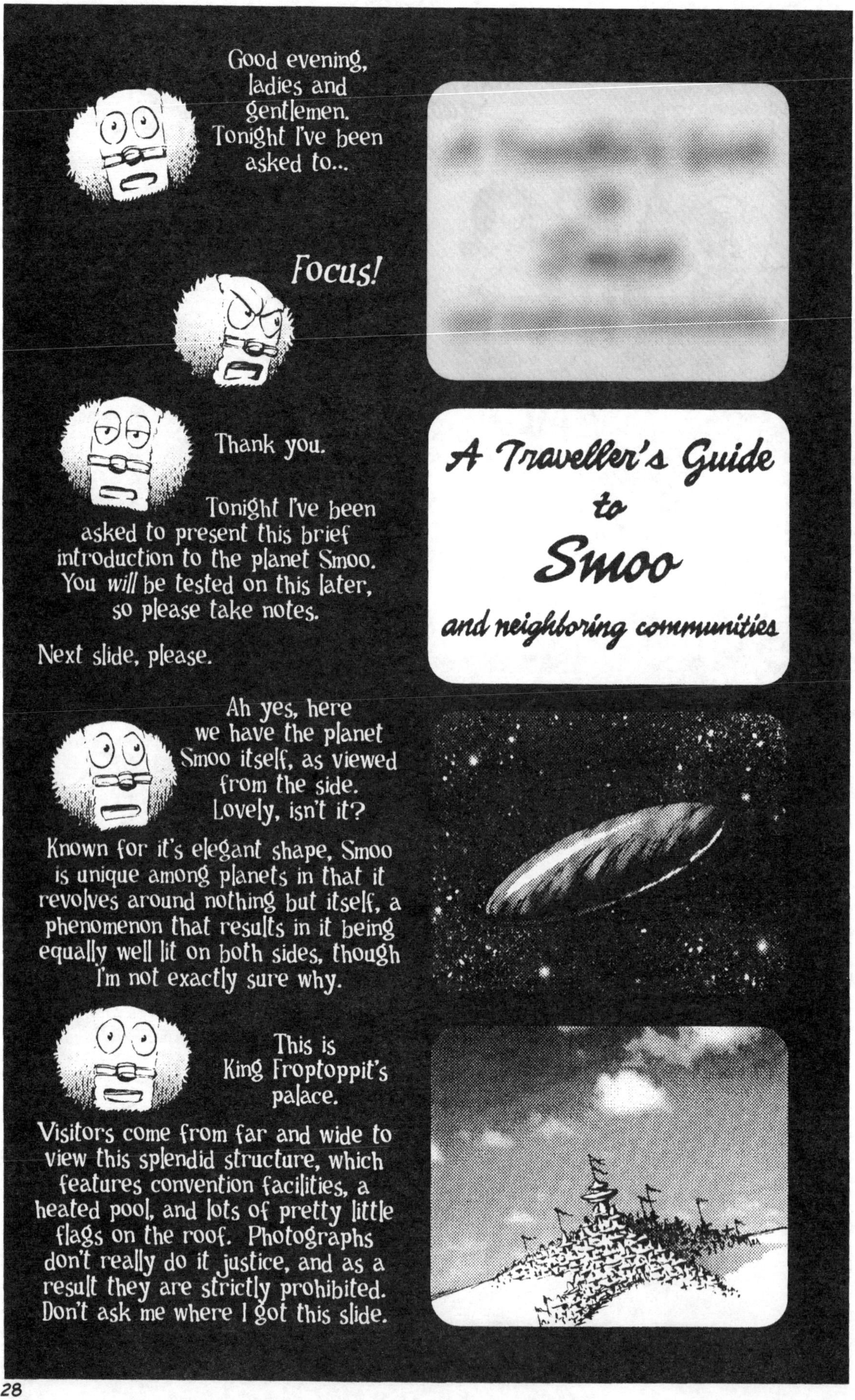
Good evening, ladies and gentlemen. Tonight I've been asked to...
Focus!
Thank you.
A Traveller's Guide to Smoo and neighboring communities
Tonight I've been asked to present this brief introduction to the planet Smoo. You *will* be tested on this later, so please take notes.
Next slide, please.
Ah yes, here we have the planet Smoo itself, as viewed from the side. Lovely, isn't it?
Known for it's elegant shape, Smoo is unique among planets in that it revolves around nothing but itself, a phenomenon that results in it being equally well lit on both sides, though I'm not exactly sure why.
This is King Froptoppit's palace.
Visitors come from far and wide to view this splendid structure, which features convention facilities, a heated pool, and lots of pretty little flags on the roof. Photographs don't really do it justice, and as a result they are strictly prohibited. Don't ask me where I got this slide.

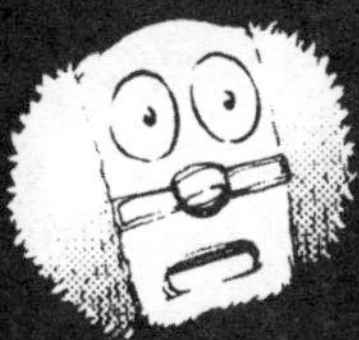

Here is King Froptoppit, famed humorist and beloved ruler of Smoo.

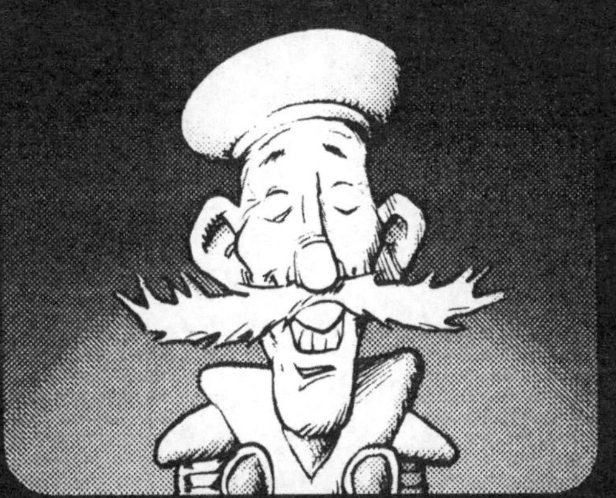

His Majesty invited me to Smoo many years ago to serve as his personal tutor, and though he hasn't excelled in any particular subject, his handwriting has improved considerably.

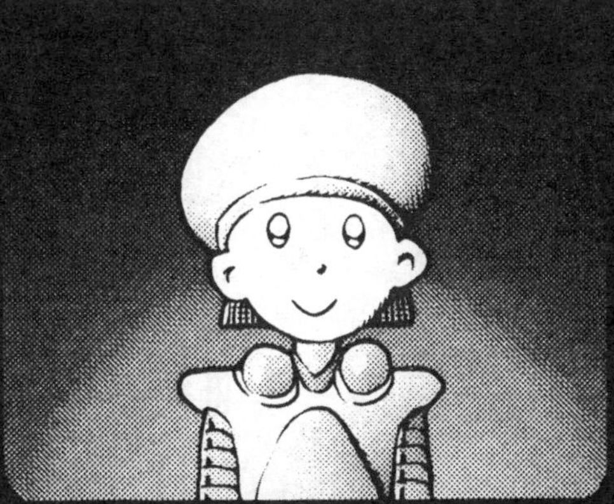

This is his son, the Prince. Now that he is of marriageable age, his father has been searching the universe for a suitable bride. We have in fact located an excellent candidate, but the wedding has had to be postponed until she has completed what is known on her planet as "the 6th grade."

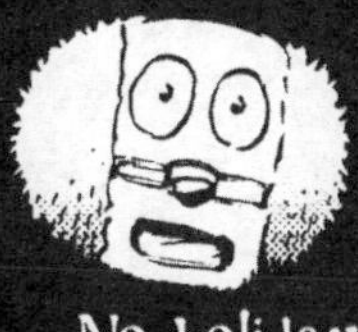

Now for some of the sights.

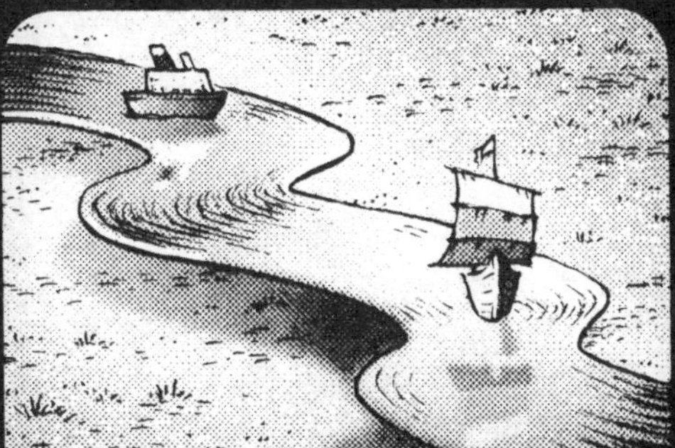

No holiday on Smoo would be complete without a visit to the Floating River of Hebbadoy. This natural marvel has flowed above the surface of Smoo for several centuries. Riverboat tours are available, except during the rainy season when they are cancelled due to the possibility of floods.

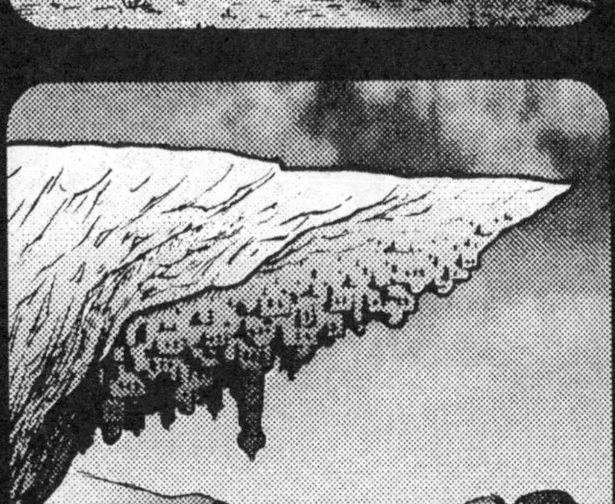

Then there is the legendary Upside Down City of Gollarondo, where people live on the underside of a cliff overlooking the Moonguzzit Sea. It's a charming town with a spectacular view, though one must be sure that all articles of clothing are firmly attached before going there, since fallen hats and such can be very difficult to retrieve.

 And here...

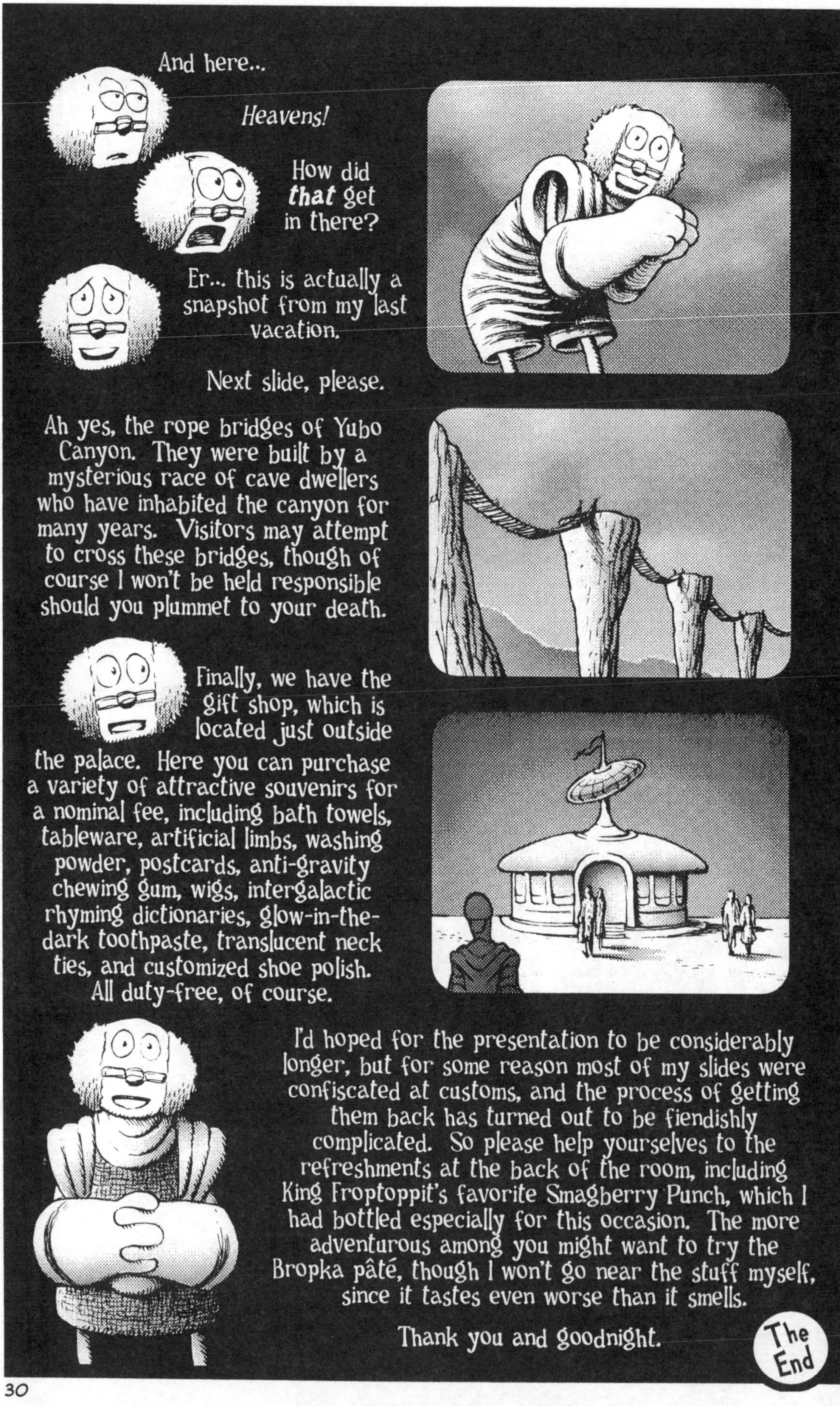

Heavens!

How did *that* get in there?

Er... this is actually a snapshot from my last vacation.

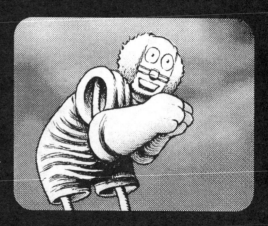

Next slide, please.

Ah yes, the rope bridges of Yubo Canyon. They were built by a mysterious race of cave dwellers who have inhabited the canyon for many years. Visitors may attempt to cross these bridges, though of course I won't be held responsible should you plummet to your death.

 Finally, we have the gift shop, which is located just outside the palace. Here you can purchase a variety of attractive souvenirs for a nominal fee, including bath towels, tableware, artificial limbs, washing powder, postcards, anti-gravity chewing gum, wigs, intergalactic rhyming dictionaries, glow-in-the-dark toothpaste, translucent neck ties, and customized shoe polish. All duty-free, of course.

 I'd hoped for the presentation to be considerably longer, but for some reason most of my slides were confiscated at customs, and the process of getting them back has turned out to be fiendishly complicated. So please help yourselves to the refreshments at the back of the room, including King Froptoppit's favorite Smagberry Punch, which I had bottled especially for this occasion. The more adventurous among you might want to try the Bropka pâté, though I won't go near the stuff myself, since it tastes even worse than it smells.

Thank you and goodnight.

 The End

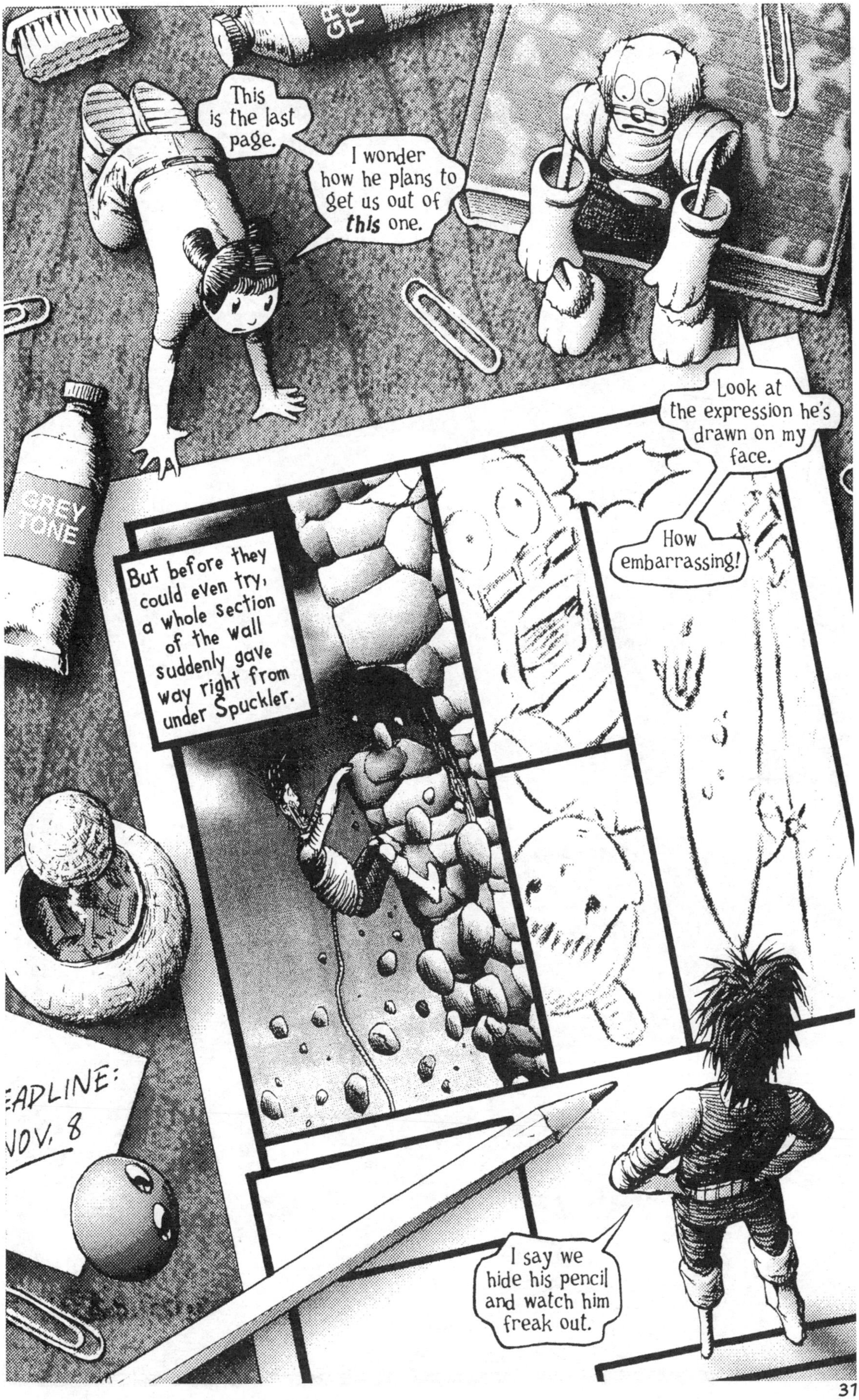
This is the last page.
I wonder how he plans to get us out of **this** one.
Look at the expression he's drawn on my face.
How embarrassing!
GREY TONE
But before they could even try, a whole section of the wall suddenly gave way right from under Spuckler.
DEADLINE: NOV. 8
I say we hide his pencil and watch him freak out.

Akiko and the Gang in "MOVIE MAYHEM"

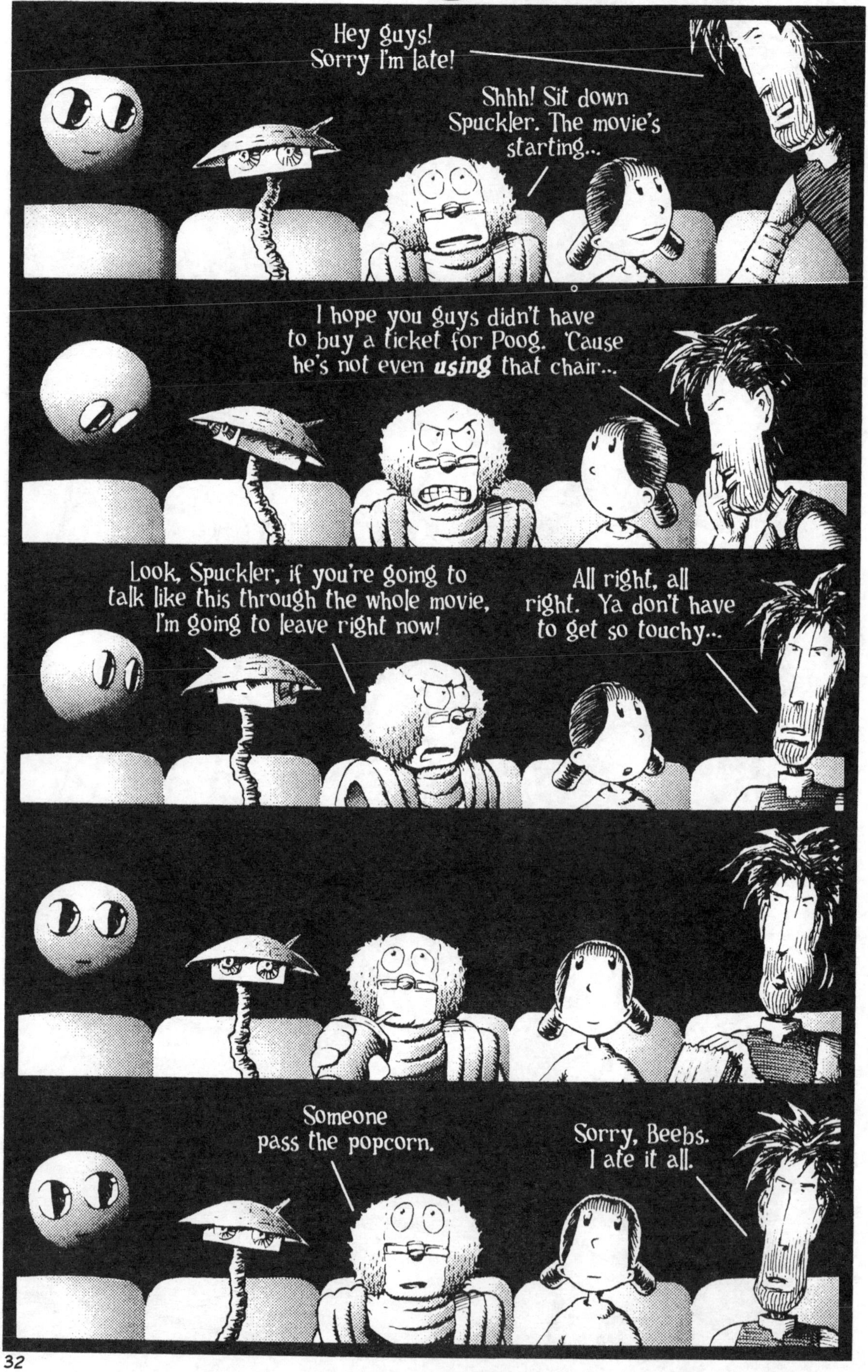
Hey guys!
Sorry I'm late!
Shhh! Sit down Spuckler. The movie's starting...
I hope you guys didn't have to buy a ticket for Poog. 'Cause he's not even *using* that chair...
Look, Spuckler, if you're going to talk like this through the whole movie, I'm going to leave right now!
All right, all right. Ya don't have to get so touchy...
Someone pass the popcorn.
Sorry, Beebs. I ate it all.

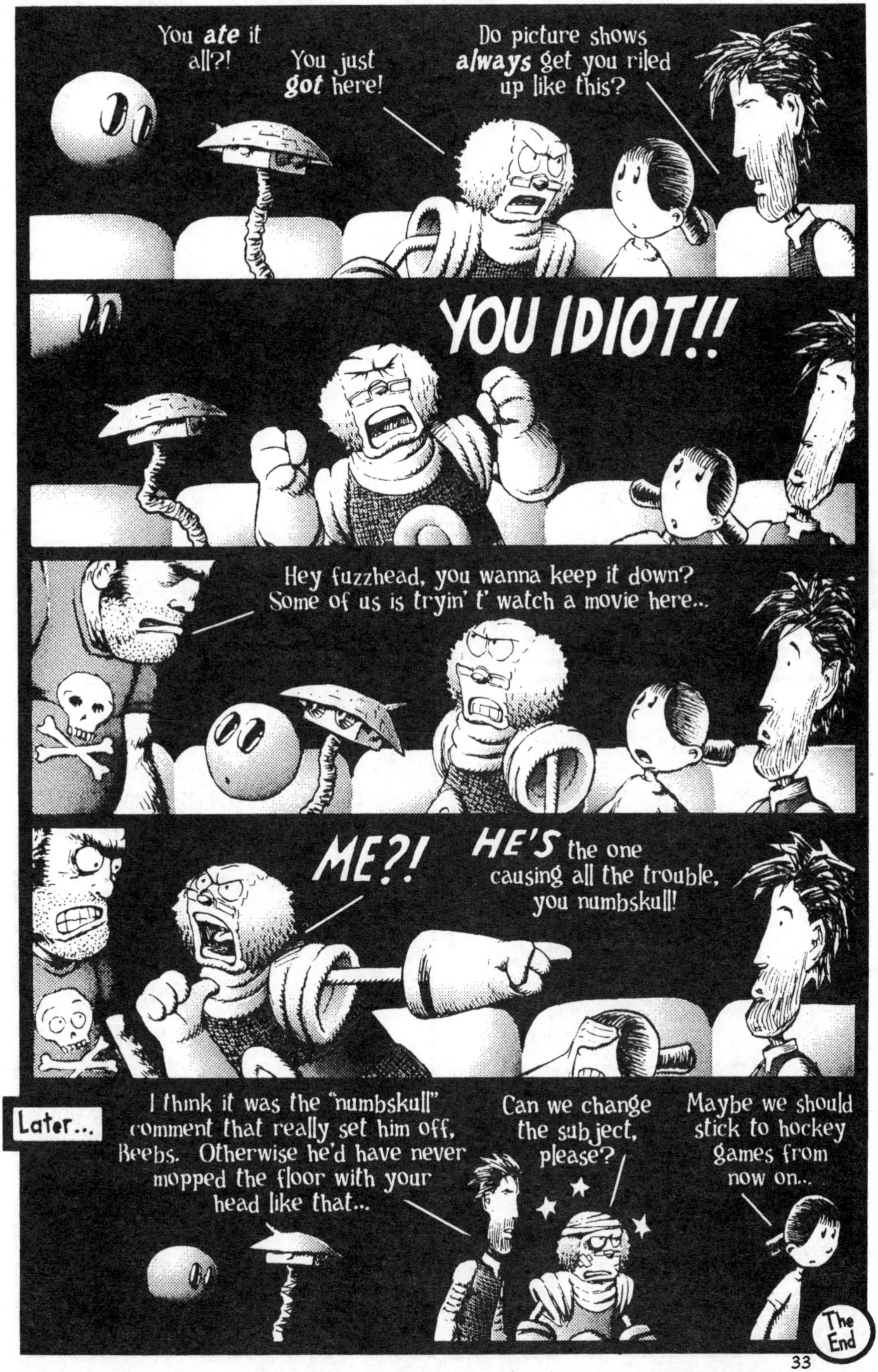
You **ate** it all?!
You just **got** here!
Do picture shows **always** get you riled up like this?
YOU IDIOT!!
Hey fuzzhead, you wanna keep it down? Some of us is tryin' t' watch a movie here..
ME?!
HE'S the one causing all the trouble, you numbskull!
Later...
I think it was the "numbskull" comment that really set him off, Beebs. Otherwise he'd have never mopped the floor with your head like that...
Can we change the subject, please?
Maybe we should stick to hockey games from now on...
The End

Me 'N 'Kiko in "Return to Sender"

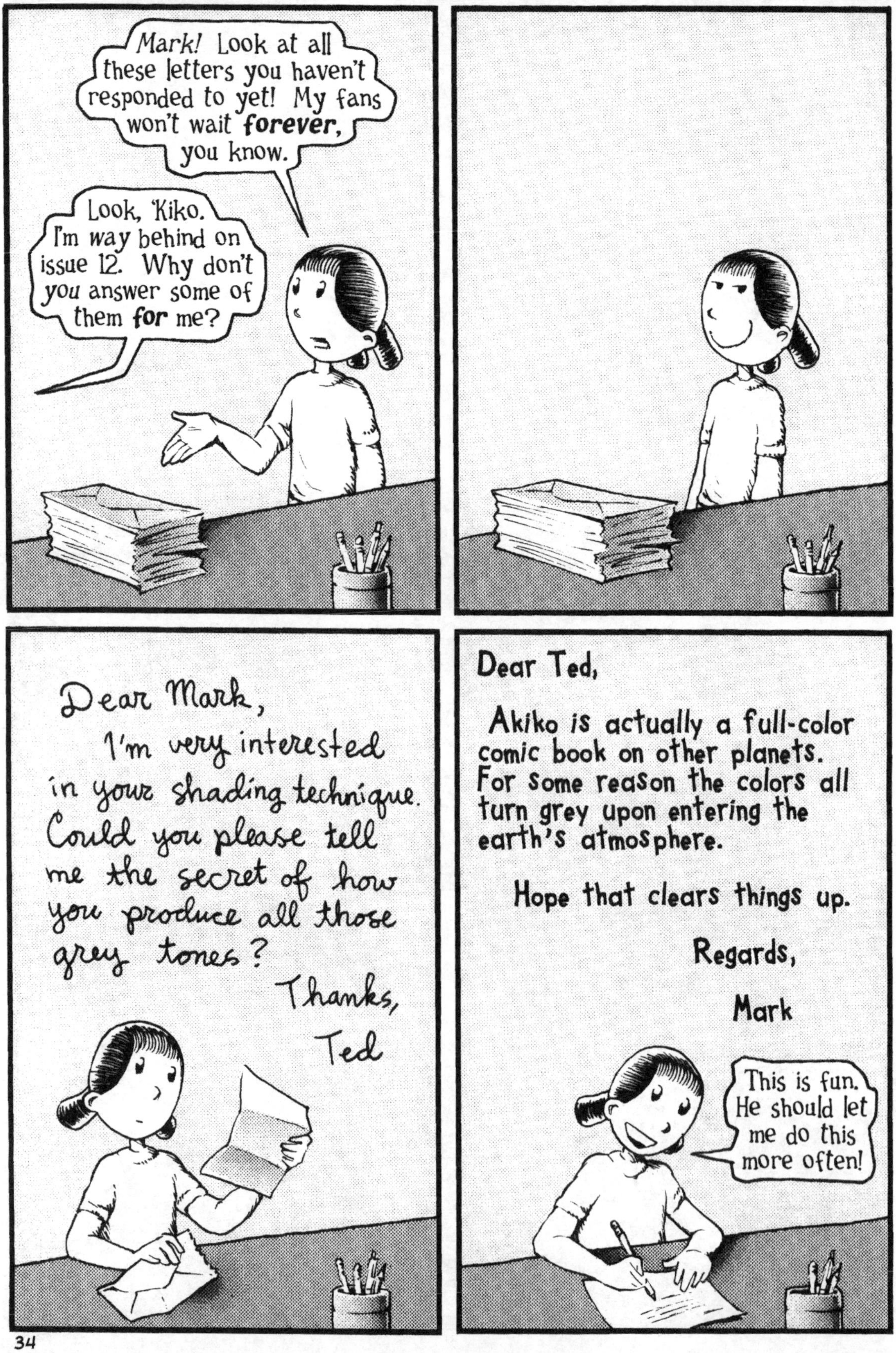
Mark! Look at all these letters you haven't responded to yet! My fans won't wait **forever**, you know.
Look, 'Kiko. I'm way behind on issue 12. Why don't *you* answer some of them **for** me?
Dear Mark,
I'm very interested in your shading technique. Could you please tell me the secret of how you produce all those grey tones?
Thanks,
Ted
Dear Ted,
Akiko is actually a full-color comic book on other planets. For some reason the colors all turn grey upon entering the earth's atmosphere.
Hope that clears things up.
Regards,
Mark
This is fun. He should let me do this more often!

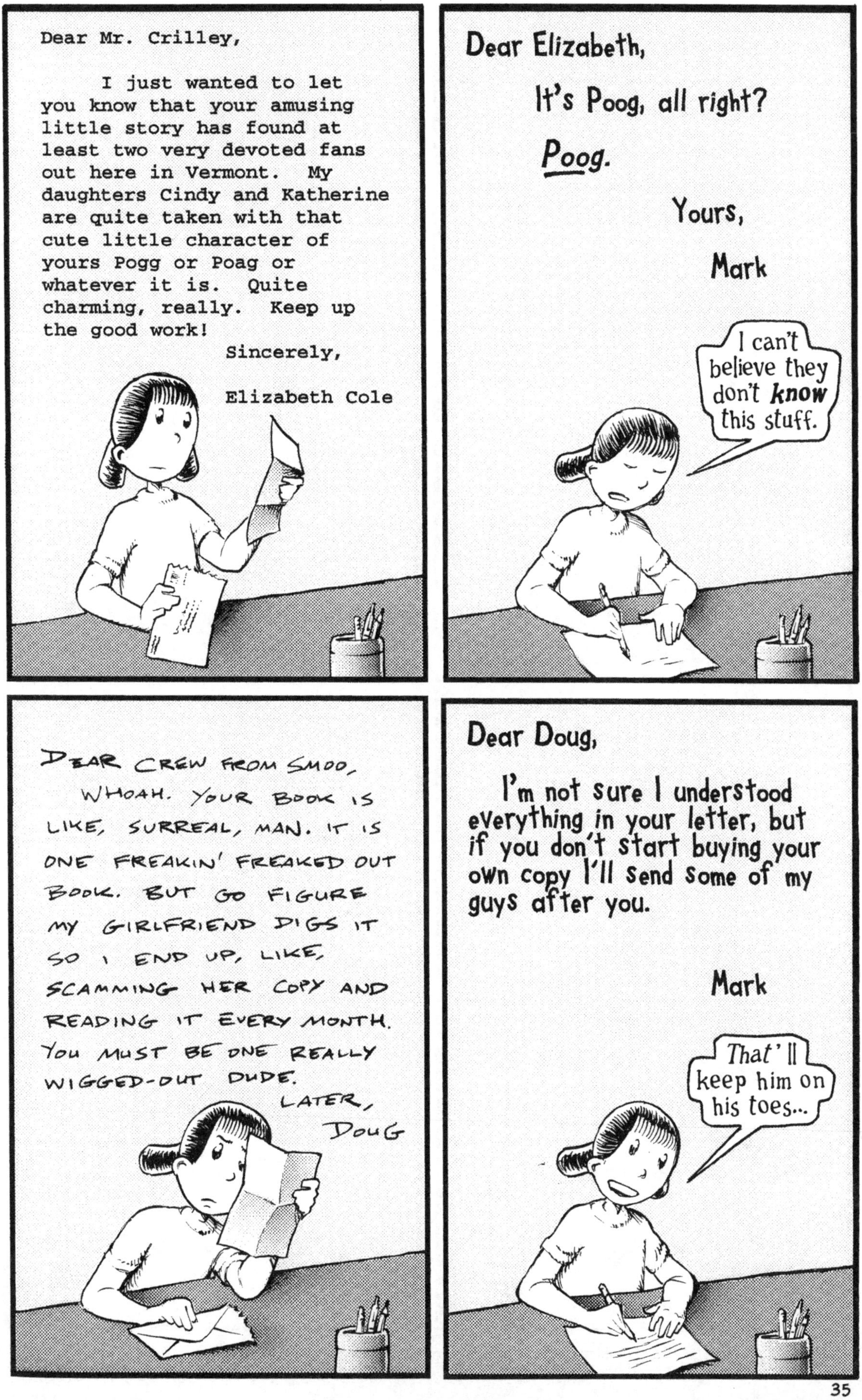
Dear Mr. Crilley,
I just wanted to let you know that your amusing little story has found at least two very devoted fans out here in Vermont. My daughters Cindy and Katherine are quite taken with that cute little character of yours Pogg or Poag or whatever it is. Quite charming, really. Keep up the good work!
Sincerely,
Elizabeth Cole
Dear Elizabeth,
It's Poog, all right?
Poog.
Yours,
Mark
I can't believe they don't *know* this stuff.
DEAR CREW FROM SMOO,
WHOAH. YOUR BOOK IS LIKE, SURREAL, MAN. IT IS ONE FREAKIN' FREAKED OUT BOOK. BUT GO FIGURE MY GIRLFRIEND DIGS IT SO I END UP, LIKE, SCAMMING HER COPY AND READING IT EVERY MONTH. YOU MUST BE ONE REALLY WIGGED-OUT DUDE.
LATER,
DOUG
Dear Doug,
I'm not sure I understood everything in your letter, but if you don't start buying your own copy I'll send some of my guys after you.
Mark
That'll keep him on his toes...

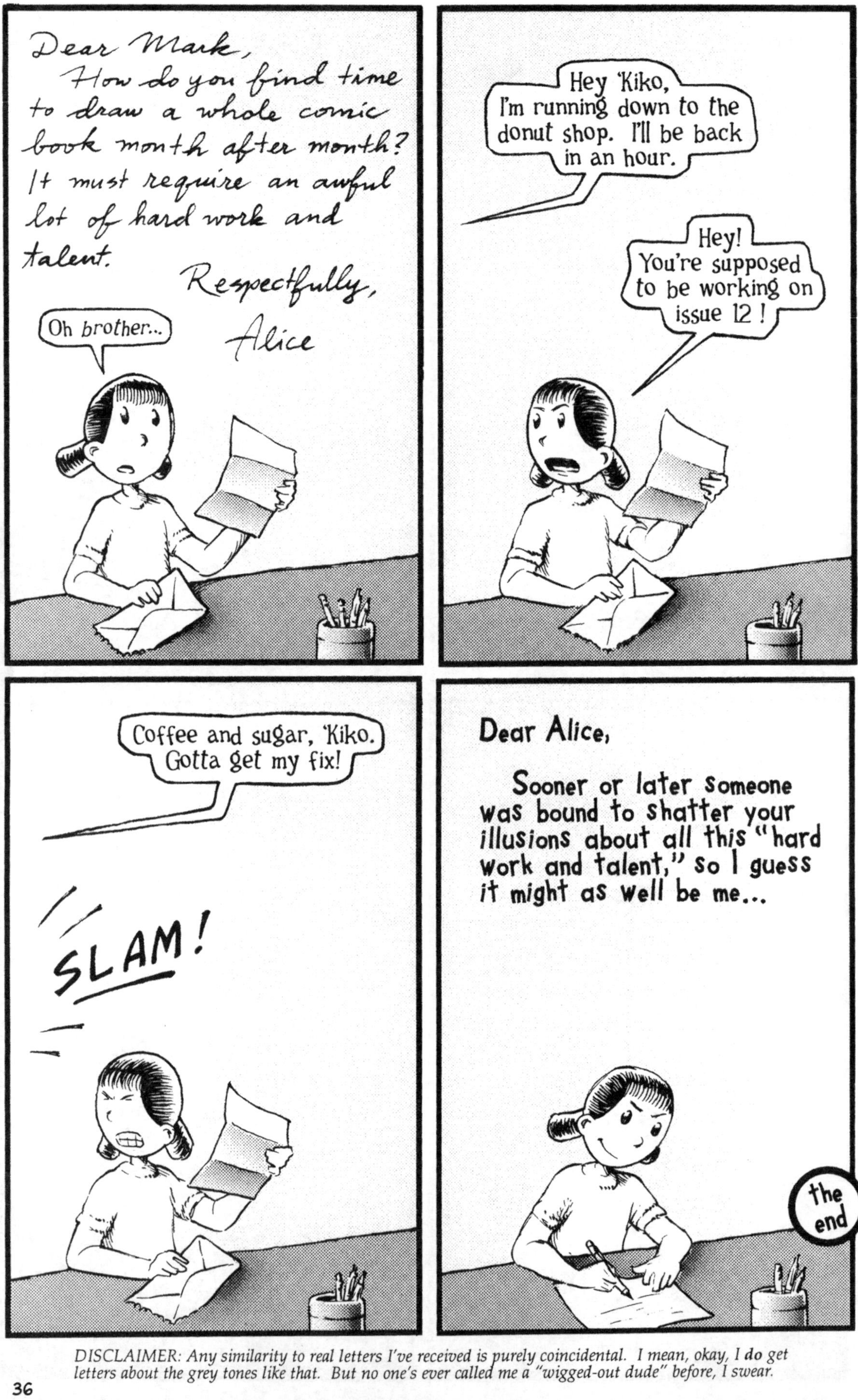
Dear Mark,
How do you find time to draw a whole comic book month after month? It must require an awful lot of hard work and talent.
Respectfully,
Alice
Oh brother...
Hey 'Kiko, I'm running down to the donut shop. I'll be back in an hour.
Hey! You're supposed to be working on issue 12!
Coffee and sugar, 'Kiko. Gotta get my fix!
SLAM!
Dear Alice,
Sooner or later someone was bound to shatter your illusions about all this "hard work and talent," so I guess it might as well be me...
the end

DISCLAIMER: Any similarity to real letters I've received is purely coincidental. I mean, okay, I do *get letters about the grey tones like that. But no one's ever called me a "wigged-out dude" before, I swear.*

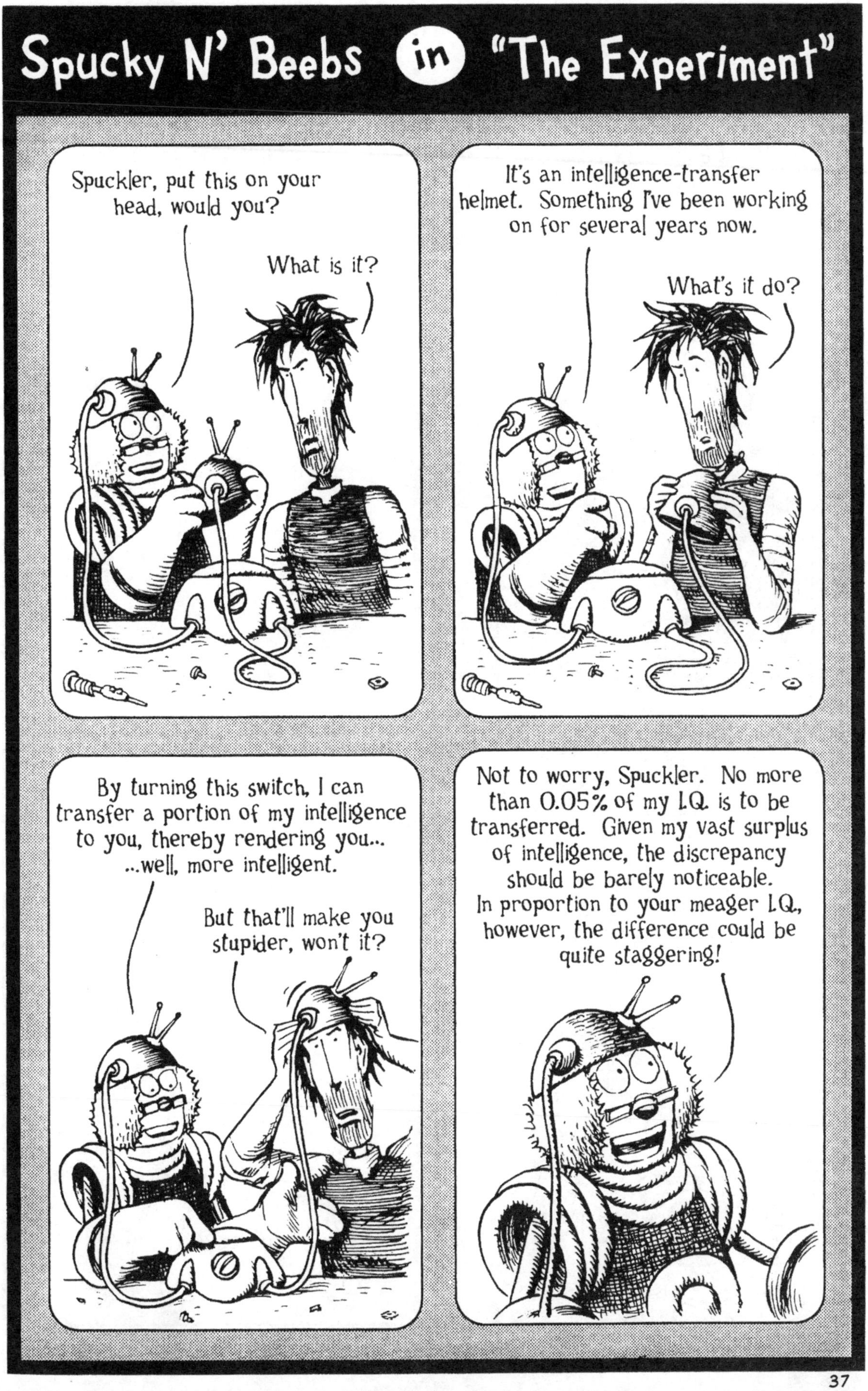
Spucky N' Beebs in "The Experiment"
Spuckler, put this on your head, would you?
What is it?
It's an intelligence-transfer helmet. Something I've been working on for several years now.
What's it do?
By turning this switch, I can transfer a portion of my intelligence to you, thereby rendering you... ...well, more intelligent.
But that'll make you stupider, won't it?
Not to worry, Spuckler. No more than 0.05% of my I.Q. is to be transferred. Given my vast surplus of intelligence, the discrepancy should be barely noticeable. In proportion to your meager I.Q., however, the difference could be quite staggering!

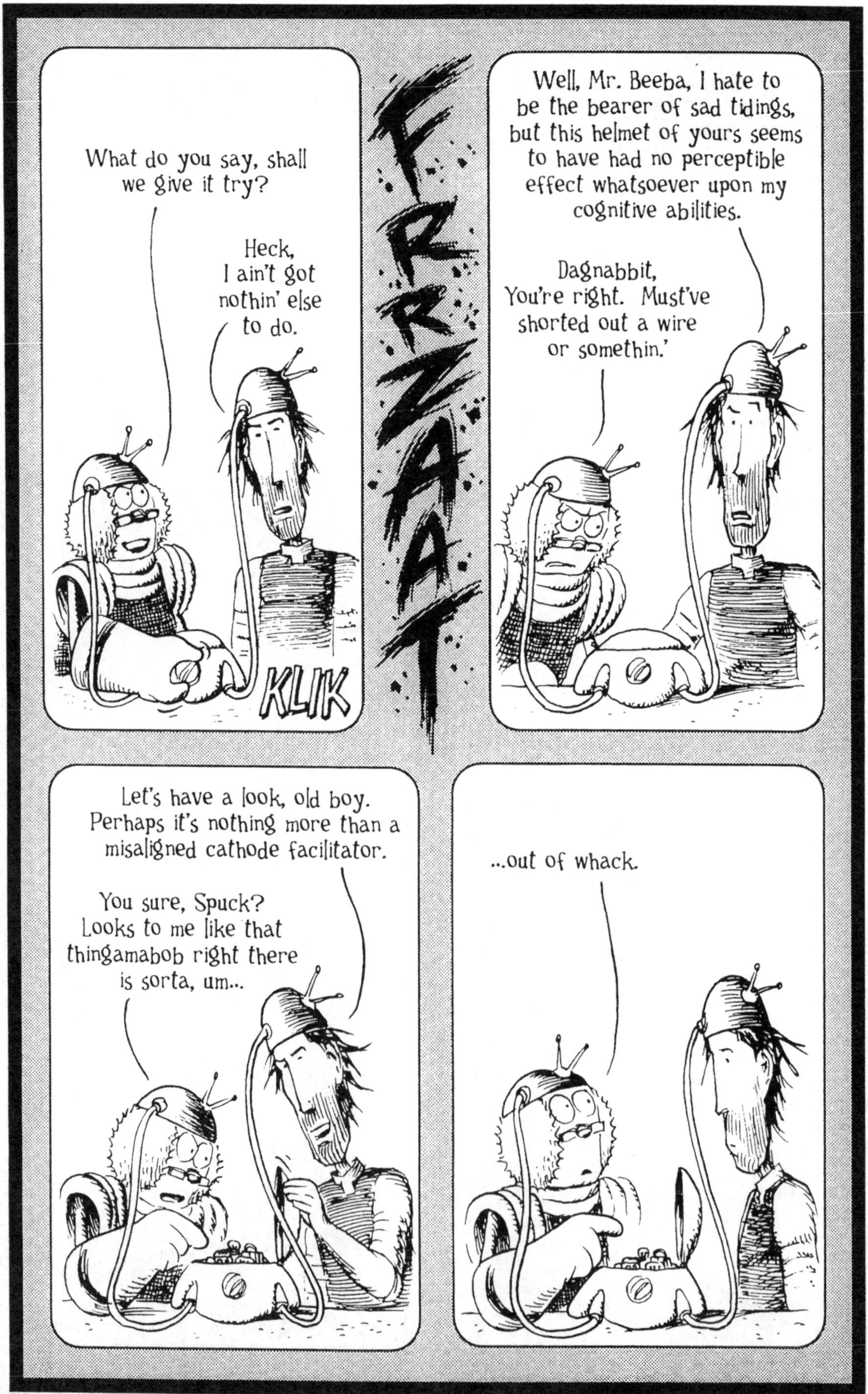
What do you say, shall we give it try?
Heck, I ain't got nothin' else to do.
KLIK
FRRZAAT
Well, Mr. Beeba, I hate to be the bearer of sad tidings, but this helmet of yours seems to have had no perceptible effect whatsoever upon my cognitive abilities.
Dagnabbit, You're right. Must've shorted out a wire or somethin.'
Let's have a look, old boy. Perhaps it's nothing more than a misaligned cathode facilitator.
You sure, Spuck? Looks to me like that thingamabob right there is sorta, um...
...out of whack.

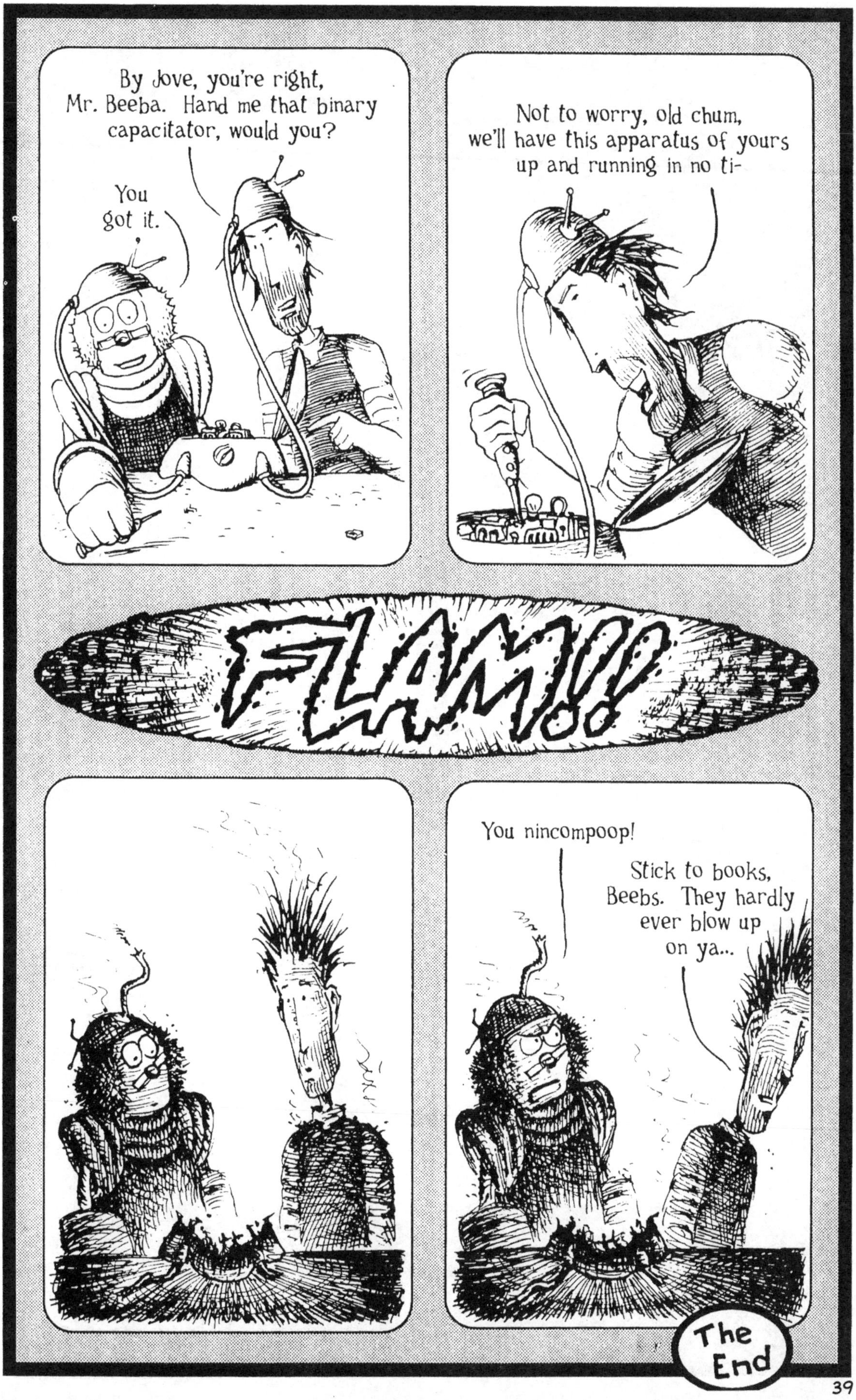
By Jove, you're right, Mr. Beeba. Hand me that binary capacitator, would you?
You got it.
Not to worry, old chum, we'll have this apparatus of yours up and running in no ti-
FLAM!!
You nincompoop!
Stick to books, Beebs. They hardly ever blow up on ya...
The End

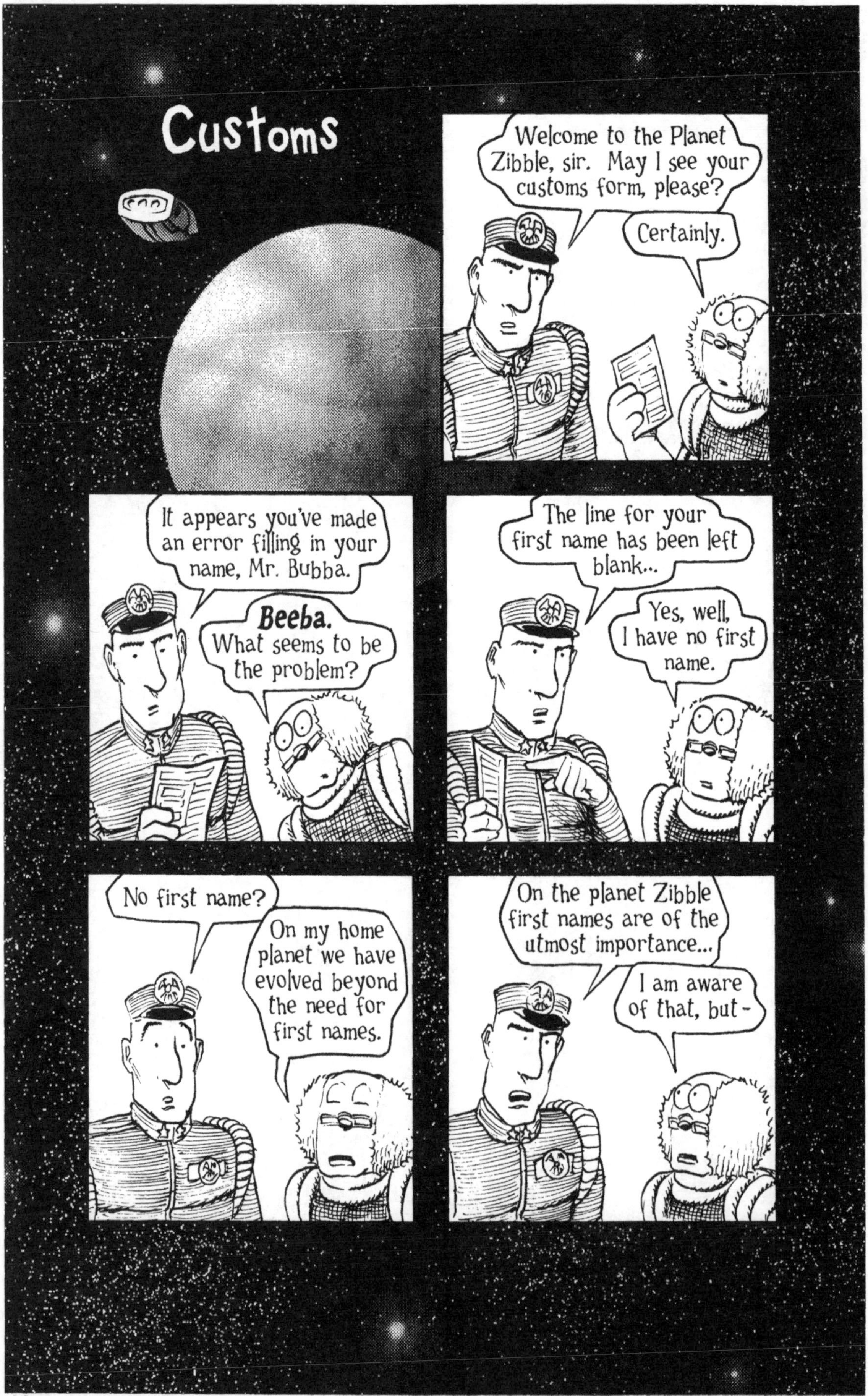
Customs
Welcome to the Planet Zibble, sir. May I see your customs form, please?
Certainly.
It appears you've made an error filling in your name, Mr. Bubba.
Beeba. What seems to be the problem?
The line for your first name has been left blank...
Yes, well, I have no first name.
No first name?
On my home planet we have evolved beyond the need for first names.
On the planet Zibble first names are of the utmost importance...
I am aware of that, but -

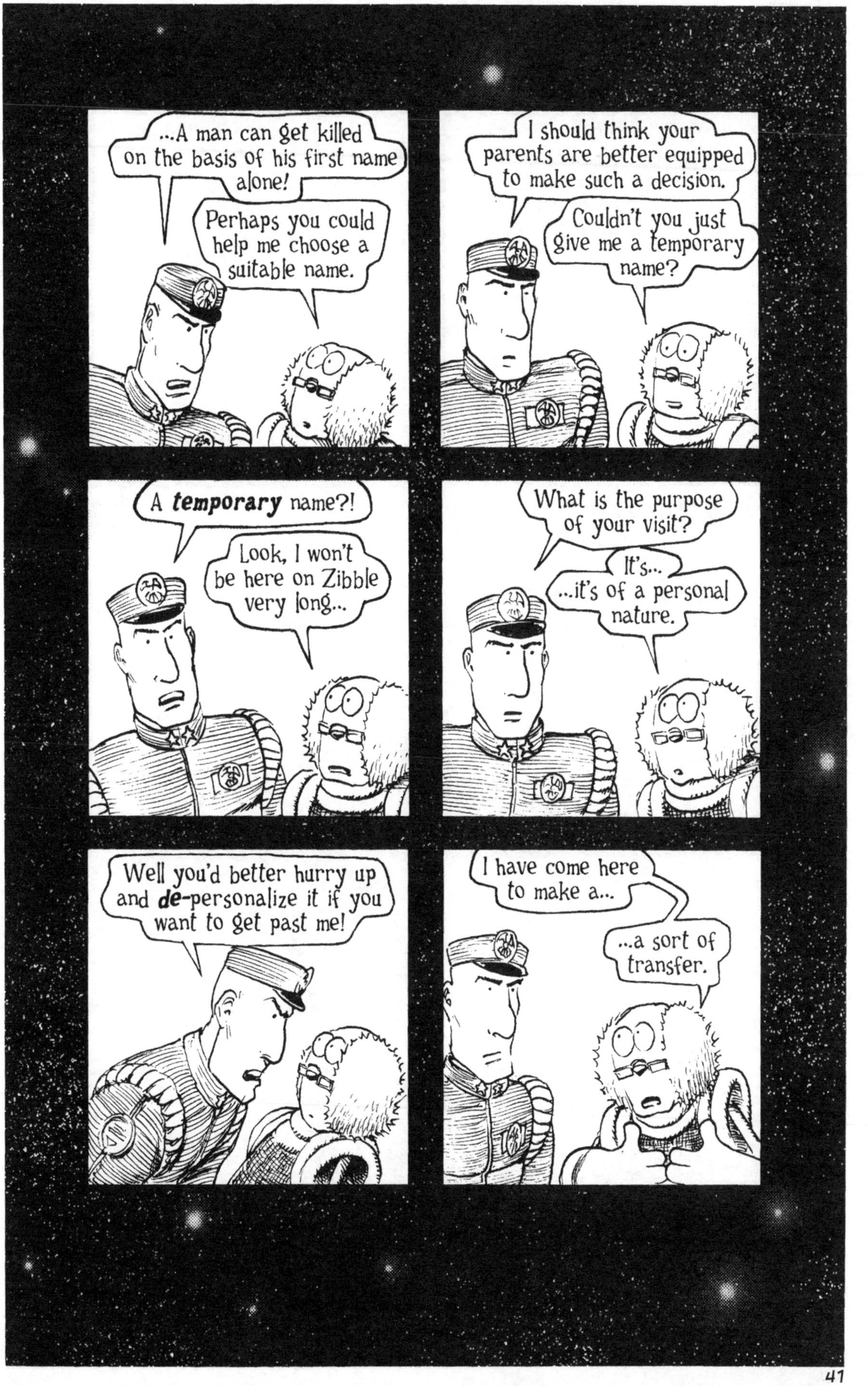
...A man can get killed on the basis of his first name alone!
Perhaps you could help me choose a suitable name.
I should think your parents are better equipped to make such a decision.
Couldn't you just give me a temporary name?
A **temporary** name?!
Look, I won't be here on Zibble very long...
What is the purpose of your visit?
It's...
...it's of a personal nature.
Well you'd better hurry up and **de**-personalize it if you want to get past me!
I have come here to make a...
...a sort of transfer.

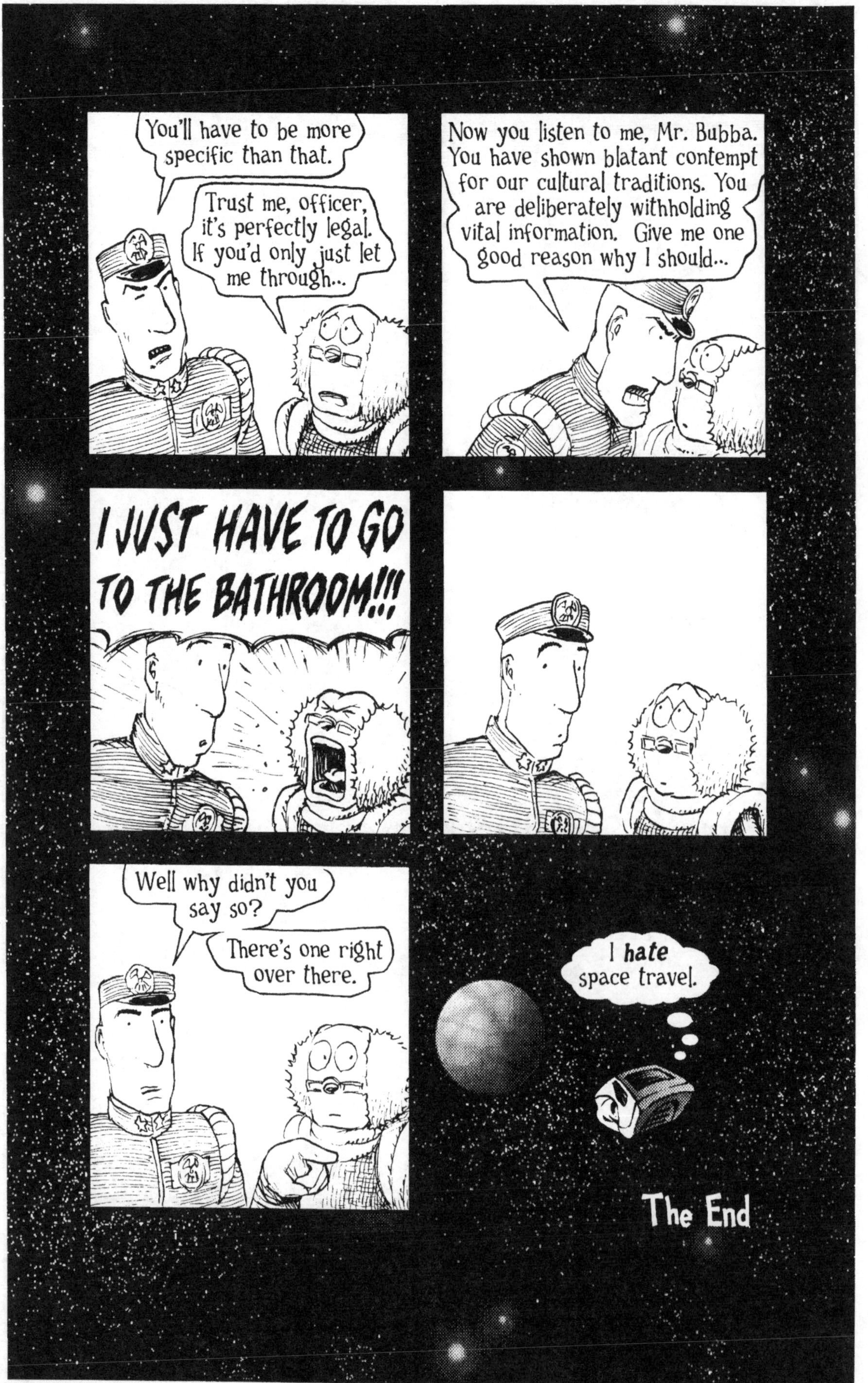
You'll have to be more specific than that.
Trust me, officer, it's perfectly legal. If you'd only just let me through...
Now you listen to me, Mr. Bubba. You have shown blatant contempt for our cultural traditions. You are deliberately withholding vital information. Give me one good reason why I should...
I JUST HAVE TO GO TO THE BATHROOM!!!
Well why didn't you say so?
There's one right over there.
I **hate** space travel.
The End

Mr. Beeba (& Akiko) in

"The Shape of Things To Come"

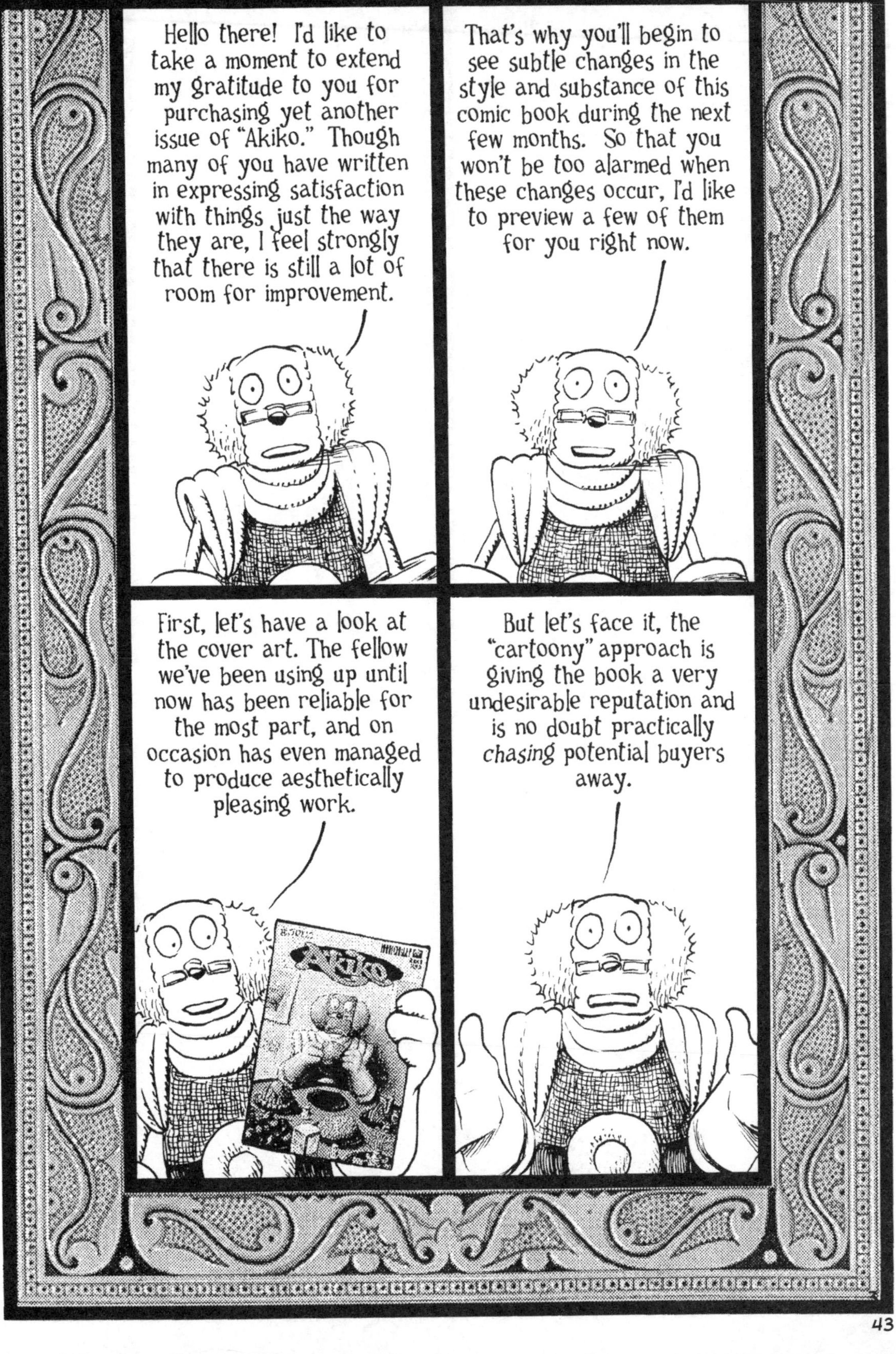

Hello there! I'd like to take a moment to extend my gratitude to you for purchasing yet another issue of "Akiko." Though many of you have written in expressing satisfaction with things just the way they are, I feel strongly that there is still a lot of room for improvement.
That's why you'll begin to see subtle changes in the style and substance of this comic book during the next few months. So that you won't be too alarmed when these changes occur, I'd like to preview a few of them for you right now.
First, let's have a look at the cover art. The fellow we've been using up until now has been reliable for the most part, and on occasion has even managed to produce aesthetically pleasing work.
Akiko
But let's face it, the "cartoony" approach is giving the book a very undesirable reputation and is no doubt practically *chasing* potential buyers away.

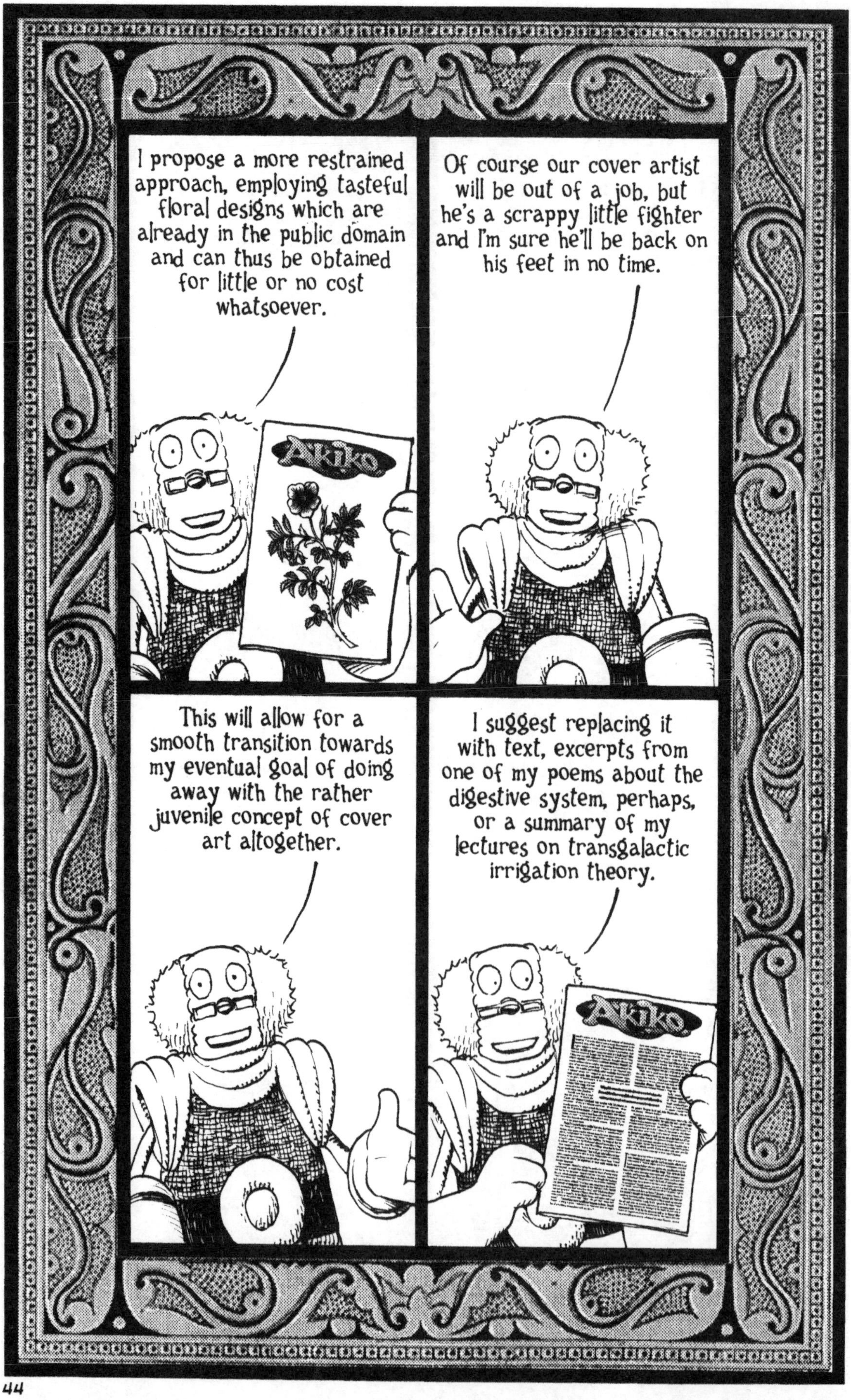
I propose a more restrained approach, employing tasteful floral designs which are already in the public domain and can thus be obtained for little or no cost whatsoever.
Akiko
Of course our cover artist will be out of a job, but he's a scrappy little fighter and I'm sure he'll be back on his feet in no time.
This will allow for a smooth transition towards my eventual goal of doing away with the rather juvenile concept of cover art altogether.
I suggest replacing it with text, excerpts from one of my poems about the digestive system, perhaps, or a summary of my lectures on transgalactic irrigation theory.
Akiko

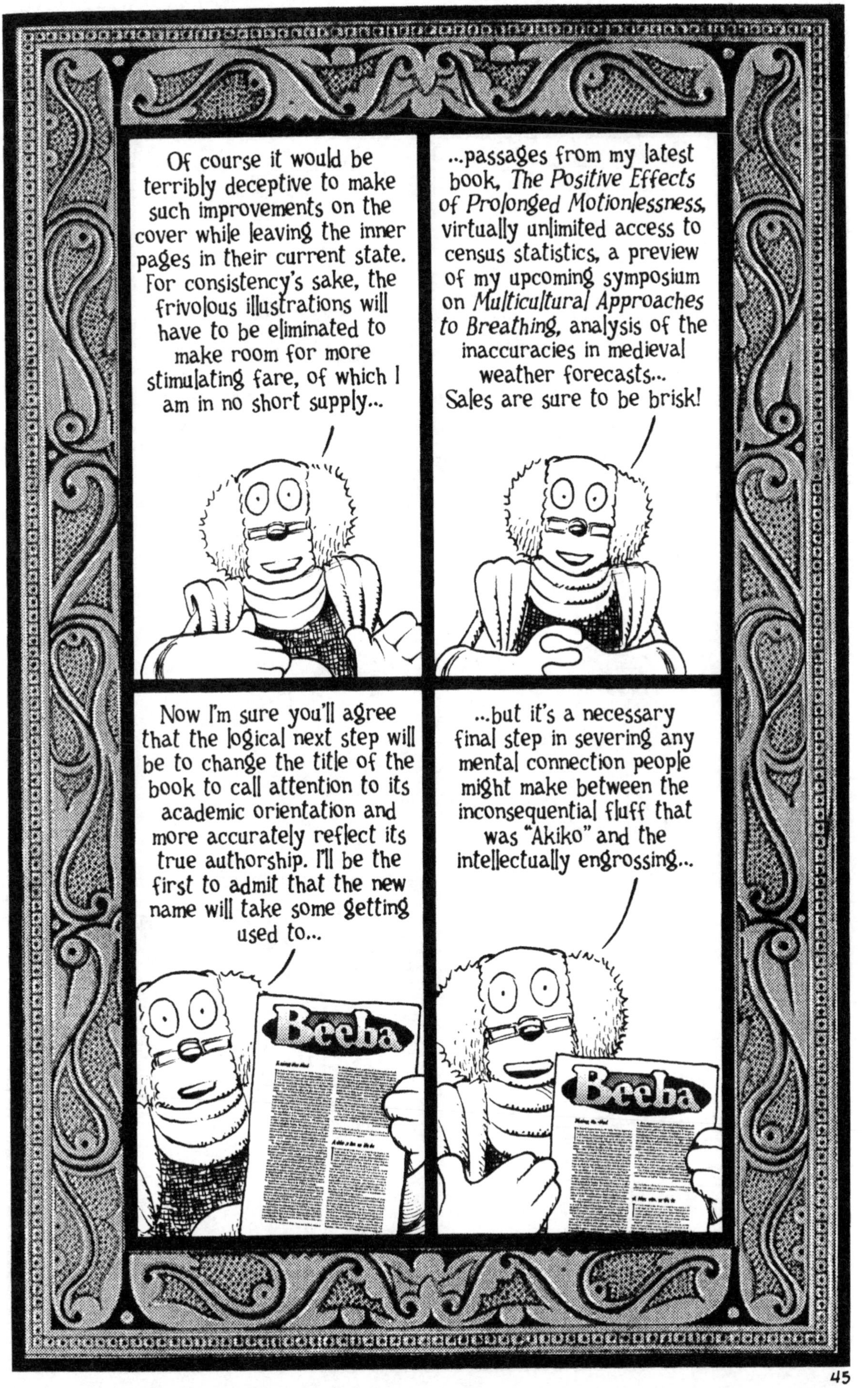
Of course it would be terribly deceptive to make such improvements on the cover while leaving the inner pages in their current state. For consistency's sake, the frivolous illustrations will have to be eliminated to make room for more stimulating fare, of which I am in no short supply...
...passages from my latest book, *The Positive Effects of Prolonged Motionlessness*, virtually unlimited access to census statistics, a preview of my upcoming symposium on *Multicultural Approaches to Breathing*, analysis of the inaccuracies in medieval weather forecasts... Sales are sure to be brisk!
Now I'm sure you'll agree that the logical next step will be to change the title of the book to call attention to its academic orientation and more accurately reflect its true authorship. I'll be the first to admit that the new name will take some getting used to...
Beeba
...but it's a necessary final step in severing any mental connection people might make between the inconsequential fluff that was "Akiko" and the intellectually engrossing...
Beeba

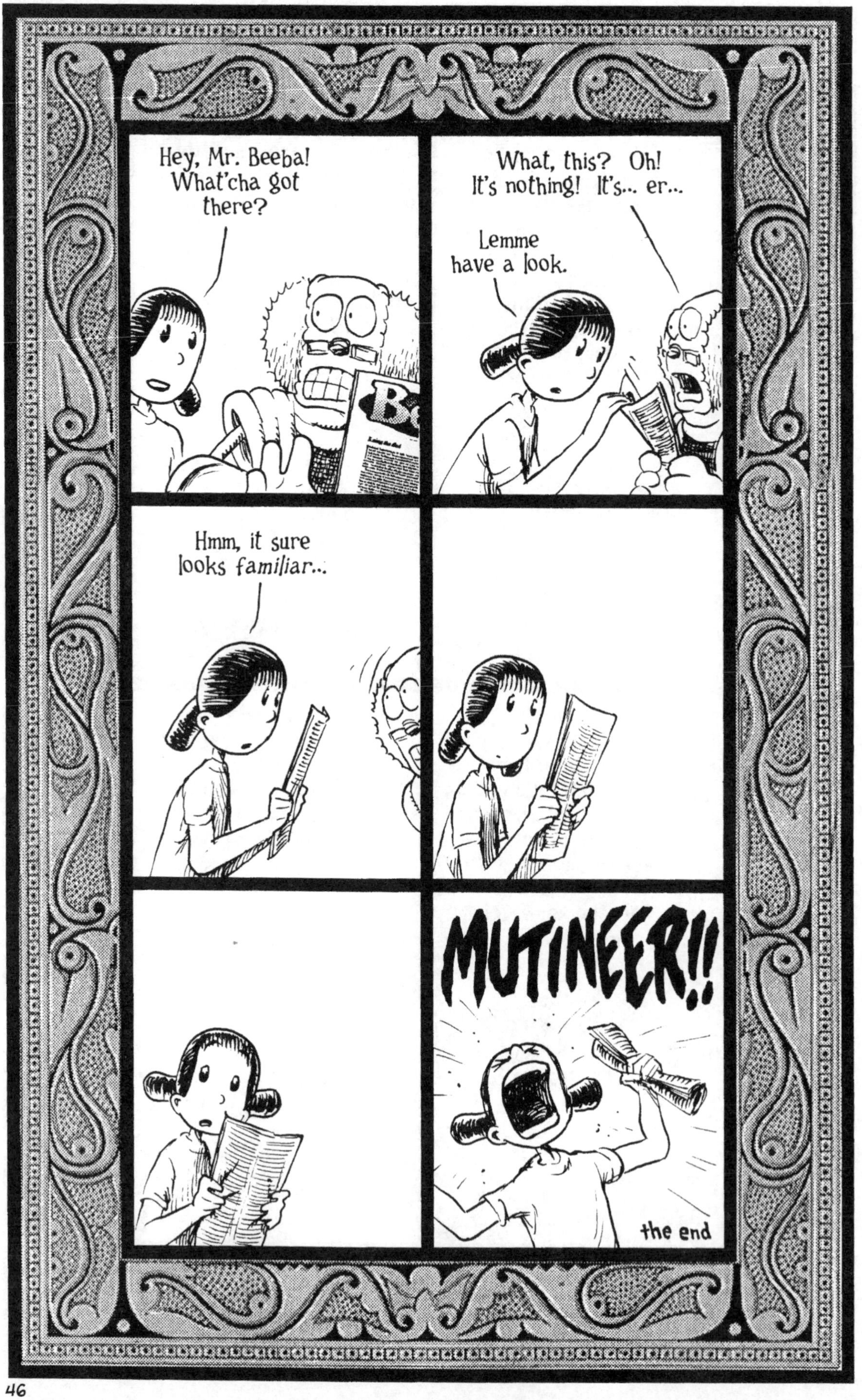

Hey, Mr. Beeba! What'cha got there?
What, this? Oh! It's nothing! It's... er...
Lemme have a look.
Hmm, it sure looks familiar...
MUTINEER!!
the end

Thirty Six Ways

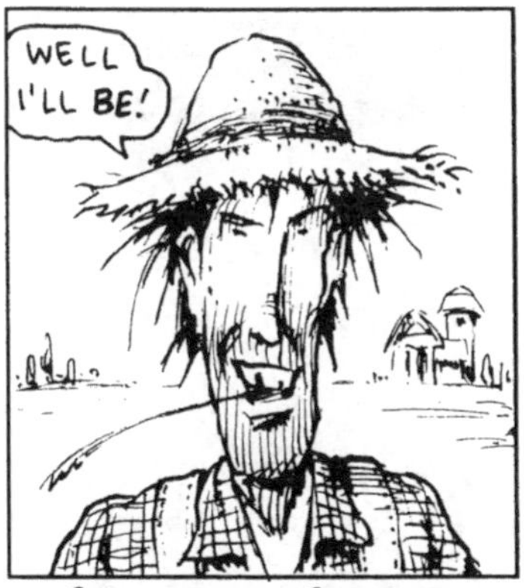
WELL I'LL BE!

Country Spuck

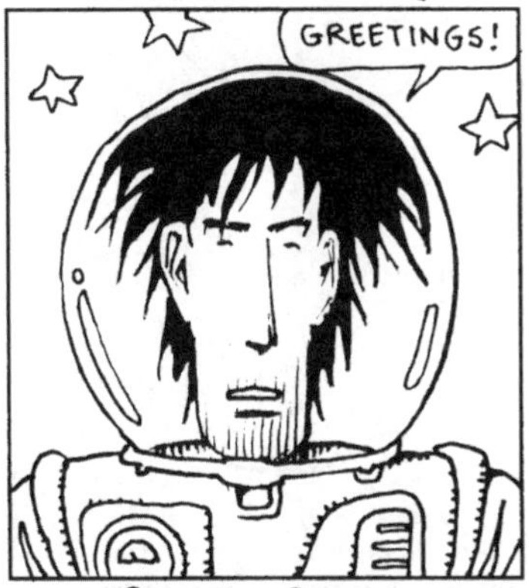
GREETINGS!

Space Spuck

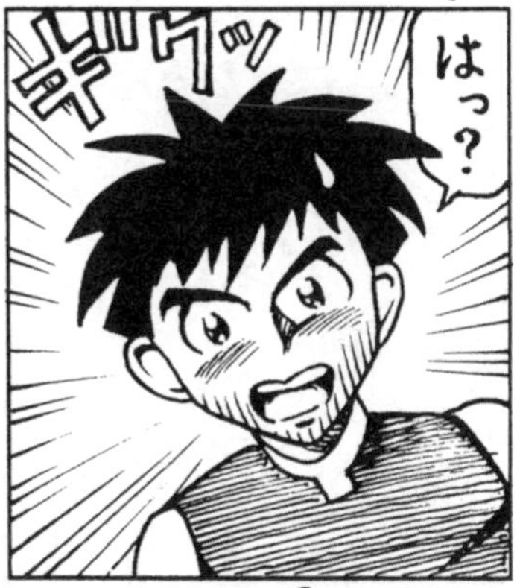
はっ?

Manga Spuck

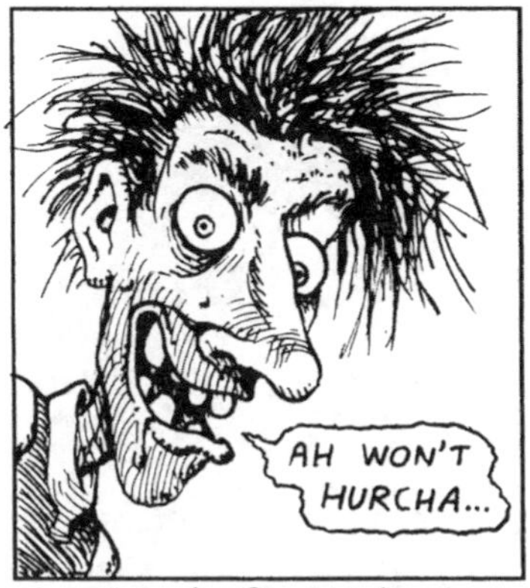
AH WON'T HURCHA...

Spuck Gone Wrong

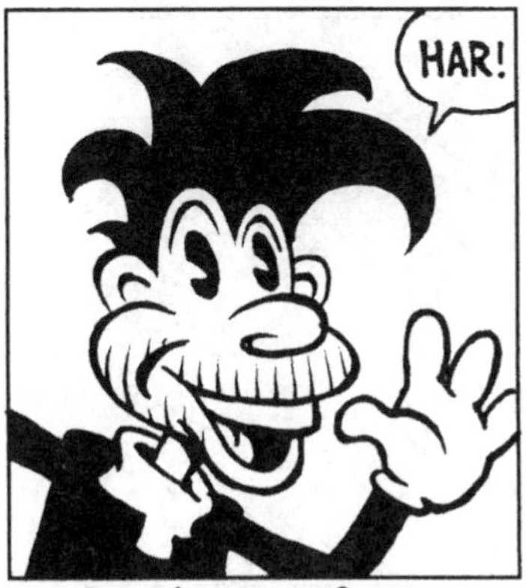
HAR!

Cartoony Spuck

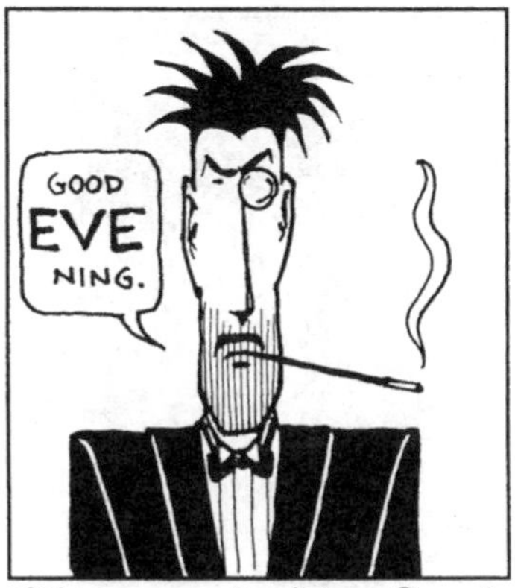
GOOD EVE NING.

Villanous Bad Guy Spuck

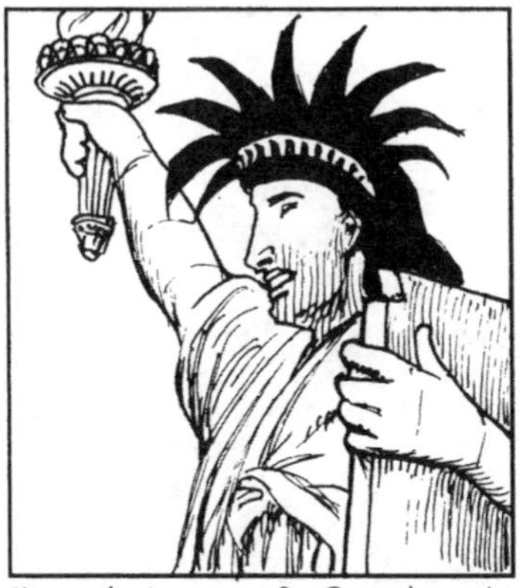

The Statue of Spuckerty

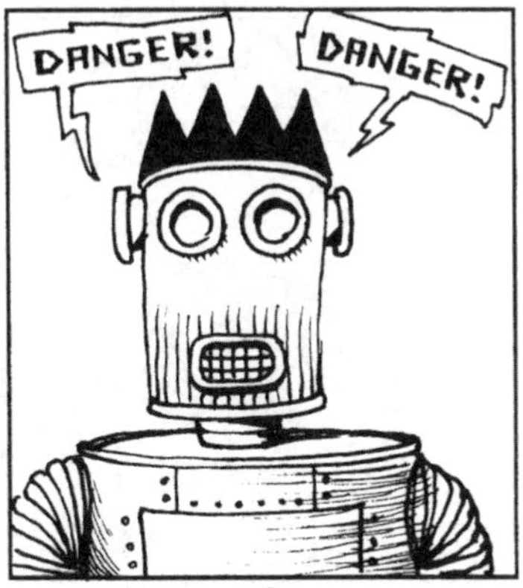
DANGER!
DANGER!

Robo Spuck

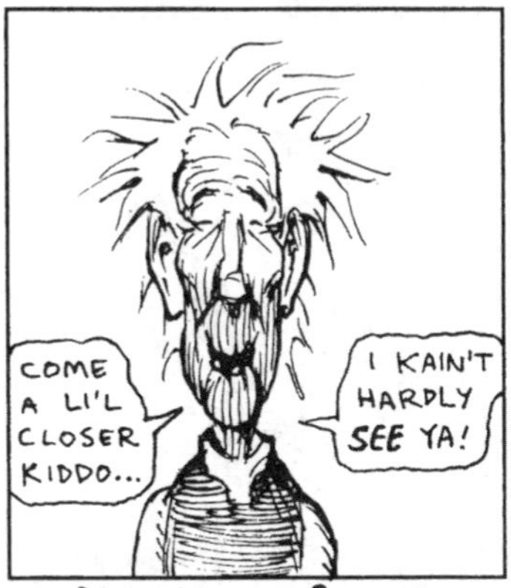
COME A LI'L CLOSER KIDDO...
I KAIN'T HARDLY SEE YA!

Old Man Spuck

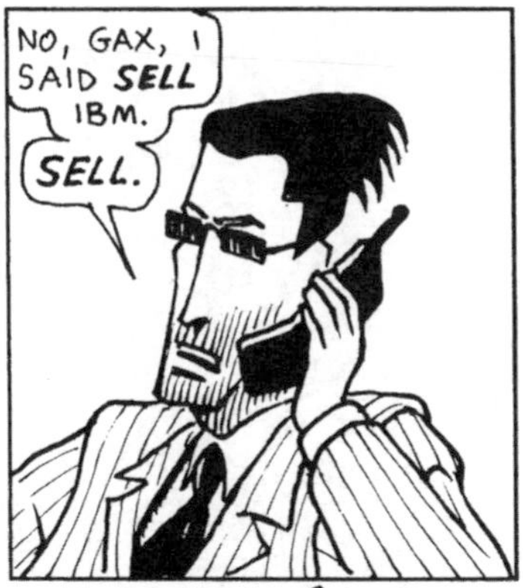
NO, GAX, I SAID SELL IBM.
SELL.

Hot Shot Spuck

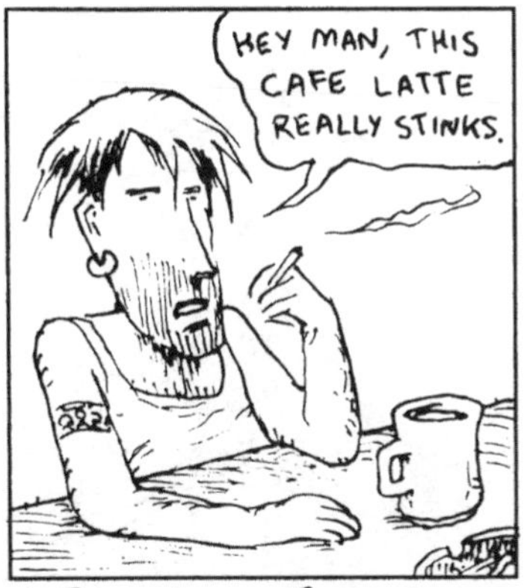
HEY MAN, THIS CAFE LATTE REALLY STINKS.

Slacker Spuck

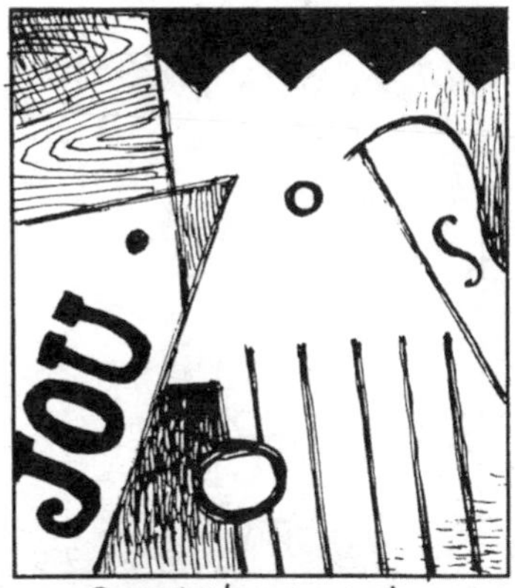

Cubist Spuck

to Draw Spuckler

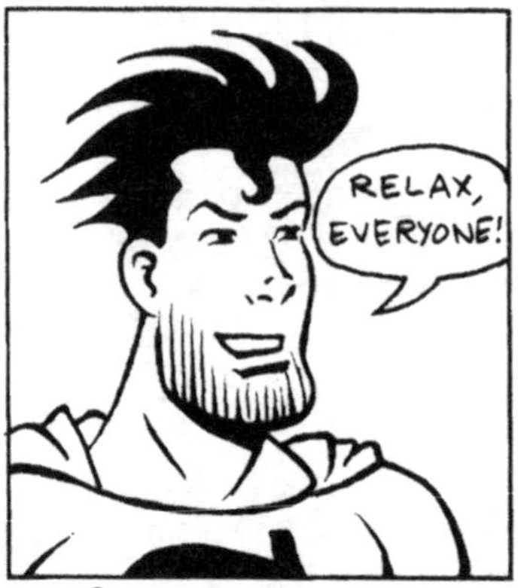
RELAX, EVERYONE!

Super spuck

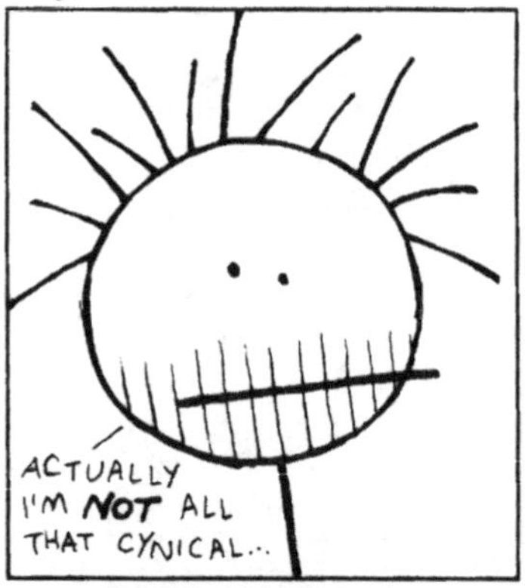
ACTUALLY I'M **NOT** ALL THAT CYNICAL...

Cynicalspuck

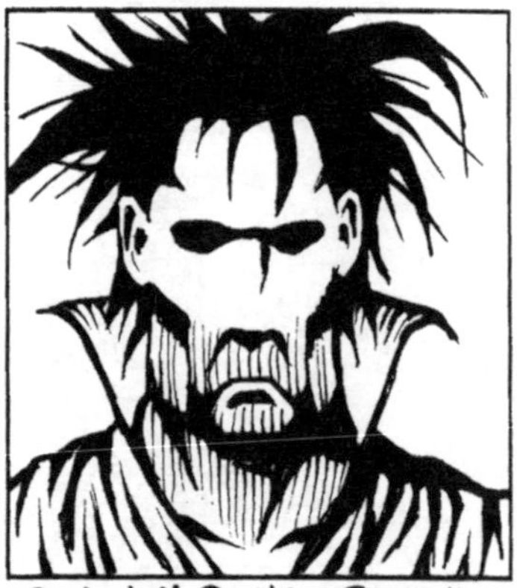

Grim 'N' Gritty Spuck

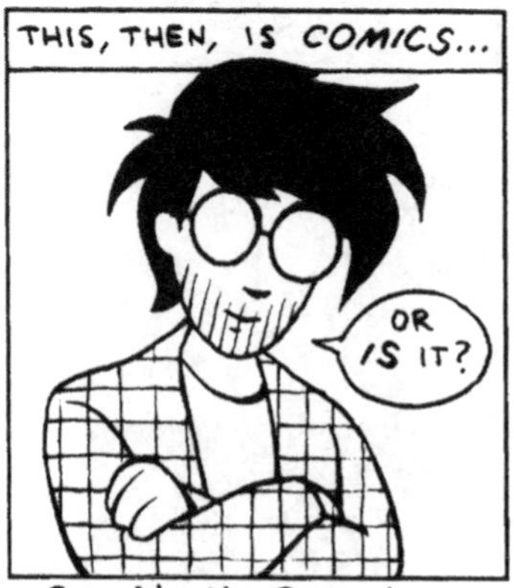
THIS, THEN, IS *COMICS*...
OR *IS* IT?

Scott McSpuck

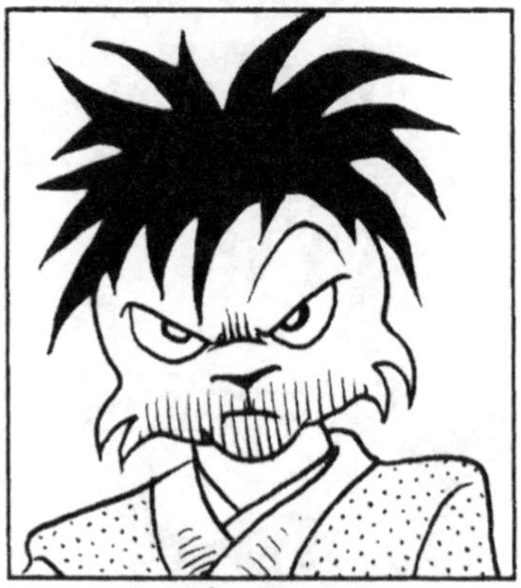

Usagi Yospucko

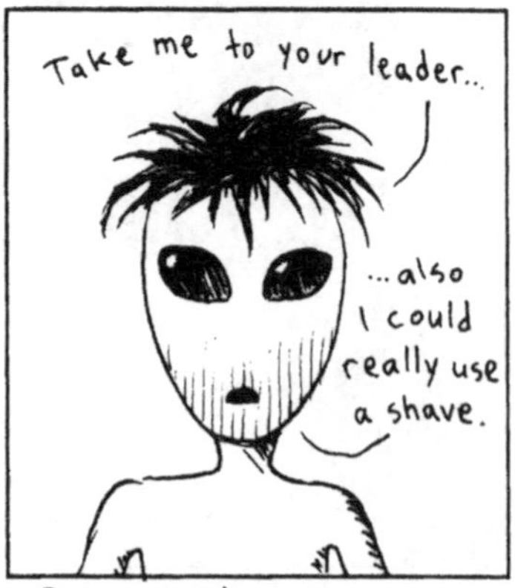
Take me to your leader...
...also I could really use a shave.

Space Alien Spuck

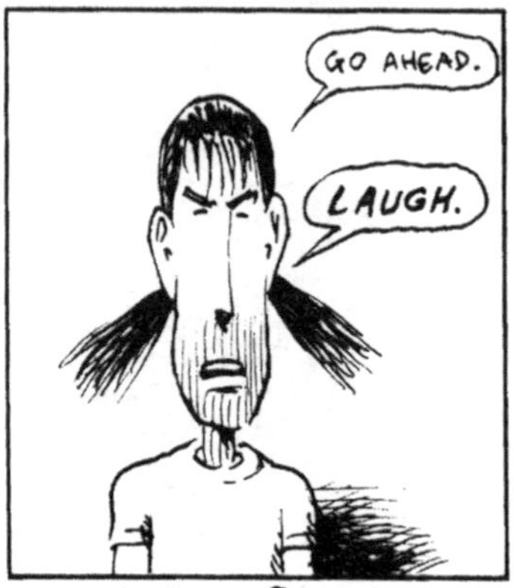
GO AHEAD.
LAUGH.

Akiko Spuck

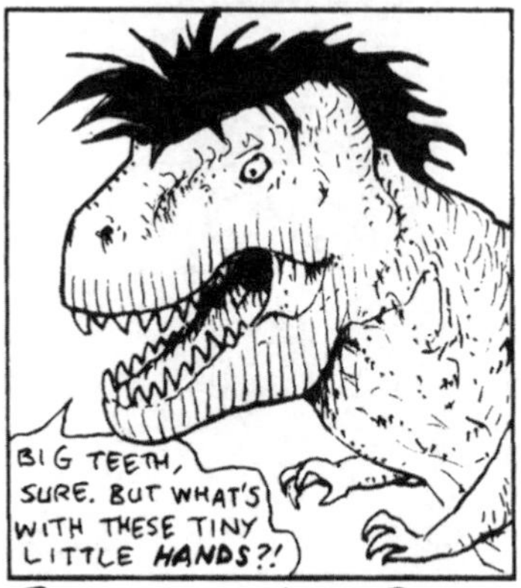
BIG TEETH, SURE. BUT WHAT'S WITH THESE TINY LITTLE *HANDS*?!

Tyrannospuckus Rex

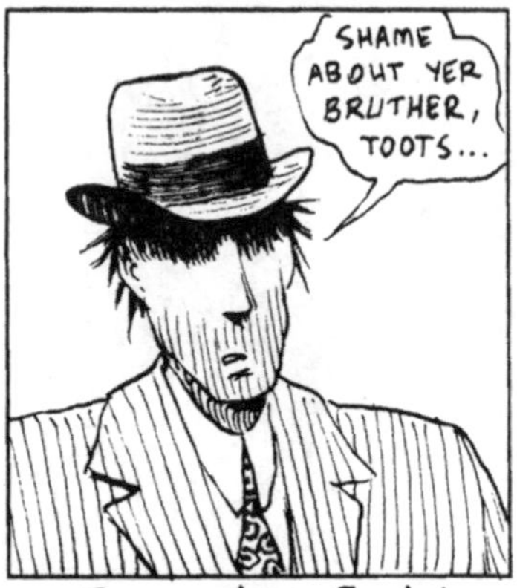
SHAME ABOUT YER BRUTHER, TOOTS...

Gangster Spuck

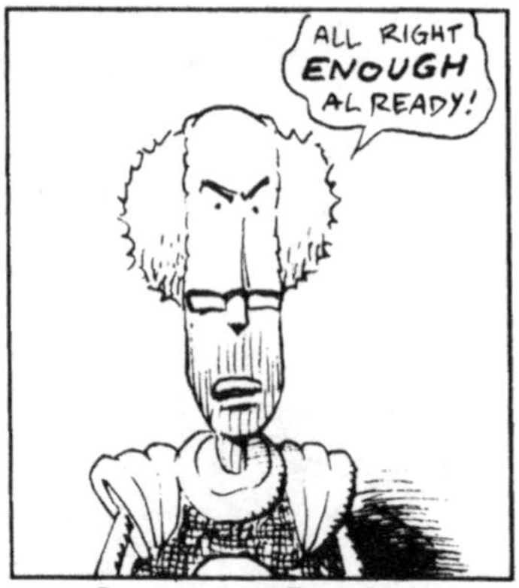
ALL RIGHT **ENOUGH** ALREADY!

Beeba Spuck

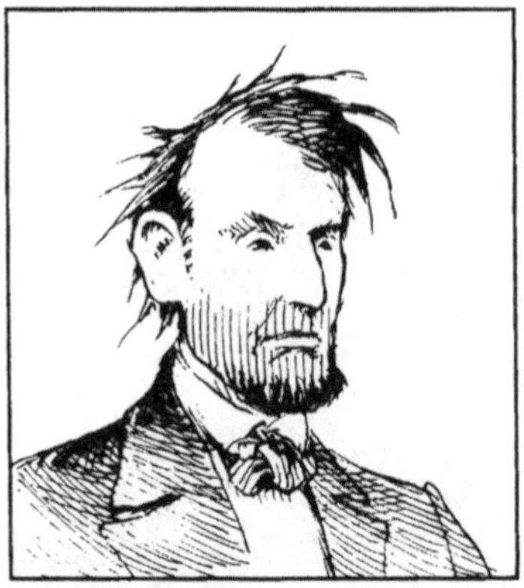

Spuckraham Lincoln

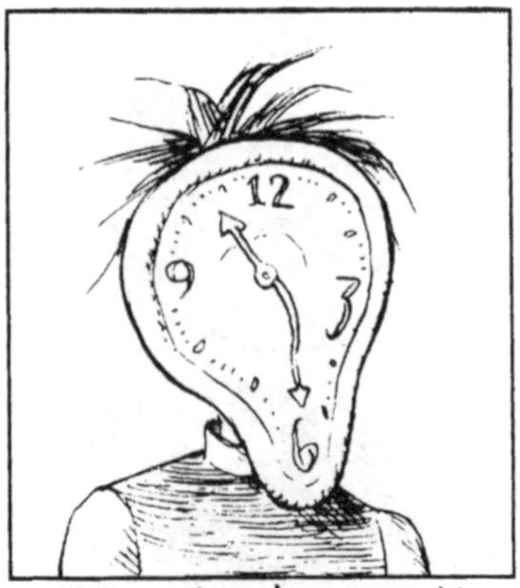
12
9
3
6

Spuckador Dali

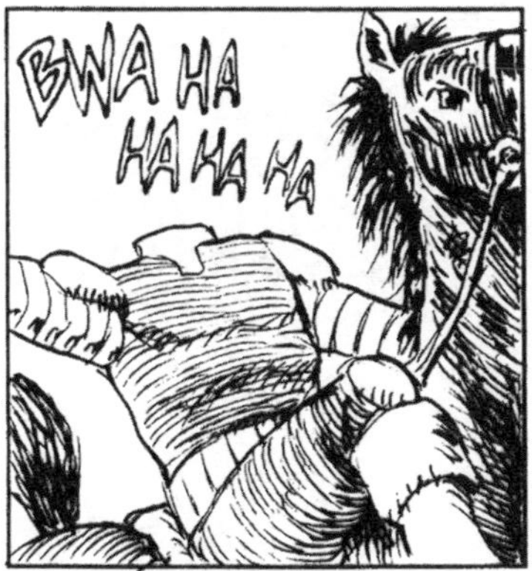
BWA HA
HA HA HA
The Headless Spuckman

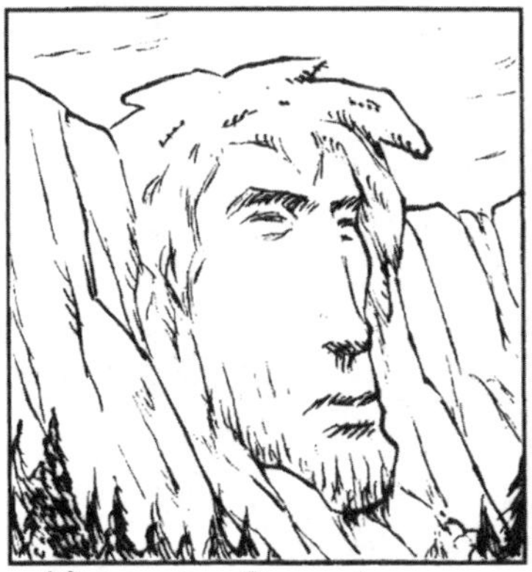
Mount Spuckmore

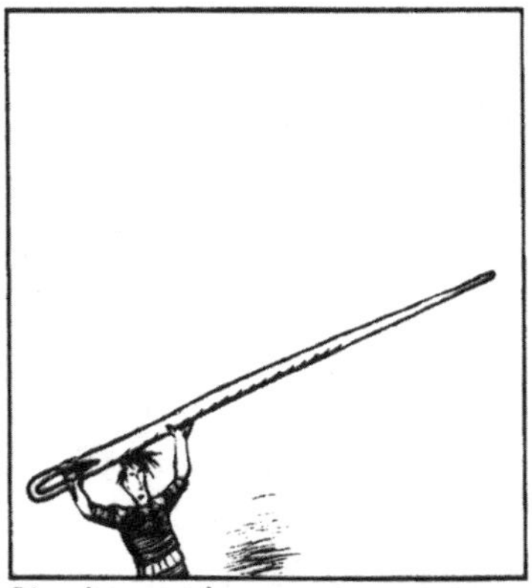
The Incredible Shrinking Spuck

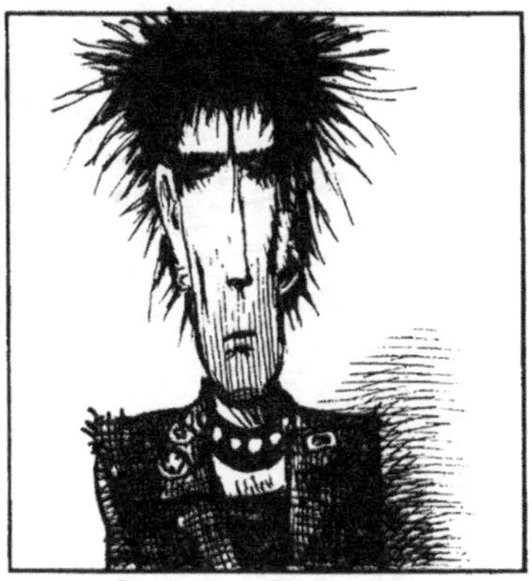
Goth Spuck

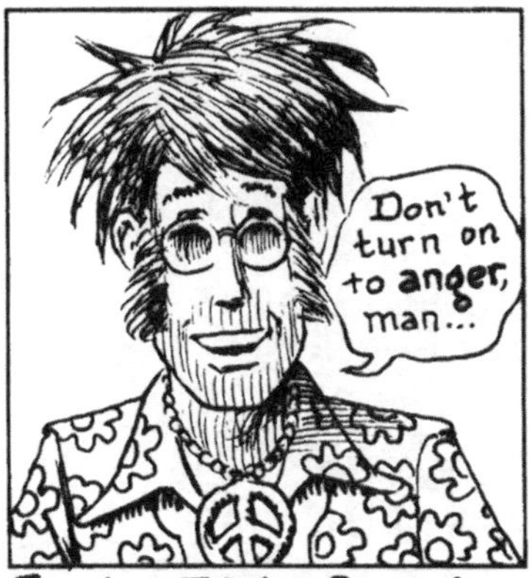
Don't turn on to anger, man...
Early 70's Spuck

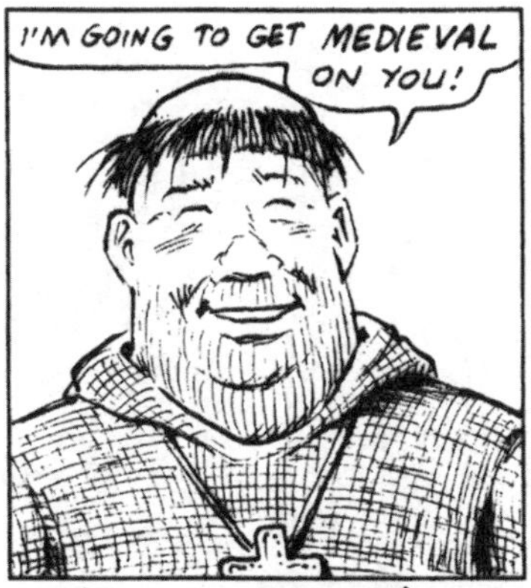
I'M GOING TO GET MEDIEVAL ON YOU!
Friar Spuck

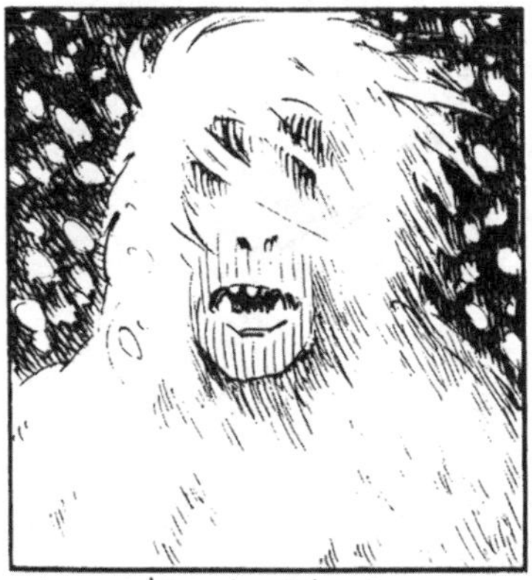
The Abominable Spuckman

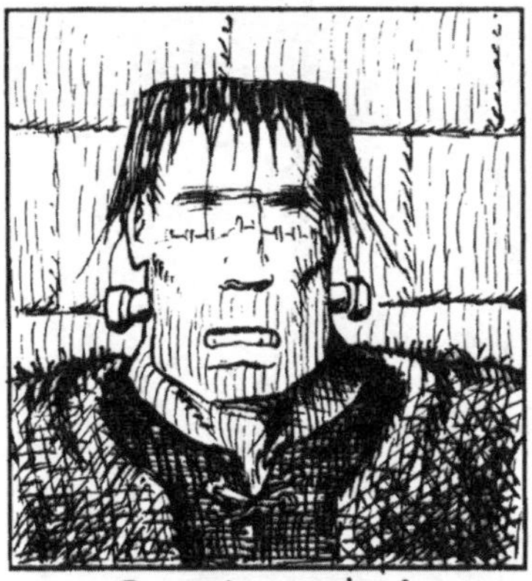
Spuckenstein

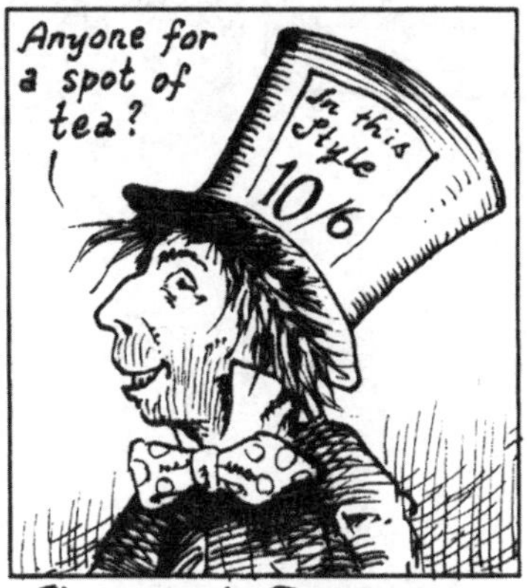
Anyone for a spot of tea?
In this Style 10/6
The Mad Spucker

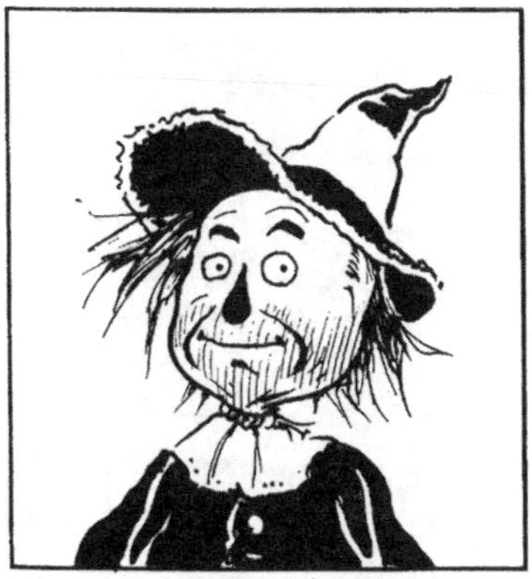
the Spuckcrow

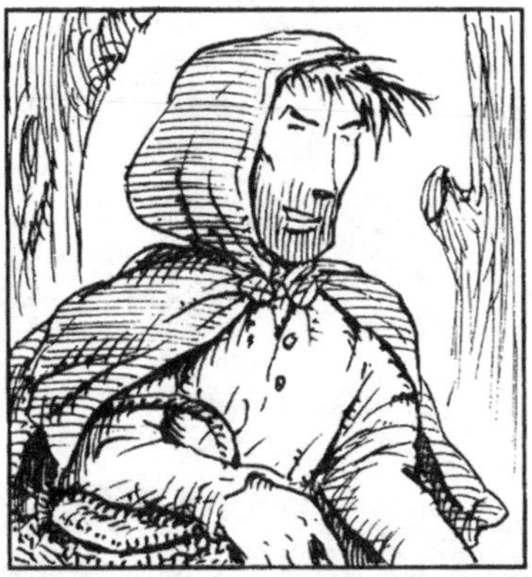
Litte Red Spuckinghood

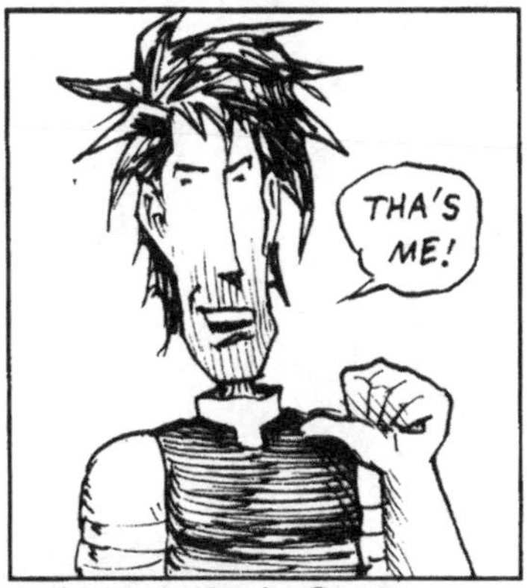
THA'S ME!
Plain Old Spuck

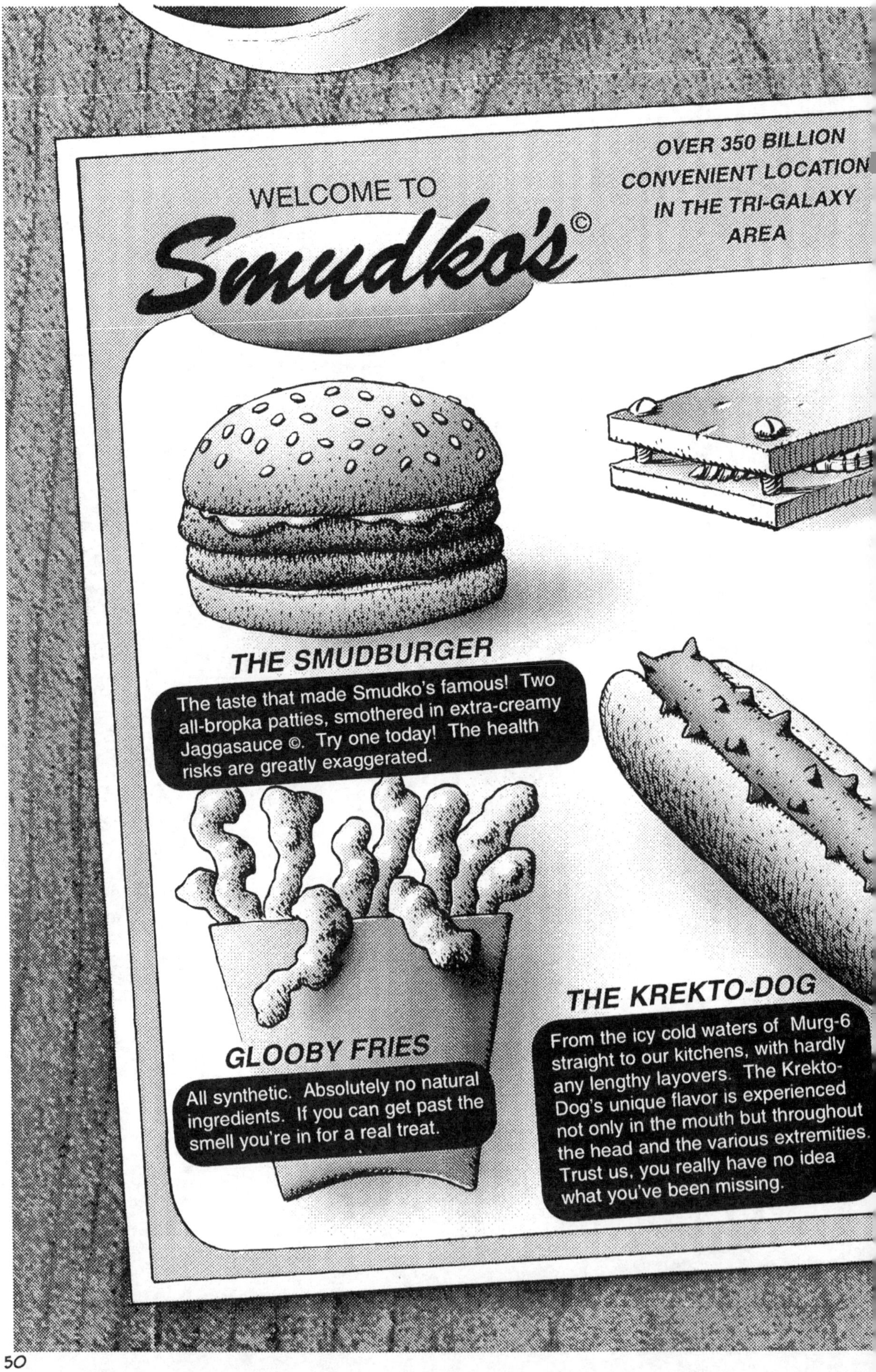
OVER 350 BILLION CONVENIENT LOCATION IN THE TRI-GALAXY AREA
WELCOME TO
Smudko's©
THE SMUDBURGER
The taste that made Smudko's famous! Two all-bropka patties, smothered in extra-creamy Jaggasauce ©. Try one today! The health risks are greatly exaggerated.
GLOOBY FRIES
All synthetic. Absolutely no natural ingredients. If you can get past the smell you're in for a real treat.
THE KREKTO-DOG
From the icy cold waters of Murg-6 straight to our kitchens, with hardly any lengthy layovers. The Krekto-Dog's unique flavor is experienced not only in the mouth but throughout the head and the various extremities. Trust us, you really have no idea what you've been missing.

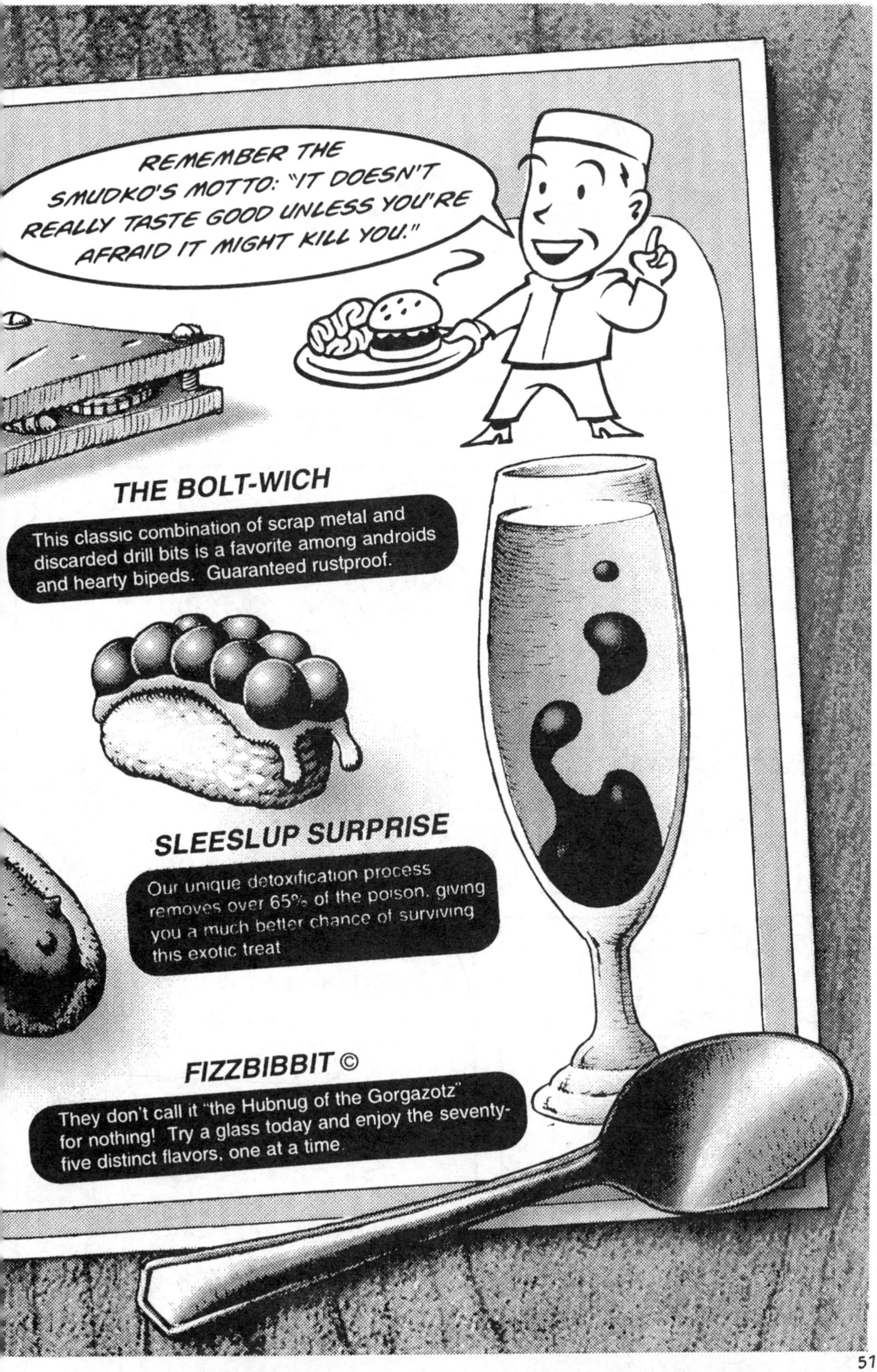
REMEMBER THE SMUDKO'S MOTTO: "IT DOESN'T REALLY TASTE GOOD UNLESS YOU'RE AFRAID IT MIGHT KILL YOU."
THE BOLT-WICH
This classic combination of scrap metal and discarded drill bits is a favorite among androids and hearty bipeds. Guaranteed rustproof.
SLEESLUP SURPRISE
Our unique detoxification process removes over 65% of the poison, giving you a much better chance of surviving this exotic treat.
FIZZBIBBIT ©
They don't call it "the Hubnug of the Gorgazotz" for nothing! Try a glass today and enjoy the seventy-five distinct flavors, one at a time.

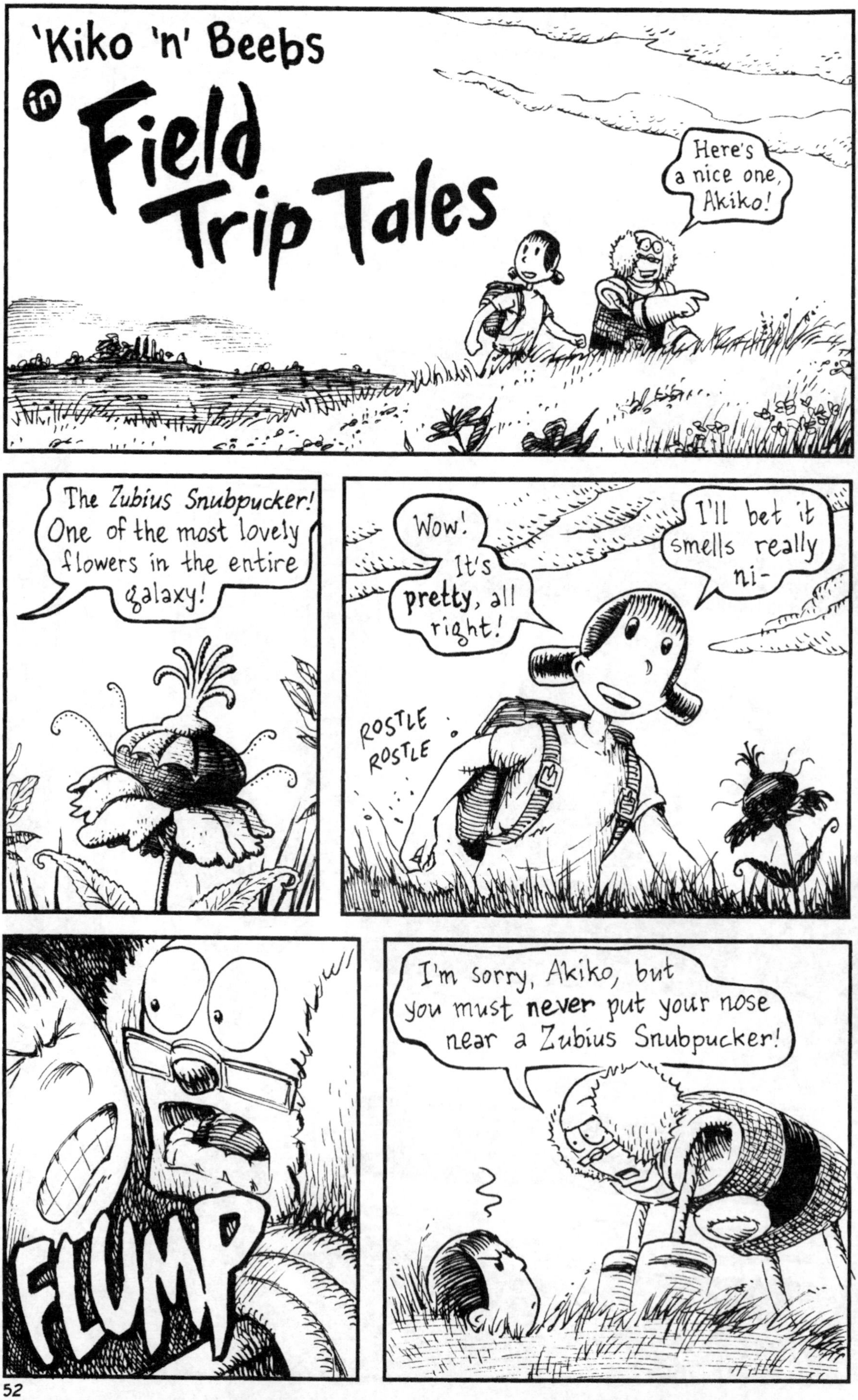
'Kiko 'n' Beebs
in
Field Trip Tales
Here's a nice one, Akiko!
The Zubius Snubpucker! One of the most lovely flowers in the entire galaxy!
Wow! It's **pretty**, all right!
I'll bet it smells really ni-
ROSTLE ROSTLE
FLUMP
I'm sorry, Akiko, but you must **never** put your nose near a Zubius Snubpucker!

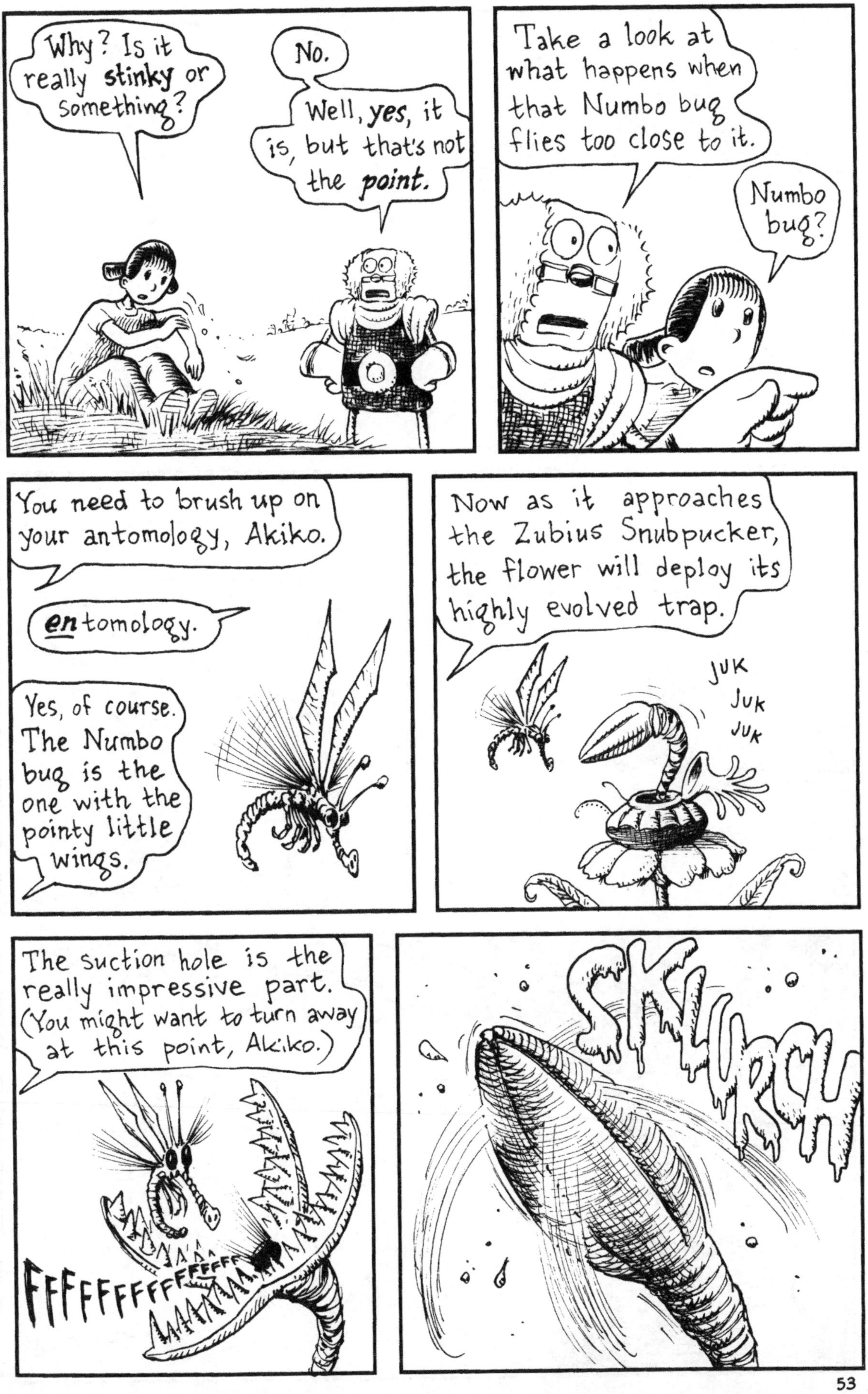
Why? Is it really **stinky** or something?
No.
Well, ***yes***, it is, but that's not the ***point***.
Take a look at what happens when that Numbo bug flies too close to it.
Numbo bug?
You need to brush up on your antomology, Akiko.
entomology.
Yes, of course. The Numbo bug is the one with the pointy little wings.
Now as it approaches the Zubius Snubpucker, the flower will deploy its highly evolved trap.
JUK
JUK
JUK
The suction hole is the really impressive part. (You might want to turn away at this point, Akiko.)
FFFFFFFFFFFFFFF
SKLURCH

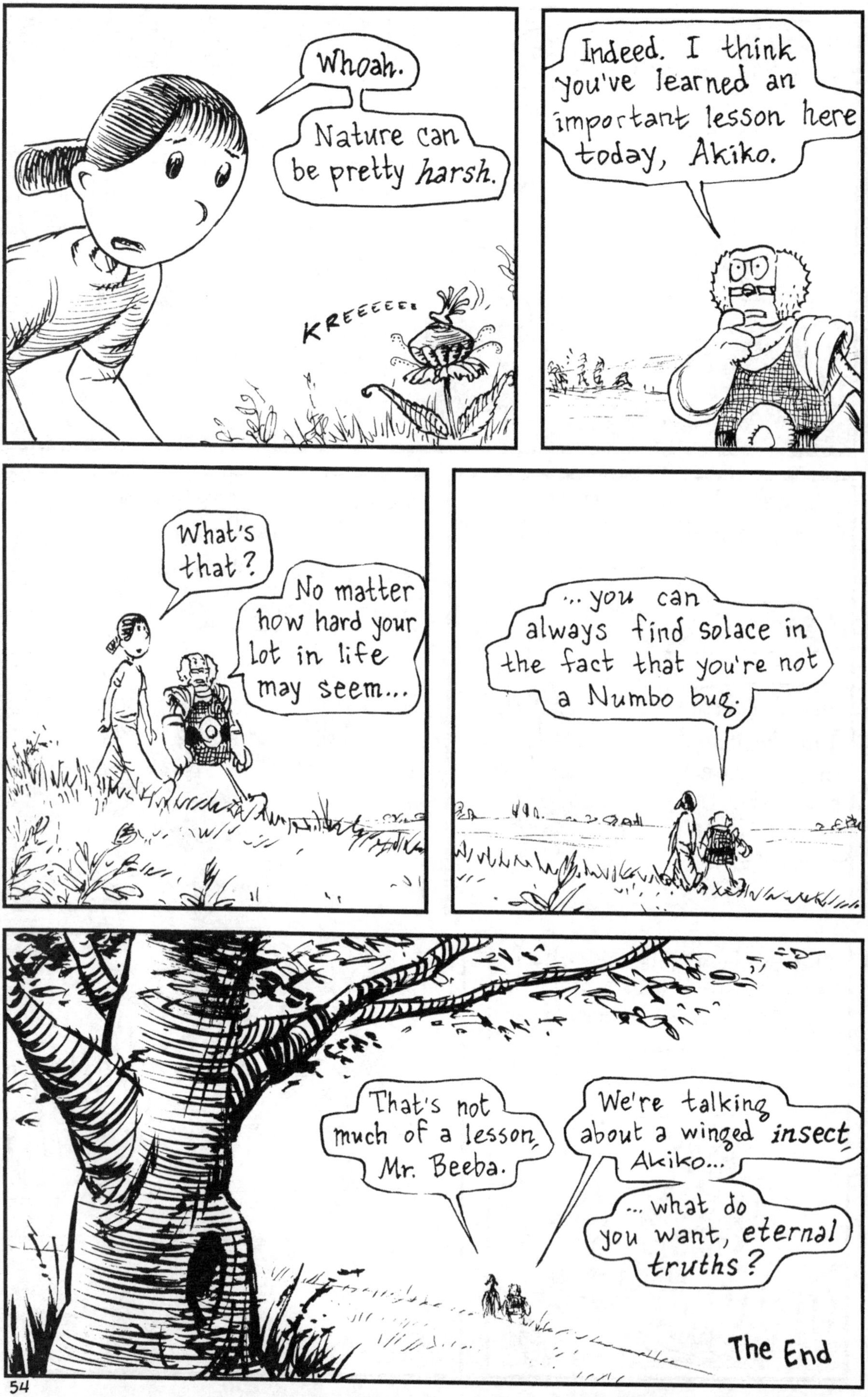
Whoah.
Nature can be pretty *harsh*.
KREEEEEE
Indeed. I think you've learned an important lesson here today, Akiko.
What's that?
No matter how hard your lot in life may seem...
...you can always find solace in the fact that you're not a Numbo bug.
That's not much of a lesson, Mr. Beeba.
We're talking about a winged *insect* Akiko...
...what do you want, eternal *truths*?
The End

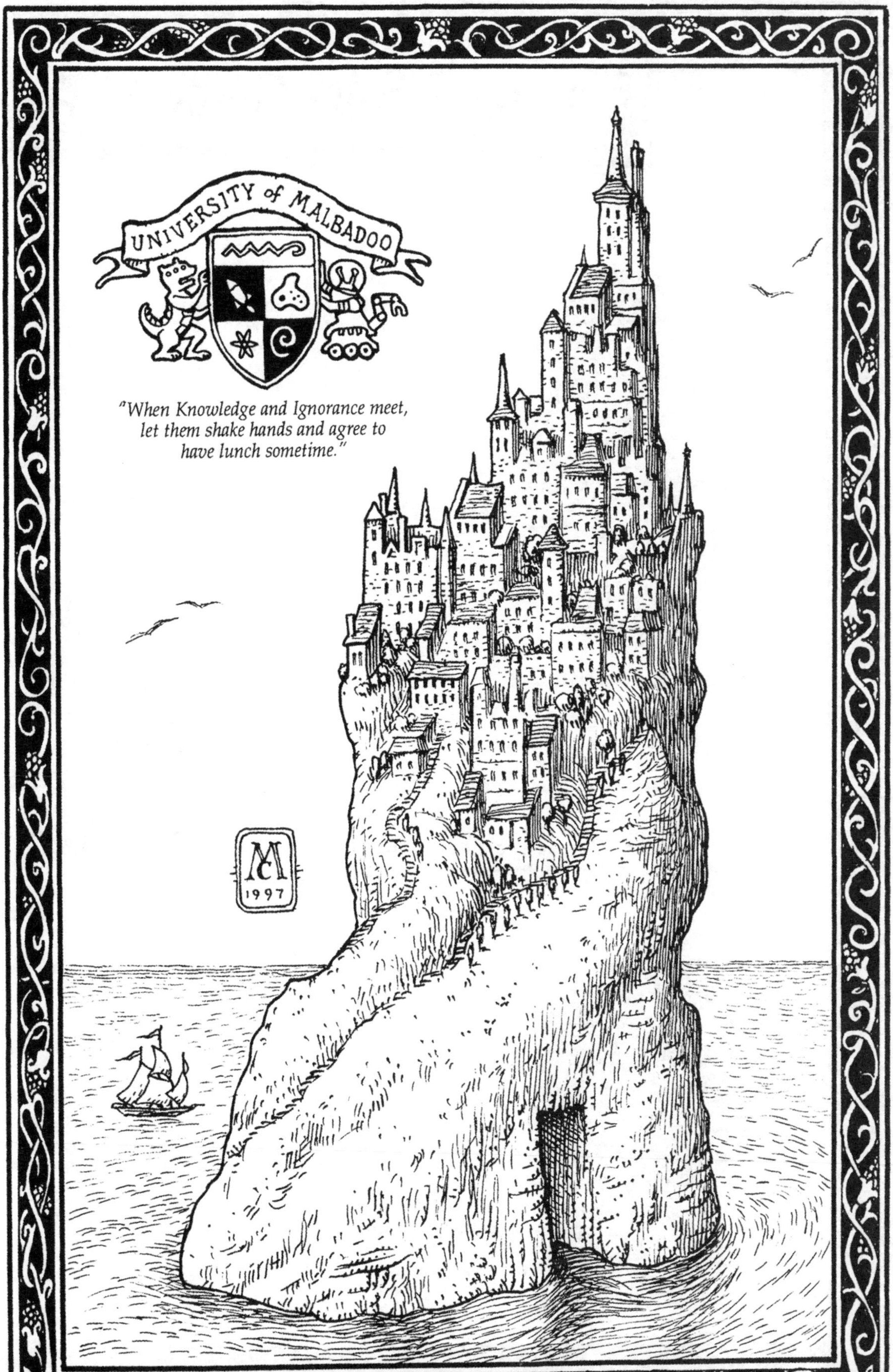
UNIVERSITY of MALBADOO
"When Knowledge and Ignorance meet,
let them shake hands and agree to
have lunch sometime."
MC
1997

A Very Silly Guide to Extr

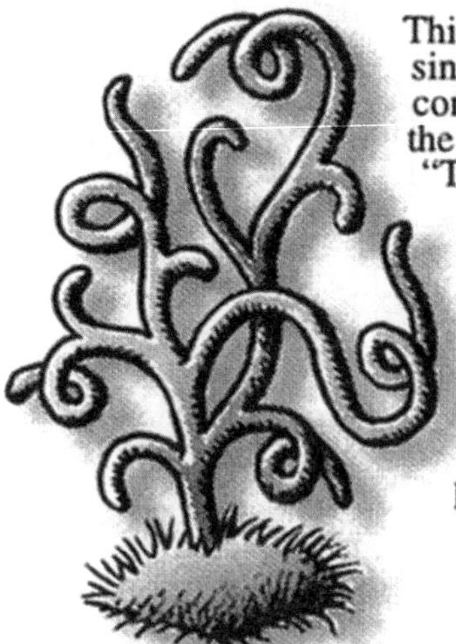

The Streptidius Hern

This remarkable plant has fascinated botanists since the dawn of time (or time immemorial, whichever comes first). The Streptidius Hern, commonly known as the "Little Hern," and known more commonly still as "That Little Plant with the Curly Things," requires neither sunlight nor water for its survival, and is thus free to grow wherever it chooses, so long as it respects zoning laws. The Streptidius Hern was named after the famous botanist, Leopold Streptidius-Hern, not because he was the first to discover the plant (as it is commonly believed), but because it was the end of the week, they were running short of names, and his had a pretty nice ring to it.

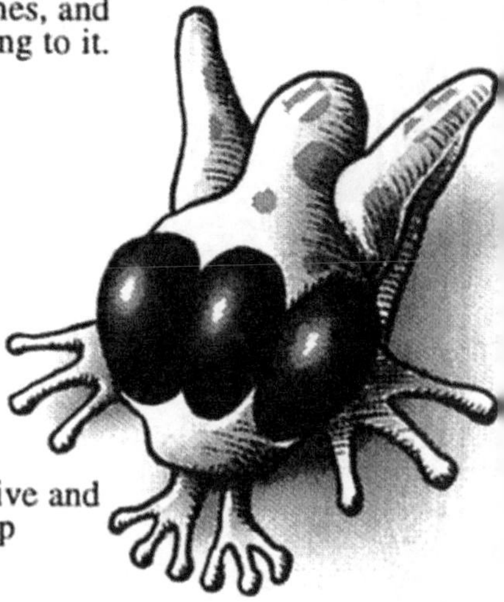

The Three-Eyed Bloy Bloy

Once a common sight along the shores of Whumpucket Swamp, the Three-Eyed Bloy Bloy has very nearly been driven into extinction by the poor quality of popular music in recent years. Thanks to a team of carefully trained conservationists (and a smaller number of conversationalists), the last few Bloy Bloys are alive and well, and are considering moving to a nicer swamp in a more convenient location.

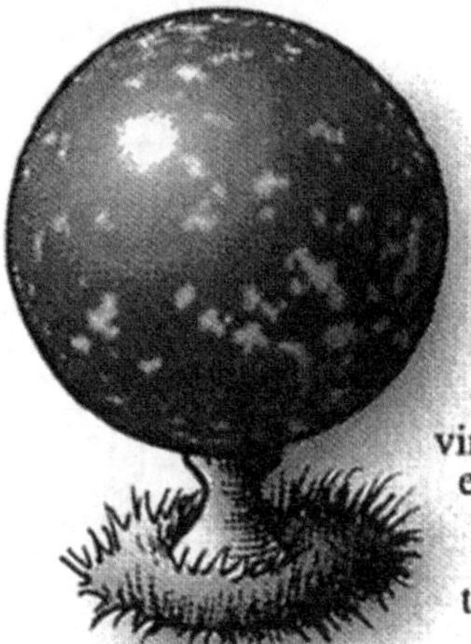

The Spotted Habnibbet-Flumoggadiller

At first glance you might mistake this rare plant for some sort of exotic mushroom. And you'd be right. That is to say, you'd be right to make the mistake. It's *not* a mushroom. But how were you to know? In actual fact it is a rare flower known as the Spotted Habnibbet-Flumoggadiller (which is virtually idertical to the *Hab*nibbet-Flumoggadiller, except for the spots). Experts theorize that the spots evolved over millions of years for no particular reason, other than to give experts something to theorize about.

...errestrial Flora & Fauna

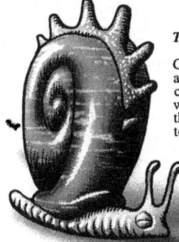

The Horned Riggbeau

Common throughout the mountains of Upper and Lower Yuzonia, the Horned Riggbeau is completely blind and thus makes its way through the world by means of a highly-refined sense of smell, though on occasion even this is insufficient, forcing it to stop and ask for directions. Once thought to possess magical properties, the shell of the Horned Riggbeau was for many years traded among Yuzonian tribesmen and witch doctors as a sort of currency; a well-crafted spear could be had for just 30 *riggbeaus*, whereas upwards of 20,000 *riggbeaus* were required for the purchase of a small motor car.

The 60-Watt Parmeesia

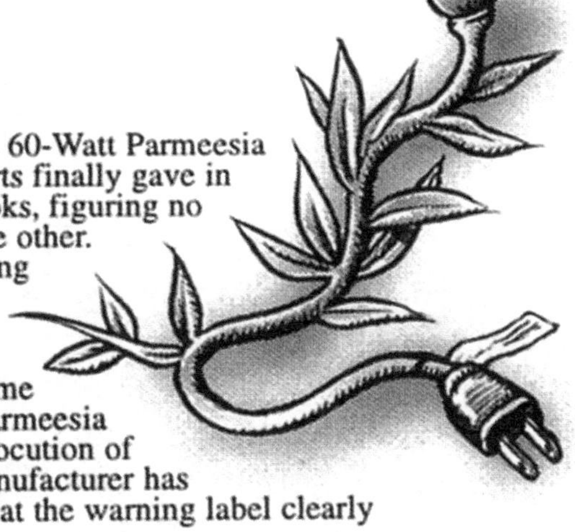

Although technically not a plant, the 60-Watt Parmeesia *looks* so much like a plant that experts finally gave in and began including it in botany books, figuring no one would really care one way or the other. Largely confined to cities and outlying suburbs, the 60-Watt Parmeesia can only rarely be found growing in the wild, and then only with the help of incredibly long extension cords. Some have called for an outright ban of Parmeesia plants, following the death by electrocution of a gardener earlier this year. The manufacturer has defended its product, pointing out that the warning label clearly advises against overwatering.

The Nublit Worm

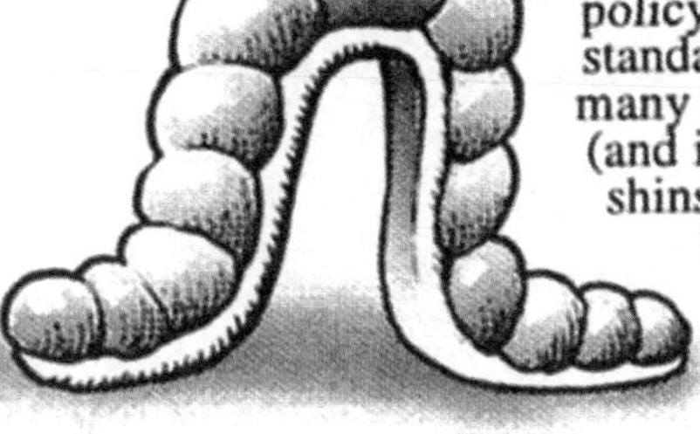

The Nublit Worm caused a sensation several years ago when it decided to locate its head in the middle of its body, in open defiance of the "one end or the other" policy which had become the animal kingdom standard. This novel approach was then copied by many other animals with varying degrees of success (and in a number of cases some very badly bruised shins). Most agree that it hasn't really helped the Nublit species as a whole, apart from the increased publicity, and that the effort would have been better spent on aquiring arms and legs, or even just a bit of body hair.

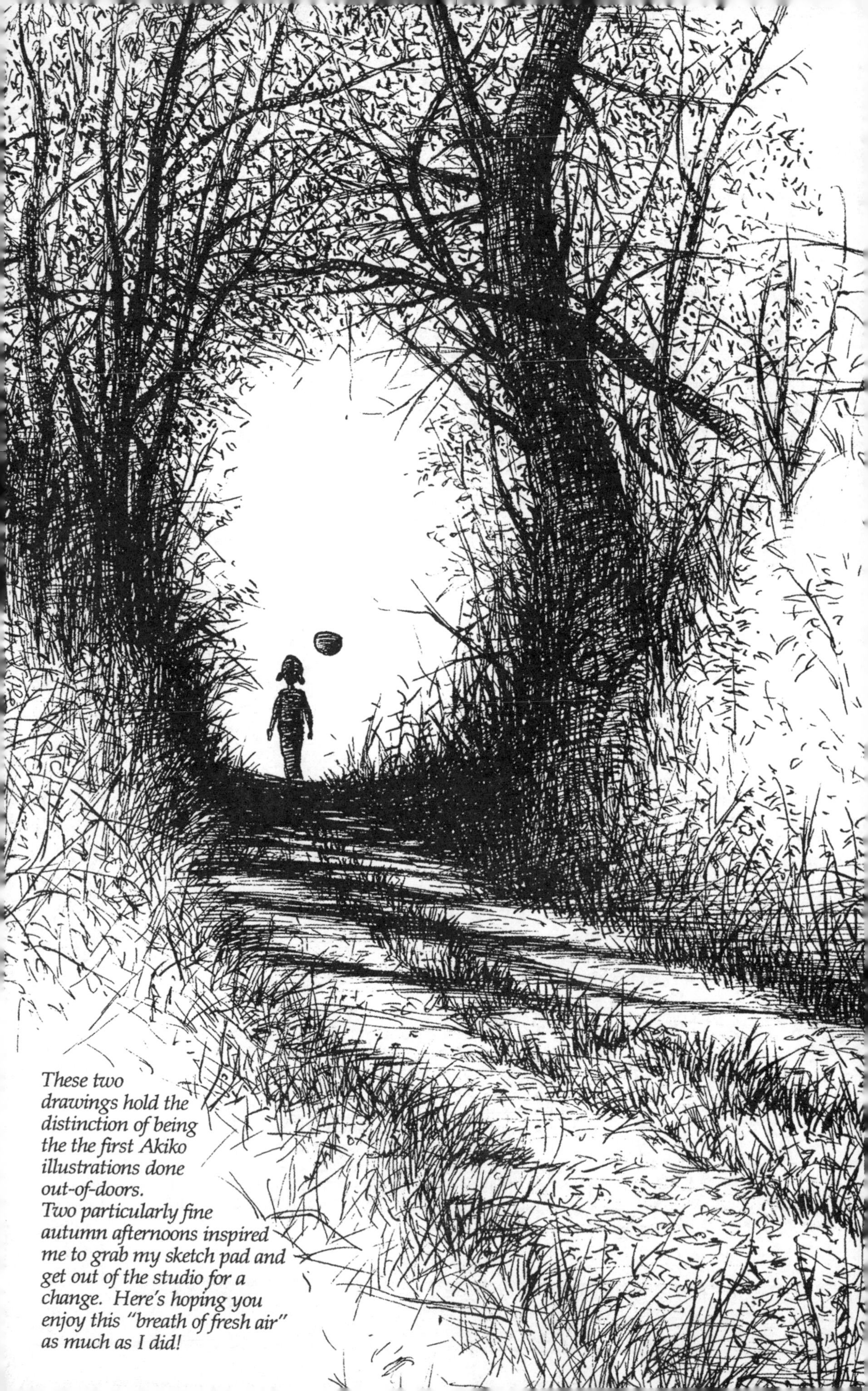

These two drawings hold the distinction of being the the first Akiko illustrations done out-of-doors. Two particularly fine autumn afternoons inspired me to grab my sketch pad and get out of the studio for a change. Here's hoping you enjoy this "breath of fresh air" as much as I did!

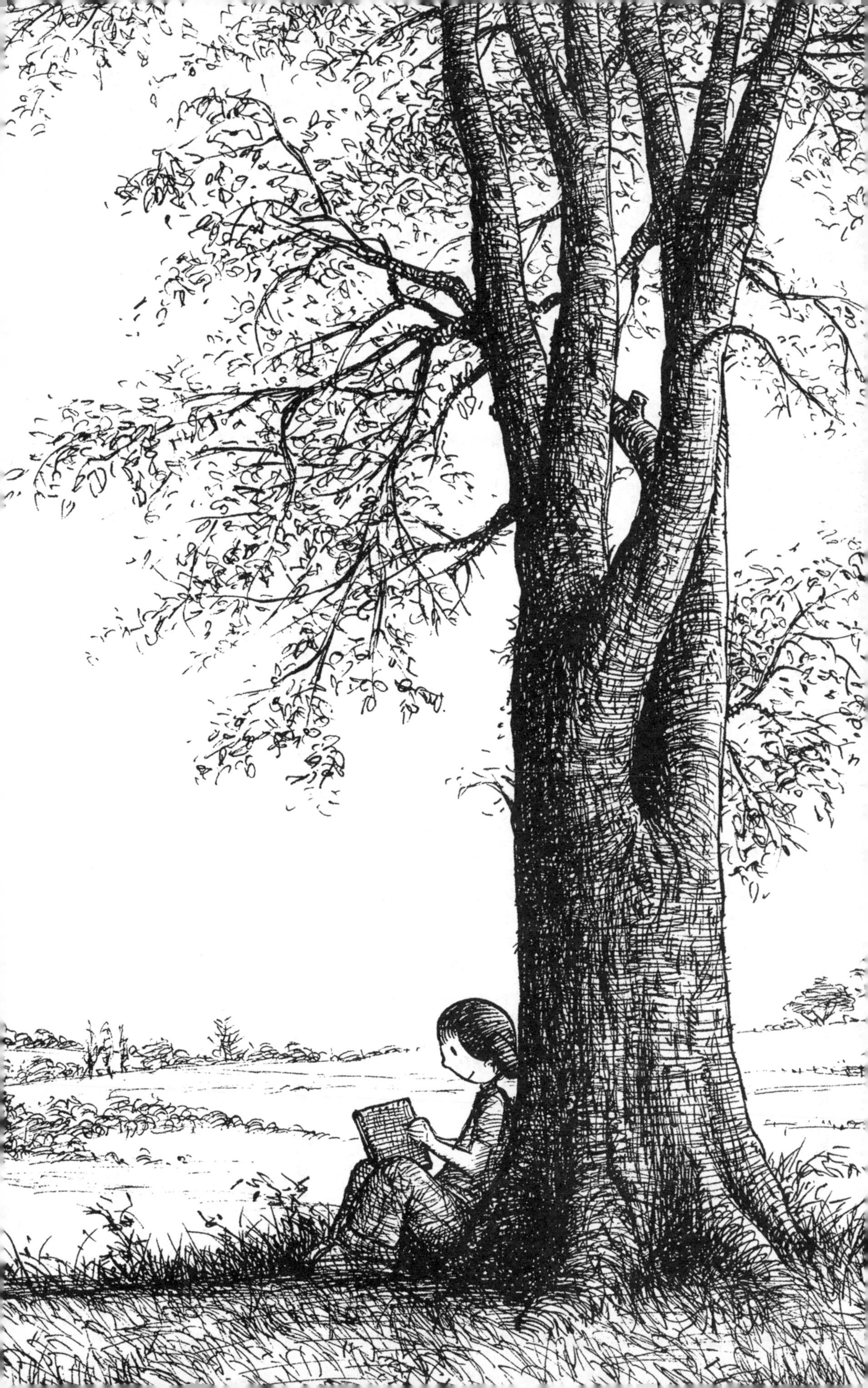

'KiKO 'n' GAX in "Man vs. Machine"

It must be pretty cool to be a robot, Gax. I mean, you never have to worry about getting sick or anything like that, do you?

NO MA'AM, ALTHOUGH I COULD BE **PROGRAMMED** TO GET SICK...

I wouldn't recommend it, Gax. Unless there's a test or something you need to get out of.

I SUPPOSE THE CLOSEST I GET TO ILLNESS IS WHEN I HAVE ONE OF MY PERIODIC BREAKDOWNS.

What's *that* like?

MOST UNPLEASANT, MA'AM. A BIT LIKE HAVING YOUR BRAIN MELT.

Eeew. That doesn't sound cool *at all.*

THERE'S NOTHING LIKE THAT FEELING WHEN THEY GET YOU UP AND RUNNING AGAIN, THOUGH.

Pretty nice, huh?

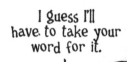

EXHILARATING, MA'AM. ESPECIALLY AFTER A GOOD OIL CHANGE: THAT **REALLY** GETS THE OLD PISTONS MOVING...

I guess I'll have to take your word for it.

IF YOU DON'T MIND ME ASKING, MA'AM, WHAT IS IT LIKE TO BE HUMAN?

Oh, it's mostly really cool, so long as you're still a kid. *Adult* humans have it pretty rough...

...at least they make it *look* that way. Always running around making phonecalls and worrying about stuff.

Some grownups look so busy half the time it's as if there's a great, big *monster* chasing them around all day.

IT SOUNDS LIKE I'M BETTER OFF AS A ROBOT, MA'AM.

Yeah, Gax. You probably are...

The End

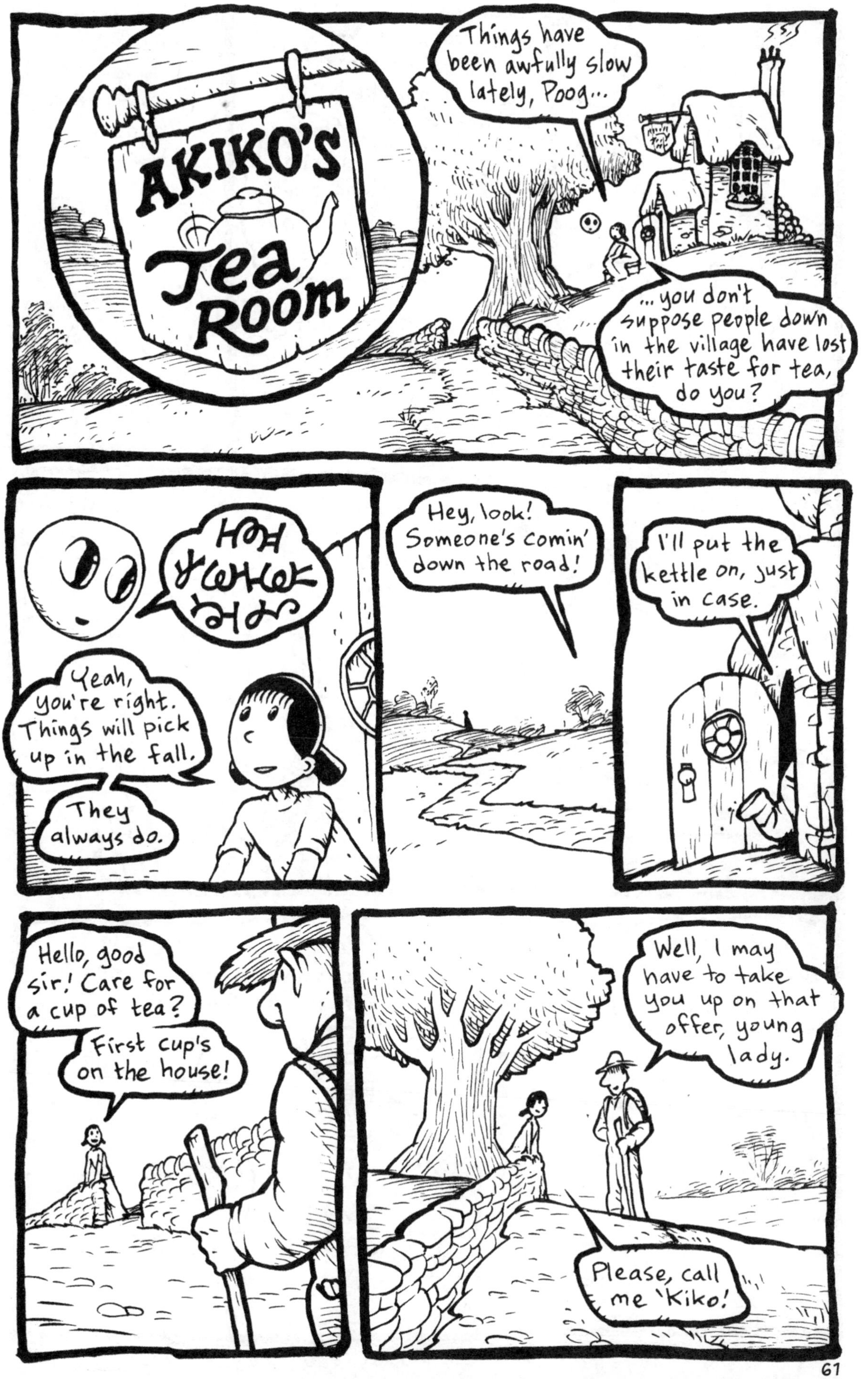
AKIKO'S Tea Room
Things have been awfully slow lately, Poog...
... you don't suppose people down in the village have lost their taste for tea, do you?
Yeah, you're right. Things will pick up in the fall.
They always do.
Hey, look! Someone's comin' down the road!
I'll put the kettle on, just in case.
Hello, good sir! Care for a cup of tea?
First cup's on the house!
Well, I may have to take you up on that offer, young lady.
Please, call me 'Kiko!

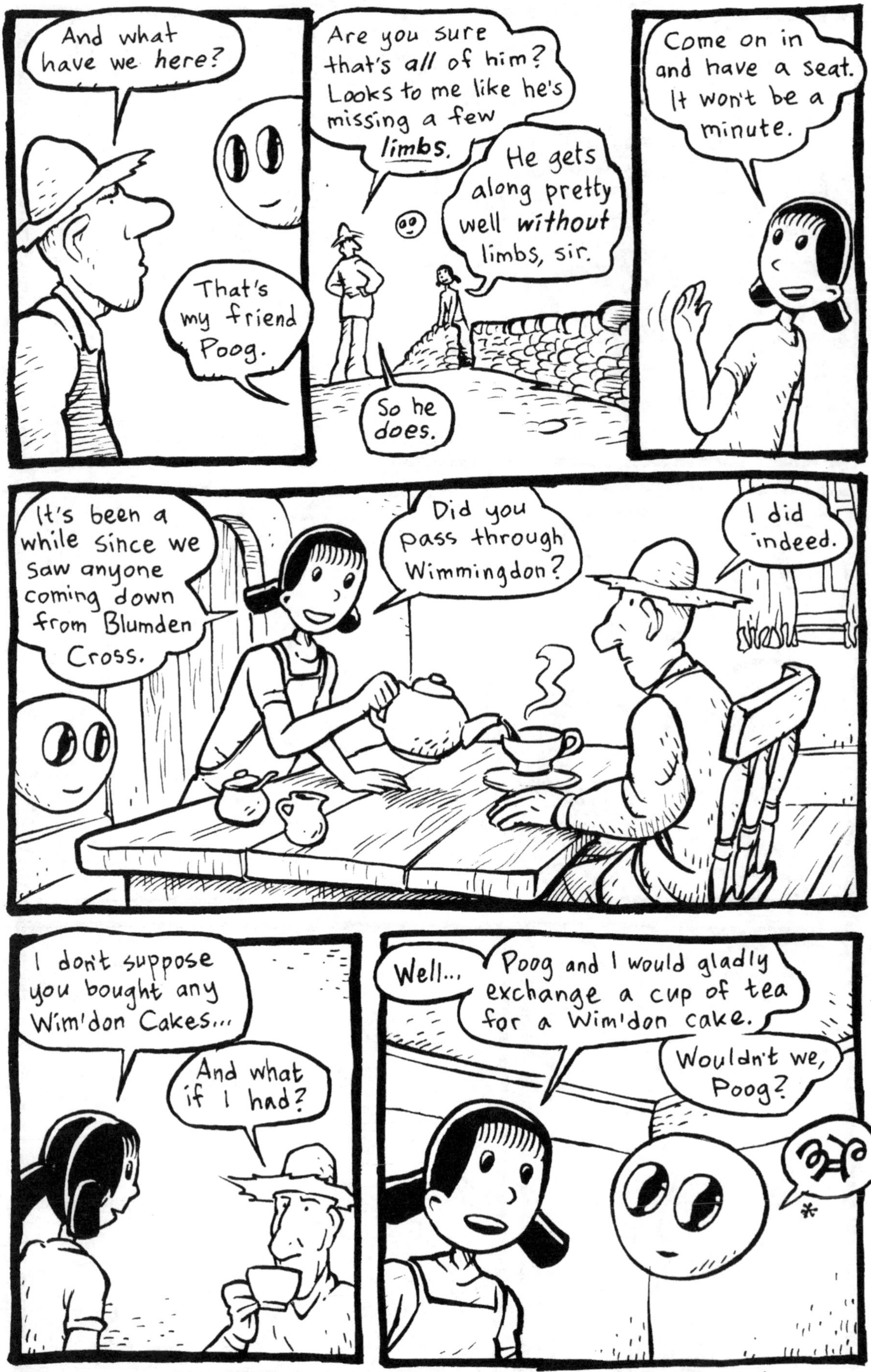
And what have we here?
That's my friend Poog.
Are you sure that's *all* of him? Looks to me like he's missing a few limbs.
He gets along pretty well *without* limbs, sir.
So he does.
Come on in and have a seat. It won't be a minute.
It's been a while since we saw anyone coming down from Blumden Cross.
Did you pass through Wimmingdon?
I did indeed.
I don't suppose you bought any Wim'don Cakes...
And what if I had?
Well...
Poog and I would gladly exchange a cup of tea for a Wim'don cake.
Wouldn't we, Poog?
*

* "Provided they're fresh."

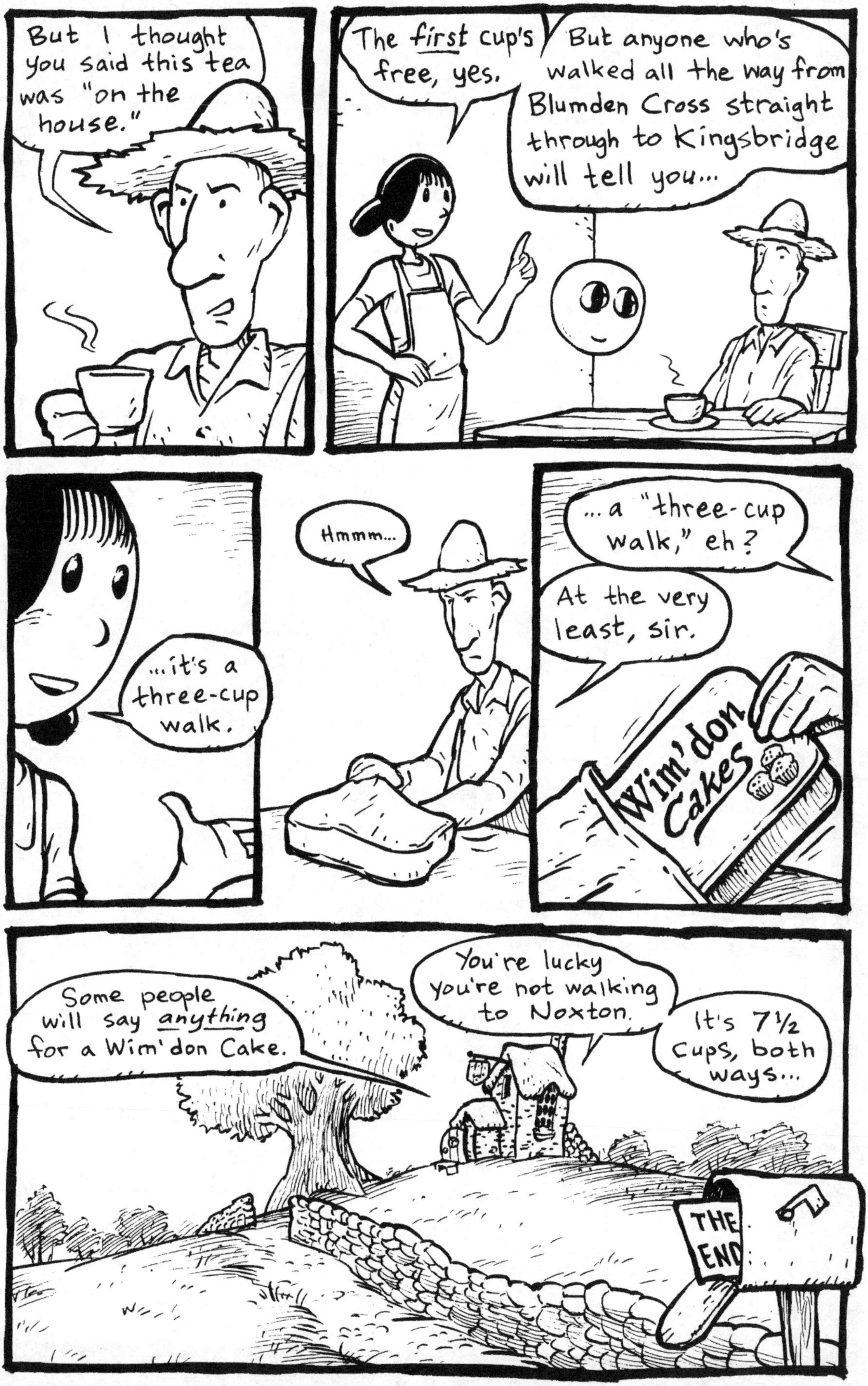

But I thought you said this tea was "on the house."
The first cup's free, yes.
But anyone who's walked all the way from Blumden Cross straight through to Kingsbridge will tell you...
...it's a three-cup walk.
Hmmm...
...a "three-cup walk," eh?
At the very least, sir.
Wim'don Cakes
Some people will say anything for a Wim'don Cake.
You're lucky you're not walking to Noxton.
It's 7½ Cups, both ways...
THE END

Okay, you've seen these guys in action, but do you really *know* these robots? Sharpen your pencils and take some notes, friends. It's time to review...

The Crew: An Introduction

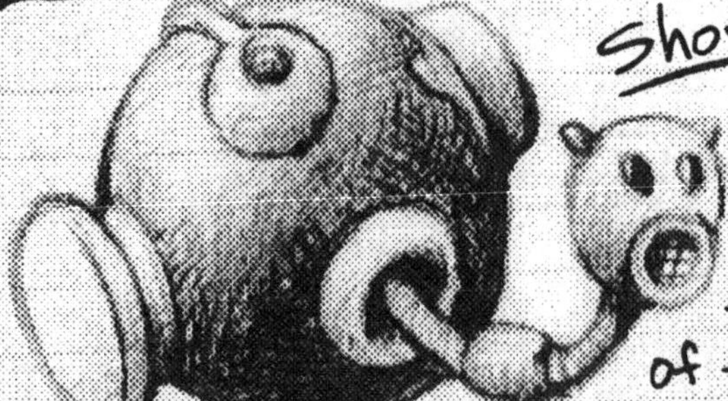

Shorpy

Sassy, sharp-tongued, & self-assured, Shorpy is a street-smart 'bot from the lower east side of the Andromeda Galaxy. He's capable of understanding seventeen different languages, and of making flippant remarks in each and every one of them.

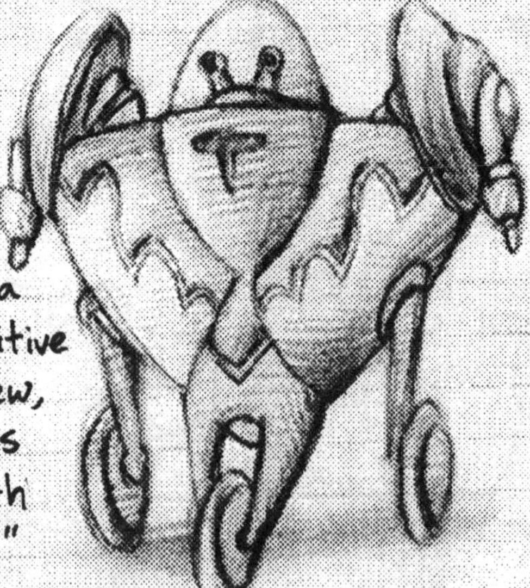

Captain Tupp

Beneath Tupp's pink-and-green exterior lies a heart of gold. Ever sensitive to the needs of his crew, Tupp's code of ethics is gravely out of step with Gothtek's "bottom line."

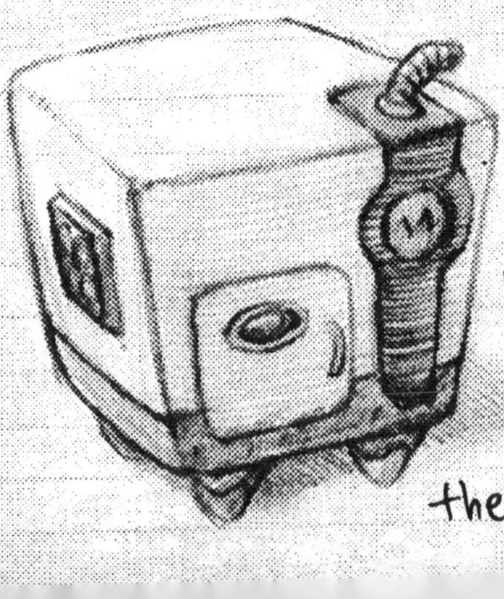

Nonk

Incapable of speech, Nonk is anything but dumb. Within his databank lies the blueprint of the entire Fognon-6, knowledge that may prove crucial to the survival of the crew.

Op-Wud

A low-cost alternative to the newer welding 'bots, Op-Wud is the sort of machine the Gothtek Corporation loves: an obedient workhorse who never questions authority. The last surviving member of a set of six, Op-Wud is on the verge of breaking down for good.

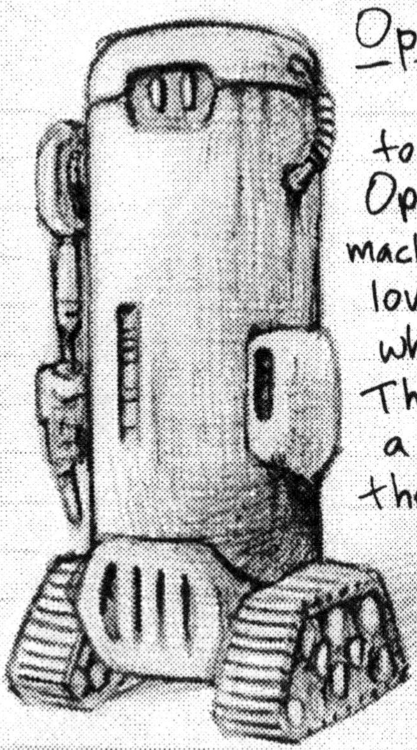

Gricks

The oldest member of the crew is also the most ill-suited for the rigors of the Fognon-6. Gricks would suffer from a split personality if not for the fact that his second head is usually half-asleep.

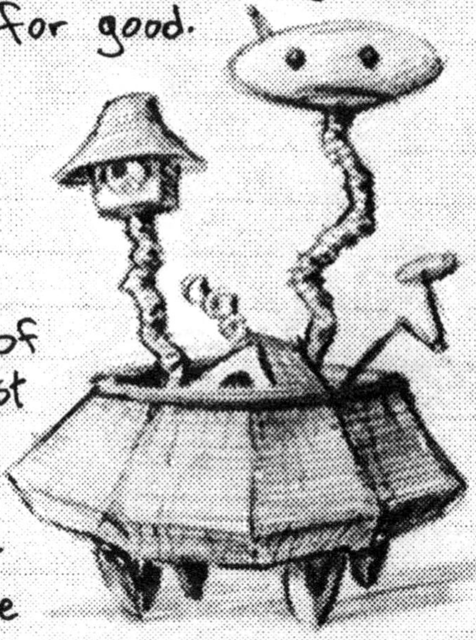

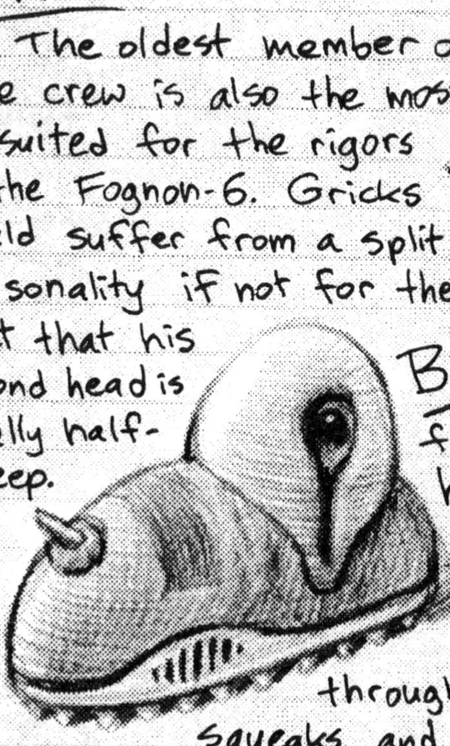

B.B.

Built for cleaning floors and exterminating household pests, B.B. is a tough little 'bot who never cracks under pressure. He converses through an odd dialect of pips, squeaks, and muffled thumps.

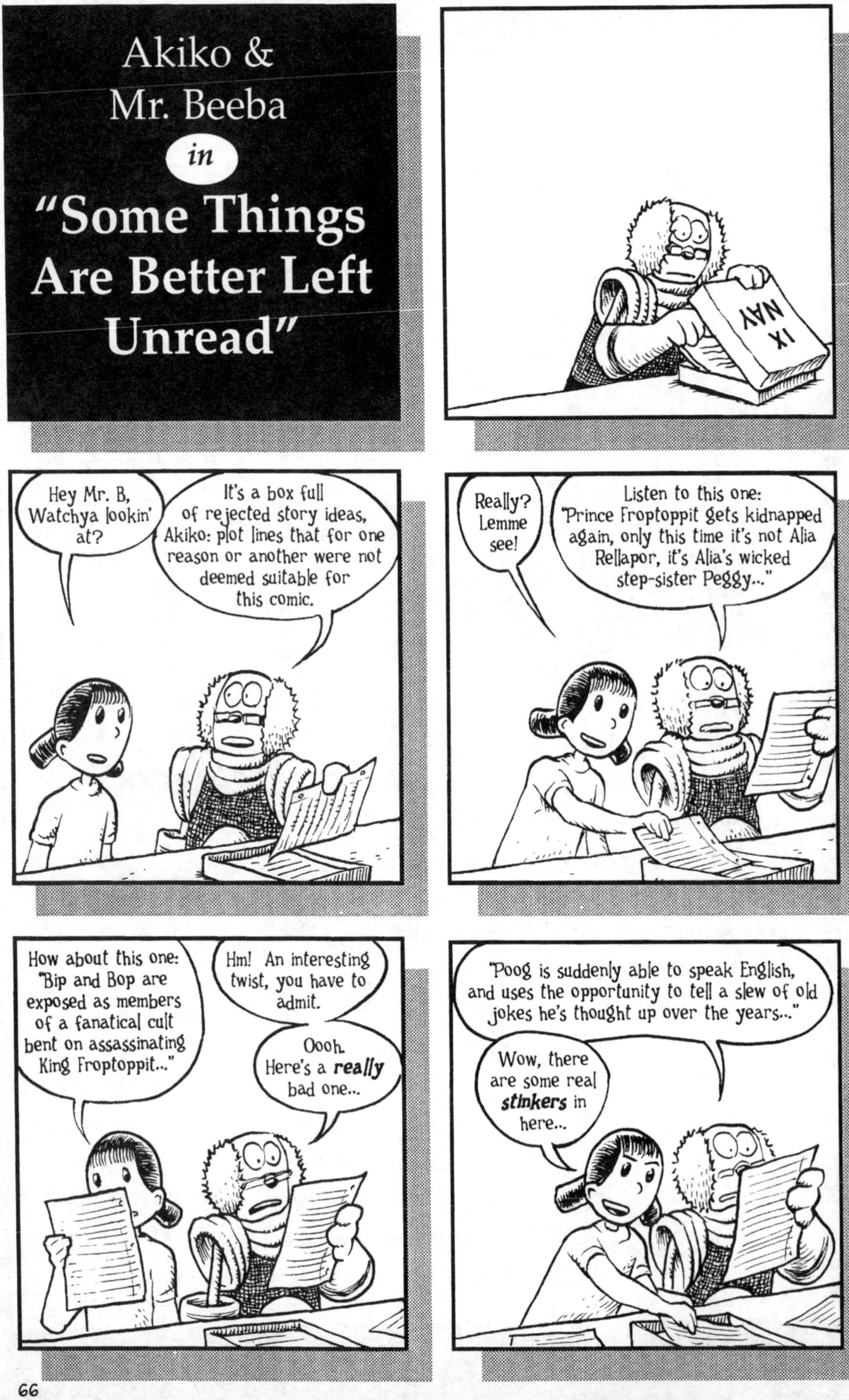
Akiko & Mr. Beeba in "Some Things Are Better Left Unread"
IX NAY
Hey Mr. B, Watchya lookin' at?
It's a box full of rejected story ideas, Akiko: plot lines that for one reason or another were not deemed suitable for this comic.
Really? Lemme see!
Listen to this one: "Prince Froptoppit gets kidnapped again, only this time it's not Alia Rellapor, it's Alia's wicked step-sister Peggy..."
How about this one: "Bip and Bop are exposed as members of a fanatical cult bent on assassinating King Froptoppit..."
Hm! An interesting twist, you have to admit.
Oooh. Here's a **really** bad one...
"Poog is suddenly able to speak English, and uses the opportunity to tell a slew of old jokes he's thought up over the years..."
Wow, there are some real **stinkers** in here...

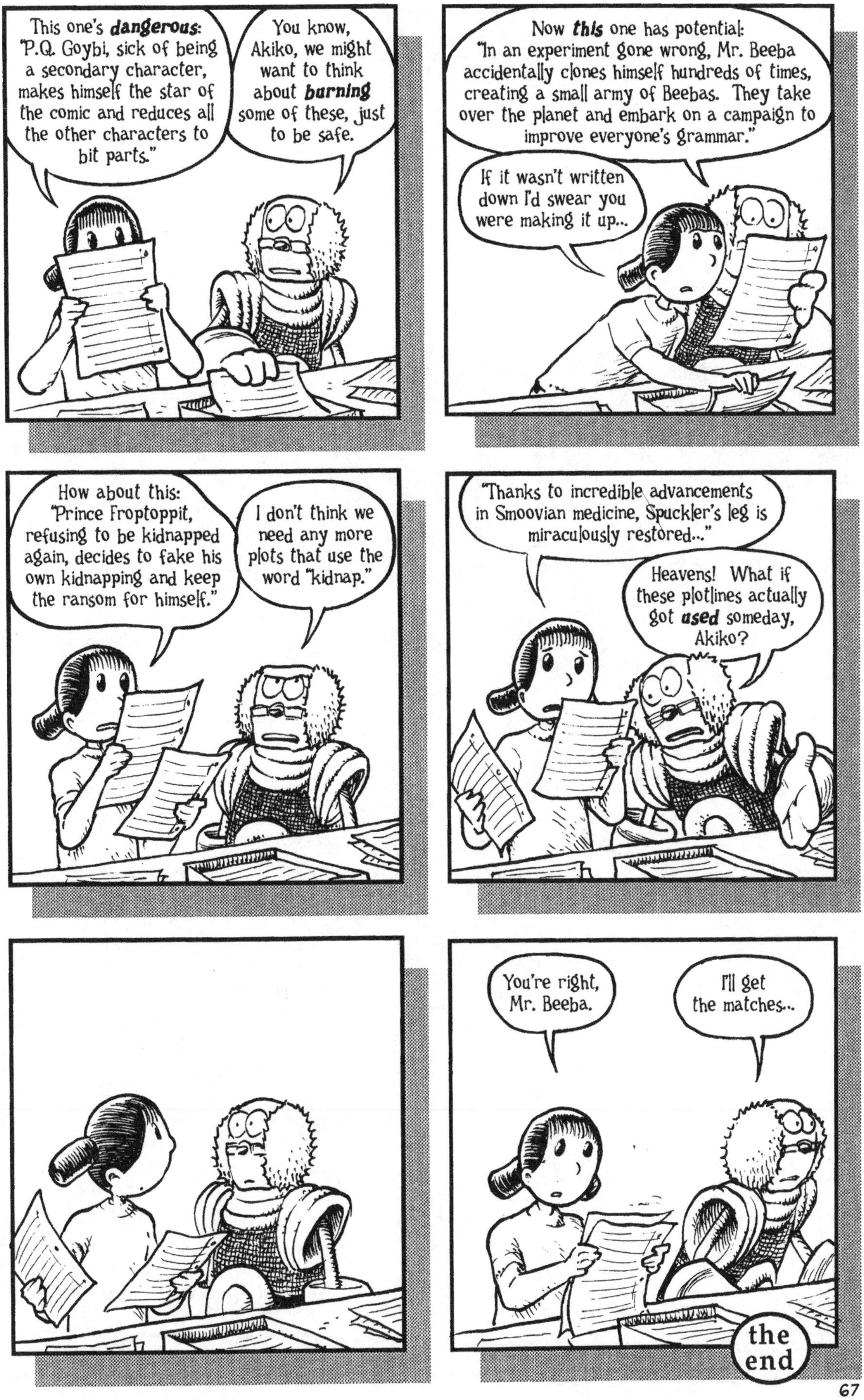
This one's **dangerous**: "P.Q. Goybi, sick of being a secondary character, makes himself the star of the comic and reduces all the other characters to bit parts."
You know, Akiko, we might want to think about **burning** some of these, just to be safe.
Now **this** one has potential: "In an experiment gone wrong, Mr. Beeba accidentally clones himself hundreds of times, creating a small army of Beebas. They take over the planet and embark on a campaign to improve everyone's grammar."
If it wasn't written down I'd swear you were making it up...
How about this: "Prince Froptoppit, refusing to be kidnapped again, decides to fake his own kidnapping and keep the ransom for himself."
I don't think we need any more plots that use the word "kidnap."
"Thanks to incredible advancements in Smoovian medicine, Spuckler's leg is miraculously restored..."
Heavens! What if these plotlines actually got **used** someday, Akiko?
You're right, Mr. Beeba.
I'll get the matches...
the end

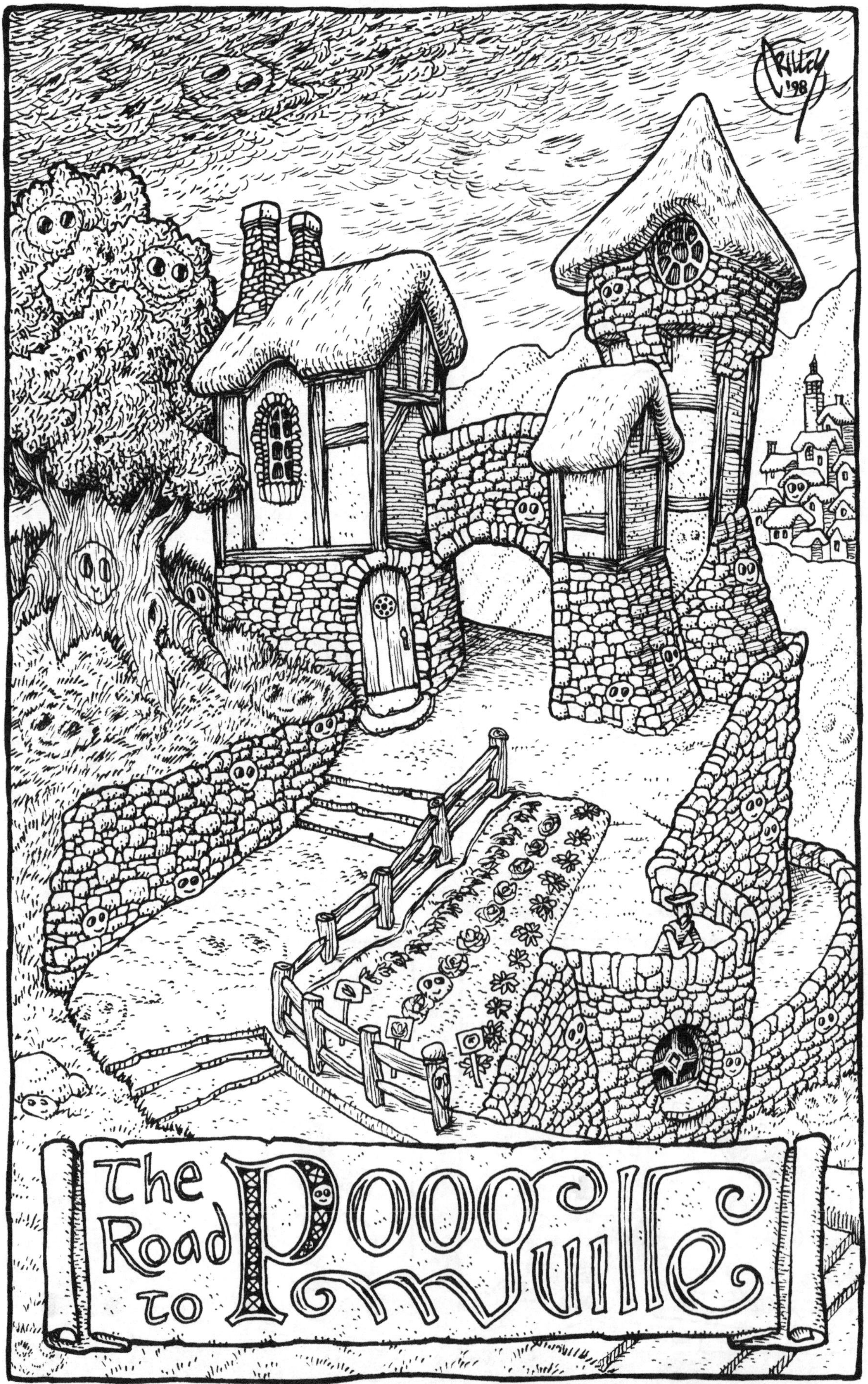
Crilley '98
The Road to Poogeville

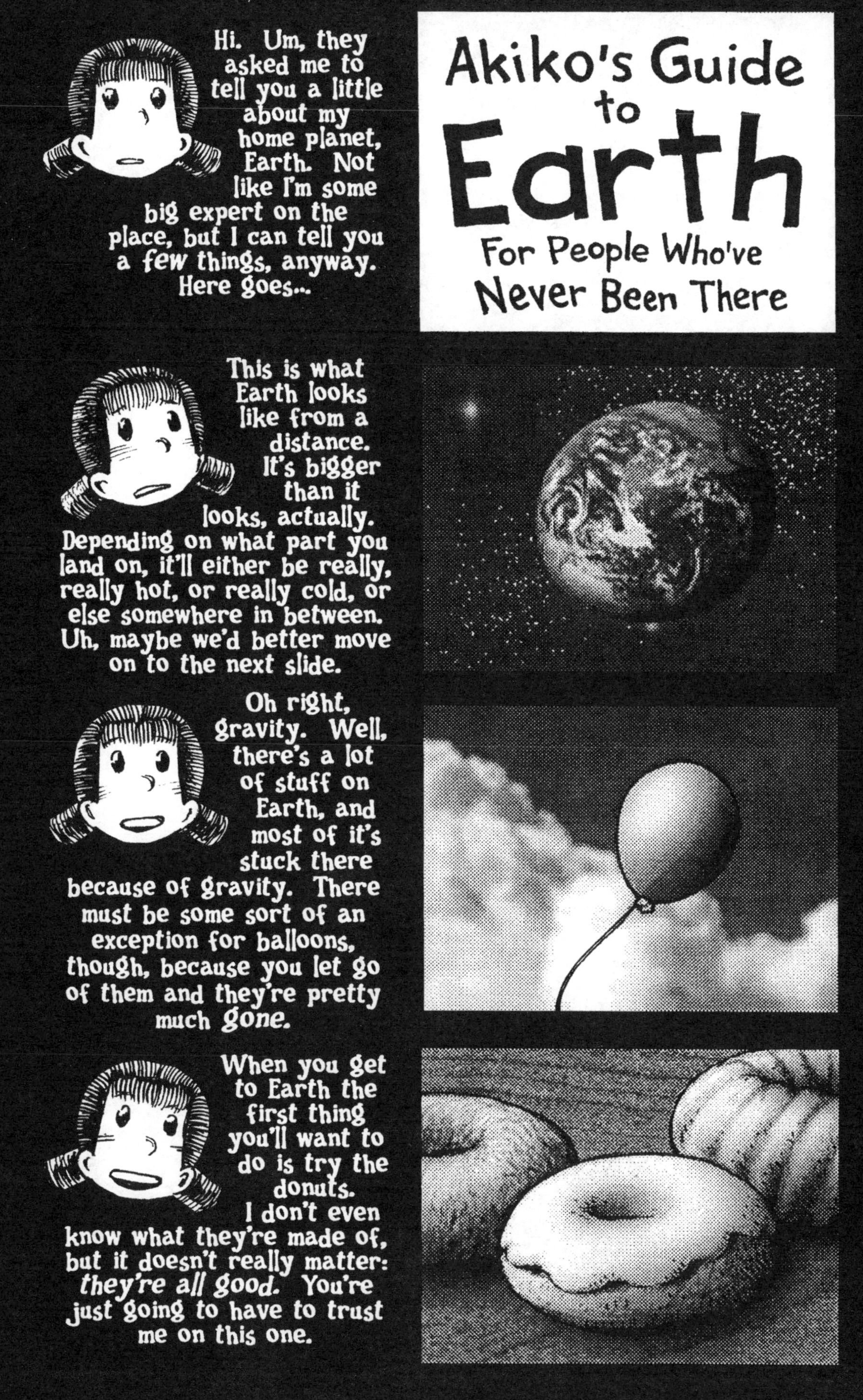
Hi. Um, they asked me to tell you a little about my home planet, Earth. Not like I'm some big expert on the place, but I can tell you a few things, anyway. Here goes...
Akiko's Guide to Earth For People Who've Never Been There
This is what Earth looks like from a distance. It's bigger than it looks, actually. Depending on what part you land on, it'll either be really, really hot, or really cold, or else somewhere in between. Uh, maybe we'd better move on to the next slide.
Oh right, gravity. Well, there's a lot of stuff on Earth, and most of it's stuck there because of gravity. There must be some sort of an exception for balloons, though, because you let go of them and they're pretty much gone.
When you get to Earth the first thing you'll want to do is try the donuts. I don't even know what they're made of, but it doesn't really matter: they're all good. You're just going to have to trust me on this one.

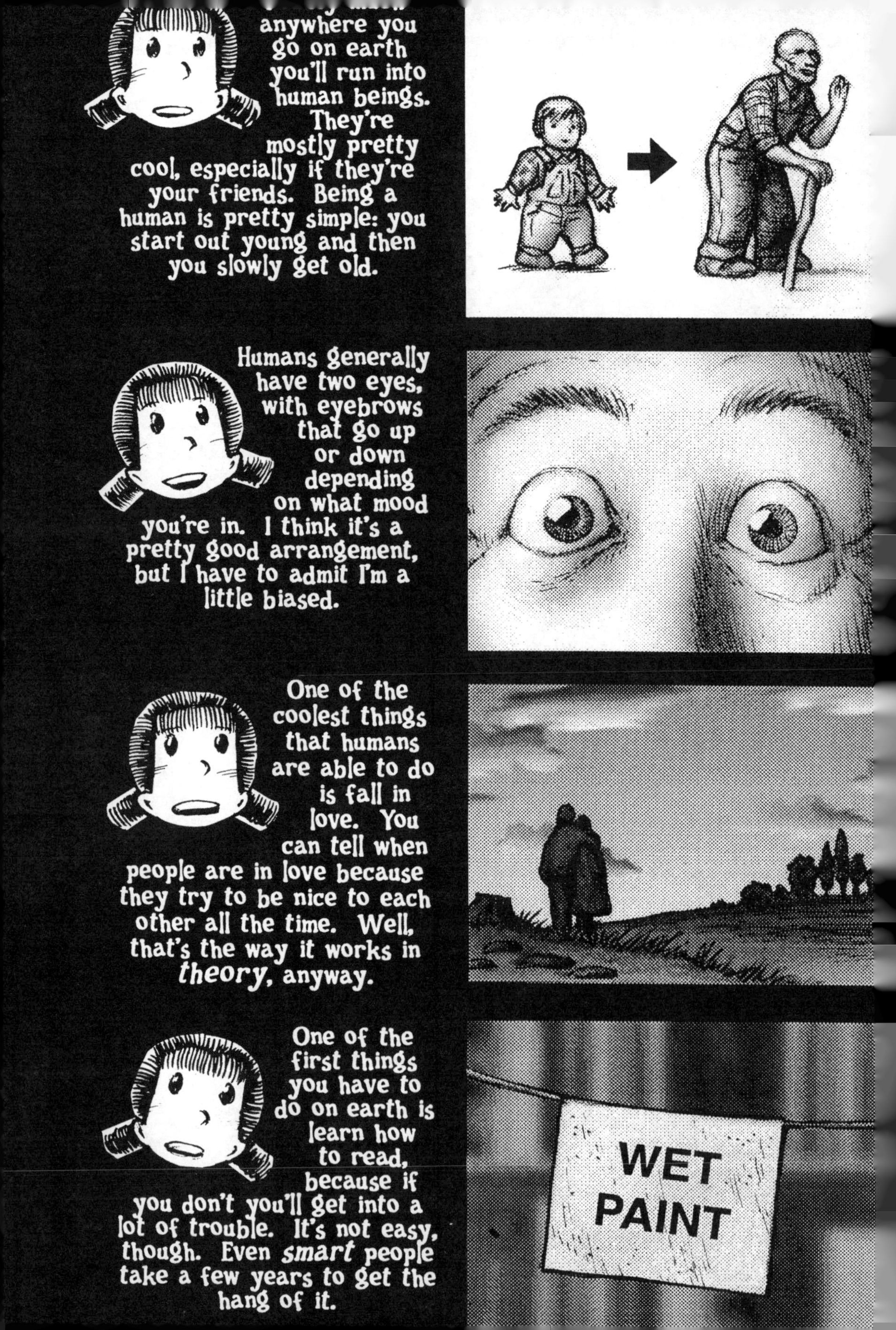

...anywhere you go on earth you'll run into human beings. They're mostly pretty cool, especially if they're your friends. Being a human is pretty simple: you start out young and then you slowly get old.

Humans generally have two eyes, with eyebrows that go up or down depending on what mood you're in. I think it's a pretty good arrangement, but I have to admit I'm a little biased.

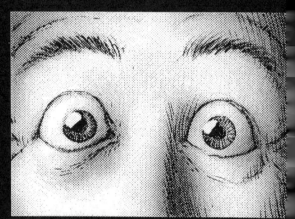

One of the coolest things that humans are able to do is fall in love. You can tell when people are in love because they try to be nice to each other all the time. Well, that's the way it works in *theory*, anyway.

One of the first things you have to do on earth is learn how to read, because if you don't you'll get into a lot of trouble. It's not easy, though. Even *smart* people take a few years to get the hang of it.

WET PAINT

I was going to tell you about money, but I'm not so sure I understand it myself. I think people invented it so they'd have a reason to work all day.

One of the best things about Earth is you get a really good view of the sun. I mean, sure, you can see it from other planets too, but it looks nicest from earth. The view from Pluto, for example, is really lousy.

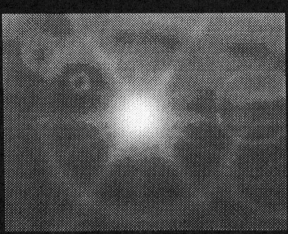

As for souvenirs, well, you could always take home a can or two of root beer. I don't know why, but I've got a feeling there's nothing else quite like it out there, and even if there is it's probably not as good.

Well, that's about it. You can see most of Earth in a day, but I'd recommend a week if you really want to see all the good stuff. It may not be the most exotic planet in the universe, but it's certainly worth a visit. I mean, it's hard enough just finding a planet that has both air *and* water. Let's not get too picky.

The End

Once upon a very long time ago...

...there lived a humble merchant by the name of Beeba. He made a meager living selling books and paintings and pieces of wood, and lived by a simple motto: "Mind your own business, or your business will own your mind." He wasn't exactly sure what it meant, but he thought it had a pretty nice ring to it, and was about as good a motto as a humble merchant like himself could wish for.

One day, when he was just settling down to make his way through a stack of old dictionaries and encyclopedias, he was interrupted by a visit from his old friend, Spuckler. Now Spuckler was a reckless fellow, who lived without regard for books or paintings, and had long forgotten his motto, if indeed he'd ever had one. But Beeba felt is was important to forgive a fellow for his lack of education, or at least to refrain from making fun of it to his face, so he'd resolved not to let Spuckler's inferiority of intellect get in the way of them being friends.

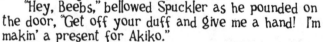

"Hey, Beebs," bellowed Spuckler as he pounded on the door, "Get off your duff and give me a hand! I'm makin' a present for Akiko."

"Hold on Spuckler, I'll be there at once!" called out Beeba, hoping to get there before Spuckler could do his door any further damage. A moment later he was on his front porch, staring in amazement at the giant boulder that Spuckler had somehow dragged to his doorstep.

"What on earth..." began Beeba.

"Now hang on, Beebs. It ain't finished yet. That's why I came here t' get your help."

"But what is it supposed to be?"

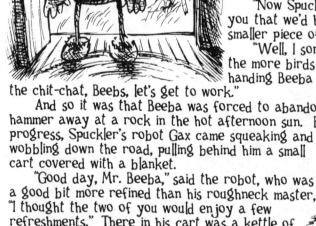

"It's a birdbath. For 'Kiko's garden." As Spuckler mopped the sweat from his forehead, Beeba tried his best to imagine how the massive piece of rock could be transformed into anything resembling a birdbath,

"Now Spuckler, my dear fellow, didn't it occur to you that we'd have been better off starting with a smaller piece of stone?"

"Well, I sorta figured that the bigger the bath, the more birds you're gonna get," replied Spuckler, handing Beeba a hammer and chisel. "Now, enough of the chit-chat, Beebs, let's get to work."

And so it was that Beeba was forced to abandon the comfort of his books in order to hammer away at a rock in the hot afternoon sun. Before they'd made very much progress, Spuckler's robot Gax came squeaking and wobbling down the road, pulling behind him a small cart covered with a blanket.

"Good day, Mr. Beeba," said the robot, who was a good bit more refined than his roughneck master, "I thought the two of you would enjoy a few refreshments." There in his cart was a kettle of tea and a plateful of biscuits. It seemed that Spuckler's little visit might not turn out to be such a bad thing after all!

"Well, now, Gax, that was mighty thoughtful of ya," said Spuckler as he tossed his mallet into the weeds, "I reckon it *is* about time for a little break." And so they enjoyed the tea and biscuits in the shade of a nearby tree, and considered the fate of their giant birdbath.

Meanwhile, Akiko was working in her garden, having a little chat with Poog. I say a *little* chat, mind you, because Poog hardly ever said a word. But Akiko had learned long ago not to question Poog's silences, and had even come to enjoy them over time.

"This ought to be a good year for roses, Poog, what with all the rain we've had lately." Poog nodded in agreement.

"I do need to keep after the weeds, though. They sprout up every time I turn my back."

Akiko got down on her hands and knees and started digging at a particularly stubborn patch of weeds near the edge of the garden. Poog hummed a little tune to keep her company.

Looking up, Akiko saw Spuckler, Gax, and Mr. Beeba trudging along the road down below, dragging behind them a huge wheelbarrow filled with rocks. Spuckler and Mr. Beeba were in the middle of a heated argument, as usual.

"I told you to hold the chisel in one place, ya dadburned idiot!"

"You were about to hammer my thumb into oblivion, Spuckler," protested Beeba, visibly exhausted from the day's labor. "It was a matter of self-defense."

"Yeah? Well thanks to your precious little thumb, we ruined Akiko's new birdbath!"

"I didn't know I *had* a new birdbath," said Akiko, as she joined them on the road.

"That's 'cause ya don't," explained Spuckler with a sigh, "Ya *almost* did, but not no more. These rocks is all that's left of it, and we're fixin' to wheel 'em on down t' the dump."

"It's just as well," smiled Akiko, "because I don't really need a birdbath."

"But I was under the impression that you were quite *fond* of birds, Akiko," said Mr. Beeba, genuinely puzzled.

"I am. The reason I don't need a birdbath because I've already *got* one." Akiko took them around to the back of the house to an old pail of water on her window ledge.

"I left this bucket out here one night when it rained. Next thing I knew the local birds had decided this would be their birdbath," Akiko explained. "It's the perfect location, too, because I can sit at the kitchen table when I'm having tea and watch them come and go."

"But Akiko, surely you need something a bit more substantial." said Mr. Beeba.

"Something bigger," agreed Spuckler. "There ain't space in that thing but for one or two birds."

"I think it's just perfect," said Akiko with a smile, "But I can tell you one thing this garden *does* need."

"What's that?"

"A wall. A nice, little wall running along the edge, just like the one down at Mrs. McGamby's."

"I've seen that wall," said Mr. Beeba, "It's made entirely of rocks, stacked one upon the other."

"Yes," said Akiko, with a rather unconvincing look of disappointment on her face, "It's a shame you're going to wheel all those rocks down to the dump..."

Spuckler grinned as he reached into the wheelbarrow and tossed a stone to Mr. Beeba. "Come on, Beebs, let's see just how well you remember how that old wall was put together."

Akiko smiled and ran back up to the house. "I'll put the kettle on."

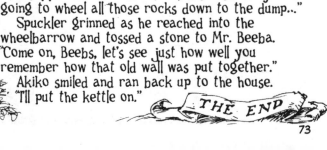

THE END

Mr. Beeba in "Doctor's Orders"

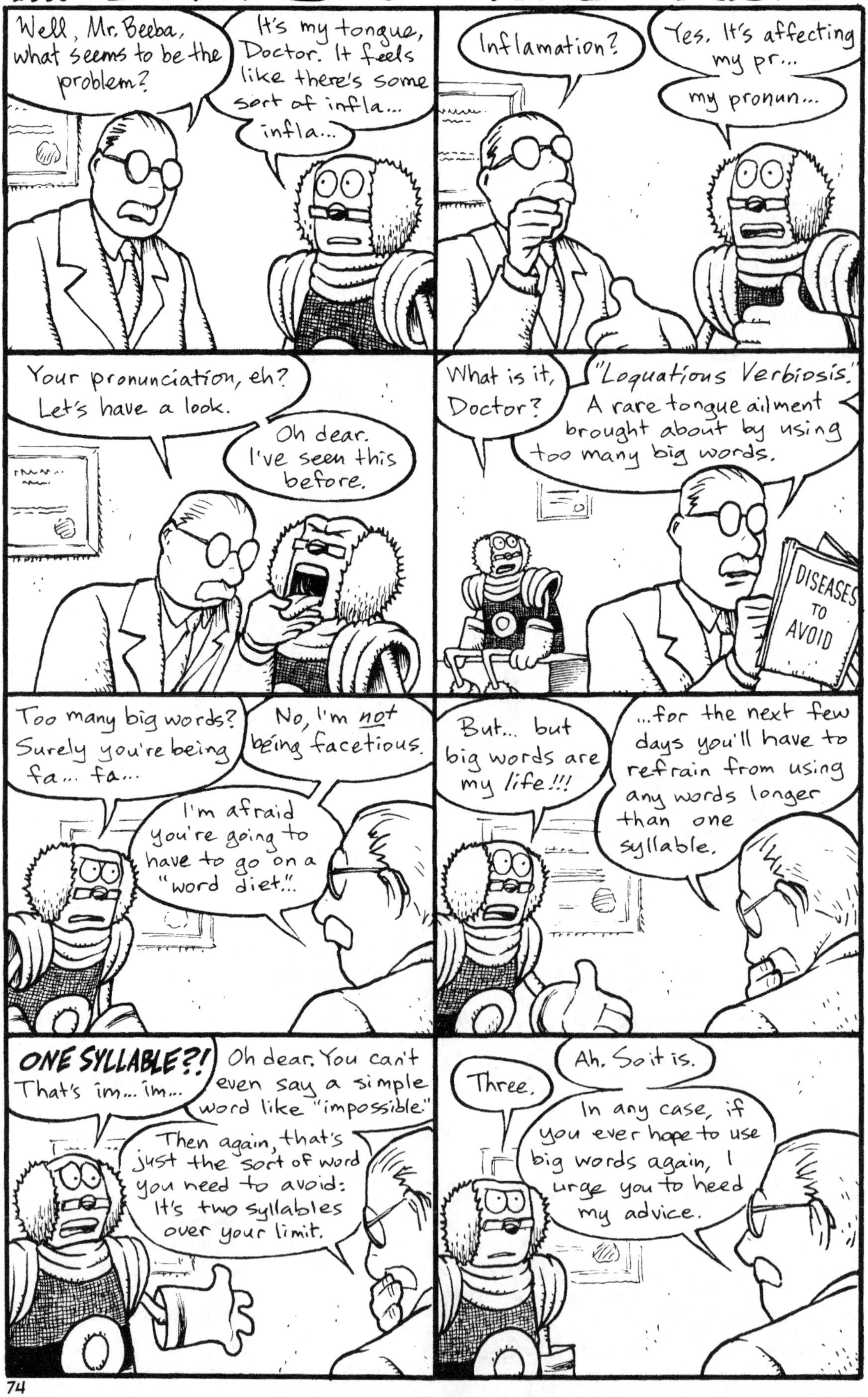

Well, Mr. Beeba, what seems to be the problem?
It's my tongue, Doctor. It feels like there's some sort of infla...
infla...
Inflamation?
Yes. It's affecting my pr...
my pronun...
Your pronunciation, eh? Let's have a look.
Oh dear. I've seen this before.
What is it, Doctor?
"Loquatious Verbiosis." A rare tongue ailment brought about by using too many big words.
DISEASES TO AVOID
Too many big words? Surely you're being fa... fa...
No, I'm not being facetious.
I'm afraid you're going to have to go on a "word diet."
But... but big words are my life!!!
...for the next few days you'll have to refrain from using any words longer than one syllable.
ONE SYLLABLE?! That's im... im...
Oh dear. You can't even say a simple word like "impossible."
Then again, that's just the sort of word you need to avoid: It's two syllables over your limit.
Three.
Ah. So it is.
In any case, if you ever hope to use big words again, I urge you to heed my advice.

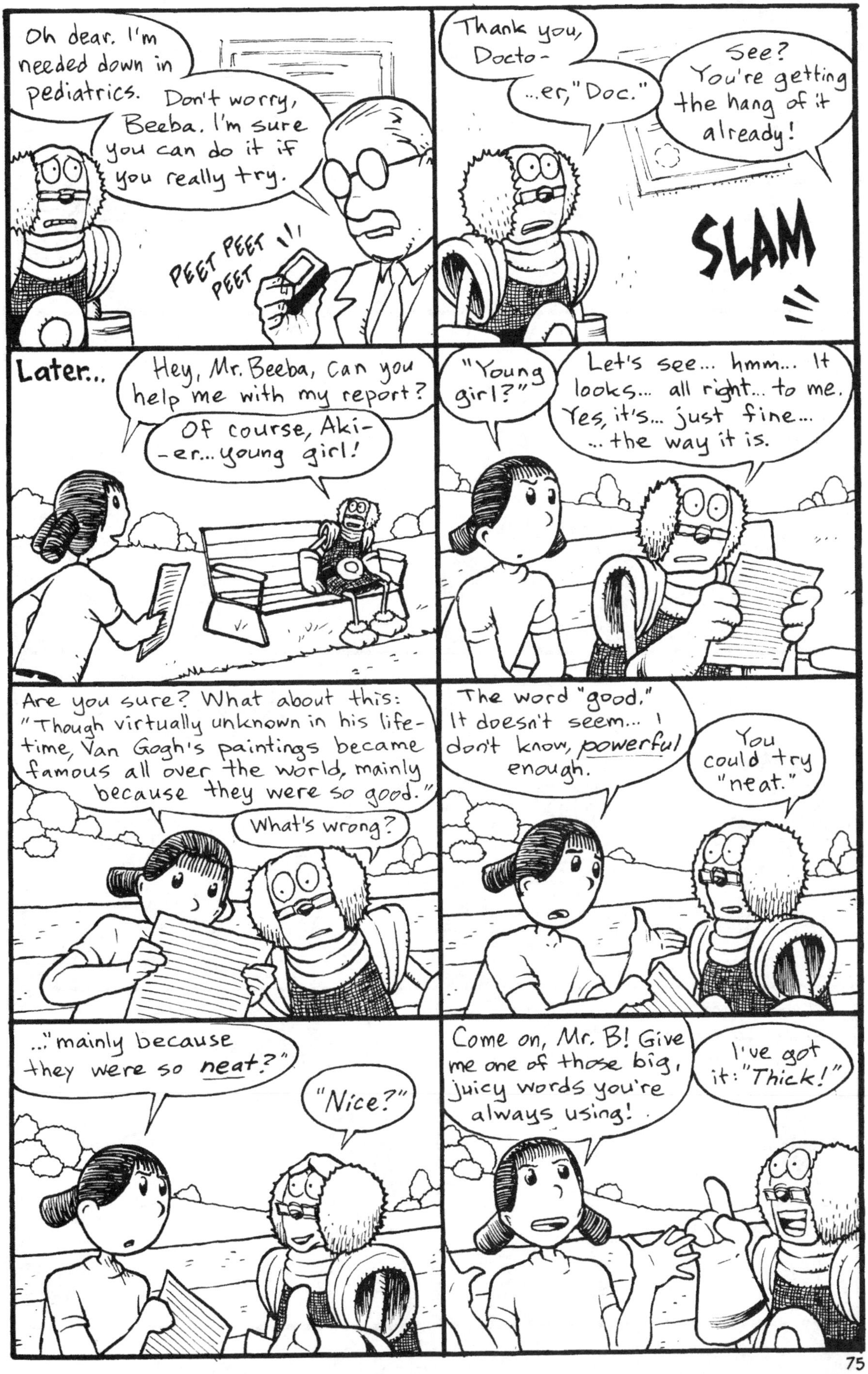
Oh dear. I'm needed down in pediatrics.
Don't worry, Beeba. I'm sure you can do it if you really try.
PEET PEET PEET
Thank you, Docto-
...er, "Doc."
See? You're getting the hang of it already!
SLAM
Later...
Hey, Mr. Beeba, can you help me with my report?
Of course, Aki- -er... young girl!
"Young girl?"
Let's see... hmm... It looks... all right... to me. Yes, it's... just fine... ...the way it is.
Are you sure? What about this: "Though virtually unknown in his lifetime, Van Gogh's paintings became famous all over the world, mainly because they were so good."
What's wrong?
The word "good." It doesn't seem... I don't know, powerful enough.
You could try "neat."
..."mainly because they were so neat?"
"Nice?"
Come on, Mr. B! Give me one of those big, juicy words you're always using!
I've got it: "Thick!"

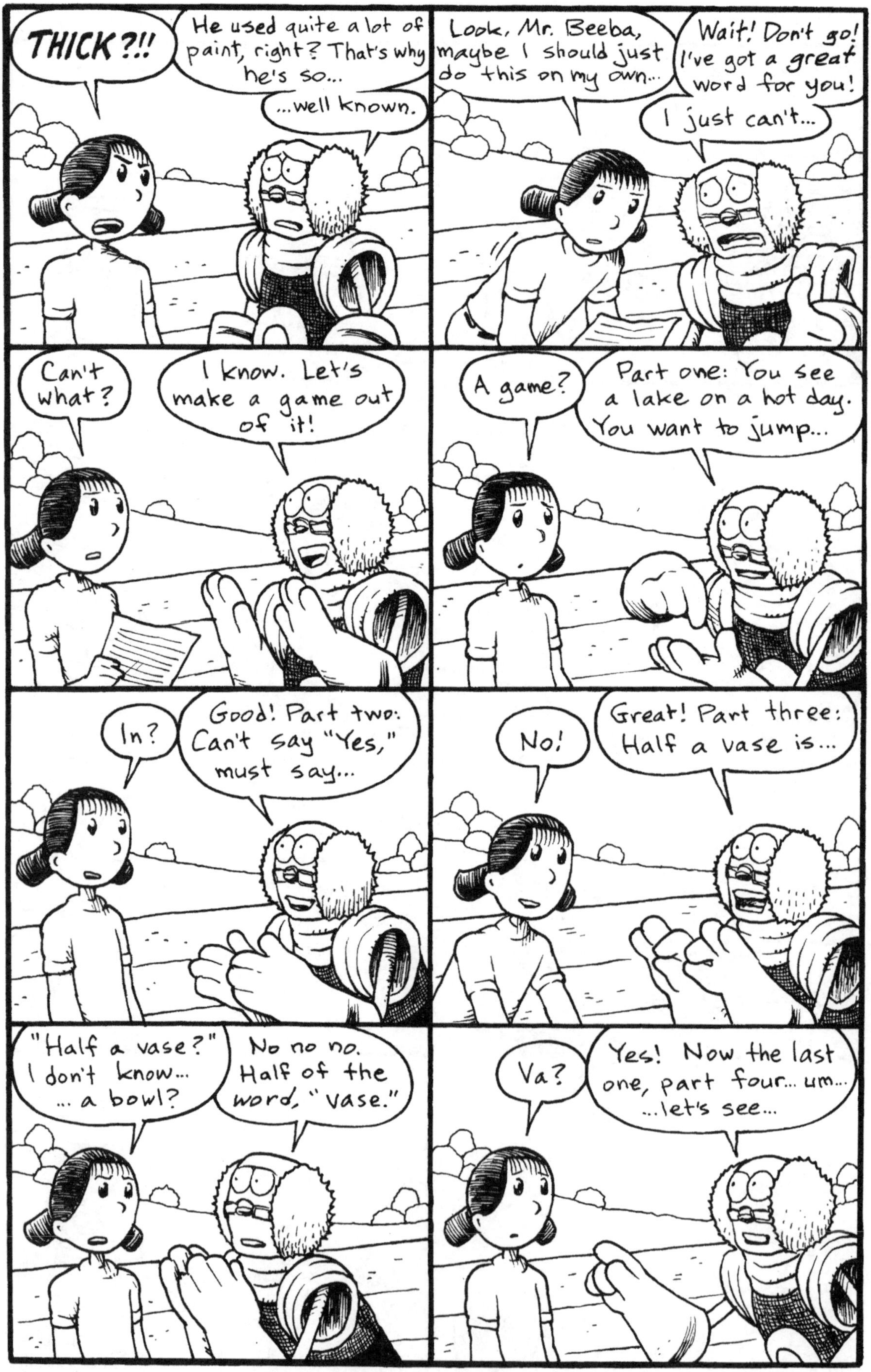
THICK?!!
He used quite a lot of paint, right? That's why he's so...
...well known.
Look, Mr. Beeba, maybe I should just do this on my own...
Wait! Don't go! I've got a great word for you!
I just can't...
Can't what?
I know. Let's make a game out of it!
A game?
Part one: You see a lake on a hot day. You want to jump...
In?
Good! Part two: Can't say "Yes," must say...
No!
Great! Part three: Half a vase is...
"Half a vase?" I don't know... ...a bowl?
No no no. Half of the word, "vase."
Va?
Yes! Now the last one, part four... um... ...let's see...

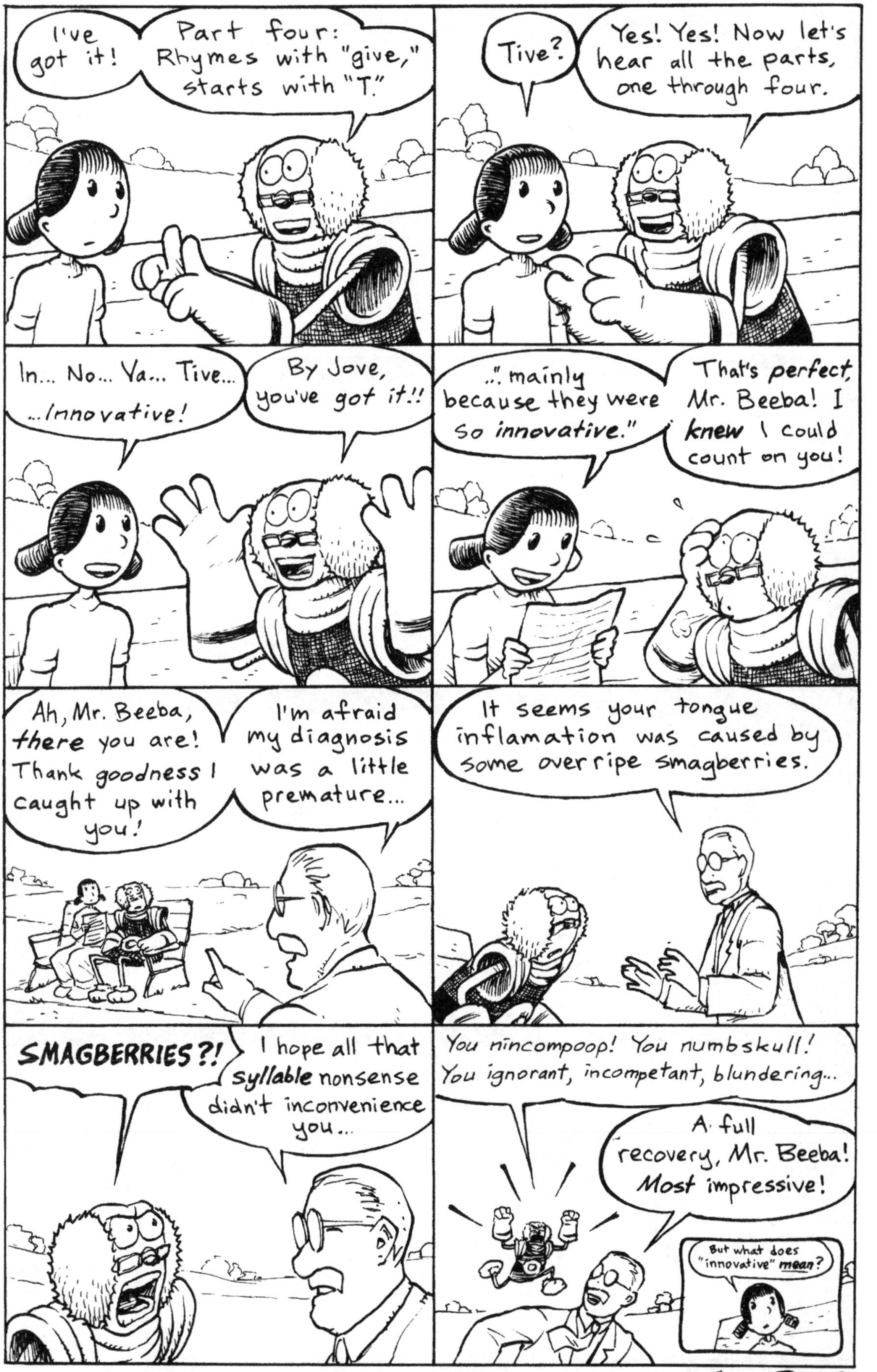
I've got it!
Part four: Rhymes with "give," starts with "T."
Tive?
Yes! Yes! Now let's hear all the parts, one through four.
In... No... Ya... Tive... ...Innovative!
By Jove, you've got it!!
..." mainly because they were so innovative."
That's perfect, Mr. Beeba! I knew I could count on you!
Ah, Mr. Beeba, there you are! Thank goodness I caught up with you!
I'm afraid my diagnosis was a little premature...
It seems your tongue inflamation was caused by some overripe smagberries.
SMAGBERRIES?!
I hope all that syllable nonsense didn't inconvenience you...
You nincompoop! You numbskull! You ignorant, incompetant, blundering...
A full recovery, Mr. Beeba! Most impressive!
But what does "innovative" mean?

The End

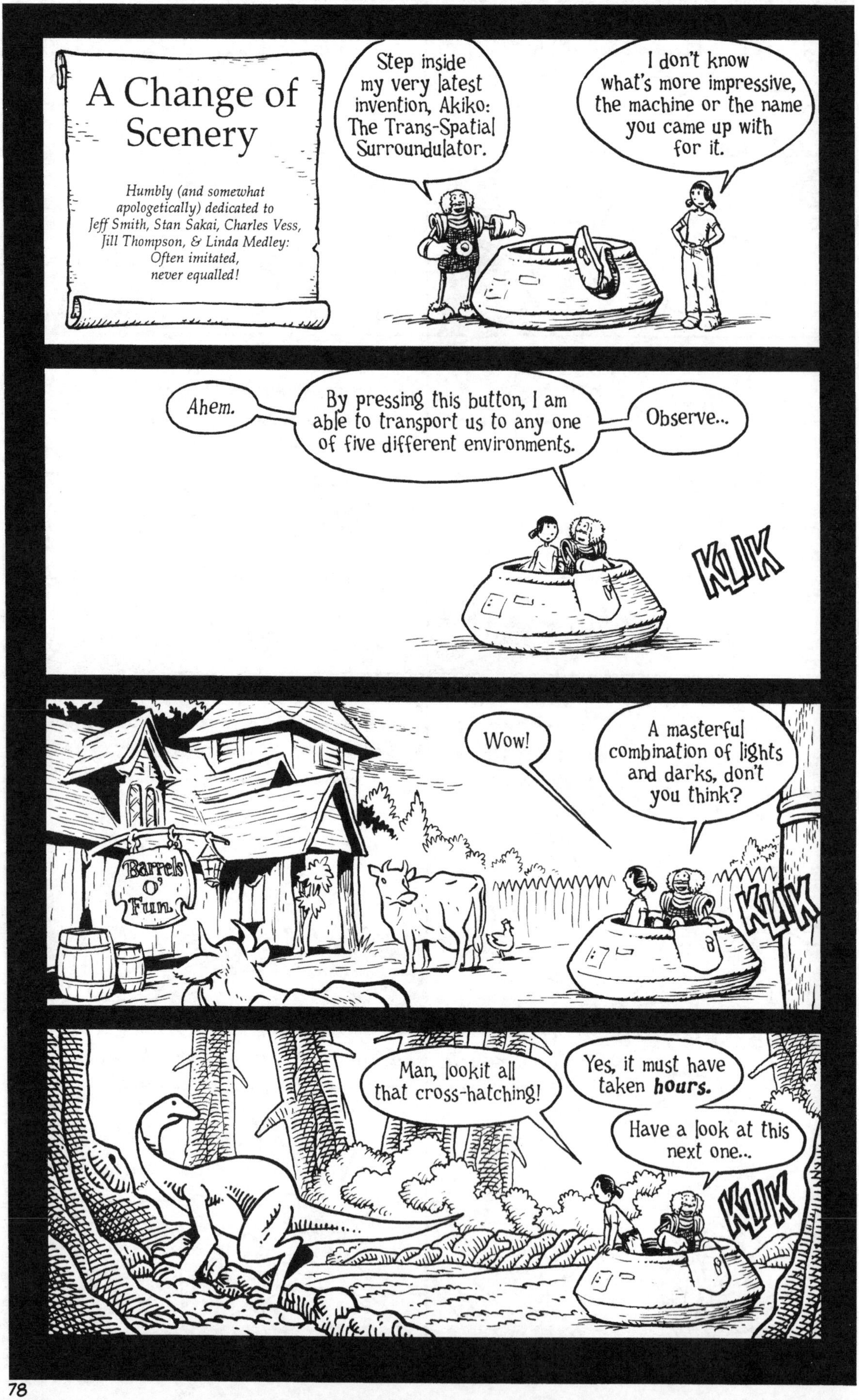
A Change of Scenery
Humbly (and somewhat apologetically) dedicated to Jeff Smith, Stan Sakai, Charles Vess, Jill Thompson, & Linda Medley: Often imitated, never equalled!
Step inside my very latest invention, Akiko: The Trans-Spatial Surroundulator.
I don't know what's more impressive, the machine or the name you came up with for it.
Ahem.
By pressing this button, I am able to transport us to any one of five different environments.
Observe...
KLIK
Barrels O' Fun
Wow!
A masterful combination of lights and darks, don't you think?
KLIK
Man, lookit all that cross-hatching!
Yes, it must have taken **hours.**
Have a look at this next one...
KLIK

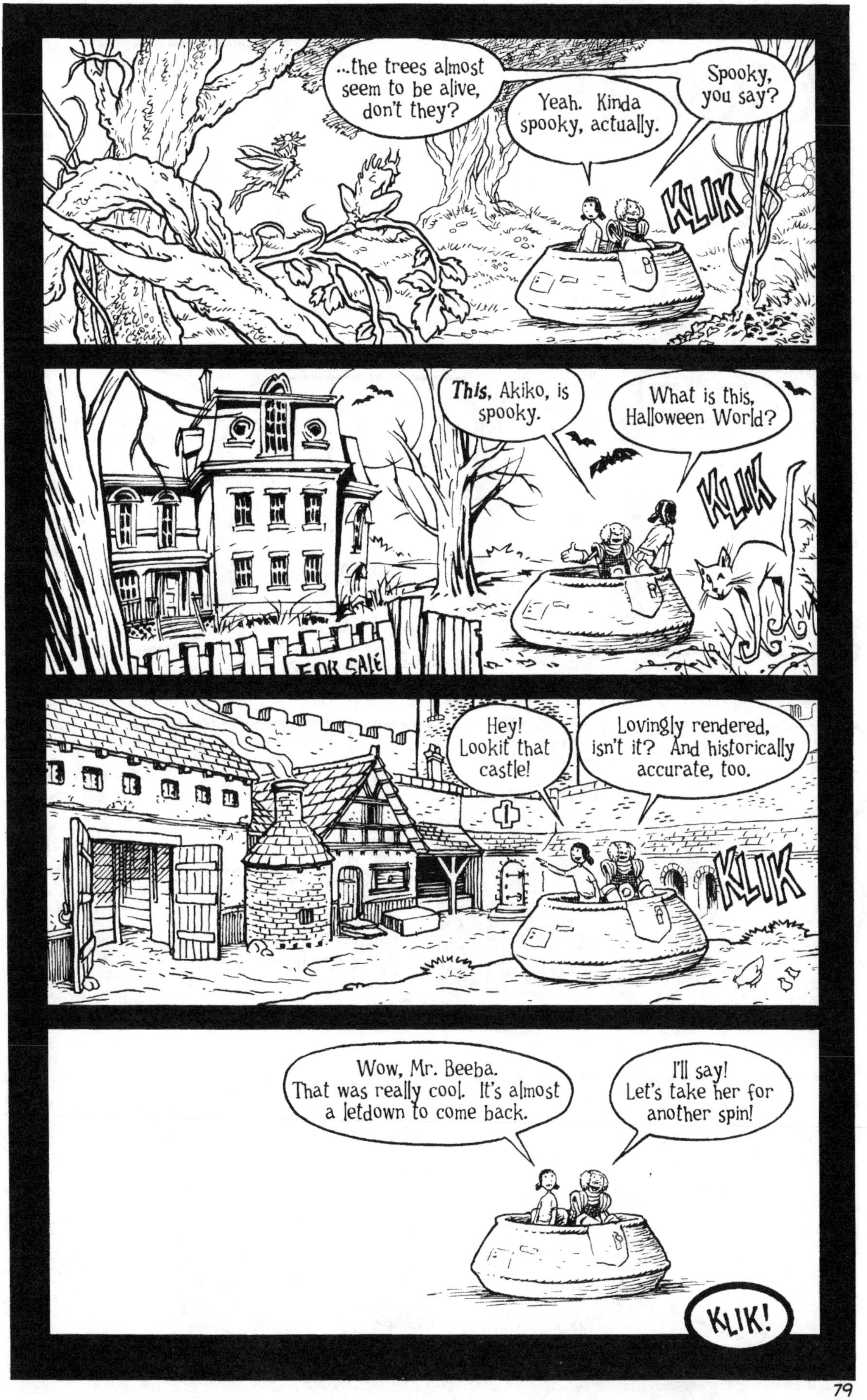
...the trees almost seem to be alive, don't they?
Yeah. Kinda spooky, actually.
Spooky, you say?
KLIK
This, Akiko, is spooky.
What is this, Halloween World?
KLIK
FOR SALE
Hey! Lookit that castle!
Lovingly rendered, isn't it? And historically accurate, too.
KLIK
Wow, Mr. Beeba. That was really cool. It's almost a letdown to come back.
I'll say! Let's take her for another spin!
KLIK!

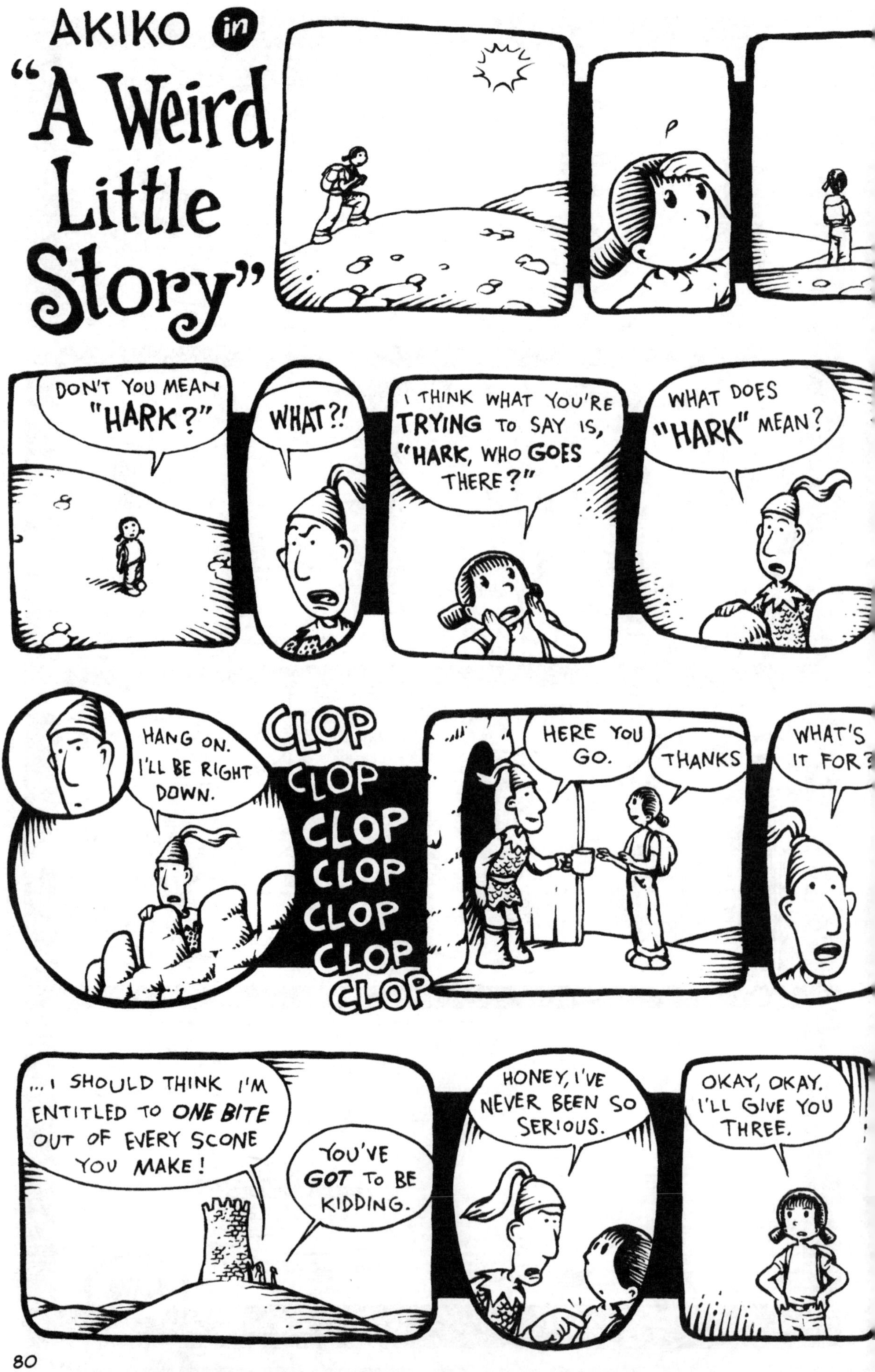
AKIKO in
"A Weird Little Story"
DON'T YOU MEAN "HARK?"
WHAT?!
I THINK WHAT YOU'RE TRYING TO SAY IS, "HARK, WHO GOES THERE?"
WHAT DOES "HARK" MEAN?
HANG ON. I'LL BE RIGHT DOWN.
CLOP CLOP CLOP CLOP CLOP CLOP CLOP
HERE YOU GO.
THANKS
WHAT'S IT FOR?
...I SHOULD THINK I'M ENTITLED TO ONE BITE OUT OF EVERY SCONE YOU MAKE!
YOU'VE GOT TO BE KIDDING.
HONEY, I'VE NEVER BEEN SO SERIOUS.
OKAY, OKAY. I'LL GIVE YOU THREE.

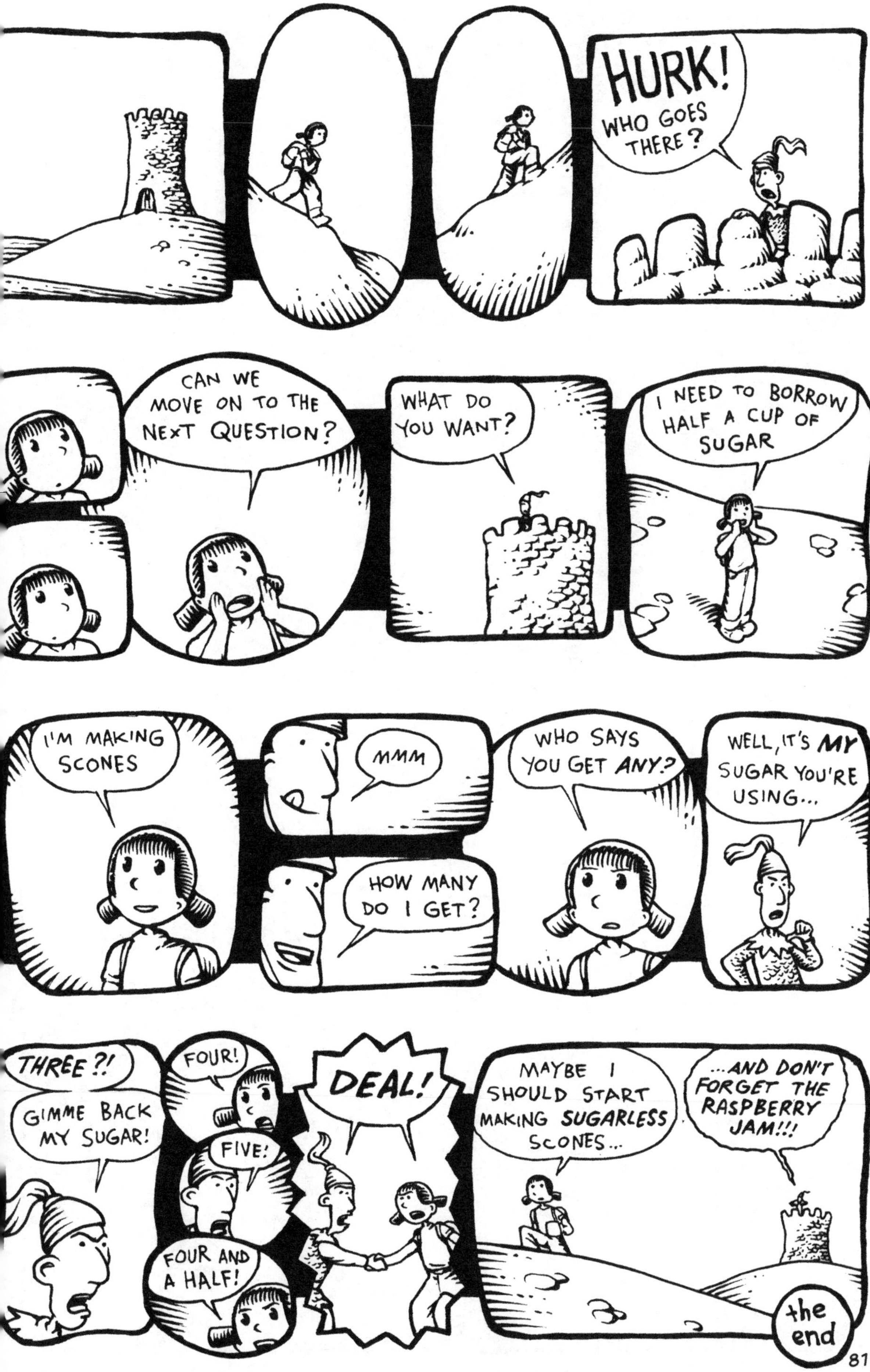
HURK!
WHO GOES THERE?
CAN WE MOVE ON TO THE NEXT QUESTION?
WHAT DO YOU WANT?
I NEED TO BORROW HALF A CUP OF SUGAR
I'M MAKING SCONES
MMM
HOW MANY DO I GET?
WHO SAYS YOU GET ANY?
WELL, IT'S MY SUGAR YOU'RE USING...
THREE?!
GIMME BACK MY SUGAR!
FOUR!
FIVE!
FOUR AND A HALF!
DEAL!
MAYBE I SHOULD START MAKING SUGARLESS SCONES...
...AND DON'T FORGET THE RASPBERRY JAM!!!
the end

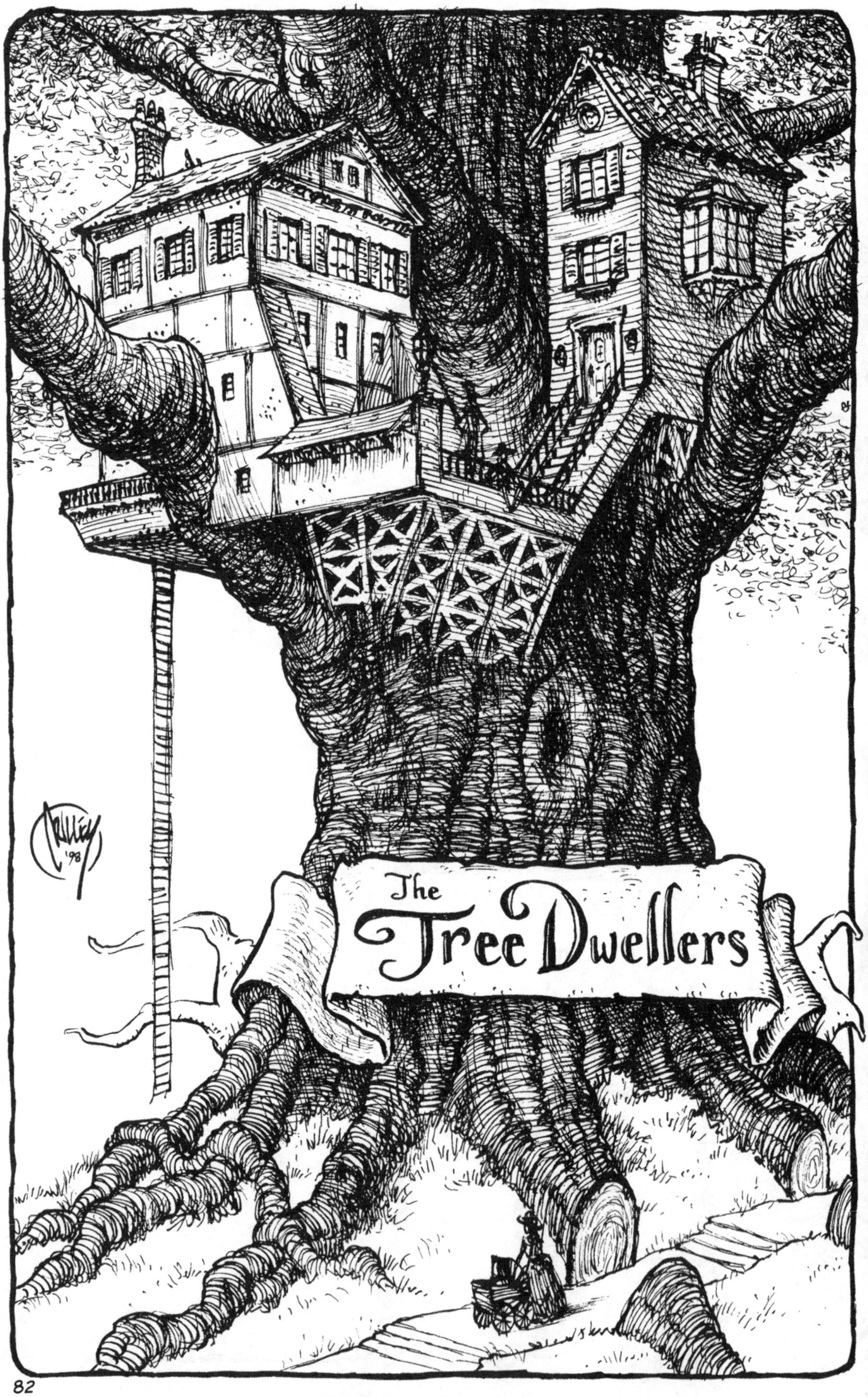
The Tree Dwellers

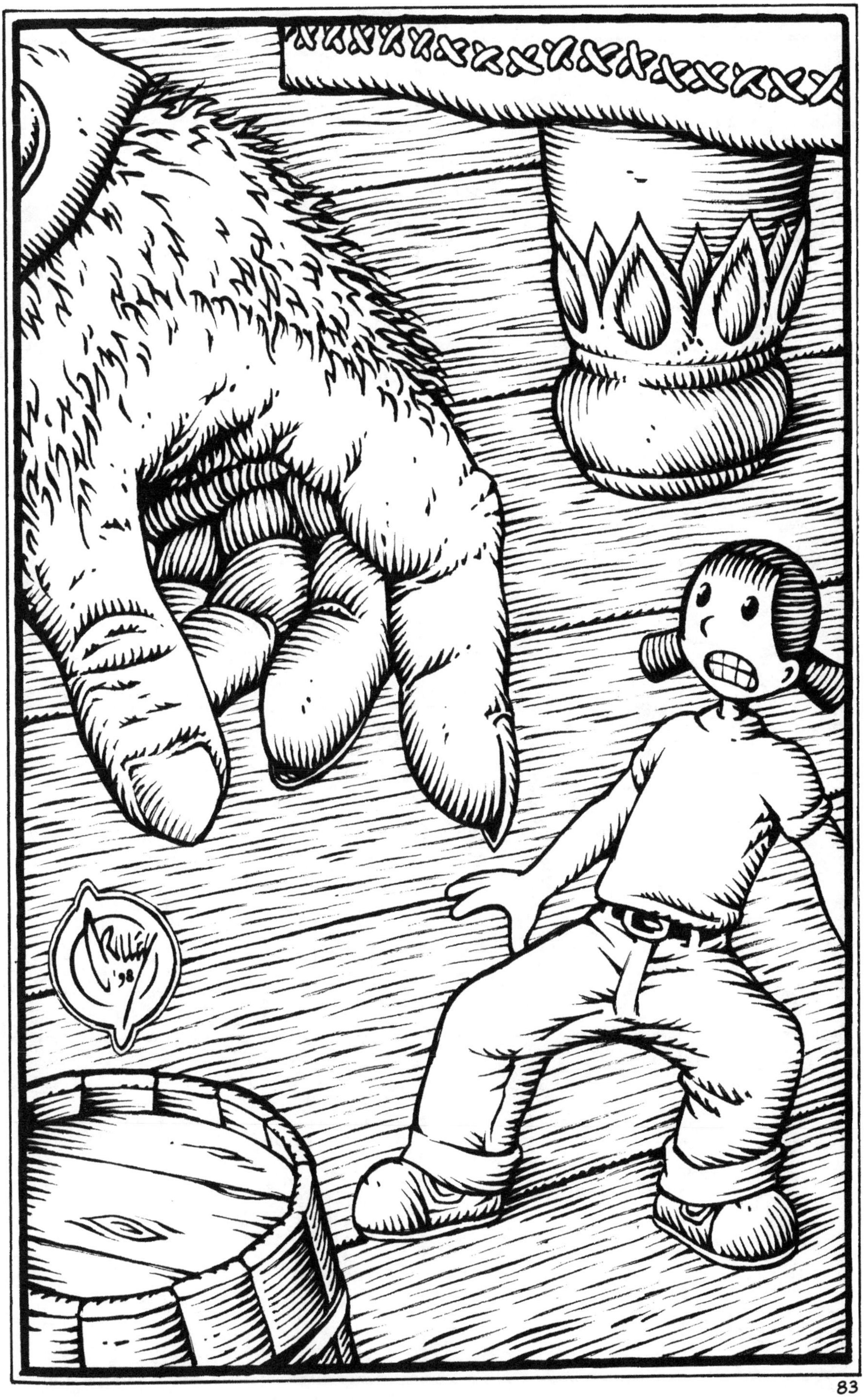

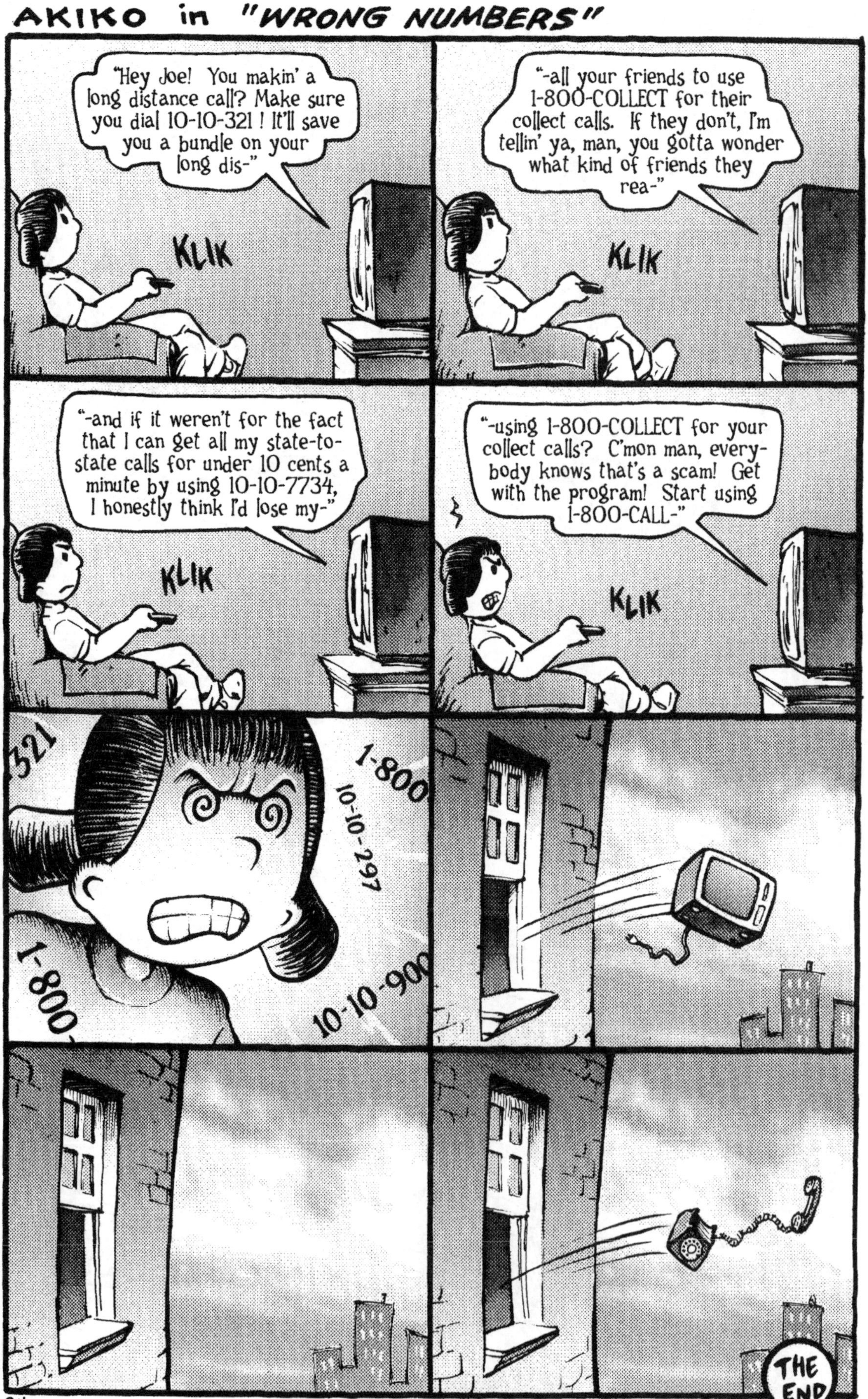
AKIKO in "WRONG NUMBERS"
"Hey Joe! You makin' a long distance call? Make sure you dial 10-10-321 ! It'll save you a bundle on your long dis-"
KLIK
"-all your friends to use 1-800-COLLECT for their collect calls. If they don't, I'm tellin' ya, man, you gotta wonder what kind of friends they rea-"
KLIK
"-and if it weren't for the fact that I can get all my state-to-state calls for under 10 cents a minute by using 10-10-7734, I honestly think I'd lose my-"
KLIK
"-using 1-800-COLLECT for your collect calls? C'mon man, every-body knows that's a scam! Get with the program! Start using 1-800-CALL-"
KLIK
321
1-800
10-10-297
1-800
10-10-900
THE END

AKIKO in "The BiG Picture"

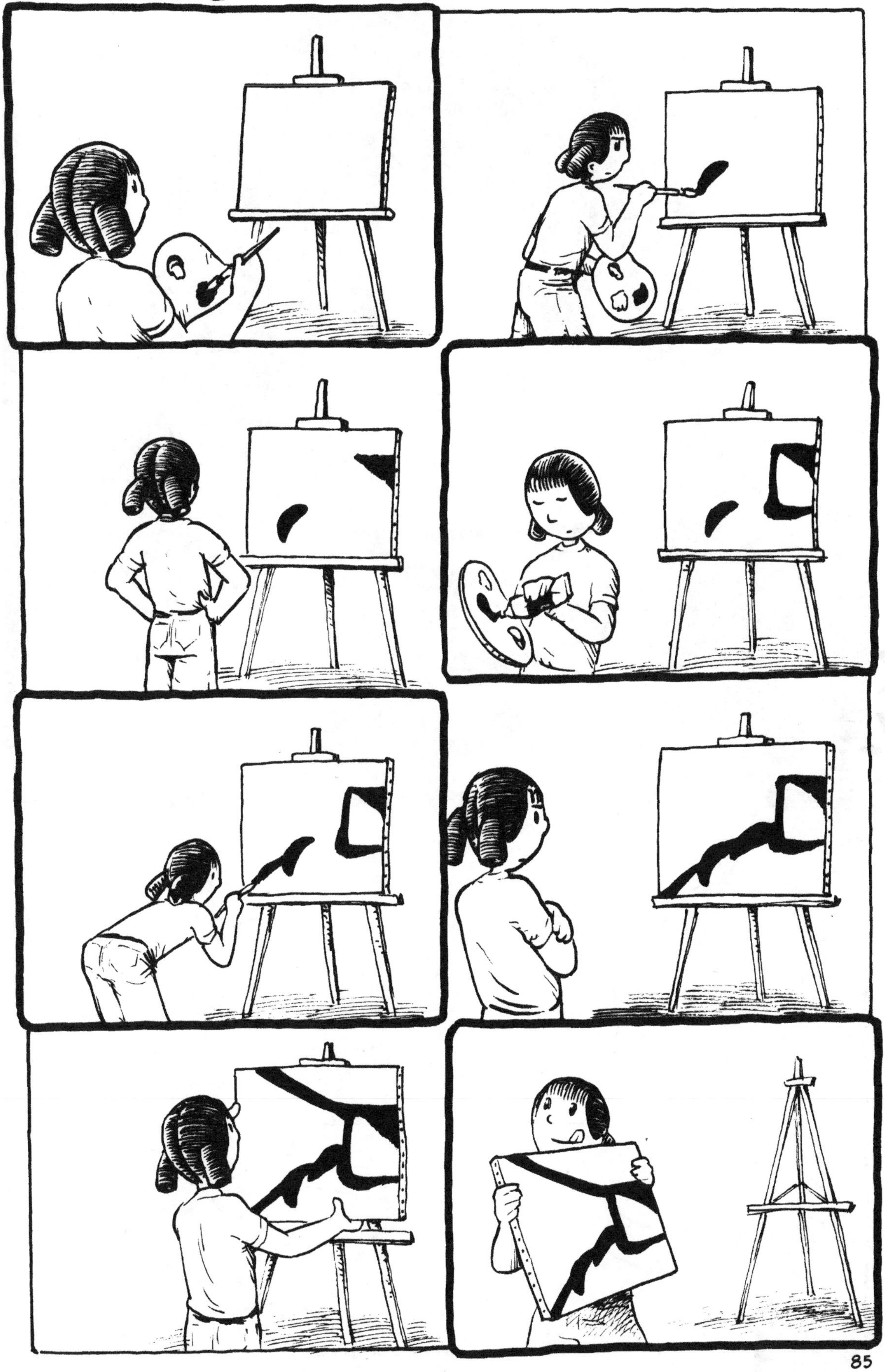

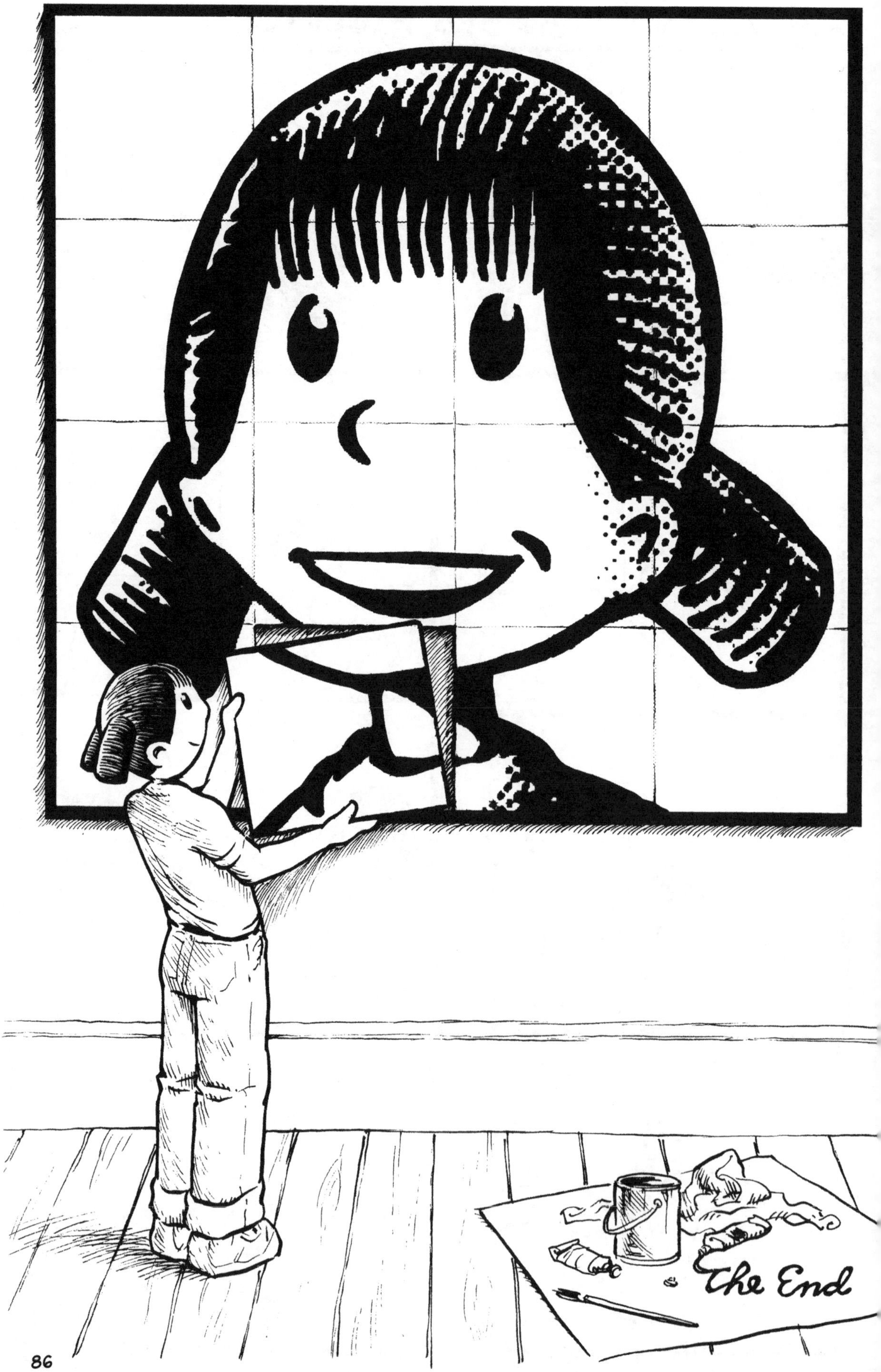
The End

planets

Planets, planets, everywhere,
Some are round, and some are square,
Some are ugly, some are nice,
Some I'd like to visit twice.

Have you heard of the Planet Thoo,
Where people's heads are filled with glue?
And every day 'bout half past four,
The King declares another war?

I much prefer the Planet Bloon,
Where every Tuesday afternoon
The Queen must practice her bassoon.
(She plays a wee bit out of tune)

Planets, planets, all around,
Some are square, and some are round,
Some are big, and some are small,
Some I do not like at all.

You wouldn't like the Planet Gway
Where people watch the news all day
And no one stops to talk to you
Because they've got Too Much to do.

I'd rather see the Planet Zwee.
(The pace is much more leisurely.)
The folks there say it isn't wrong
To stay in bed all morning long.

Planets, planets, everywhere,
Some are round, and some are square,
Some are ugly, some are nice,
Some I'd like to visit twice.

You won't believe the Planet Whyze
Where yogurt walks and butter flies
And muffins dress in silk and lace.
(It *is* a most peculiar place.)

But still it beats the Planet Traw
Where laughing is against the law
And children aren't allowed to play
Or smile more than once a day.

Planets, planets, all around,
Some are square, and some are round,
Some are big, and some are small,
Some I do not like at all.

I'll bet that you have never heard
Of people on the planet Squird,
And how they take their morning tea
A little bit too seriously.

You'd best avoid the Planet Kwight
Where people think they're always right,
And if your views aren't *apropos*
They're not afraid to tell you so.

Planets, planets, everywhere,
Some are round, and some are square,
Some are ugly, and some are nice,
Some I'd like to visit twice.

I once went to the Planet Flunn
(The 16th planet from the sun)
And there I searched from pole to pole
And never even met a soul.

From there I went to the Planet Plarrs
Where homes are built of candy bars
And there's a pond where you can wade
Up to your knees in lemonade.

Planets, planets, all around,
Some are square, and some are round,
Some are East, and some are West,
One is different from the rest.

Of course I mean the Planet Earth,
And my opinion, for what it's worth,
Is that it's lovely, through and through.

(But *I* prefer the planet Smoo.)

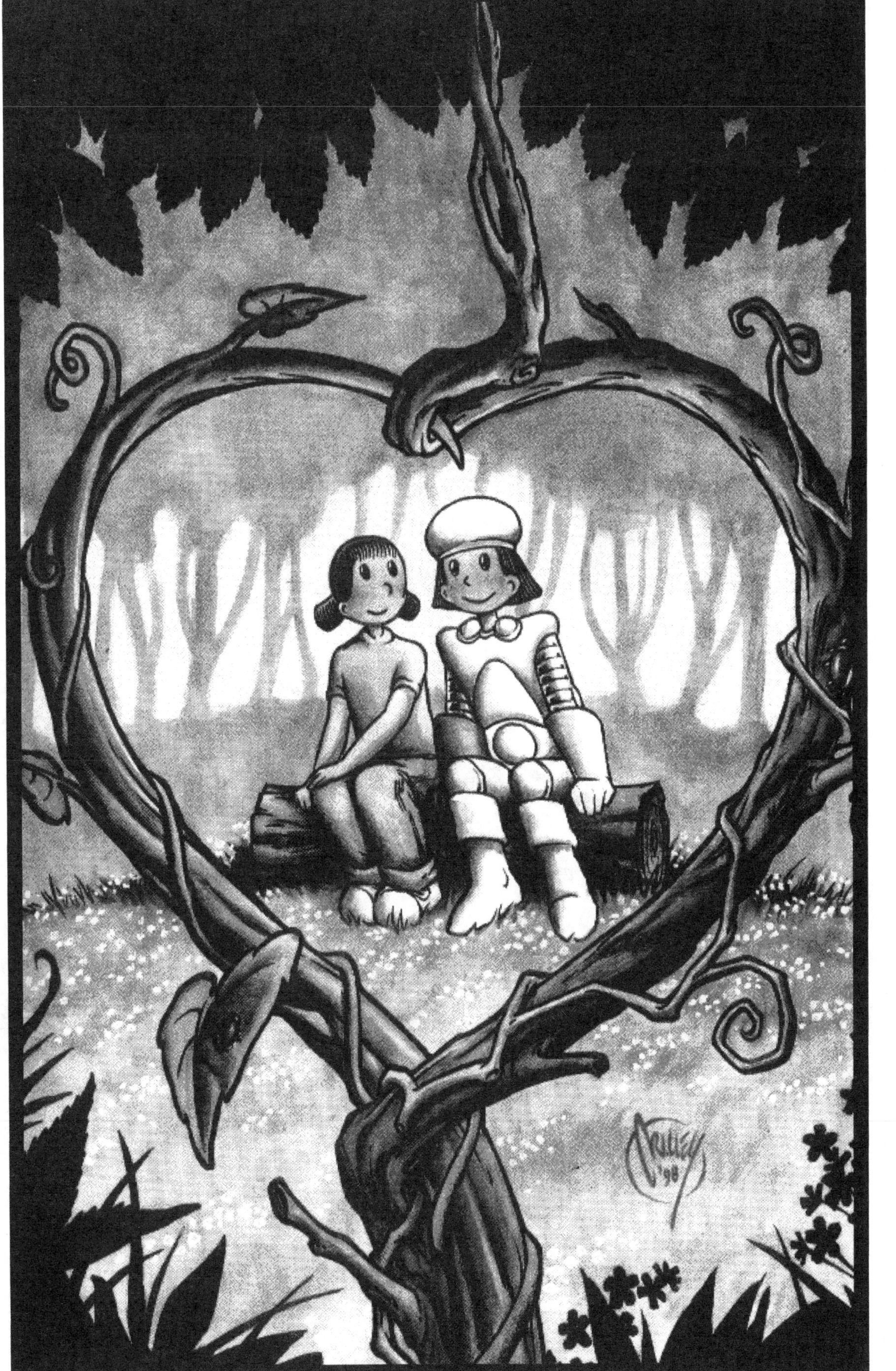

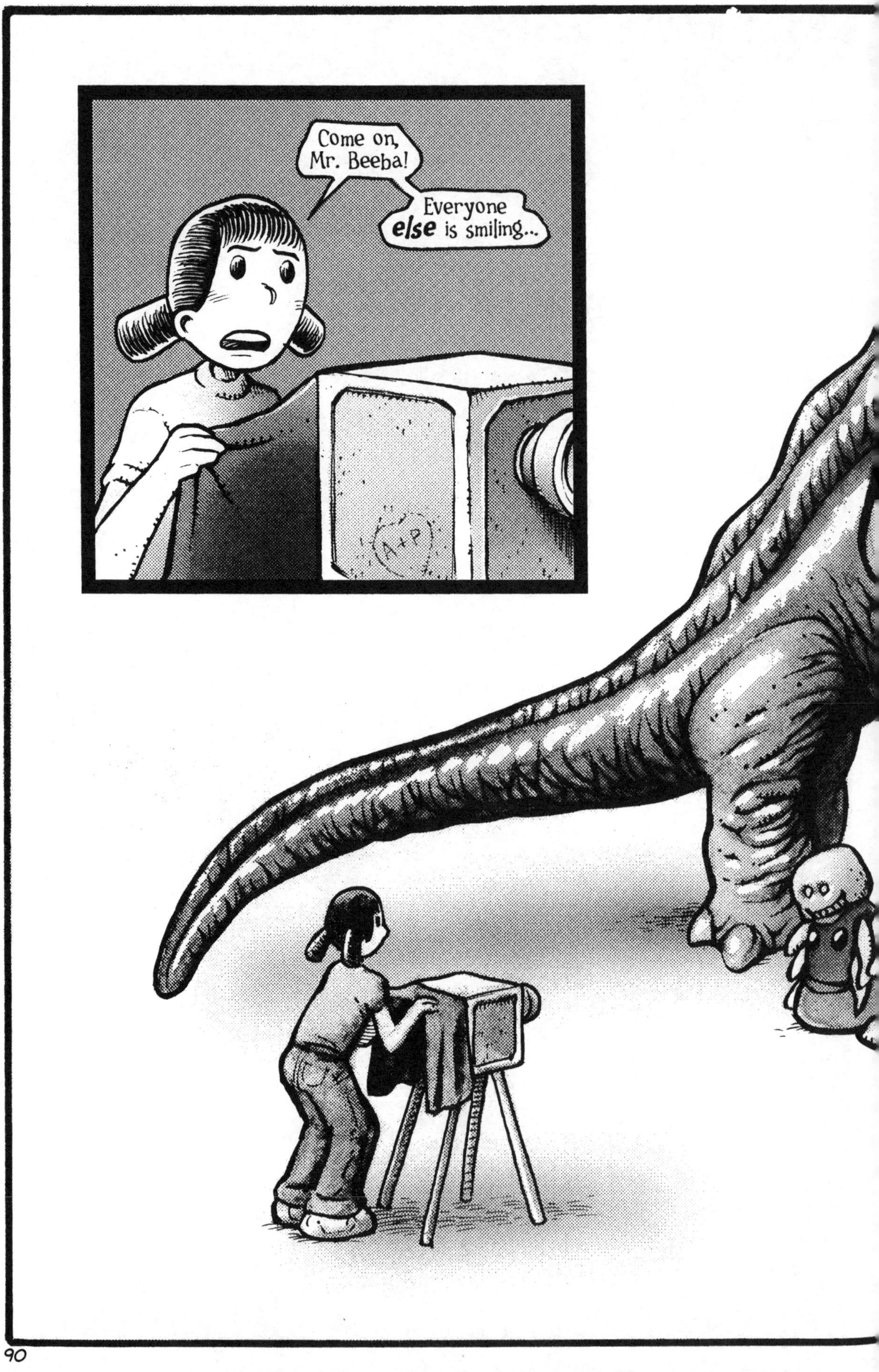
Come on, Mr. Beeba!
Everyone *else* is smiling...
A+P

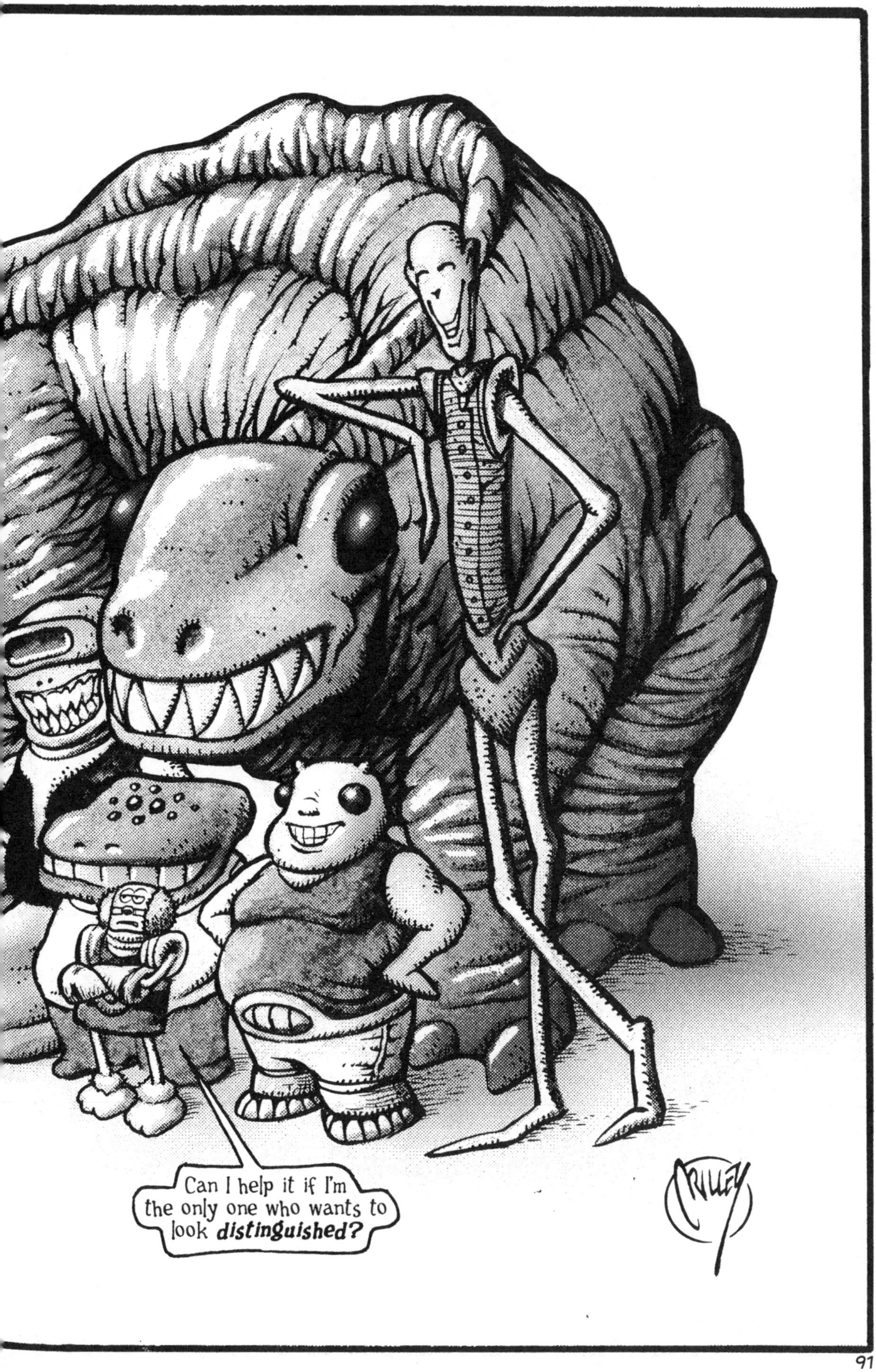
Can I help it if I'm the only one who wants to look **distinguished?**
CRILLEY

Spuckler *in* "Spuckler vs. Spuckler"

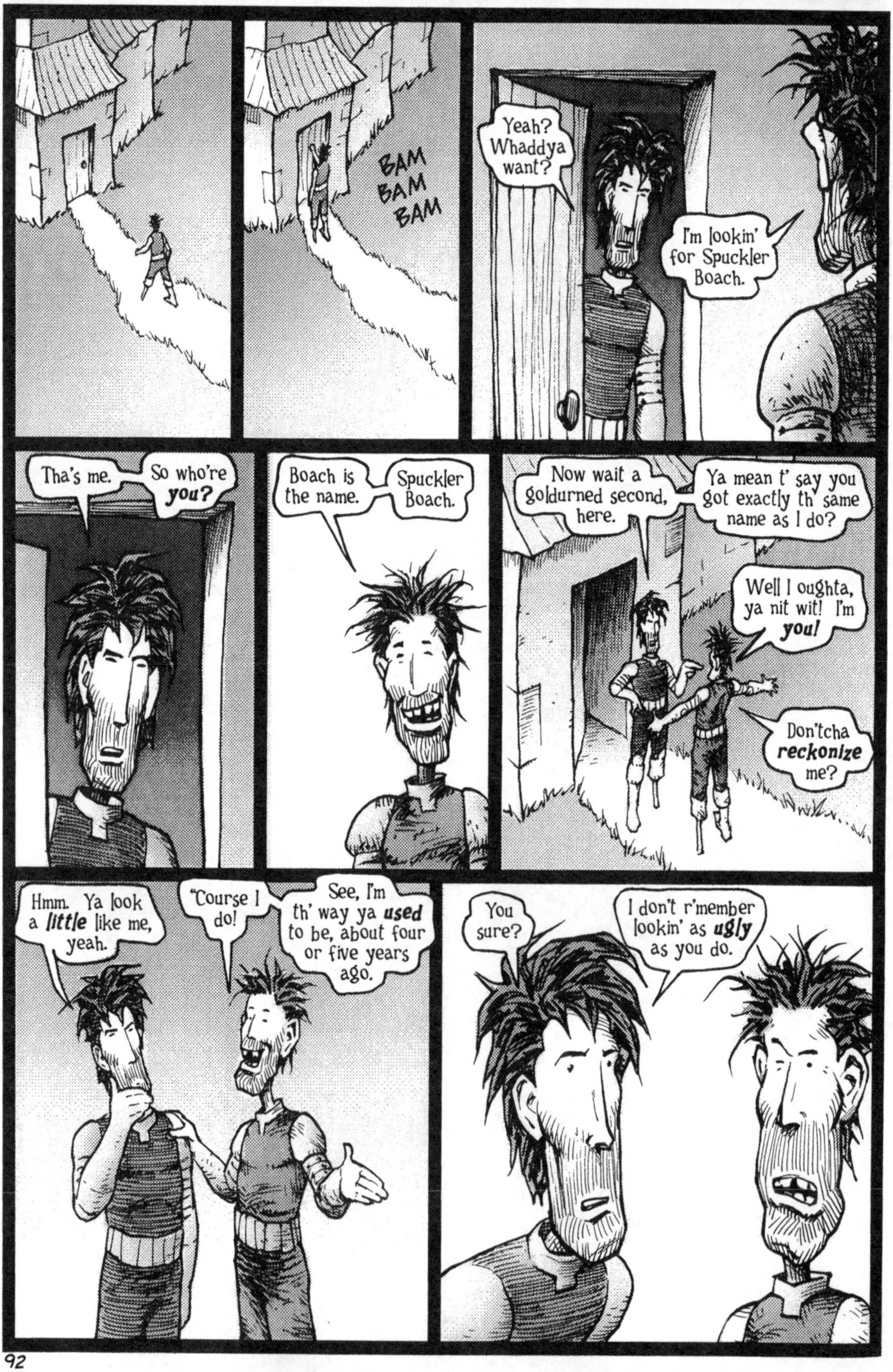

BAM
BAM
BAM
Yeah? Whaddya want?
I'm lookin' for Spuckler Boach.
Tha's me.
So who're *you?*
Boach is the name.
Spuckler Boach.
Now wait a goldurned second, here.
Ya mean t' say you got exactly th' same name as I do?
Well I oughta, ya nit wit! I'm *you!*
Don'tcha *reckonize* me?
Hmm. Ya look a *little* like me, yeah.
"Course I do!
See, I'm th' way ya *used* to be, about four or five years ago.
You sure?
I don't r'member lookin' as *ugly* as you do.

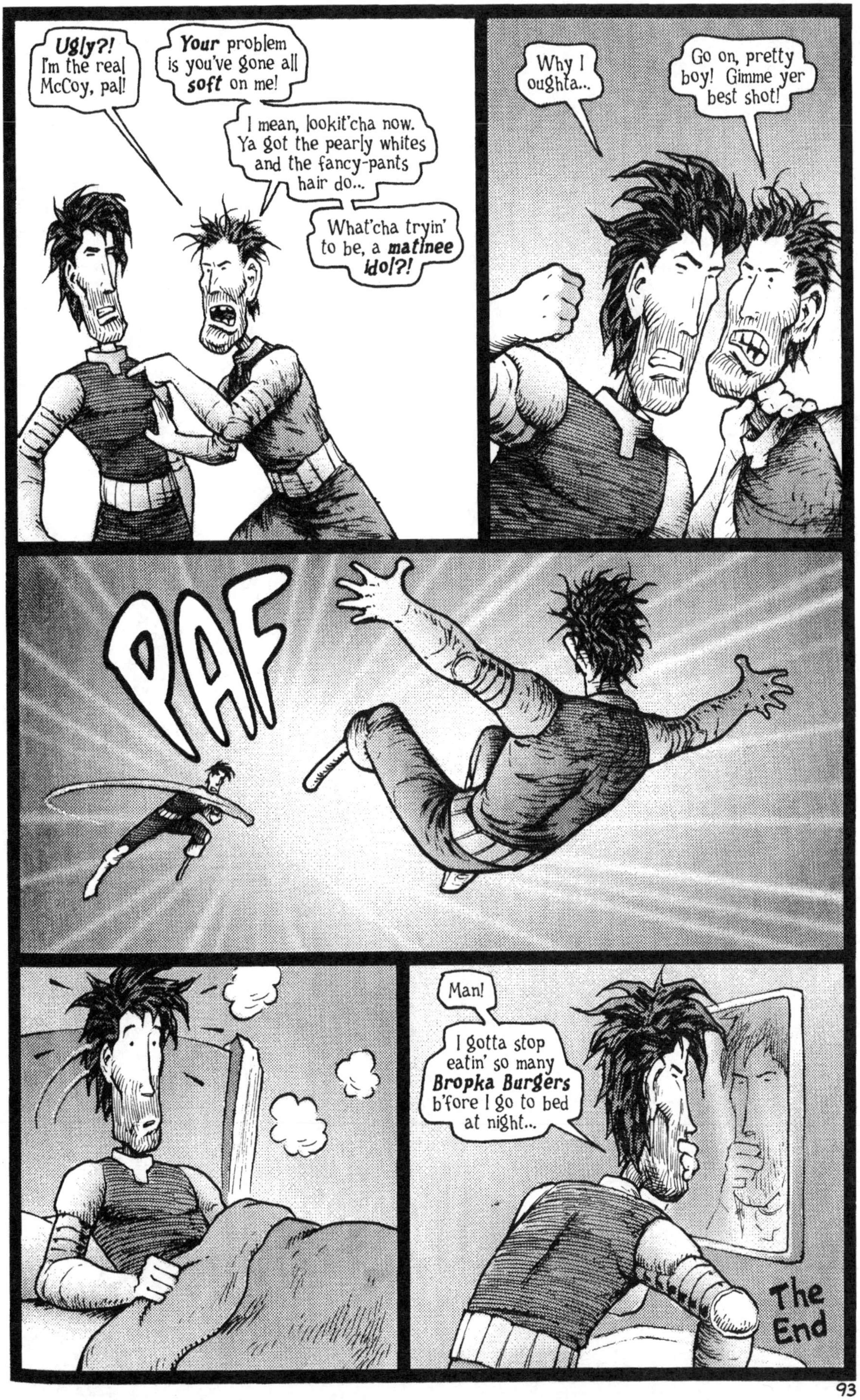
Ugly?! I'm the real McCoy, pal!
Your problem is you've gone all soft on me!
I mean, lookit'cha now. Ya got the pearly whites and the fancy-pants hair do...
What'cha tryin' to be, a matinee idol?!
Why I oughta...
Go on, pretty boy! Gimme yer best shot!
PAF
Man!
I gotta stop eatin' so many Bropka Burgers b'fore I go to bed at night...
The End

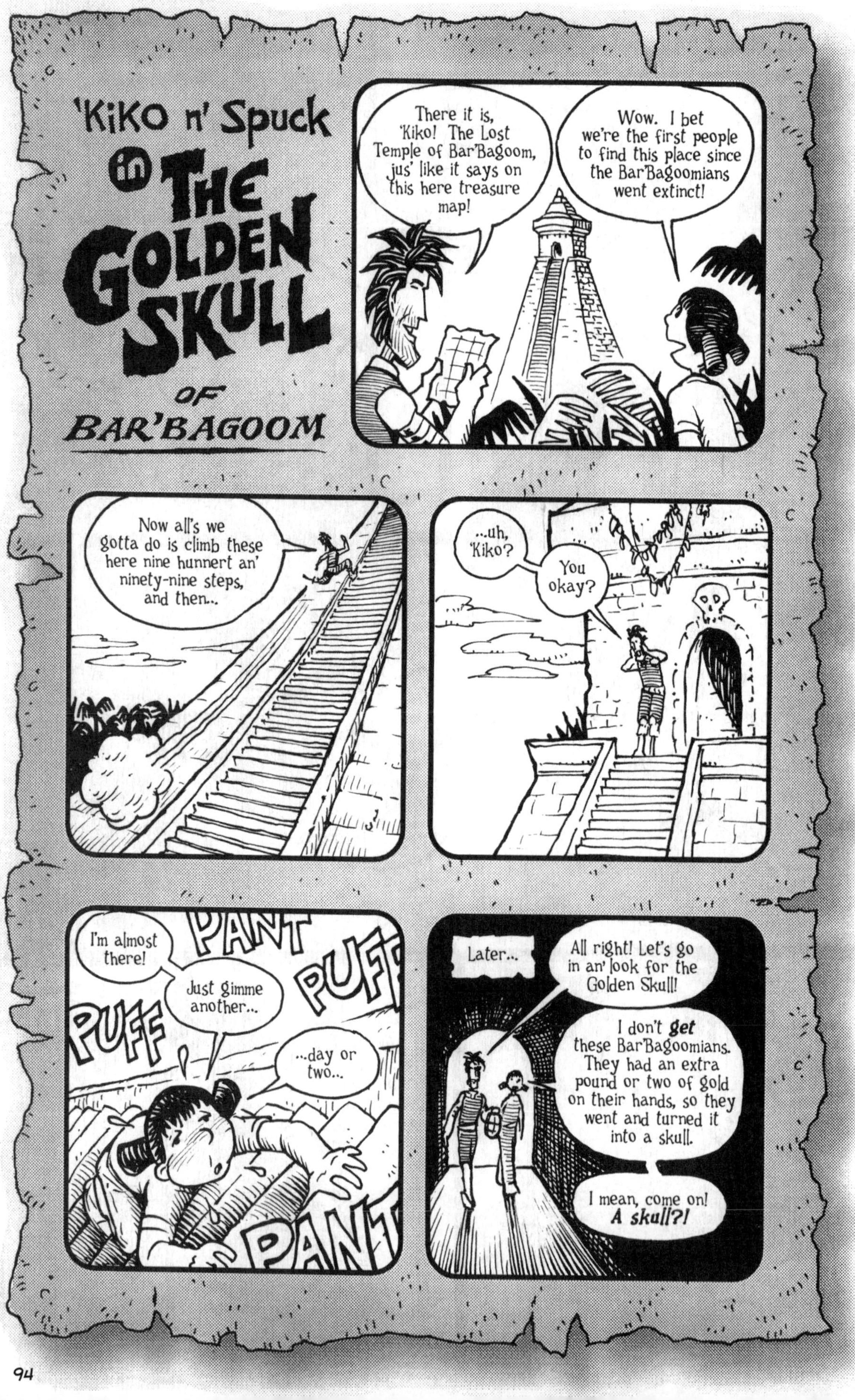
'KiKO n' Spuck
in
THE GOLDEN SKULL
OF
BAR'BAGOOM
There it is, 'Kiko! The Lost Temple of Bar'Bagoom, jus' like it says on this here treasure map!
Wow. I bet we're the first people to find this place since the Bar'Bagoomians went extinct!
Now all's we gotta do is climb these here nine hunnert an' ninety-nine steps, and then...
...uh, 'Kiko?
You okay?
I'm almost there!
PANT
PUFF
PUFF
Just gimme another...
...day or two...
PANT
Later...
All right! Let's go in an' look for the Golden Skull!
I don't **get** these Bar'Bagoomians. They had an extra pound or two of gold on their hands, so they went and turned it into a skull.
I mean, come on! ***A skull?!***

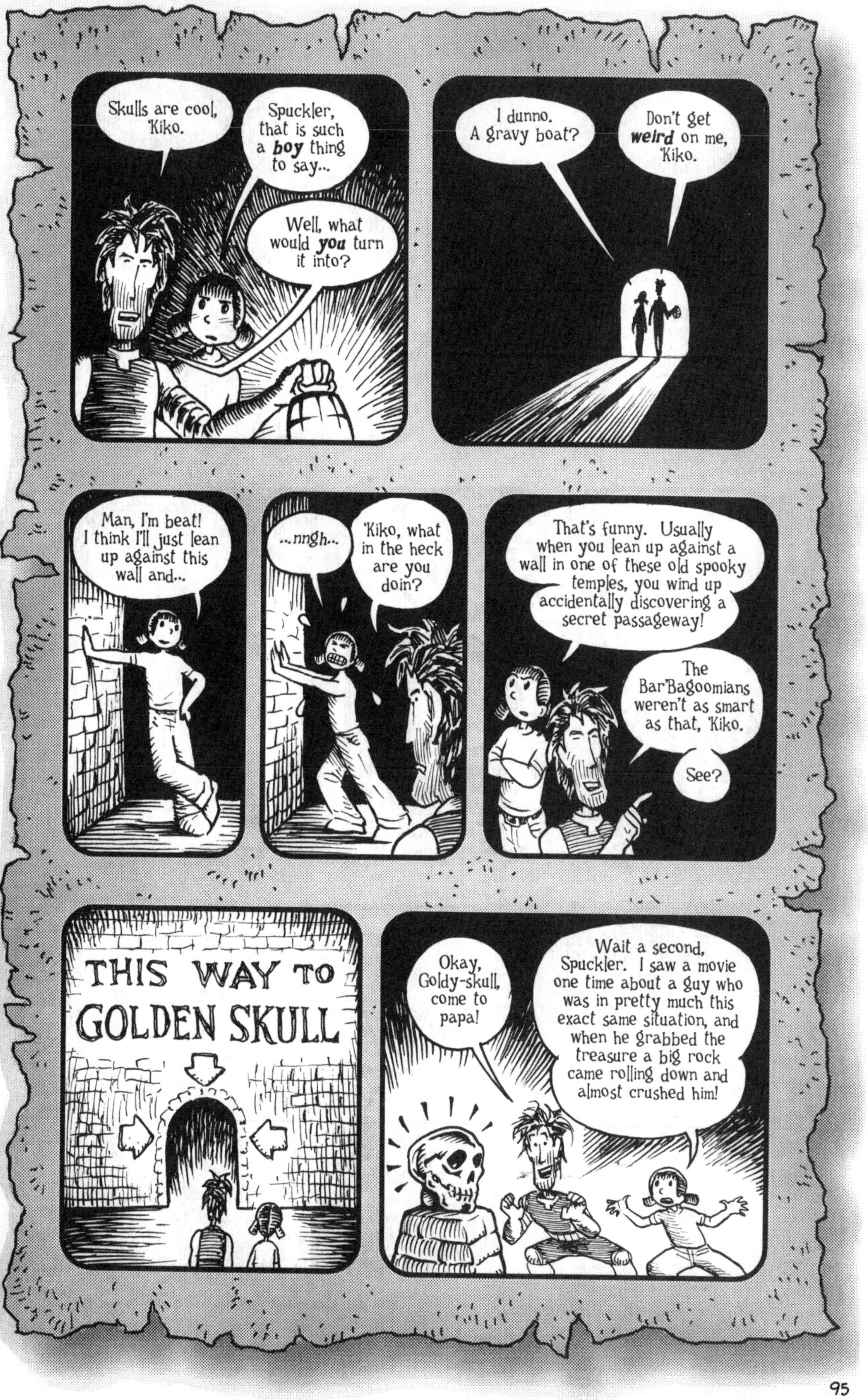

Skulls are cool, 'Kiko.
Spuckler, that is such a **boy** thing to say...
Well, what would **you** turn it into?
I dunno. A gravy boat?
Don't get **weird** on me, 'Kiko.
Man, I'm beat! I think I'll just lean up against this wall and...
...nngh...
'Kiko, what in the heck are you doin?
That's funny. Usually when you lean up against a wall in one of these old spooky temples, you wind up accidentally discovering a secret passageway!
The Bar'Bagoomians weren't as smart as that, 'Kiko.
See?
THIS WAY TO GOLDEN SKULL
Okay, Goldy-skull, come to papa!
Wait a second, Spuckler. I saw a movie one time about a guy who was in pretty much this exact same situation, and when he grabbed the treasure a big rock came rolling down and almost crushed him!

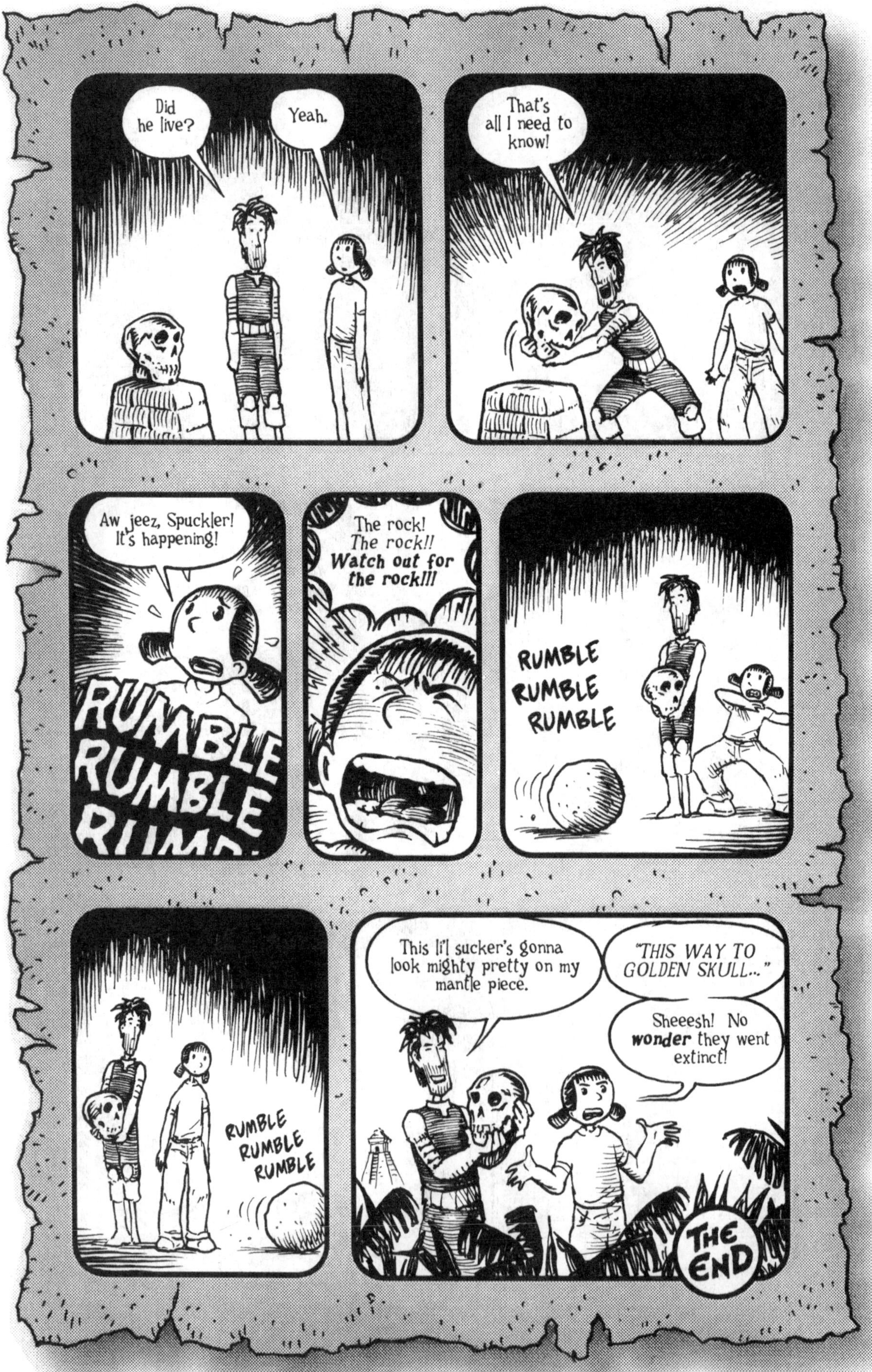
Did he live?
Yeah.
That's all I need to know!
Aw jeez, Spuckler! It's happening!
RUMBLE RUMBLE
The rock! The rock!! Watch out for the rock!!!
RUMBLE RUMBLE RUMBLE
RUMBLE RUMBLE RUMBLE
This li'l sucker's gonna look mighty pretty on my mantle piece.
"THIS WAY TO GOLDEN SKULL..."
Sheeesh! No wonder they went extinct!
THE END

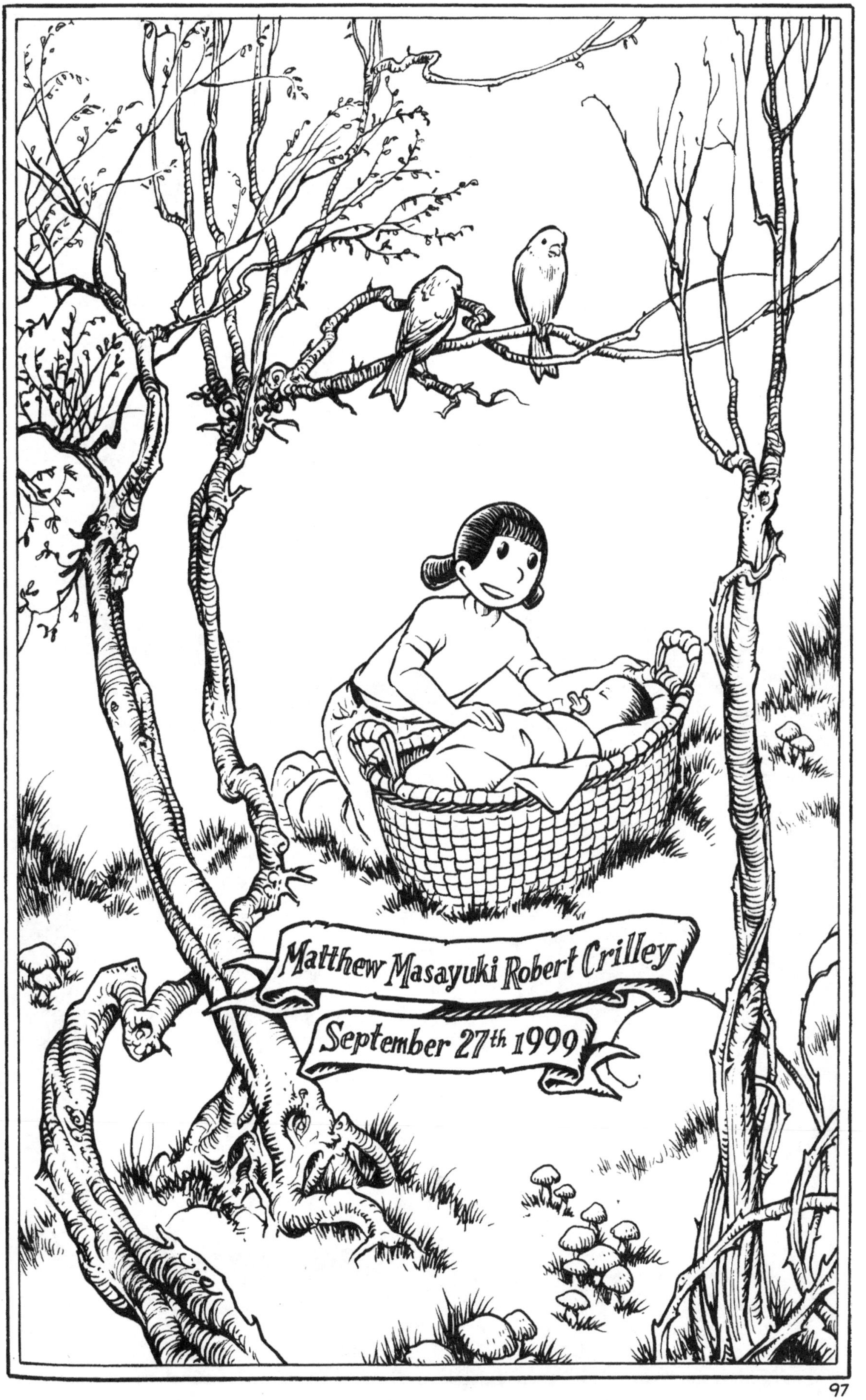
Matthew Masayuki Robert Crilley
September 27th 1999

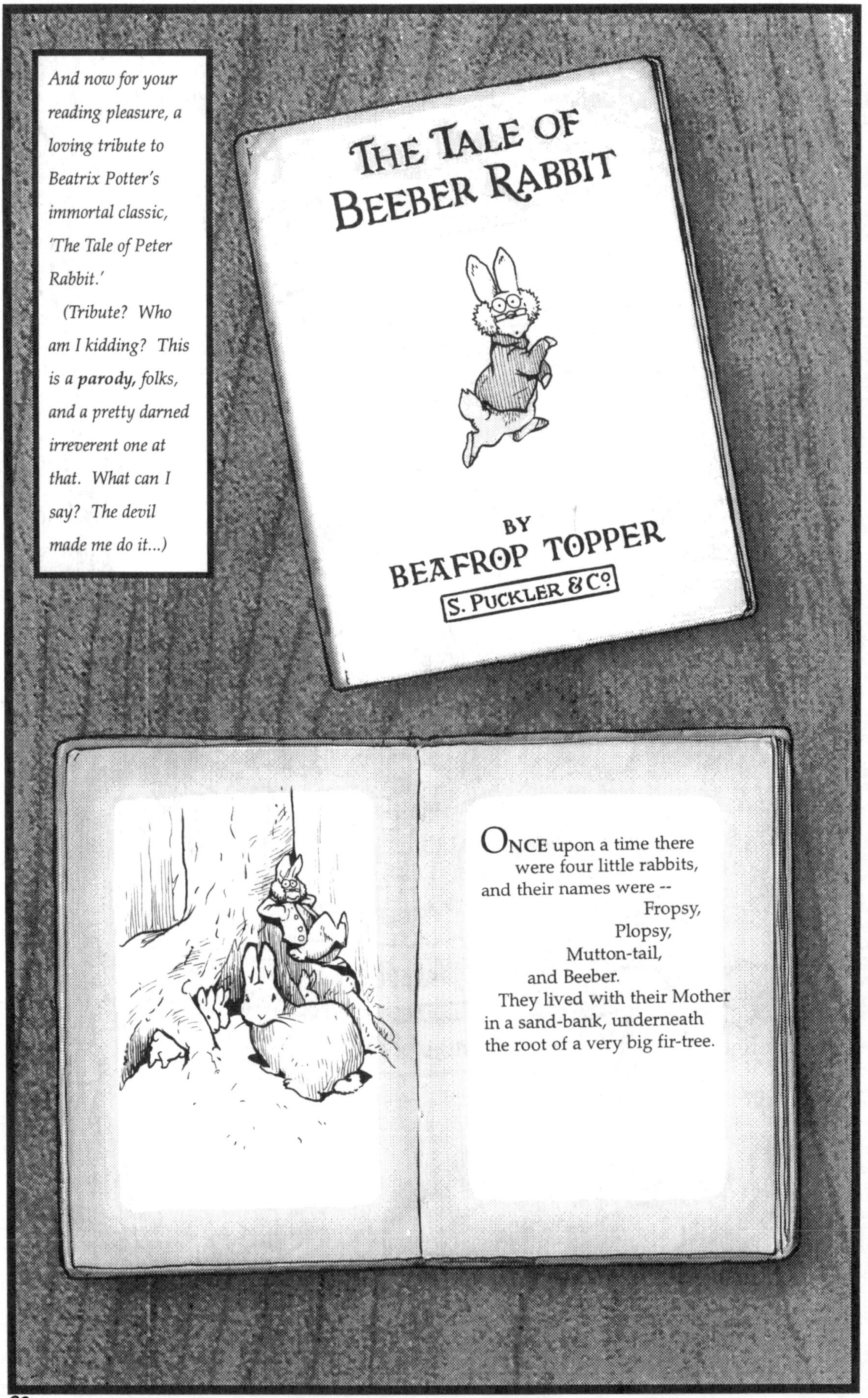
And now for your reading pleasure, a loving tribute to Beatrix Potter's immortal classic, 'The Tale of Peter Rabbit.'
(Tribute? Who am I kidding? This is a **parody,** folks, and a pretty darned irreverent one at that. What can I say? The devil made me do it...)
THE TALE OF BEEBER RABBIT
BY
BEAFROP TOPPER
S. PUCKLER & Co
ONCE upon a time there were four little rabbits, and their names were --
Fropsy,
Plopsy,
Mutton-tail,
and Beeber.
They lived with their Mother in a sand-bank, underneath the root of a very big fir-tree.

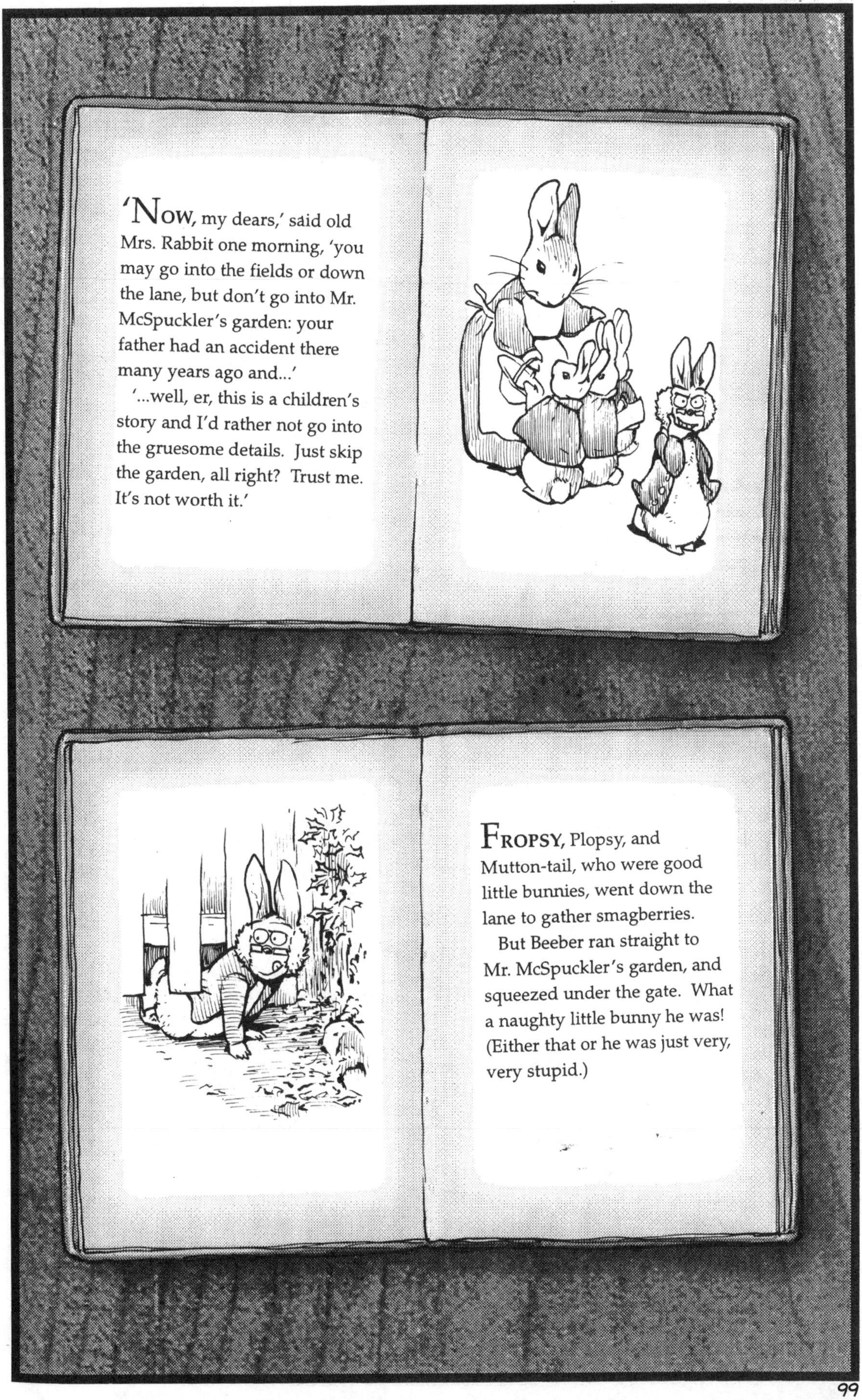
'Now, my dears,' said old Mrs. Rabbit one morning, 'you may go into the fields or down the lane, but don't go into Mr. McSpuckler's garden: your father had an accident there many years ago and...'
'...well, er, this is a children's story and I'd rather not go into the gruesome details. Just skip the garden, all right? Trust me. It's not worth it.'
Fropsy, Plopsy, and Mutton-tail, who were good little bunnies, went down the lane to gather smagberries.
But Beeber ran straight to Mr. McSpuckler's garden, and squeezed under the gate. What a naughty little bunny he was! (Either that or he was just very, very stupid.)

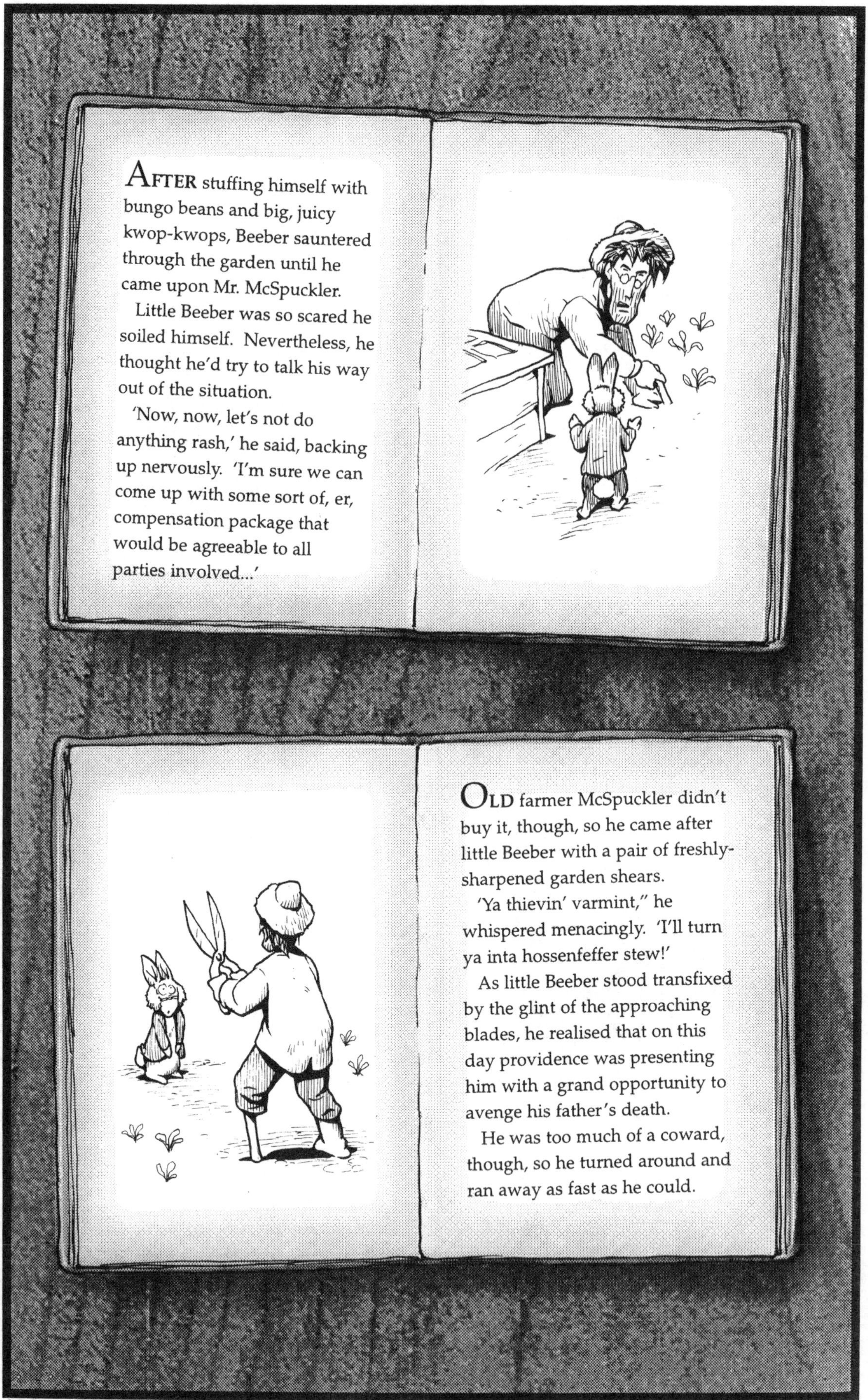
AFTER stuffing himself with bungo beans and big, juicy kwop-kwops, Beeber sauntered through the garden until he came upon Mr. McSpuckler.
Little Beeber was so scared he soiled himself. Nevertheless, he thought he'd try to talk his way out of the situation.
'Now, now, let's not do anything rash,' he said, backing up nervously. 'I'm sure we can come up with some sort of, er, compensation package that would be agreeable to all parties involved...'
OLD farmer McSpuckler didn't buy it, though, so he came after little Beeber with a pair of freshly-sharpened garden shears.
'Ya thievin' varmint," he whispered menacingly. 'I'll turn ya inta hossenfeffer stew!'
As little Beeber stood transfixed by the glint of the approaching blades, he realised that on this day providence was presenting him with a grand opportunity to avenge his father's death.
He was too much of a coward, though, so he turned around and ran away as fast as he could.

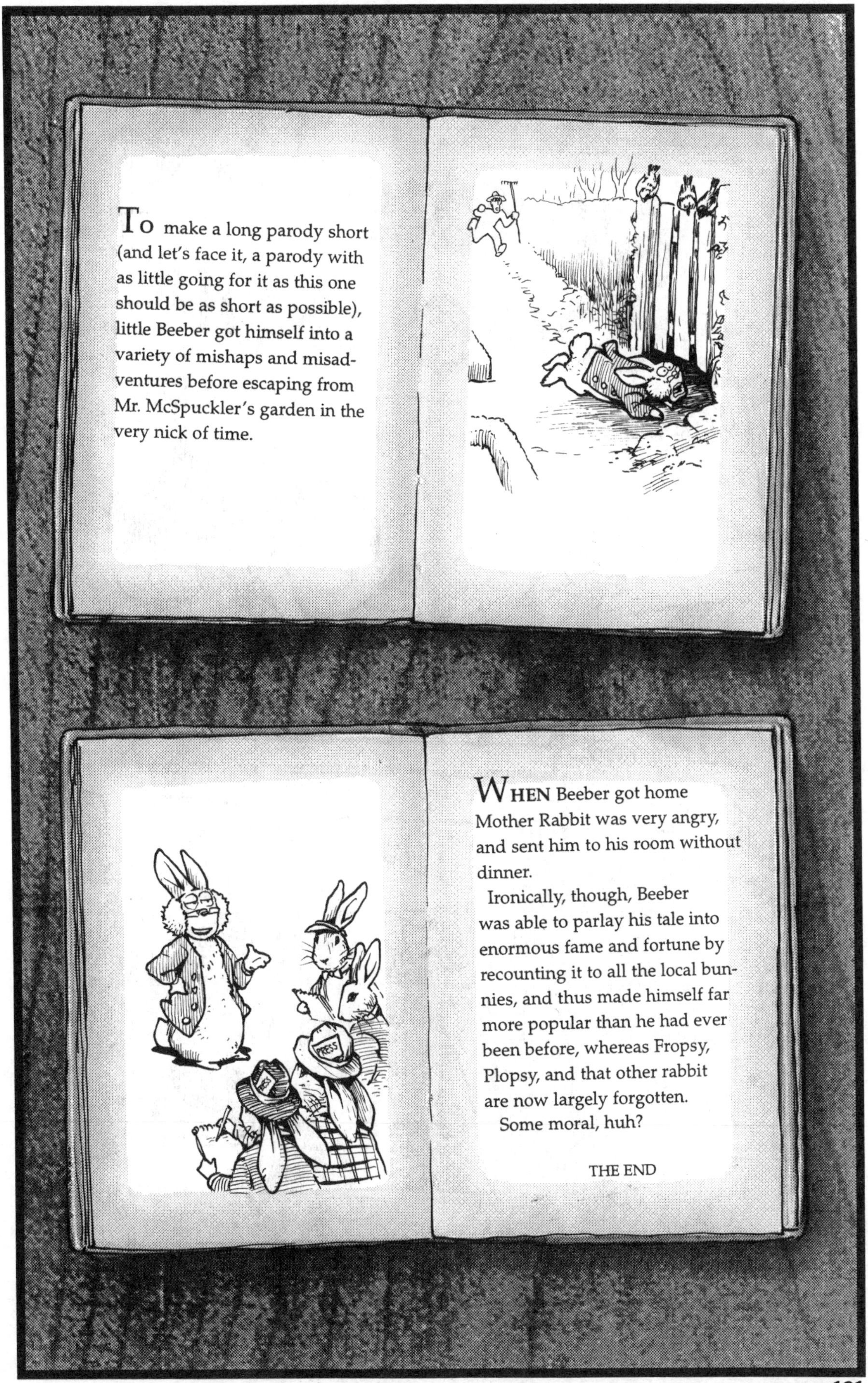
To make a long parody short (and let's face it, a parody with as little going for it as this one should be as short as possible), little Beeber got himself into a variety of mishaps and misadventures before escaping from Mr. McSpuckler's garden in the very nick of time.
PRESS
PRESS
WHEN Beeber got home Mother Rabbit was very angry, and sent him to his room without dinner.
Ironically, though, Beeber was able to parlay his tale into enormous fame and fortune by recounting it to all the local bunnies, and thus made himself far more popular than he had ever been before, whereas Fropsy, Plopsy, and that other rabbit are now largely forgotten.
Some moral, huh?
THE END

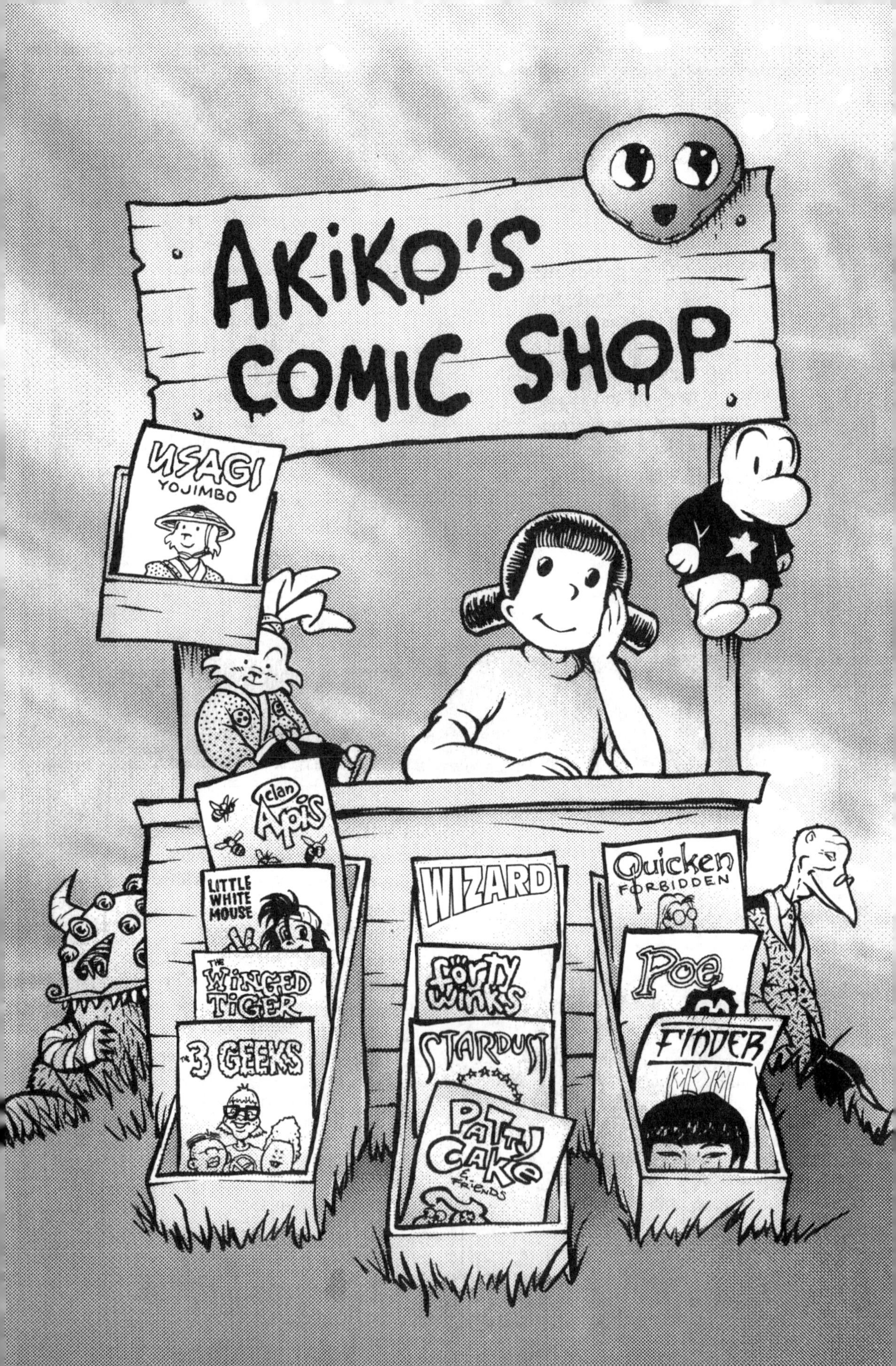
AKIKO'S
COMIC SHOP
USAGI YOJIMBO
clan Apis
LITTLE WHITE MOUSE
THE WINGED TIGER
THE 3 GEEKS
WIZARD
forty winks
STARDUST
PATTY CAKE & FRIENDS
Quicken FORBIDDEN
Poe
FINDER

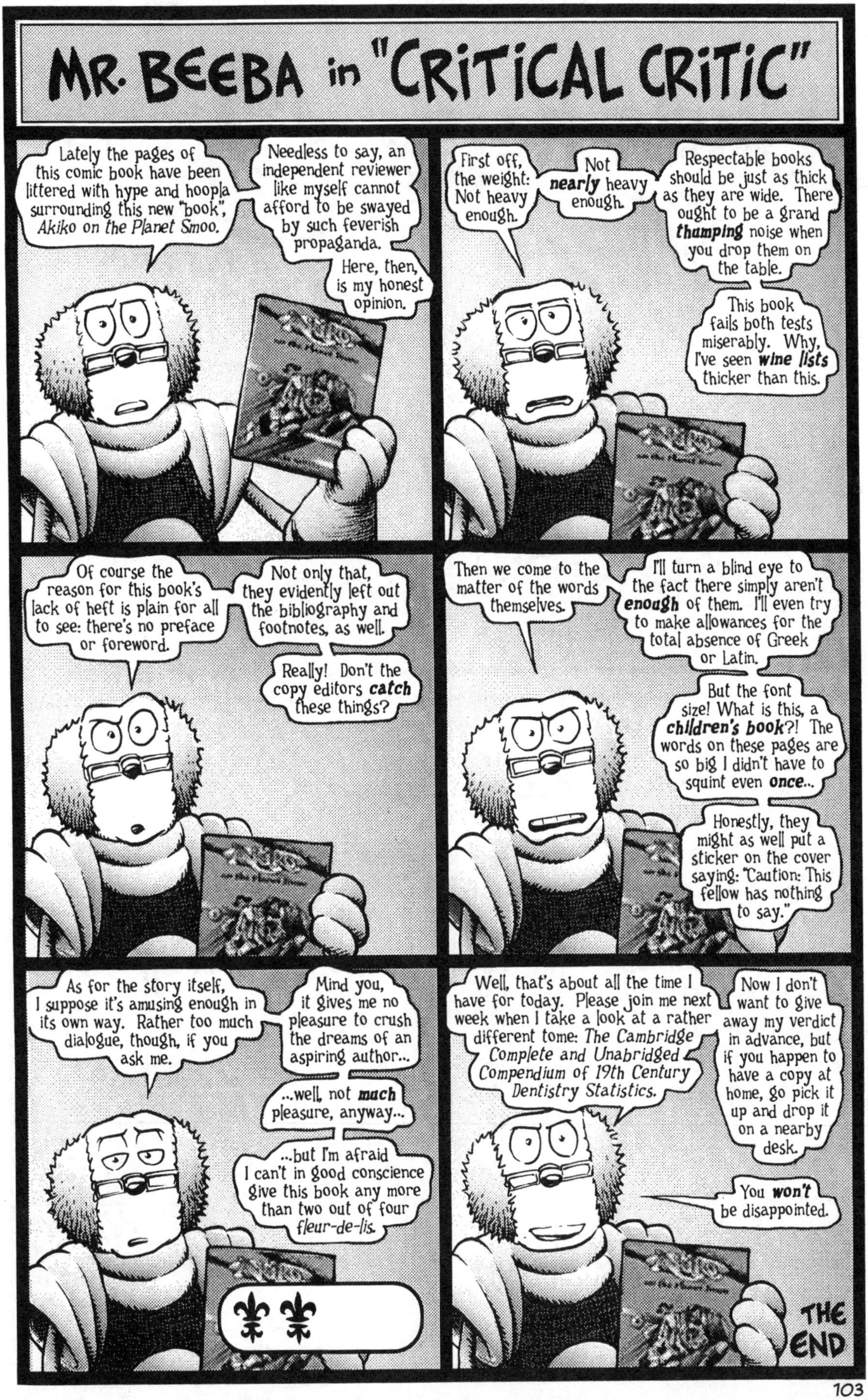
MR. BEEBA in "CRITICAL CRITIC"
Lately the pages of this comic book have been littered with hype and hoopla surrounding this new "book", Akiko on the Planet Smoo.
Needless to say, an independent reviewer like myself cannot afford to be swayed by such feverish propaganda.
Here, then, is my honest opinion.
First off, the weight: Not heavy enough.
Not nearly heavy enough.
Respectable books should be just as thick as they are wide. There ought to be a grand thumping noise when you drop them on the table.
This book fails both tests miserably. Why, I've seen wine lists thicker than this.
Of course the reason for this book's lack of heft is plain for all to see: there's no preface or foreword.
Not only that, they evidently left out the bibliography and footnotes, as well.
Really! Don't the copy editors catch these things?
Then we come to the matter of the words themselves.
I'll turn a blind eye to the fact there simply aren't enough of them. I'll even try to make allowances for the total absence of Greek or Latin.
But the font size! What is this, a children's book?! The words on these pages are so big I didn't have to squint even once...
Honestly, they might as well put a sticker on the cover saying: "Caution: This fellow has nothing to say."
As for the story itself, I suppose it's amusing enough in its own way. Rather too much dialogue, though, if you ask me.
Mind you, it gives me no pleasure to crush the dreams of an aspiring author...
...well, not much pleasure, anyway...
...but I'm afraid I can't in good conscience give this book any more than two out of four fleur-de-lis.
Well, that's about all the time I have for today. Please join me next week when I take a look at a rather different tome: The Cambridge Complete and Unabridged Compendium of 19th Century Dentistry Statistics.
Now I don't want to give away my verdict in advance, but if you happen to have a copy at home, go pick it up and drop it on a nearby desk.
You won't be disappointed.
THE END

THIS STORY IS DEDICATED TO MY PARENTS-IN-LAW, KOJI & MINAE HIRABAYASHI

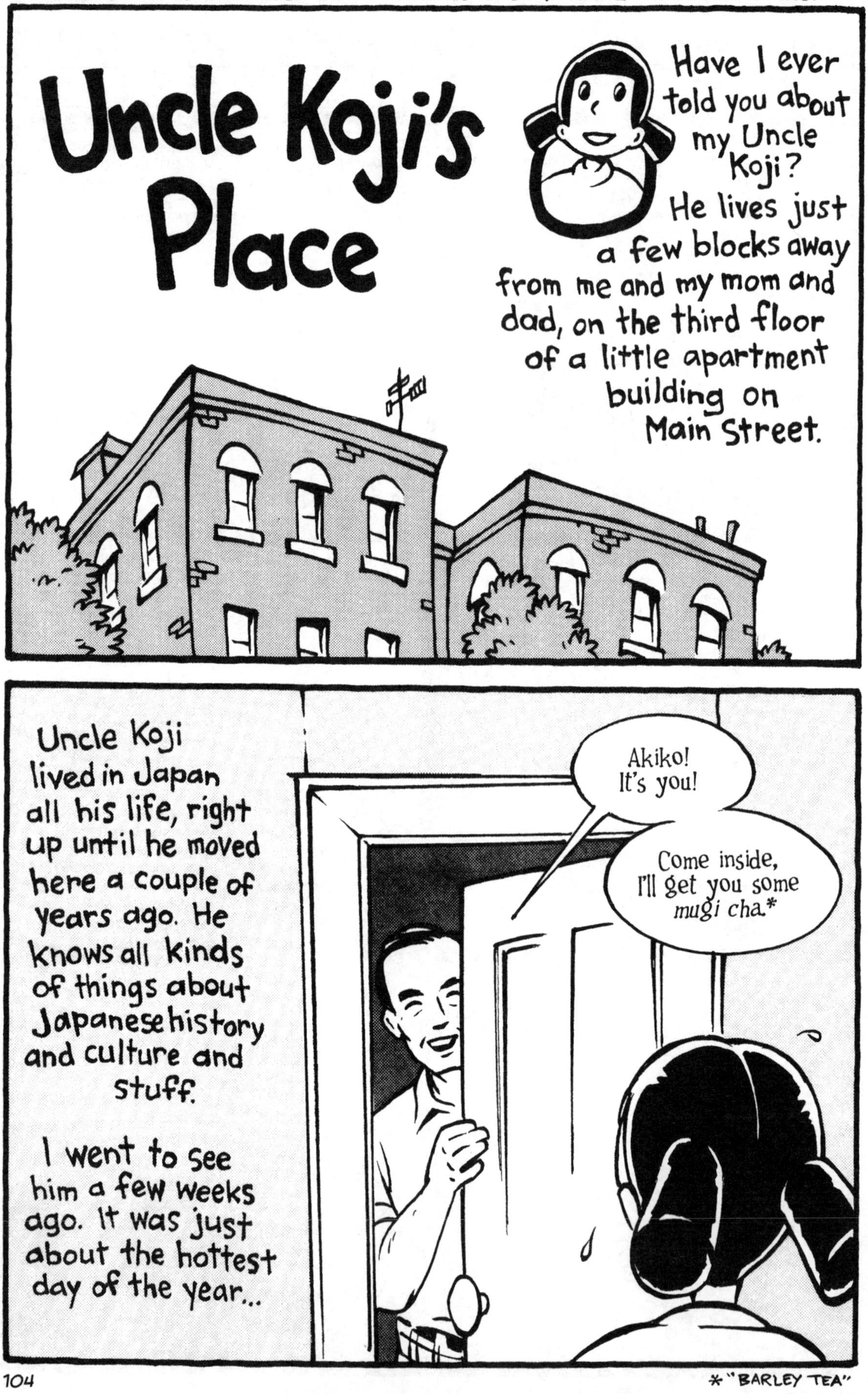
Uncle Koji's Place
Have I ever told you about my Uncle Koji? He lives just a few blocks away from me and my mom and dad, on the third floor of a little apartment building on Main Street.
Uncle Koji lived in Japan all his life, right up until he moved here a couple of years ago. He knows all kinds of things about Japanese history and culture and stuff.
I went to see him a few weeks ago. It was just about the hottest day of the year...
Akiko! It's you!
Come inside, I'll get you some *mugi cha*.*

* "BARLEY TEA"

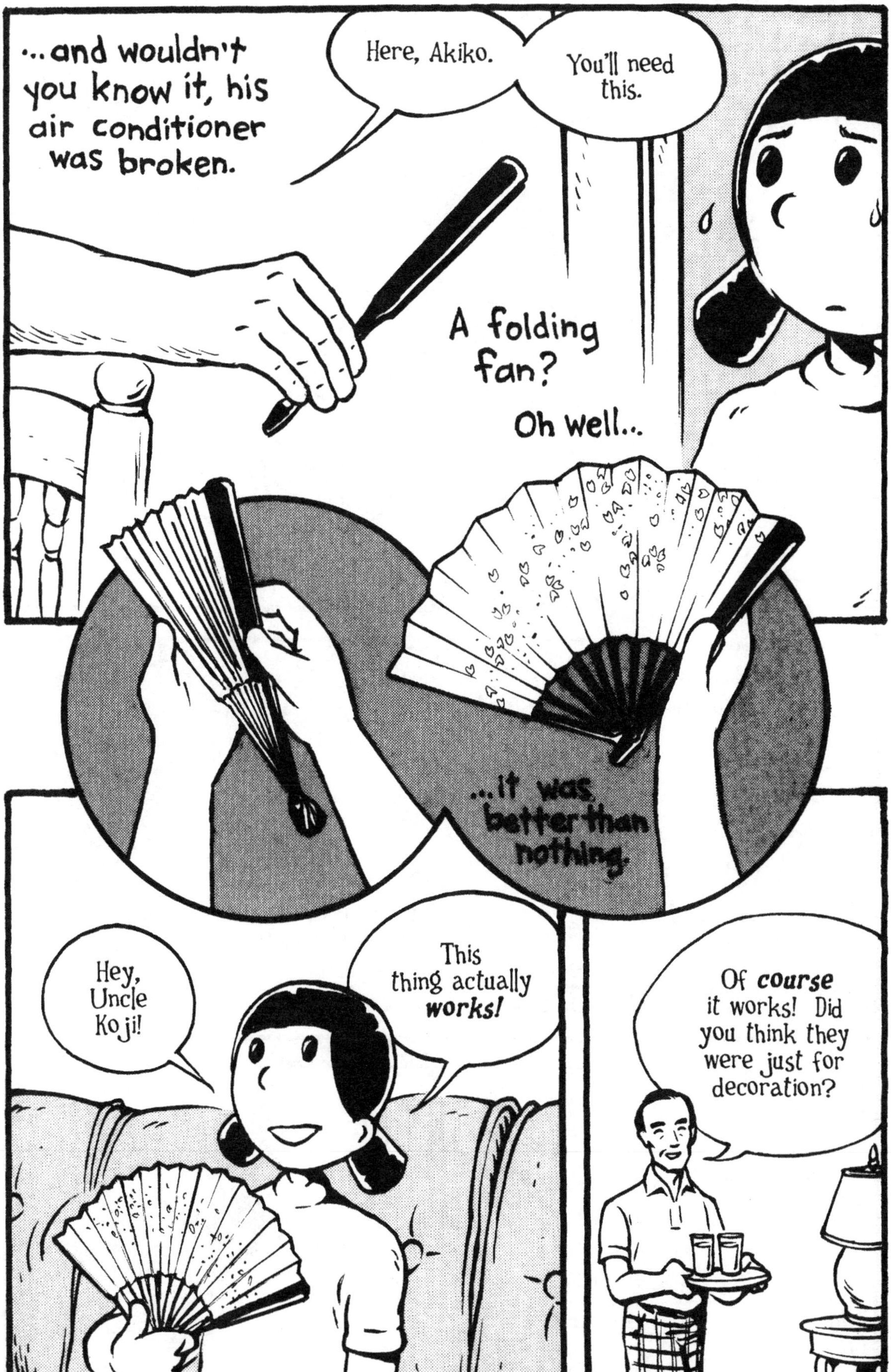
...and wouldn't you know it, his air conditioner was broken.
Here, Akiko.
You'll need this.
A folding fan?
Oh well...
...it was better than nothing.
Hey, Uncle Koji!
This thing actually *works!*
Of **course** it works! Did you think they were just for decoration?

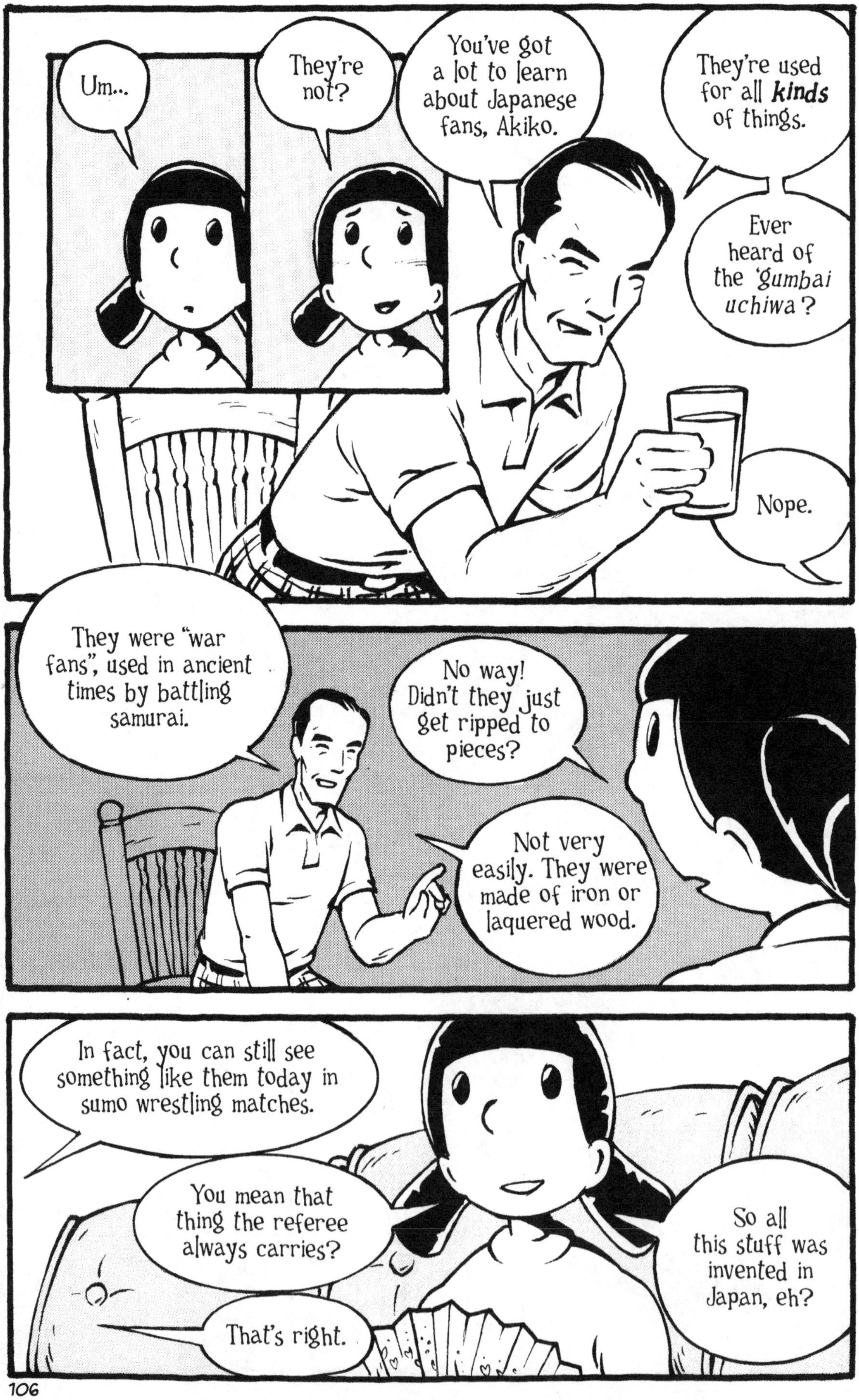
Um...
They're not?
You've got a lot to learn about Japanese fans, Akiko.
They're used for all **kinds** of things.
Ever heard of the 'gumbai uchiwa'?
Nope.
They were "war fans", used in ancient times by battling samurai.
No way! Didn't they just get ripped to pieces?
Not very easily. They were made of iron or laquered wood.
In fact, you can still see something like them today in sumo wrestling matches.
You mean that thing the referee always carries?
That's right.
So all this stuff was invented in Japan, eh?

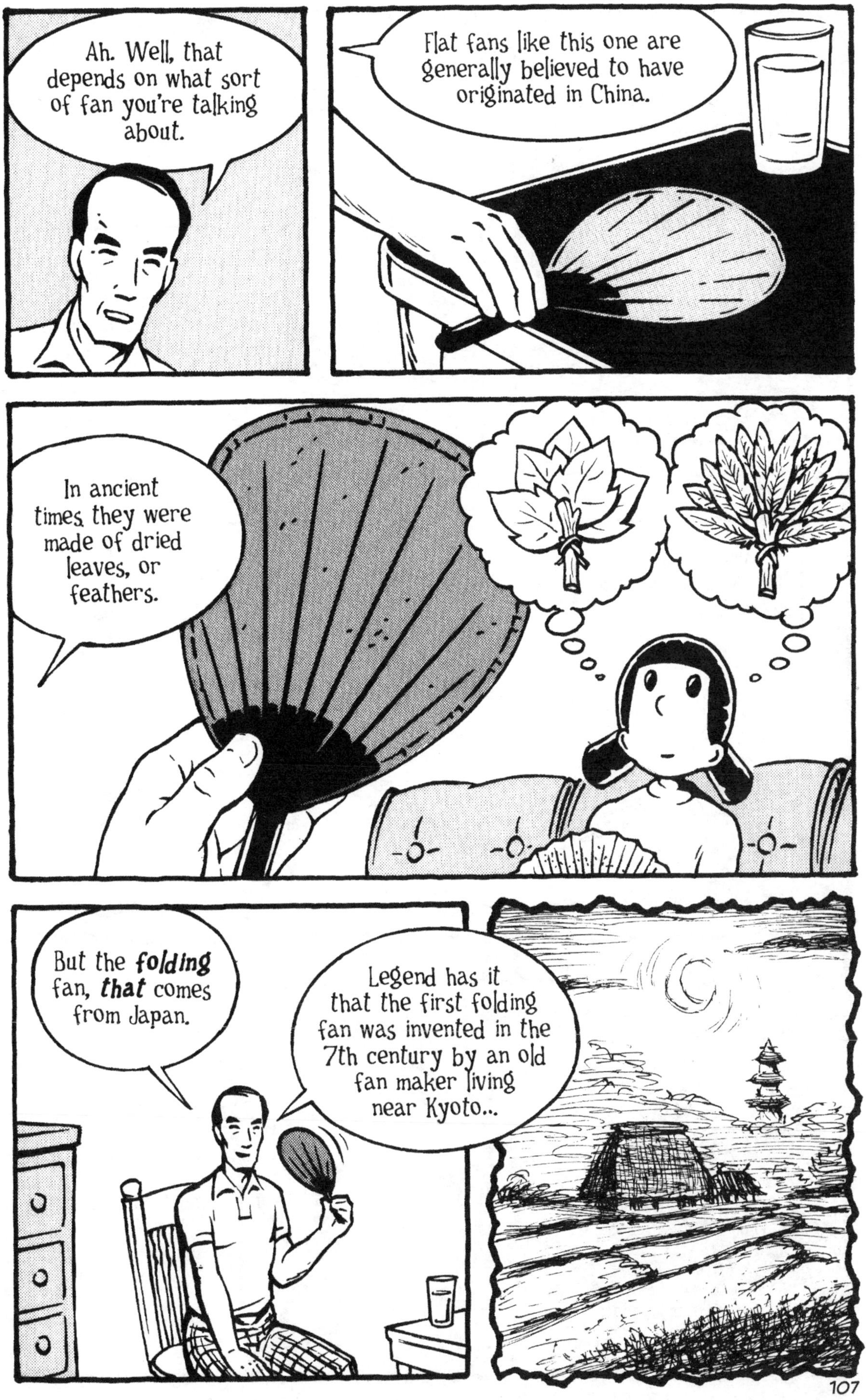
Ah. Well, that depends on what sort of fan you're talking about.
Flat fans like this one are generally believed to have originated in China.
In ancient times they were made of dried leaves, or feathers.
But the ***folding*** fan, ***that*** comes from Japan.
Legend has it that the first folding fan was invented in the 7th century by an old fan maker living near Kyoto...

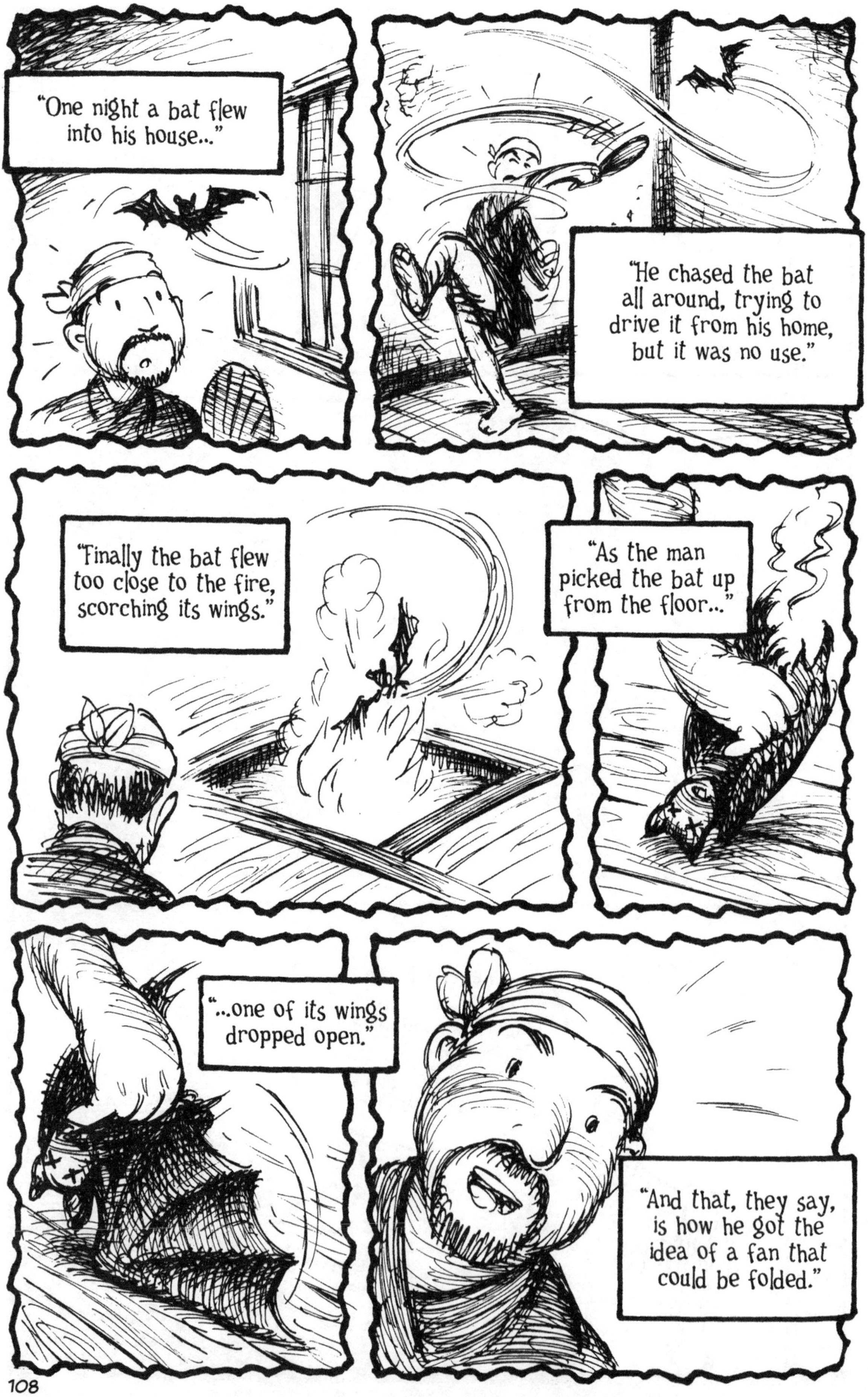
"One night a bat flew into his house..."
"He chased the bat all around, trying to drive it from his home, but it was no use."
"Finally the bat flew too close to the fire, scorching its wings."
"As the man picked the bat up from the floor..."
"...one of its wings dropped open."
"And that, they say, is how he got the idea of a fan that could be folded."

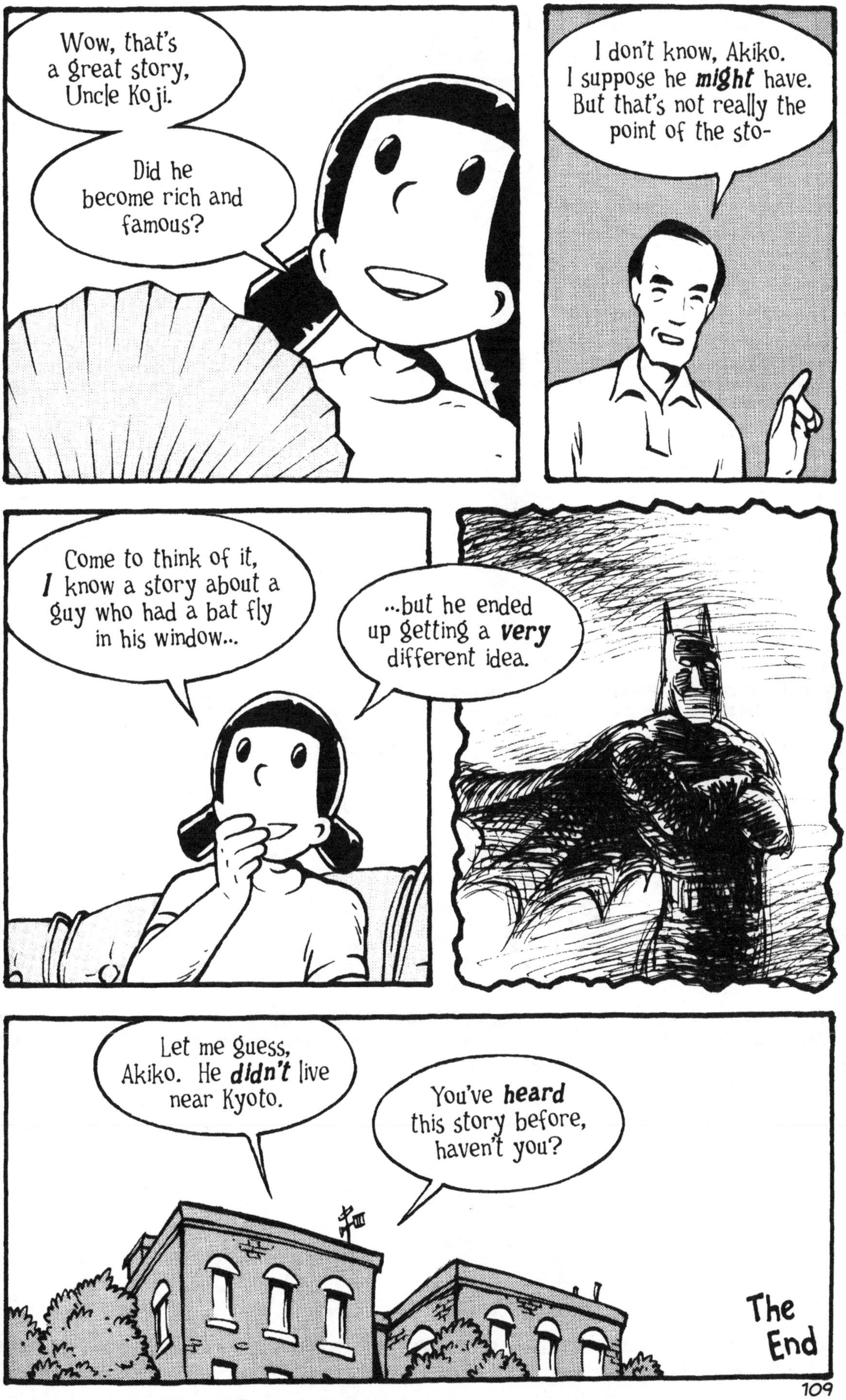
Wow, that's a great story, Uncle Koji.
Did he become rich and famous?
I don't know, Akiko. I suppose he **might** have. But that's not really the point of the sto-
Come to think of it, *I* know a story about a guy who had a bat fly in his window...
...but he ended up getting a **very** different idea.
Let me guess, Akiko. He **didn't** live near Kyoto.
You've **heard** this story before, haven't you?
The End

INFORMATION IN THIS STORY COMES FROM THE TRADITIONAL ARTS OF JAPAN, BY H. BATTERSON BOGER

AKIKO'S PLAYHOUSE

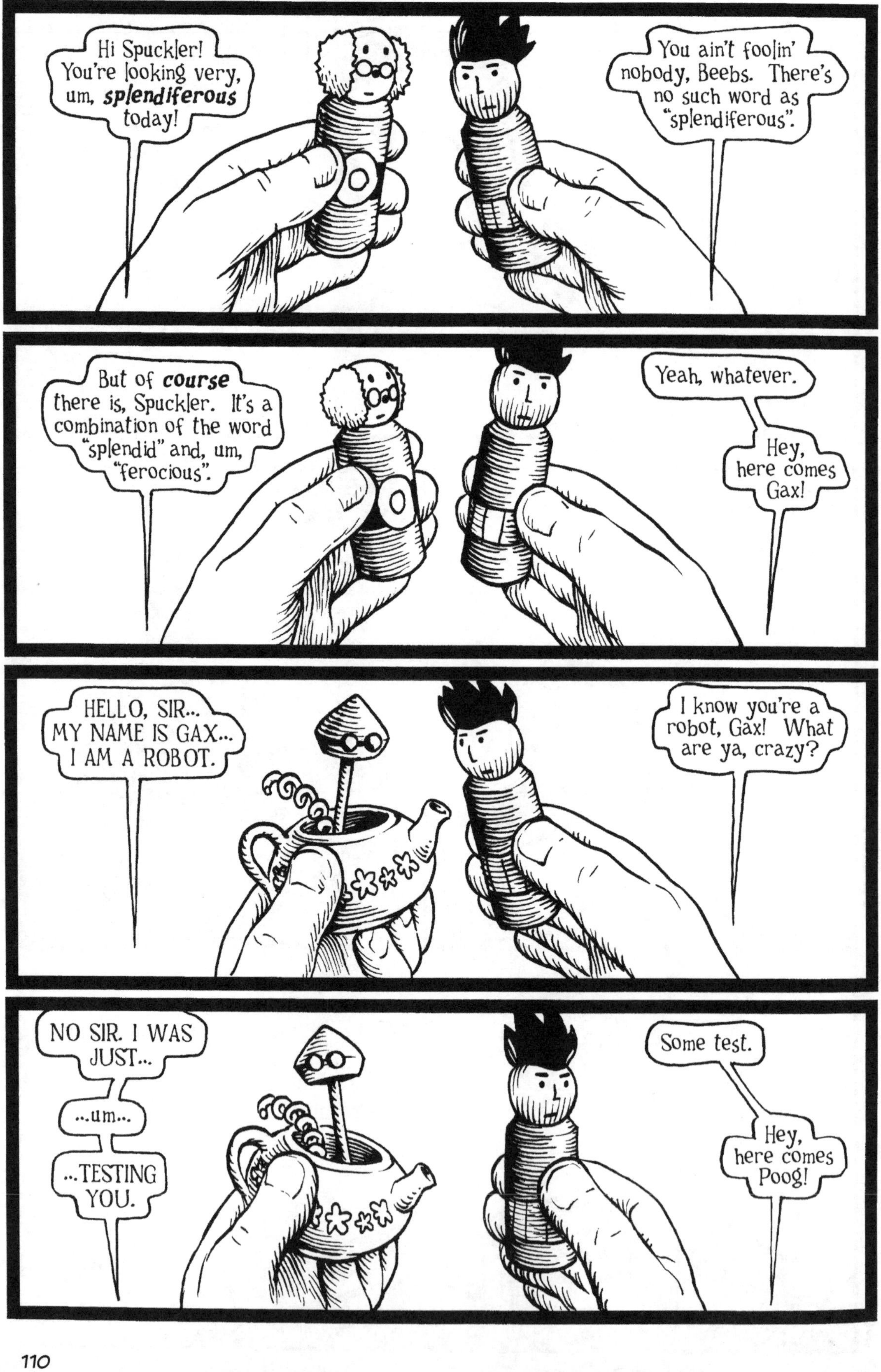

Hi Spuckler! You're looking very, um, **splendiferous** today!
You ain't foolin' nobody, Beebs. There's no such word as "splendiferous".
But of **course** there is, Spuckler. It's a combination of the word "splendid" and, um, "ferocious".
Yeah, whatever.
Hey, here comes Gax!
HELLO, SIR... MY NAME IS GAX... I AM A ROBOT.
I know you're a robot, Gax! What are ya, crazy?
NO SIR. I WAS JUST...
...um...
...TESTING YOU.
Some test.
Hey, here comes Poog!

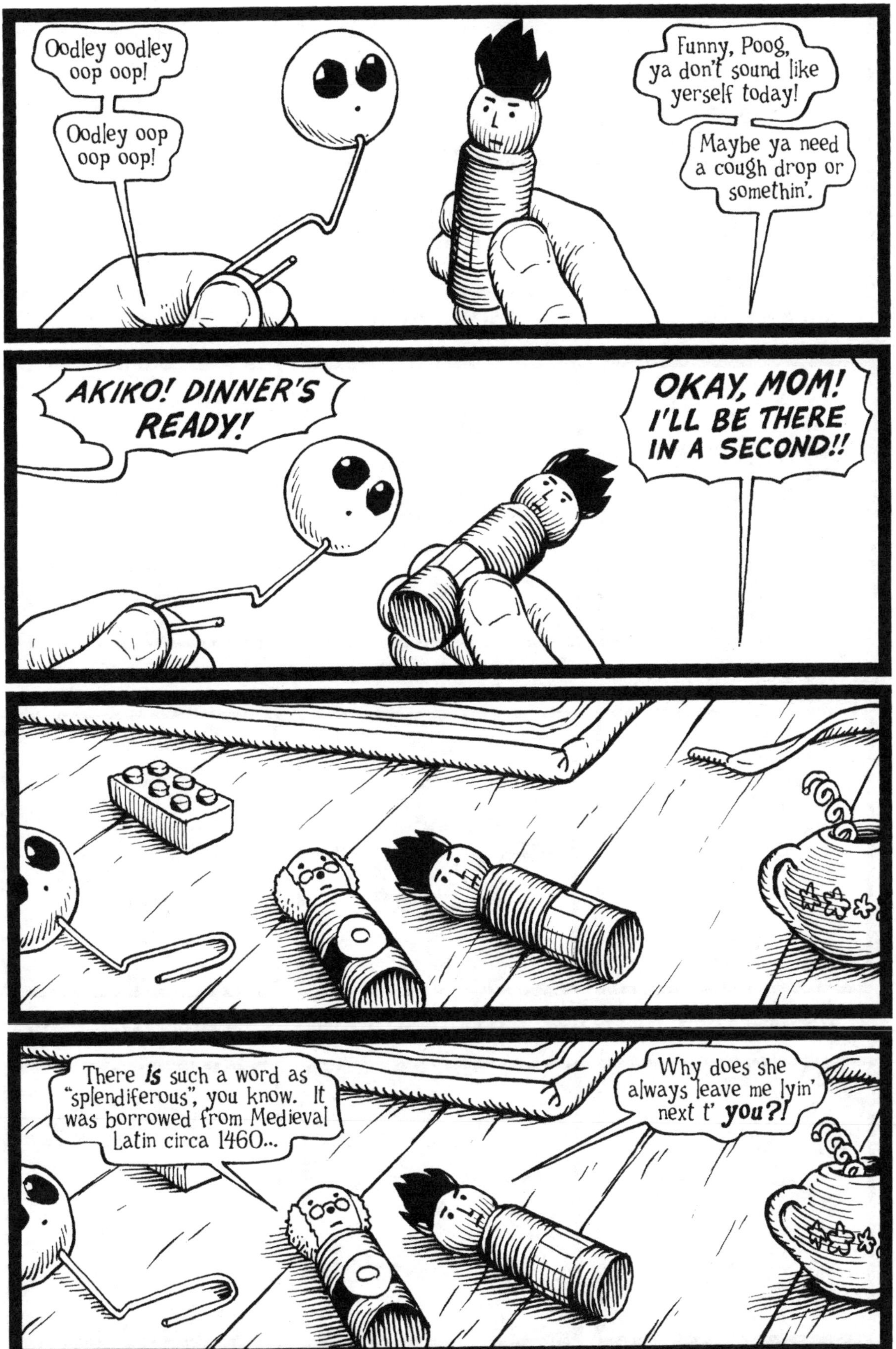

Oodley oodley oop oop!
Oodley oop oop oop!
Funny, Poog, ya don't sound like yerself today!
Maybe ya need a cough drop or somethin'.
AKIKO! DINNER'S READY!
OKAY, MOM! I'LL BE THERE IN A SECOND!!
There *is* such a word as "splendiferous", you know. It was borrowed from Medieval Latin circa 1460...
Why does she always leave me lyin' next t' ***you?!***

THE END

24 WAYS TO DRAW GAX

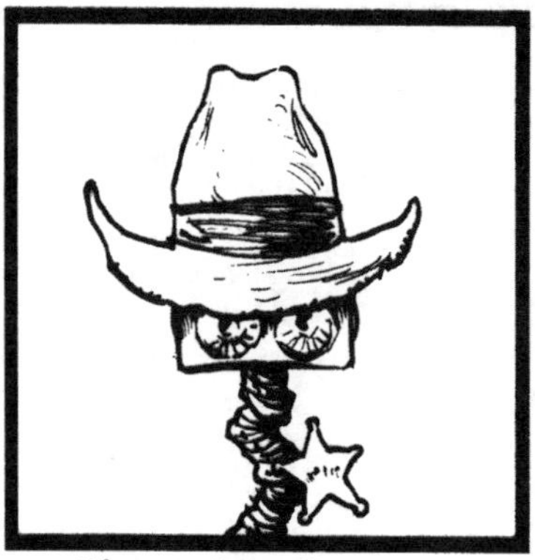
Sheriff Gax

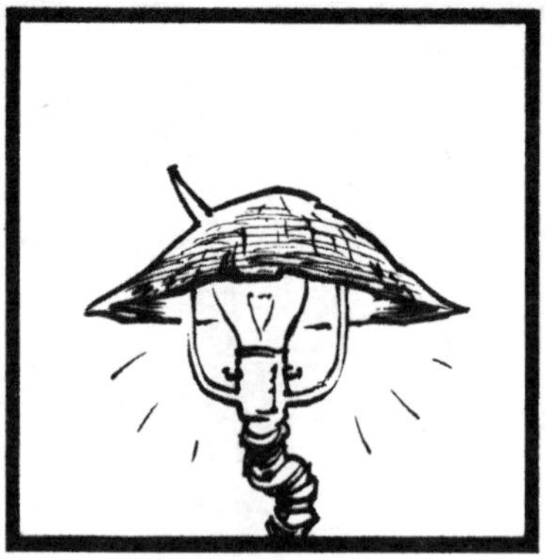
Gax Lamp

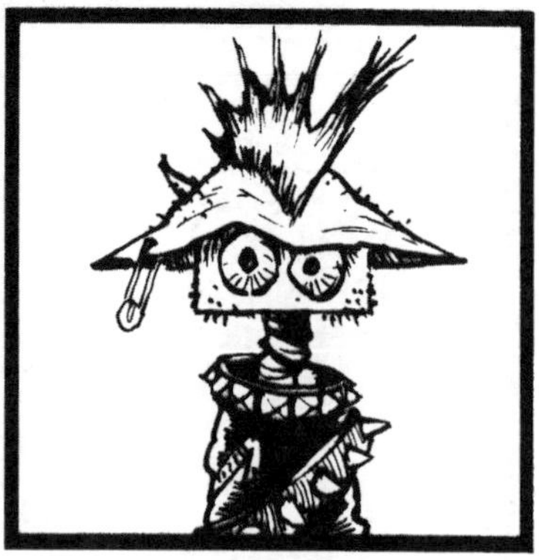
Punk Gax

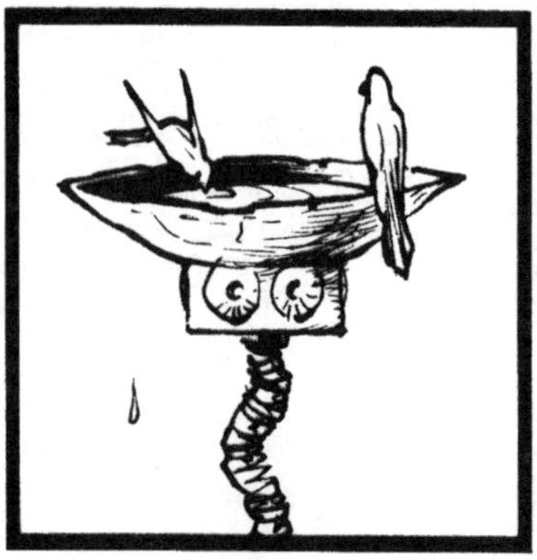
Bird Bath Gax

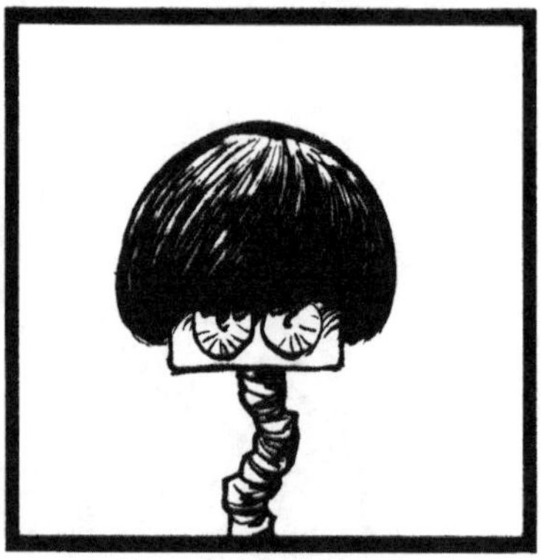
Beatle Gax

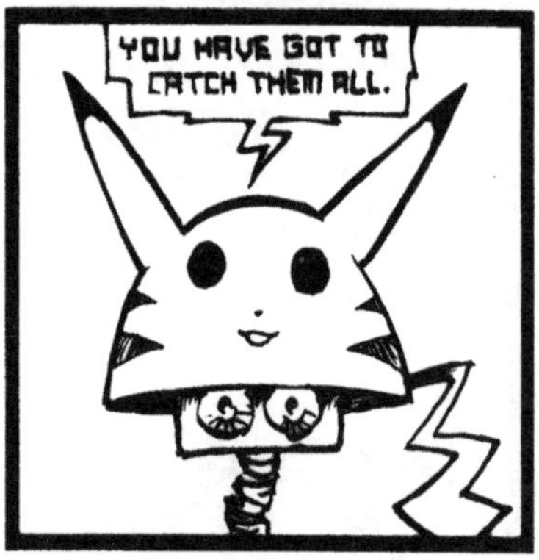
YOU HAVE GOT TO CATCH THEM ALL.
Pokémon Gax

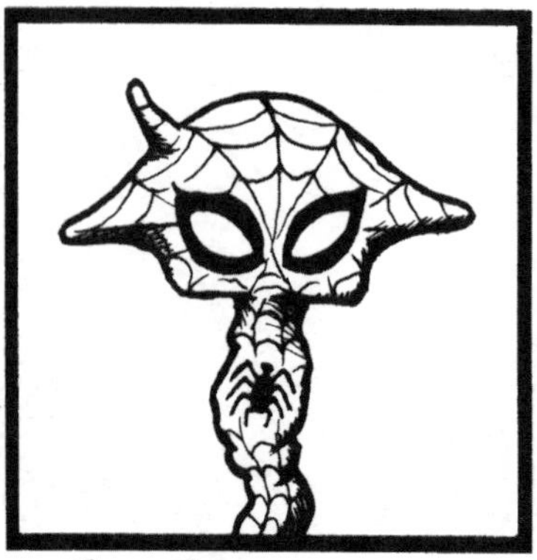
Spidergax

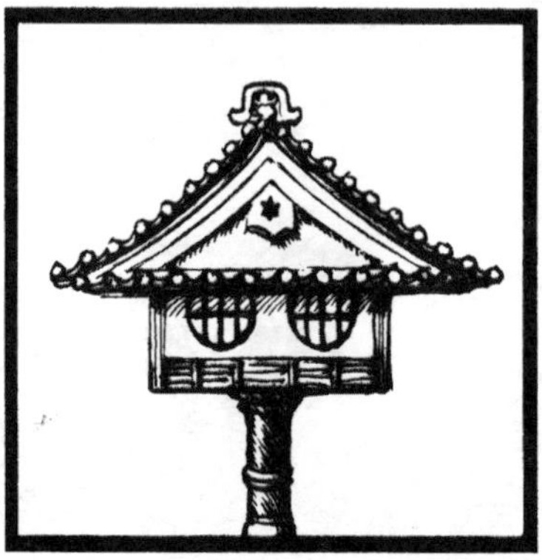
Eastern Architecture Gax

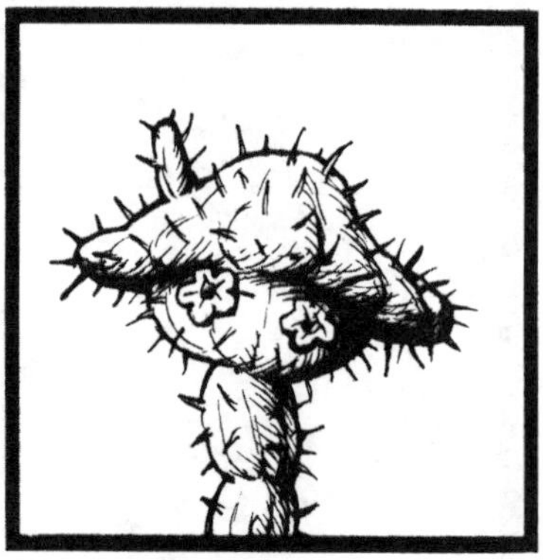
Gactus

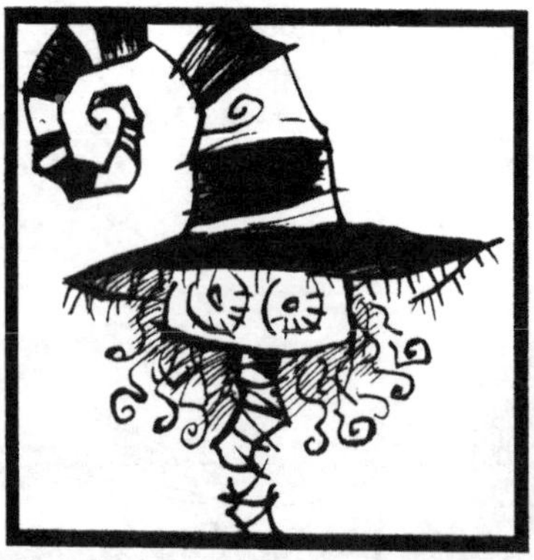
The Scary Gaxmother

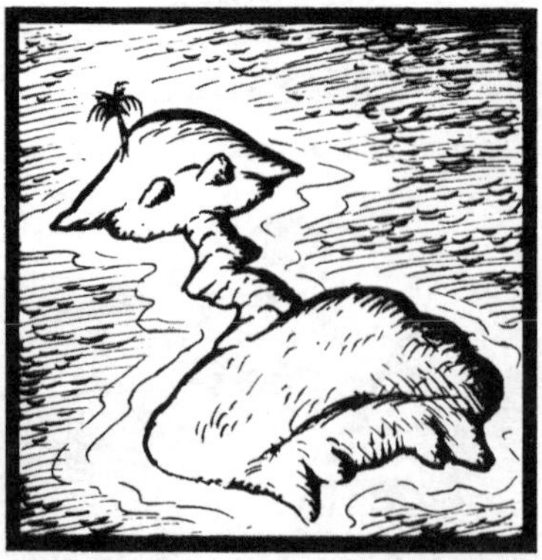
Desert Island Gax

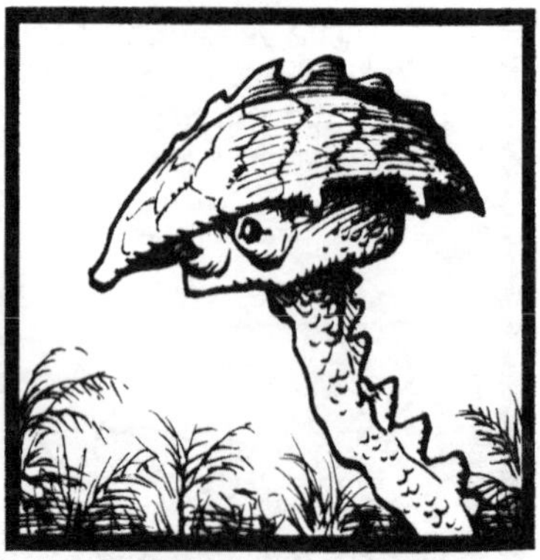
Tyrannosaurus Gax

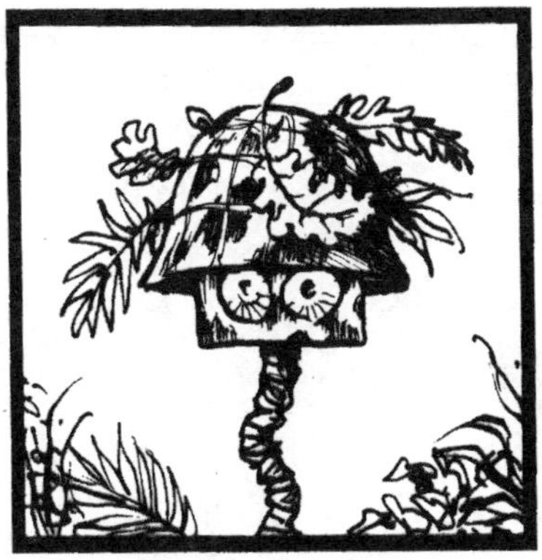
G.I. Gax

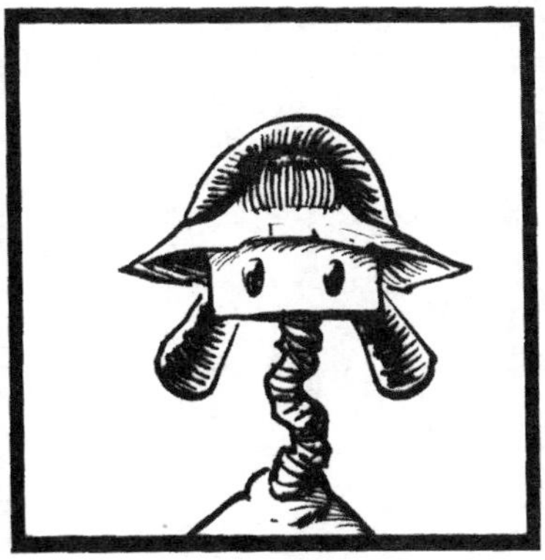
'Kiko Gax

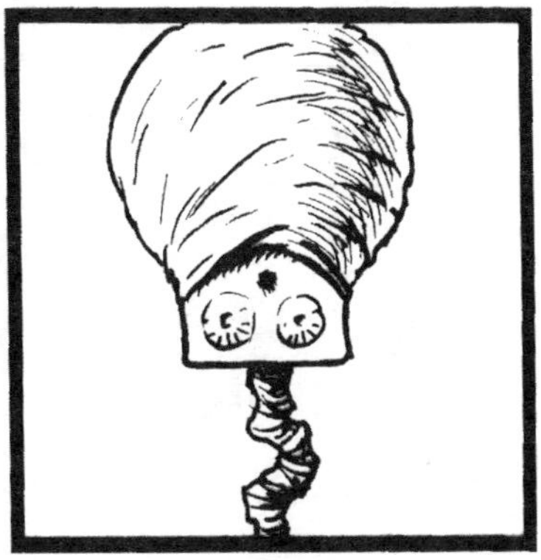
Indian Gax

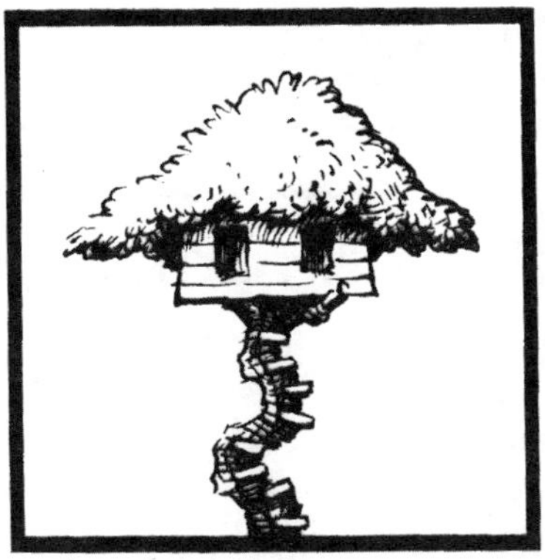
Treehouse Gax

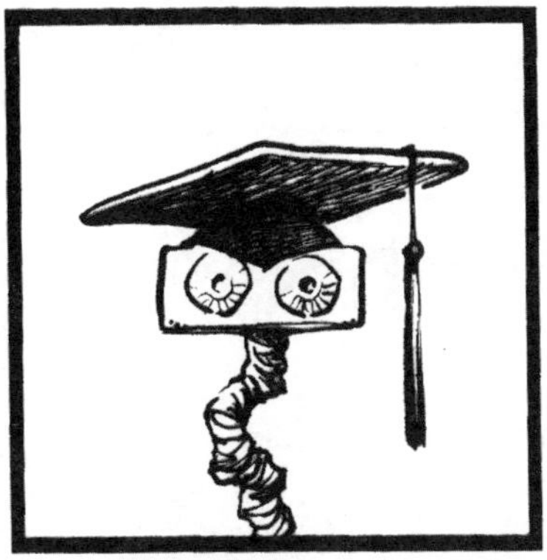
College Grad Gax

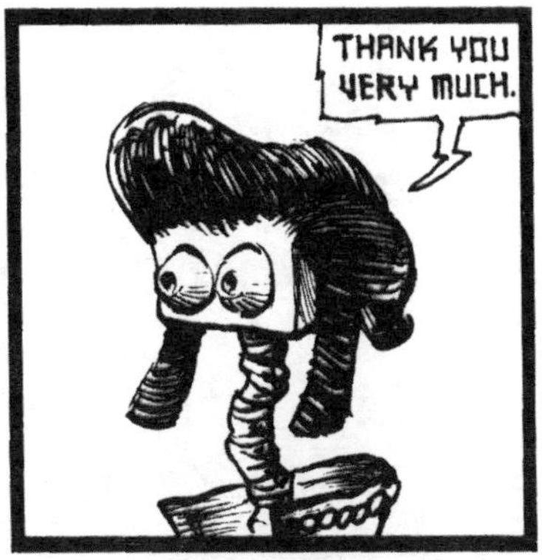
THANK YOU VERY MUCH.
Elvis Gaxley

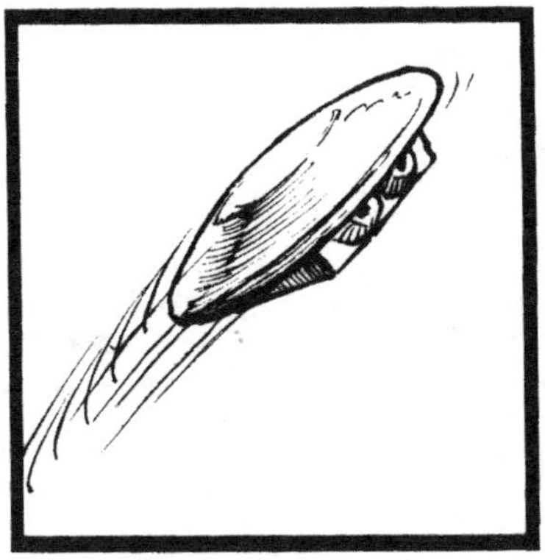
Frisbee Gax

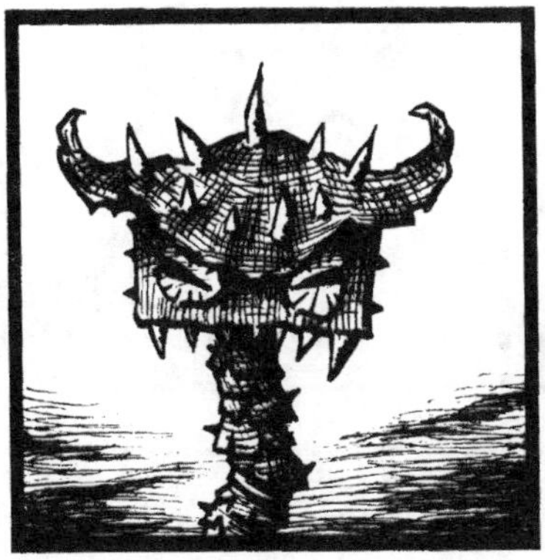
Evil Scary Gax

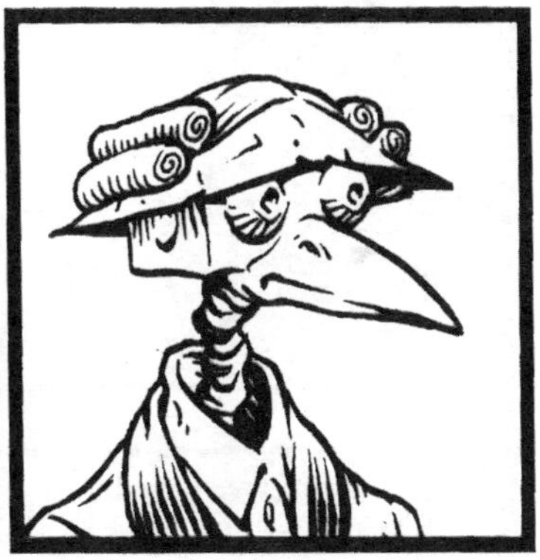
Gaxham Adjutant

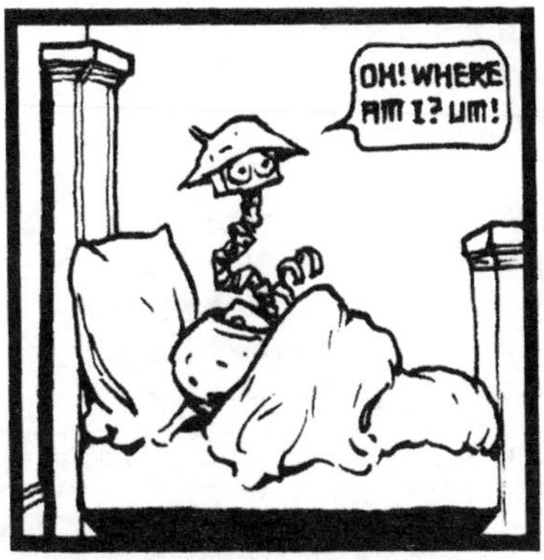
OH! WHERE AM I? UM!
Little Nemo Gax

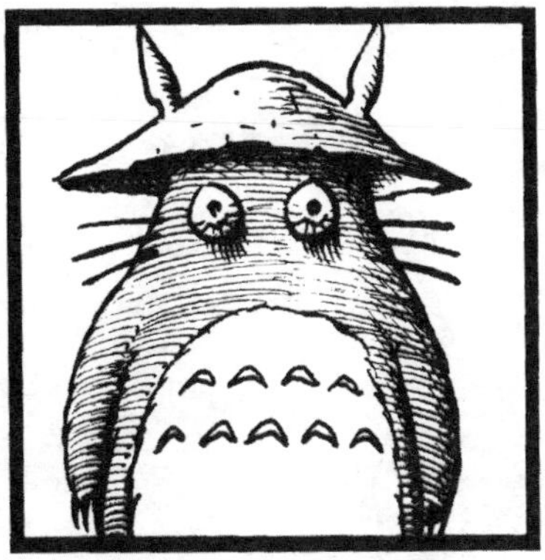
Totoro Gax

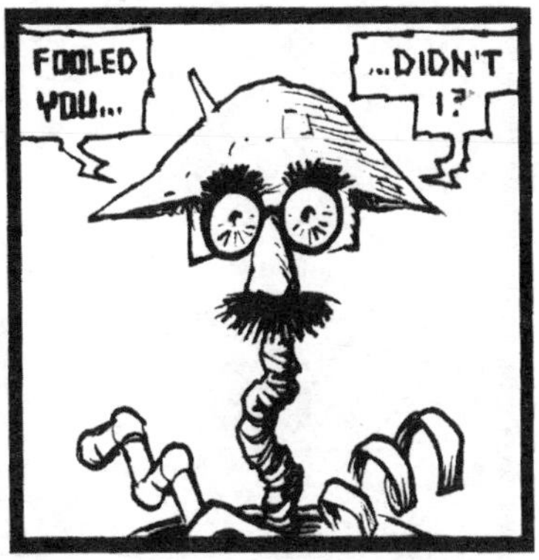
FOOLED YOU...
...DIDN'T I?
Gax in Disguise

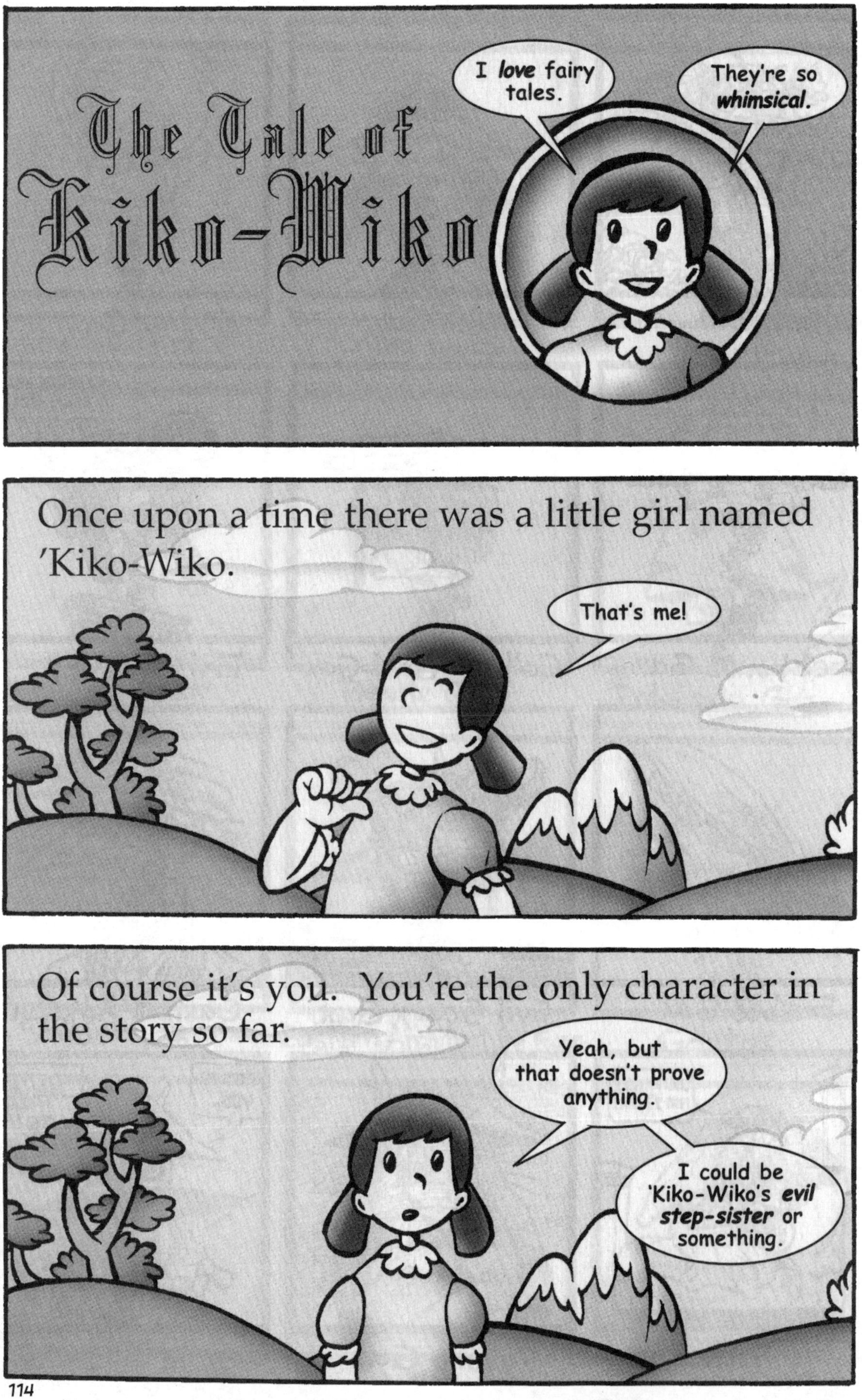
The Tale of Kiko-Wiko
I love fairy tales.
They're so whimsical.
Once upon a time there was a little girl named 'Kiko-Wiko.
That's me!
Of course it's you. You're the only character in the story so far.
Yeah, but that doesn't prove anything.
I could be 'Kiko-Wiko's evil step-sister or something.

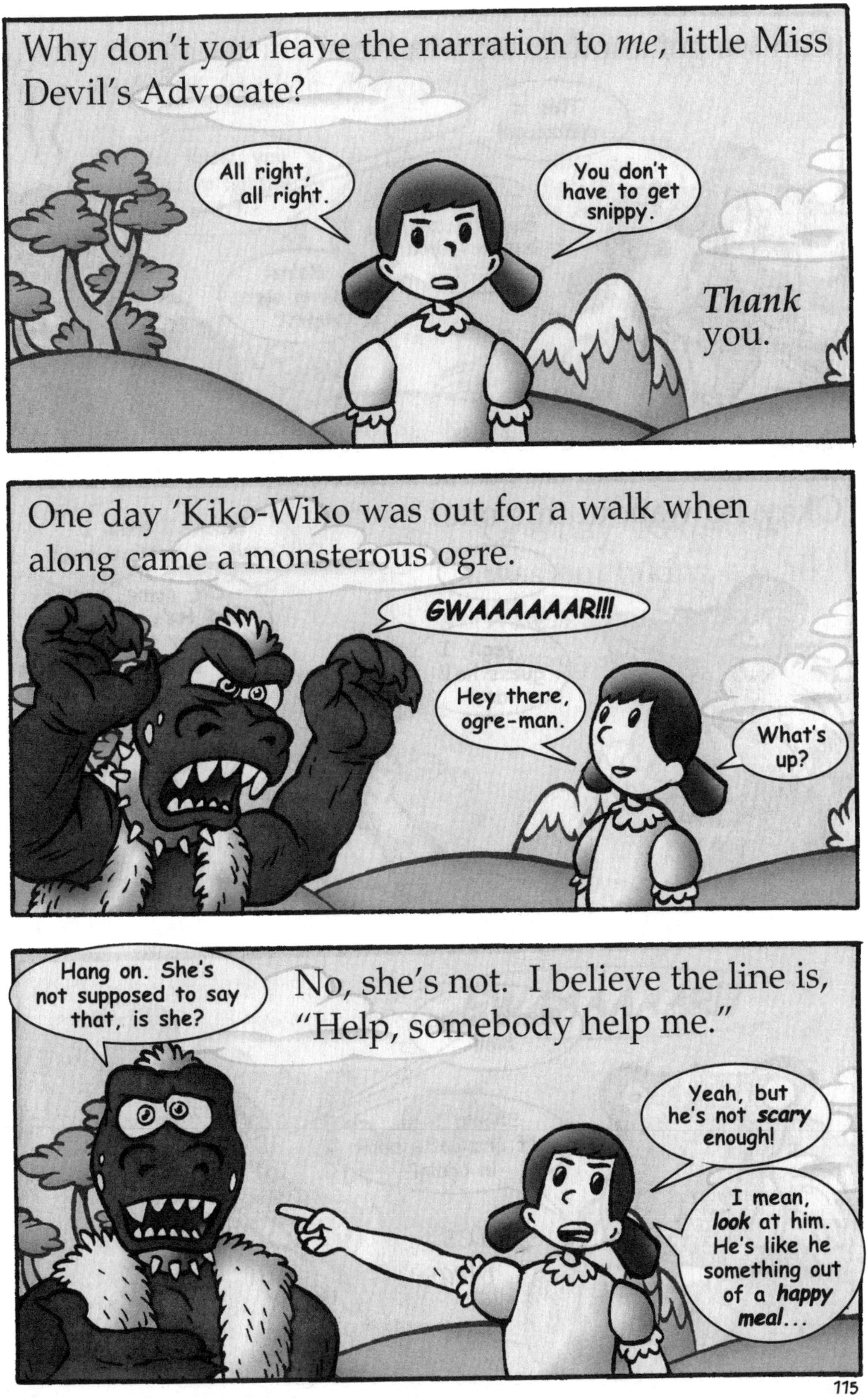
Why don't you leave the narration to *me*, little Miss Devil's Advocate?
All right, all right.
You don't have to get snippy.
Thank you.
One day 'Kiko-Wiko was out for a walk when along came a monsterous ogre.
GWAAAAAAR!!!
Hey there, ogre-man.
What's up?
Hang on. She's not supposed to say that, is she?
No, she's not. I believe the line is, "Help, somebody help me."
Yeah, but he's not *scary* enough!
I mean, *look* at him. He's like he something out of a *happy meal*...

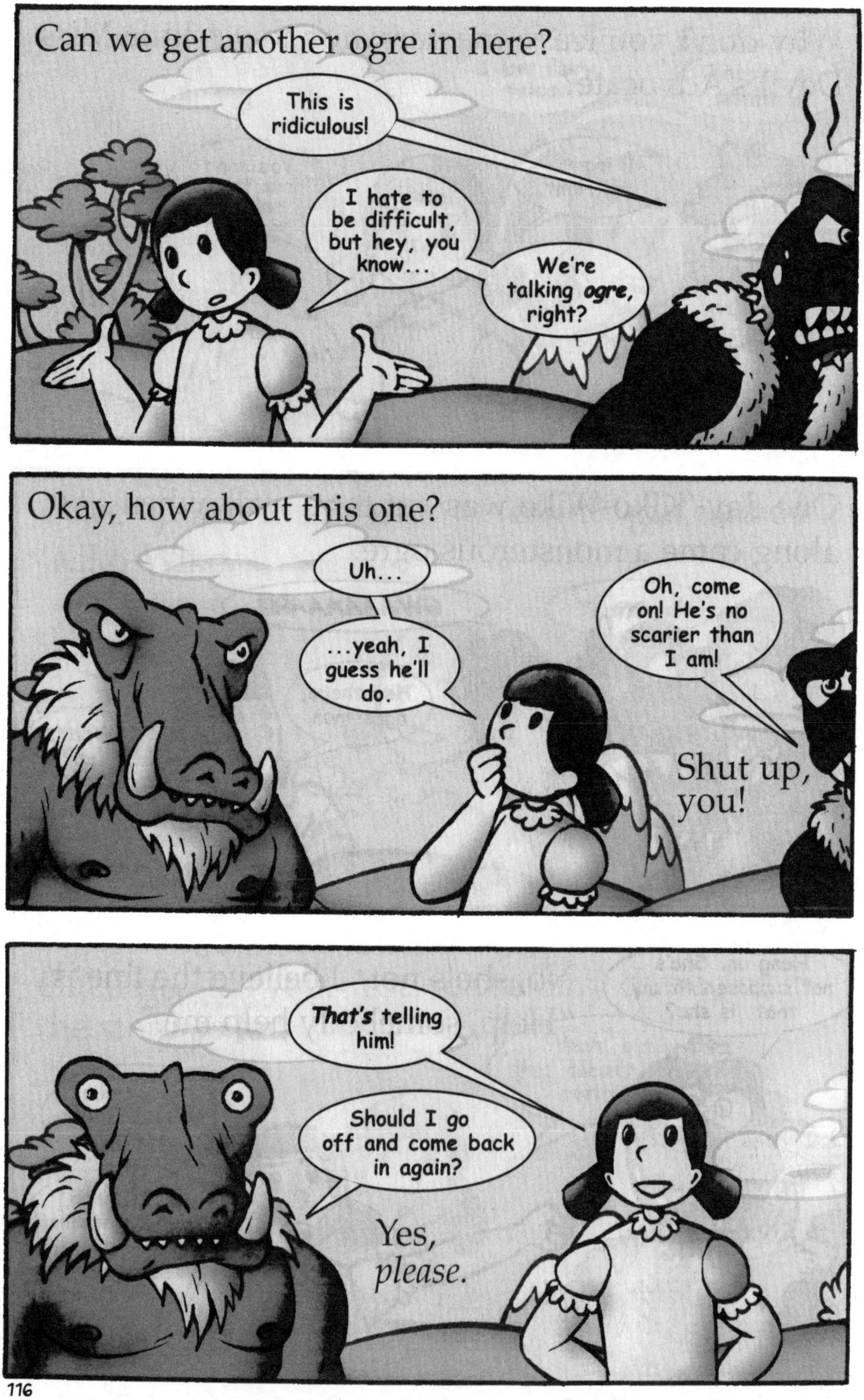
Can we get another ogre in here?
This is ridiculous!
I hate to be difficult, but hey, you know...
We're talking *ogre*, right?
Okay, how about this one?
Uh...
...yeah, I guess he'll do.
Oh, come on! He's no scarier than I am!
Shut up, you!
That's telling him!
Should I go off and come back in again?
Yes, *please*.

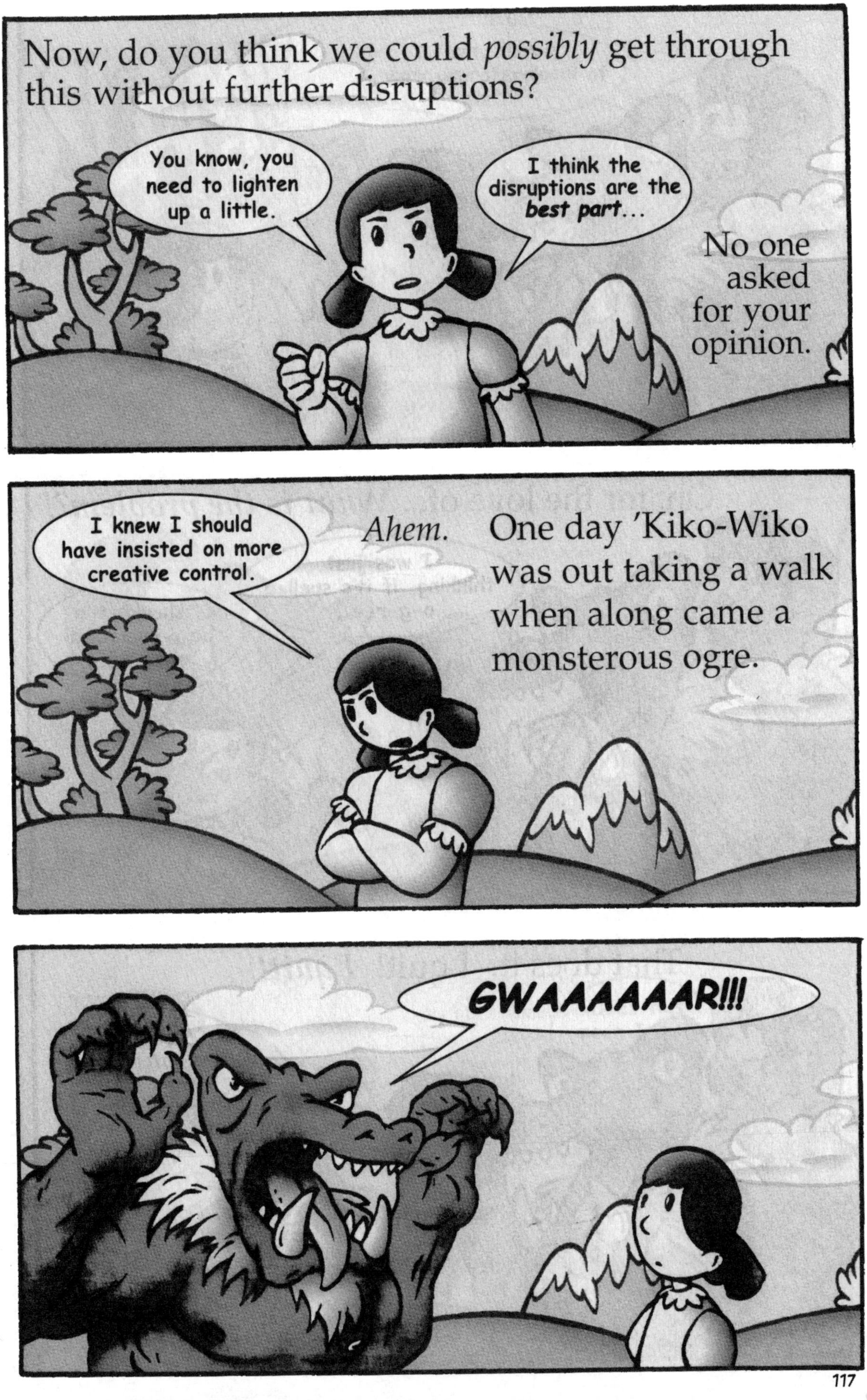
Now, do you think we could *possibly* get through this without further disruptions?
You know, you need to lighten up a little.
I think the disruptions are the *best part*...
No one asked for your opinion.
I knew I should have insisted on more creative control.
Ahem.
One day 'Kiko-Wiko was out taking a walk when along came a monsterous ogre.
GWAAAAAAR!!!

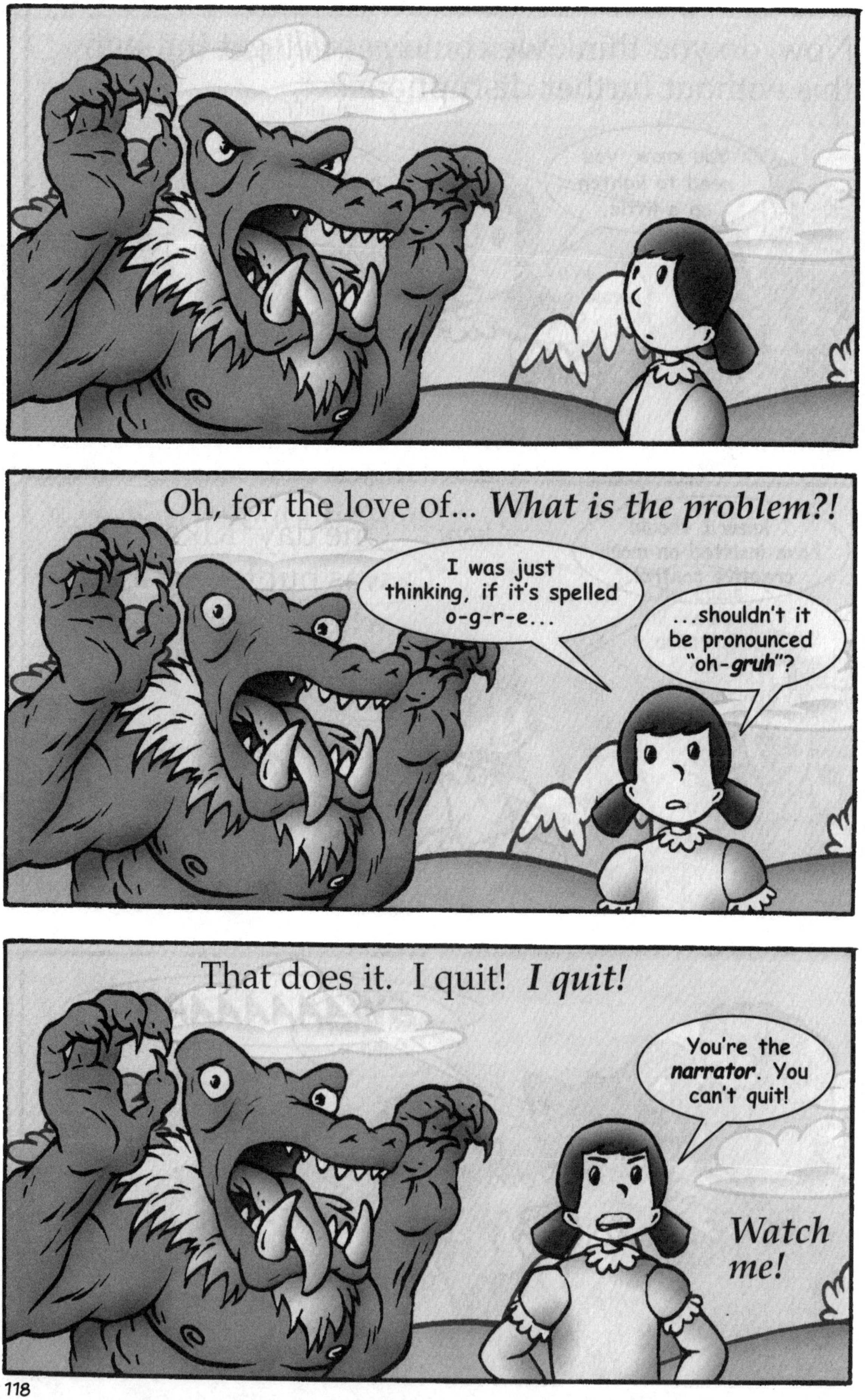
Oh, for the love of... *What is the problem?!*
I was just thinking, if it's spelled o-g-r-e...
...shouldn't it be pronounced "oh-*gruh*"?
That does it. I quit! *I quit!*
You're the *narrator*. You can't quit!
Watch me!

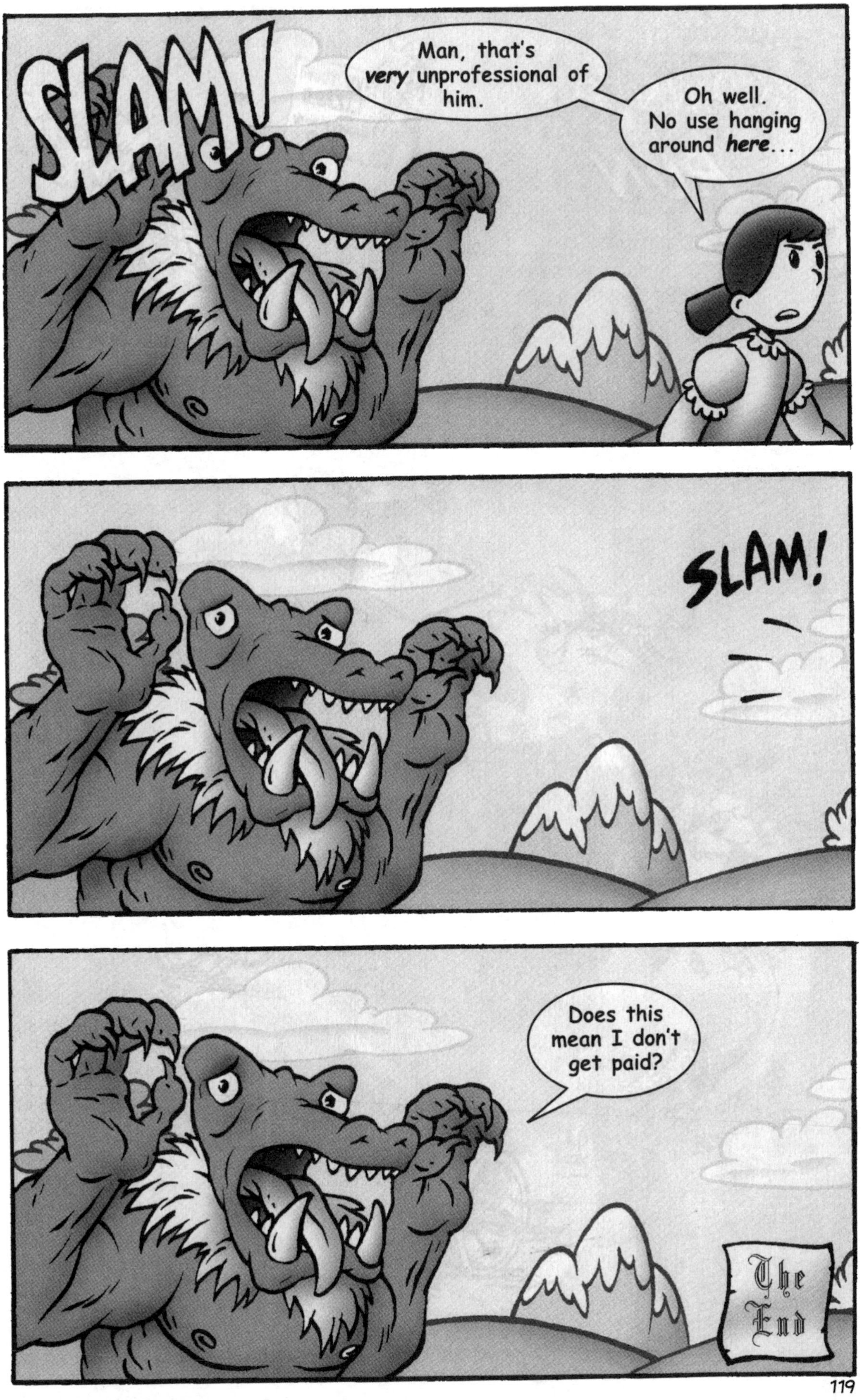
SLAM!
Man, that's *very* unprofessional of him.
Oh well. No use hanging around *here*...
SLAM!
Does this mean I don't get paid?
The End

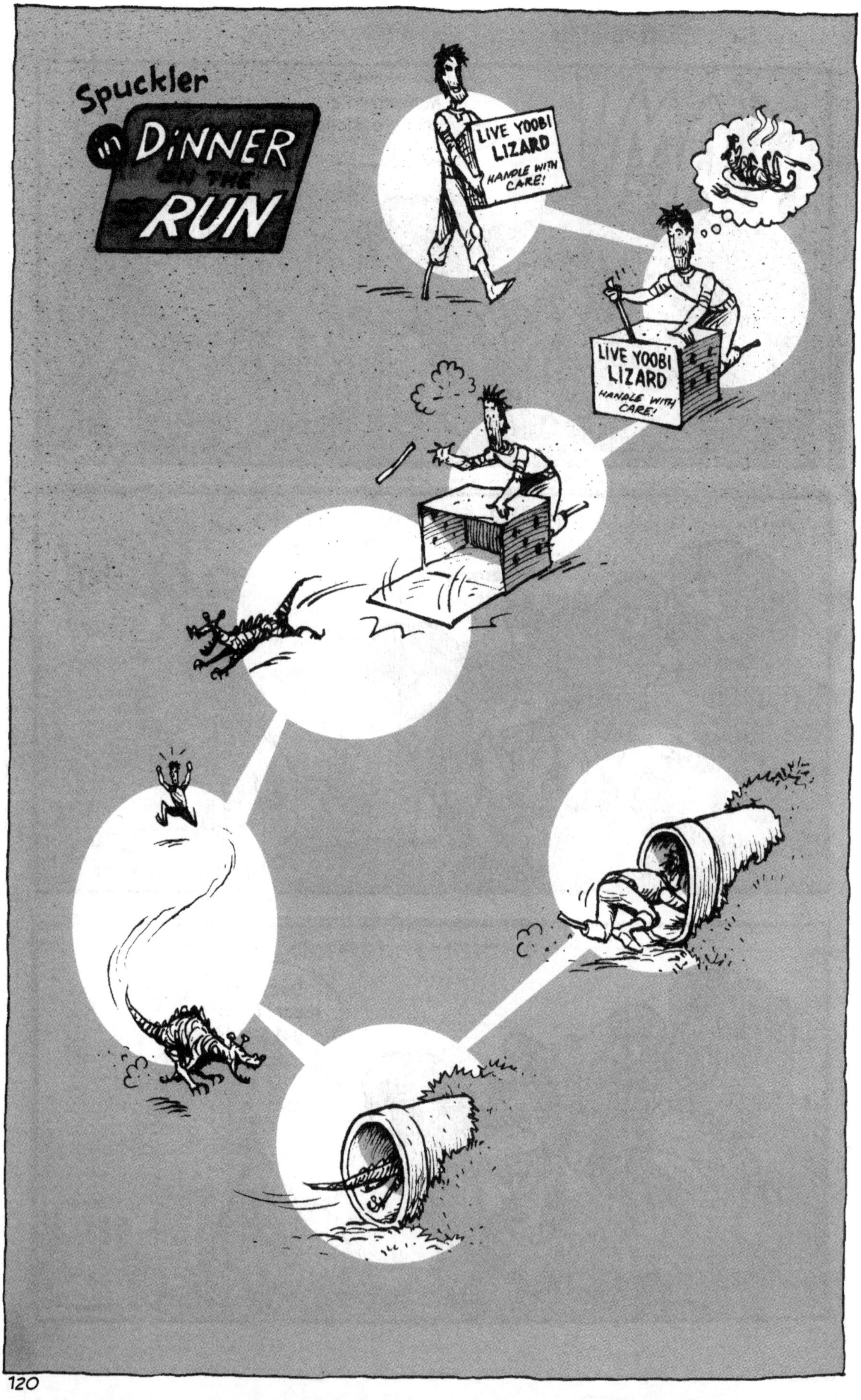
Spuckler
in DINNER ON THE RUN
LIVE YOOBI LIZARD
HANDLE WITH CARE!
LIVE YOOBI LIZARD
HANDLE WITH CARE!

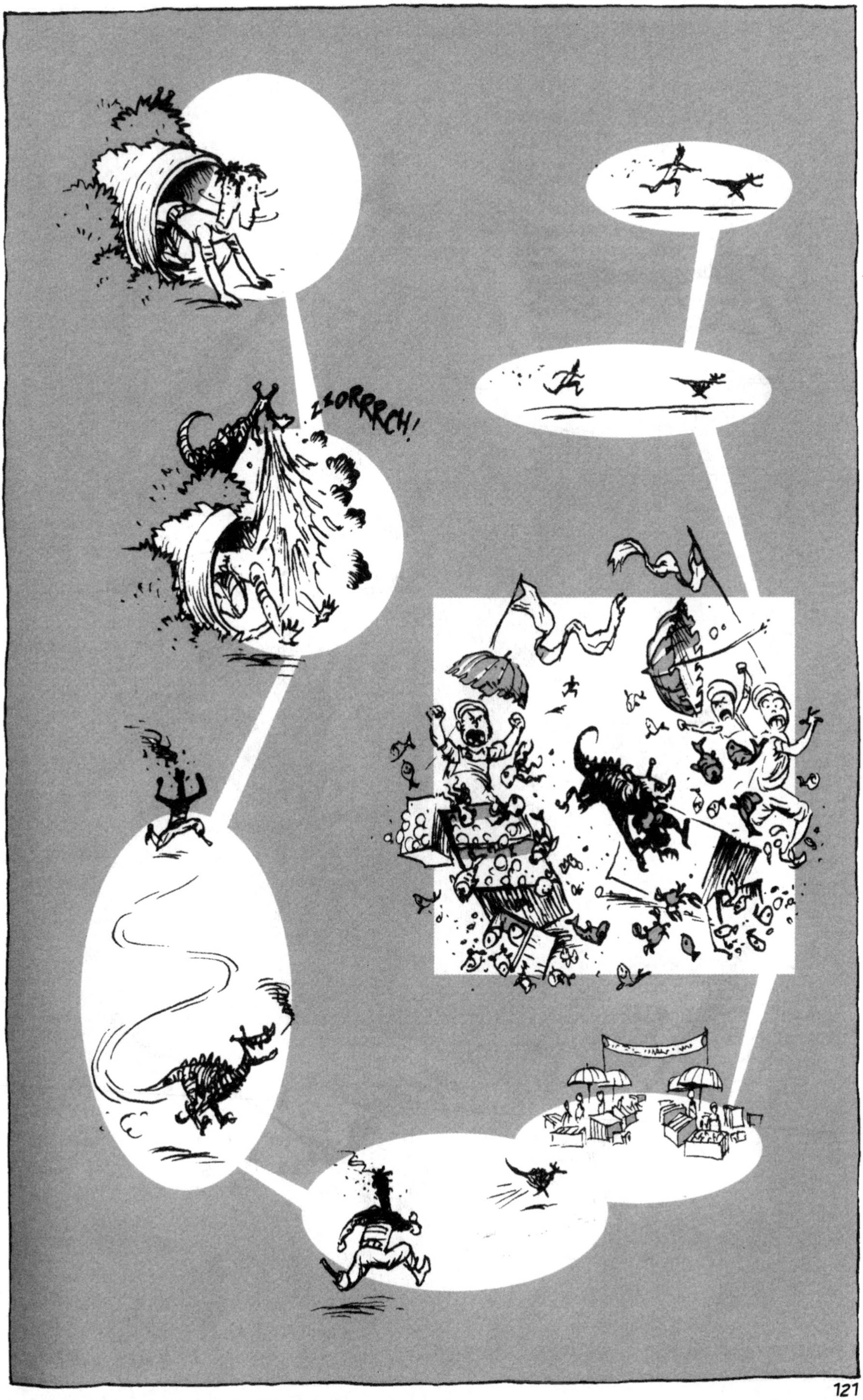
ZZORRRCH!

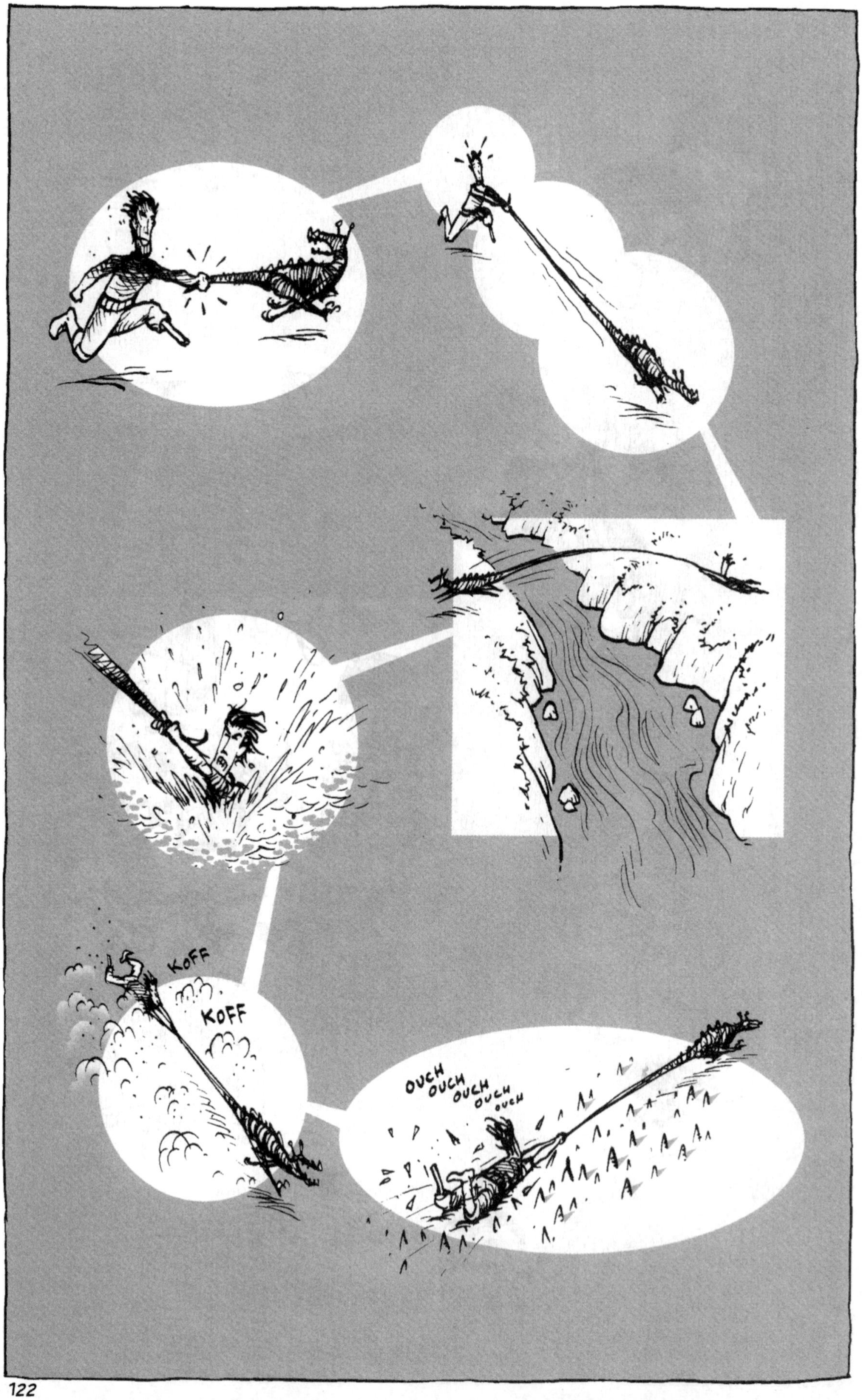
KOFF
KOFF
OUCH
OUCH
OUCH
OUCH
OUCH

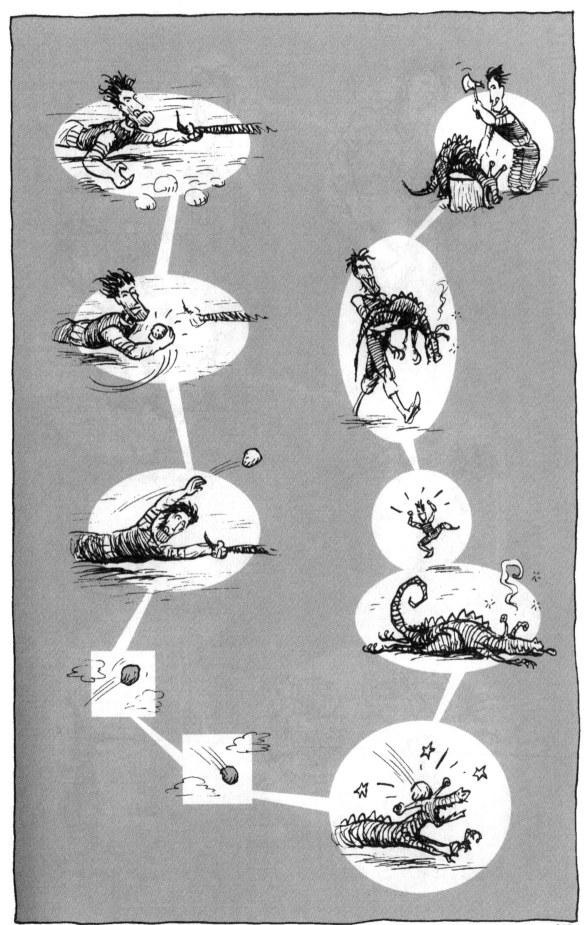

123

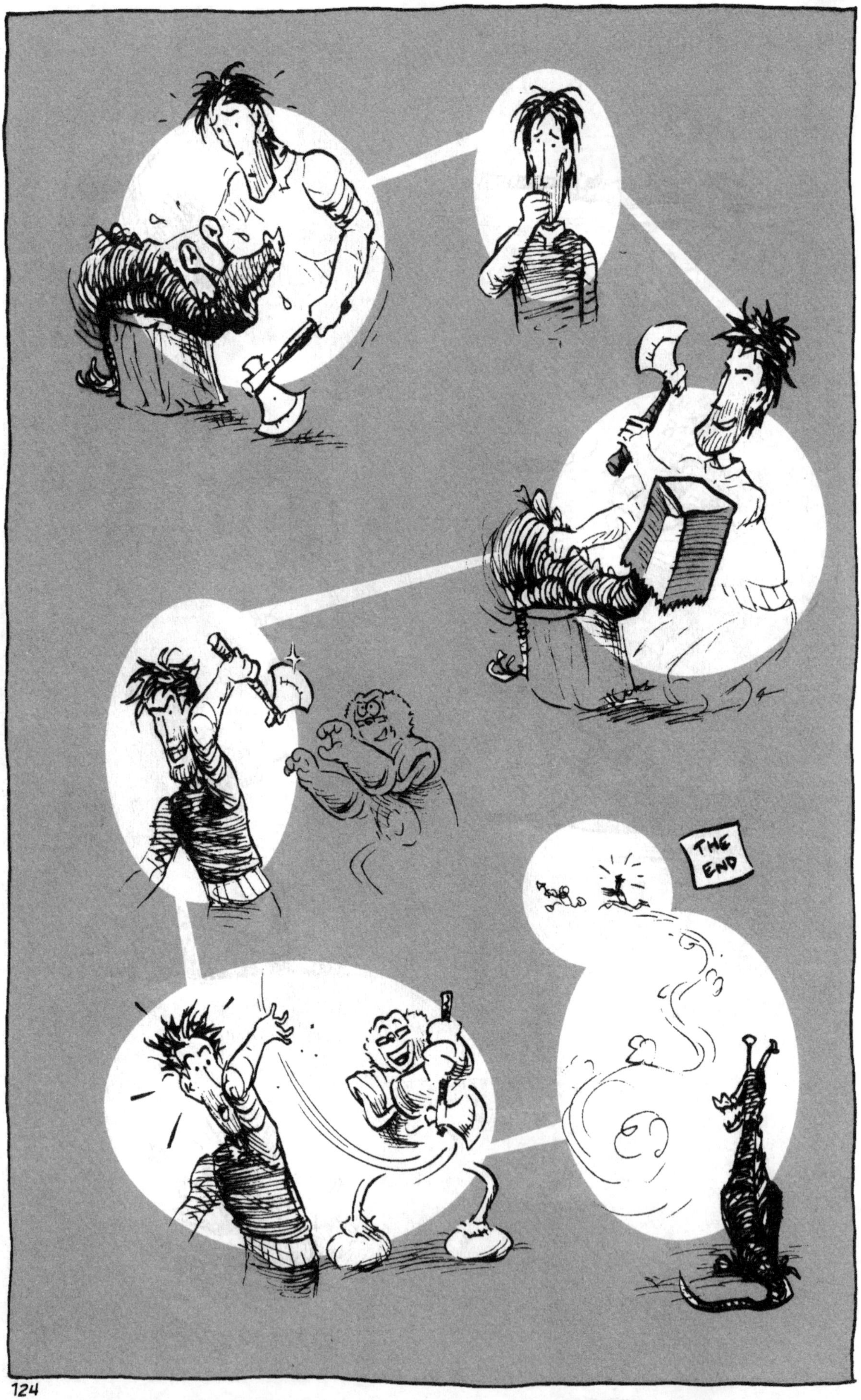
THE
END

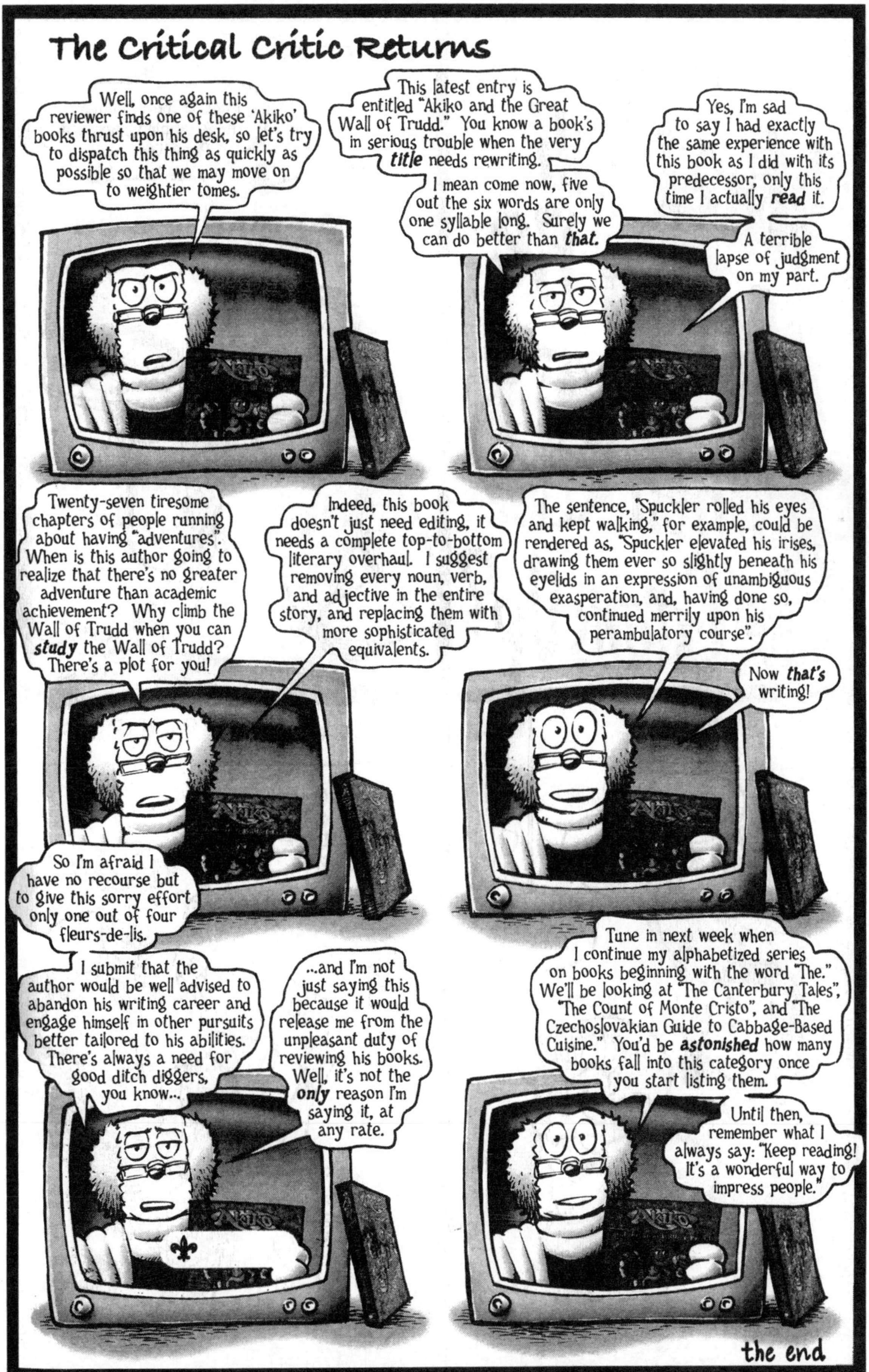
The Critical Critic Returns
Well, once again this reviewer finds one of these 'Akiko' books thrust upon his desk, so let's try to dispatch this thing as quickly as possible so that we may move on to weightier tomes.
This latest entry is entitled "Akiko and the Great Wall of Trudd." You know a book's in serious trouble when the very *title* needs rewriting.
I mean come now, five out the six words are only one syllable long. Surely we can do better than *that.*
Yes, I'm sad to say I had exactly the same experience with this book as I did with its predecessor, only this time I actually *read* it.
A terrible lapse of judgment on my part.
Twenty-seven tiresome chapters of people running about having "adventures". When is this author going to realize that there's no greater adventure than academic achievement? Why climb the Wall of Trudd when you can *study* the Wall of Trudd? There's a plot for you!
Indeed, this book doesn't just need editing, it needs a complete top-to-bottom literary overhaul. I suggest removing every noun, verb, and adjective in the entire story, and replacing them with more sophisticated equivalents.
The sentence, "Spuckler rolled his eyes and kept walking," for example, could be rendered as, "Spuckler elevated his irises, drawing them ever so slightly beneath his eyelids in an expression of unambiguous exasperation, and, having done so, continued merrily upon his perambulatory course".
Now *that's* writing!
So I'm afraid I have no recourse but to give this sorry effort only one out of four fleurs-de-lis.
I submit that the author would be well advised to abandon his writing career and engage himself in other pursuits better tailored to his abilities. There's always a need for good ditch diggers, you know...
...and I'm not just saying this because it would release me from the unpleasant duty of reviewing his books. Well, it's not the *only* reason I'm saying it, at any rate.
Tune in next week when I continue my alphabetized series on books beginning with the word "The." We'll be looking at "The Canterbury Tales", "The Count of Monte Cristo", and "The Czechoslovakian Guide to Cabbage-Based Cuisine." You'd be *astonished* how many books fall into this category once you start listing them.
Until then, remember what I always say: "Keep reading! It's a wonderful way to impress people."
the end

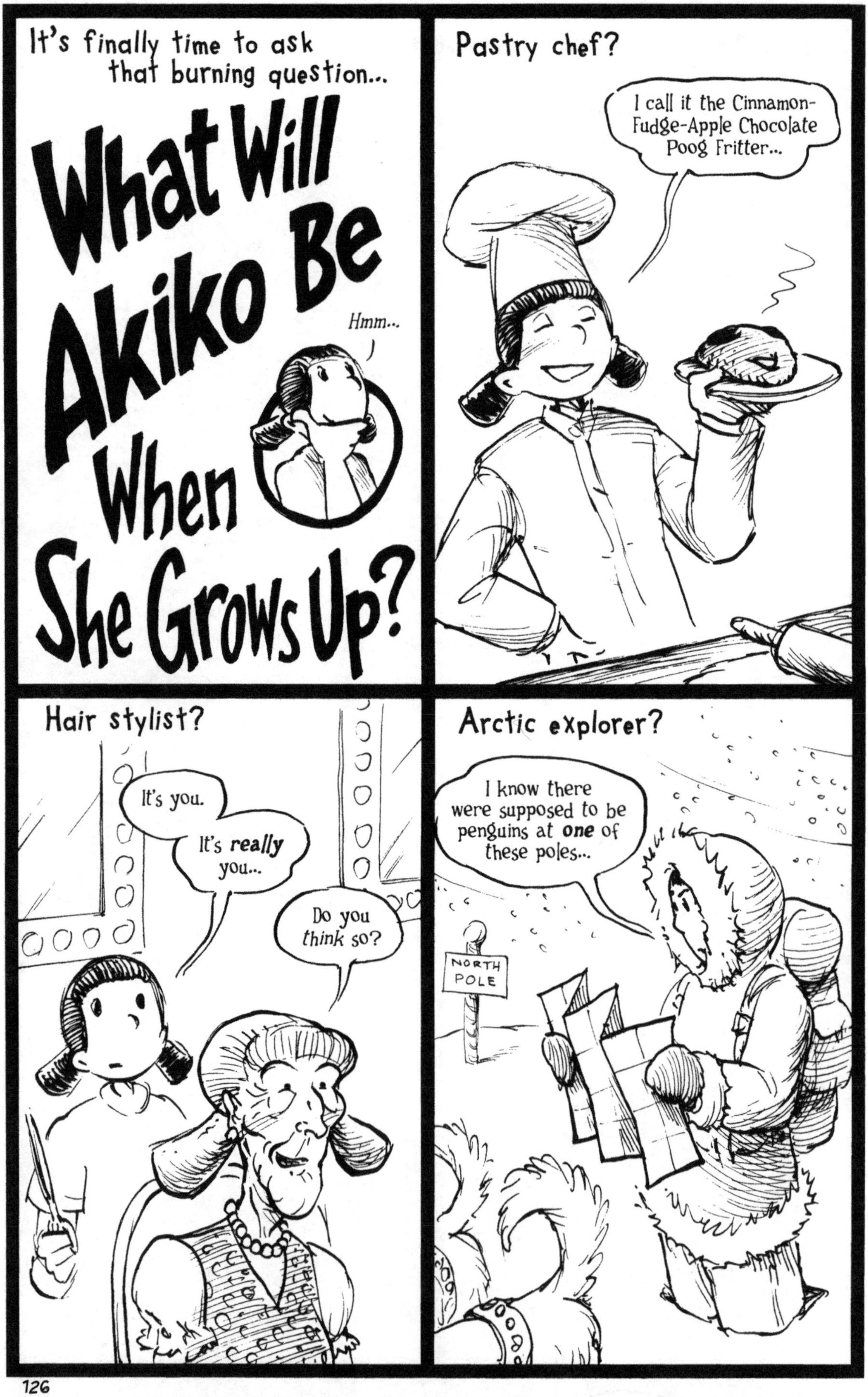
It's finally time to ask that burning question...
What Will Akiko Be When She Grows Up?
Hmm...
Pastry chef?
I call it the Cinnamon-Fudge-Apple Chocolate Poog Fritter...
Hair stylist?
It's you.
It's *really* you...
Do you *think* so?
Arctic explorer?
I know there were supposed to be penguins at **one** of these poles...
NORTH POLE

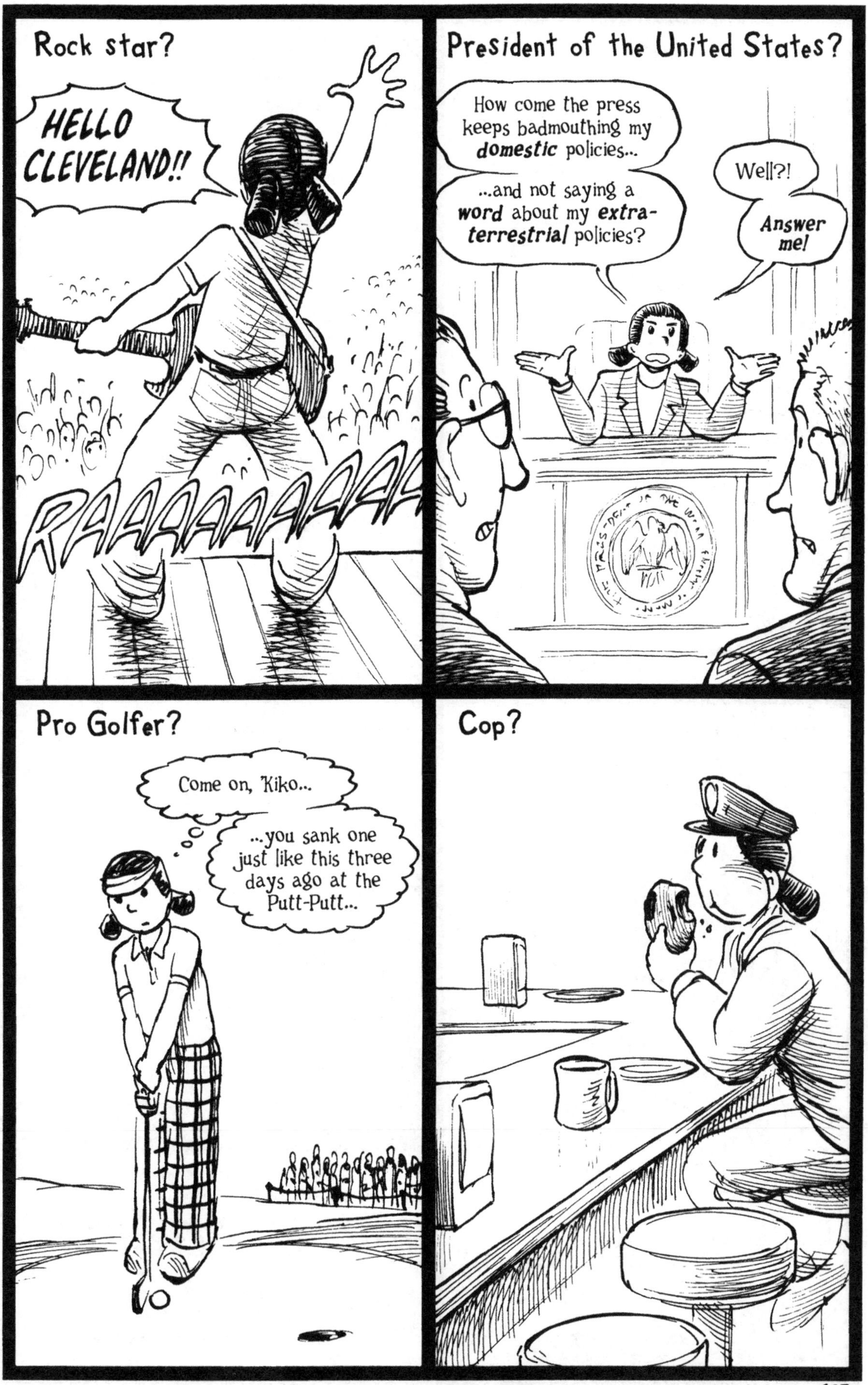
Rock star?
HELLO CLEVELAND!!
RAAAAAAAAAA
President of the United States?
How come the press keeps badmouthing my domestic policies...
...and not saying a word about my extra-terrestrial policies?
Well?!
Answer me!
Pro Golfer?
Come on, Kiko...
...you sank one just like this three days ago at the Putt-Putt...
Cop?

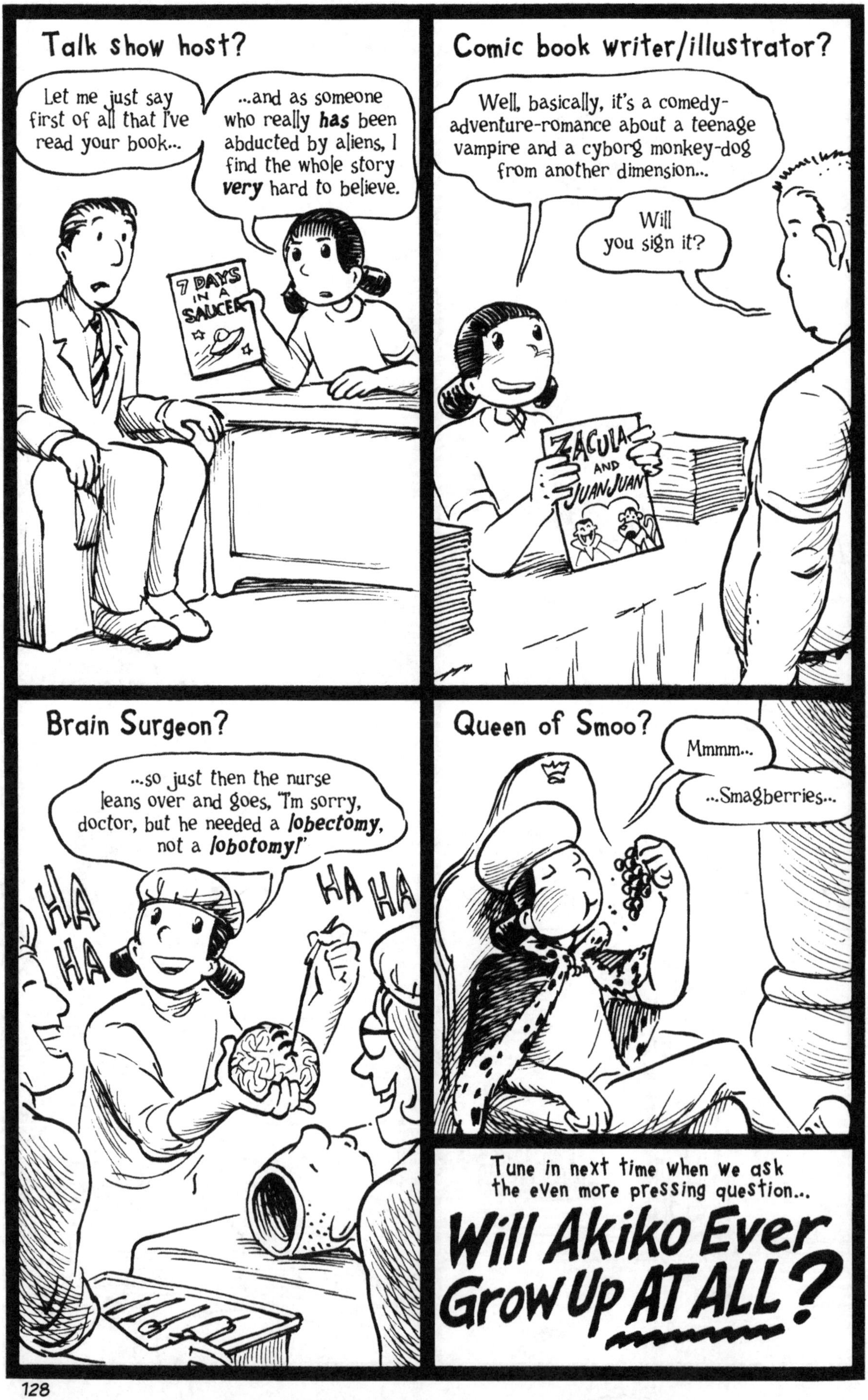
Talk show host?
Let me just say first of all that I've read your book...
...and as someone who really **has** been abducted by aliens, I find the whole story **very** hard to believe.
7 DAYS IN A SAUCER
Comic book writer/illustrator?
Well, basically, it's a comedy-adventure-romance about a teenage vampire and a cyborg monkey-dog from another dimension...
Will you sign it?
ZACULA AND JUAN JUAN
Brain Surgeon?
...so just then the nurse leans over and goes, "I'm sorry, doctor, but he needed a **lobectomy**, not a **lobotomy**!"
HA HA
HA HA
Queen of Smoo?
Mmmm...
...Smagberries...
Tune in next time when we ask the even more pressing question...
Will Akiko Ever Grow Up AT ALL?

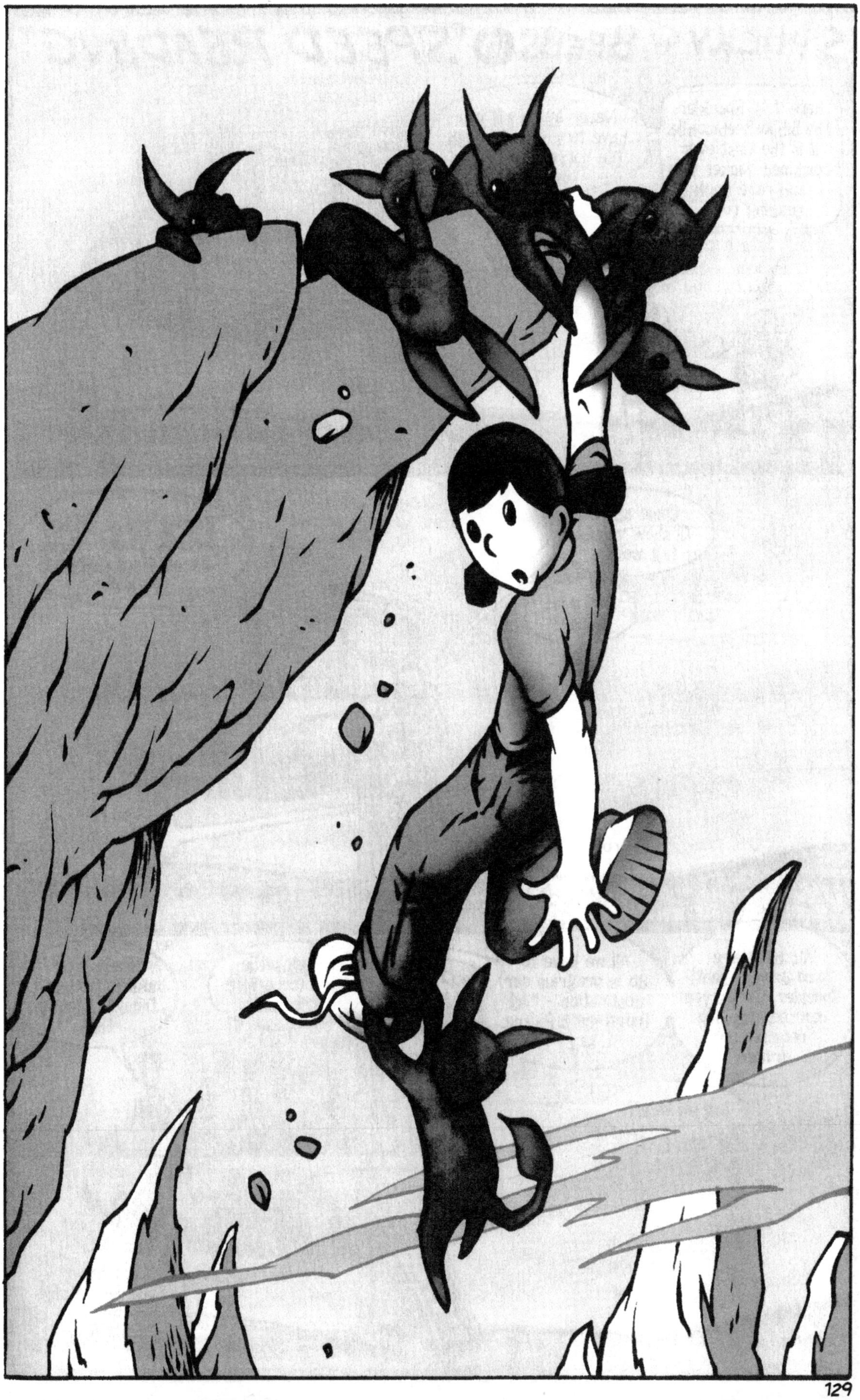

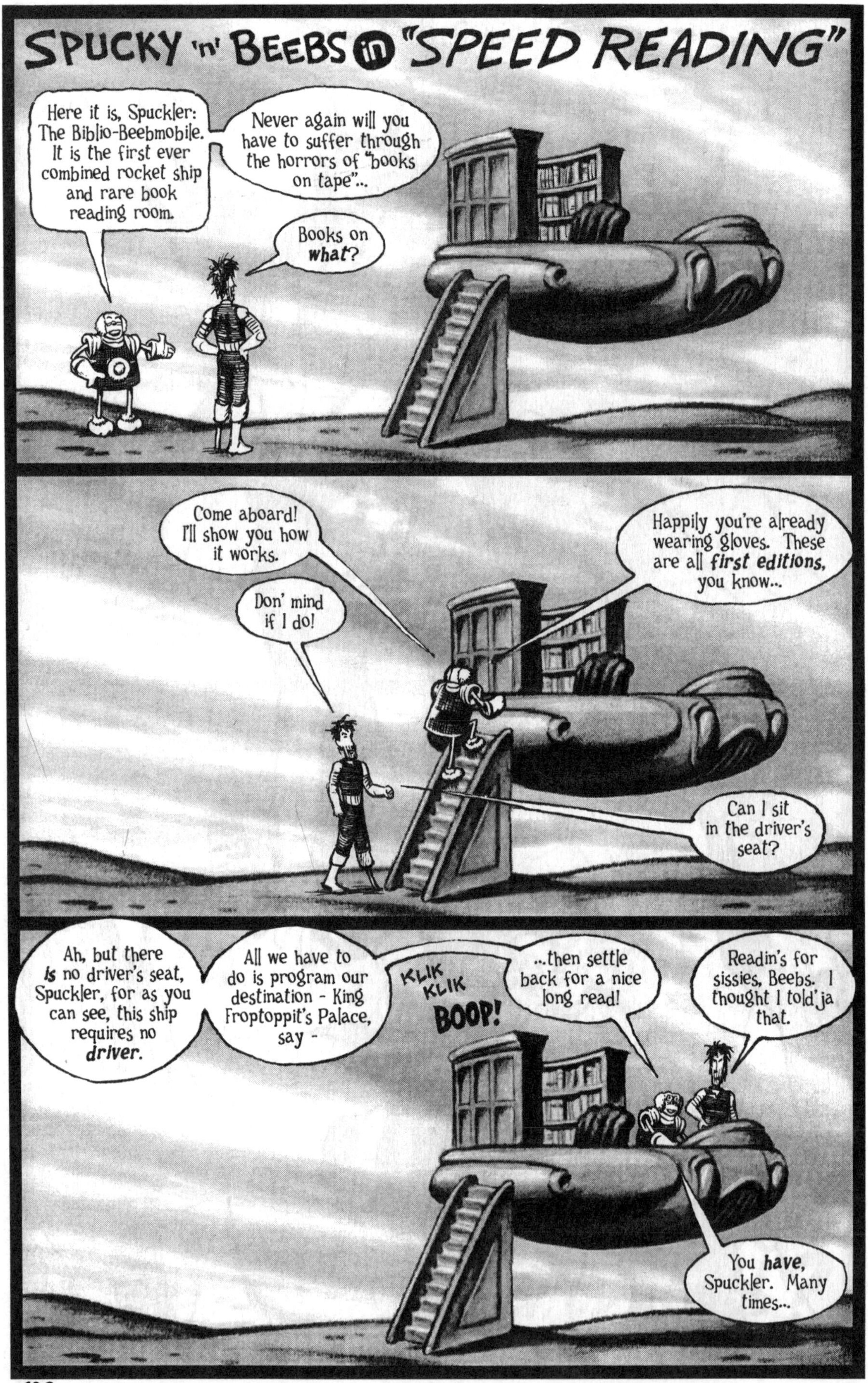
SPUCKY 'n' BEEBS in "SPEED READING"
Here it is, Spuckler: The Biblio-Beebmobile. It is the first ever combined rocket ship and rare book reading room.
Never again will you have to suffer through the horrors of "books on tape"...
Books on what?
Come aboard! I'll show you how it works.
Happily you're already wearing gloves. These are all first editions, you know...
Don' mind if I do!
Can I sit in the driver's seat?
Ah, but there is no driver's seat, Spuckler, for as you can see, this ship requires no driver.
All we have to do is program our destination - King Froptoppit's Palace, say -
KLIK KLIK BOOP!
...then settle back for a nice long read!
Readin's for sissies, Beebs. I thought I told'ja that.
You have, Spuckler. Many times...

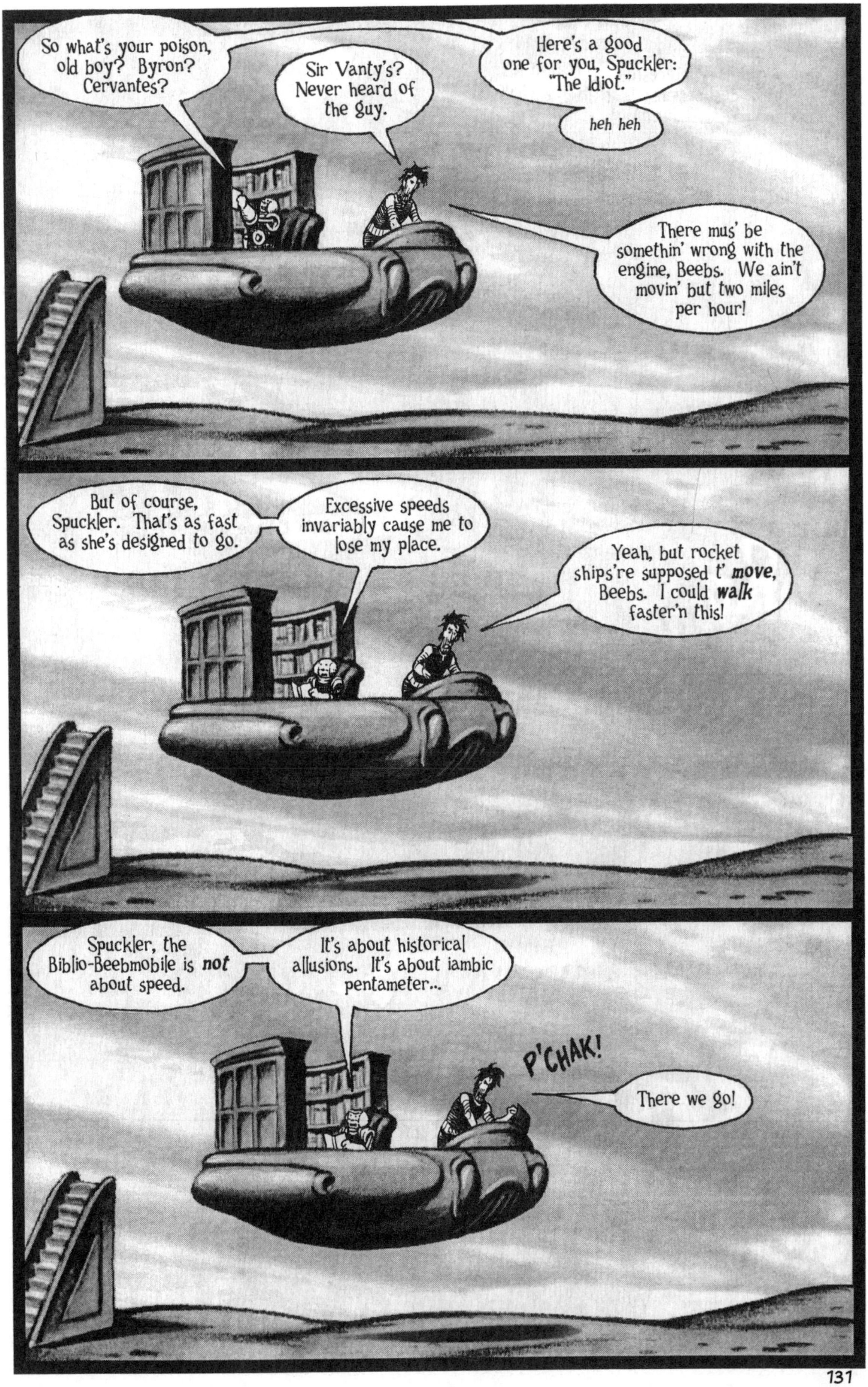
So what's your poison, old boy? Byron? Cervantes?
Sir Vanty's? Never heard of the guy.
Here's a good one for you, Spuckler: "The Idiot."
heh heh
There mus' be somethin' wrong with the engine, Beebs. We ain't movin' but two miles per hour!
But of course, Spuckler. That's as fast as she's designed to go.
Excessive speeds invariably cause me to lose my place.
Yeah, but rocket ships're supposed t' *move*, Beebs. I could *walk* faster'n this!
Spuckler, the Biblio-Beebmobile is *not* about speed.
It's about historical allusions. It's about iambic pentameter...
P'CHAK!
There we go!

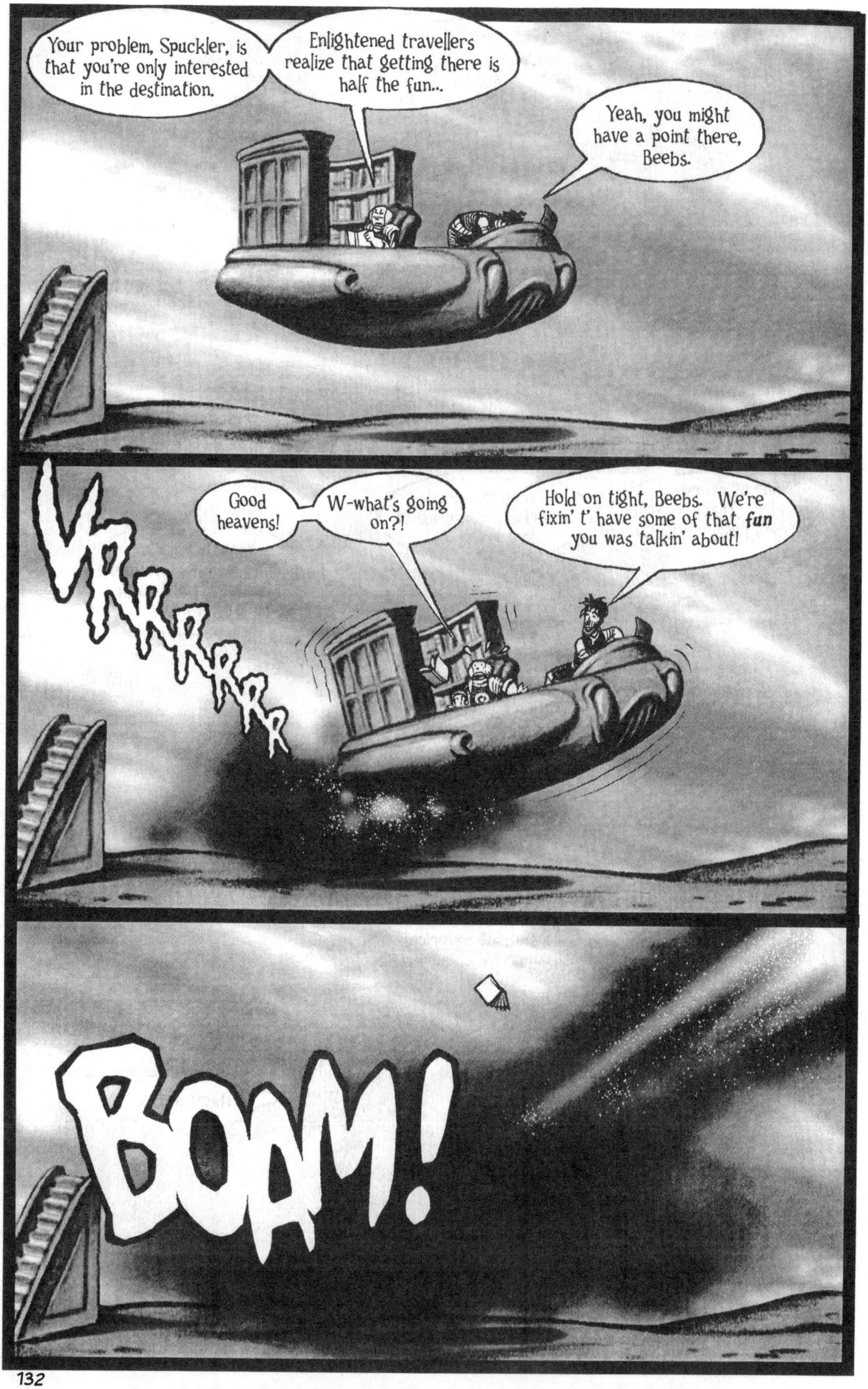
Your problem, Spuckler, is that you're only interested in the destination.
Enlightened travellers realize that getting there is half the fun...
Yeah, you might have a point there, Beebs.
VRRRRRRR
Good heavens!
W-what's going on?!
Hold on tight, Beebs. We're fixin' t' have some of that **fun** you was talkin' about!
BOAM!

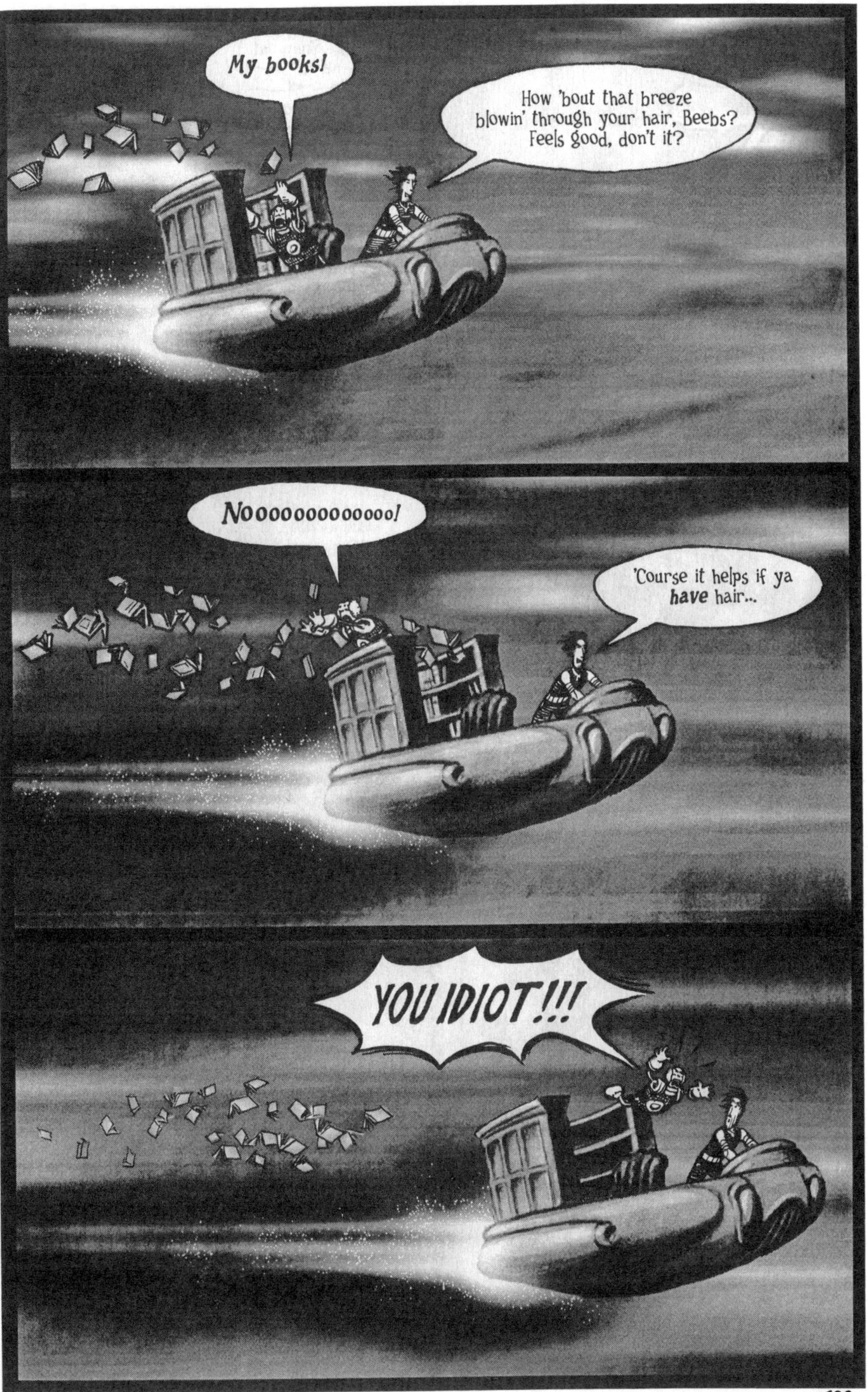
My books!
How 'bout that breeze blowin' through your hair, Beebs? Feels good, don't it?
Noooooooooooooo!
'Course it helps if ya **have** hair...
YOU IDIOT!!!

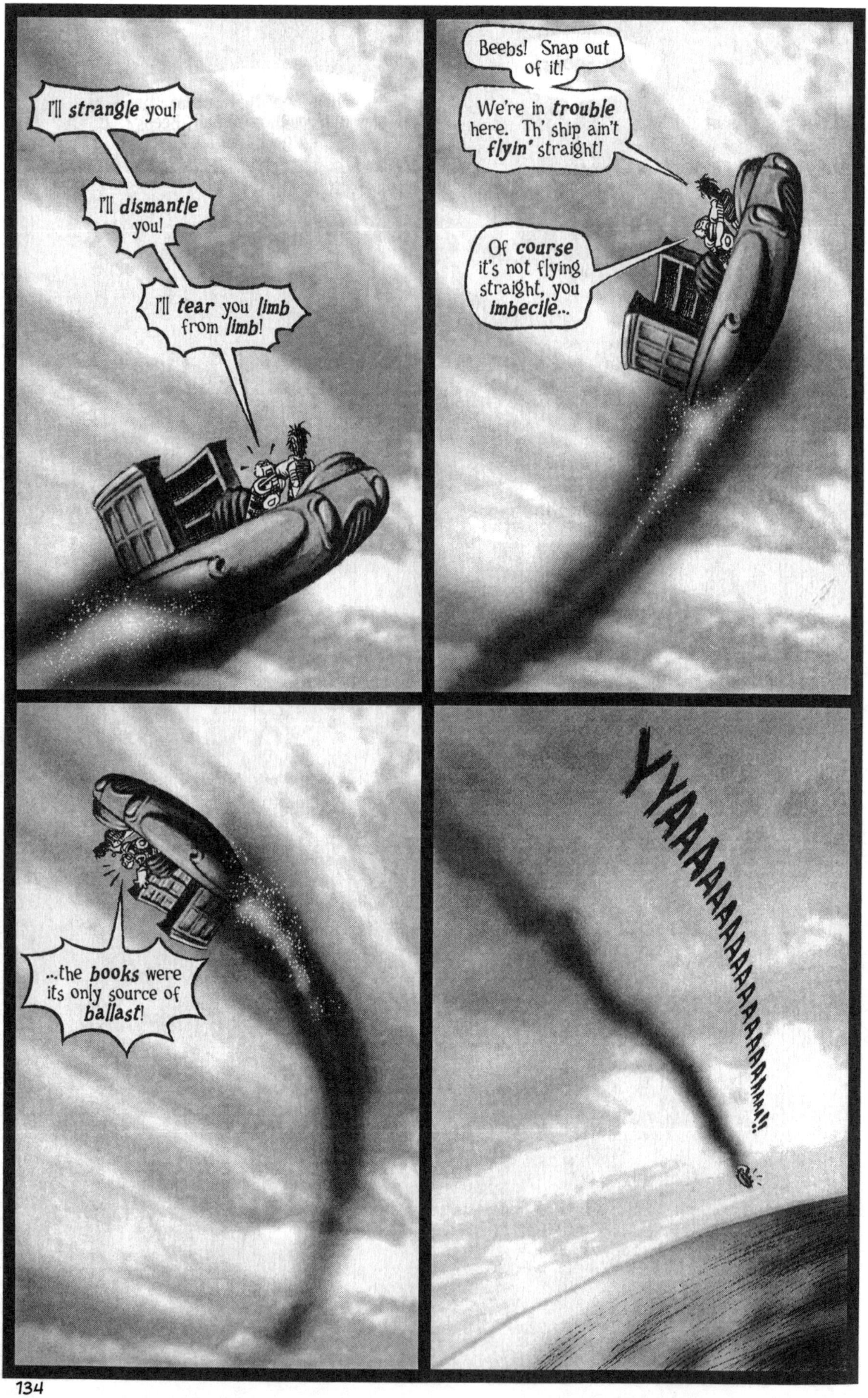
I'll strangle you!
I'll dismantle you!
I'll tear you limb from limb!
Beebs! Snap out of it!
We're in trouble here. Th' ship ain't flyin' straight!
Of course it's not flying straight, you imbecile...
...the books were its only source of ballast!
YYAAAAAAAAAAAAAAAAAAAAA!!

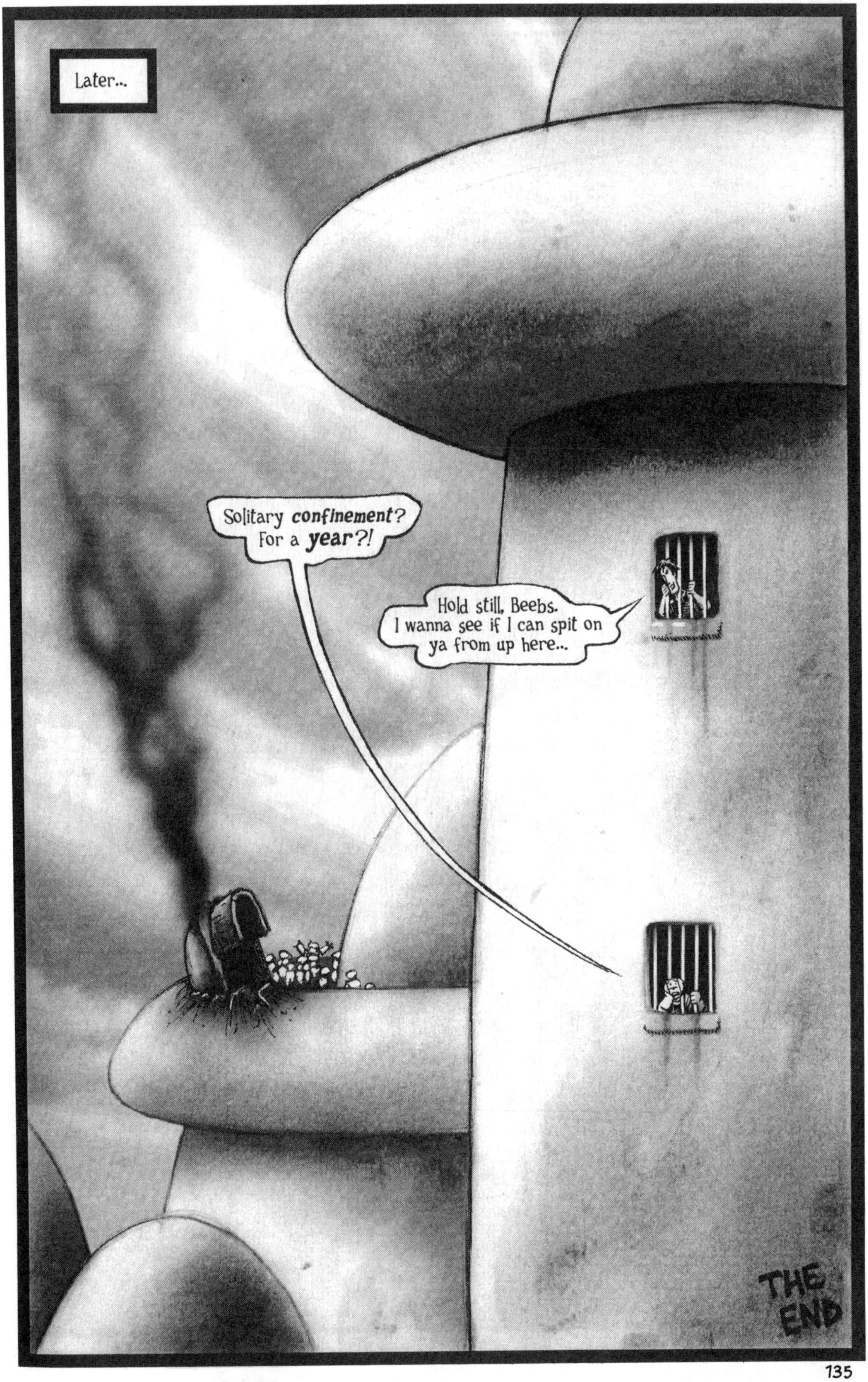
Later...
Solitary confinement? For a year?!
Hold still, Beebs. I wanna see if I can spit on ya from up here...
THE END

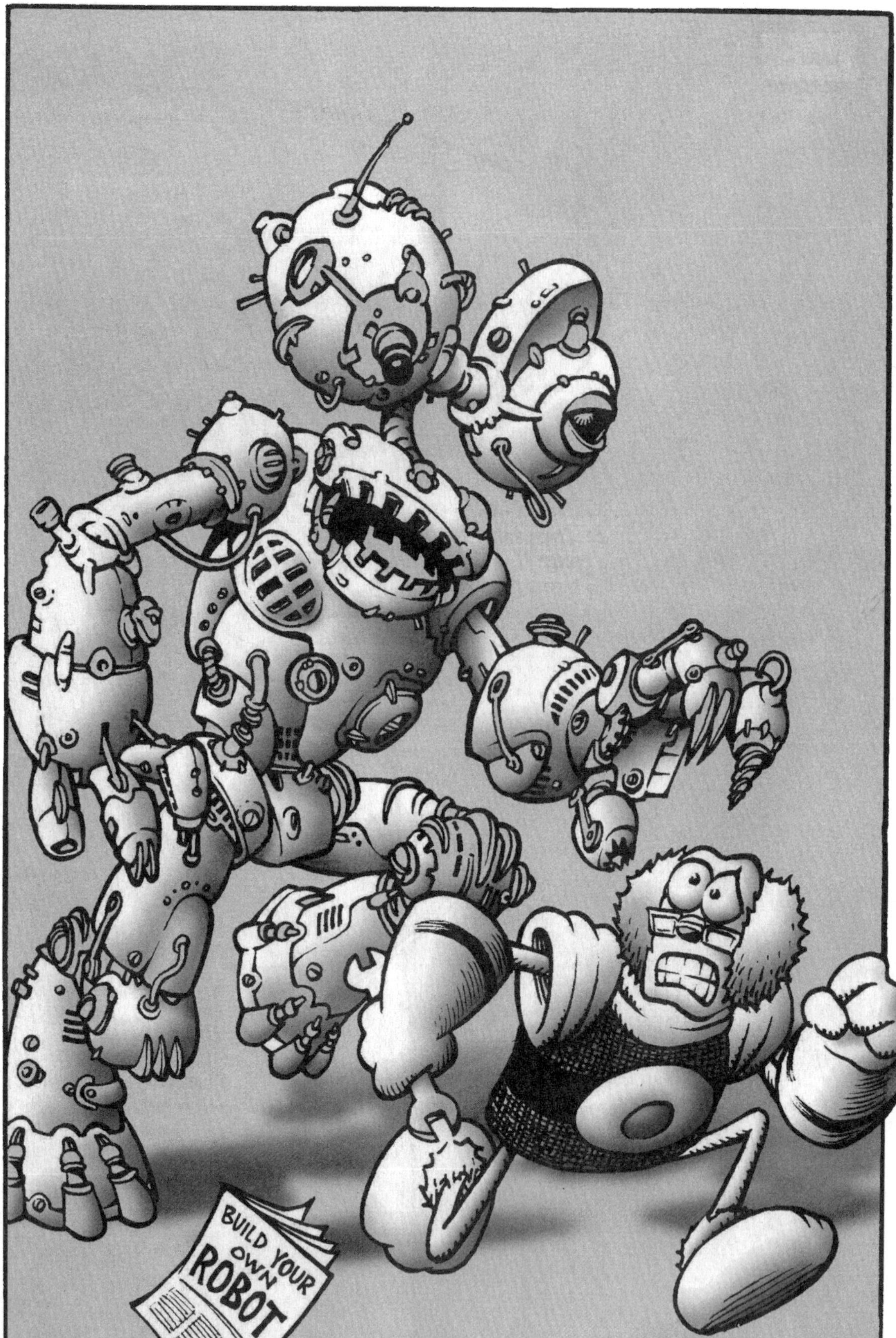
BUILD YOUR OWN ROBOT

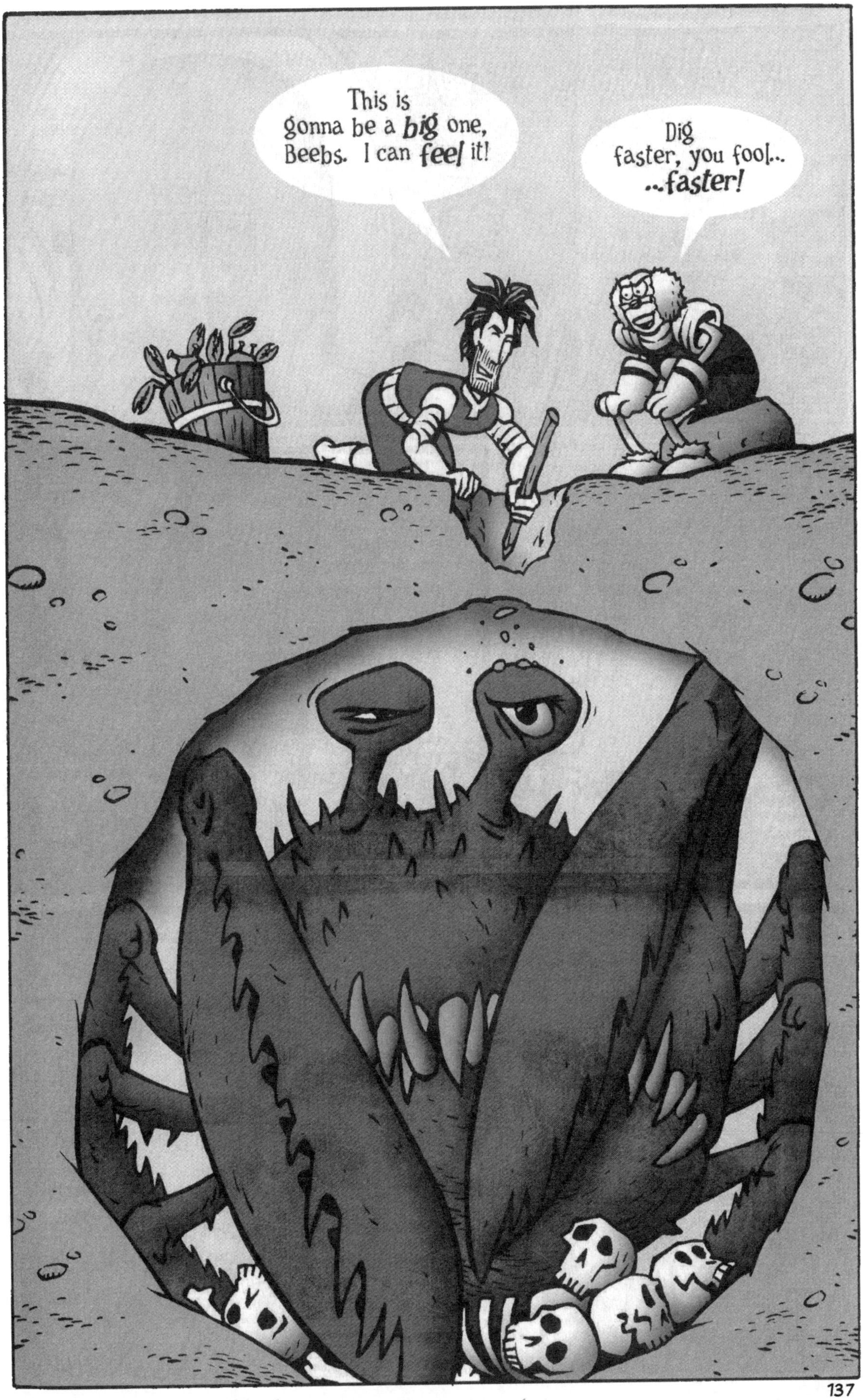
This is gonna be a big one, Beebs. I can feel it!
Dig faster, you fool... ...faster!

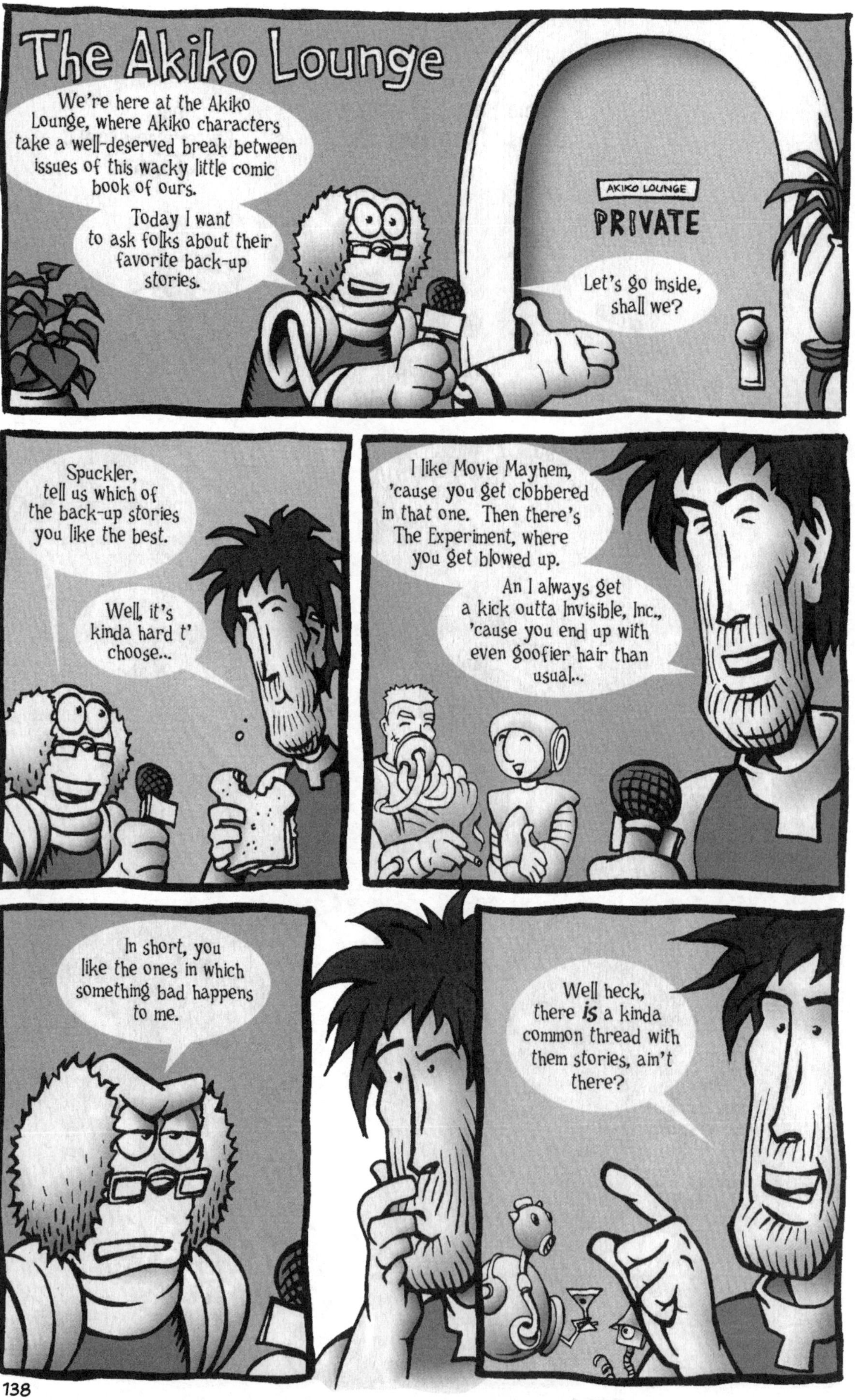
The Akiko Lounge
We're here at the Akiko Lounge, where Akiko characters take a well-deserved break between issues of this wacky little comic book of ours.
Today I want to ask folks about their favorite back-up stories.
AKIKO LOUNGE
PRIVATE
Let's go inside, shall we?
Spuckler, tell us which of the back-up stories you like the best.
Well, it's kinda hard t' choose...
I like Movie Mayhem, 'cause you get clobbered in that one. Then there's The Experiment, where you get blowed up.
An I always get a kick outta Invisible, Inc., 'cause you end up with even goofier hair than usual...
In short, you like the ones in which something bad happens to me.
Well heck, there *is* a kinda common thread with them stories, ain't there?

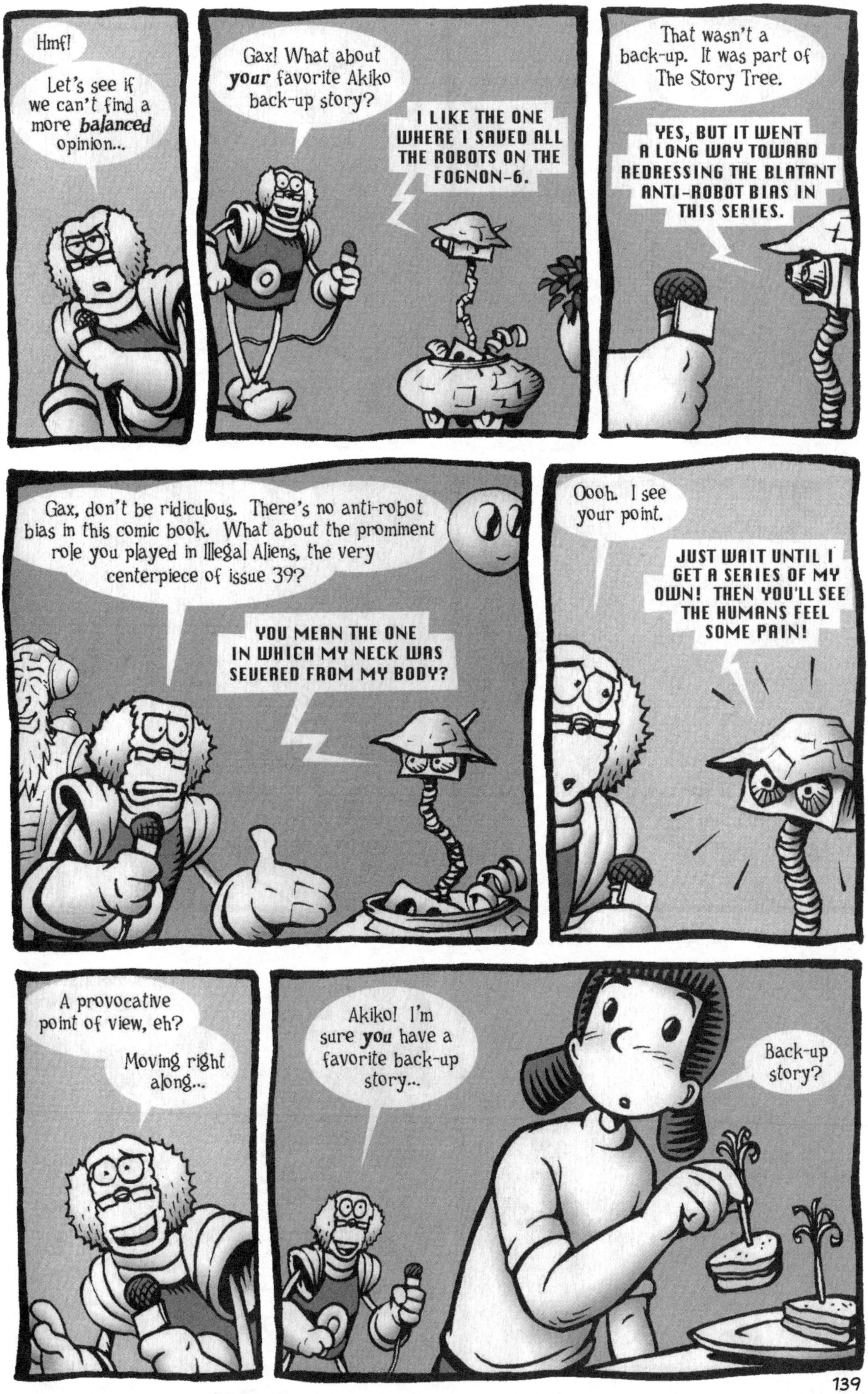
Hmf!
Let's see if we can't find a more **balanced** opinion...
Gax! What about **your** favorite Akiko back-up story?
I LIKE THE ONE WHERE I SAVED ALL THE ROBOTS ON THE FOGNON-6.
That wasn't a back-up. It was part of The Story Tree.
YES, BUT IT WENT A LONG WAY TOWARD REDRESSING THE BLATANT ANTI-ROBOT BIAS IN THIS SERIES.
Gax, don't be ridiculous. There's no anti-robot bias in this comic book. What about the prominent role you played in Illegal Aliens, the very centerpiece of issue 39?
YOU MEAN THE ONE IN WHICH MY NECK WAS SEVERED FROM MY BODY?
Oooh. I see your point.
JUST WAIT UNTIL I GET A SERIES OF MY OWN! THEN YOU'LL SEE THE HUMANS FEEL SOME PAIN!
A provocative point of view, eh?
Moving right along...
Akiko! I'm sure **you** have a favorite back-up story...
Back-up story?

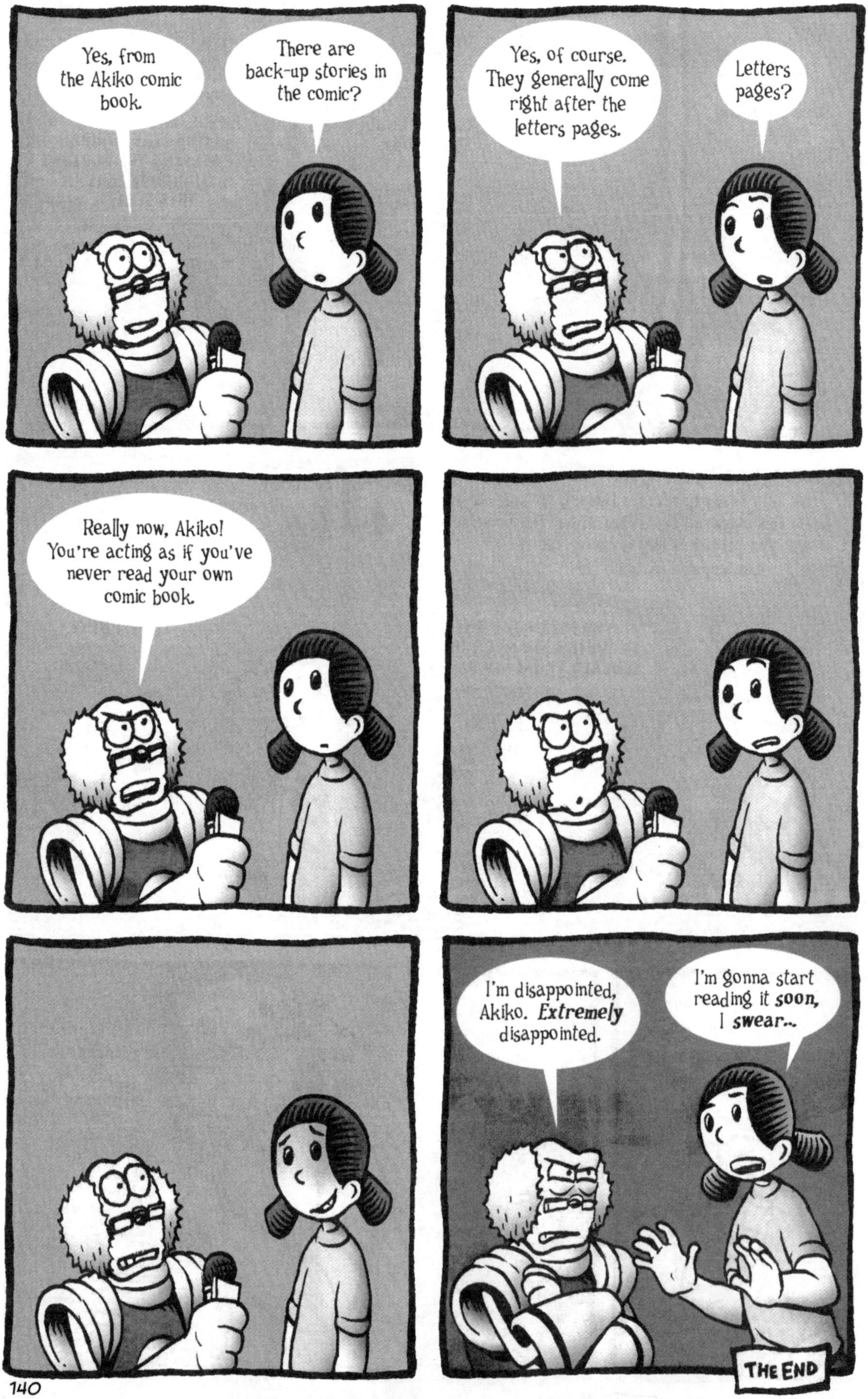
Yes, from the Akiko comic book.
There are back-up stories in the comic?
Yes, of course. They generally come right after the letters pages.
Letters pages?
Really now, Akiko! You're acting as if you've never read your own comic book.
I'm disappointed, Akiko. *Extremely* disappointed.
I'm gonna start reading it ***soon,*** I ***swear...***
THE END

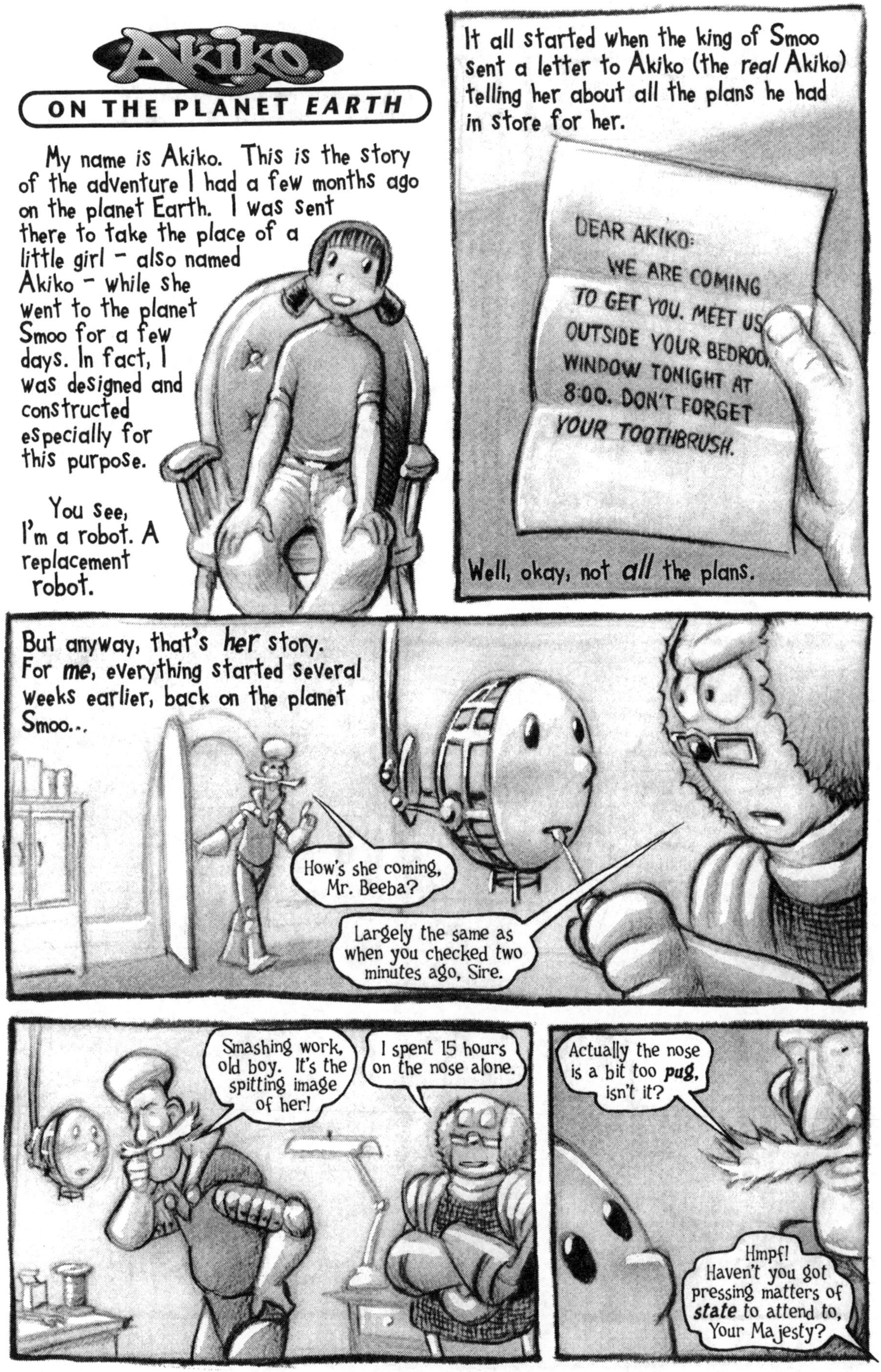
Akiko
ON THE PLANET EARTH
My name is Akiko. This is the story of the adventure I had a few months ago on the planet Earth. I was sent there to take the place of a little girl - also named Akiko - while she went to the planet Smoo for a few days. In fact, I was designed and constructed especially for this purpose.
You see, I'm a robot. A replacement robot.
It all started when the king of Smoo sent a letter to Akiko (the *real* Akiko) telling her about all the plans he had in store for her.
DEAR AKIKO:
WE ARE COMING TO GET YOU. MEET US OUTSIDE YOUR BEDROO WINDOW TONIGHT AT 8:00. DON'T FORGET YOUR TOOTHBRUSH.
Well, okay, not *all* the plans.
But anyway, that's *her* story. For *me*, everything started several weeks earlier, back on the planet Smoo...
How's she coming, Mr. Beeba?
Largely the same as when you checked two minutes ago, Sire.
Smashing work, old boy. It's the spitting image of her!
I spent 15 hours on the nose alone.
Actually the nose is a bit too *pug*, isn't it?
Hmpf! Haven't you got pressing matters of *state* to attend to, Your Majesty?

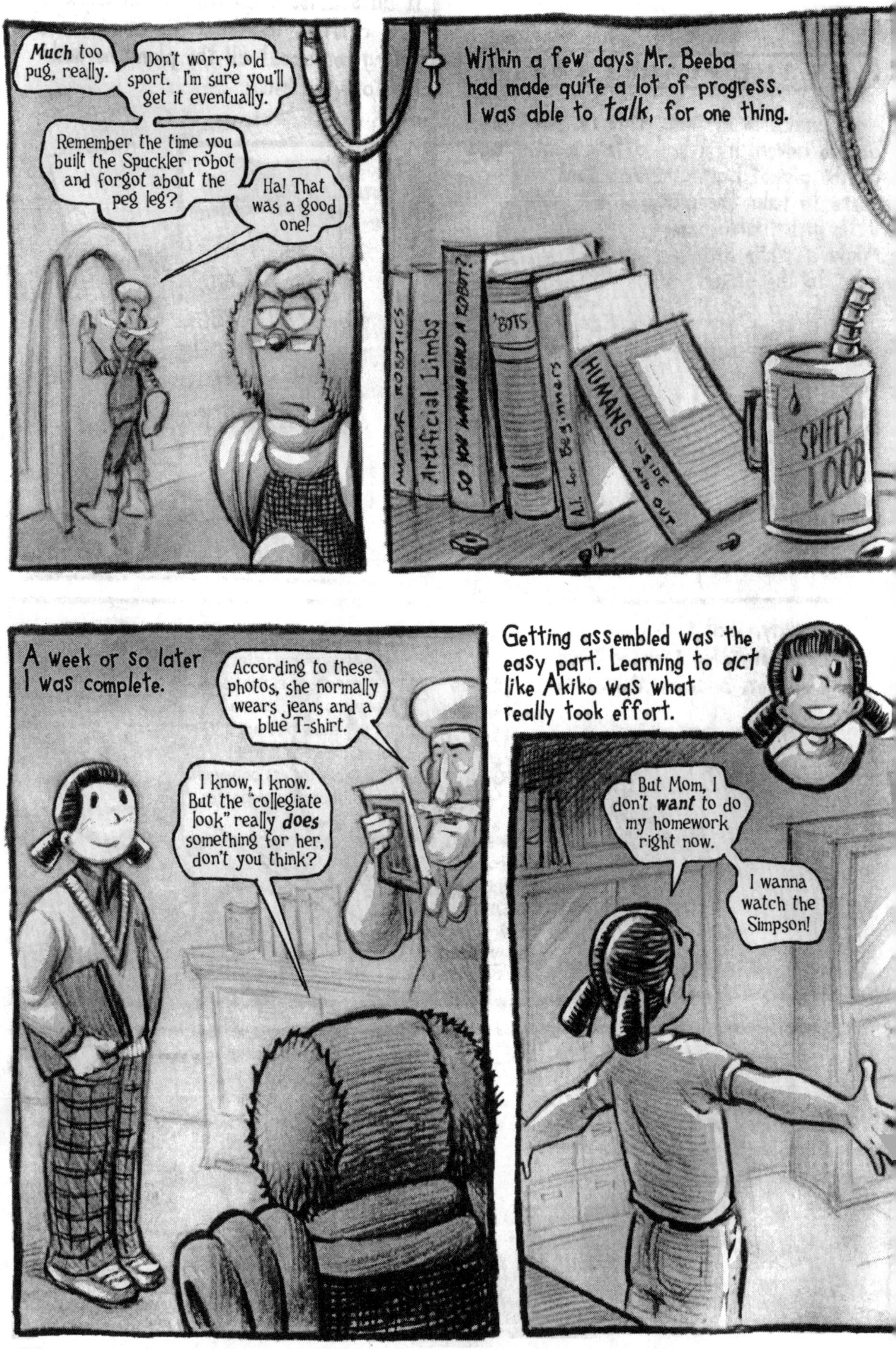

Much too pug, really.
Don't worry, old sport. I'm sure you'll get it eventually.
Remember the time you built the Spuckler robot and forgot about the peg leg?
Ha! That was a good one!
Within a few days Mr. Beeba had made quite a lot of progress. I was able to talk, for one thing.
AMATEUR ROBOTICS
Artificial Limbs
SO YOU WANNA BUILD A ROBOT?
'BOTS
A.I. for Beginners
HUMANS INSIDE AND OUT
SPIFFY LOOB
A week or so later I was complete.
According to these photos, she normally wears jeans and a blue T-shirt.
I know, I know. But the "collegiate look" really does something for her, don't you think?
Getting assembled was the easy part. Learning to act like Akiko was what really took effort.
But Mom, I don't want to do my homework right now.
I wanna watch the Simpson!

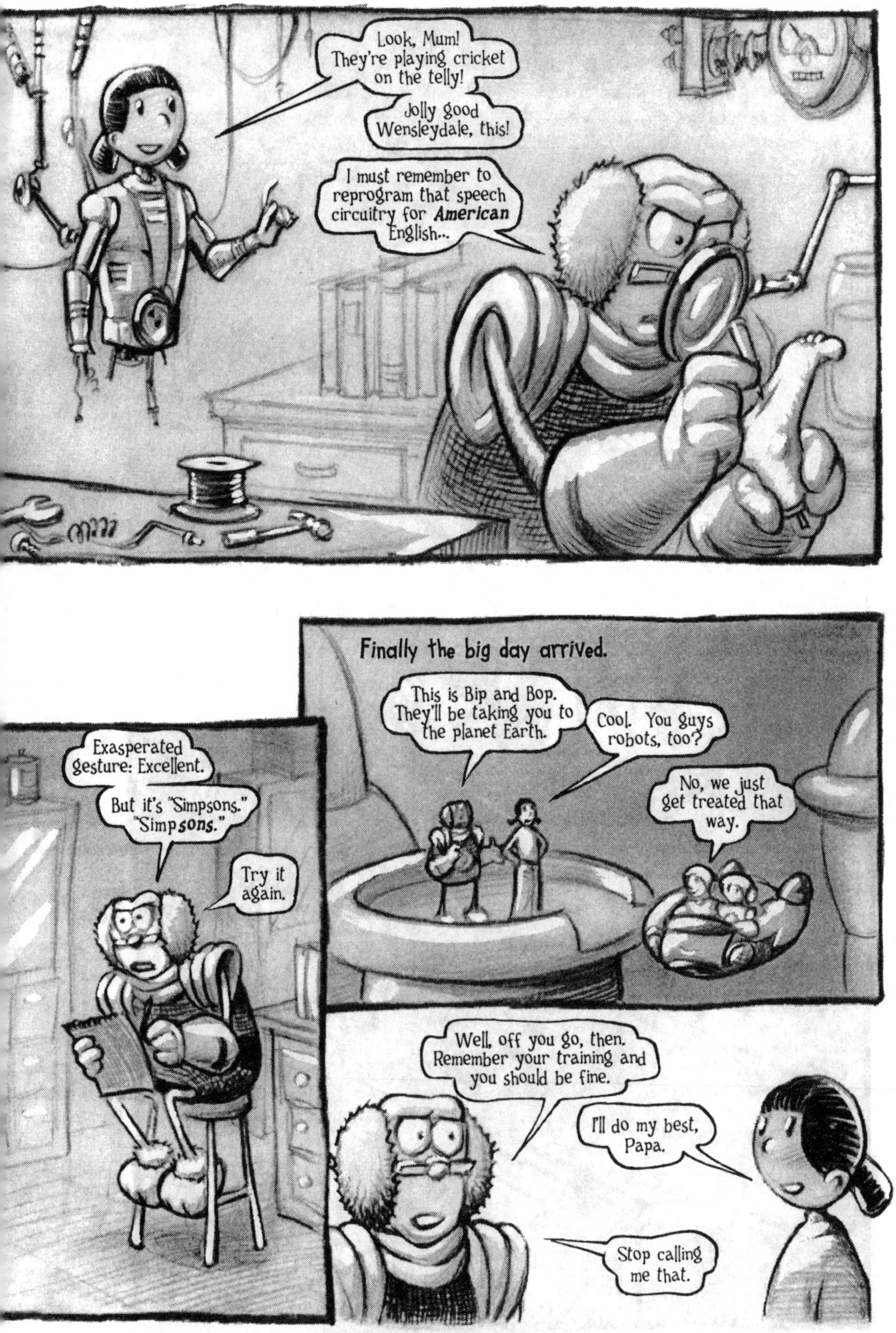
Look, Mum! They're playing cricket on the telly!
Jolly good Wensleydale, this!
I must remember to reprogram that speech circuitry for **American** English...
Exasperated gesture: Excellent.
But it's "Simpsons." "Simp*sons*."
Try it again.
Finally the big day arrived.
This is Bip and Bop. They'll be taking you to the planet Earth.
Cool. You guys robots, too?
No, we just get treated that way.
Well, off you go, then. Remember your training and you should be fine.
I'll do my best, Papa.
Stop calling me that.

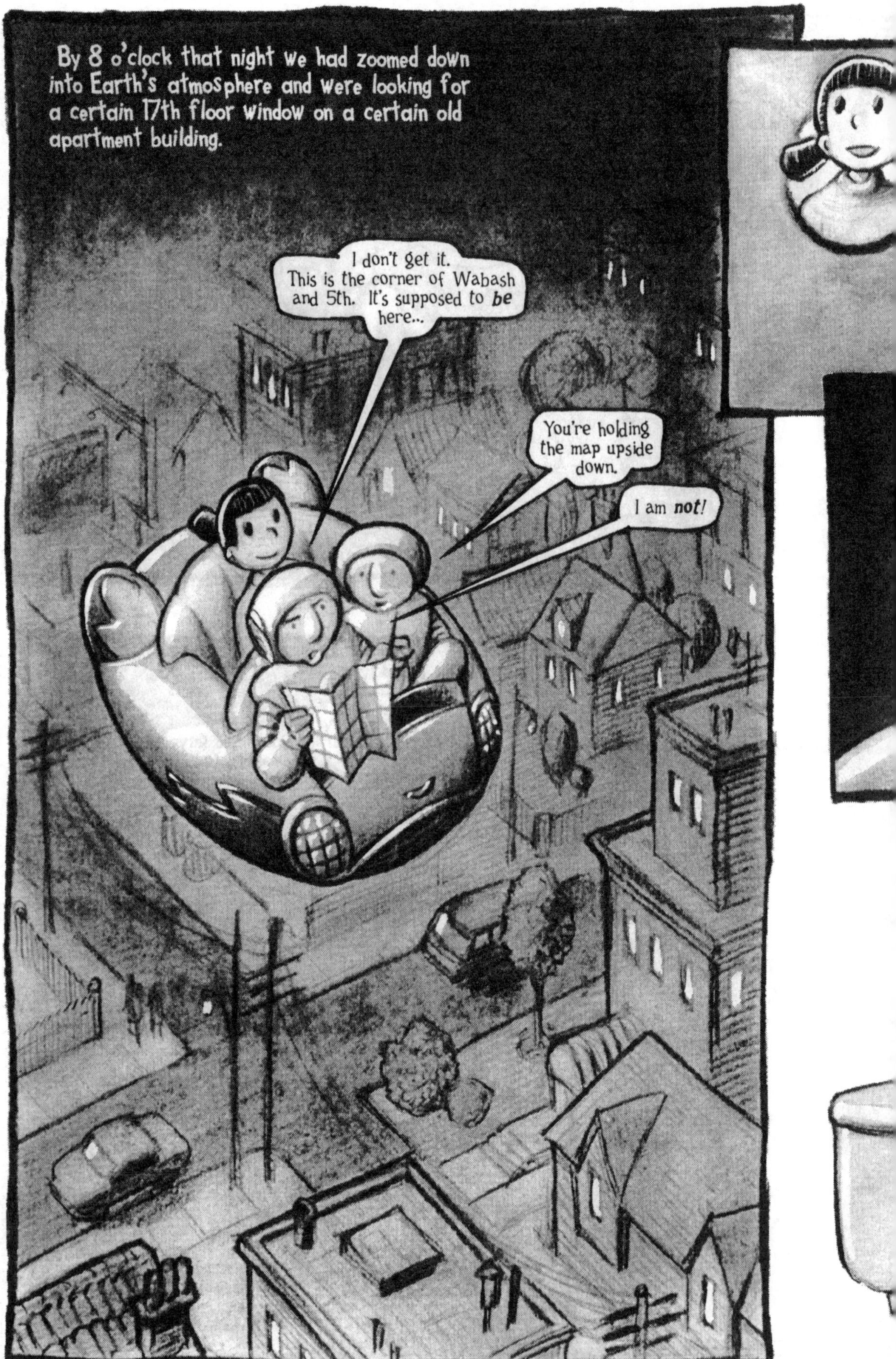
By 8 o'clock that night we had zoomed down into Earth's atmosphere and were looking for a certain 17th floor window on a certain old apartment building.
I don't get it. This is the corner of Wabash and 5th. It's supposed to *be* here...
You're holding the map upside down.
I am ***not!***

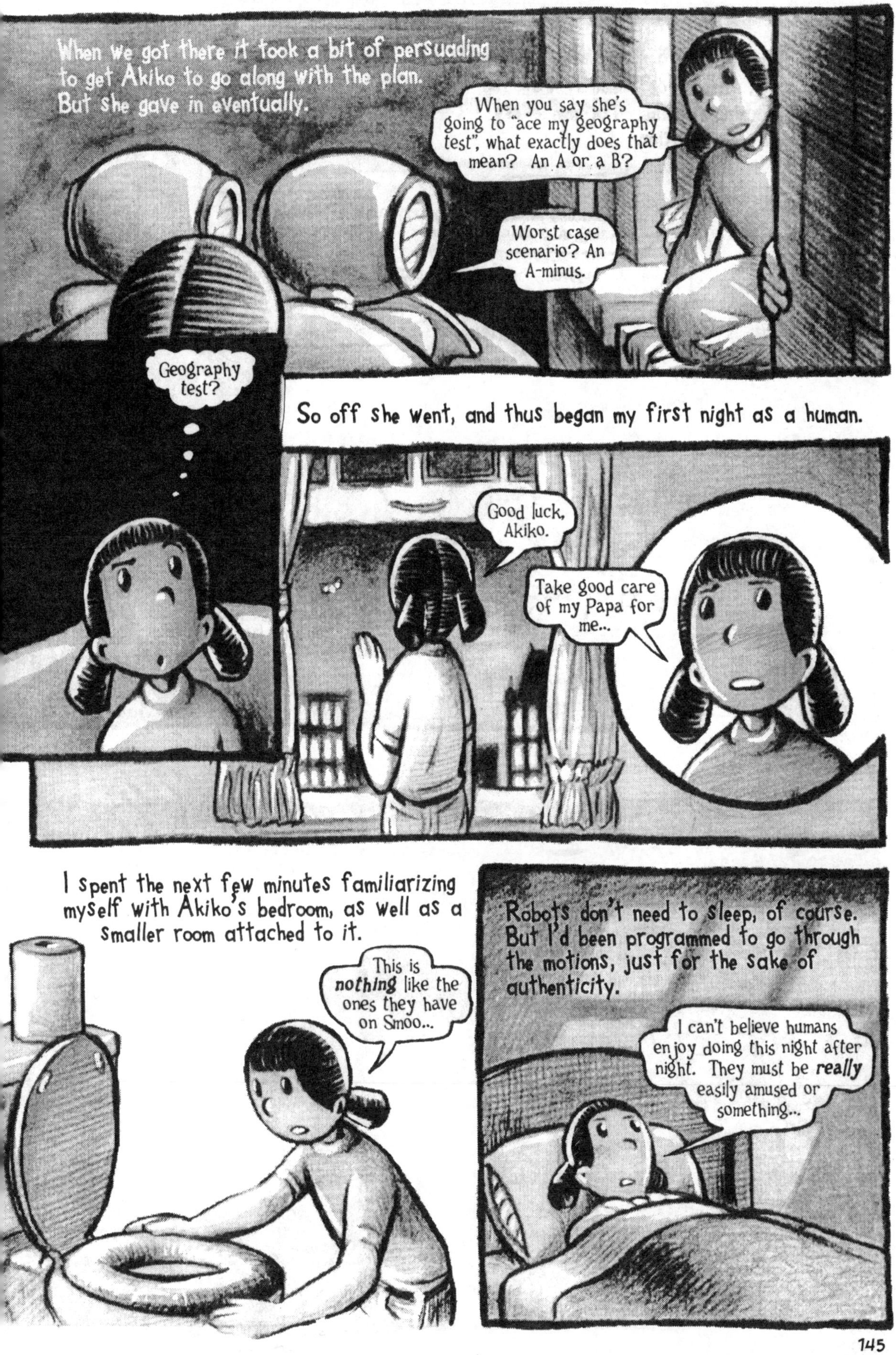

When we got there it took a bit of persuading to get Akiko to go along with the plan. But she gave in eventually.
When you say she's going to "ace my geography test", what exactly does that mean? An A or a B?
Worst case scenario? An A-minus.
Geography test?
So off she went, and thus began my first night as a human.
Good luck, Akiko.
Take good care of my Papa for me...
I spent the next few minutes familiarizing myself with Akiko's bedroom, as well as a smaller room attached to it.
This is *nothing* like the ones they have on Smoo...
Robots don't need to sleep, of course. But I'd been programmed to go through the motions, just for the sake of authenticity.
I can't believe humans enjoy doing this night after night. They must be *really* easily amused or something...

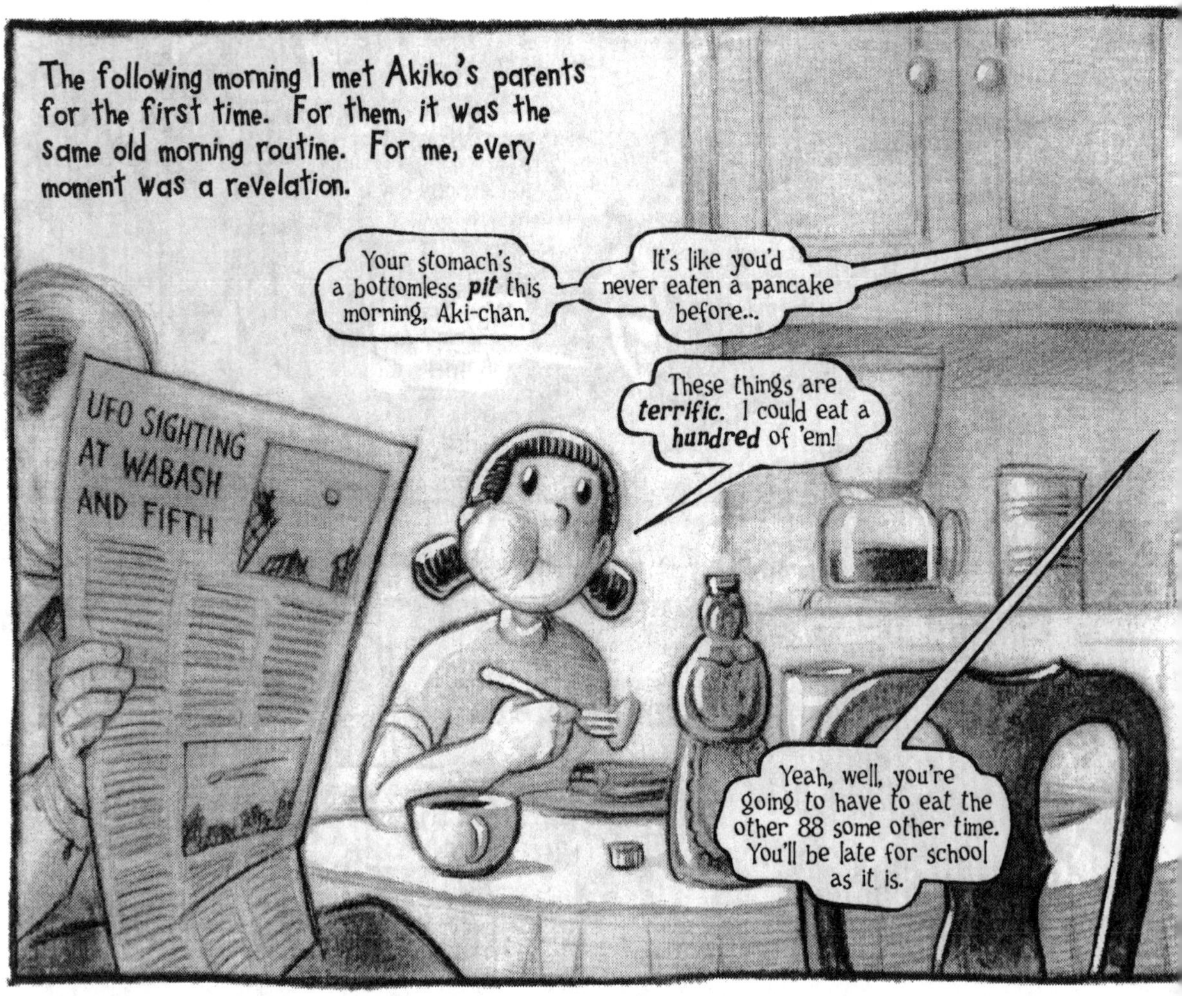
The following morning I met Akiko's parents for the first time. For them, it was the same old morning routine. For me, every moment was a revelation.
UFO SIGHTING AT WABASH AND FIFTH
Your stomach's a bottomless *pit* this morning, Aki-chan.
It's like you'd never eaten a pancake before...
These things are **terrific**. I could eat a **hundred** of 'em!
Yeah, well, you're going to have to eat the other 88 some other time. You'll be late for school as it is.

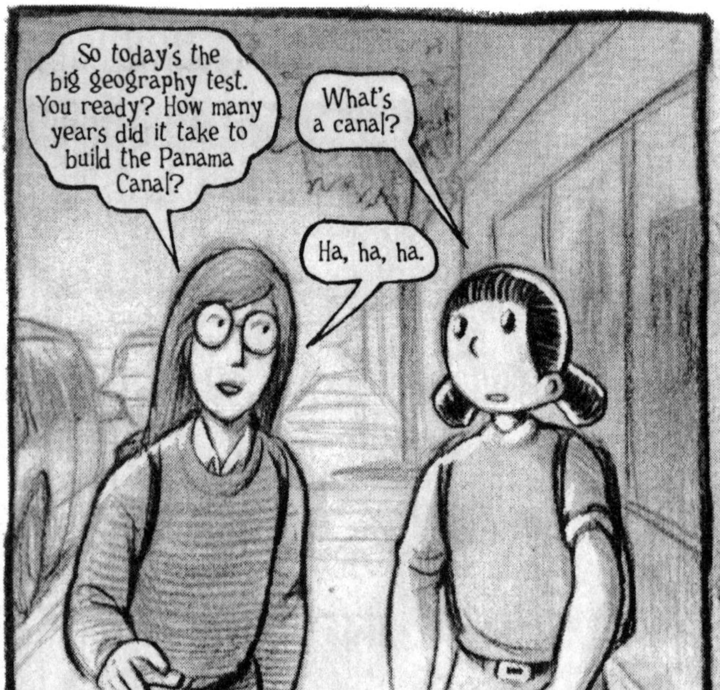
So today's the big geography test. You ready? How many years did it take to build the Panama Canal?
What's a canal?
Ha, ha, ha.

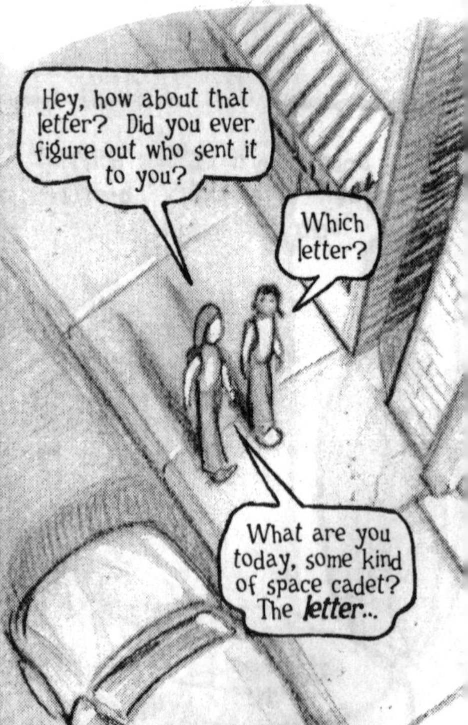
Hey, how about that letter? Did you ever figure out who sent it to you?
Which letter?
What are you today, some kind of space cadet? The ***letter***...

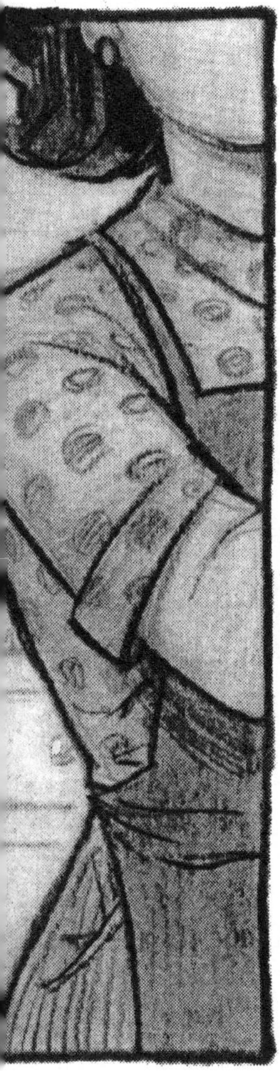

School. I'd almost forgotten! I had to meet Akiko's friend Melissa on the sixth floor so we could walk to Middleton Elementary together. At first I was afraid she'd spot tiny tell tale differences between me and the real Akiko...

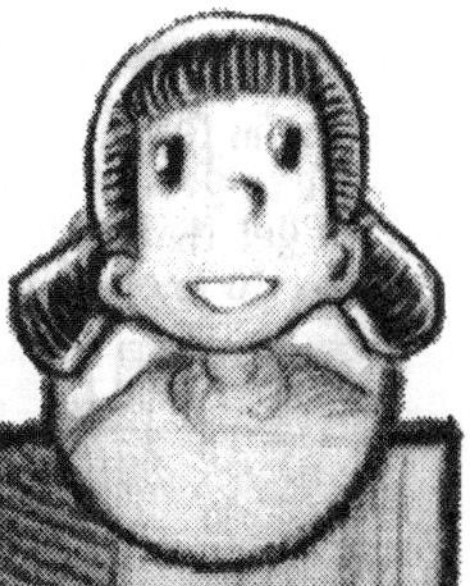

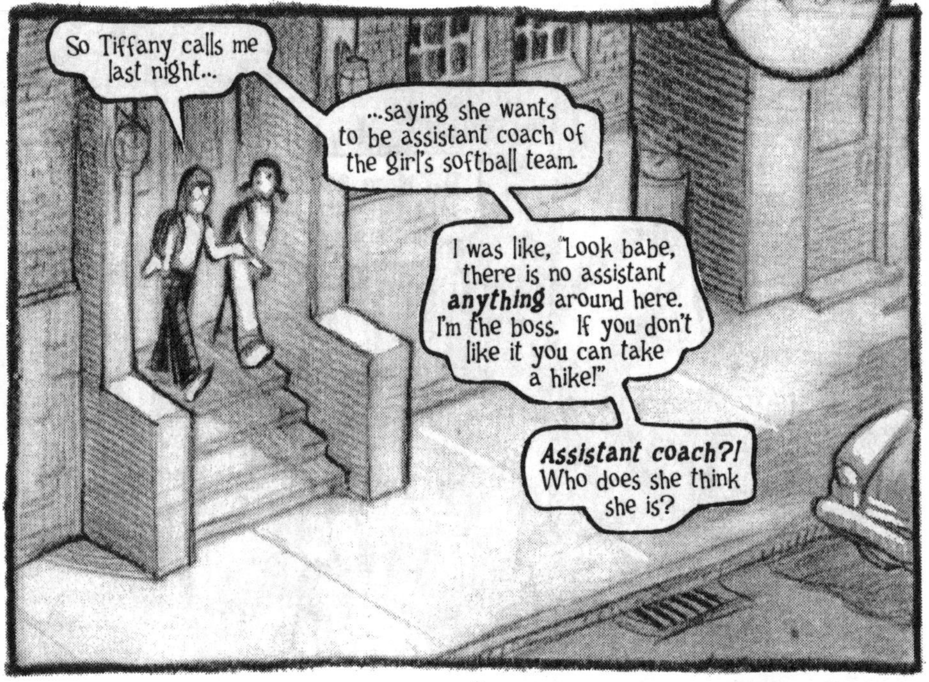
So Tiffany calls me last night...
...saying she wants to be assistant coach of the girl's softball team.
I was like, "Look babe, there is no assistant **anything** around here. I'm the boss. If you don't like it you can take a hike!"
Assistant coach?! Who does she think she is?

Fortunately for me, human beings don't tend to notice stuff like that because they're too busy focusing on ***themselves.***

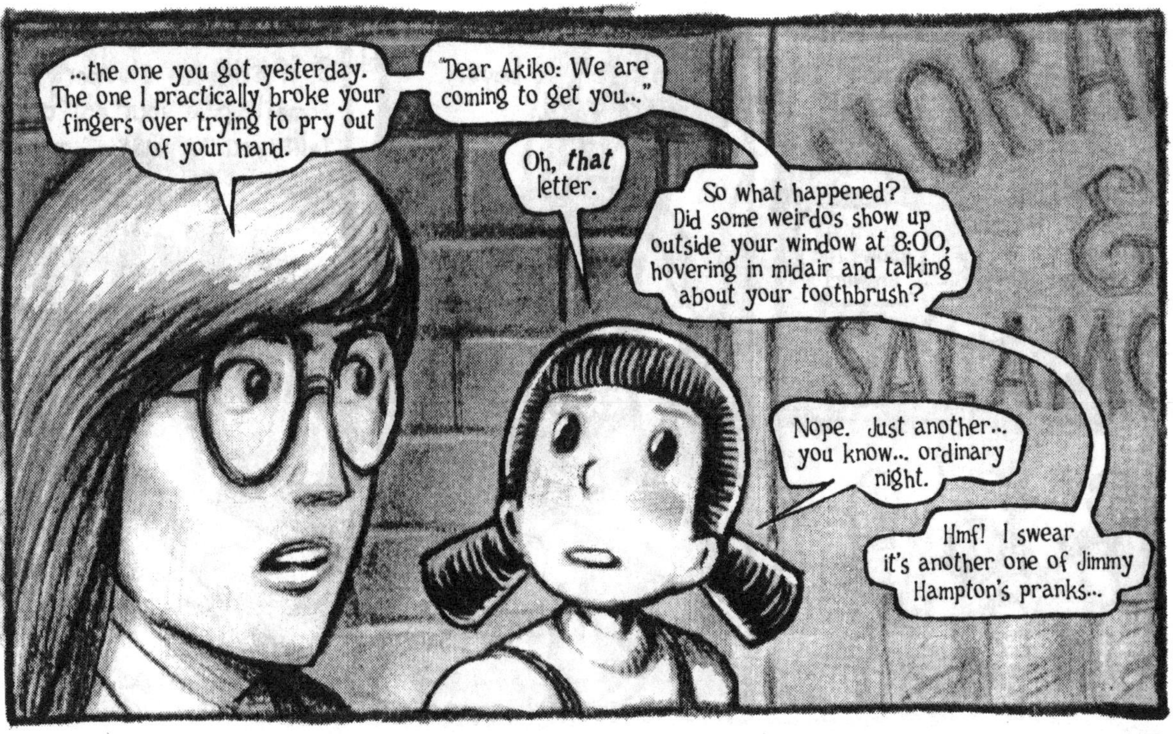
...the one you got yesterday. The one I practically broke your fingers over trying to pry out of your hand.
"Dear Akiko: We are coming to get you..."
Oh, ***that*** letter.
So what happened? Did some weirdos show up outside your window at 8:00, hovering in midair and talking about your toothbrush?
Nope. Just another... you know... ordinary night.
Hmf! I swear it's another one of Jimmy Hampton's pranks...

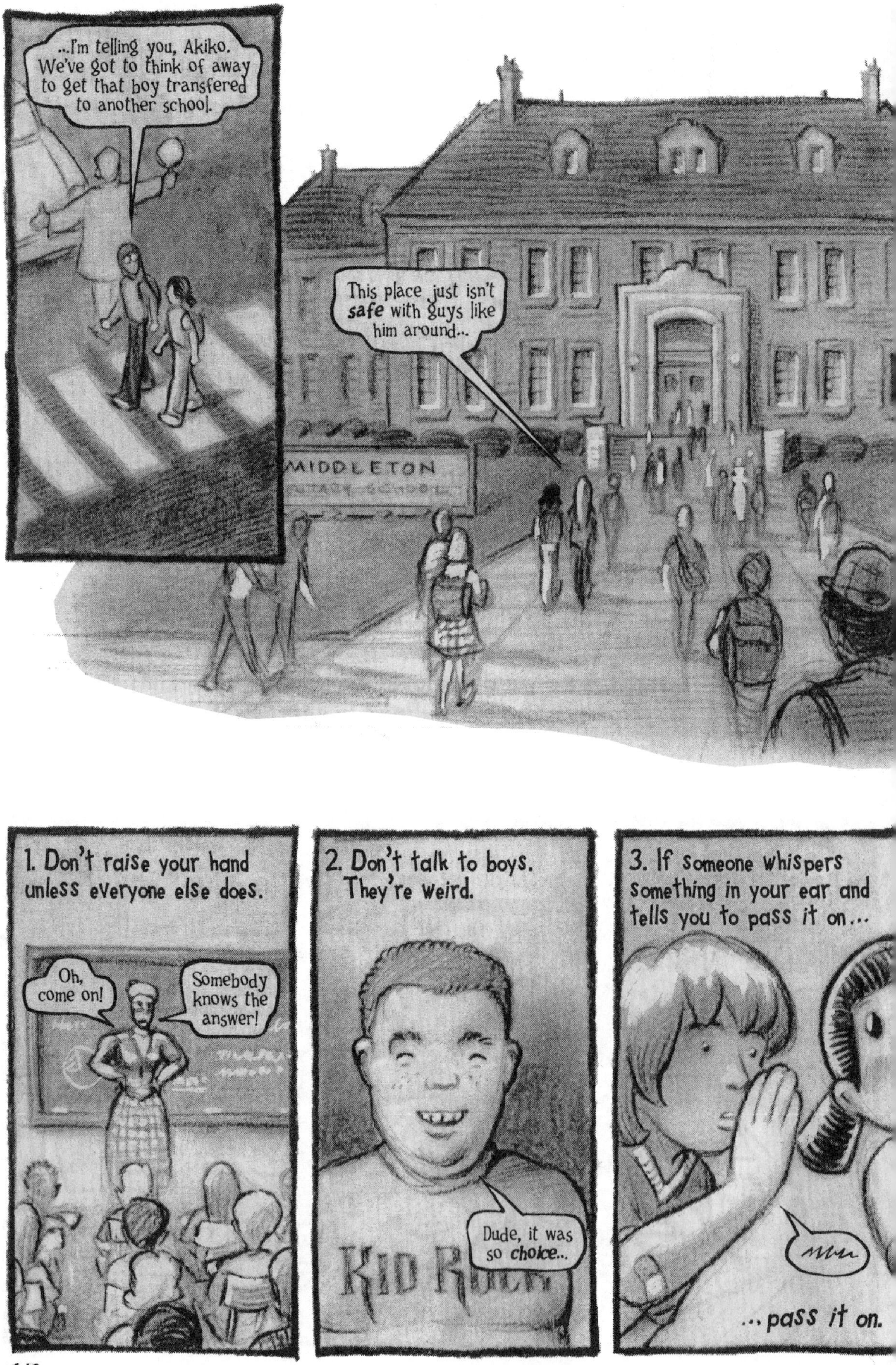

...I'm telling you, Akiko. We've got to think of away to get that boy transfered to another school.
This place just isn't *safe* with guys like him around...
MIDDLETON
1. Don't raise your hand unless everyone else does.
Oh, come on!
Somebody knows the answer!
2. Don't talk to boys. They're weird.
Dude, it was so *choice*...
3. If someone whispers something in your ear and tells you to pass it on...
...pass it on.

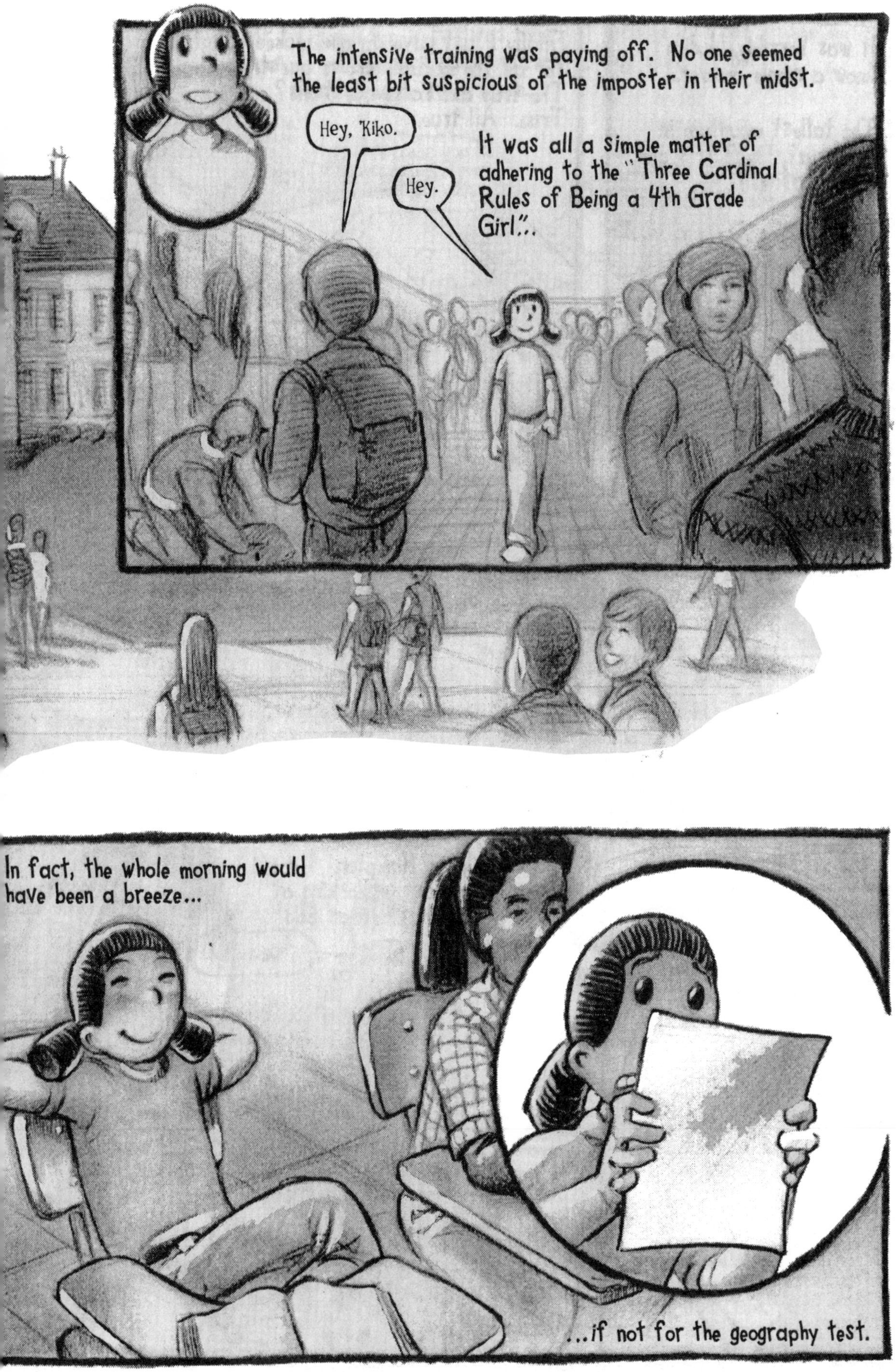

The intensive training was paying off. No one seemed the least bit suspicious of the imposter in their midst.
Hey, 'Kiko.
Hey.
It was all a simple matter of adhering to the "Three Cardinal Rules of Being a 4th Grade Girl."..
In fact, the whole morning would have been a breeze...
...if not for the geography test.

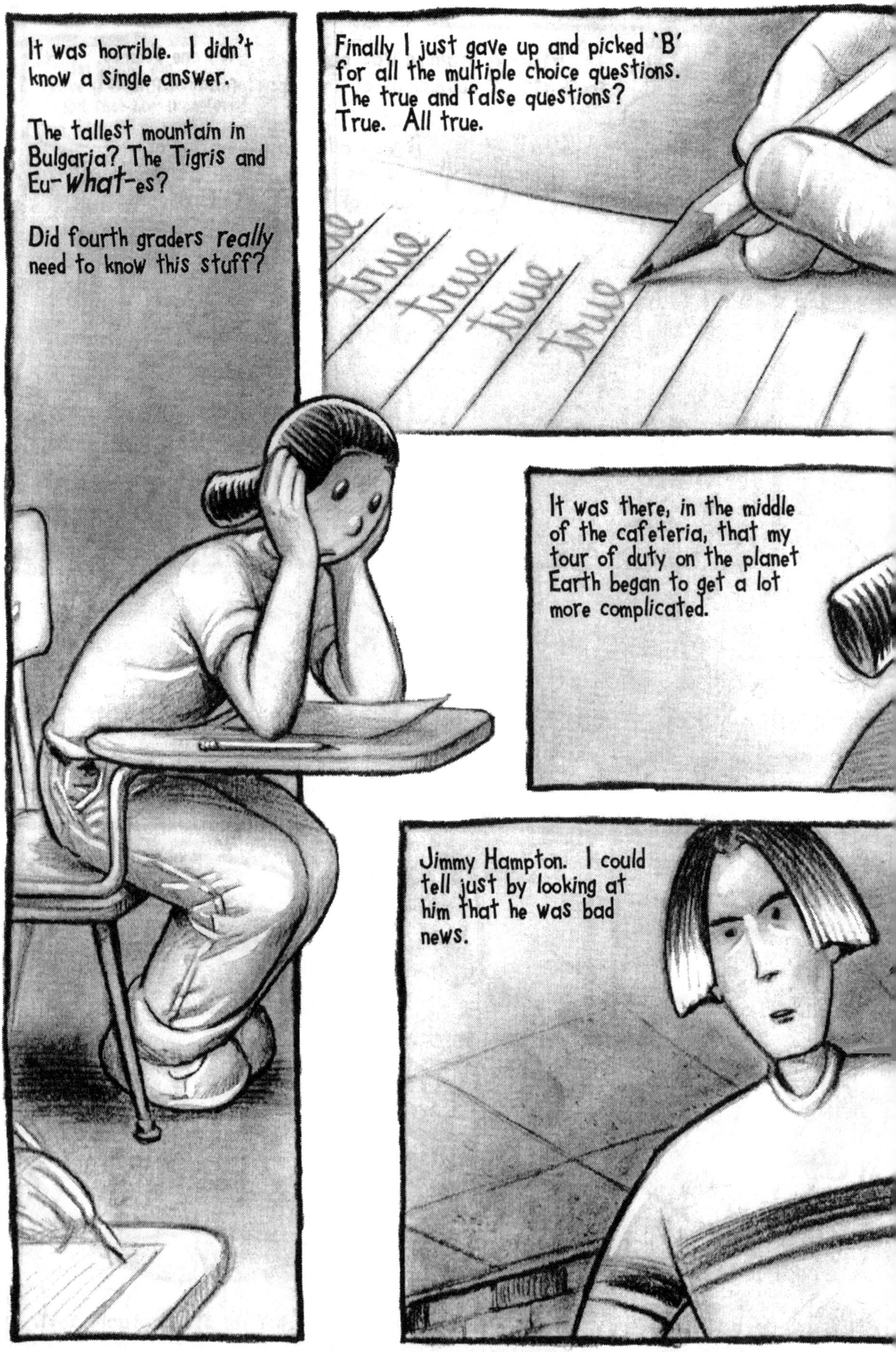
It was horrible. I didn't know a single answer.
The tallest mountain in Bulgaria? The Tigris and Eu-*What*-es?
Did fourth graders *really* need to know this stuff?
Finally I just gave up and picked 'B' for all the multiple choice questions. The true and false questions? True. All true.
true
true
true
true
It was there, in the middle of the cafeteria, that my tour of duty on the planet Earth began to get a lot more complicated.
Jimmy Hampton. I could tell just by looking at him that he was bad news.

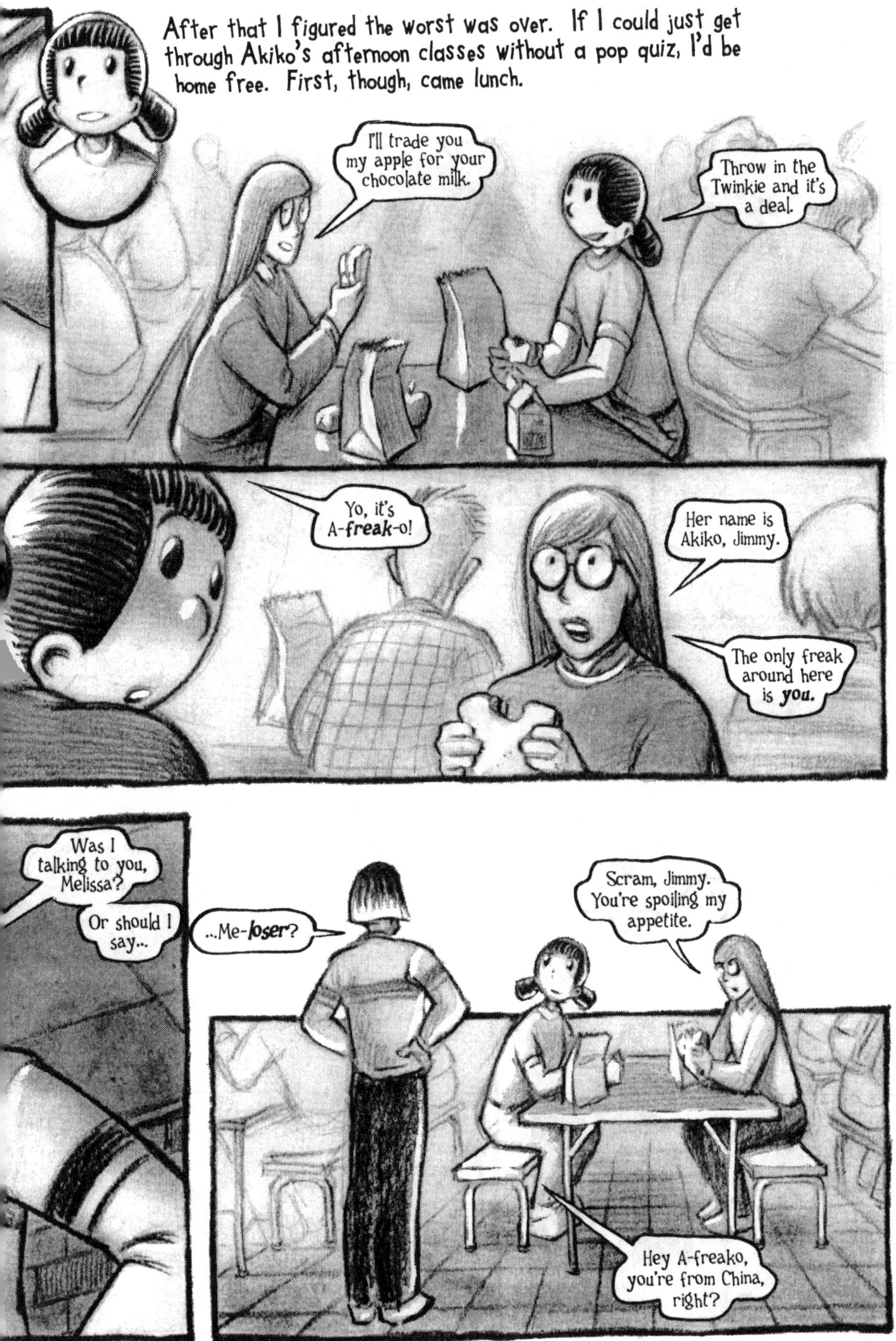
After that I figured the worst was over. If I could just get through Akiko's afternoon classes without a pop quiz, I'd be home free. First, though, came lunch.
I'll trade you my apple for your chocolate milk.
Throw in the Twinkie and it's a deal.
Yo, it's A-**freak**-o!
Her name is Akiko, Jimmy.
The only freak around here is ***you.***
Was I talking to you, Melissa?
Or should I say...
...Me-***loser***?
Scram, Jimmy. You're spoiling my appetite.
Hey A-freako, you're from China, right?

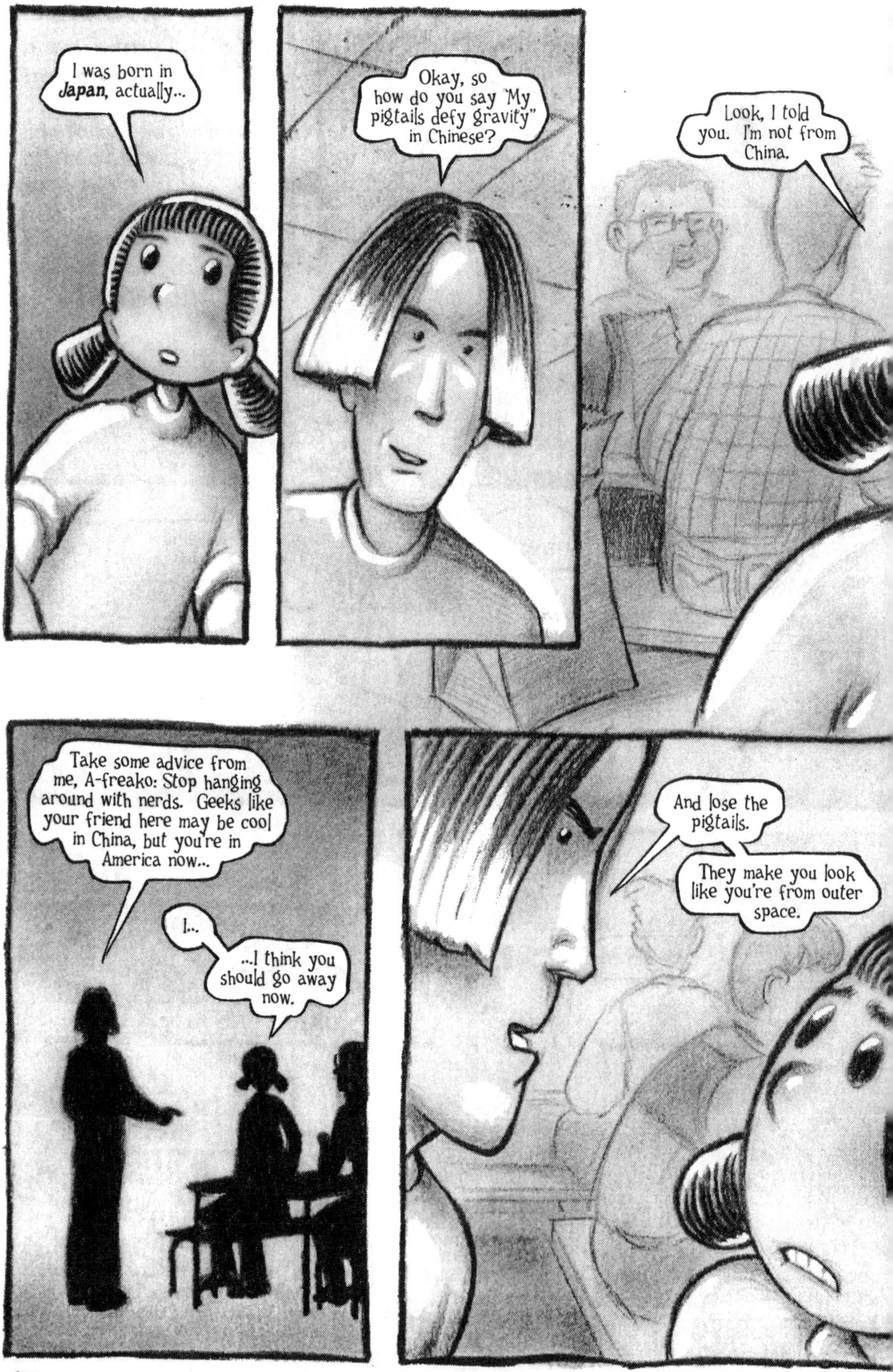

I was born in **Japan**, actually...
Okay, so how do you say "My pigtails defy gravity" in Chinese?
Look, I told you. I'm not from China.
Take some advice from me, A-freako: Stop hanging around with nerds. Geeks like your friend here may be cool in China, but you're in America now...
I...
...I think you should go away now.
And lose the pigtails.
They make you look like you're from outer space.

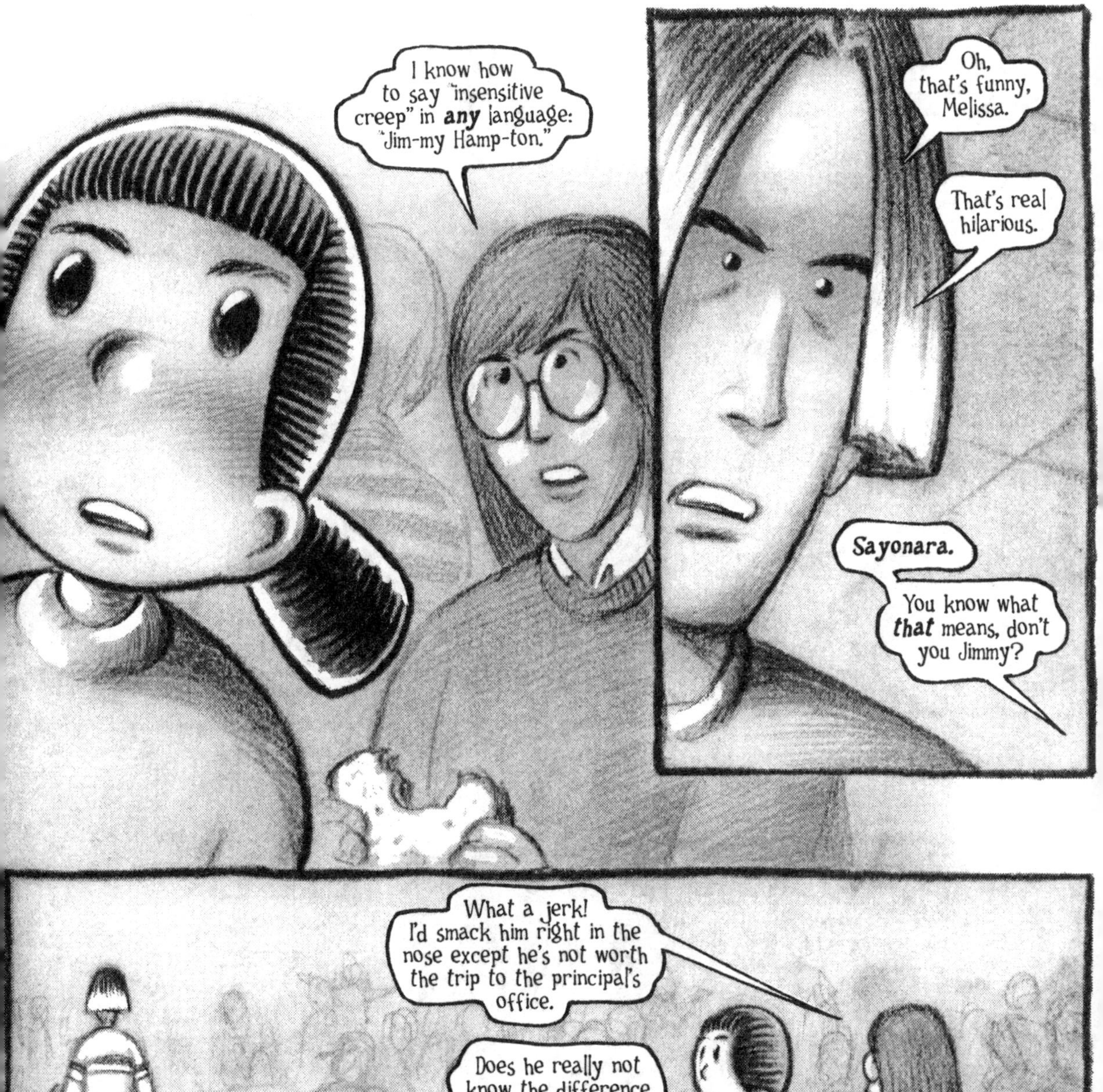
I know how to say "insensitive creep" in **any** language: "Jim-my Hamp-ton."
Oh, that's funny, Melissa.
That's real hilarious.
Sayonara.
You know what ***that*** means, don't you Jimmy?

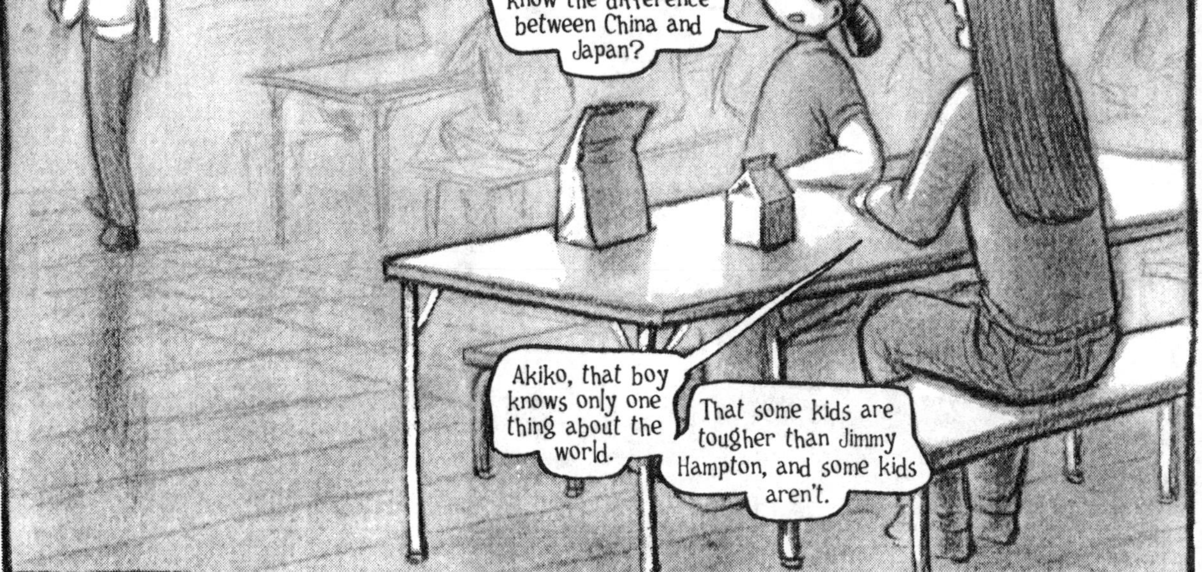
What a jerk! I'd smack him right in the nose except he's not worth the trip to the principal's office.
Does he really not know the difference between China and Japan?
Akiko, that boy knows only one thing about the world.
That some kids are tougher than Jimmy Hampton, and some kids aren't.

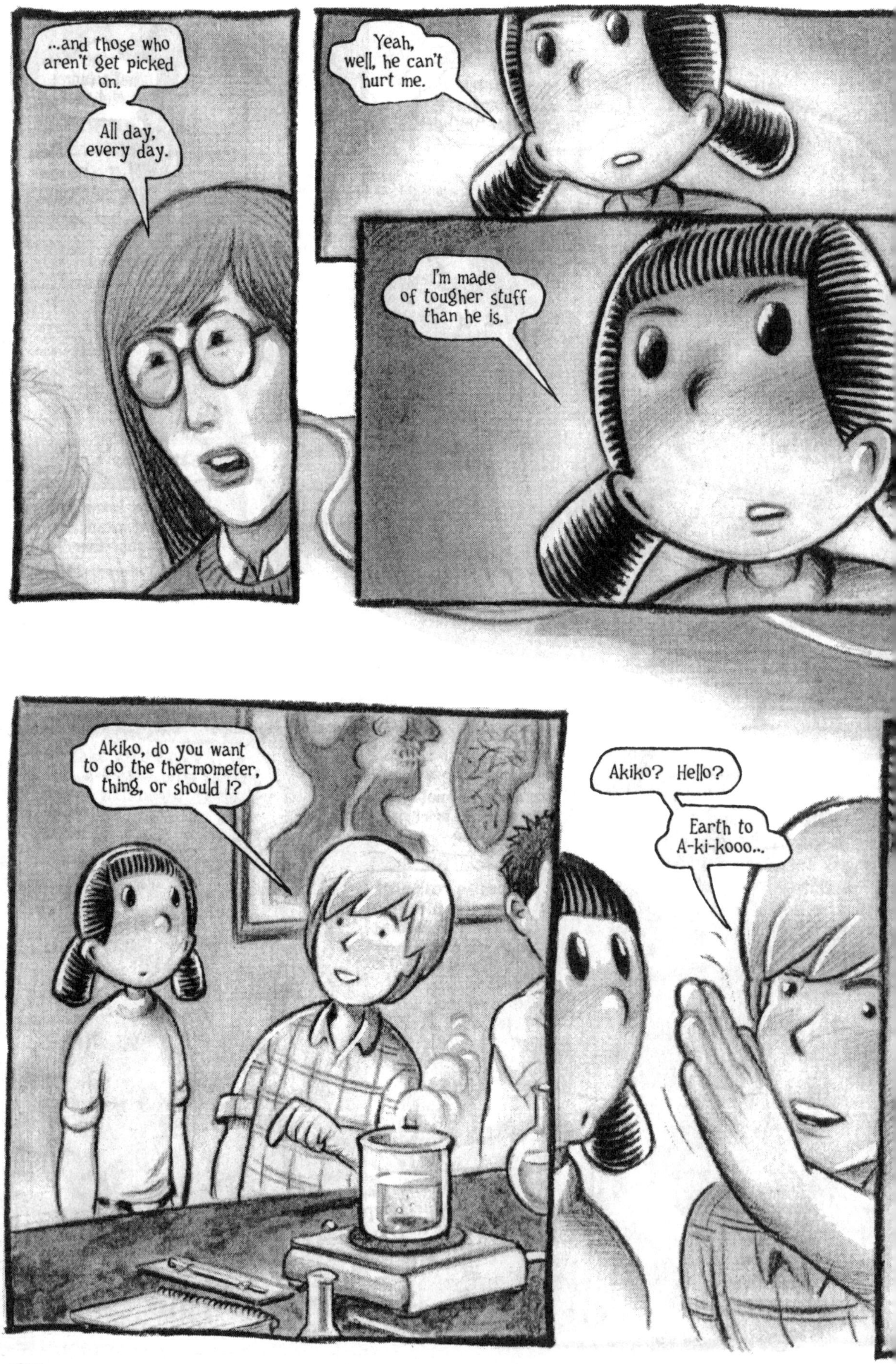
...and those who aren't get picked on.
All day, every day.
Yeah, well, he can't hurt me.
I'm made of tougher stuff than he is.
Akiko, do you want to do the thermometer, thing, or should I?
Akiko? Hello?
Earth to A-ki-kooo...

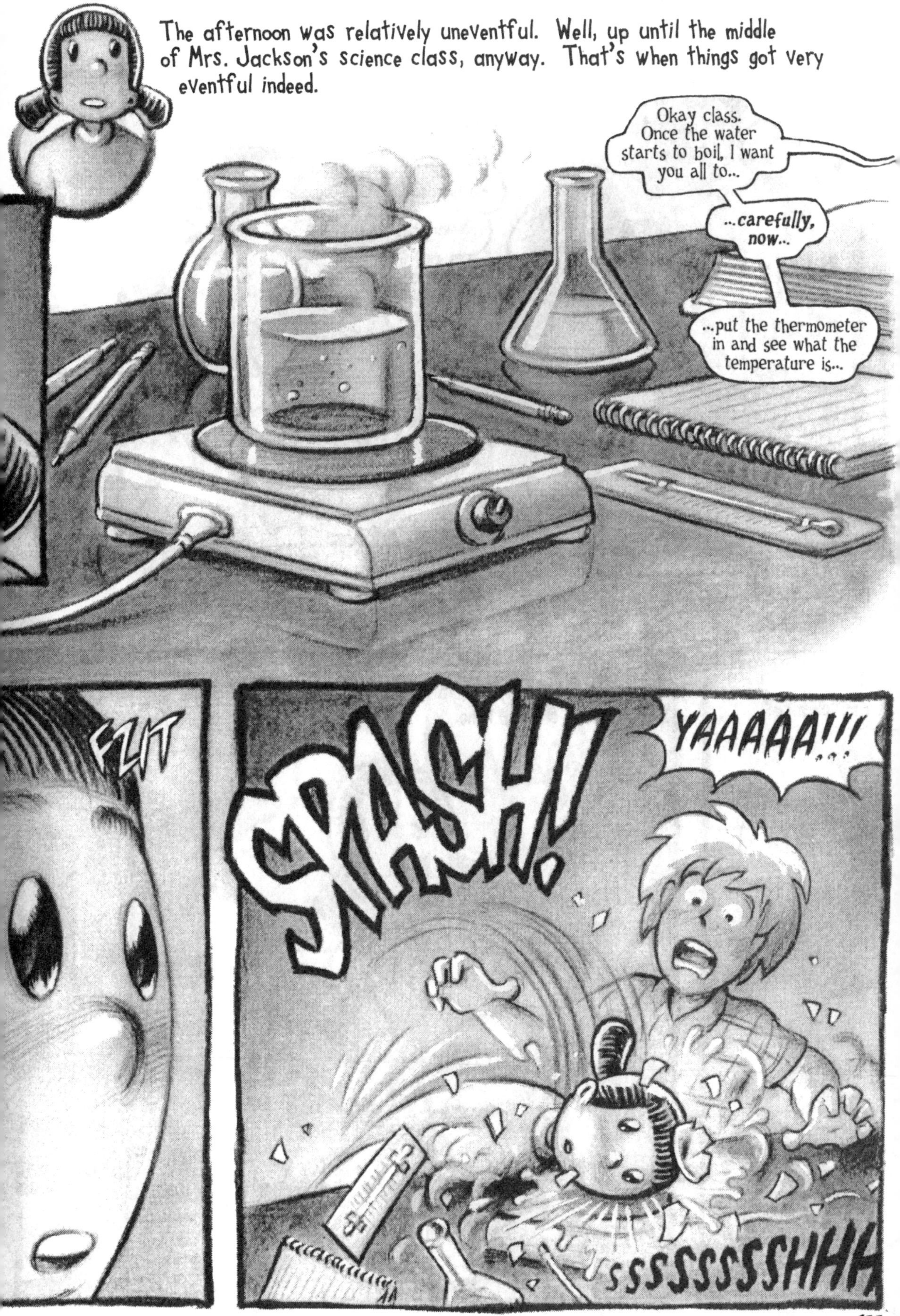
The afternoon was relatively uneventful. Well, up until the middle of Mrs. Jackson's science class, anyway. That's when things got very eventful indeed.
Okay class. Once the water starts to boil, I want you all to...
...carefully, now...
...put the thermometer in and see what the temperature is...
FZIT
SPASH!
YAAAAA!!!
SSSSSSSSHHH

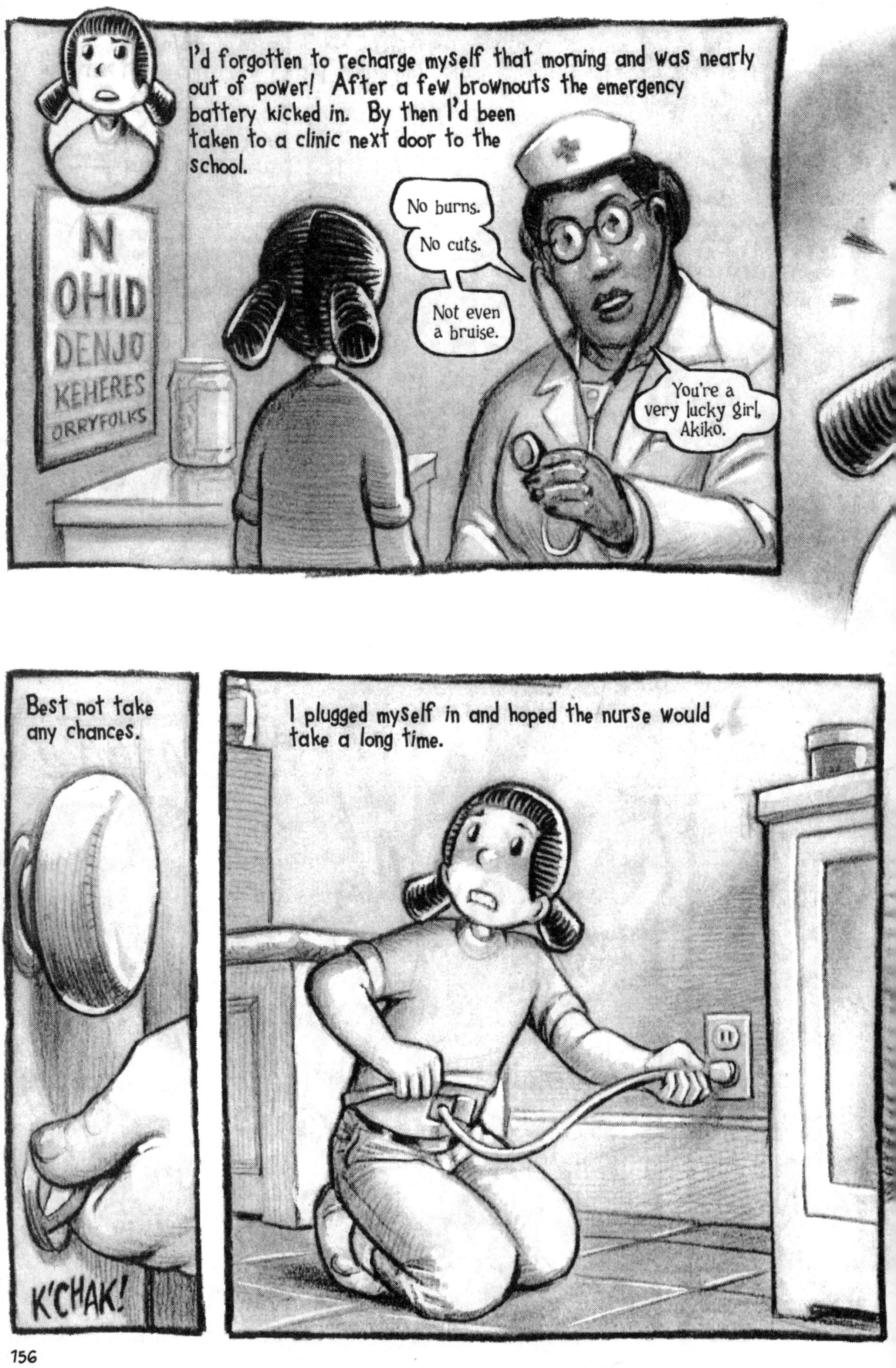
I'd forgotten to recharge myself that morning and was nearly out of power! After a few brownouts the emergency battery kicked in. By then I'd been taken to a clinic next door to the school.
N
OHID
DENJO
KEHERES
ORRYFOLKS
No burns.
No cuts.
Not even a bruise.
You're a very lucky girl, Akiko.
Best not take any chances.
K'CHAK!
I plugged myself in and hoped the nurse would take a long time.

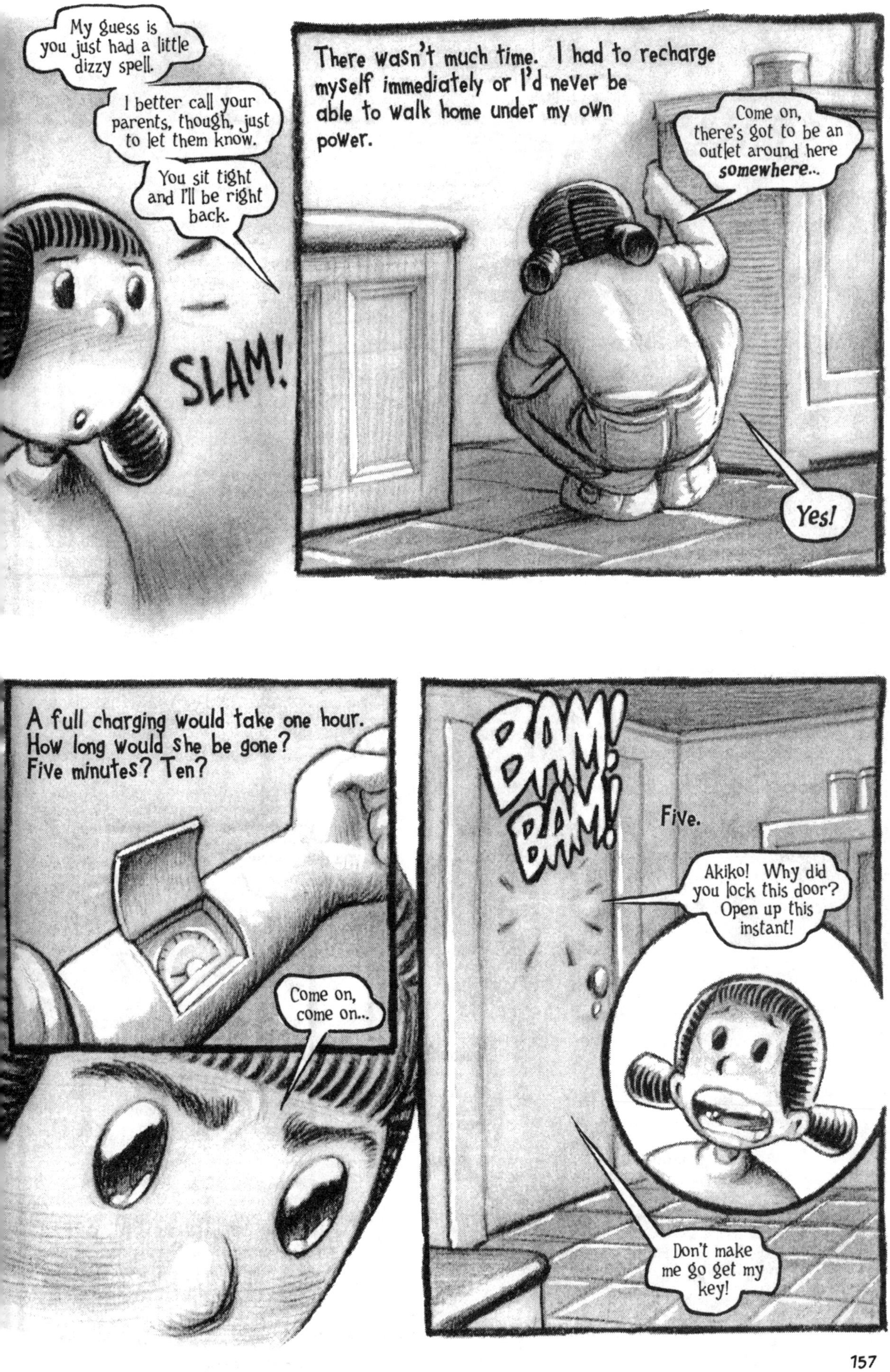
My guess is you just had a little dizzy spell.
I better call your parents, though, just to let them know.
You sit tight and I'll be right back.
SLAM!
There wasn't much time. I had to recharge myself immediately or I'd never be able to walk home under my own power.
Come on, there's got to be an outlet around here *somewhere*...
Yes!
A full charging would take one hour. How long would she be gone? Five minutes? Ten?
Come on, come on...
BAM! BAM!
Five.
Akiko! Why did you lock this door? Open up this instant!
Don't make me go get my key!

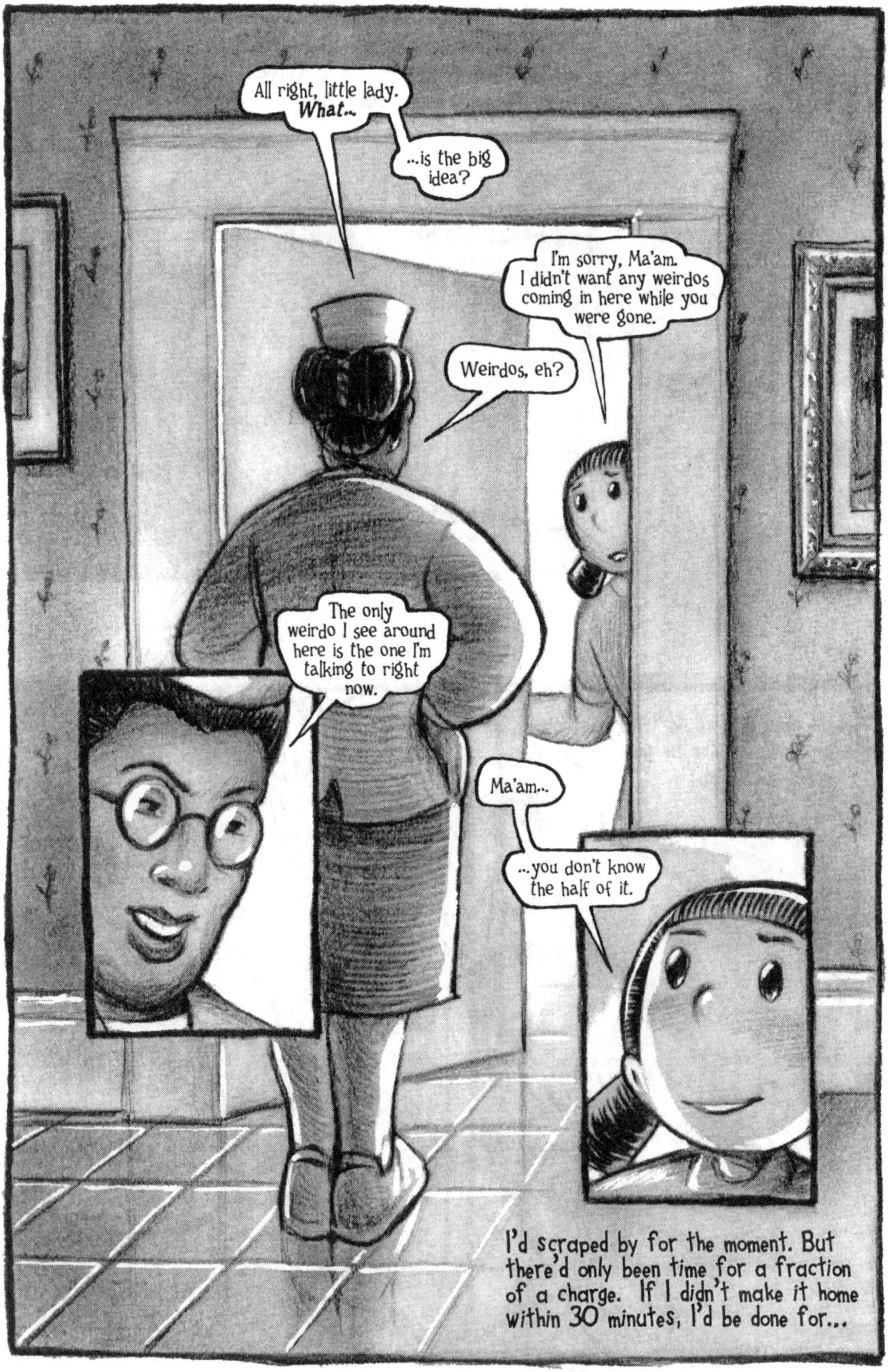
All right, little lady. *What...*
...is the big idea?
I'm sorry, Ma'am. I didn't want any weirdos coming in here while you were gone.
Weirdos, eh?
The only weirdo I see around here is the one I'm talking to right now.
Ma'am...
...you don't know the half of it.
I'd scraped by for the moment. But there'd only been time for a fraction of a charge. If I didn't make it home within 30 minutes, I'd be done for...

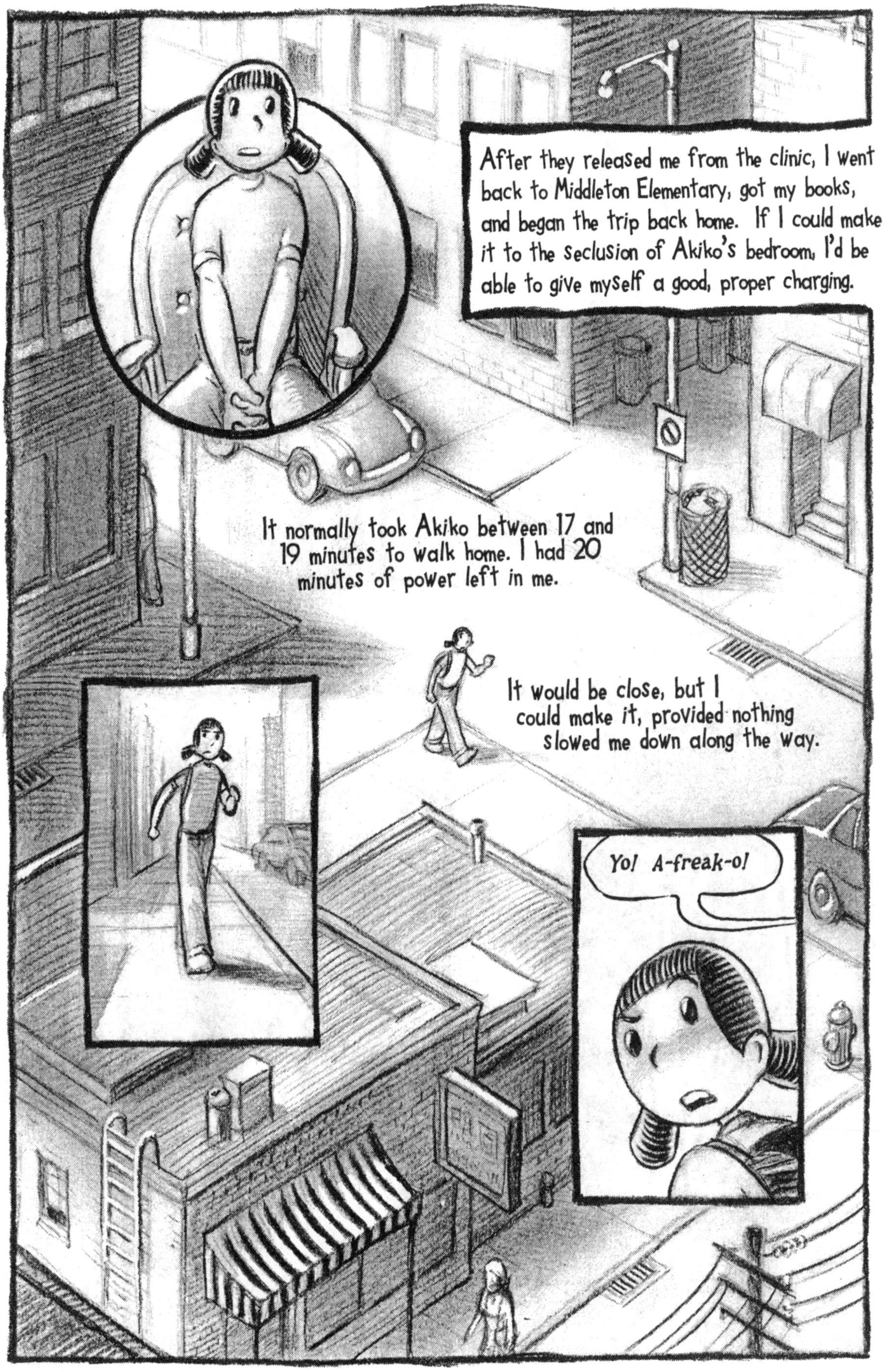
After they released me from the clinic, I went back to Middleton Elementary, got my books, and began the trip back home. If I could make it to the seclusion of Akiko's bedroom, I'd be able to give myself a good, proper charging.
It normally took Akiko between 17 and 19 minutes to walk home. I had 20 minutes of power left in me.
It would be close, but I could make it, provided nothing slowed me down along the way.
Yo! A-freak-o!

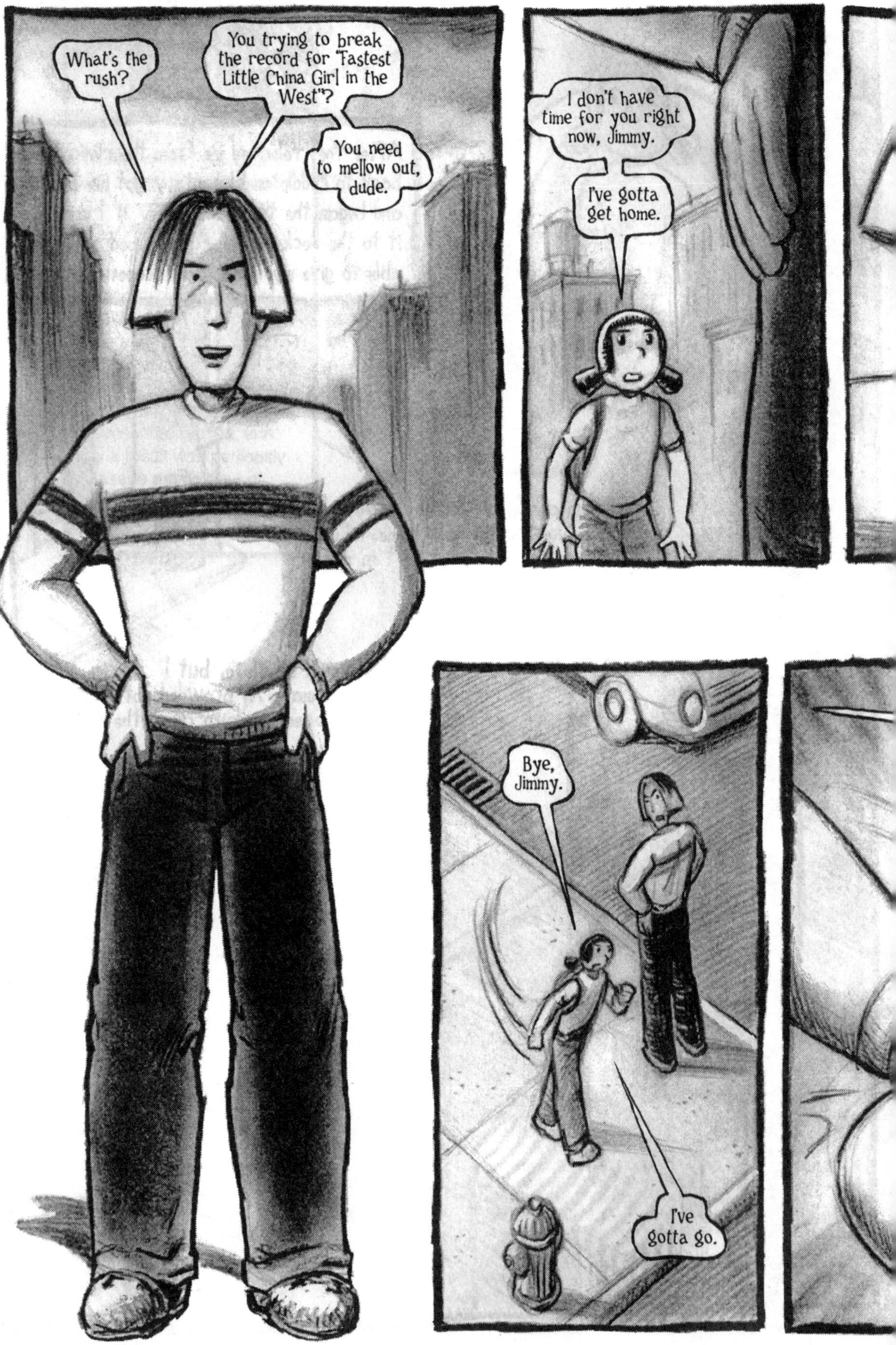
What's the rush?
You trying to break the record for "Fastest Little China Girl in the West"?
You need to mellow out, dude.
I don't have time for you right now, Jimmy.
I've gotta get home.
Bye, Jimmy.
I've gotta go.

I hear you, like, *fainted* during science class today.

So what's the problem?

Forget to eat your Rice Krispies this morning?

Get it? *Rice*... ...Krispies...

That's not funny.

Now step aside.

Freak-o, freak-o...

You've gotta learn some manners. I'm trying to be *friendly* here.

I was down to sixteen minutes of power, with at least a fifteen minute walk ahead of me.

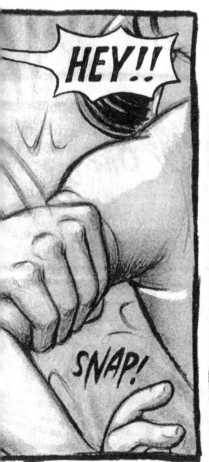

HEY!!

SNAP!

I'm *talking* to you, Freak-o.

You can't just walk away from me.

You're being rude, do you know that?

Very rude.

Now, that may be the way you do things in China...

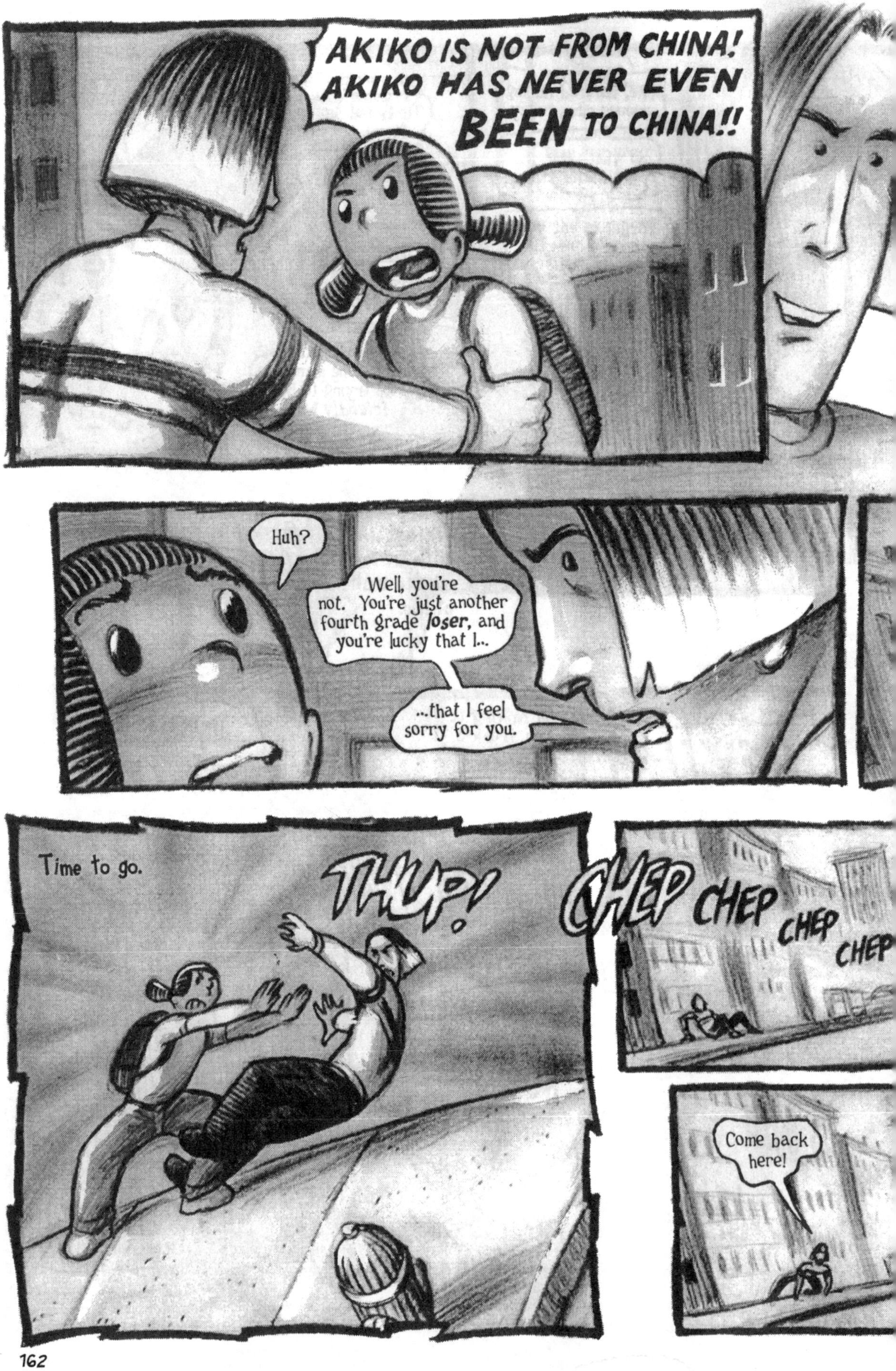
AKIKO IS NOT FROM CHINA! AKIKO HAS NEVER EVEN BEEN TO CHINA!!
Huh?
Well, you're not. You're just another fourth grade loser, and you're lucky that I...
...that I feel sorry for you.
Time to go.
THUP!
CHEP CHEP CHEP CHEP
Come back here!

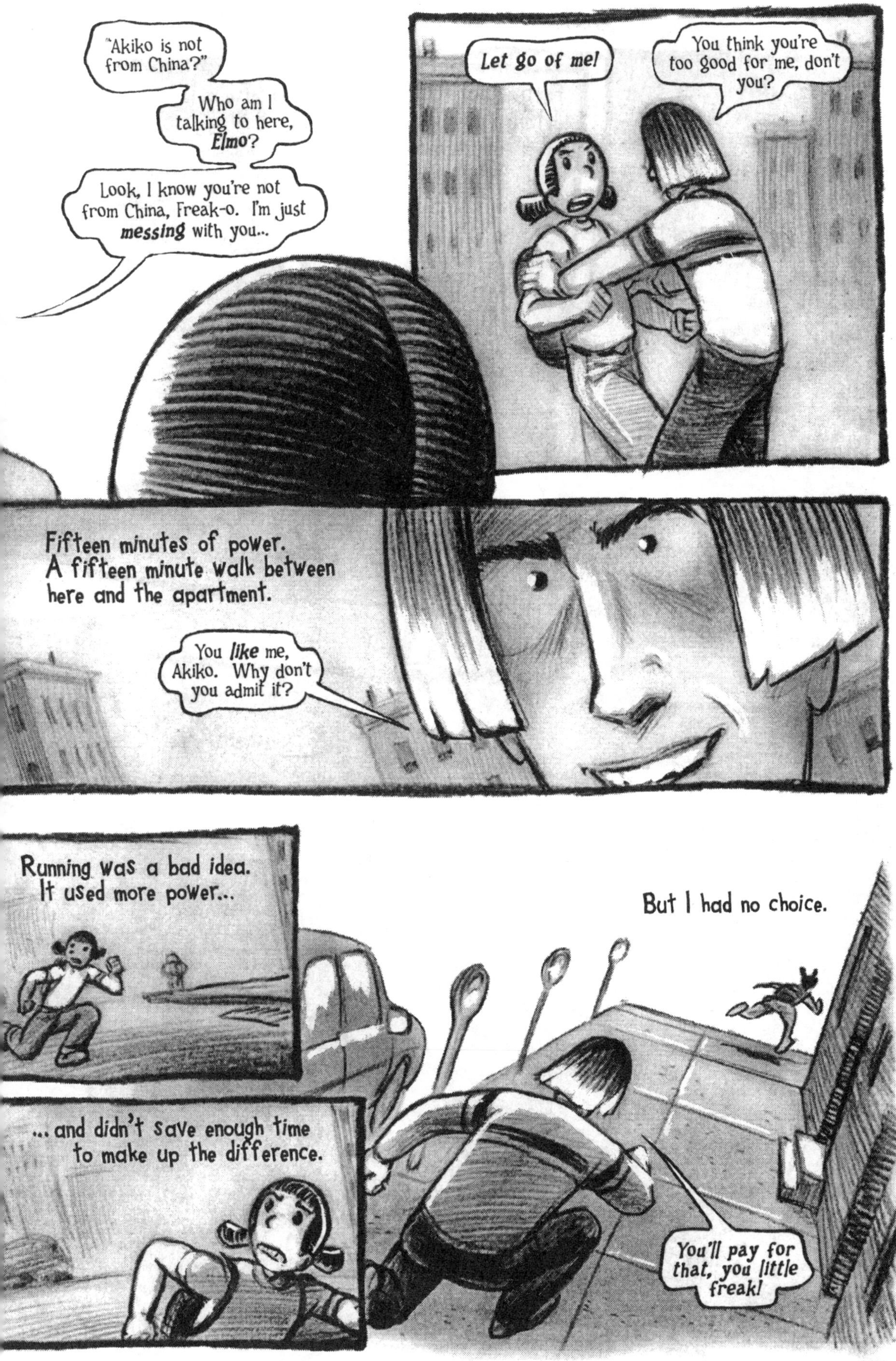
"Akiko is not from China?"
Who am I talking to here, Elmo?
Look, I know you're not from China, Freak-o. I'm just messing with you...
Let go of me!
You think you're too good for me, don't you?
Fifteen minutes of power. A fifteen minute walk between here and the apartment.
You like me, Akiko. Why don't you admit it?
Running was a bad idea. It used more power...
But I had no choice.
...and didn't save enough time to make up the difference.
You'll pay for that, you little freak!

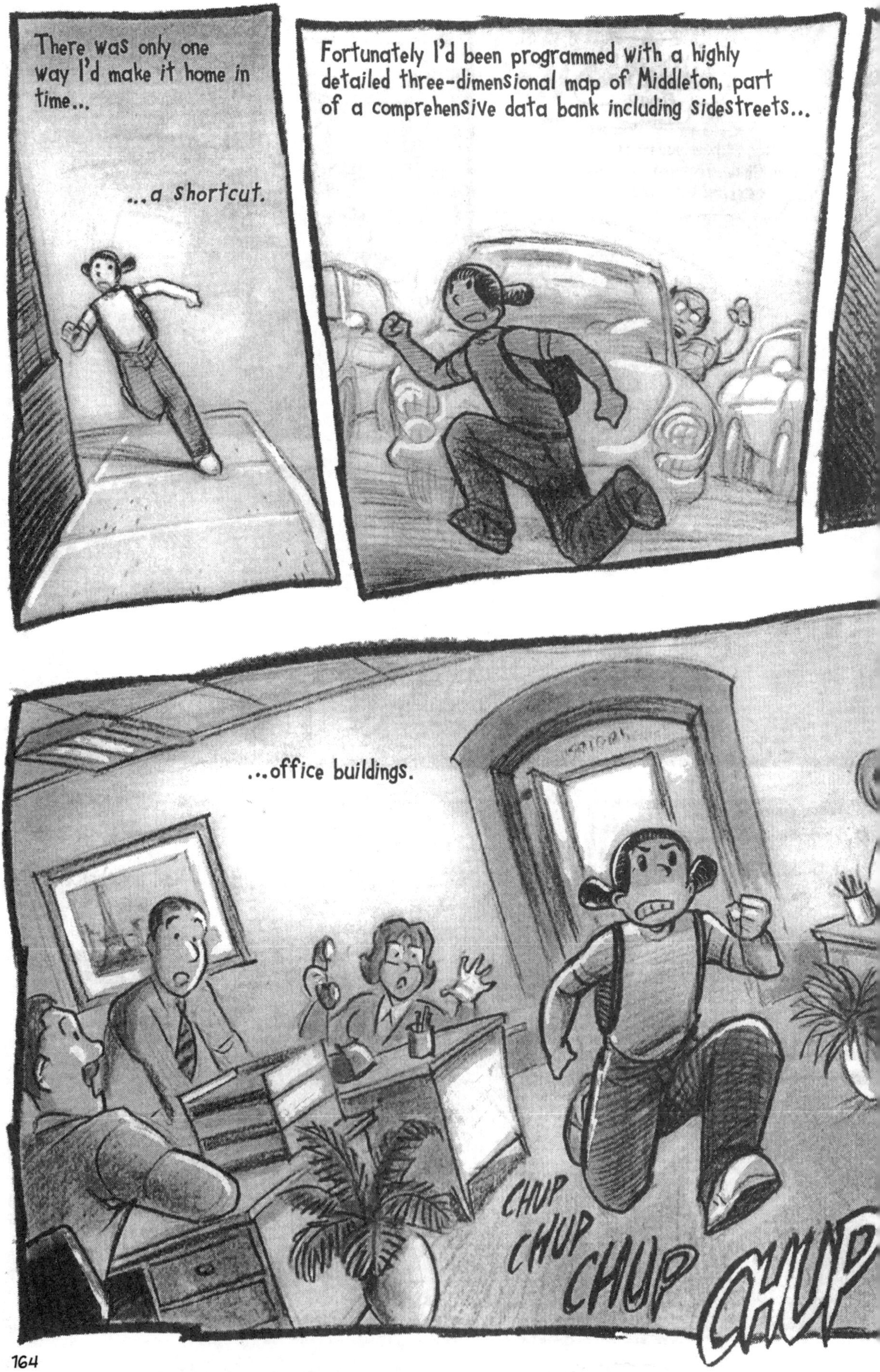
There was only one way I'd make it home in time...
...a shortcut.
Fortunately I'd been programmed with a highly detailed three-dimensional map of Middleton, part of a comprehensive data bank including sidestreets...
...office buildings.
CHUP
CHUP
CHUP
CHUP

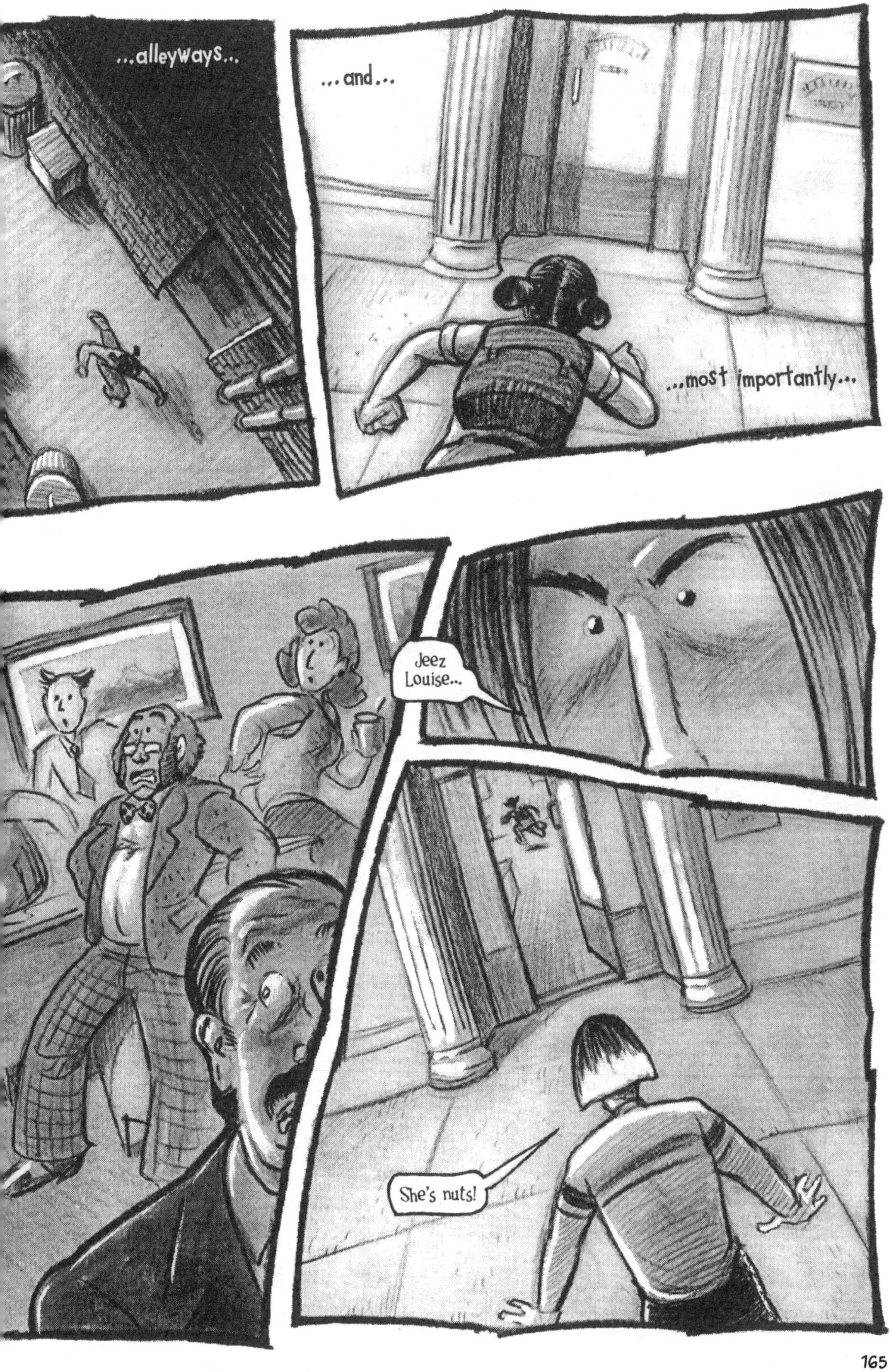
...alleyways...
...and...
...most importantly...
Jeez Louise...
She's nuts!

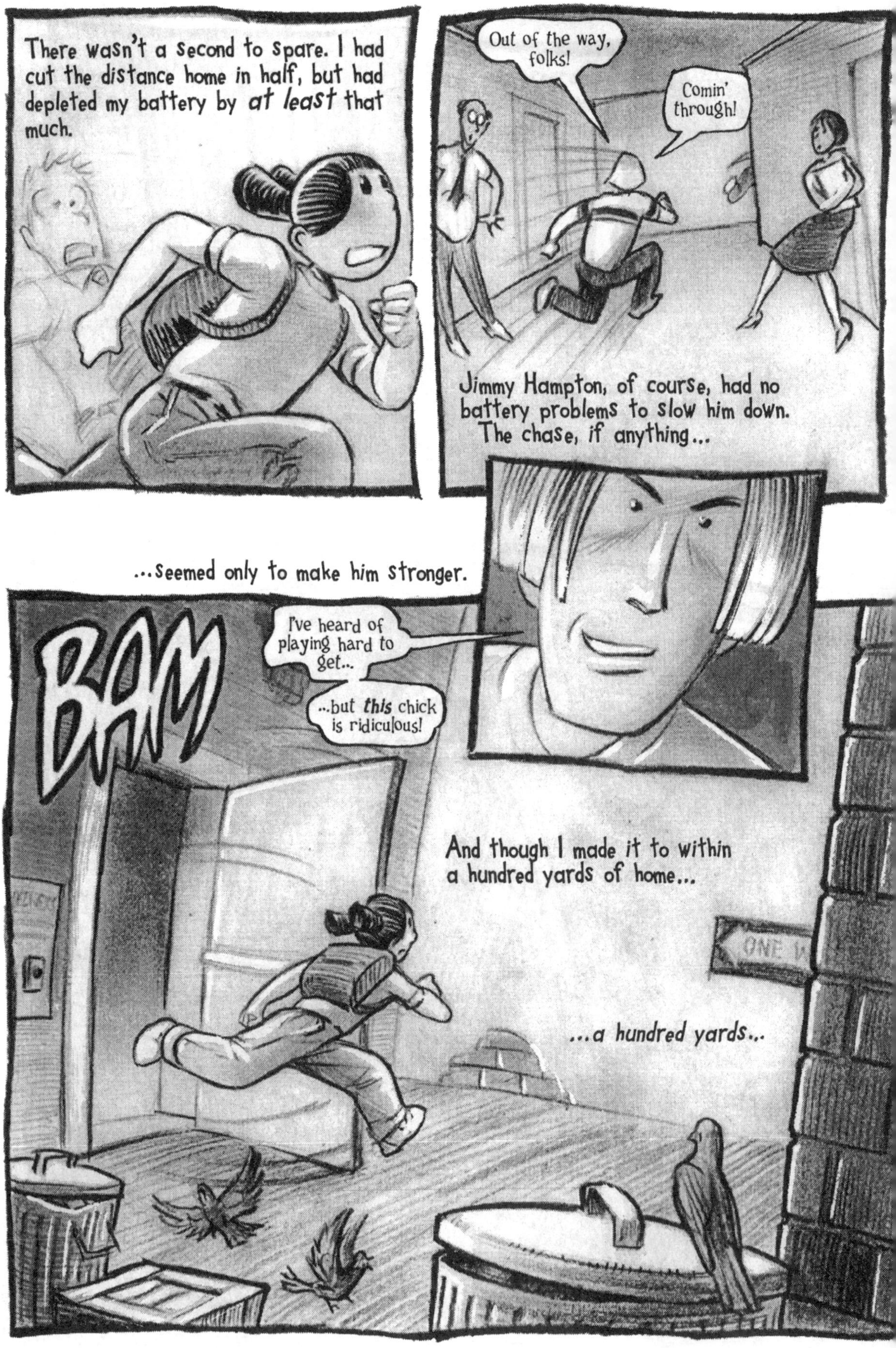
There wasn't a second to spare. I had cut the distance home in half, but had depleted my battery by *at least* that much.
Out of the way, folks!
Comin' through!
Jimmy Hampton, of course, had no battery problems to slow him down. The chase, if anything...
...seemed only to make him stronger.
BAM
I've heard of playing hard to get...
...but *this* chick is ridiculous!
And though I made it to within a hundred yards of home...
ONE W
...a hundred yards...

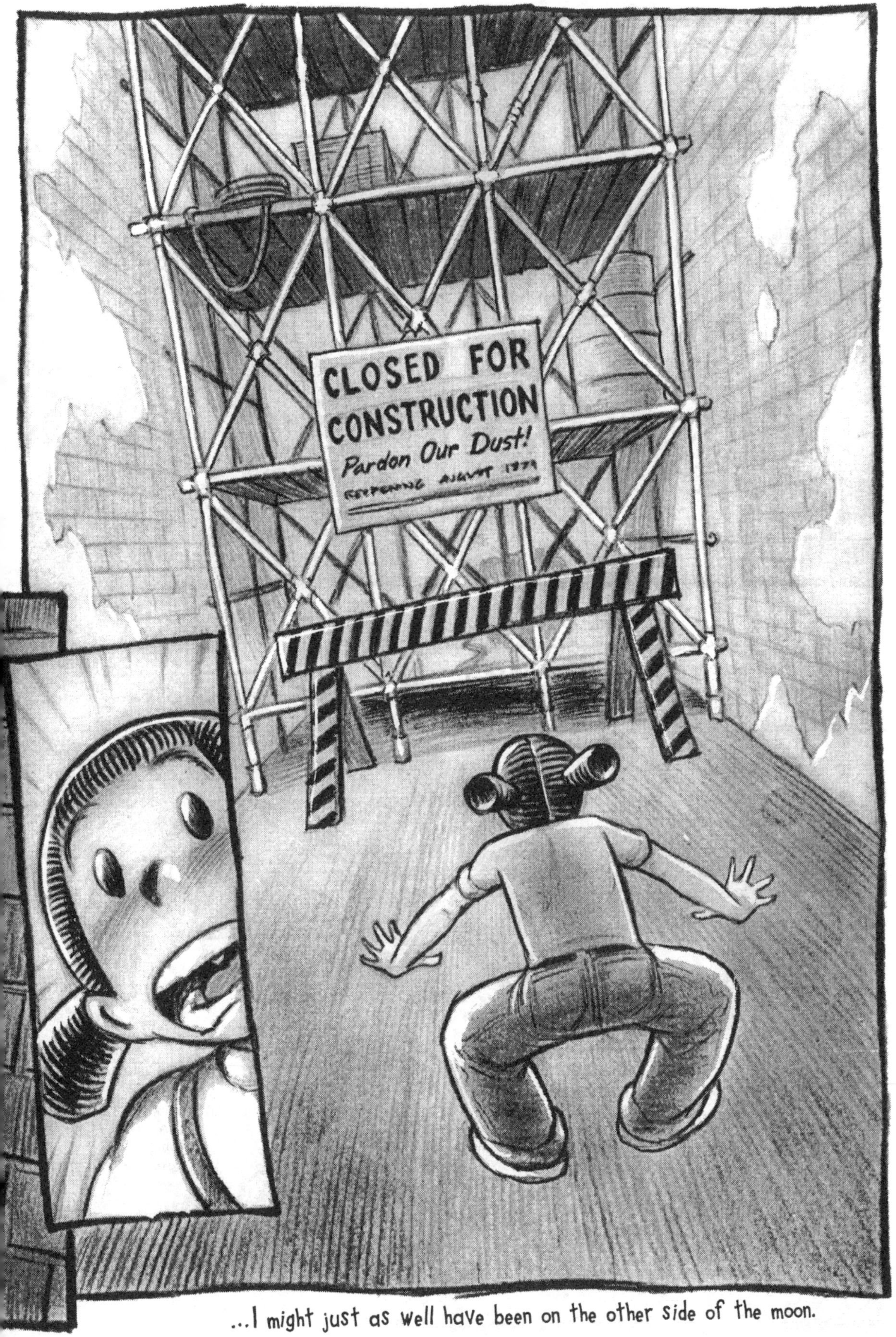
CLOSED FOR
CONSTRUCTION
Pardon Our Dust!

...I might just as well have been on the other side of the moon.

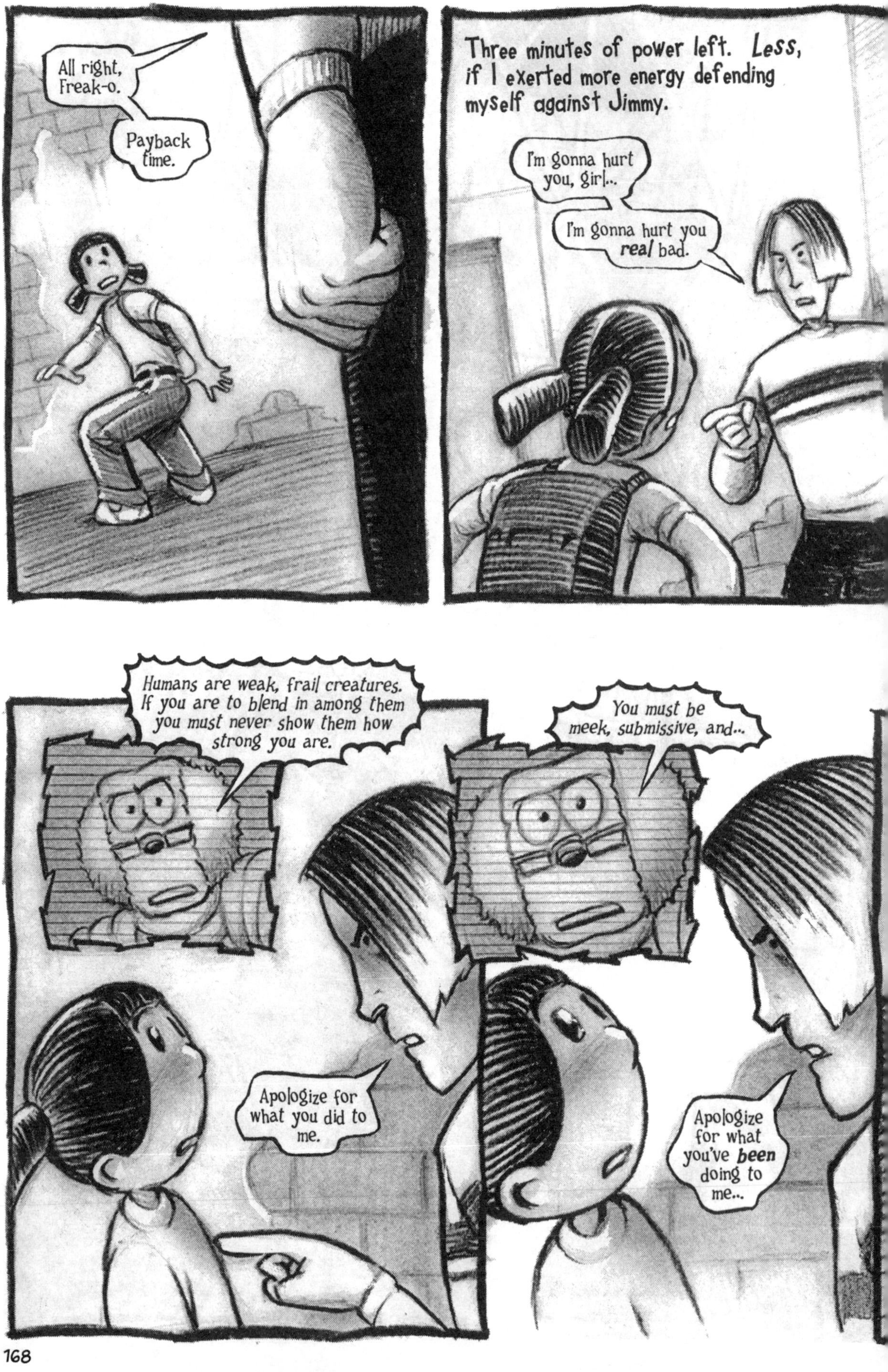
All right, Freak-o.
Payback time.
Three minutes of power left. *Less*, if I exerted more energy defending myself against Jimmy.
I'm gonna hurt you, girl...
I'm gonna hurt you **real** bad.
Humans are weak, frail creatures. If you are to blend in among them you must never show them how strong you are.
Apologize for what you did to me.
You must be meek, submissive, and...
Apologize for what you've **been** doing to me...

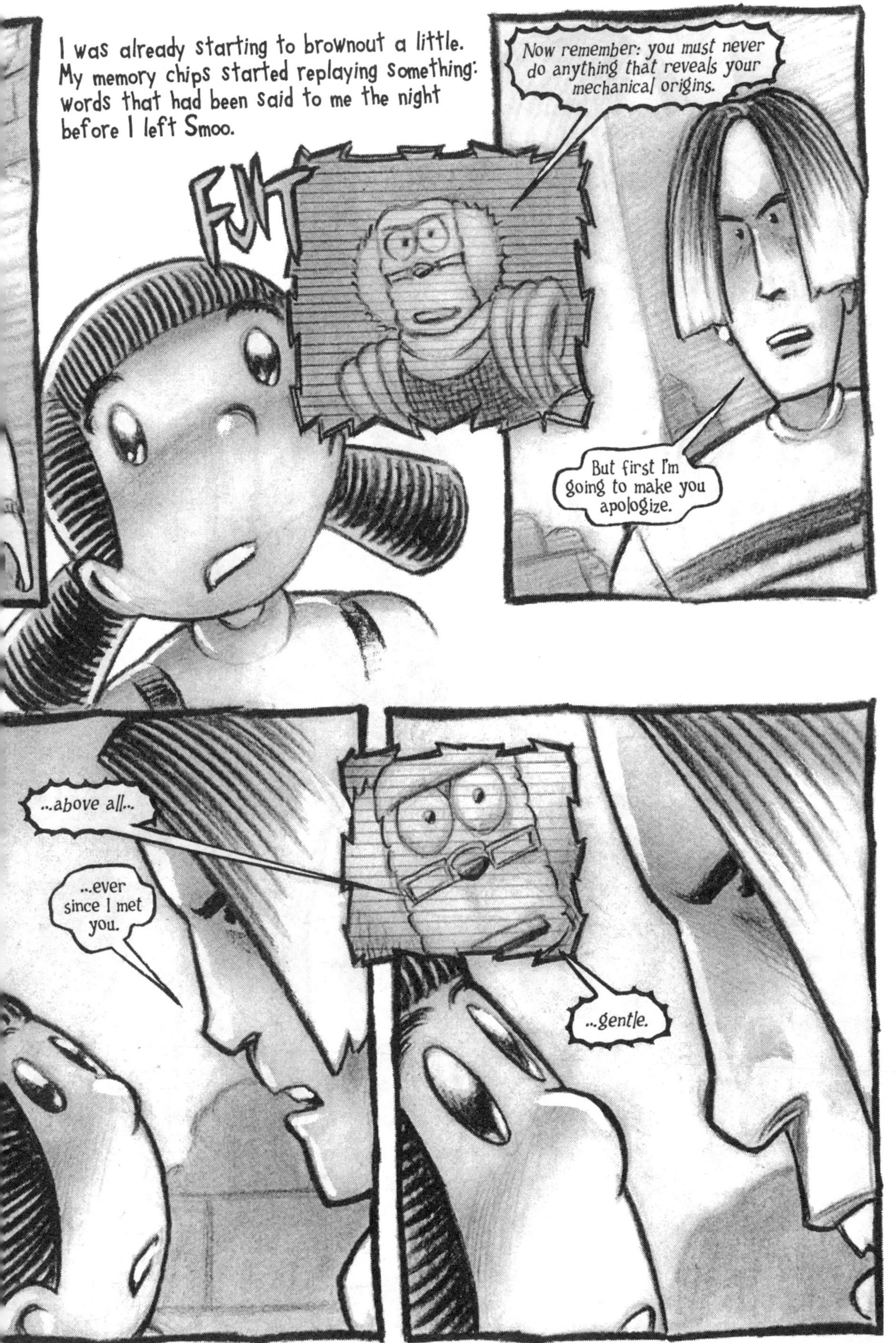
I was already starting to brownout a little. My memory chips started replaying something: words that had been said to me the night before I left Smoo.
FJIT
Now remember: you must never do anything that reveals your mechanical origins.
But first I'm going to make you apologize.
...above all...
...ever since I met you.
...gentle.

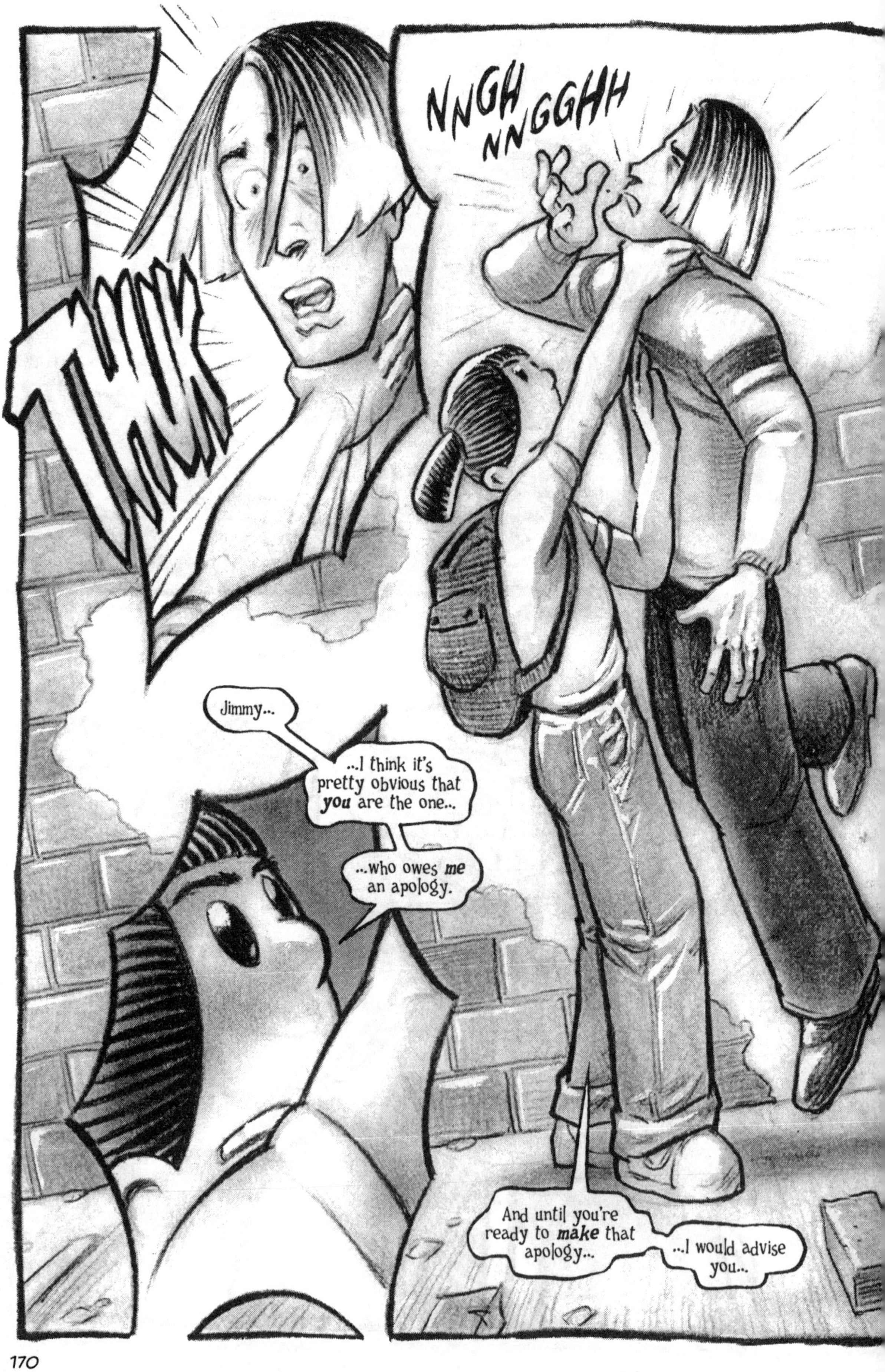
THUNK
NNGH NNGGHH
Jimmy...
...I think it's pretty obvious that *you* are the one...
...who owes *me* an apology.
And until you're ready to *make* that apology...
...I would advise you...

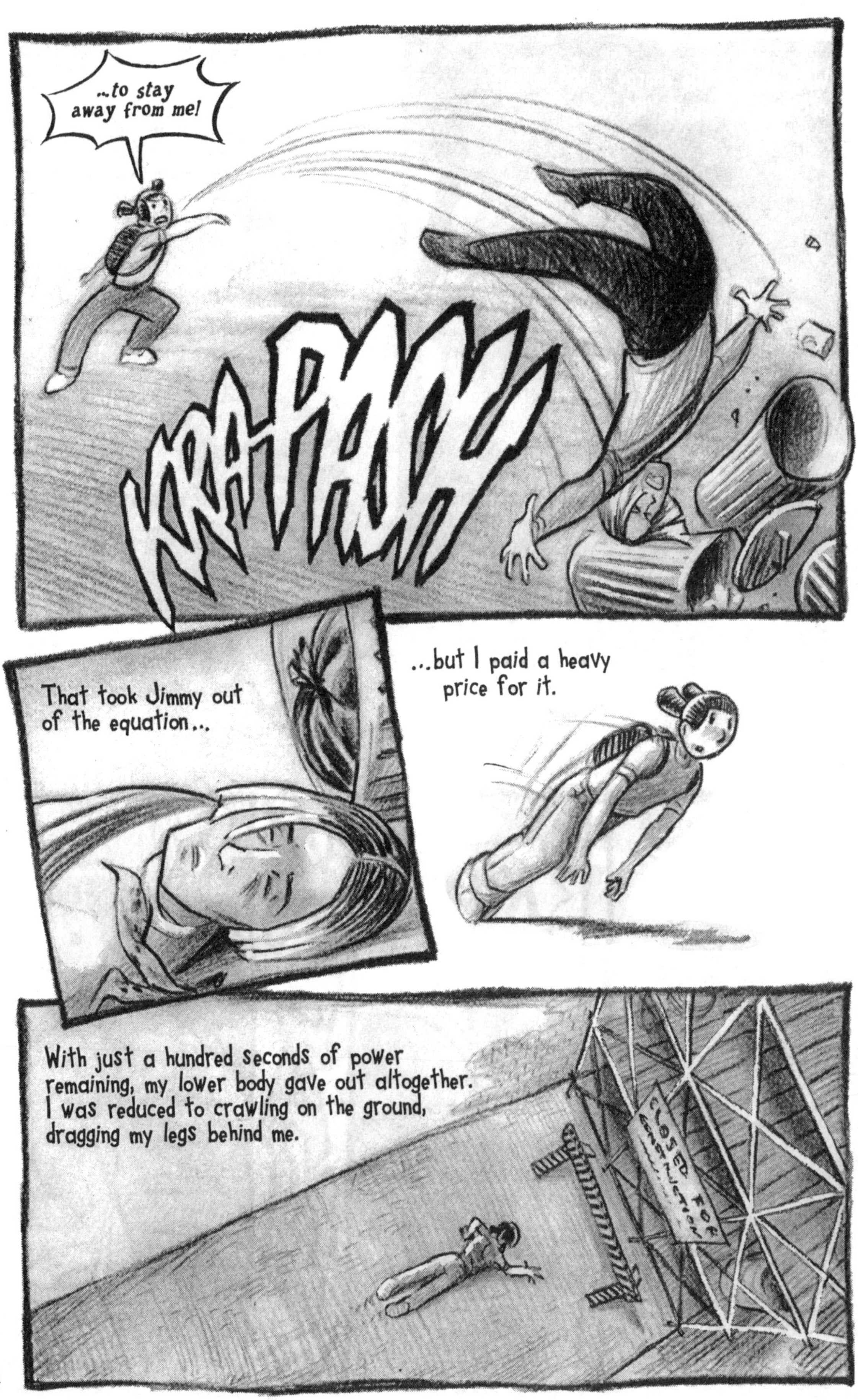
...to stay away from me!
KRA-PACK
That took Jimmy out of the equation...
...but I paid a heavy price for it.
With just a hundred seconds of power remaining, my lower body gave out altogether. I was reduced to crawling on the ground, dragging my legs behind me.
CLOSED FOR CONSTRUCTION

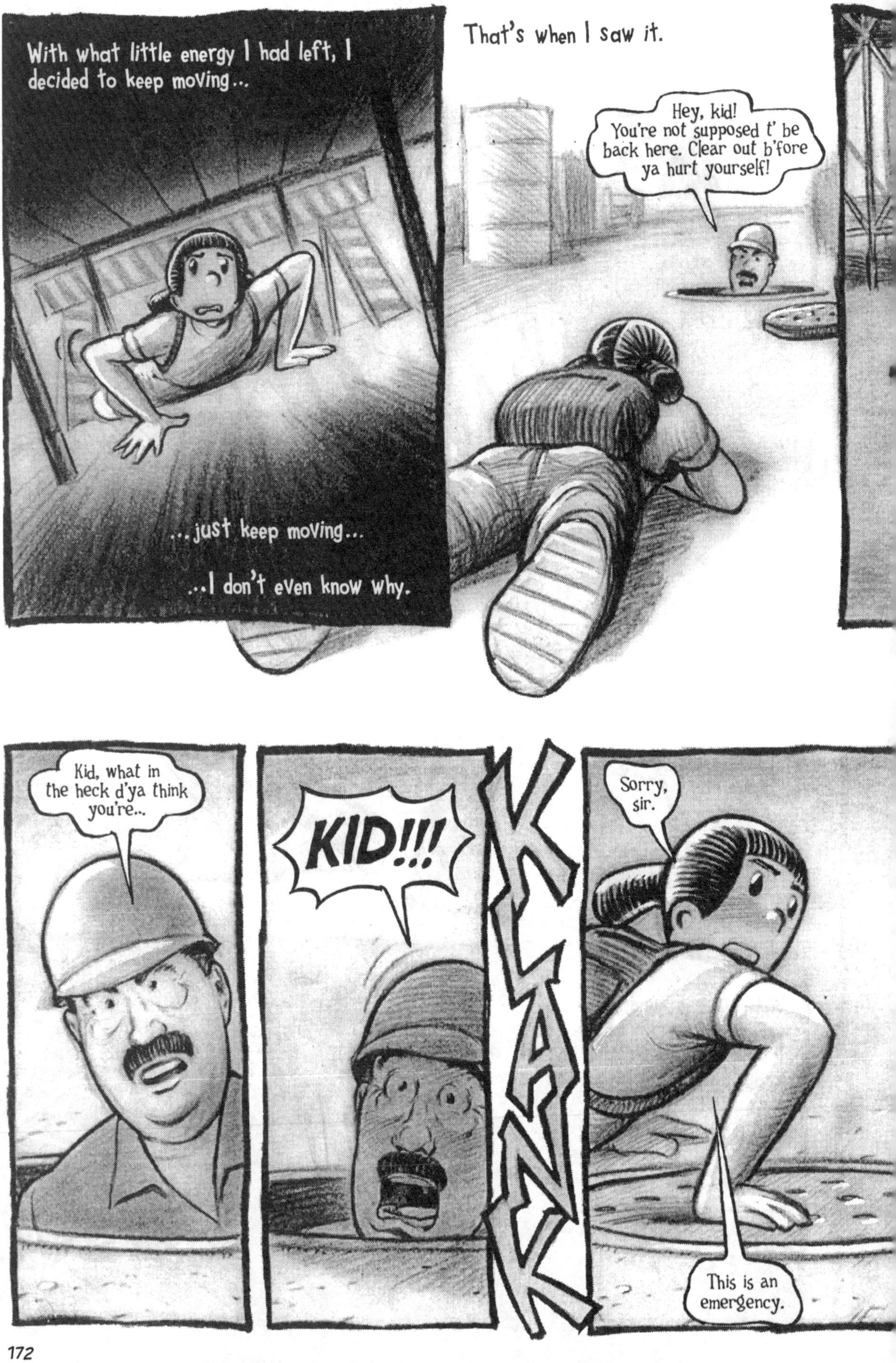
With what little energy I had left, I decided to keep moving...
...just keep moving...
...I don't even know why.
That's when I saw it.
Hey, kid! You're not supposed t' be back here. Clear out b'fore ya hurt yourself!
Kid, what in the heck d'ya think you're..
KID!!!
KLANK
Sorry, sir.
This is an emergency.

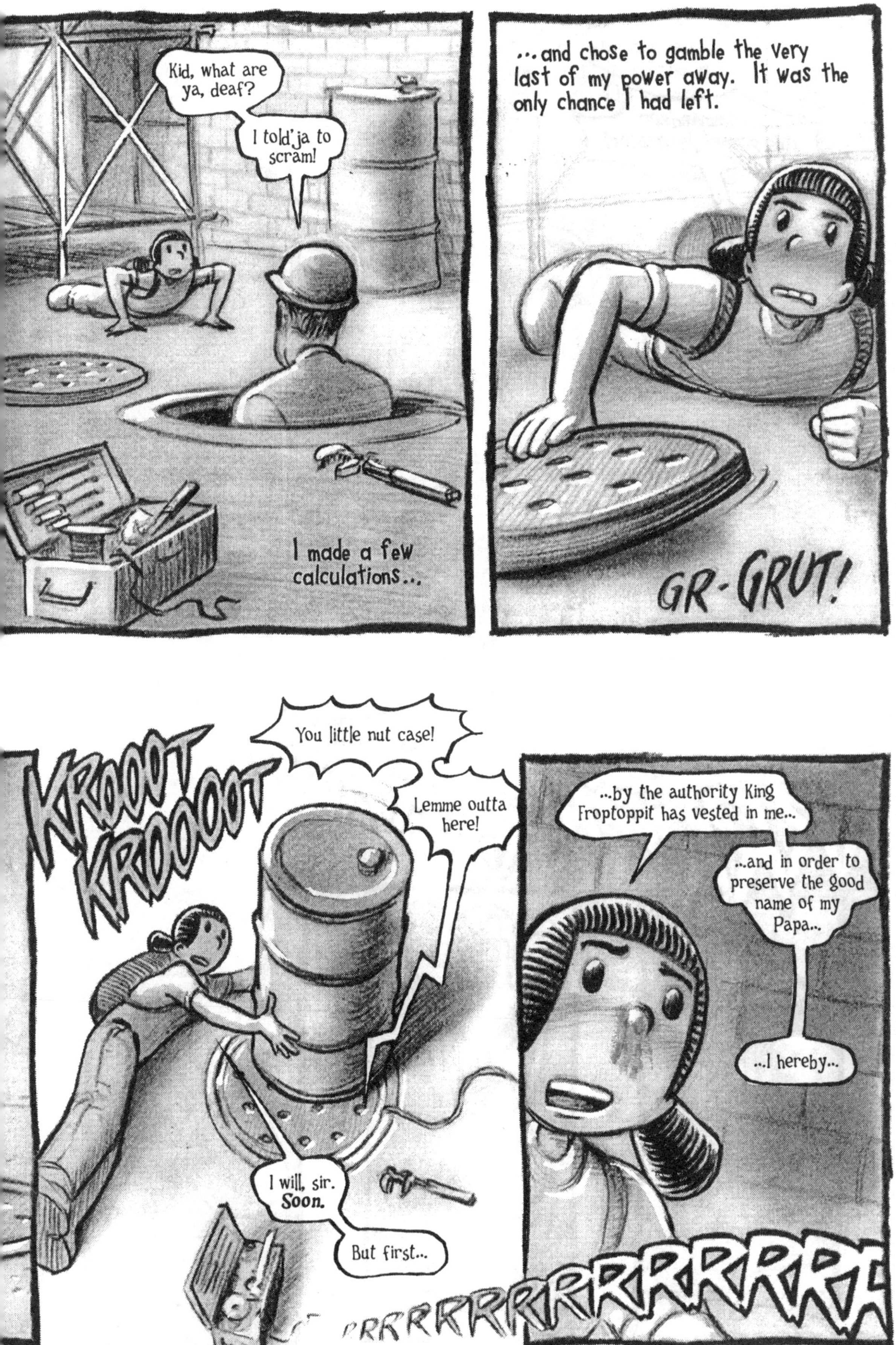
Kid, what are ya, deaf?
I told'ja to scram!
I made a few calculations...
...and chose to gamble the very last of my power away. It was the only chance I had left.
GR-GRUT!
KROOOT KROOOOT
You little nut case!
Lemme outta here!
I will, sir. **Soon.**
But first...
...by the authority King Froptoppit has vested in me...
...and in order to preserve the good name of my Papa...
...I hereby...
RRRRRRRRRRRRRRRRRA

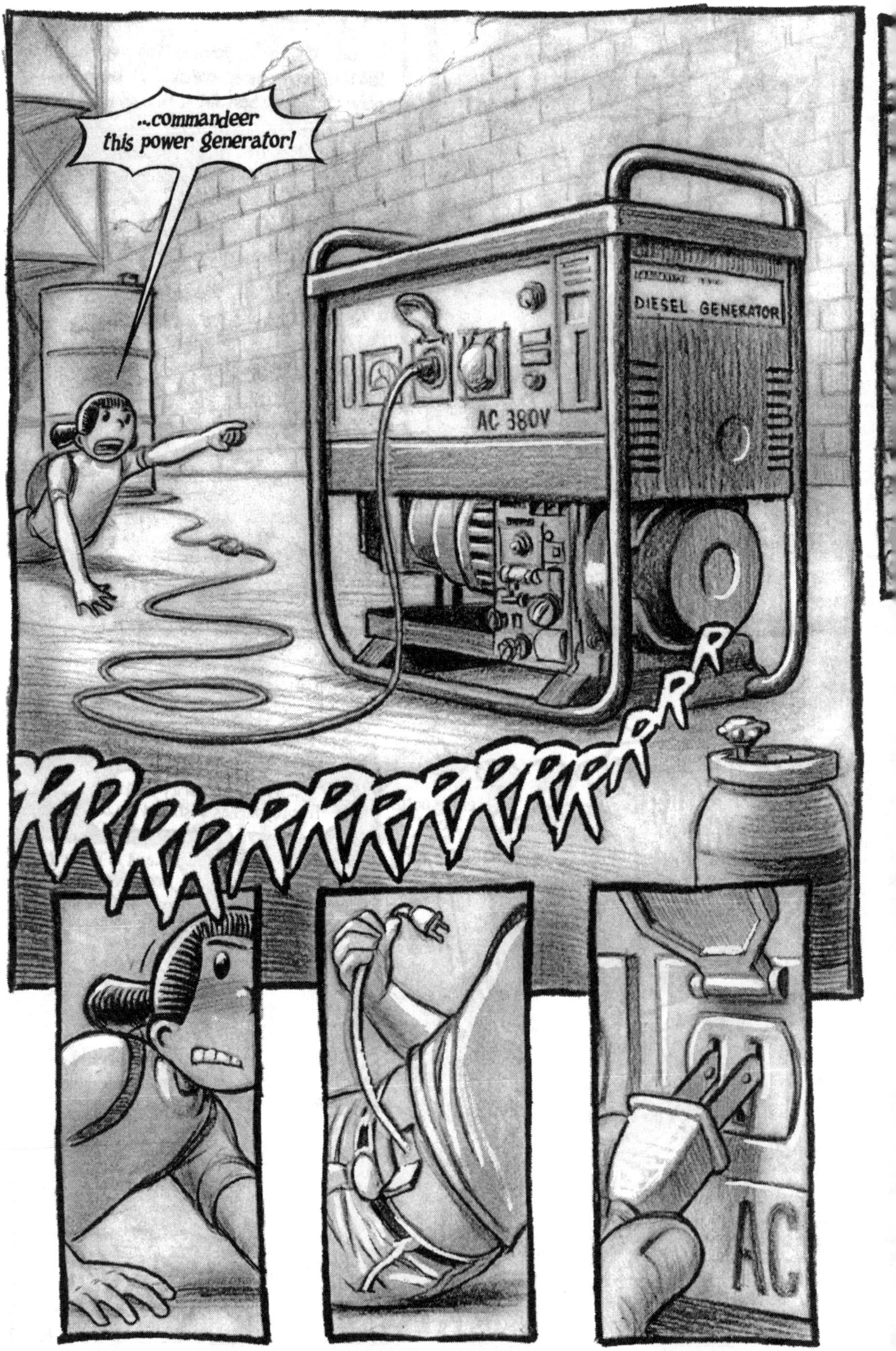
...commandeer this power generator!
DIESEL GENERATOR
AC 380V
RRRRRRRRRRRRRRRRRRRRR
AC

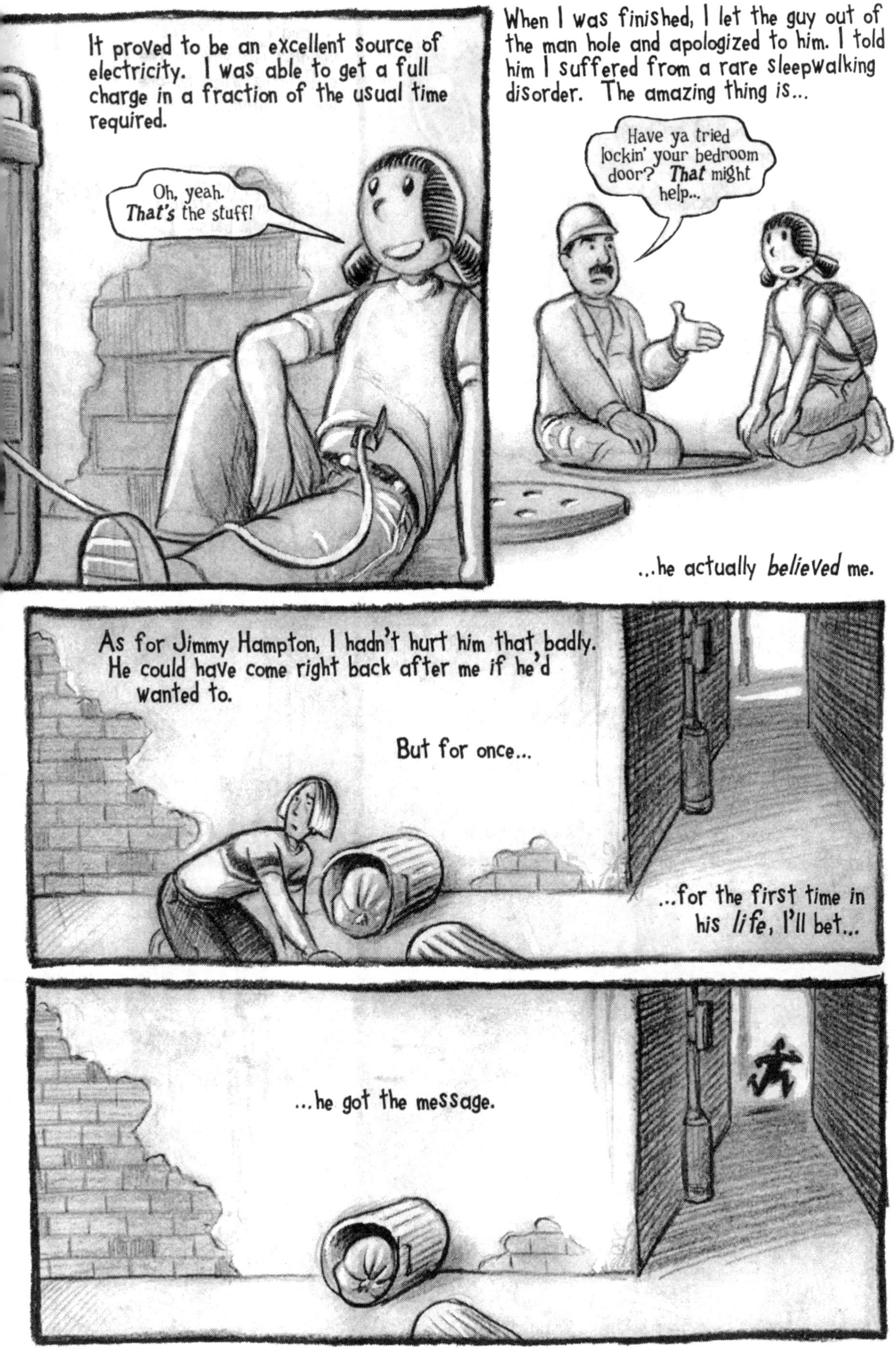
It proved to be an excellent source of electricity. I was able to get a full charge in a fraction of the usual time required.
Oh, yeah. *That's* the stuff!
When I was finished, I let the guy out of the man hole and apologized to him. I told him I suffered from a rare sleepwalking disorder. The amazing thing is...
Have ya tried lockin' your bedroom door? *That* might help...
...he actually *believed* me.
As for Jimmy Hampton, I hadn't hurt him that badly. He could have come right back after me if he'd wanted to.
But for once...
...for the first time in his *life*, I'll bet...
...he got the message.

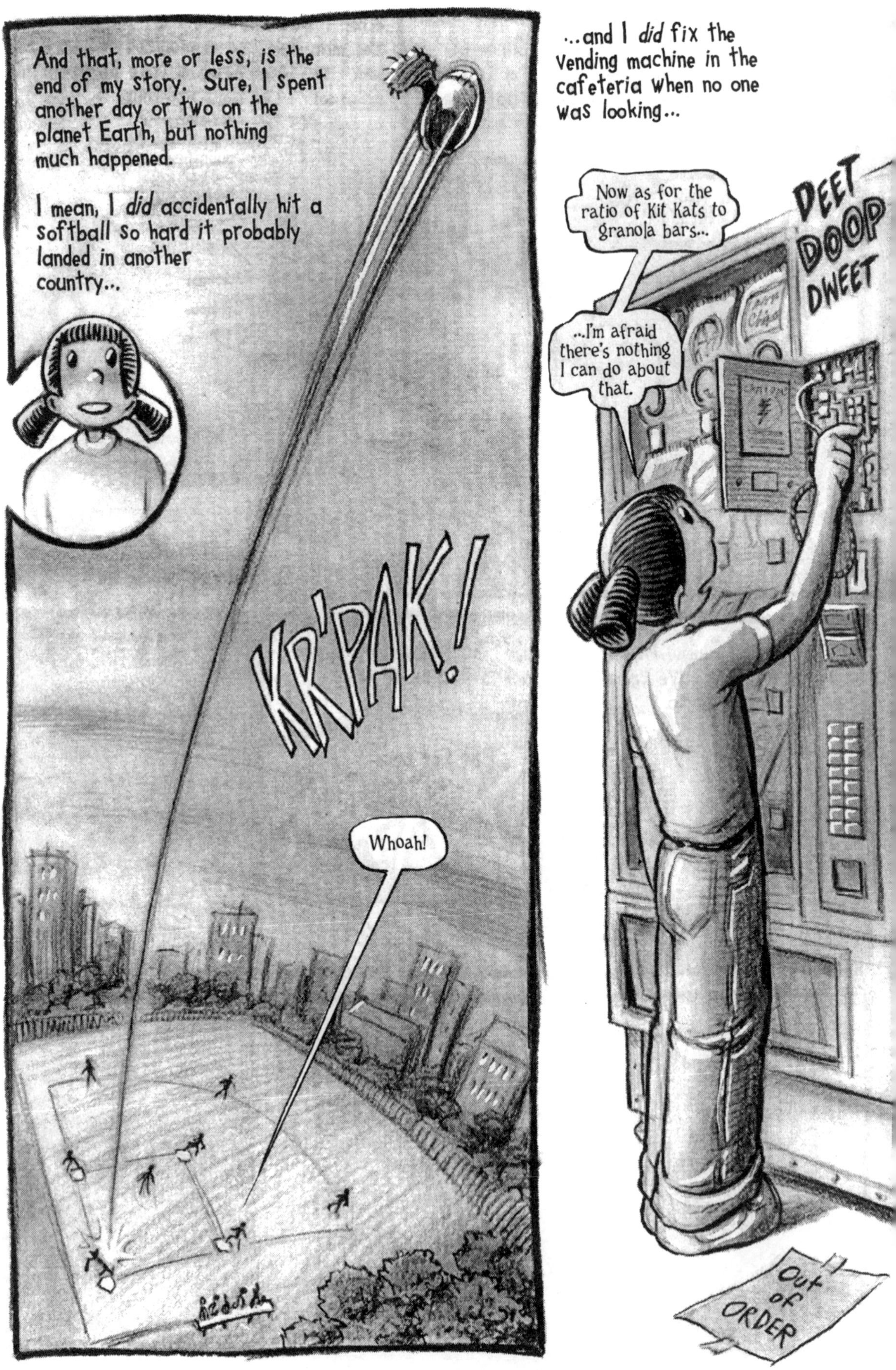
And that, more or less, is the end of my story. Sure, I spent another day or two on the planet Earth, but nothing much happened.
I mean, I *did* accidentally hit a softball so hard it probably landed in another country...
KR'PAK!
Whoah!
...and I *did* fix the vending machine in the cafeteria when no one was looking...
Now as for the ratio of Kit Kats to granola bars...
...I'm afraid there's nothing I can do about that.
DEET DOOP DWEET
Out of ORDER

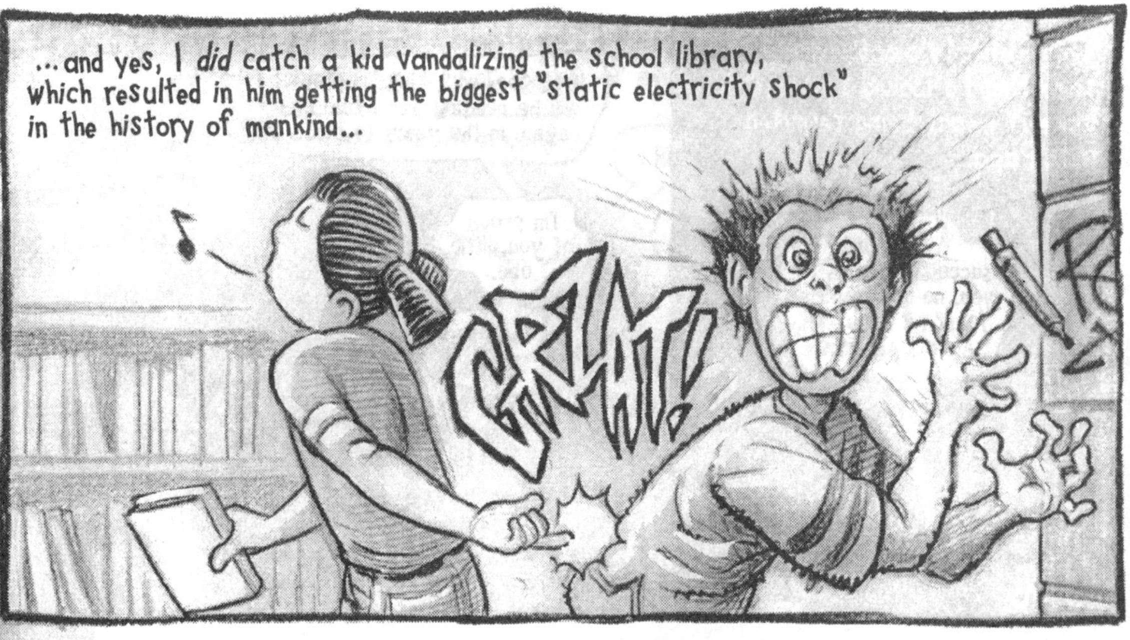
...and yes, I *did* catch a kid vandalizing the school library, which resulted in him getting the biggest "static electricity shock" in the history of mankind...
CRZAT!

...but come on, you don't want to hear about boring stuff like *that*, do you?

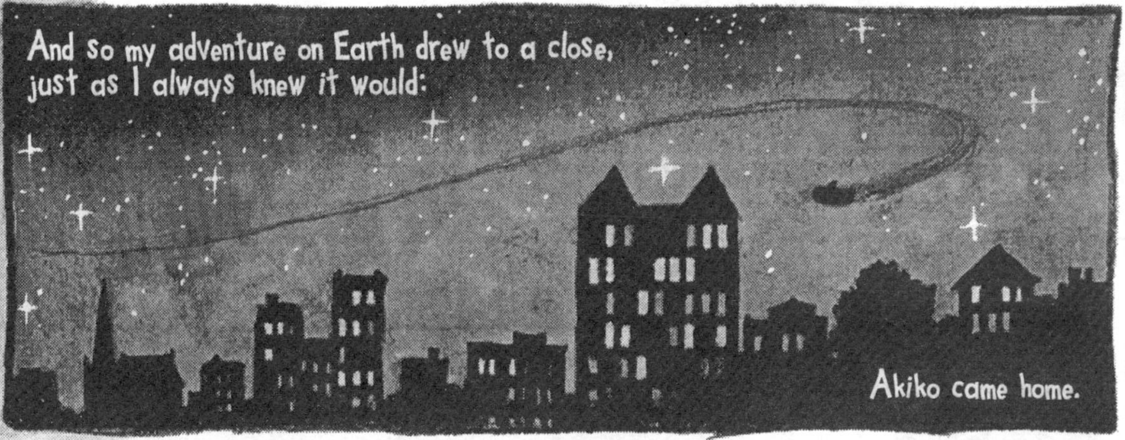
And so my adventure on Earth drew to a close, just as I always knew it would:
Akiko came home.

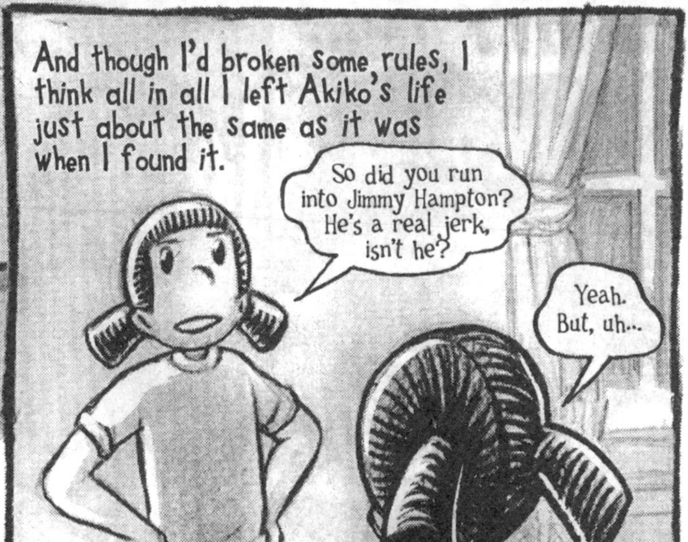
And though I'd broken some rules, I think all in all I left Akiko's life just about the same as it was when I found it.
So did you run into Jimmy Hampton? He's a real jerk, isn't he?
Yeah. But, uh...

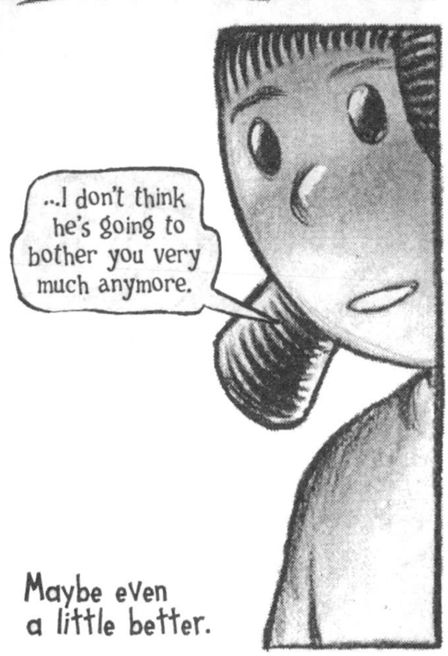
...I don't think he's going to bother you very much anymore.
Maybe even a little better.

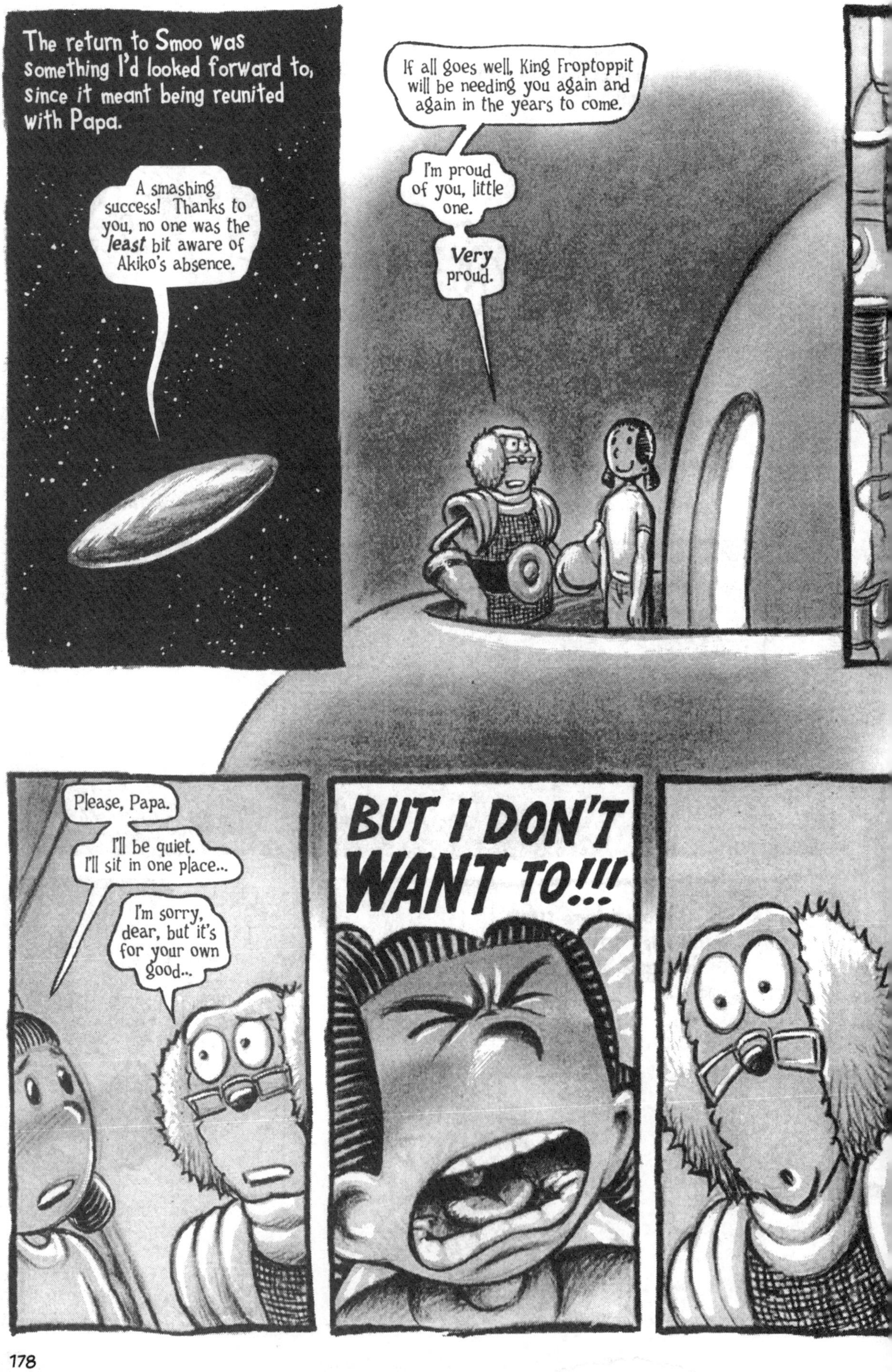

The return to Smoo was something I'd looked forward to, since it meant being reunited with Papa.
A smashing success! Thanks to you, no one was the *least* bit aware of Akiko's absence.
If all goes well, King Froptoppit will be needing you again and again in the years to come.
I'm proud of you, little one.
Very proud.
Please, Papa.
I'll be quiet. I'll sit in one place...
I'm sorry, dear, but it's for your own good...
BUT I DON'T WANT TO!!!

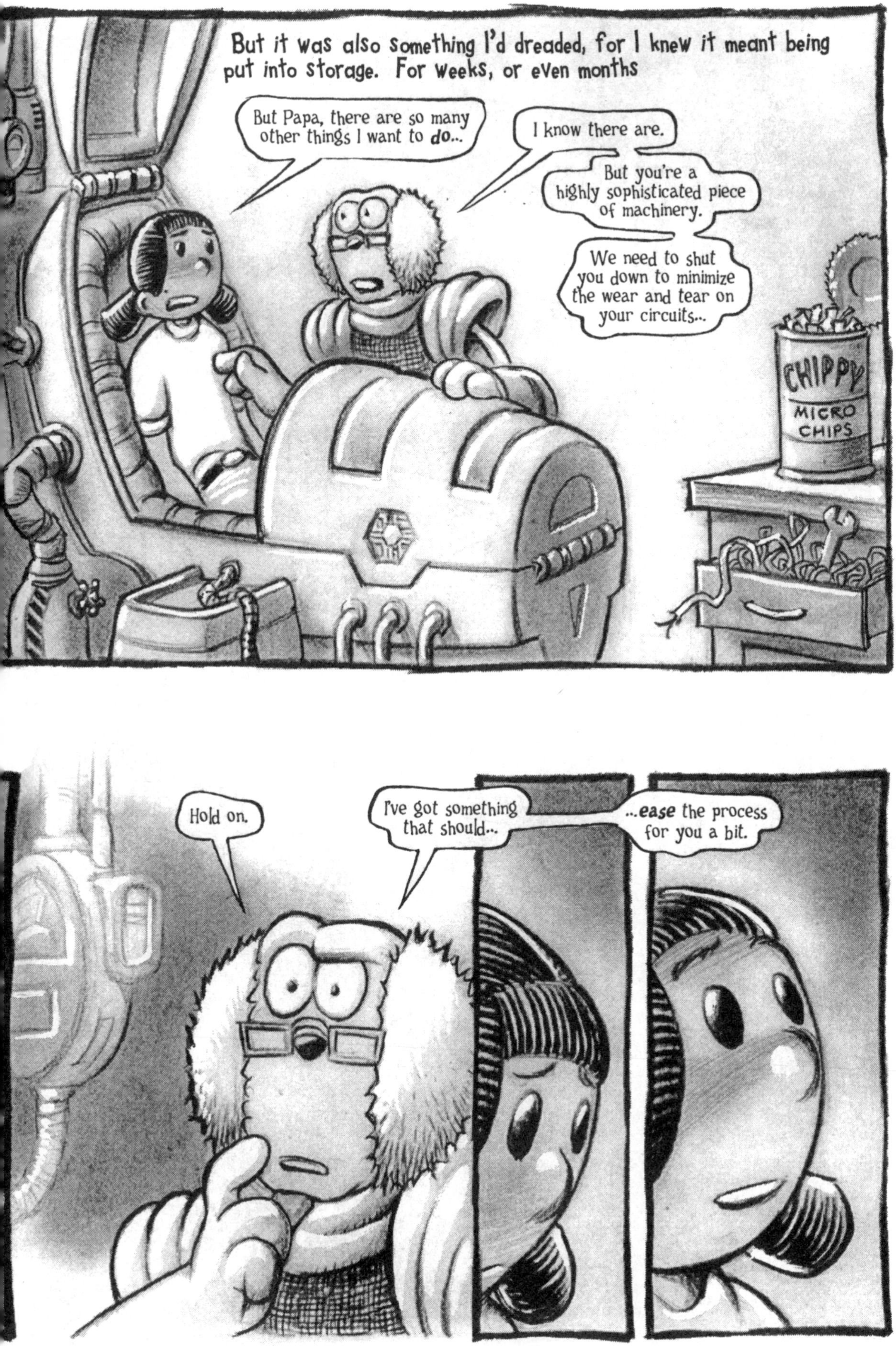
But it was also something I'd dreaded, for I knew it meant being put into storage. For weeks, or even months
But Papa, there are so many other things I want to *do*...
I know there are.
But you're a highly sophisticated piece of machinery.
We need to shut you down to minimize the wear and tear on your circuits...
CHIPPY
MICRO CHIPS
Hold on.
I've got something that should...
...*ease* the process for you a bit.

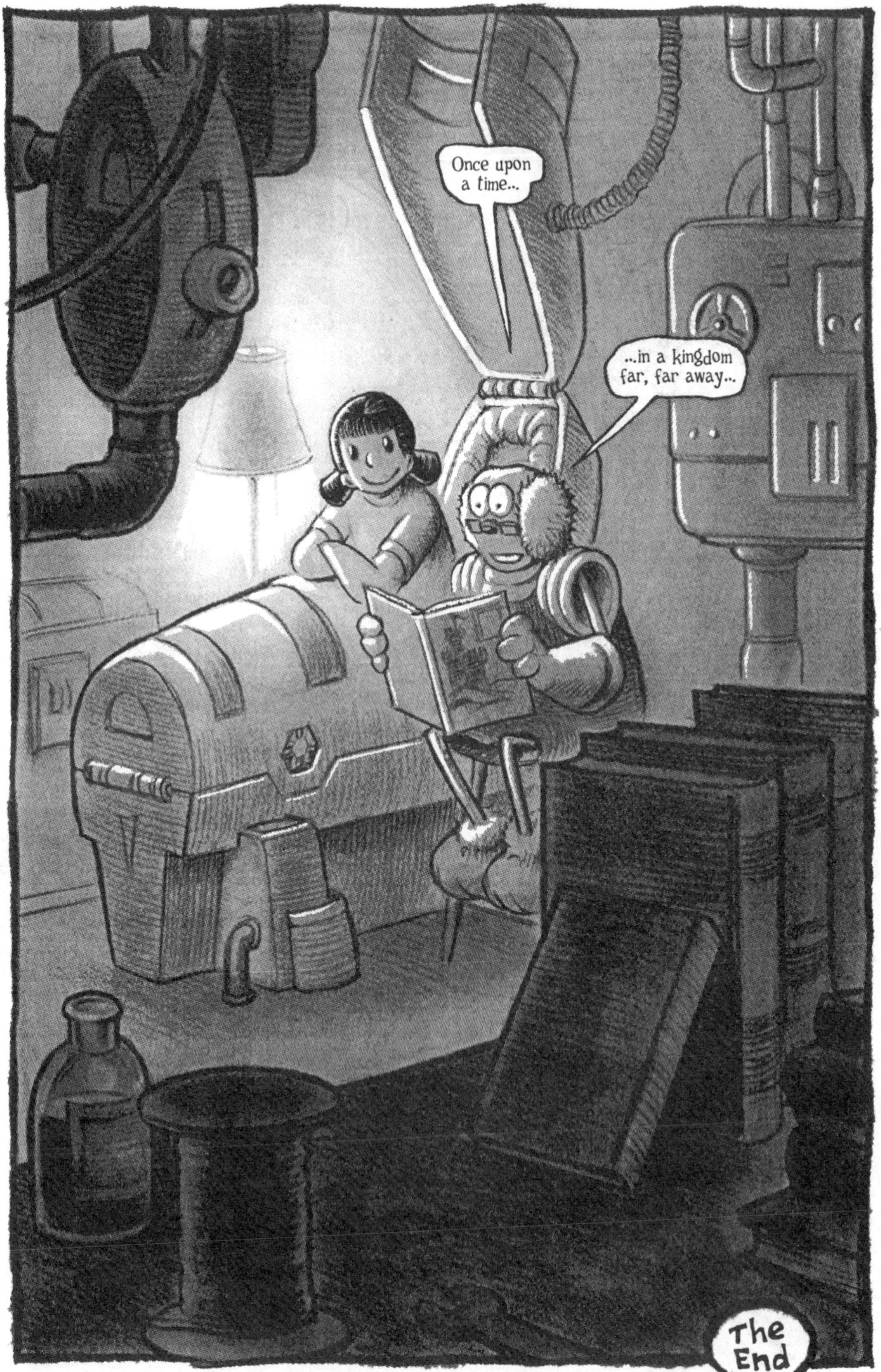
Once upon a time...
...in a kingdom far, far away...
The End

BEEBA 'n' GAX in "FACE VALUE"

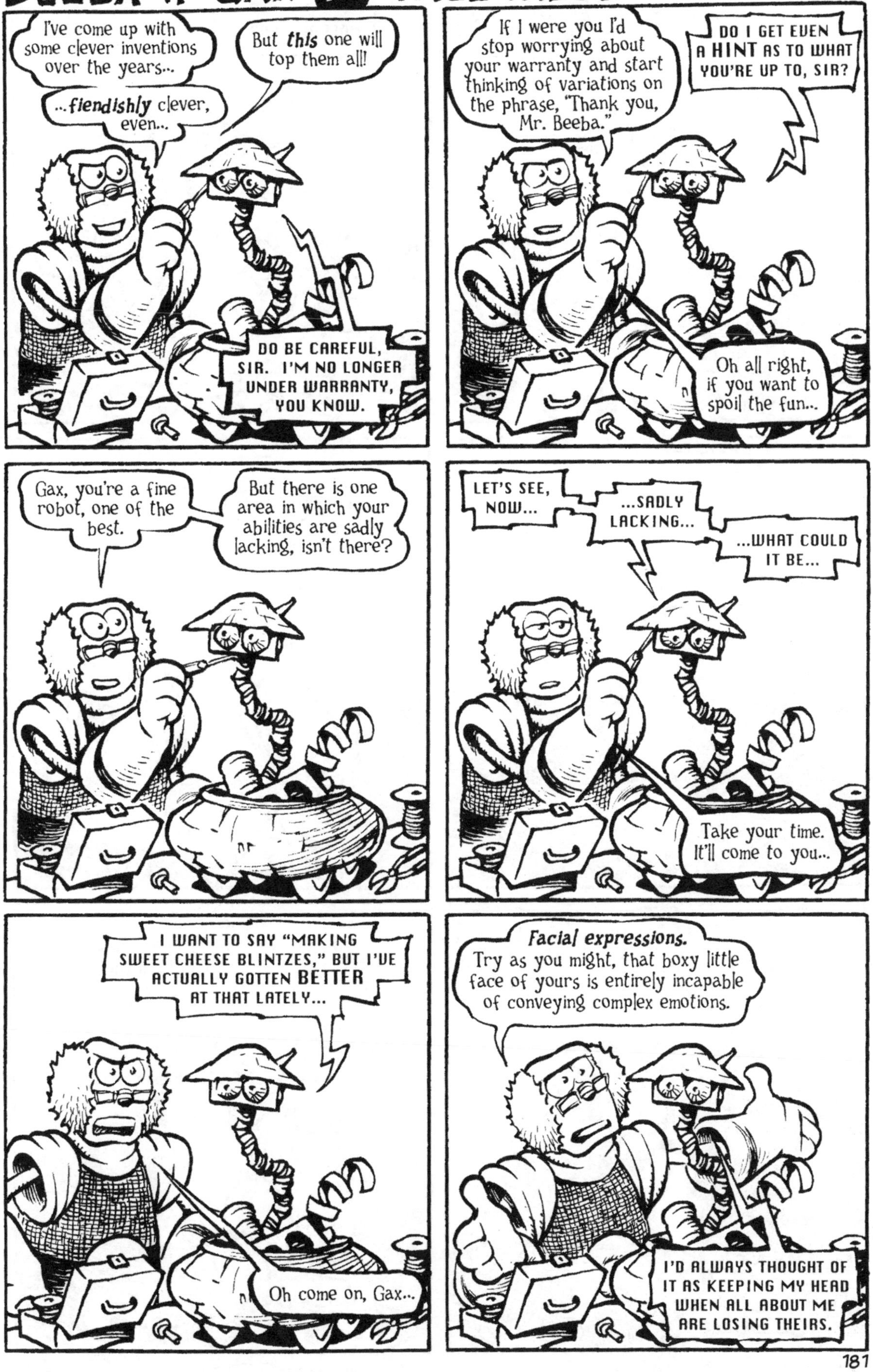
I've come up with some clever inventions over the years...
...*fiendishly* clever, even...
But *this* one will top them all!
DO BE CAREFUL, SIR. I'M NO LONGER UNDER WARRANTY, YOU KNOW.
If I were you I'd stop worrying about your warranty and start thinking of variations on the phrase, "Thank you, Mr. Beeba."
DO I GET EVEN A **HINT** AS TO WHAT YOU'RE UP TO, SIR?
Oh all right, if you want to spoil the fun...
Gax, you're a fine robot, one of the best.
But there is one area in which your abilities are sadly lacking, isn't there?
LET'S SEE, NOW...
...SADLY LACKING...
...WHAT COULD IT BE...
Take your time. It'll come to you...
I WANT TO SAY "MAKING SWEET CHEESE BLINTZES," BUT I'VE ACTUALLY GOTTEN **BETTER** AT THAT LATELY...
Oh come on, Gax...
Facial expressions. Try as you might, that boxy little face of yours is entirely incapable of conveying complex emotions.
I'D ALWAYS THOUGHT OF IT AS KEEPING MY HEAD WHEN ALL ABOUT ME ARE LOSING THEIRS.

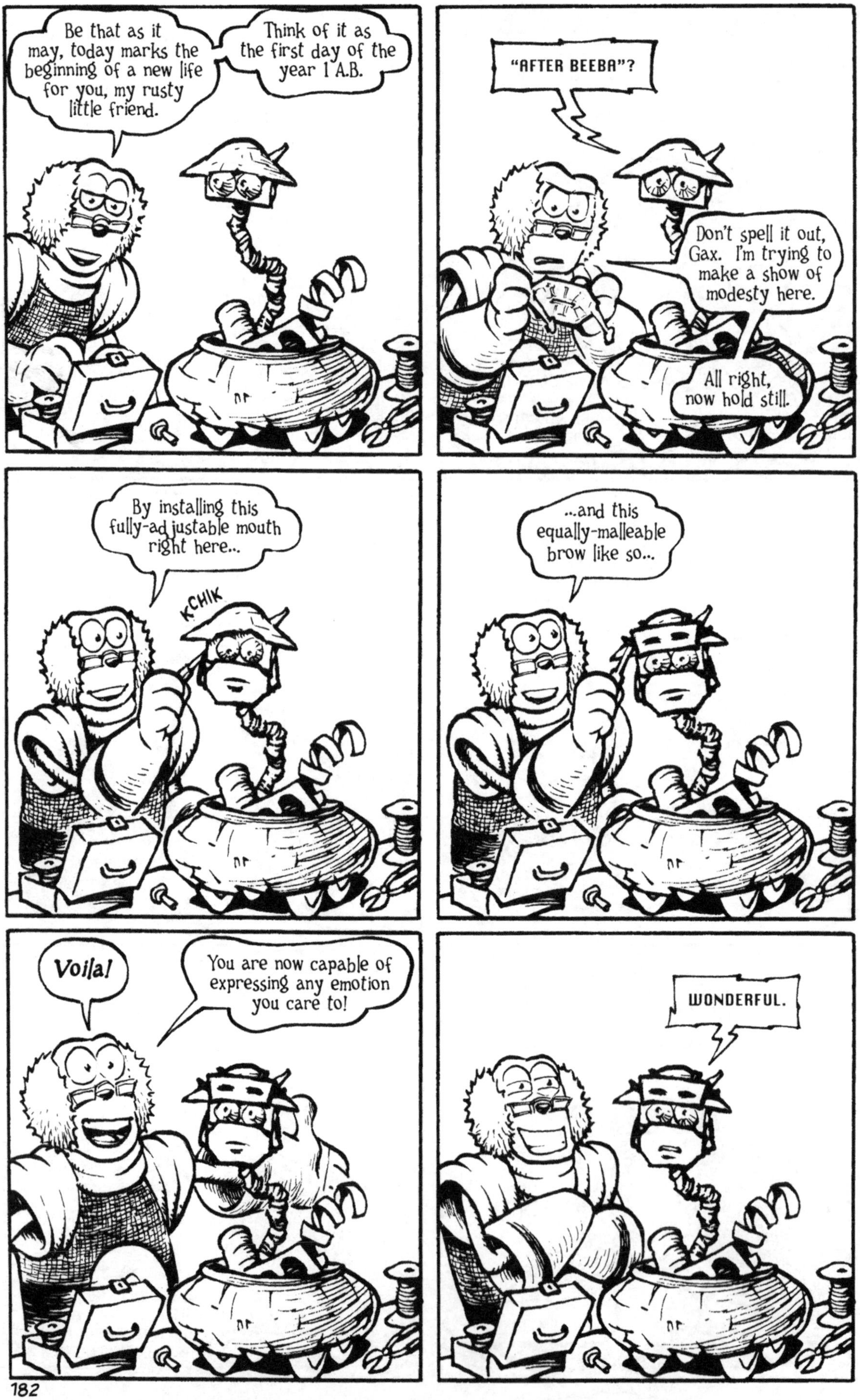
Be that as it may, today marks the beginning of a new life for you, my rusty little friend.
Think of it as the first day of the year 1 A.B.
"AFTER BEEBA"?
Don't spell it out, Gax. I'm trying to make a show of modesty here.
All right, now hold still.
By installing this fully-adjustable mouth right here...
KCHIK
...and this equally-malleable brow like so...
Voila!
You are now capable of expressing any emotion you care to!
WONDERFUL.

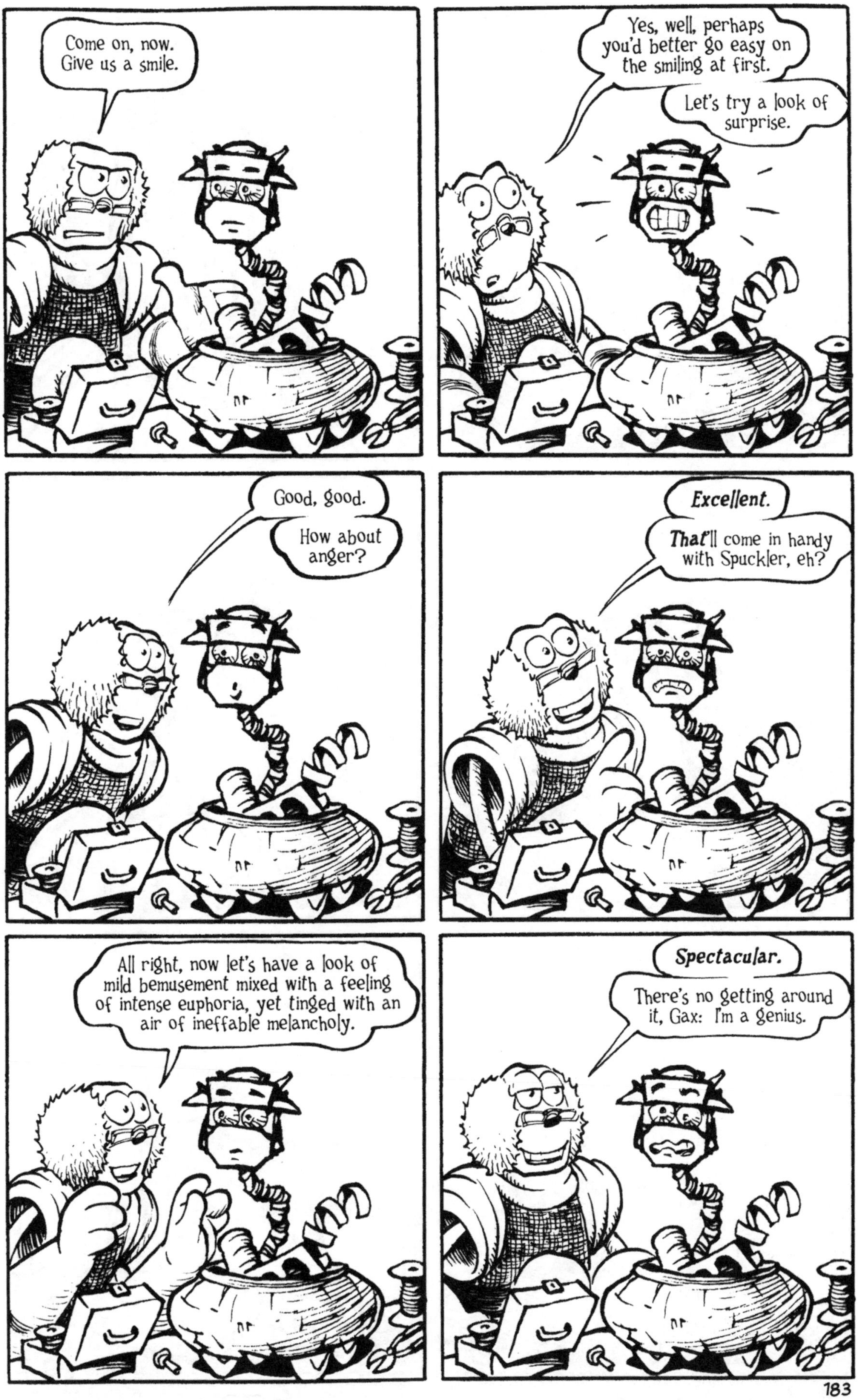
Come on, now. Give us a smile.
Yes, well, perhaps you'd better go easy on the smiling at first.
Let's try a look of surprise.
Good, good.
How about anger?
Excellent.
That'll come in handy with Spuckler, eh?
All right, now let's have a look of mild bemusement mixed with a feeling of intense euphoria, yet tinged with an air of ineffable melancholy.
Spectacular.
There's no getting around it, Gax: I'm a genius.

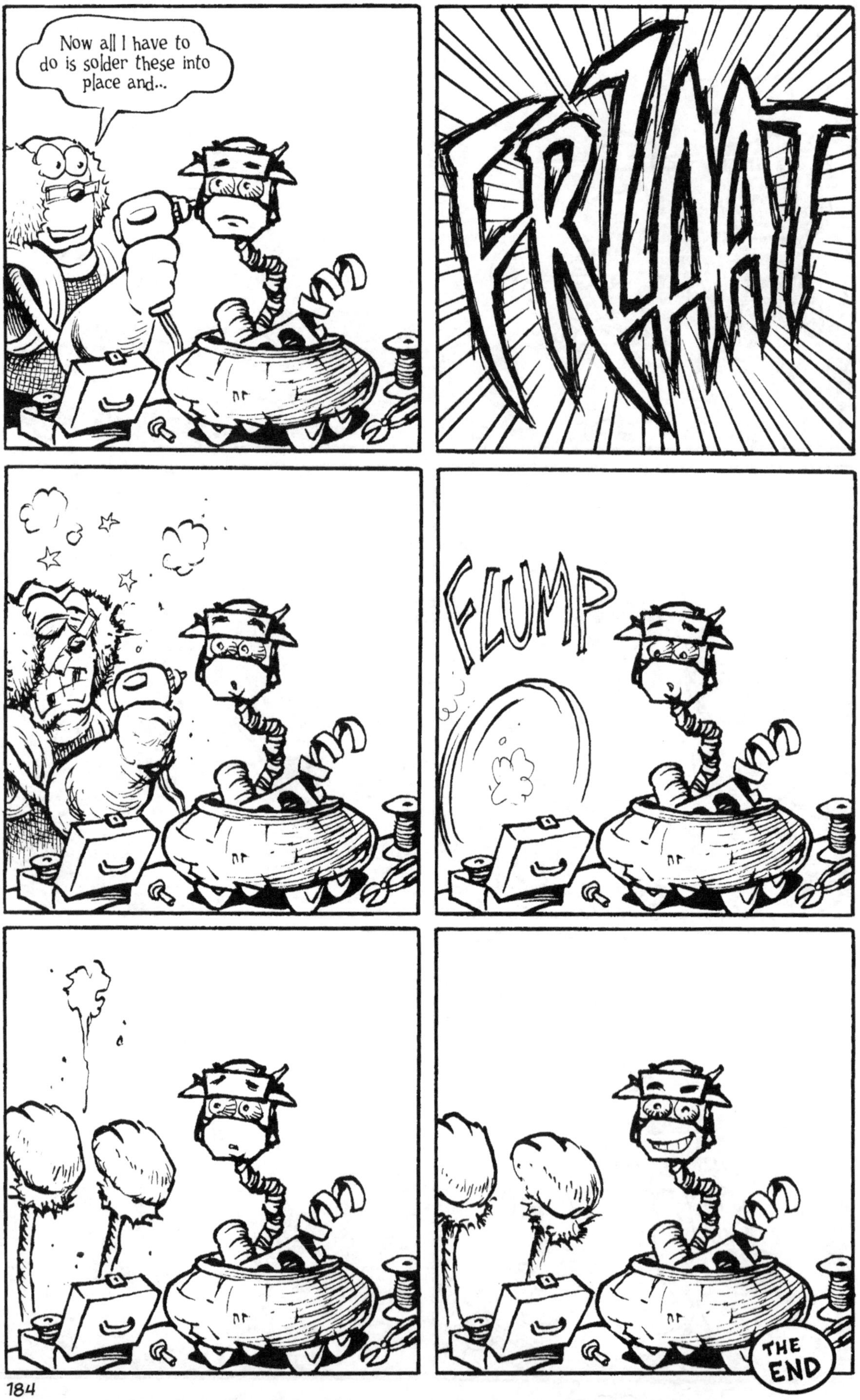
Now all I have to do is solder these into place and...
FRZAAT
FLUMP
THE END

LAST PAGE PRODUCTIONS presents:

'KIKO'S BLUE JEANS
A CLOSER LOOK!

SMAGBERRY JUICE STAINS
"Shout" it out? If only it were that easy.

TOP SECRET HOMING BEACON
Installed at the behest of Mr. Beeba, this chip-embedded button allows Akiko's Smoovian friends to locate her wherever she happens to be on the planet Earth.

(Or locate her *blue jeans*, at any rate.)

SLIGHT TEAR
From Akiko's tussle with the Living Castle of Gamgor. (Torn further during Akiko's tussle with Loza Throck.) (And crash landing in rural Japan didn't exactly help, either.)

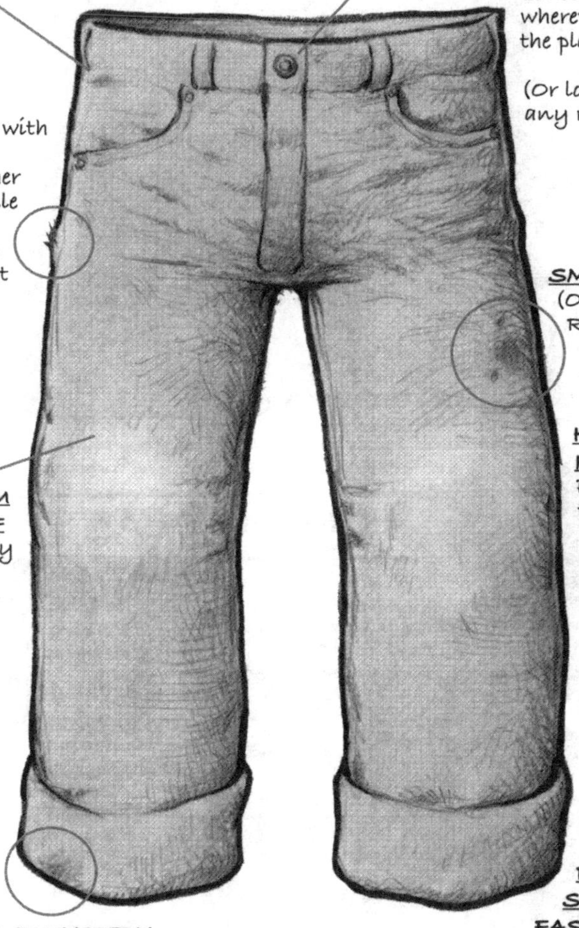

SMUDBURGER GREASE
(Or was it the Moolo Rings?)

HYPER-REINFORCED KNEE SWATCHES
Perfectly camouflaged threads of pure Trutanium (Spuckler's idea) make this area on both legs all but invulnerable to normal wear and tear.

(Akiko's knees, sadly, are just as bruise-able as they've ever been.)

FORMER SITE OF GRASS STAINS FROM MIMBURKEN'S BLUFF
This area mysteriously cleared up during the trip to the Farflux Dimension. (The smell, oddly enough, is still there.)

OIL SPLOTCH, THE ORIGIN OF WHICH REMAINS SHROUDED IN MYSTERY
Remember the time they were climbing the Great Wall of Trudd, and Akiko fainted, and she fell off the wall, and the only thing still holding her up there was this rope tangled around her ankles, and then Spuckler fell too, and then Akiko climbed up on top of Gax and he carried her all the way up to the top of the wall? Well, this oil splotch has nothing to do with *any* of that, and in fact I'm pretty sure it was just something she picked up while goofing around in a parking lot somewhere.

ROLLED JEANS: SHORT LEGS OR FASHION STATEMENT?
History will be the judge.

COMMENT MADE BY AKIKO'S MOTHER AT LEAST ONCE EVERY THREE DAYS:
"Darling, it's nothing personal, honestly, but please, *PLEASE* let us buy you a new pair of Levi's."

AKIKO'S RESPONSE:
"These jeans and I have been through a *lot* together, Mom. I can't just toss them out!

I *could* use a new light-blue T-shirt, though."

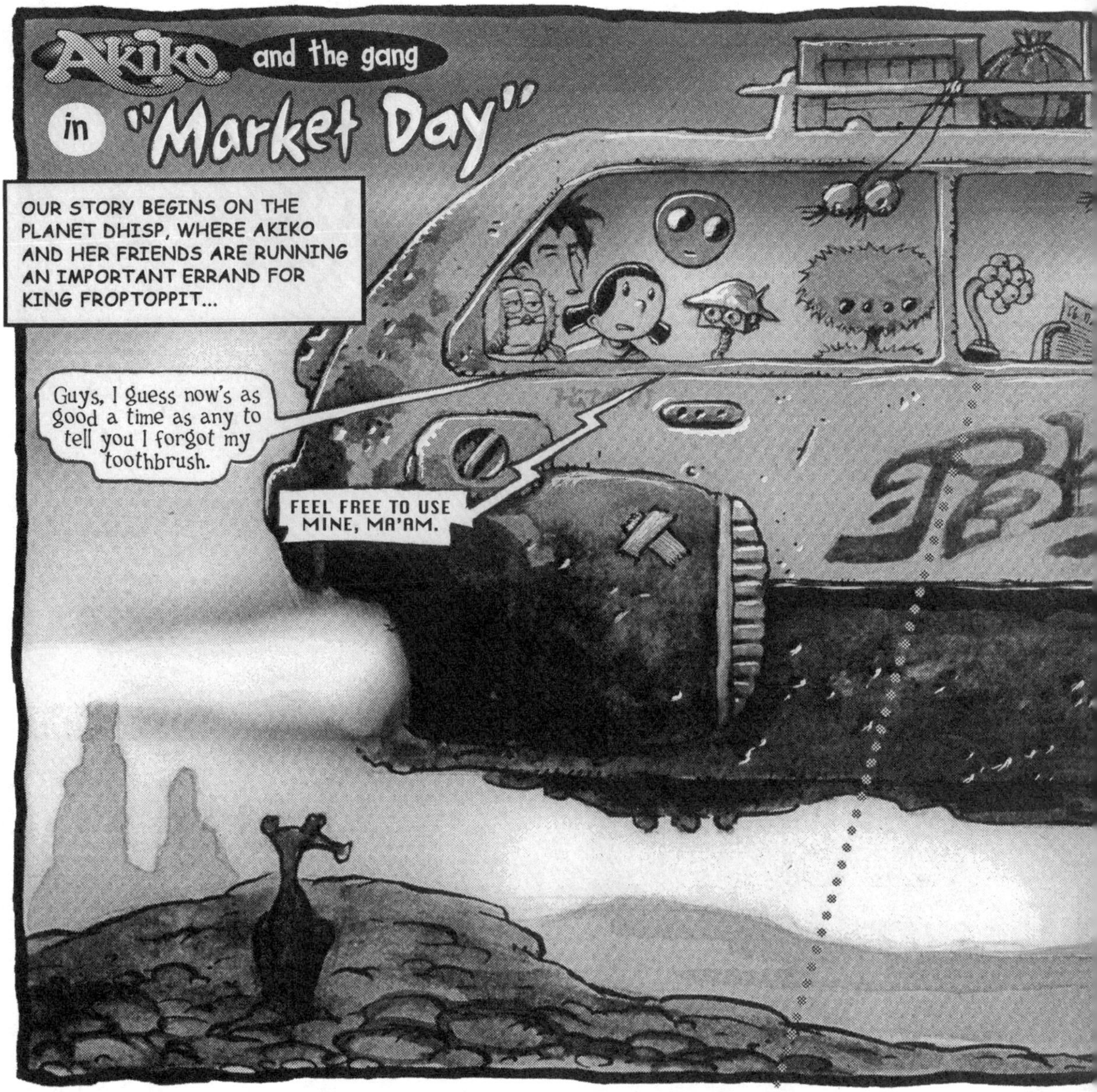
Akiko and the gang
in "Market Day"
OUR STORY BEGINS ON THE PLANET DHISP, WHERE AKIKO AND HER FRIENDS ARE RUNNING AN IMPORTANT ERRAND FOR KING FROPTOPPIT...
Guys, I guess now's as good a time as any to tell you I forgot my toothbrush.
FEEL FREE TO USE MINE, MA'AM.

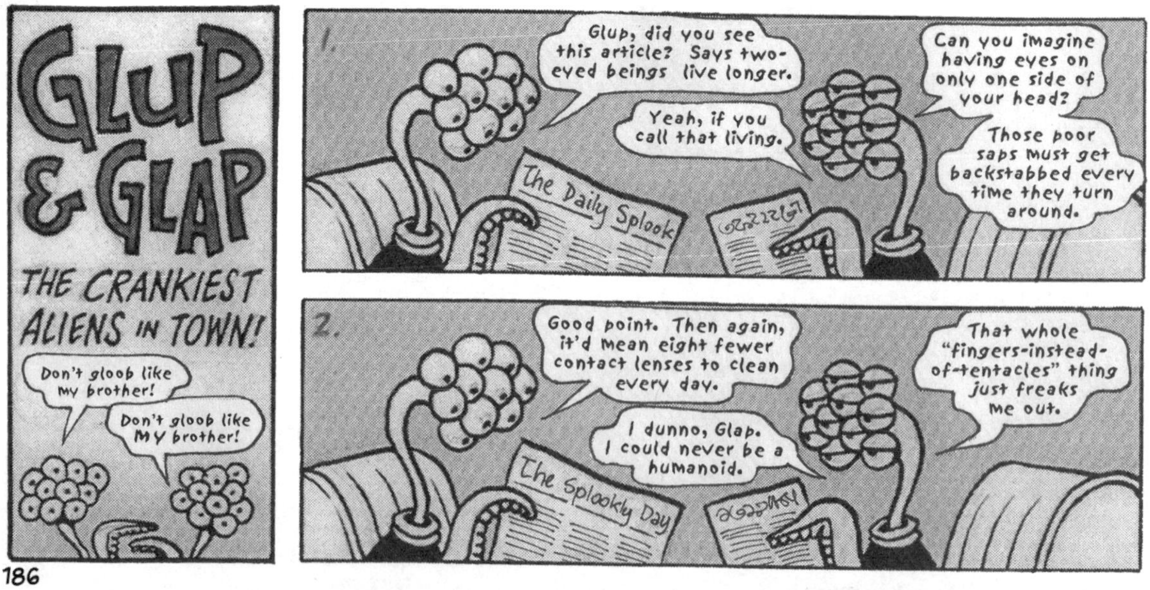
GLUP & GLAP
THE CRANKIEST ALIENS IN TOWN!
Don't gloob like my brother!
Don't gloob like MY brother!
1.
Glup, did you see this article? Says two-eyed beings live longer.
Yeah, if you call that living.
Can you imagine having eyes on only one side of your head?
Those poor saps must get backstabbed every time they turn around.
The Daily Splook
2.
Good point. Then again, it'd mean eight fewer contact lenses to clean every day.
I dunno, Glap. I could never be a humanoid.
That whole "fingers-instead-of-tentacles" thing just freaks me out.
The Splookly Day

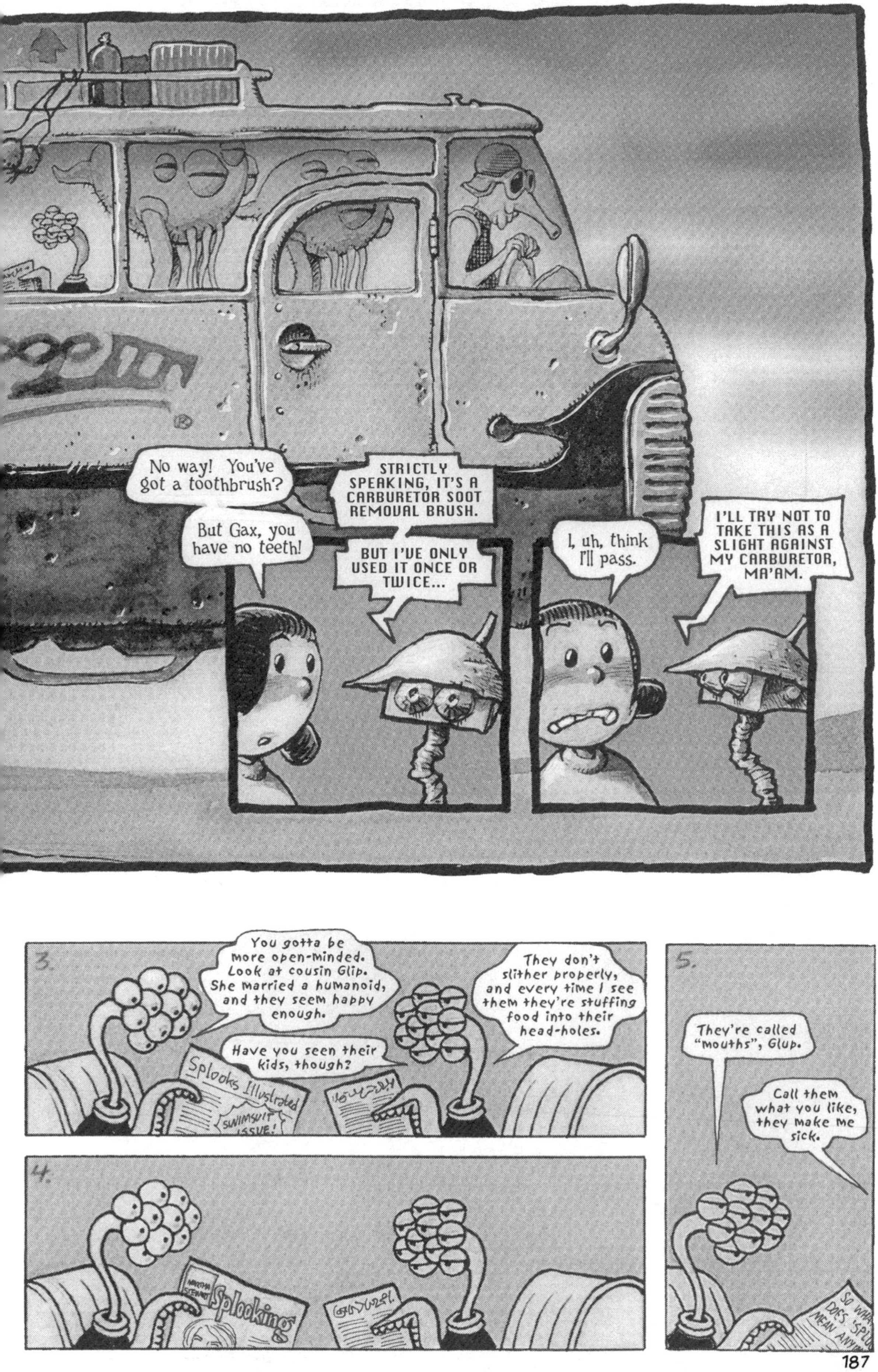
No way! You've got a toothbrush?
STRICTLY SPEAKING, IT'S A CARBURETOR SOOT REMOVAL BRUSH.
But Gax, you have no teeth!
BUT I'VE ONLY USED IT ONCE OR TWICE...
I, uh, think I'll pass.
I'LL TRY NOT TO TAKE THIS AS A SLIGHT AGAINST MY CARBURETOR, MA'AM.
3.
You gotta be more open-minded. Look at cousin Glip. She married a humanoid, and they seem happy enough.
Have you seen their kids, though?
They don't slither properly, and every time I see them they're stuffing food into their head-holes.
Splooks Illustrated
SWIMSUIT ISSUE!
4.
Splookings
5.
They're called "mouths", Glup.
Call them what you like, they make me sick.

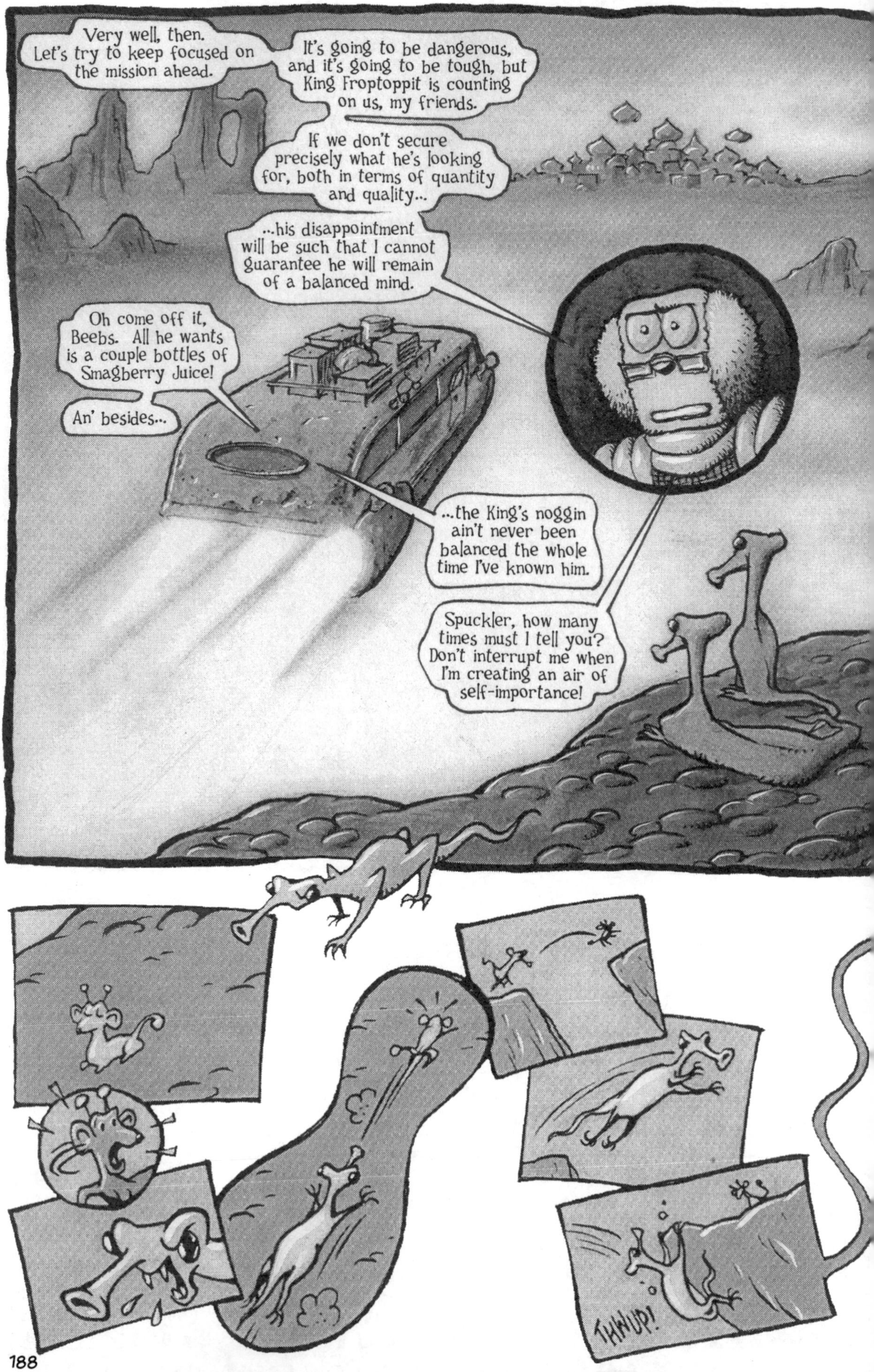
Very well, then. Let's try to keep focused on the mission ahead.
It's going to be dangerous, and it's going to be tough, but King Froptoppit is counting on us, my friends.
If we don't secure precisely what he's looking for, both in terms of quantity and quality...
...his disappointment will be such that I cannot guarantee he will remain of a balanced mind.
Oh come off it, Beebs. All he wants is a couple bottles of Smagberry Juice!
An' besides...
...the King's noggin ain't never been balanced the whole time I've known him.
Spuckler, how many times must I tell you? Don't interrupt me when I'm creating an air of self-importance!
THWUP!

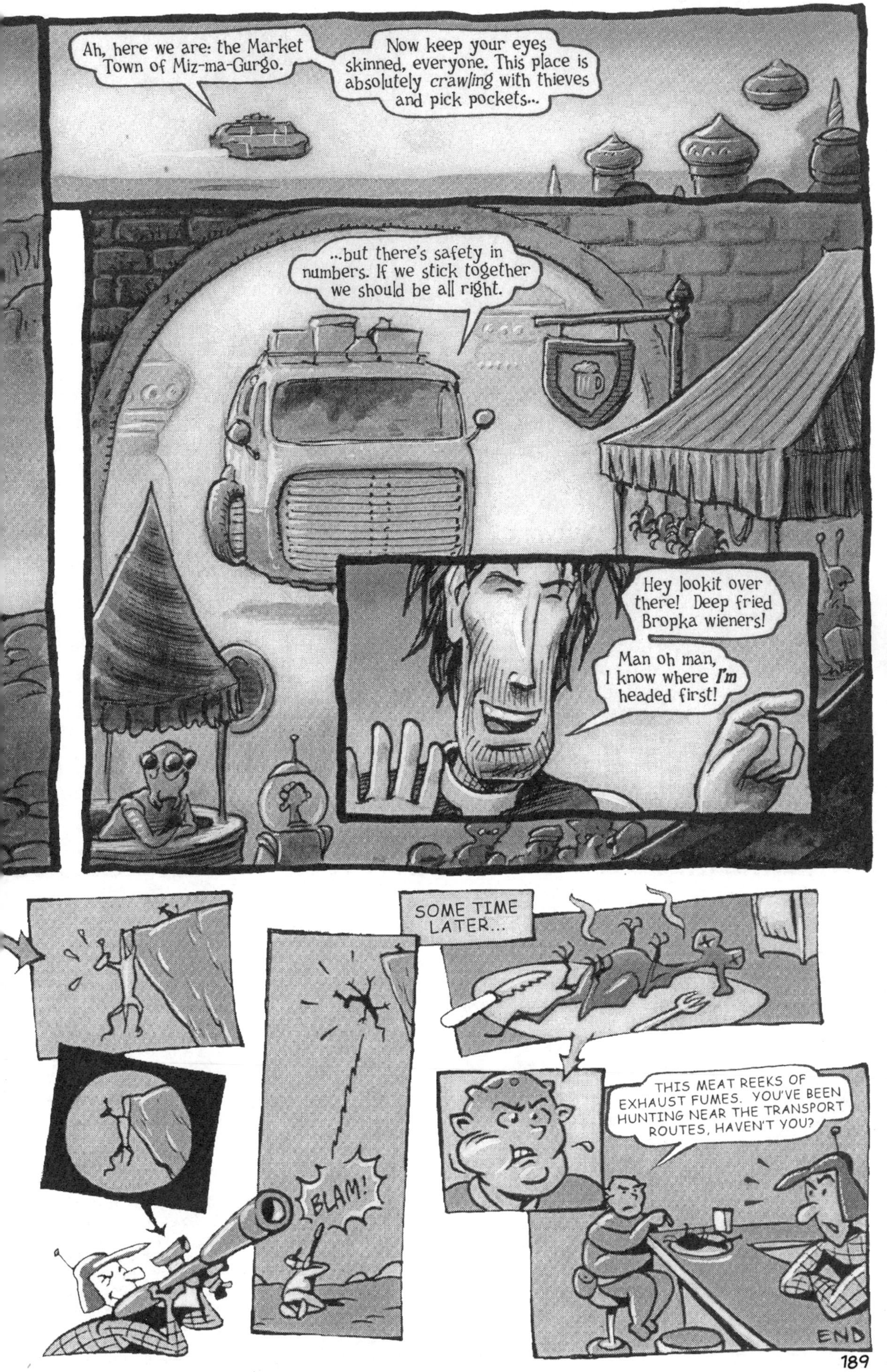
Ah, here we are: the Market Town of Miz-ma-Gurgo.
Now keep your eyes skinned, everyone. This place is absolutely *crawling* with thieves and pick pockets...
...but there's safety in numbers. If we stick together we should be all right.
Hey lookit over there! Deep fried Bropka wieners!
Man oh man, I know where ***I'm*** headed first!
BLAM!
SOME TIME LATER...
THIS MEAT REEKS OF EXHAUST FUMES. YOU'VE BEEN HUNTING NEAR THE TRANSPORT ROUTES, HAVEN'T YOU?
END

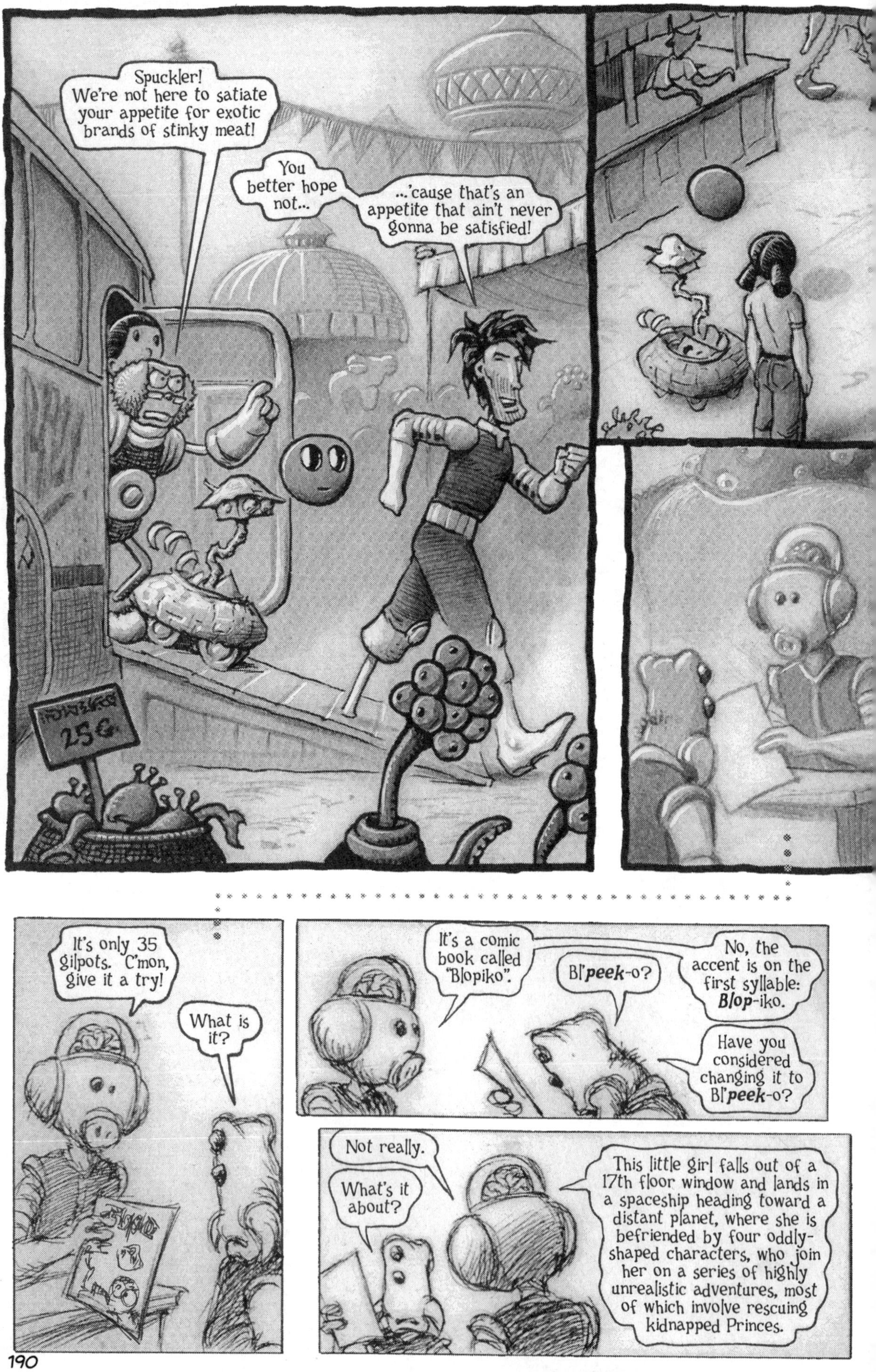
Spuckler! We're not here to satiate your appetite for exotic brands of stinky meat!
You better hope not...
...'cause that's an appetite that ain't never gonna be satisfied!
It's only 35 gilpots. C'mon, give it a try!
What is it?
It's a comic book called "Blopiko".
Bl'**peek**-o?
No, the accent is on the first syllable: ***Blop***-iko.
Have you considered changing it to Bl'**peek**-o?
Not really.
What's it about?
This little girl falls out of a 17th floor window and lands in a spaceship heading toward a distant planet, where she is befriended by four oddly-shaped characters, who join her on a series of highly unrealistic adventures, most of which involve rescuing kidnapped Princes.

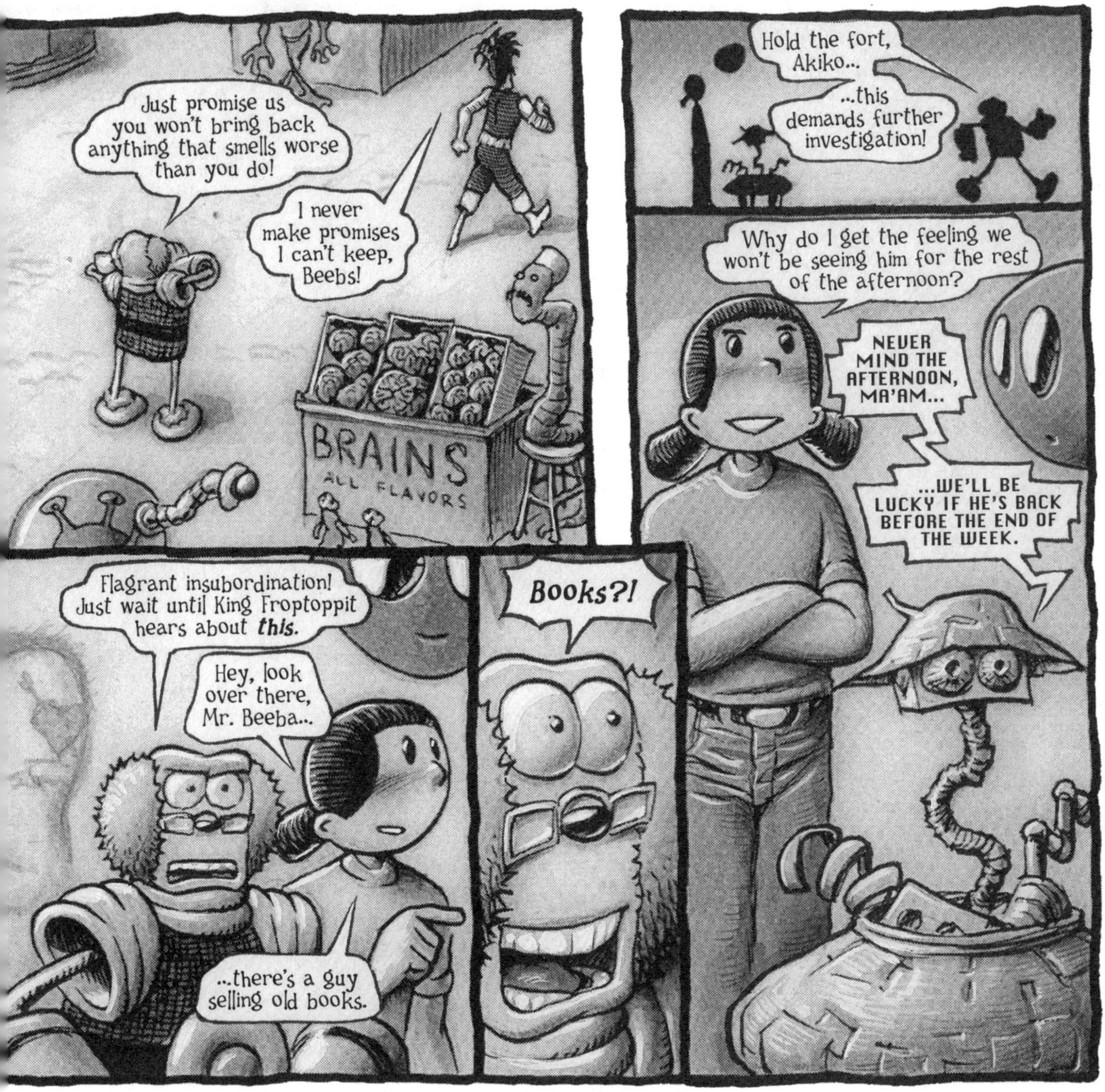
Just promise us you won't bring back anything that smells worse than you do!
I never make promises I can't keep, Beebs!
BRAINS ALL FLAVORS
Hold the fort, Akiko...
...this demands further investigation!
Why do I get the feeling we won't be seeing him for the rest of the afternoon?
NEVER MIND THE AFTERNOON, MA'AM...
...WE'LL BE LUCKY IF HE'S BACK BEFORE THE END OF THE WEEK.
Flagrant insubordination! Just wait until King Froptoppit hears about **this**.
Hey, look over there, Mr. Beeba...
...there's a guy selling old books.
Books?!

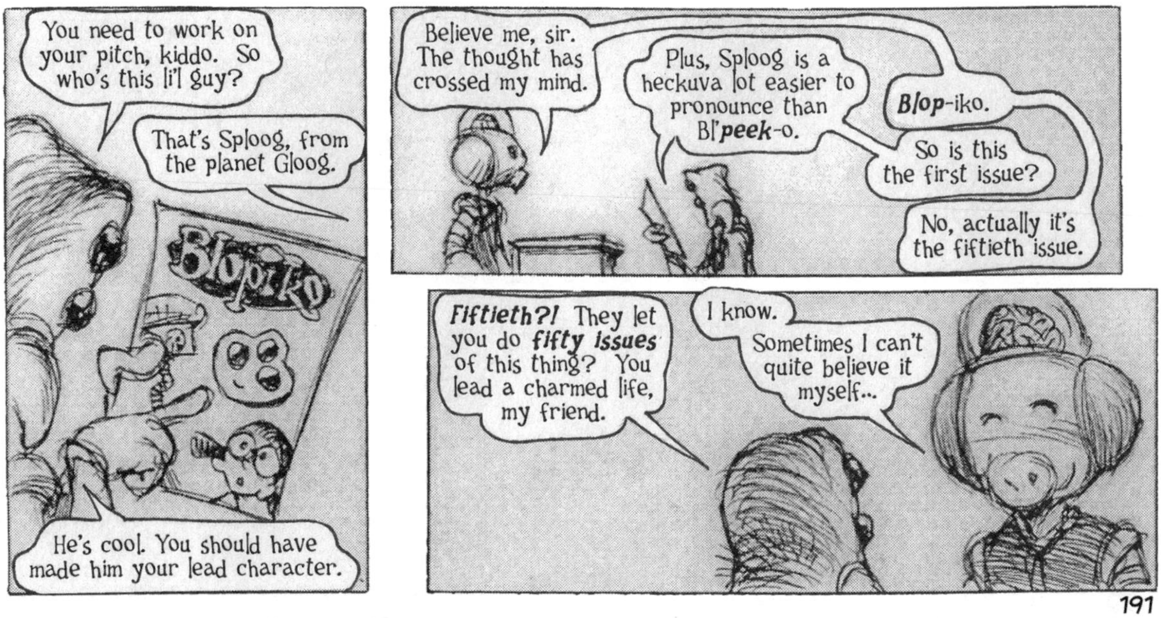
You need to work on your pitch, kiddo. So who's this li'l guy?
That's Sploog, from the planet Gloog.
He's cool. You should have made him your lead character.
Believe me, sir. The thought has crossed my mind.
Plus, Sploog is a heckuva lot easier to pronounce than Bl'**peek**-o.
Blop-iko.
So is this the first issue?
No, actually it's the fiftieth issue.
Fiftieth?! They let you do **fifty issues** of this thing? You lead a charmed life, my friend.
I know.
Sometimes I can't quite believe it myself...

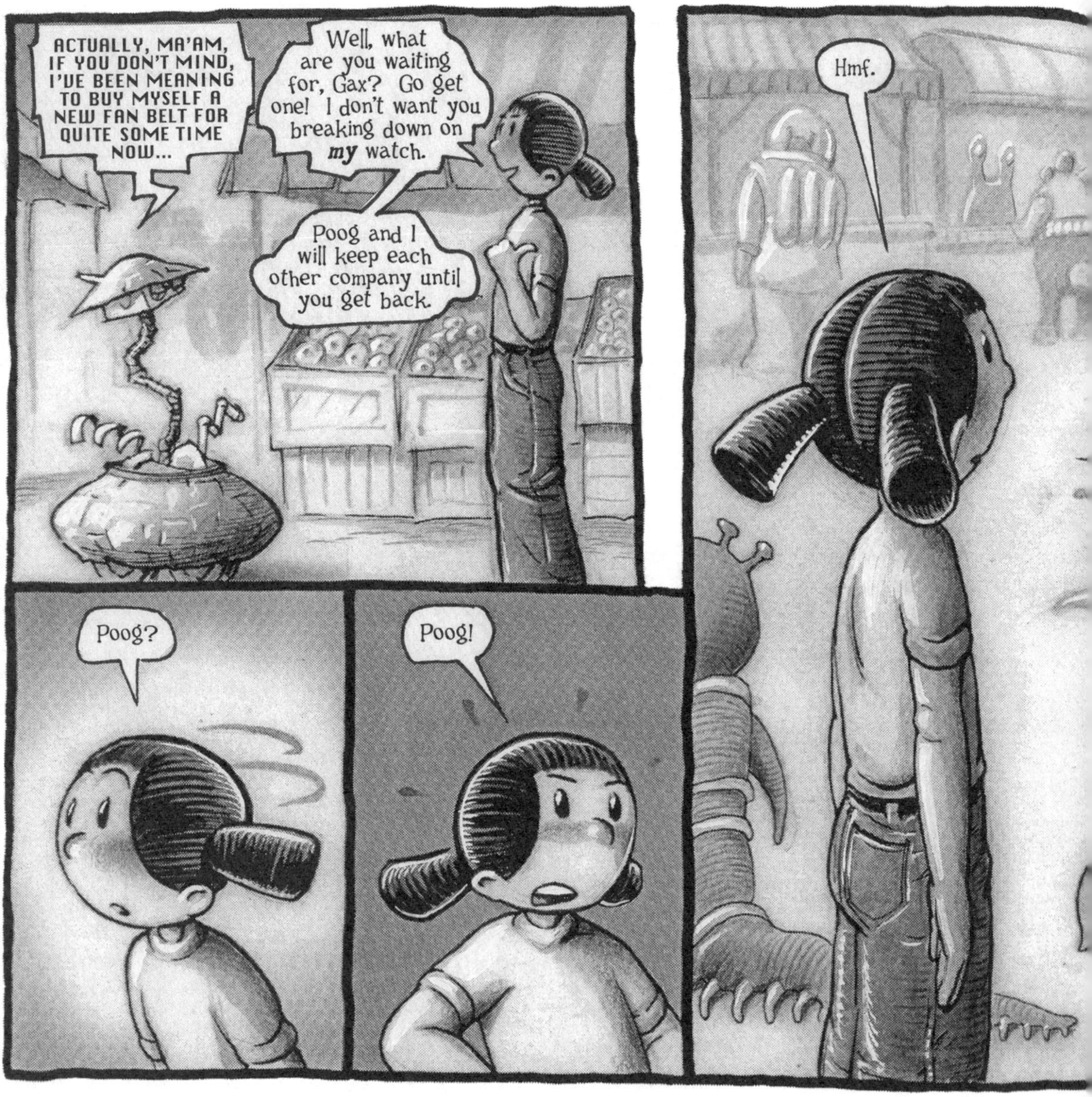
ACTUALLY, MA'AM, IF YOU DON'T MIND, I'VE BEEN MEANING TO BUY MYSELF A NEW FAN BELT FOR QUITE SOME TIME NOW...
Well, what are you waiting for, Gax? Go get one! I don't want you breaking down on *my* watch.
Poog and I will keep each other company until you get back.
Hmf.
Poog?
Poog!

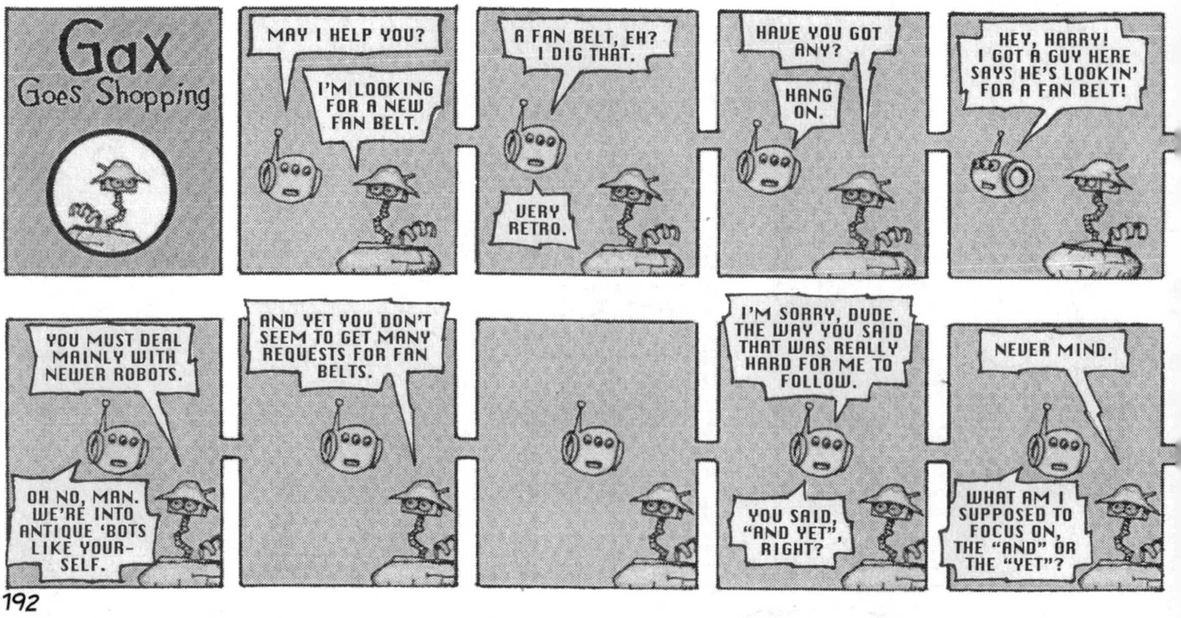
Gax Goes Shopping
MAY I HELP YOU?
I'M LOOKING FOR A NEW FAN BELT.
A FAN BELT, EH? I DIG THAT.
VERY RETRO.
HAVE YOU GOT ANY?
HANG ON.
HEY, HARRY! I GOT A GUY HERE SAYS HE'S LOOKIN' FOR A FAN BELT!
YOU MUST DEAL MAINLY WITH NEWER ROBOTS.
OH NO, MAN. WE'RE INTO ANTIQUE 'BOTS LIKE YOUR-SELF.
AND YET YOU DON'T SEEM TO GET MANY REQUESTS FOR FAN BELTS.
I'M SORRY, DUDE. THE WAY YOU SAID THAT WAS REALLY HARD FOR ME TO FOLLOW.
YOU SAID, "AND YET", RIGHT?
NEVER MIND.
WHAT AM I SUPPOSED TO FOCUS ON, THE "AND" OR THE "YET"?

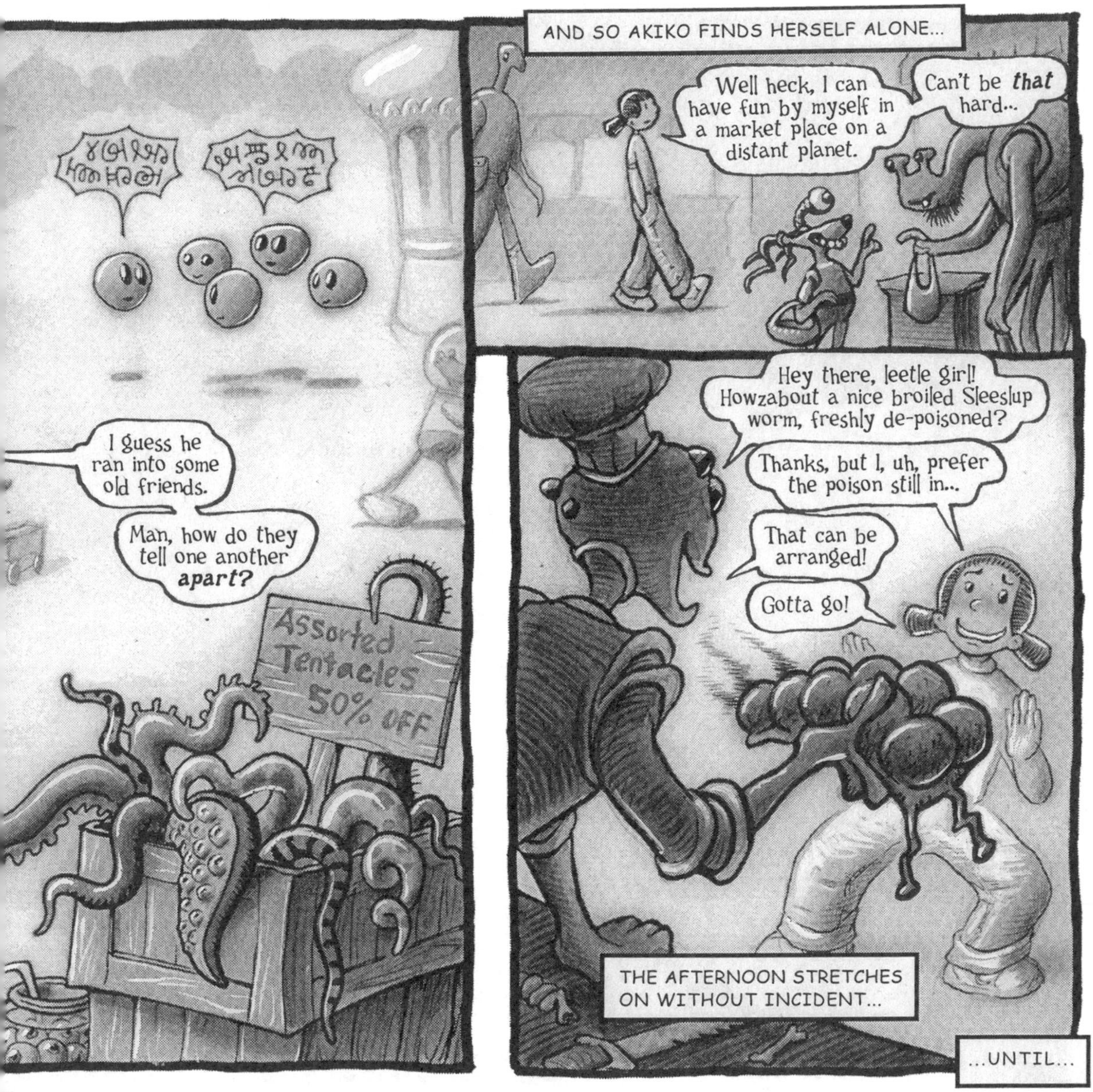
I guess he ran into some old friends.
Man, how do they tell one another *apart?*
Assorted Tentacles 50% OFF
AND SO AKIKO FINDS HERSELF ALONE...
Well heck, I can have fun by myself in a market place on a distant planet.
Can't be *that* hard...
Hey there, leetle girl! Howzabout a nice broiled Sleeslup worm, freshly de-poisoned?
Thanks, but I, uh, prefer the poison still in...
That can be arranged!
Gotta go!
THE AFTERNOON STRETCHES ON WITHOUT INCIDENT...
...UNTIL...

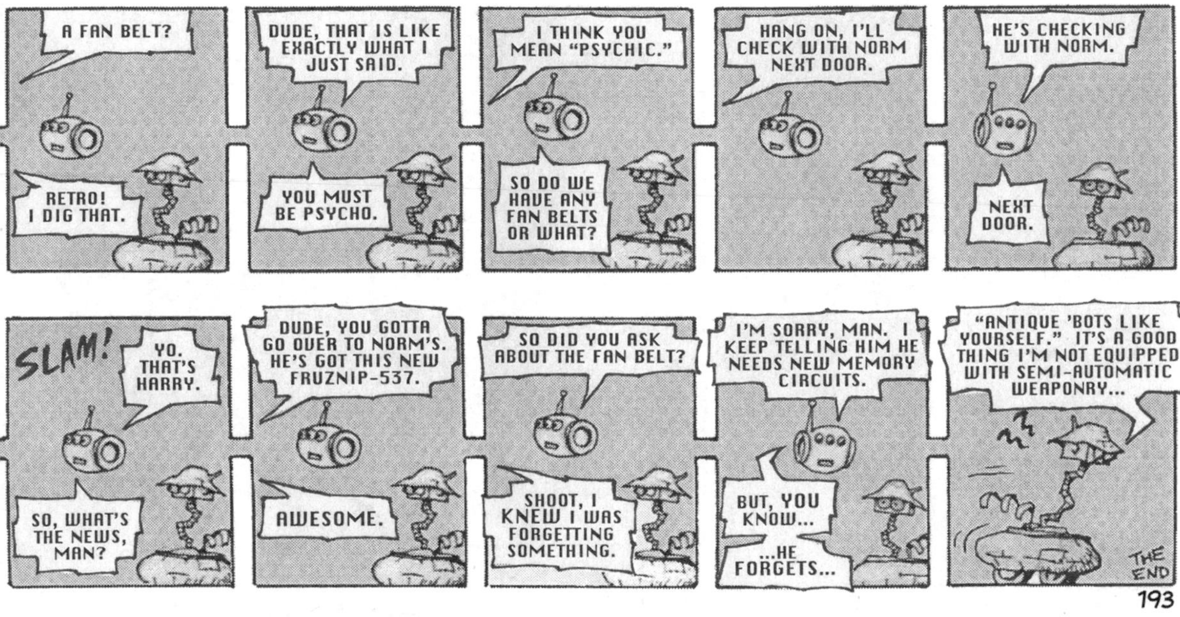
A FAN BELT?
RETRO! I DIG THAT.
DUDE, THAT IS LIKE EXACTLY WHAT I JUST SAID.
YOU MUST BE PSYCHO.
I THINK YOU MEAN "PSYCHIC."
SO DO WE HAVE ANY FAN BELTS OR WHAT?
HANG ON, I'LL CHECK WITH NORM NEXT DOOR.
HE'S CHECKING WITH NORM.
NEXT DOOR.
SLAM!
YO. THAT'S HARRY.
SO, WHAT'S THE NEWS, MAN?
DUDE, YOU GOTTA GO OVER TO NORM'S. HE'S GOT THIS NEW FRUZNIP-537.
AWESOME.
SO DID YOU ASK ABOUT THE FAN BELT?
SHOOT, I KNEW I WAS FORGETTING SOMETHING.
I'M SORRY, MAN. I KEEP TELLING HIM HE NEEDS NEW MEMORY CIRCUITS.
BUT, YOU KNOW...
...HE FORGETS...
"ANTIQUE 'BOTS LIKE YOURSELF." IT'S A GOOD THING I'M NOT EQUIPPED WITH SEMI-AUTOMATIC WEAPONRY...
THE END

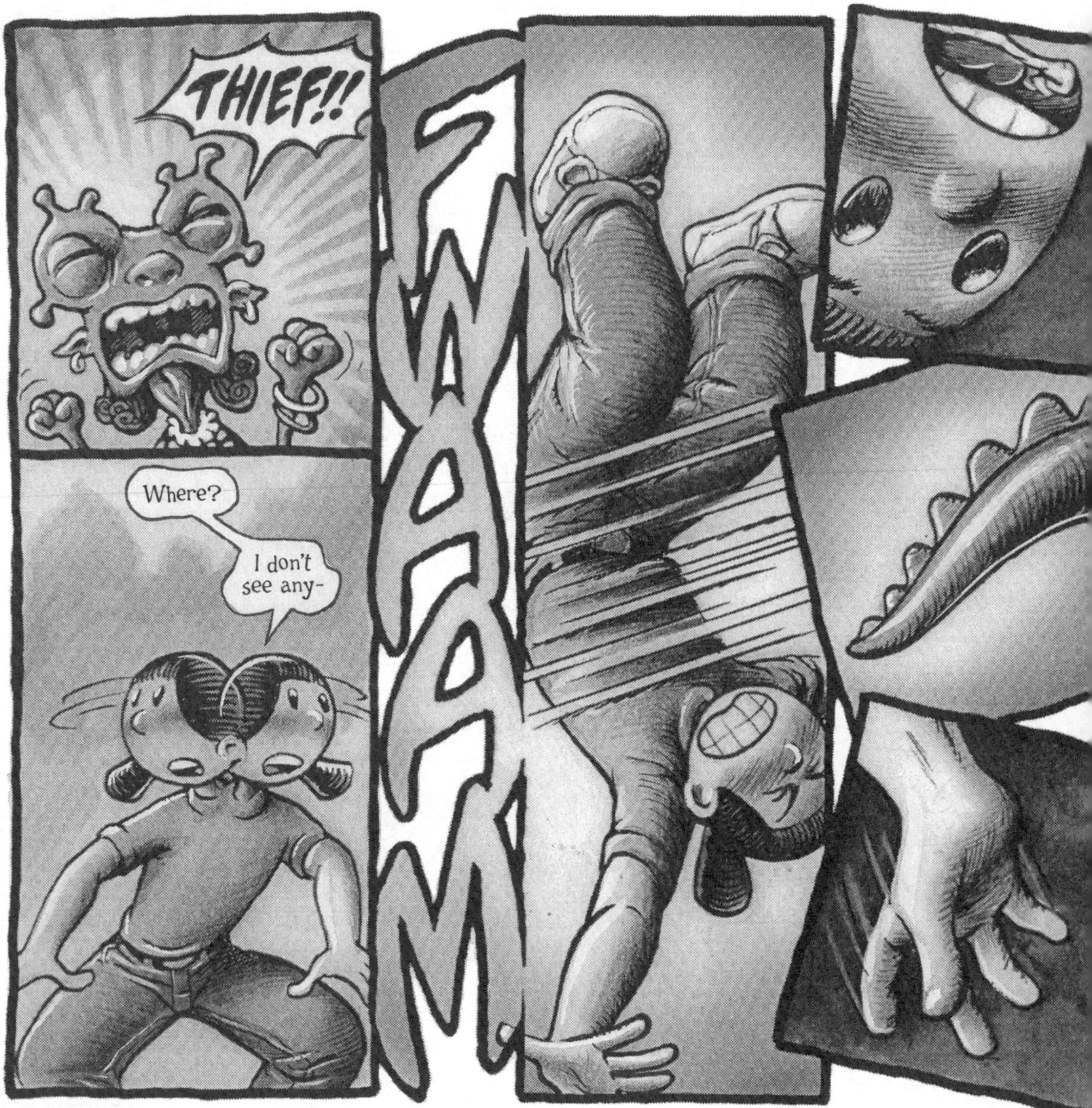
THIEF!!
Where?
I don't see any-

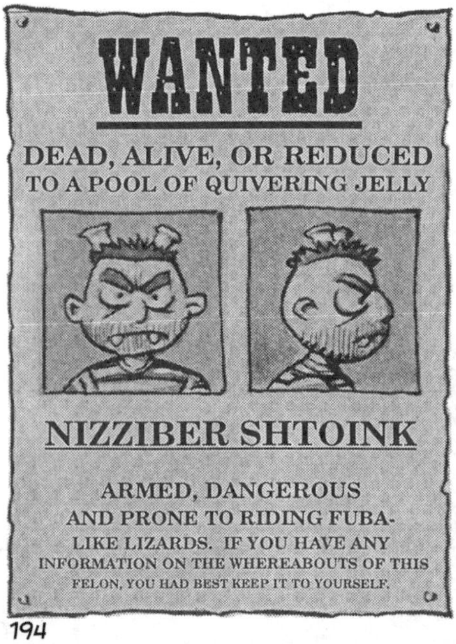
WANTED
DEAD, ALIVE, OR REDUCED TO A POOL OF QUIVERING JELLY
NIZZIBER SHTOINK
ARMED, DANGEROUS AND PRONE TO RIDING FUBA-LIKE LIZARDS. IF YOU HAVE ANY INFORMATION ON THE WHEREABOUTS OF THIS FELON, YOU HAD BEST KEEP IT TO YOURSELF.

A BRIEF HISTORY OF HIS PREVIOUS EXPLOITS:

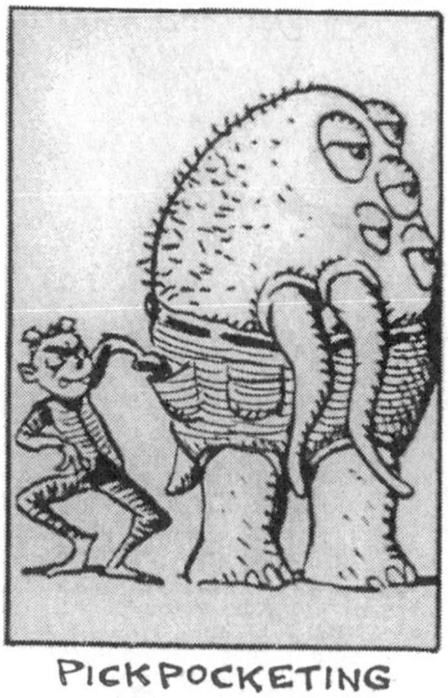

PICKPOCKETING

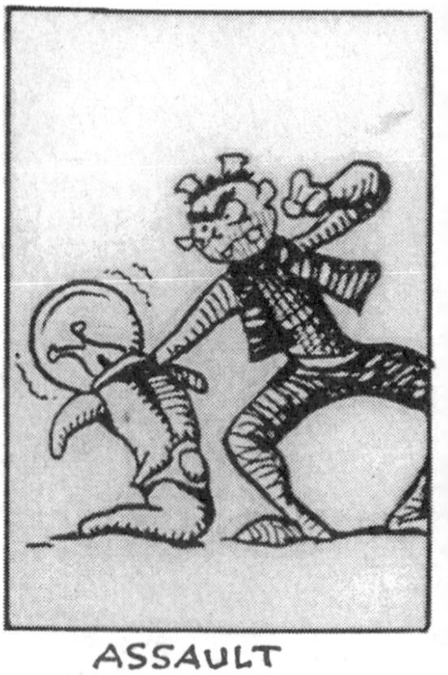

ASSAULT

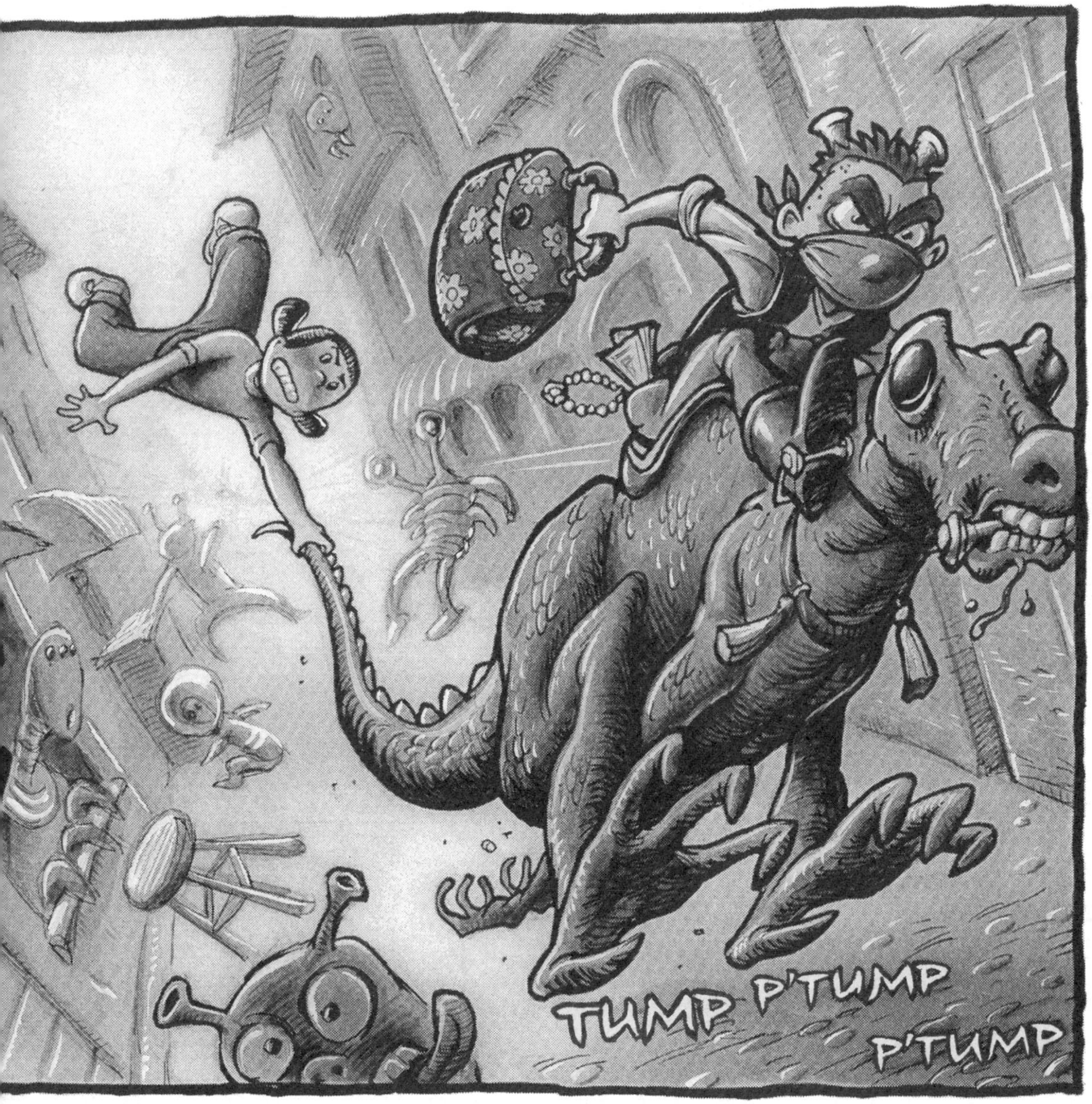

TUMP P'TUMP
P'TUMP

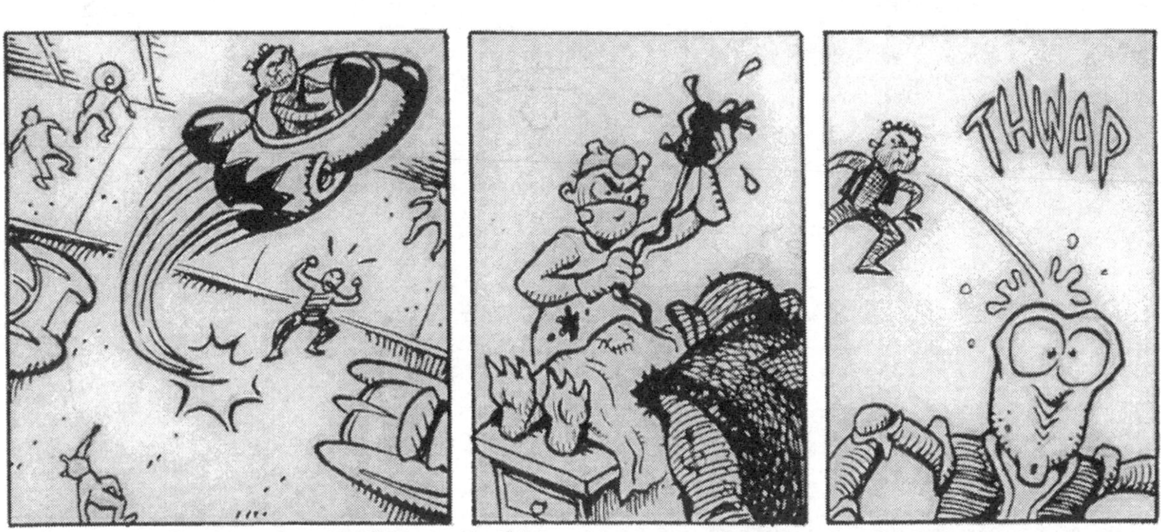

THWAP

GRAND THEFT ROCKET ILLEGAL ORGAN TRANSPLANTS EXCESSIVE SPITTING

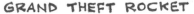

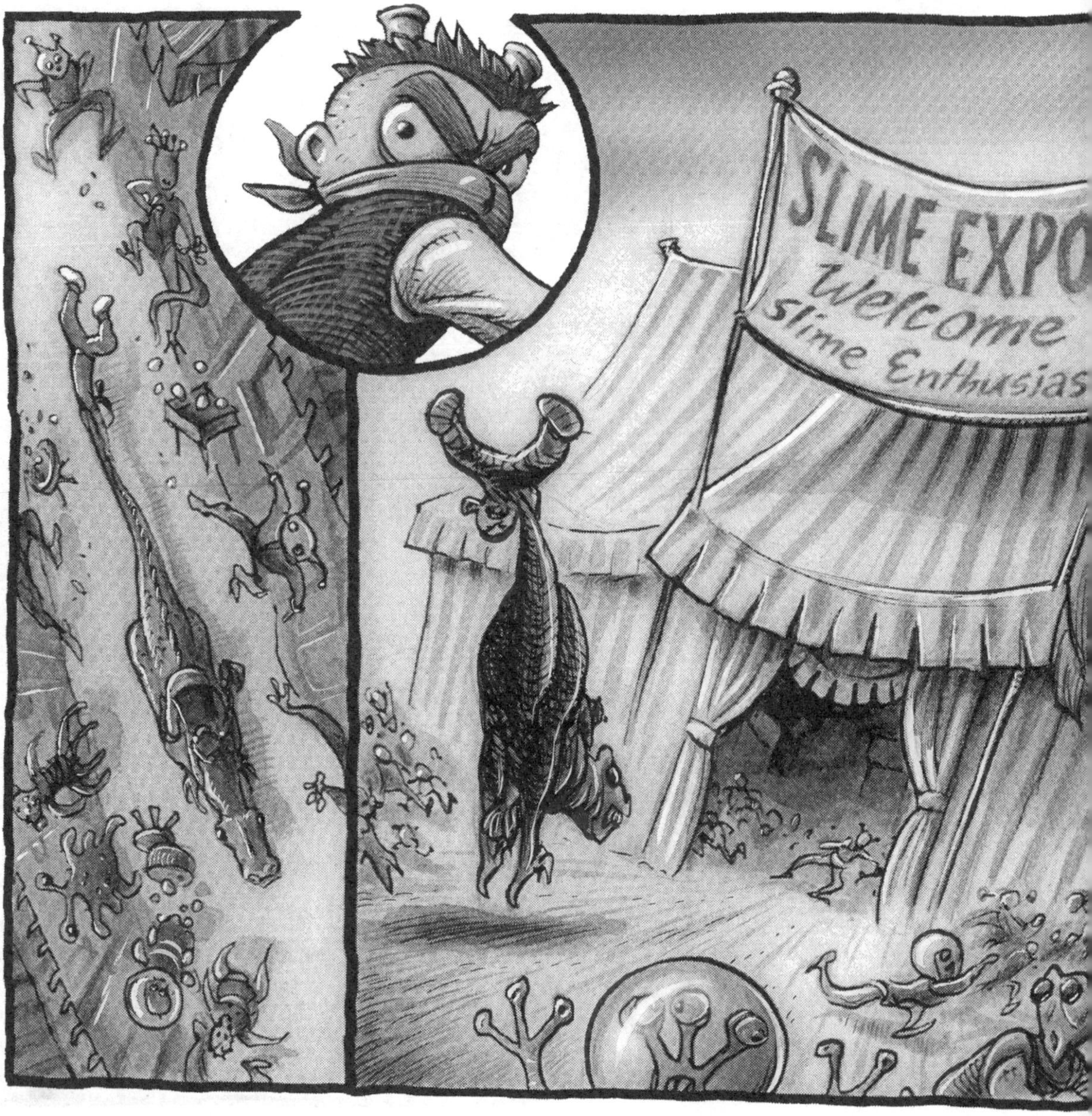
SLIME EXPO
Welcome
slime Enthusias

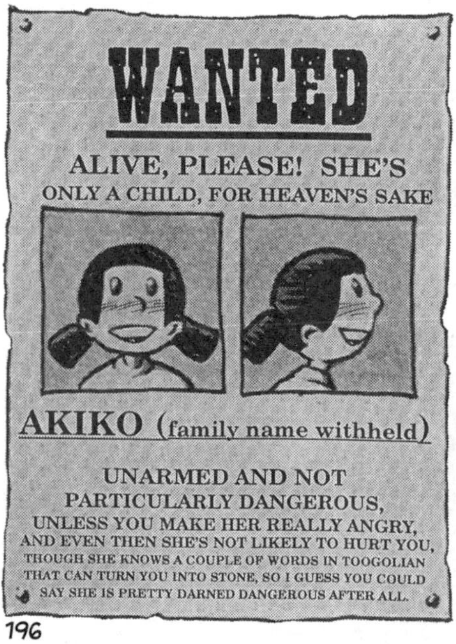
WANTED
ALIVE, PLEASE! SHE'S
ONLY A CHILD, FOR HEAVEN'S SAKE
AKIKO (family name withheld)
UNARMED AND NOT
PARTICULARLY DANGEROUS,
UNLESS YOU MAKE HER REALLY ANGRY,
AND EVEN THEN SHE'S NOT LIKELY TO HURT YOU,
THOUGH SHE KNOWS A COUPLE OF WORDS IN TOOGOLIAN
THAT CAN TURN YOU INTO STONE, SO I GUESS YOU COULD
SAY SHE IS PRETTY DARNED DANGEROUS AFTER ALL.

A BRIEF HISTORY OF HER PREVIOUS EXPLOITS:

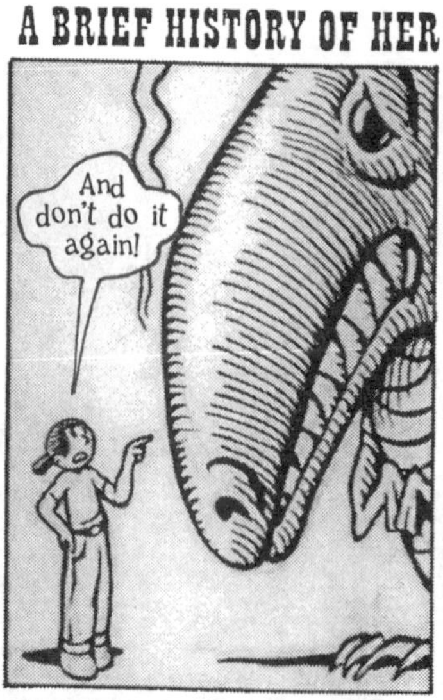
And don't do it again!

SCOLDING JAGGASAURS

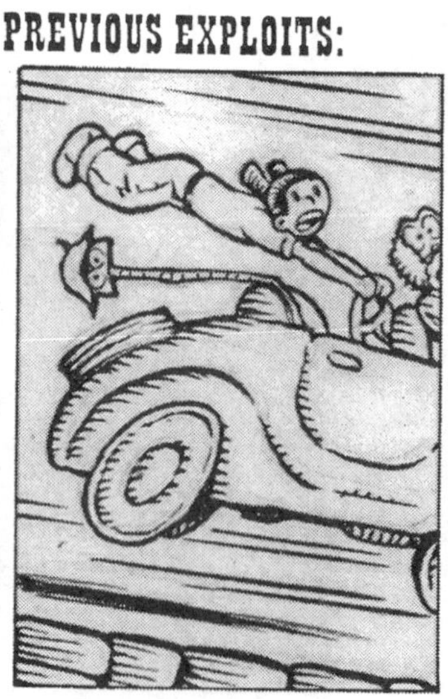

BACKSEAT DRIVING

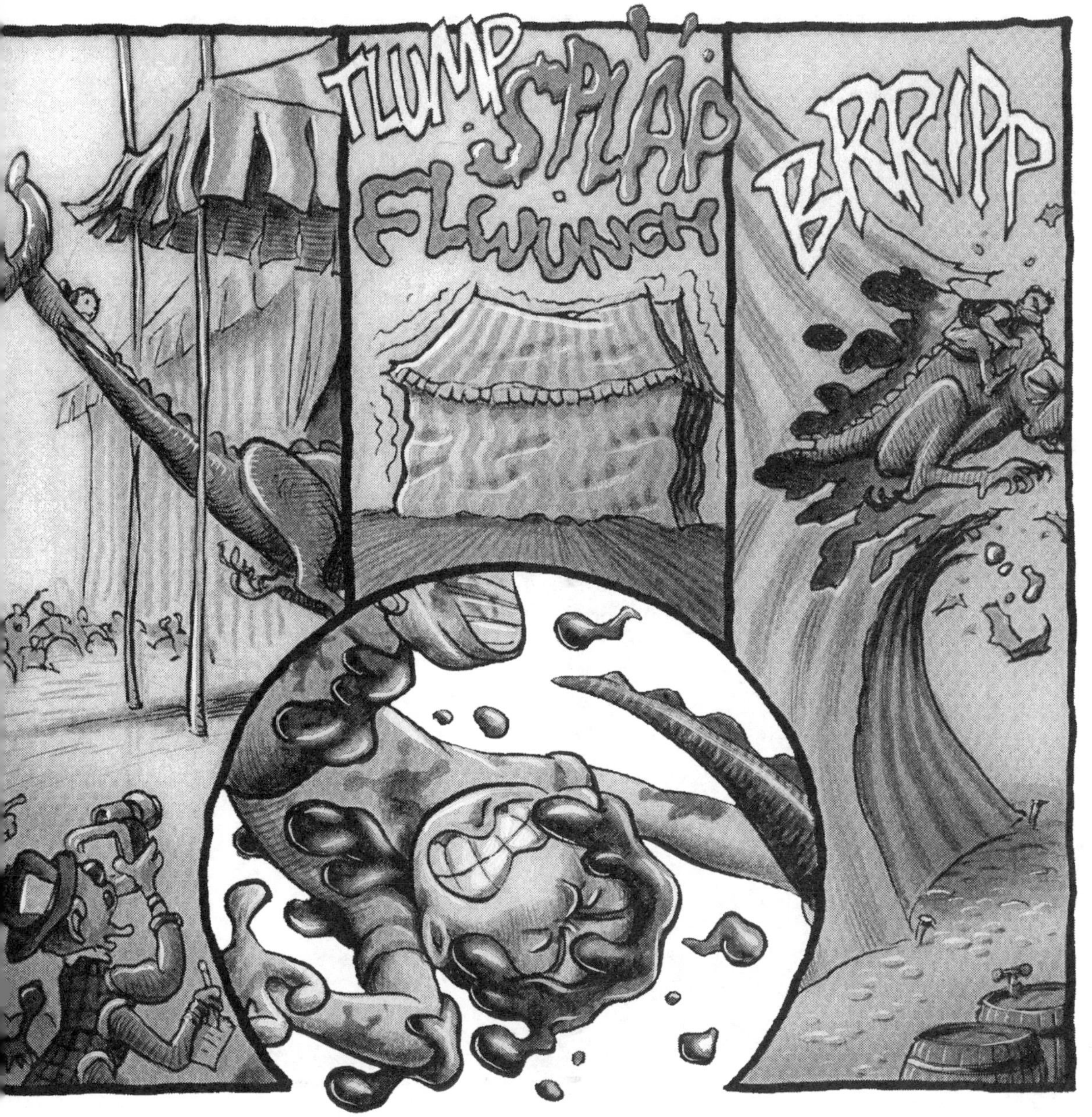
TLUMP
SPLAP
FLWUNCH
BRRIPP

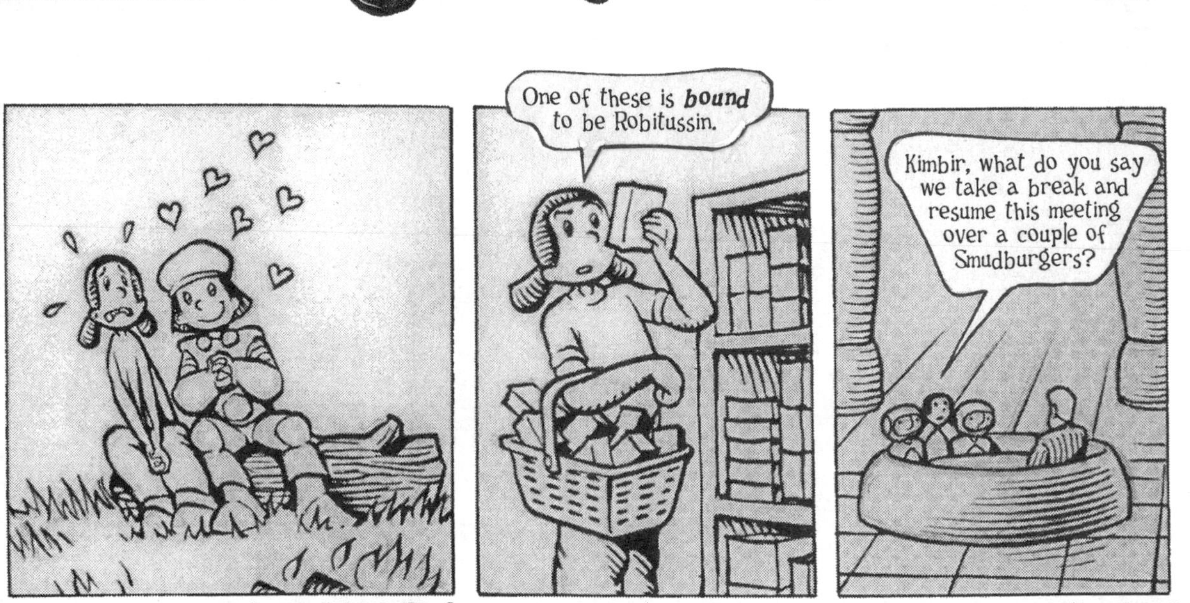
One of these is ***bound*** to be Robitussin.
Kimbir, what do you say we take a break and resume this meeting over a couple of Smudburgers?

TURNING DOWN MARRIAGE PROPOSALS   SHOPPING IN JAPAN   CLINCHING DEALS IN OUTER SPACE

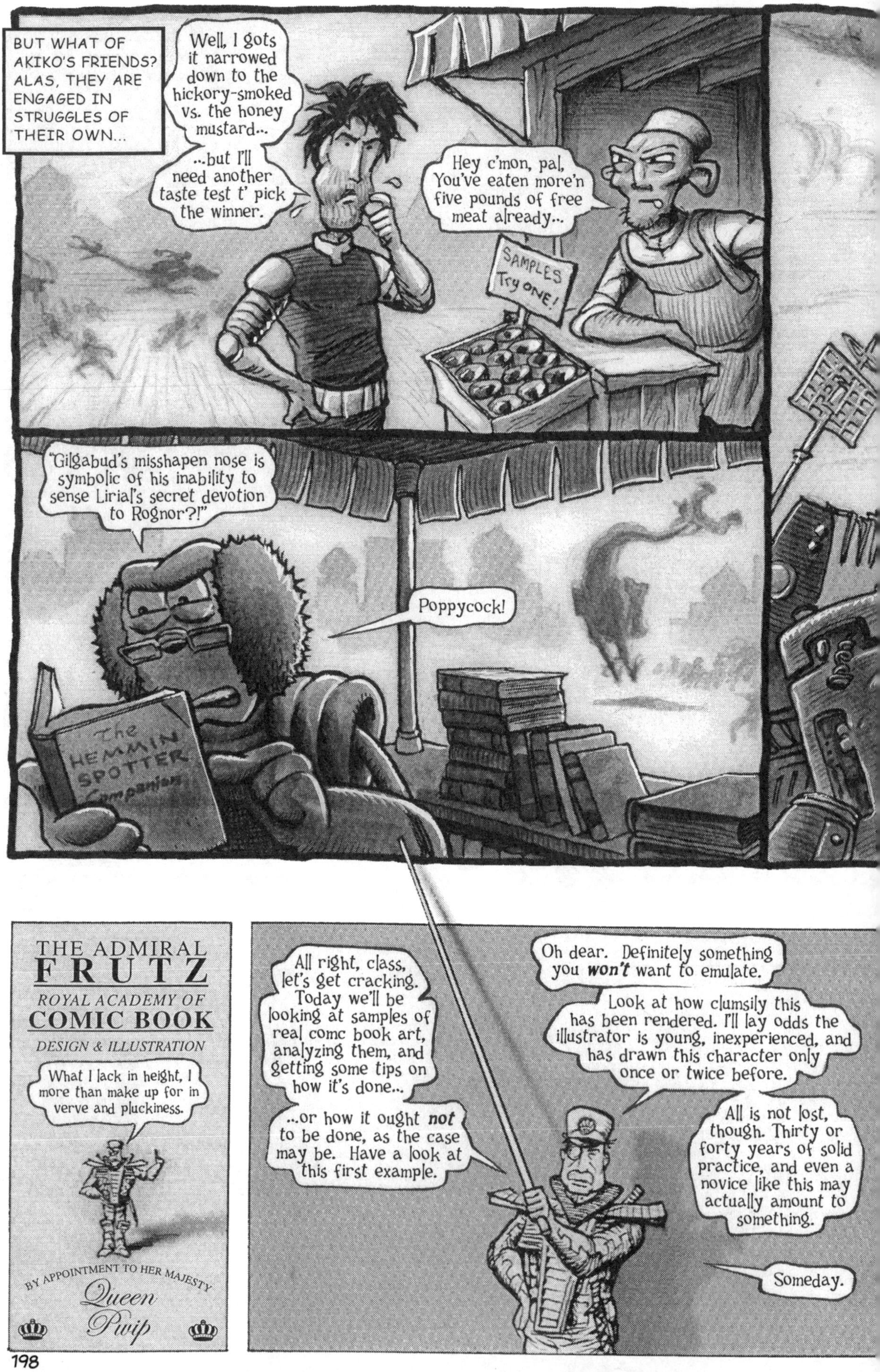
BUT WHAT OF AKIKO'S FRIENDS? ALAS, THEY ARE ENGAGED IN STRUGGLES OF THEIR OWN...
Well, I gots it narrowed down to the hickory-smoked vs. the honey mustard...
...but I'll need another taste test t' pick the winner.
Hey c'mon, pal, You've eaten more'n five pounds of free meat already...
SAMPLES Try ONE!
"Gilgabud's misshapen nose is symbolic of his inability to sense Lirial's secret devotion to Rognor?!"
Poppycock!
The HEMMIN SPOTTER Companion
THE ADMIRAL FRUTZ ROYAL ACADEMY OF COMIC BOOK DESIGN & ILLUSTRATION
What I lack in height, I more than make up for in verve and pluckiness.
BY APPOINTMENT TO HER MAJESTY Queen Pwip
All right, class, let's get cracking. Today we'll be looking at samples of real comc book art, analyzing them, and getting some tips on how it's done...
...or how it ought *not* to be done, as the case may be. Have a look at this first example.
Oh dear. Definitely something you *won't* want to emulate.
Look at how clumsily this has been rendered. I'll lay odds the illustrator is young, inexperienced, and has drawn this character only once or twice before.
All is not lost, though. Thirty or forty years of solid practice, and even a novice like this may actually amount to something.
Someday.

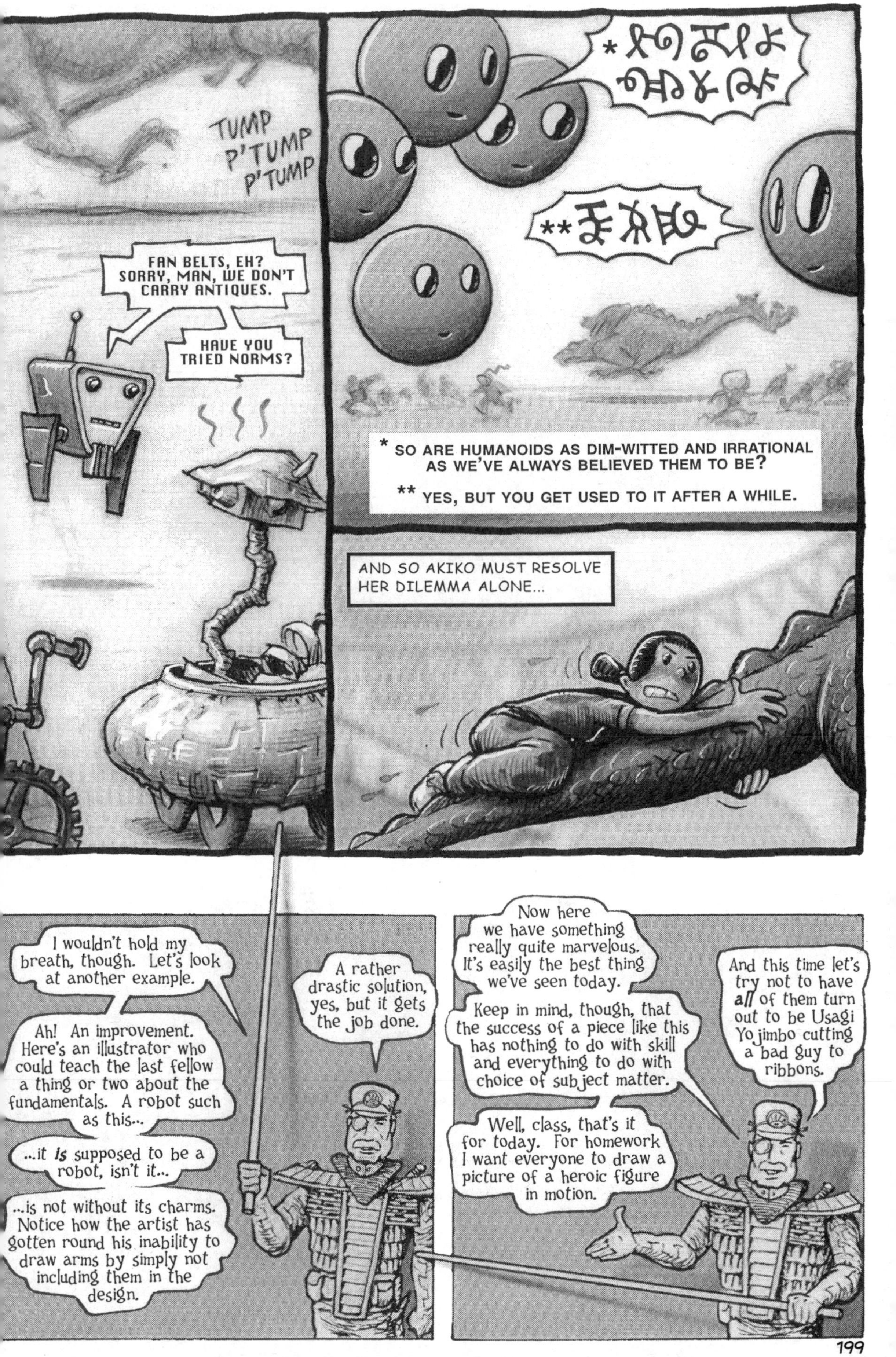
TUMP P'TUMP P'TUMP
FAN BELTS, EH? SORRY, MAN, WE DON'T CARRY ANTIQUES.
HAVE YOU TRIED NORMS?
* SO ARE HUMANOIDS AS DIM-WITTED AND IRRATIONAL AS WE'VE ALWAYS BELIEVED THEM TO BE?
** YES, BUT YOU GET USED TO IT AFTER A WHILE.
AND SO AKIKO MUST RESOLVE HER DILEMMA ALONE...
I wouldn't hold my breath, though. Let's look at another example.
Ah! An improvement. Here's an illustrator who could teach the last fellow a thing or two about the fundamentals. A robot such as this...
...it *is* supposed to be a robot, isn't it...
...is not without its charms. Notice how the artist has gotten round his inability to draw arms by simply not including them in the design.
A rather drastic solution, yes, but it gets the job done.
Now here we have something really quite marvelous. It's easily the best thing we've seen today.
Keep in mind, though, that the success of a piece like this has nothing to do with skill and everything to do with choice of subject matter.
Well, class, that's it for today. For homework I want everyone to draw a picture of a heroic figure in motion.
And this time let's try not to have *all* of them turn out to be Usagi Yojimbo cutting a bad guy to ribbons.

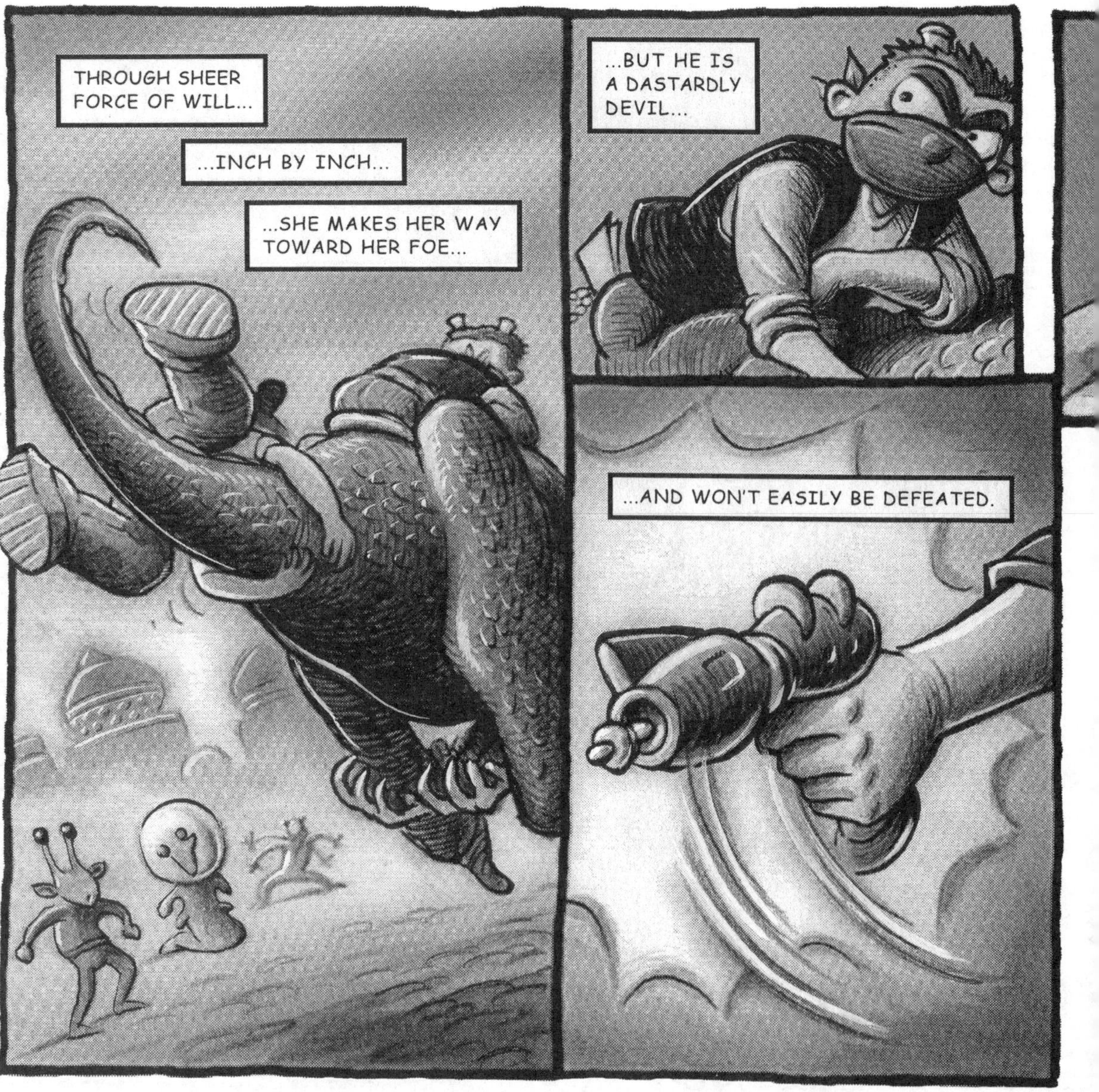
THROUGH SHEER FORCE OF WILL...
...INCH BY INCH...
...SHE MAKES HER WAY TOWARD HER FOE...
...BUT HE IS A DASTARDLY DEVIL...
...AND WON'T EASILY BE DEFEATED.

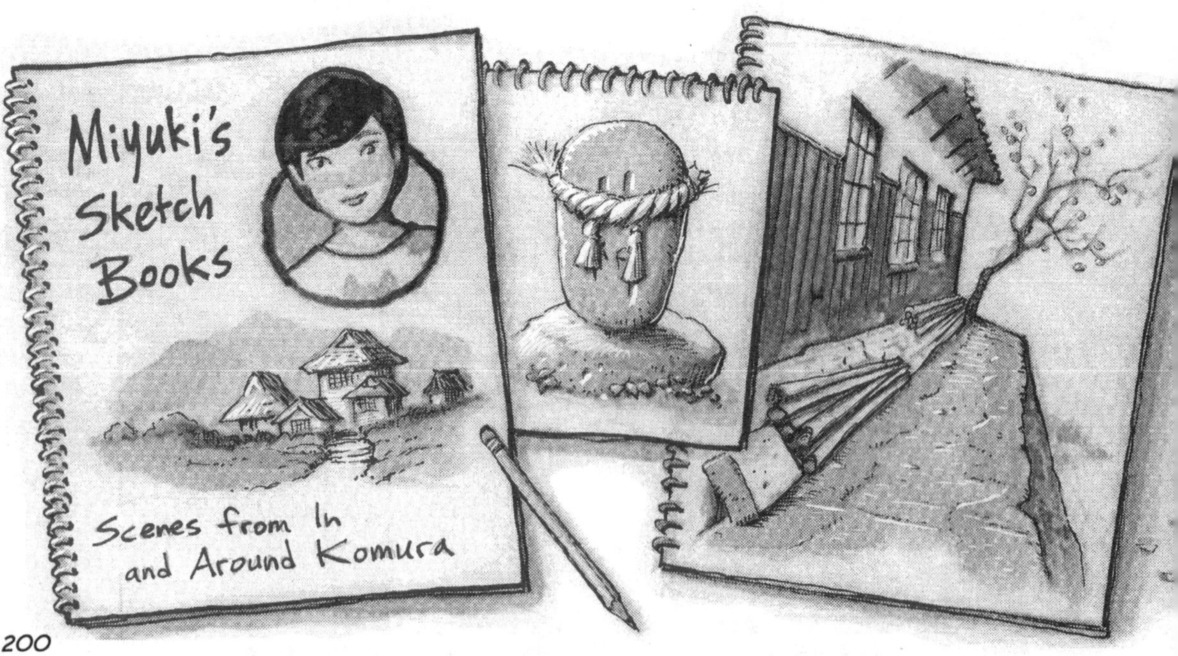
Miyuki's Sketch Books
Scenes from In and Around Komura

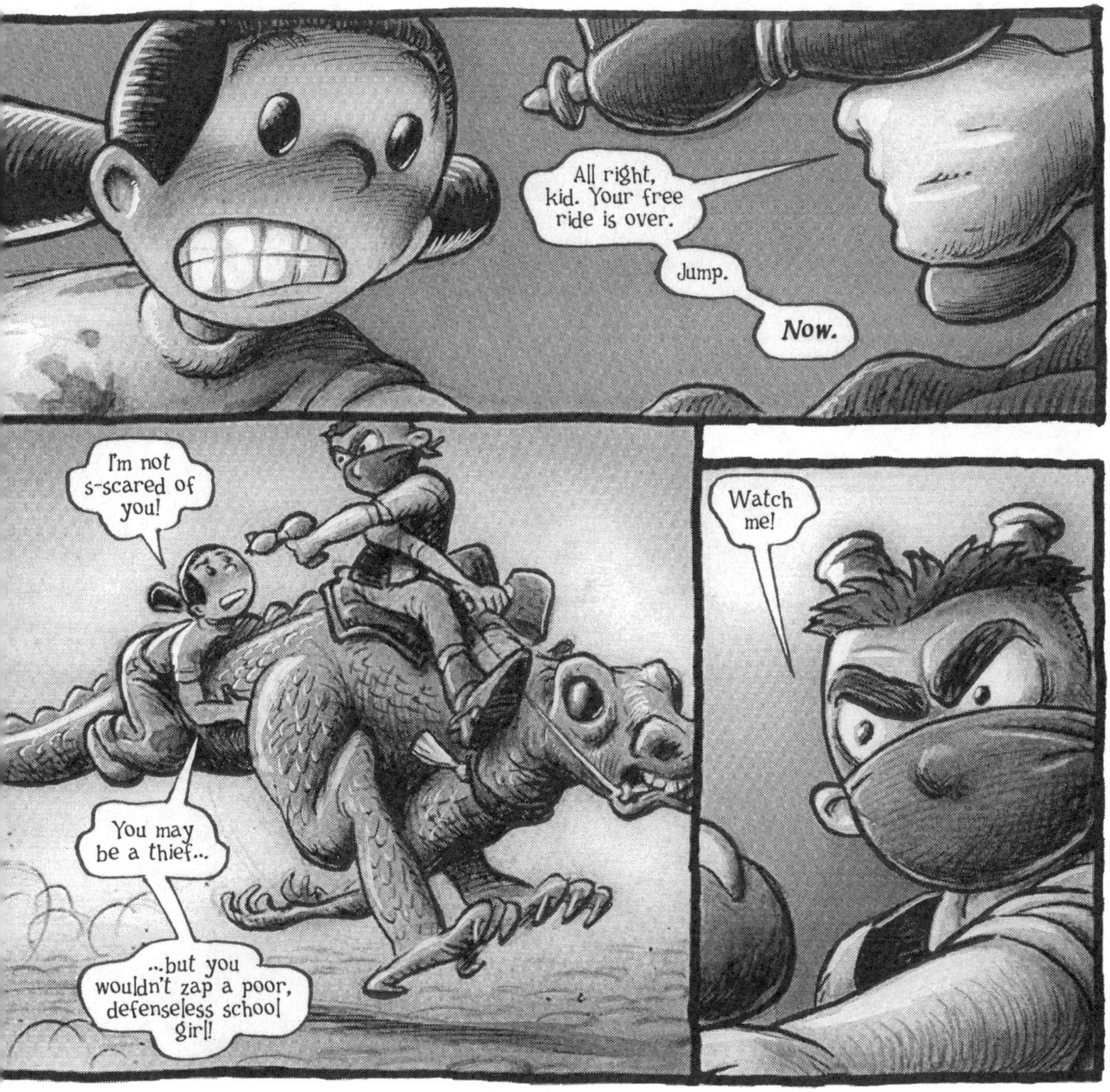
All right, kid. Your free ride is over.
Jump.
Now.
I'm not s-scared of you!
You may be a thief...
...but you wouldn't zap a poor, defenseless school girl!
Watch me!

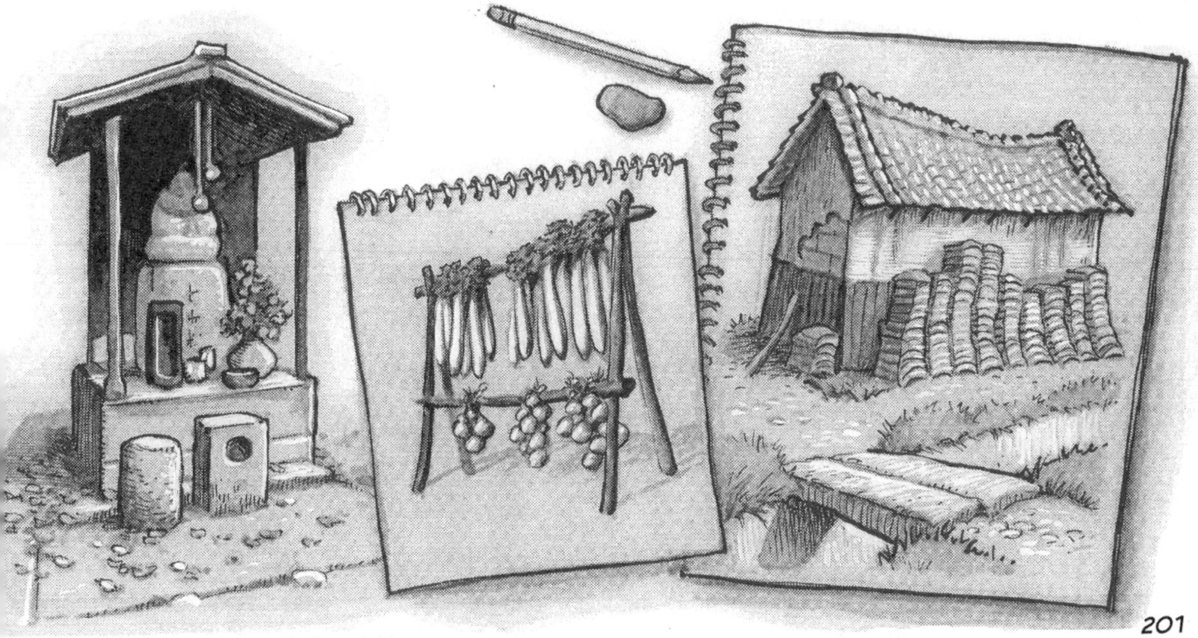

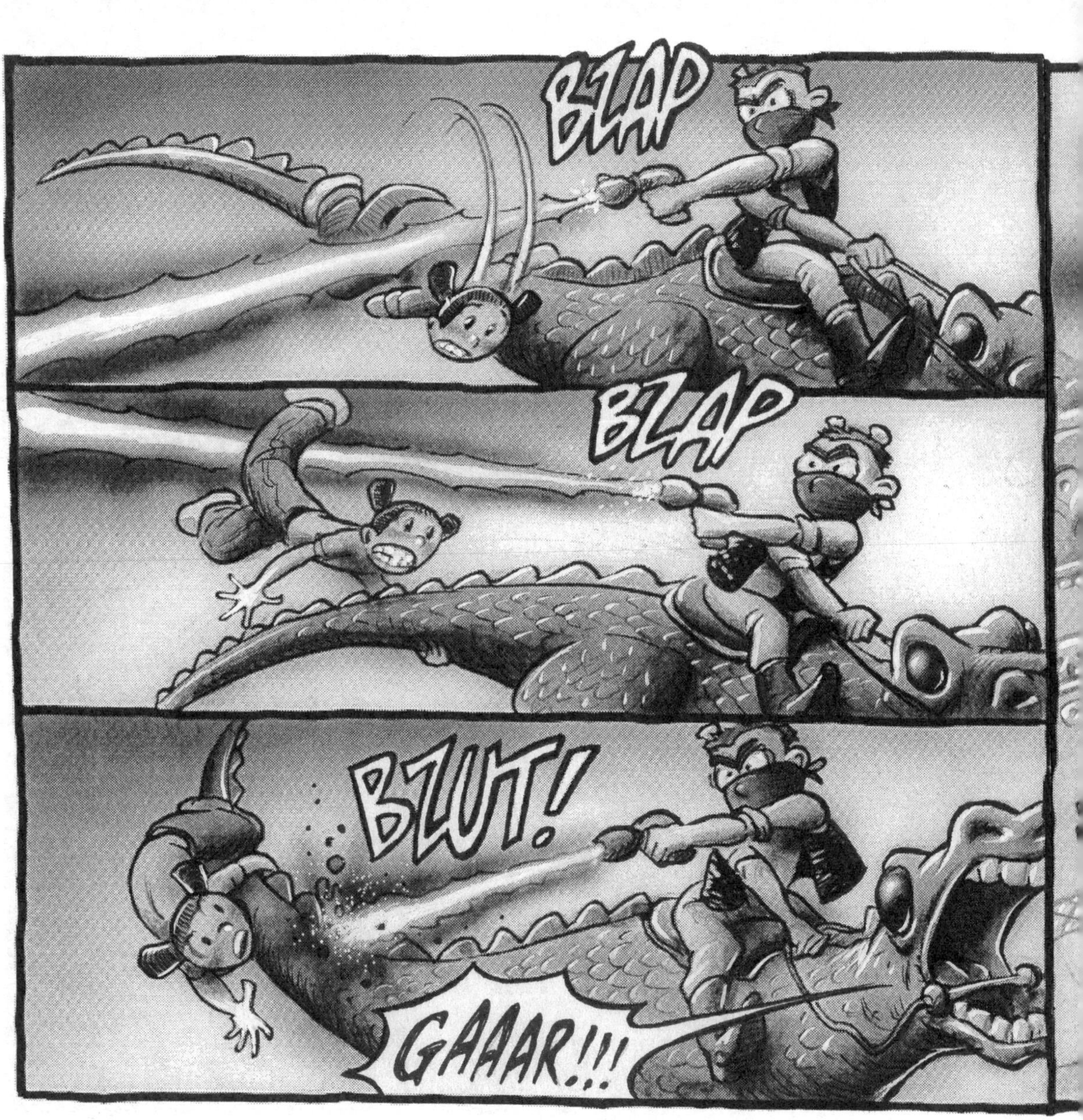
BZAP
BZAP
BZUT!
GAAAR!!!

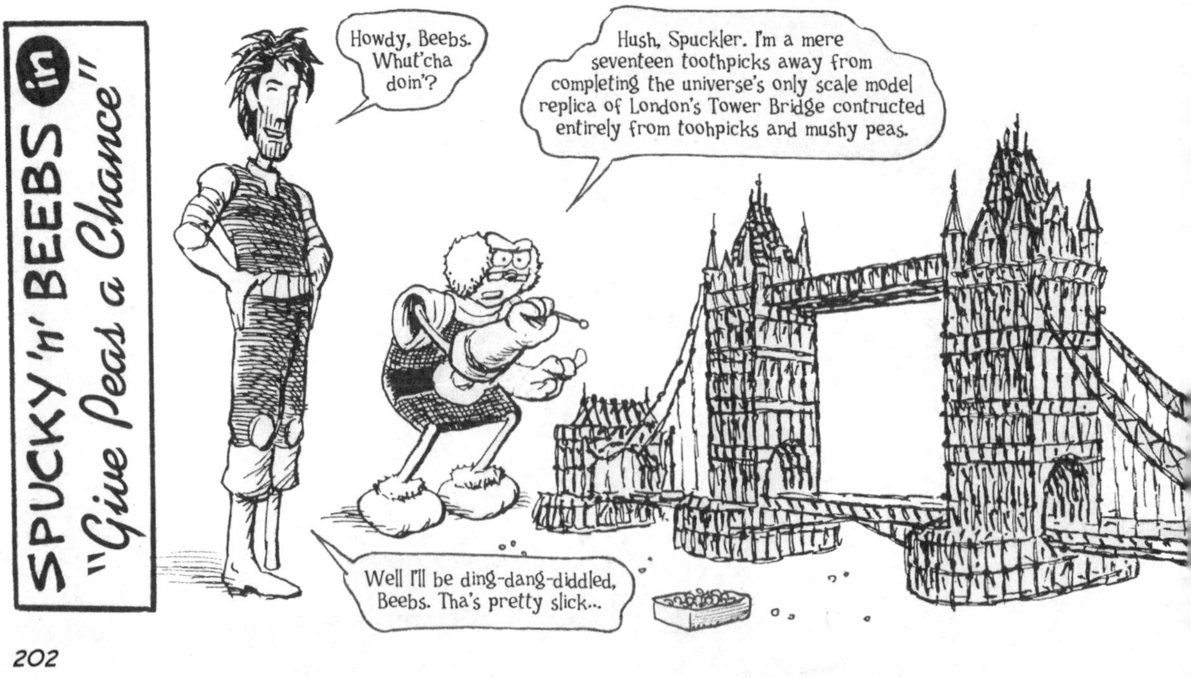
SPUCKY 'n' BEEBS in "Give Peas a Chance"
Howdy, Beebs. Whut'cha doin'?
Hush, Spuckler. I'm a mere seventeen toothpicks away from completing the universe's only scale model replica of London's Tower Bridge contructed entirely from toohpicks and mushy peas.
Well I'll be ding-dang-diddled, Beebs. Tha's pretty slick...

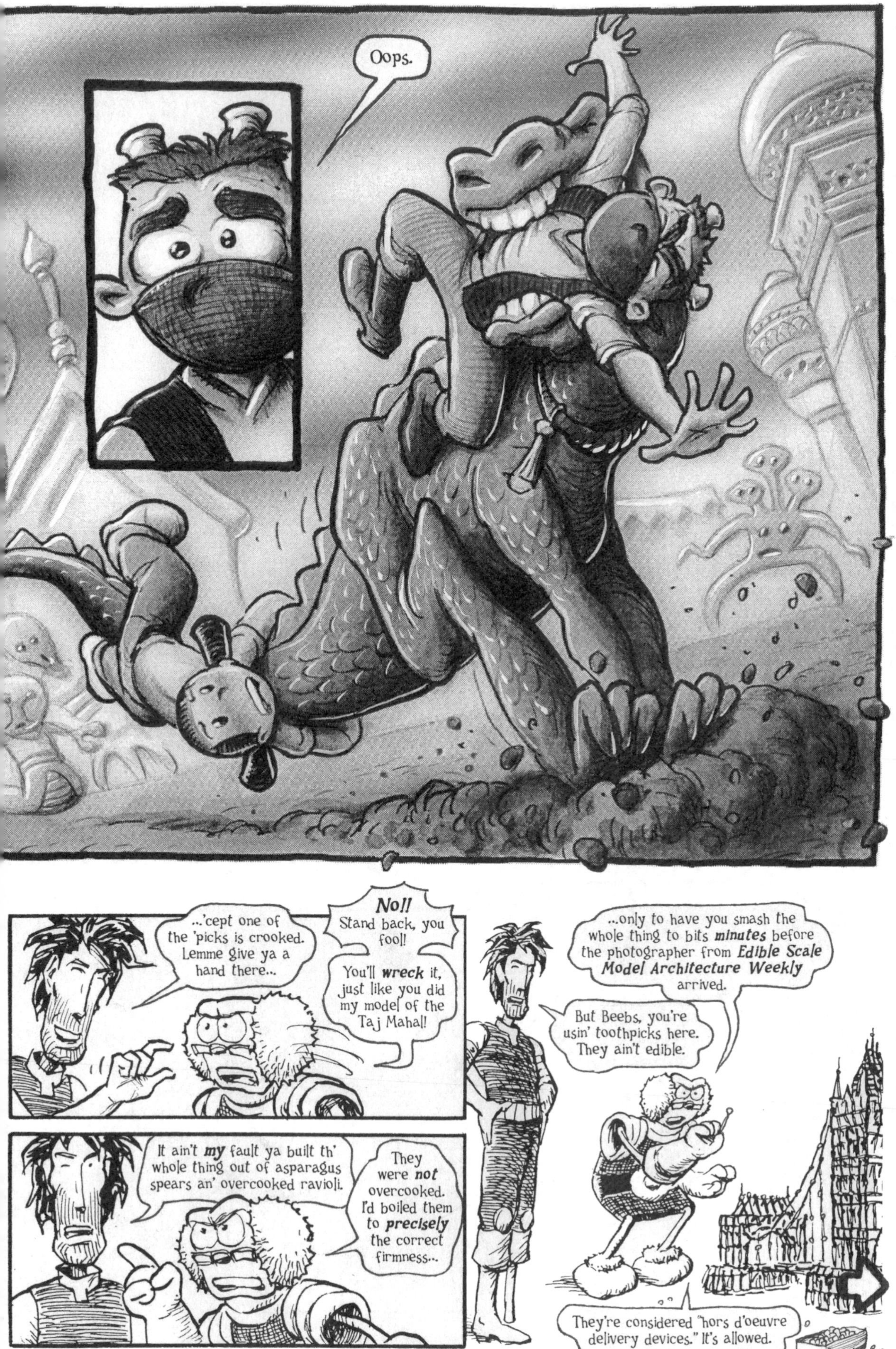
Oops.
...'cept one of the 'picks is crooked. Lemme give ya a hand there...
No!! Stand back, you fool!
You'll wreck it, just like you did my model of the Taj Mahal!
It ain't my fault ya built th' whole thing out of asparagus spears an' overcooked ravioli.
They were not overcooked. I'd boiled them to precisely the correct firmness...
...only to have you smash the whole thing to bits minutes before the photographer from Edible Scale Model Architecture Weekly arrived.
But Beebs, you're usin' toothpicks here. They ain't edible.
They're considered "hors d'oeuvre delivery devices." It's allowed.

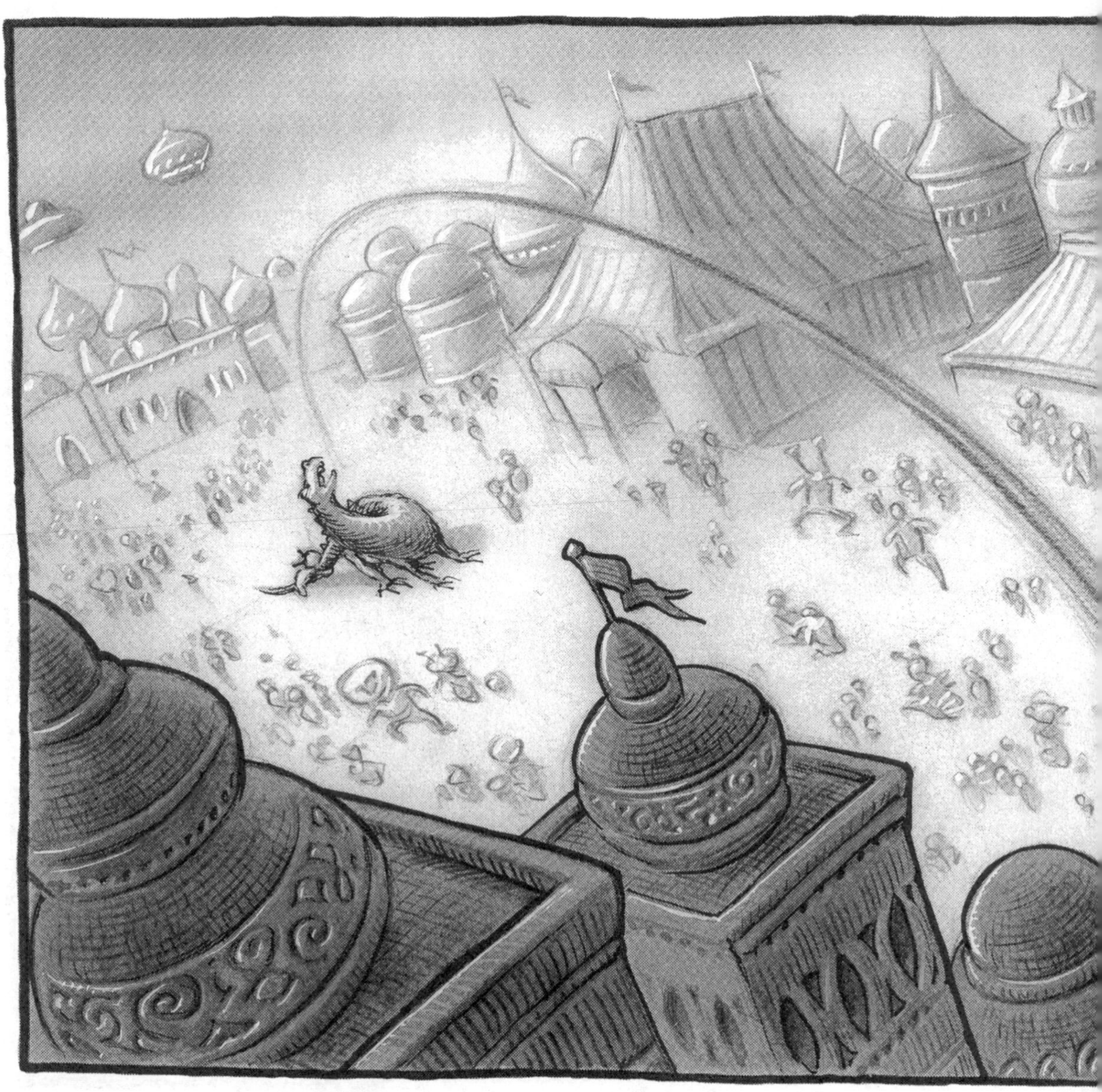

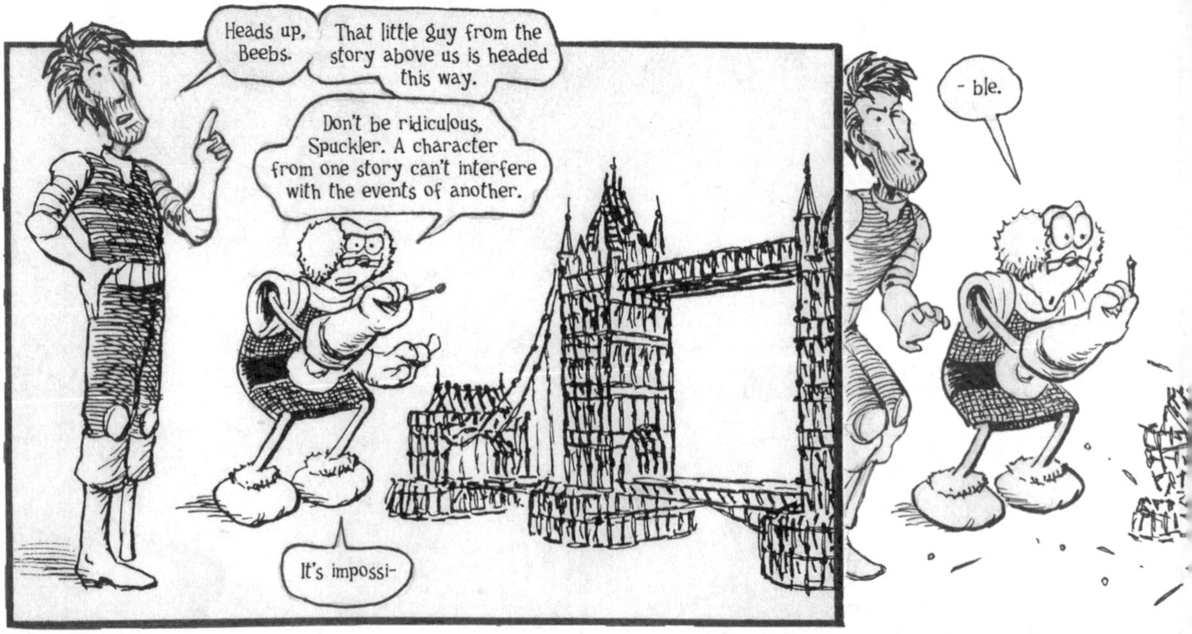
Heads up, Beebs.
That little guy from the story above us is headed this way.
Don't be ridiculous, Spuckler. A character from one story can't interfere with the events of another.
It's impossi-
- ble.

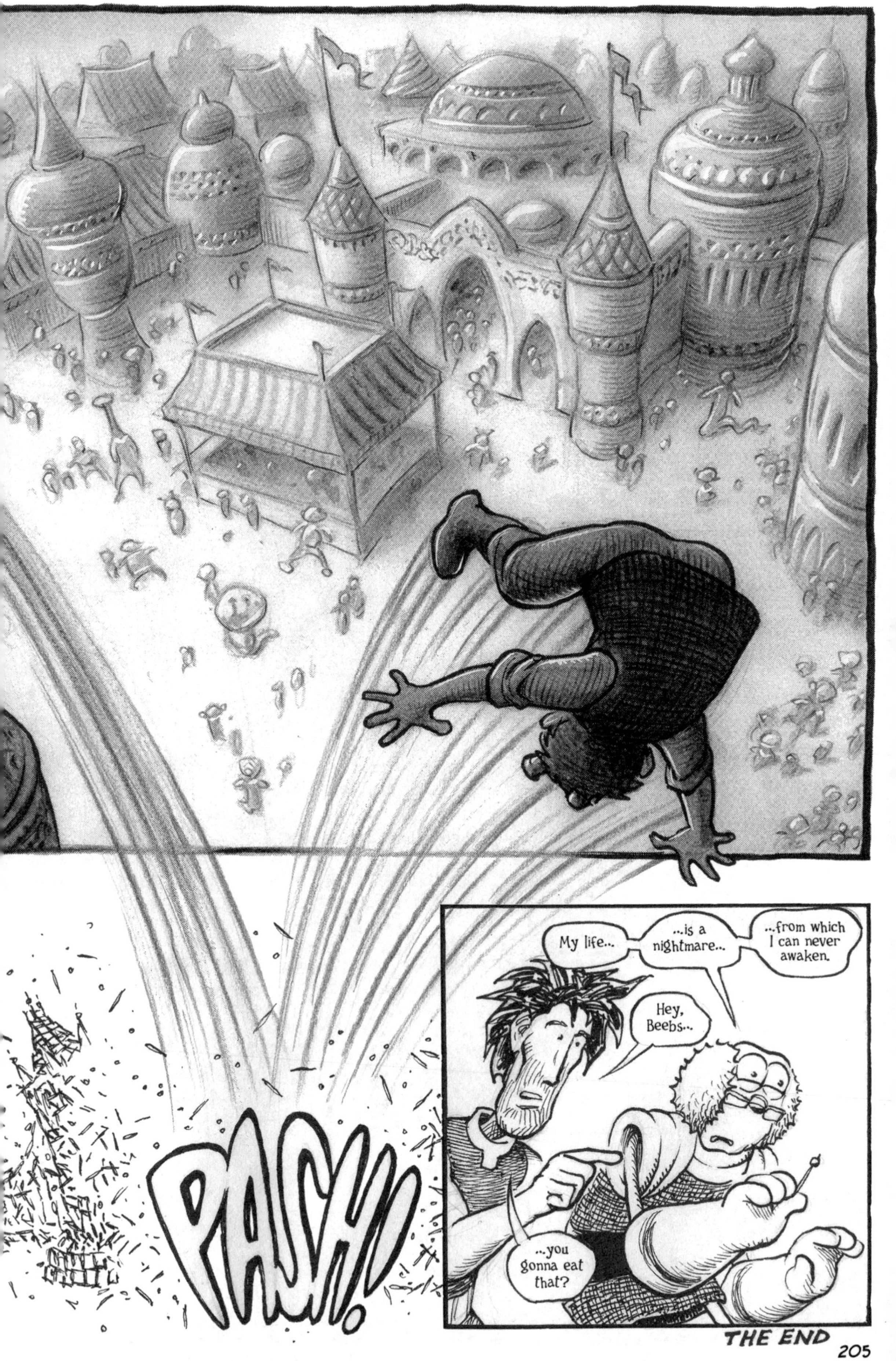
PASH!
My life...
...is a nightmare...
...from which I can never awaken.
Hey, Beebs...
...you gonna eat that?

THE END

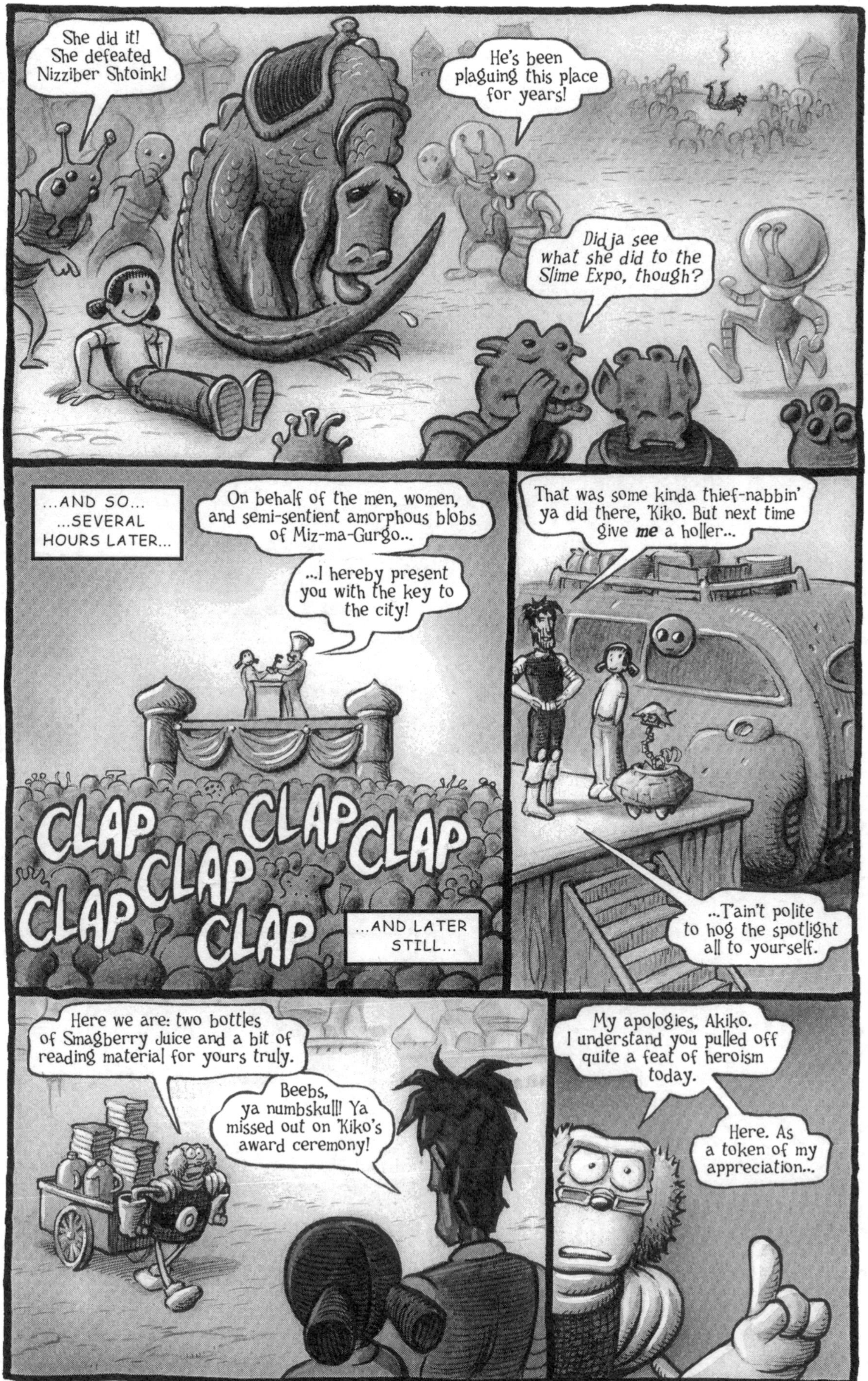
She did it! She defeated Nizziber Shtoink!
He's been plaguing this place for years!
Didja see what she did to the Slime Expo, though?
...AND SO... ...SEVERAL HOURS LATER...
On behalf of the men, women, and semi-sentient amorphous blobs of Miz-ma-Gurgo...
...I hereby present you with the key to the city!
CLAP CLAP CLAP CLAP CLAP CLAP
...AND LATER STILL...
That was some kinda thief-nabbin' ya did there, 'Kiko. But next time give **me** a holler...
...T'ain't polite to hog the spotlight all to yourself.
Here we are: two bottles of Smagberry Juice and a bit of reading material for yours truly.
Beebs, ya numbskull! Ya missed out on 'Kiko's award ceremony!
My apologies, Akiko. I understand you pulled off quite a feat of heroism today.
Here. As a token of my appreciation...

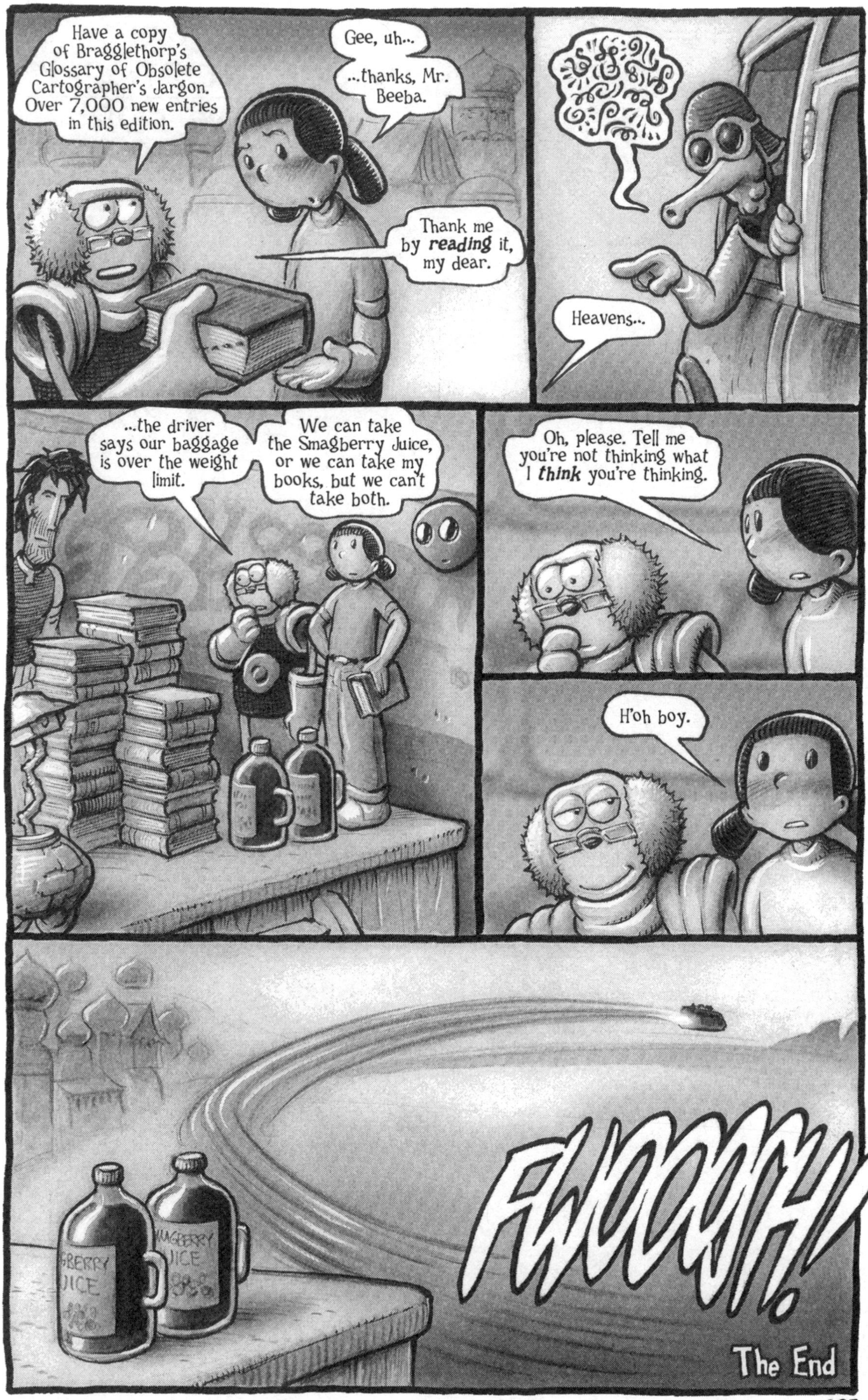
Have a copy of Braggléthorp's Glossary of Obsolete Cartographer's Jargon. Over 7,000 new entries in this edition.
Gee, uh...
...thanks, Mr. Beeba.
Thank me by **reading** it, my dear.
Heavens...
...the driver says our baggage is over the weight limit.
We can take the Smagberry Juice, or we can take my books, but we can't take both.
Oh, please. Tell me you're not thinking what I **think** you're thinking.
H'oh boy.
FWOOOOSH!
The End

Akiko

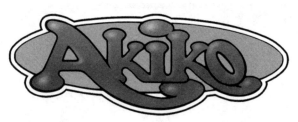

AKIKO & PRINCE FROPTOPPIT

DESIGNS FOR ANIMATED SERIES

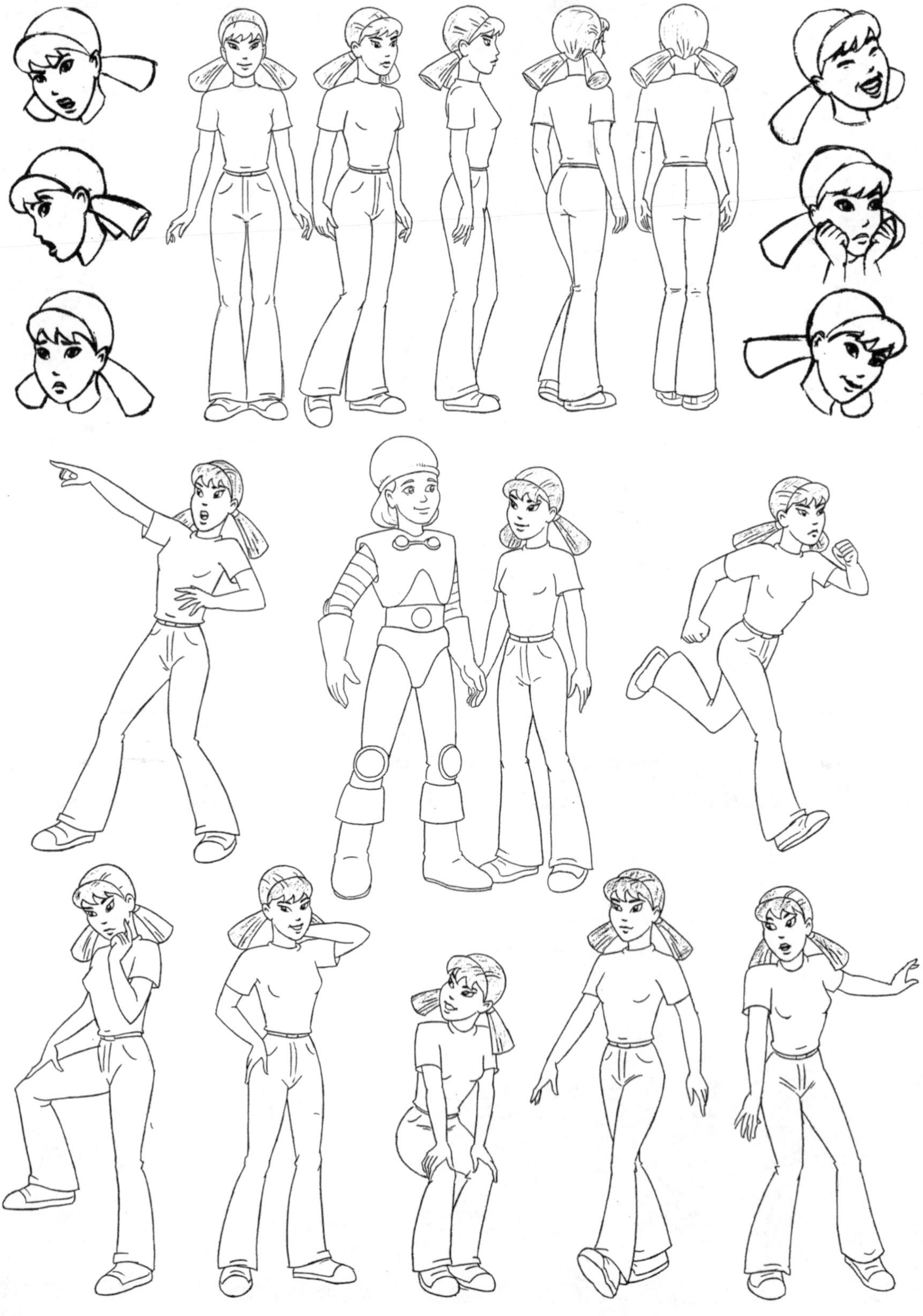

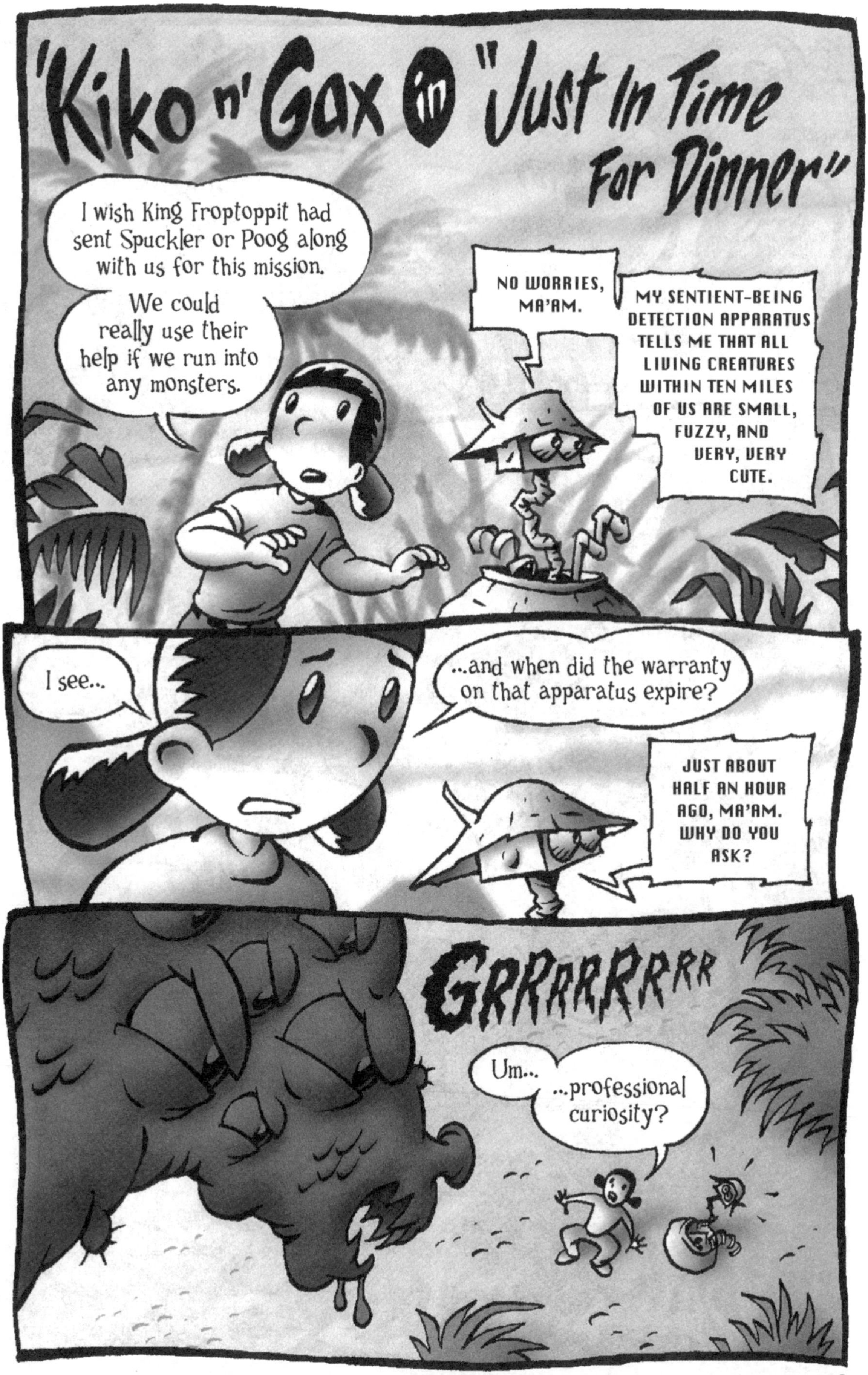

'Kiko n' Gax in "Just In Time For Dinner"
I wish King Froptoppit had sent Spuckler or Poog along with us for this mission.
We could really use their help if we run into any monsters.
NO WORRIES, MA'AM.
MY SENTIENT-BEING DETECTION APPARATUS TELLS ME THAT ALL LIVING CREATURES WITHIN TEN MILES OF US ARE SMALL, FUZZY, AND VERY, VERY CUTE.
I see...
...and when did the warranty on that apparatus expire?
JUST ABOUT HALF AN HOUR AGO, MA'AM. WHY DO YOU ASK?
GRRRRRRRR
Um...
...professional curiosity?

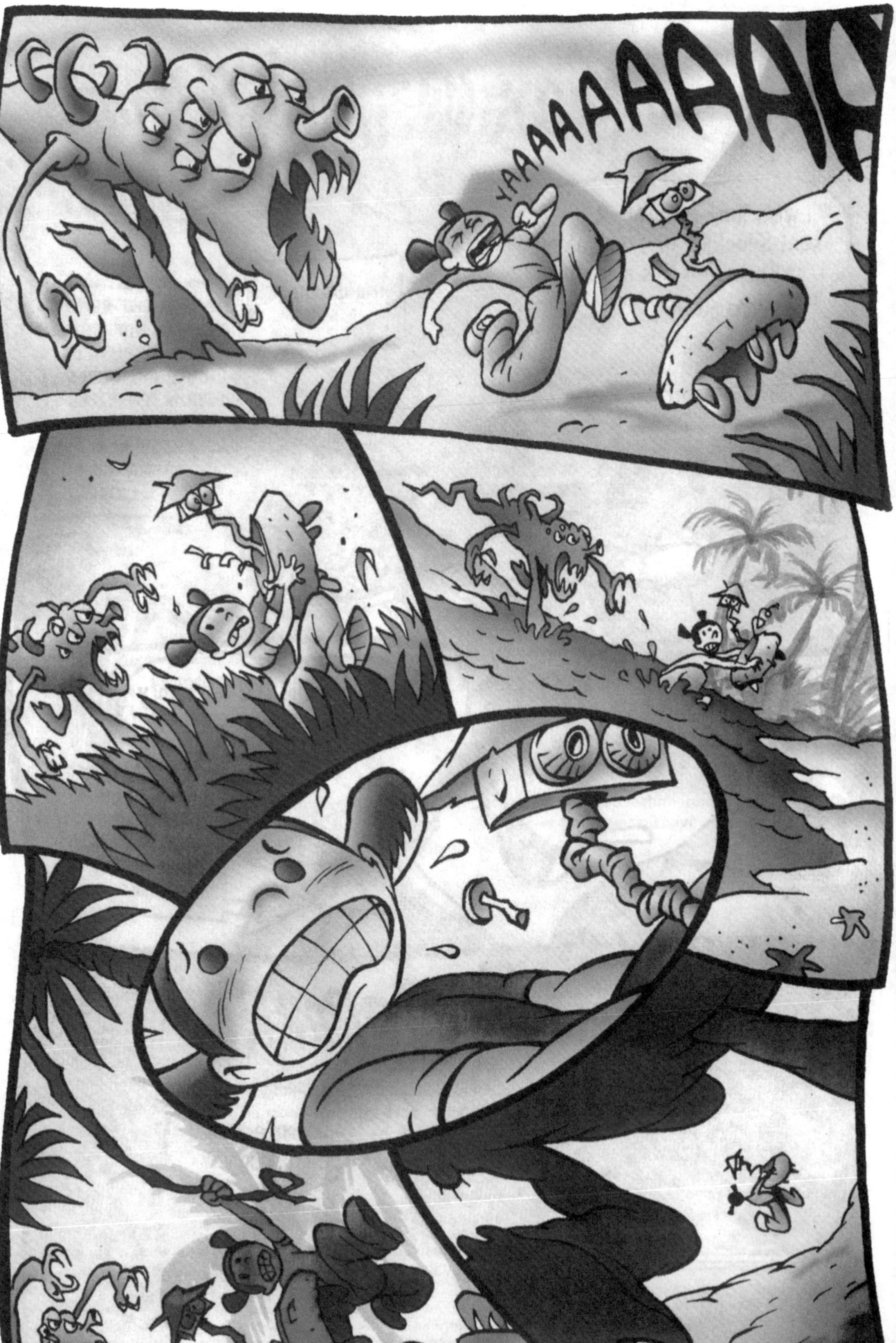
YAAAAAAAAAAA

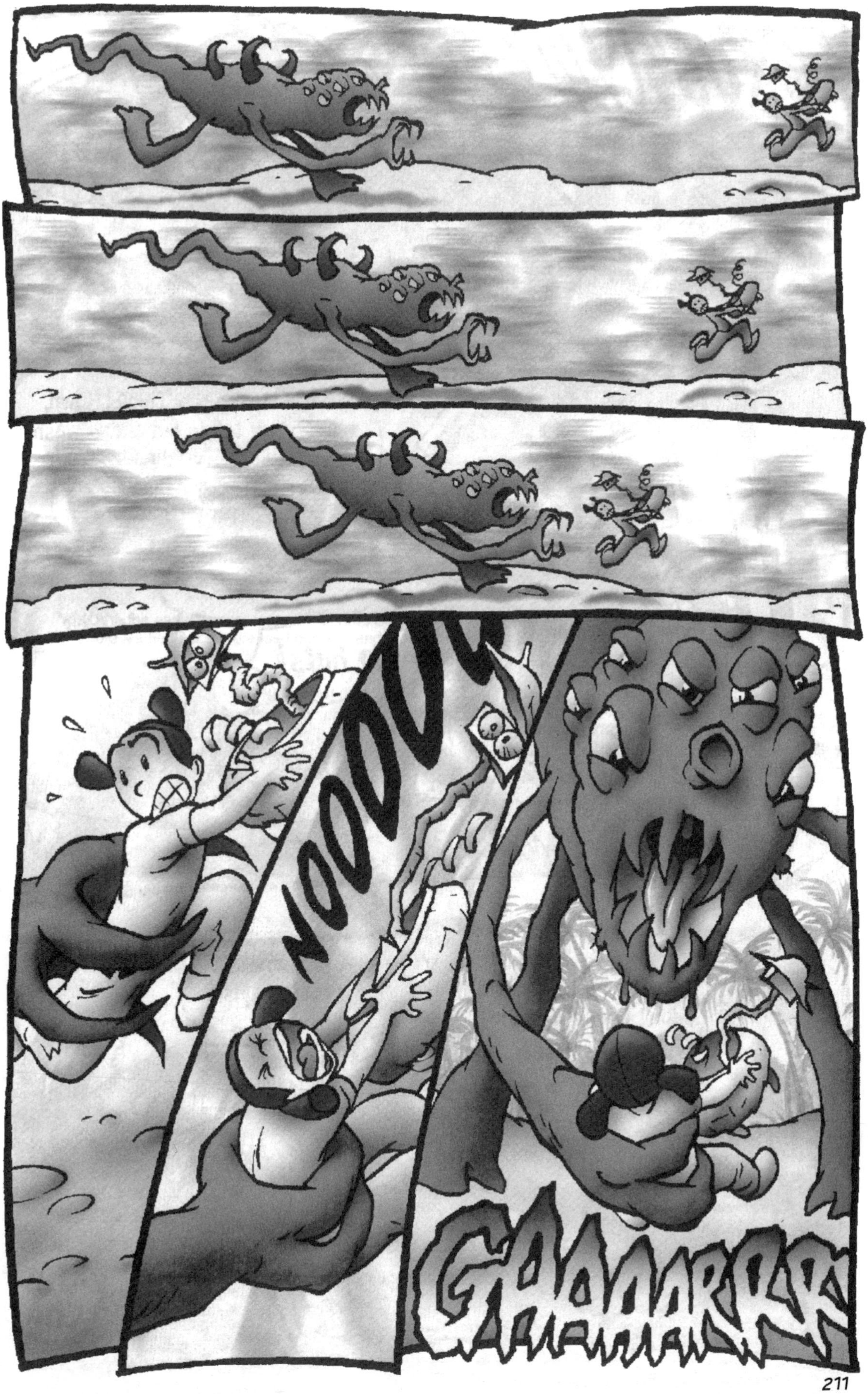
NOOOO
GAAAARRR

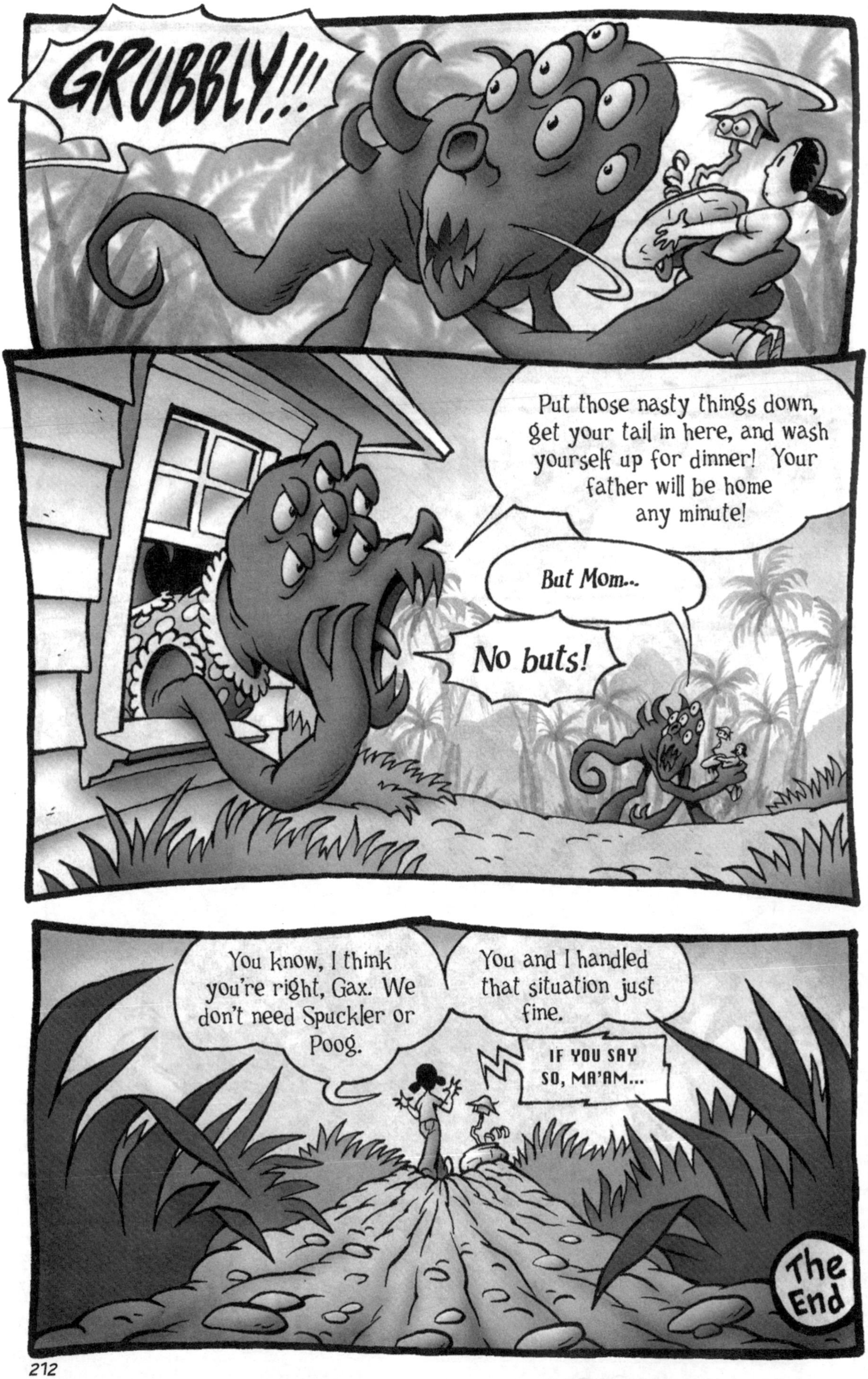
GRUBBLY!!!
Put those nasty things down, get your tail in here, and wash yourself up for dinner! Your father will be home any minute!
But Mom...
No buts!
You know, I think you're right, Gax. We don't need Spuckler or Poog.
You and I handled that situation just fine.
IF YOU SAY SO, MA'AM...
The End

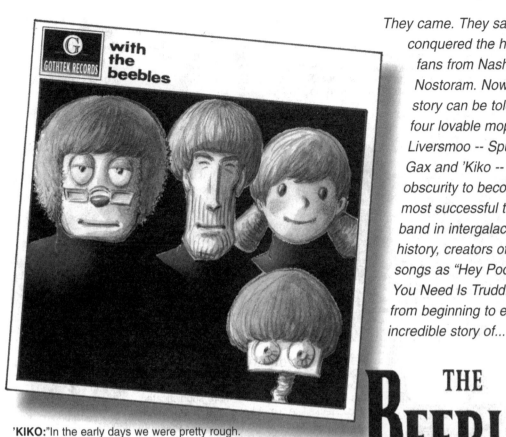

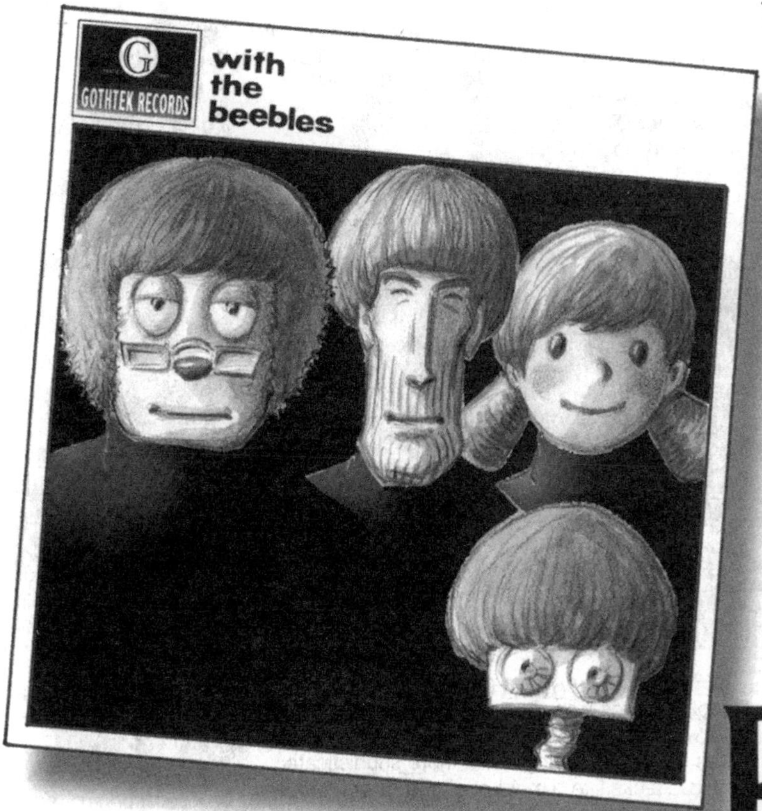
G
GOTHTEK RECORDS
with the beebles

They came. They saw. They conquered the hearts of fans from Nashville to Nostoram. Now at last the story can be told of how four lovable moptops from Liversmoo -- Spuck, Beebs, Gax and 'Kiko -- rose from obscurity to become the most successful throck n' roll band in intergalactic music history, creators of such hits songs as "Hey Poog" and "All You Need Is Trudd." Here it is, from beginning to end, the incredible story of...

THE BEEBLES

'KIKO:"In the early days we were pretty rough. We wore leather jackets, greased our hair, and ate Bropka jerky. Well, Spuck did, anyway. That was back when we were playing the Gamgor Club, a dingy little dive on the lower east side of Liversmoo."

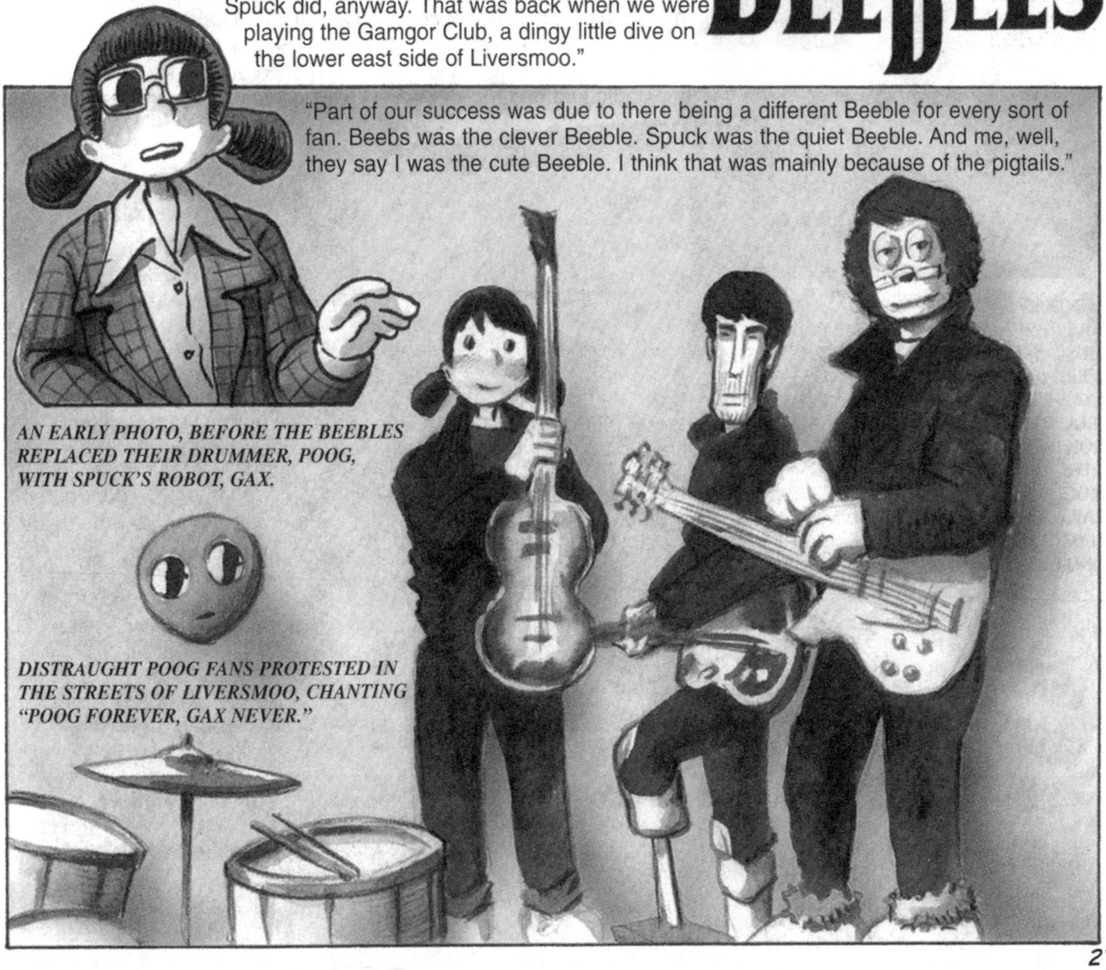

"Part of our success was due to there being a different Beeble for every sort of fan. Beebs was the clever Beeble. Spuck was the quiet Beeble. And me, well, they say I was the cute Beeble. I think that was mainly because of the pigtails."

AN EARLY PHOTO, BEFORE THE BEEBLES REPLACED THEIR DRUMMER, POOG, WITH SPUCK'S ROBOT, GAX.

DISTRAUGHT POOG FANS PROTESTED IN THE STREETS OF LIVERSMOO, CHANTING "POOG FOREVER, GAX NEVER."

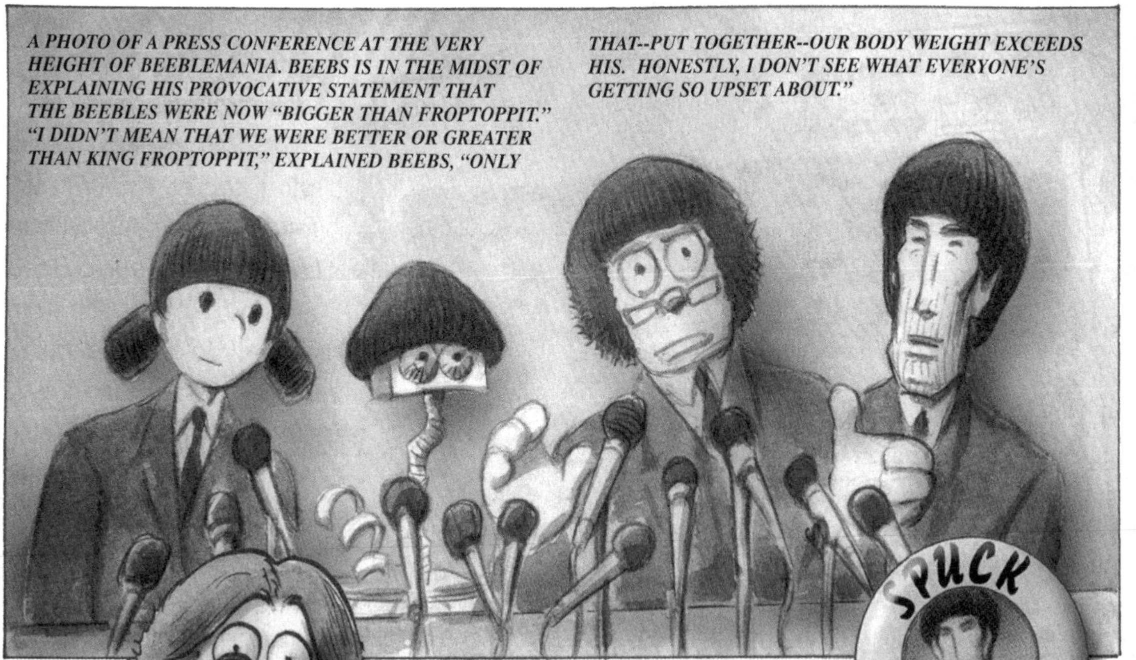

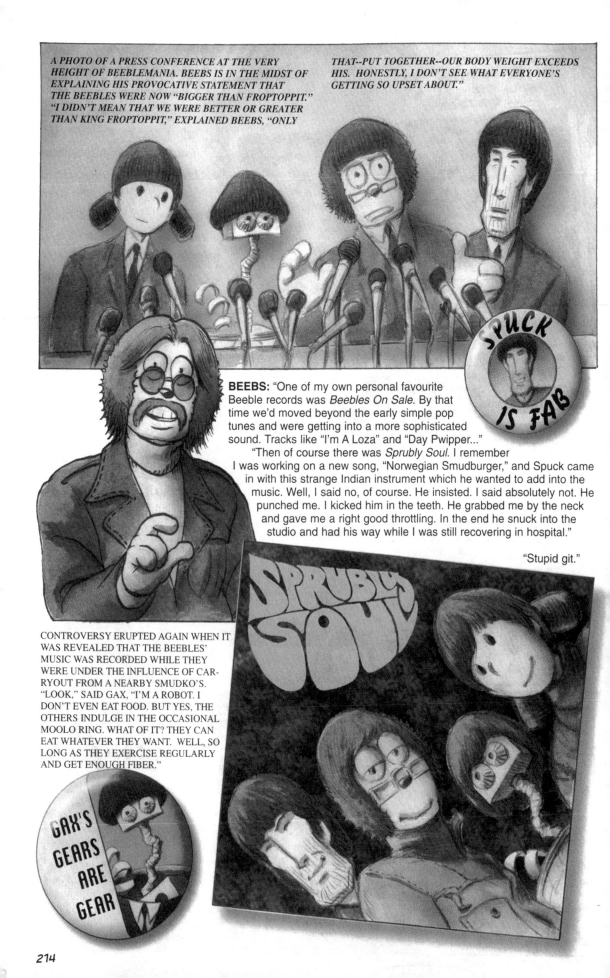

A PHOTO OF A PRESS CONFERENCE AT THE VERY HEIGHT OF BEEBLEMANIA. BEEBS IS IN THE MIDST OF EXPLAINING HIS PROVOCATIVE STATEMENT THAT THE BEEBLES WERE NOW "BIGGER THAN FROPTOPPIT." "I DIDN'T MEAN THAT WE WERE BETTER OR GREATER THAN KING FROPTOPPIT," EXPLAINED BEEBS, "ONLY THAT--PUT TOGETHER--OUR BODY WEIGHT EXCEEDS HIS. HONESTLY, I DON'T SEE WHAT EVERYONE'S GETTING SO UPSET ABOUT."

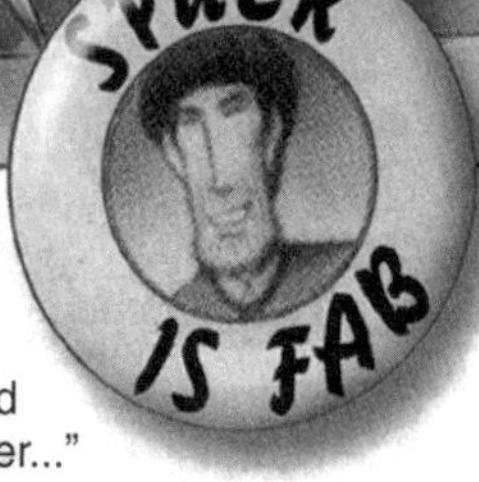
SPUCK
IS FAB

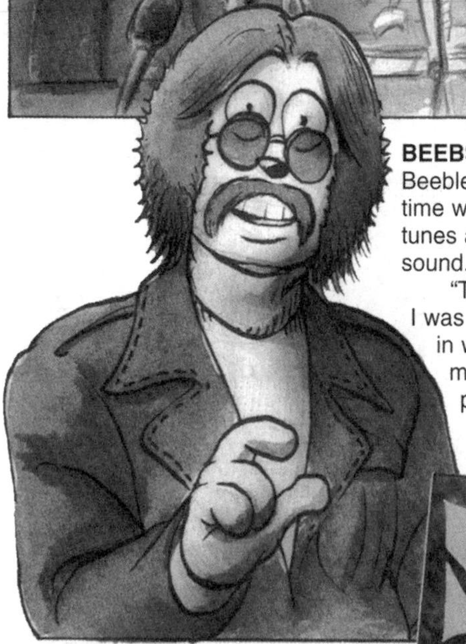

BEEBS: "One of my own personal favourite Beeble records was *Beebles On Sale*. By that time we'd moved beyond the early simple pop tunes and were getting into a more sophisticated sound. Tracks like "I'm A Loza" and "Day Pwipper..."

"Then of course there was *Sprubly Soul*. I remember I was working on a new song, "Norwegian Smudburger," and Spuck came in with this strange Indian instrument which he wanted to add into the music. Well, I said no, of course. He insisted. I said absolutely not. He punched me. I kicked him in the teeth. He grabbed me by the neck and gave me a right good throttling. In the end he snuck into the studio and had his way while I was still recovering in hospital."

"Stupid git."

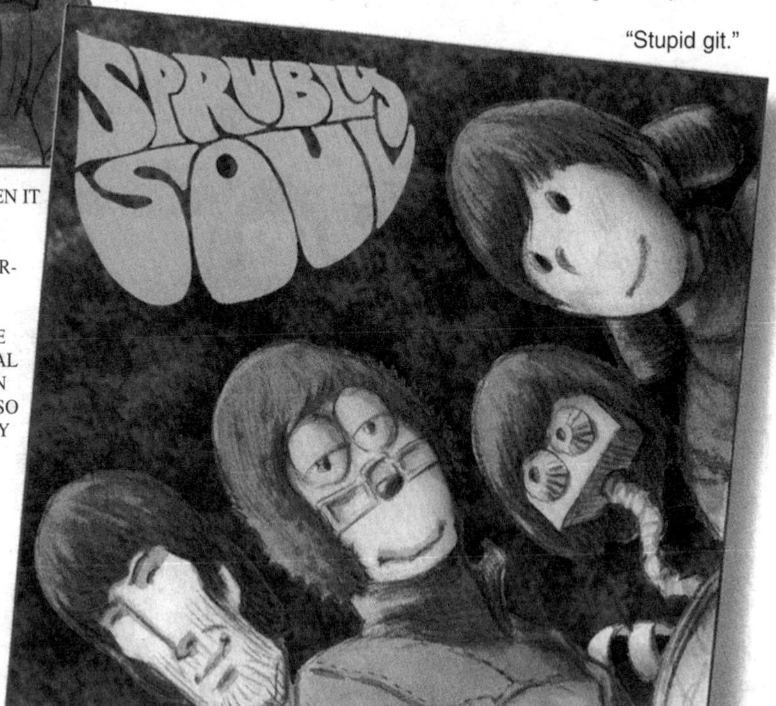
SPRUBLY
SOUL

CONTROVERSY ERUPTED AGAIN WHEN IT WAS REVEALED THAT THE BEEBLES' MUSIC WAS RECORDED WHILE THEY WERE UNDER THE INFLUENCE OF CARRYOUT FROM A NEARBY SMUDKO'S. "LOOK," SAID GAX, "I'M A ROBOT. I DON'T EVEN EAT FOOD. BUT YES, THE OTHERS INDULGE IN THE OCCASIONAL MOOLO RING. WHAT OF IT? THEY CAN EAT WHATEVER THEY WANT. WELL, SO LONG AS THEY EXERCISE REGULARLY AND GET ENOUGH FIBER."

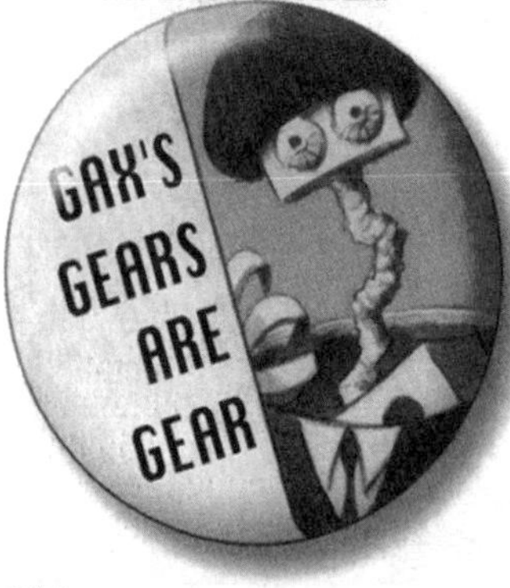
GAX'S
GEARS
ARE
GEAR

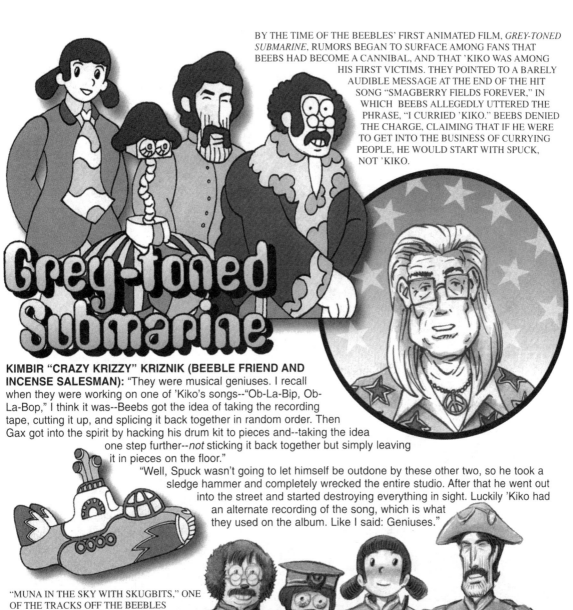

BY THE TIME OF THE BEEBLES' FIRST ANIMATED FILM, *GREY-TONED SUBMARINE*, RUMORS BEGAN TO SURFACE AMONG FANS THAT BEEBS HAD BECOME A CANNIBAL, AND THAT 'KIKO WAS AMONG HIS FIRST VICTIMS. THEY POINTED TO A BARELY AUDIBLE MESSAGE AT THE END OF THE HIT SONG "SMAGBERRY FIELDS FOREVER," IN WHICH BEEBS ALLEGEDLY UTTERED THE PHRASE, "I CURRIED 'KIKO." BEEBS DENIED THE CHARGE, CLAIMING THAT IF HE WERE TO GET INTO THE BUSINESS OF CURRYING PEOPLE, HE WOULD START WITH SPUCK, NOT 'KIKO.

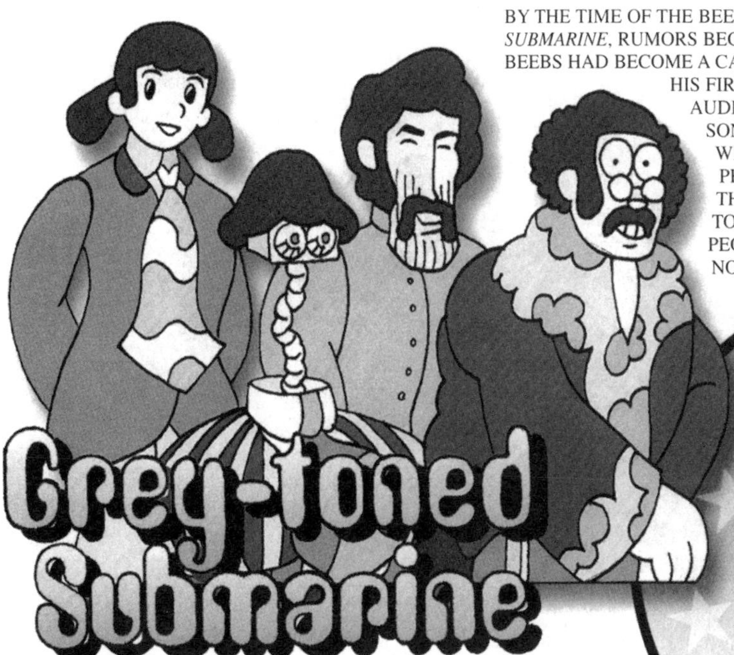

Grey-toned Submarine

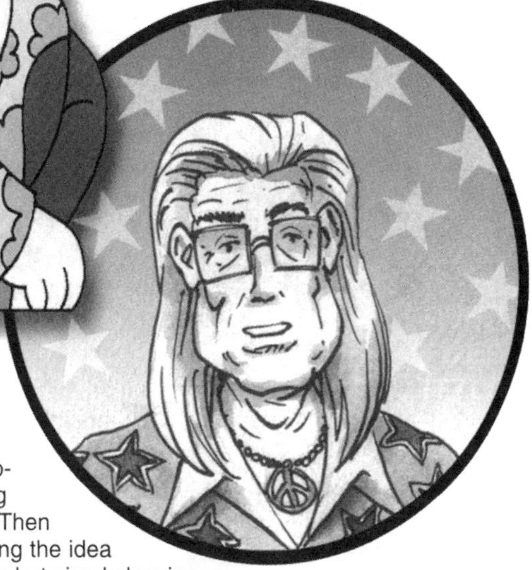

KIMBIR "CRAZY KRIZZY" KRIZNIK (BEEBLE FRIEND AND INCENSE SALESMAN): "They were musical geniuses. I recall when they were working on one of 'Kiko's songs--"Ob-La-Bip, Ob-La-Bop," I think it was--Beebs got the idea of taking the recording tape, cutting it up, and splicing it back together in random order. Then Gax got into the spirit by hacking his drum kit to pieces and--taking the idea one step further--*not* sticking it back together but simply leaving it in pieces on the floor."

"Well, Spuck wasn't going to let himself be outdone by these other two, so he took a sledge hammer and completely wrecked the entire studio. After that he went out into the street and started destroying everything in sight. Luckily 'Kiko had an alternate recording of the song, which is what they used on the album. Like I said: Geniuses."

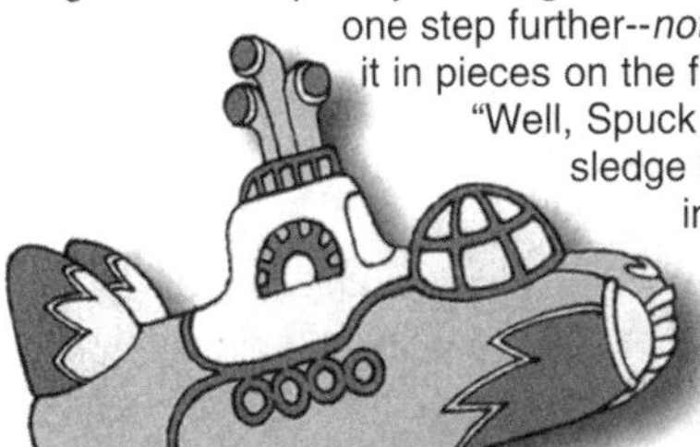

"MUNA IN THE SKY WITH SKUGBITS," ONE OF THE TRACKS OFF THE BEEBLES LANDMARK ALBUM *ADMIRAL FRUTZ'S HOMELY WARTS CREAM BAND*, INCLUDED THE LINE, "GOTGAZZER FUBAS APPEAR ON THE SHORE / WAITING TO MAKE YOU GO 'WAY." WHEN ASKED THE MEANING OF SUCH LYRICS, BEEBS REPLIED, "GET OFF MY FOOT." (SOME INTERPRET THIS METAPHORICALLY. OTHERS SUSPECT THE REPORTER WAS STANDING ON BEEBS'S FOOT WHEN HE ASKED THE QUESTION.)

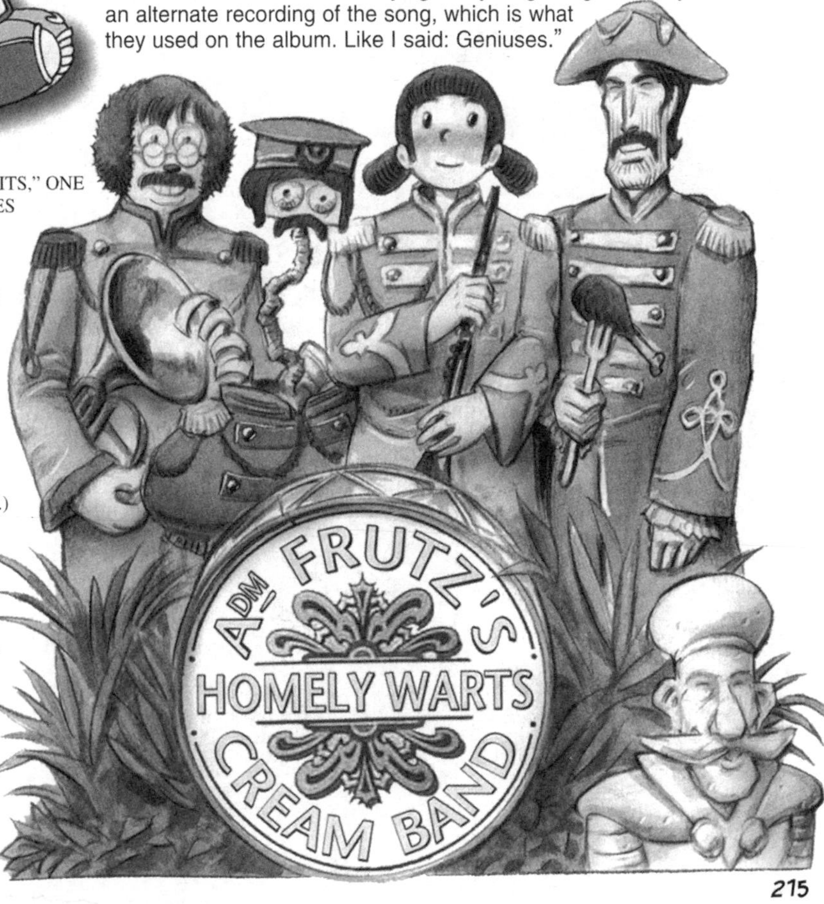
ADM FRUTZ'S
HOMELY WARTS
CREAM BAND

THE MAHARISHI MAHESH GOYBI, INDIAN GURU AND SUBJECT OF THE BEEBLES SONG, "GOYBI YOU'RE A RICH MAN."

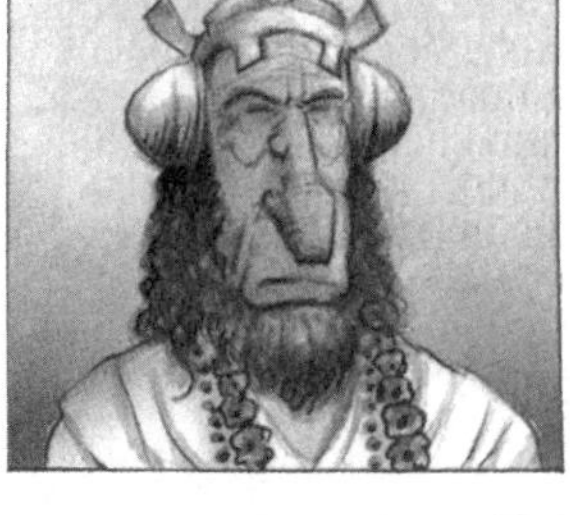

WHEN BEEBS FELL MADLY IN LOVE WITH AVANT-GARDE JAPANESE ARTIST MIYUKI SOHO, A NEW TENSION ENTERED INTO THE GROUP, DUE MOSTLY TO THE FACT THAT--TRY AS THEY MIGHT--THE OTHER BEEBLES COULDN'T GROW THEIR HAIR AS LONG AS HERS. BEEBS RESPONDED BY WRITING "THE BALLAD OF BEEBS AND MIYUKI," A HIGHLY PERSONAL SONG THAT NO ONE UNDERSTOOD, BEEBS INCLUDED.

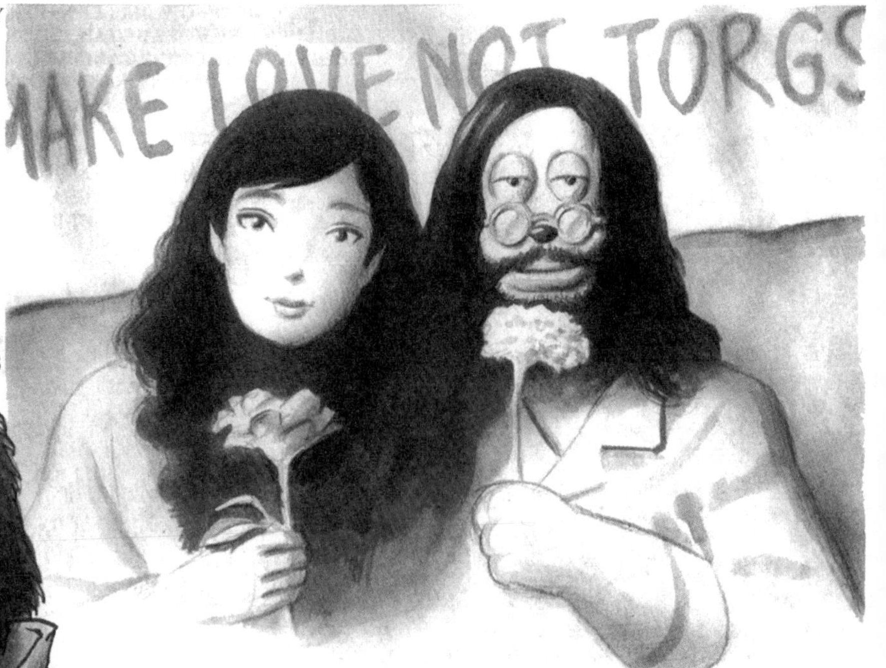

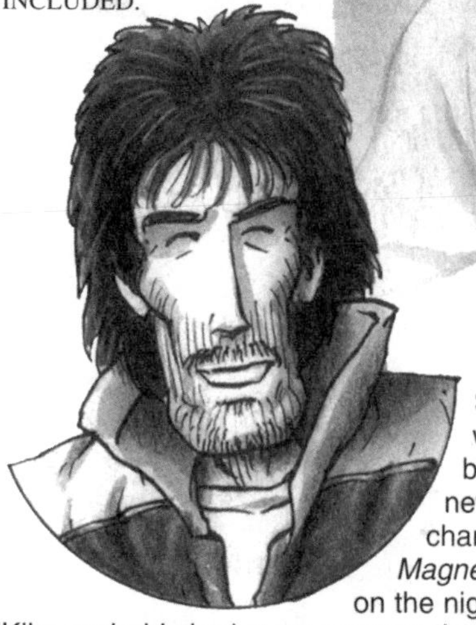

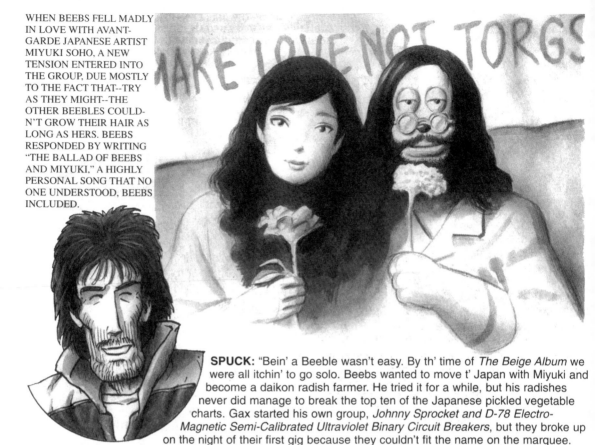

SPUCK: "Bein' a Beeble wasn't easy. By th' time of *The Beige Album* we were all itchin' to go solo. Beebs wanted to move t' Japan with Miyuki and become a daikon radish farmer. He tried it for a while, but his radishes never did manage to break the top ten of the Japanese pickled vegetable charts. Gax started his own group, *Johnny Sprocket and D-78 Electro-Magnetic Semi-Calibrated Ultraviolet Binary Circuit Breakers*, but they broke up on the night of their first gig because they couldn't fit the name on the marquee. 'Kiko probably had more success than any of us. She started a line of clothing--blue jeans and light-blue T-shirts, mainly--and got rich enough to retire before she'd even finished the seventh grade. Me, I did what I was always meant t' do: raise bropkas. The market stinks almost as bad as the meat itself. But I'm my own boss, an' the job description don't include showerin'."

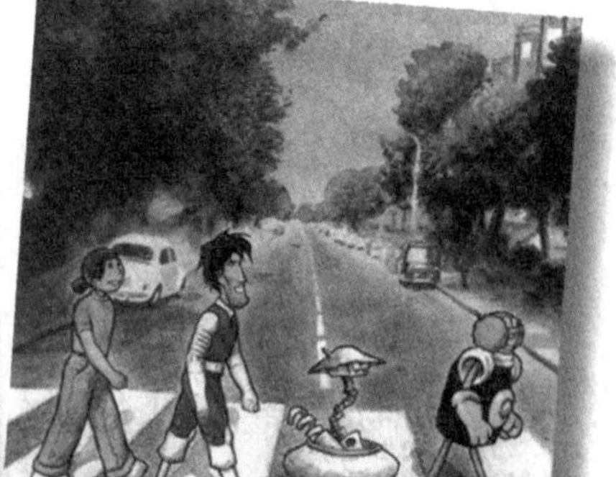

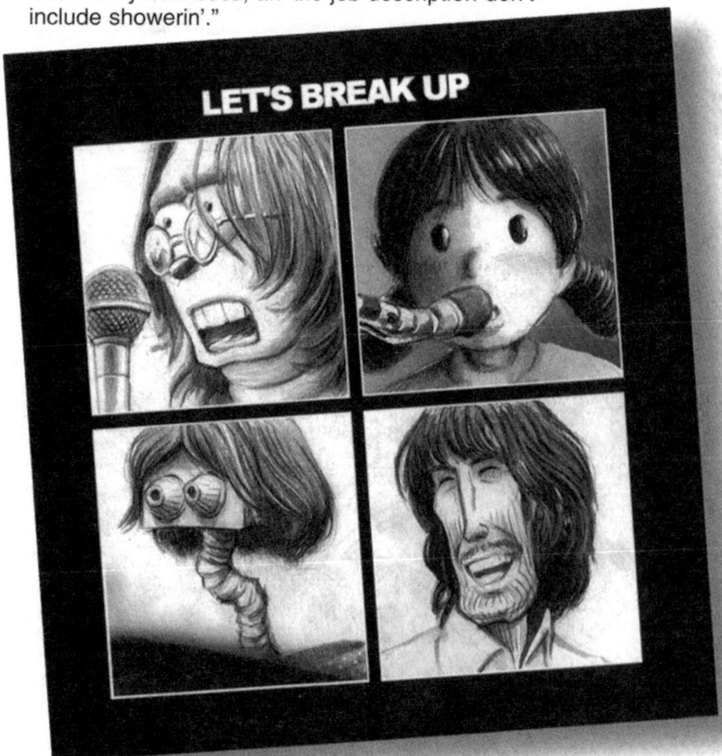
LET'S BREAK UP

THE BEEBLES FOLLOWED UP THEIR *YABBY ROAD* ALBUM WITH THE ENIGMATICALLY TITLED *LET'S BREAK UP.* BEEBLES FANS IMMEDIATELY BEGAN SPECULATING ABOUT WHAT THEIR NEXT RECORD WOULD BE CALLED, BUT GOT A RUDE SHOCK WHEN THE GROUP SPLIT UP A FORTNIGHT LATER. WHAT FOLLOWED WAS A QUAGMIRE OF LAWSUITS, COUNTERSUITS, AND REGRETTABLE WARDROBE CHOICES. STILL, THE BEEBLES MUSICAL LEGACY LIVES ON. AS BEEBS HIMSELF SAID, "LOOK, WE WERE JUST A BUNCH OF LADS WHO GOT TOGETHER AND BECAME RICHER AND MORE SUCCESSFUL THAN ANY OTHER GROUP IN THE HISTORY OF MUSIC. I DON'T SEE WHAT ALL THE FUSS IS ABOUT."

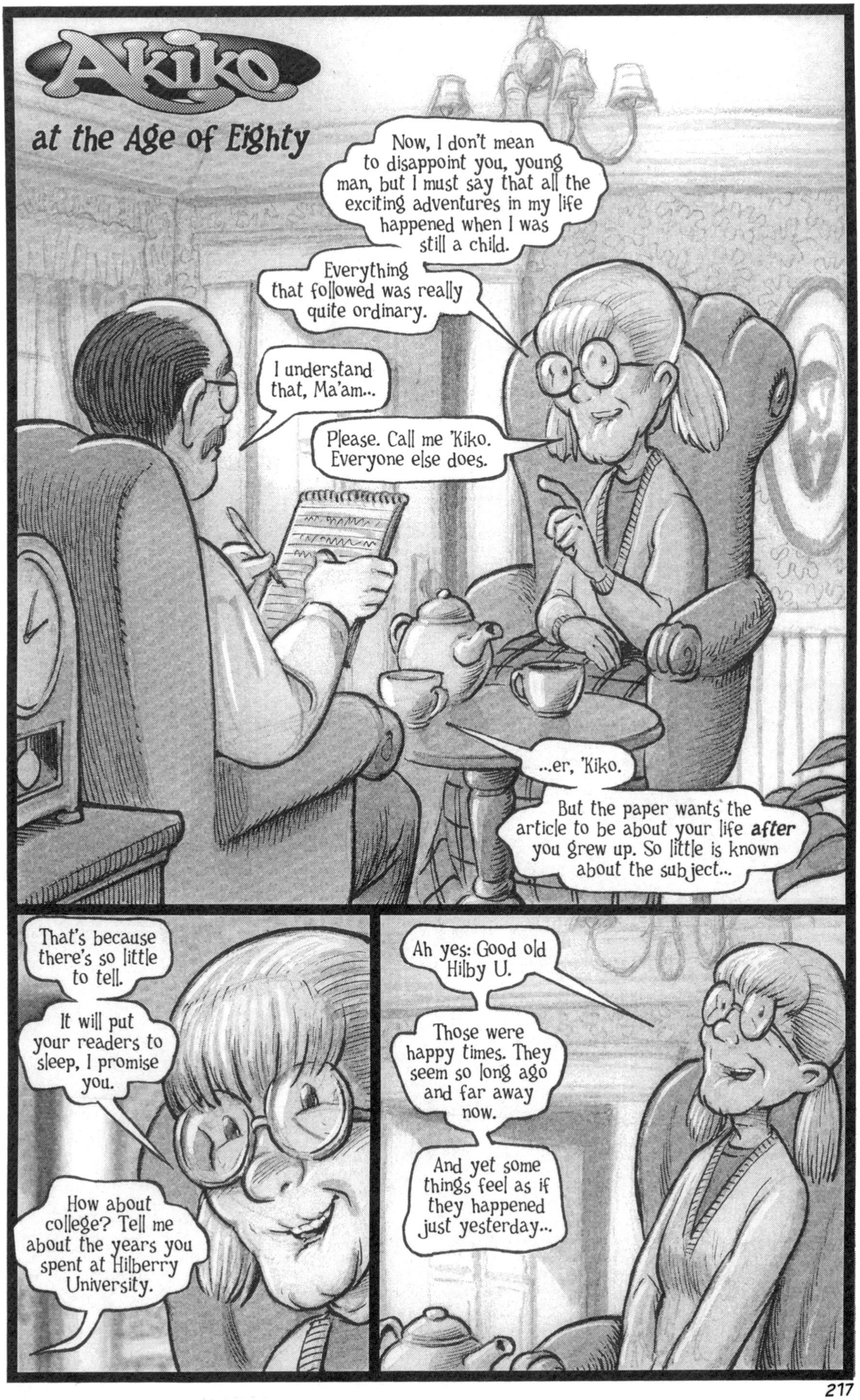
Akiko
at the Age of Eighty
Now, I don't mean to disappoint you, young man, but I must say that all the exciting adventures in my life happened when I was still a child.
Everything that followed was really quite ordinary.
I understand that, Ma'am...
Please. Call me 'Kiko. Everyone else does.
...er, 'Kiko.
But the paper wants the article to be about your life after you grew up. So little is known about the subject...
That's because there's so little to tell.
It will put your readers to sleep, I promise you.
How about college? Tell me about the years you spent at Hilberry University.
Ah yes: Good old Hilby U.
Those were happy times. They seem so long ago and far away now.
And yet some things feel as if they happened just yesterday...

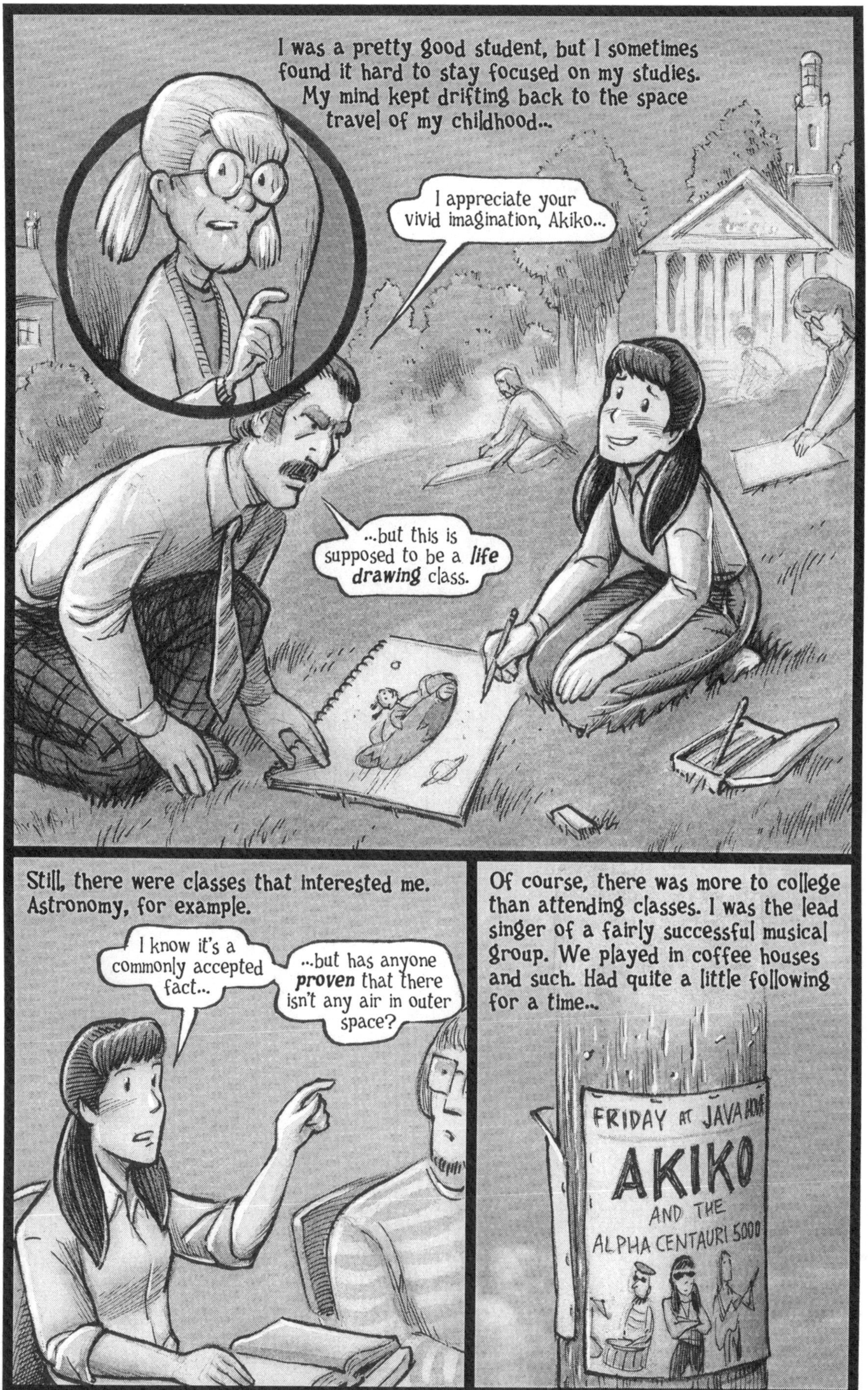
I was a pretty good student, but I sometimes found it hard to stay focused on my studies. My mind kept drifting back to the space travel of my childhood...
I appreciate your vivid imagination, Akiko...
...but this is supposed to be a *life drawing* class.
Still, there were classes that interested me. Astronomy, for example.
I know it's a commonly accepted fact...
...but has anyone *proven* that there isn't any air in outer space?
Of course, there was more to college than attending classes. I was the lead singer of a fairly successful musical group. We played in coffee houses and such. Had quite a little following for a time...
FRIDAY AT JAVA
AKIKO
AND THE
ALPHA CENTAURI 5000

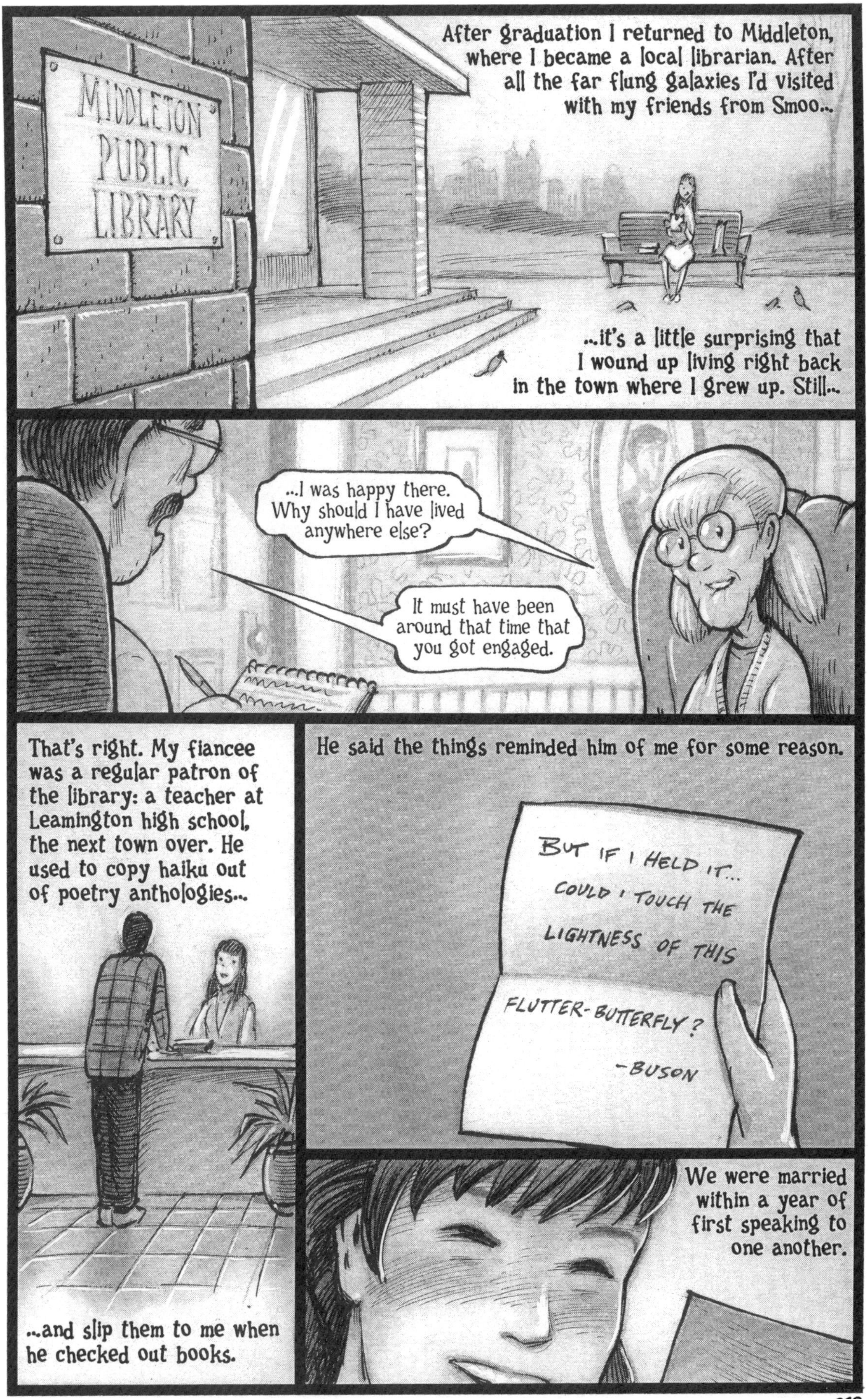
After graduation I returned to Middleton, where I became a local librarian. After all the far flung galaxies I'd visited with my friends from Smoo...
MIDDLETON PUBLIC LIBRARY
...it's a little surprising that I wound up living right back in the town where I grew up. Still...
...I was happy there. Why should I have lived anywhere else?
It must have been around that time that you got engaged.
That's right. My fiancee was a regular patron of the library: a teacher at Leamington high school, the next town over. He used to copy haiku out of poetry anthologies...
...and slip them to me when he checked out books.
He said the things reminded him of me for some reason.
BUT IF I HELD IT... COULD I TOUCH THE LIGHTNESS OF THIS FLUTTER-BUTTERFLY? -BUSON
We were married within a year of first speaking to one another.

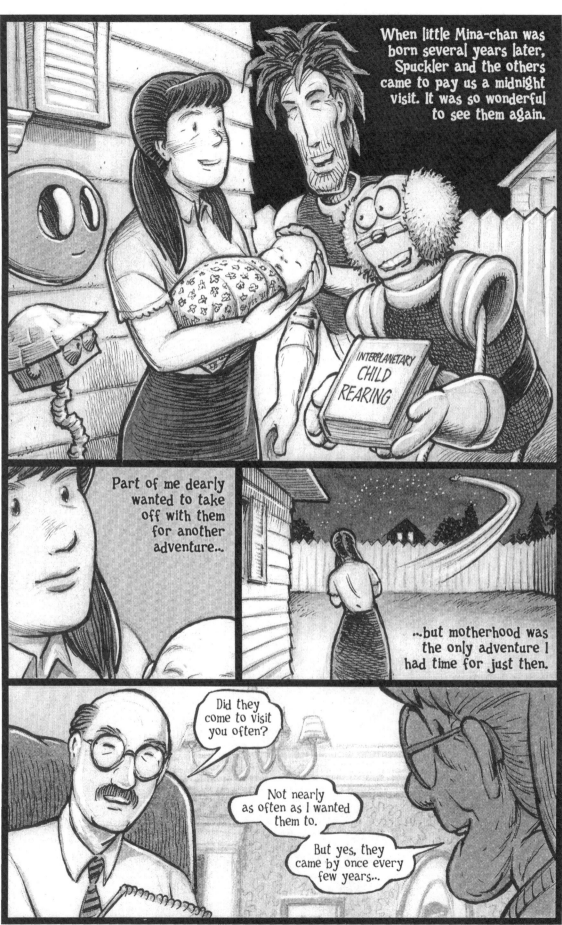

When little Mina-chan was born several years later, Spuckler and the others came to pay us a midnight visit. It was so wonderful to see them again.

INTERPLANETARY CHILD REARING

Part of me dearly wanted to take off with them for another adventure...

...but motherhood was the only adventure I had time for just then.

Did they come to visit you often?

Not nearly as often as I wanted them to.

But yes, they came by once every few years...

Once I arranged for them to join my family on a camping trip. Mina was eight or nine by then, nearly as old as I'd been when I made my first trip to Smoo.

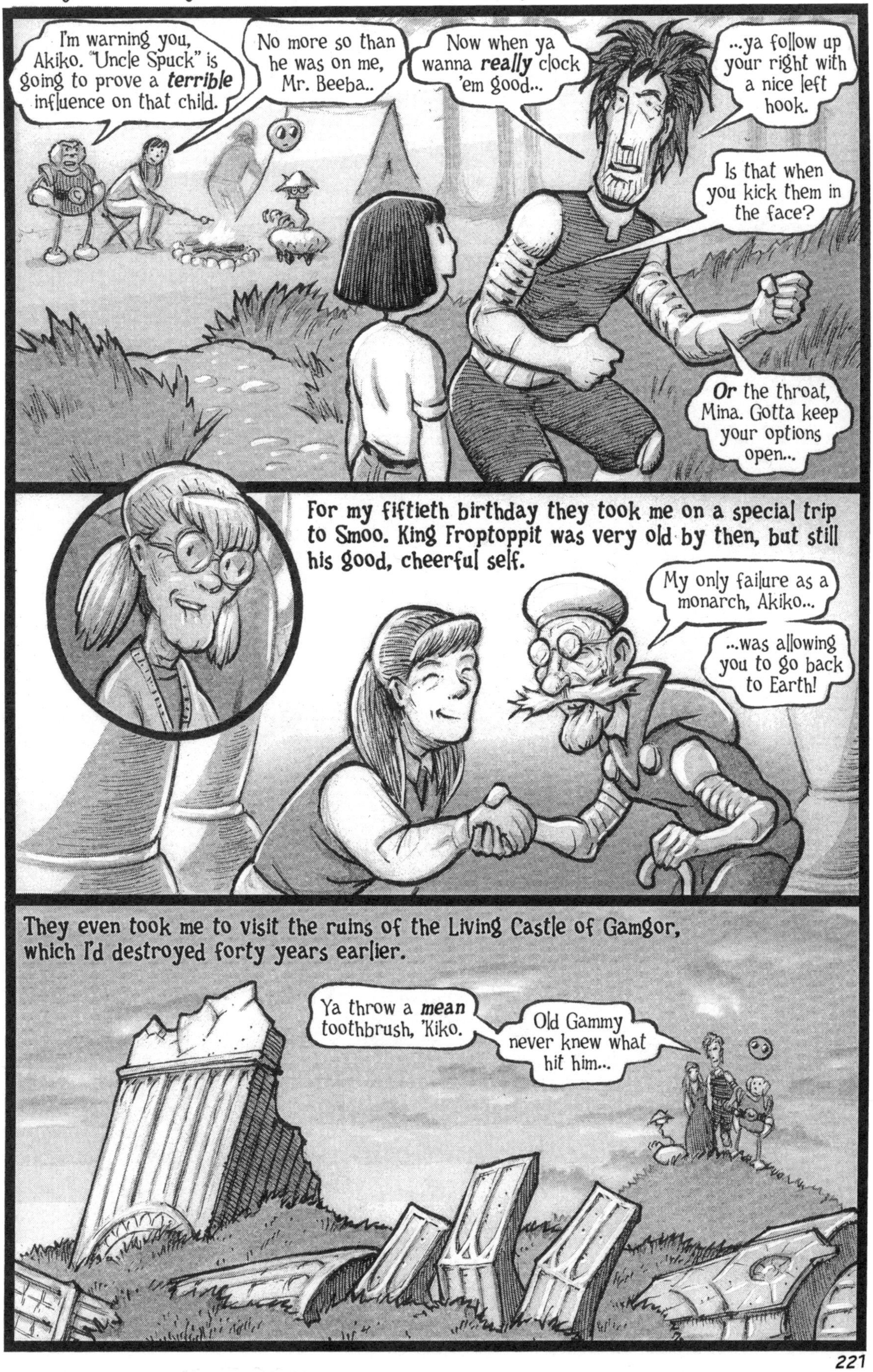

I'm warning you, Akiko. "Uncle Spuck" is going to prove a *terrible* influence on that child.
No more so than he was on me, Mr. Beeba..
Now when ya wanna *really* clock 'em good...
...ya follow up your right with a nice left hook.
Is that when you kick them in the face?
Or the throat, Mina. Gotta keep your options open...
For my fiftieth birthday they took me on a special trip to Smoo. King Froptoppit was very old by then, but still his good, cheerful self.
My only failure as a monarch, Akiko...
...was allowing you to go back to Earth!
They even took me to visit the ruins of the Living Castle of Gamgor, which I'd destroyed forty years earlier.
Ya throw a *mean* toothbrush, 'Kiko.
Old Gammy never knew what hit him...

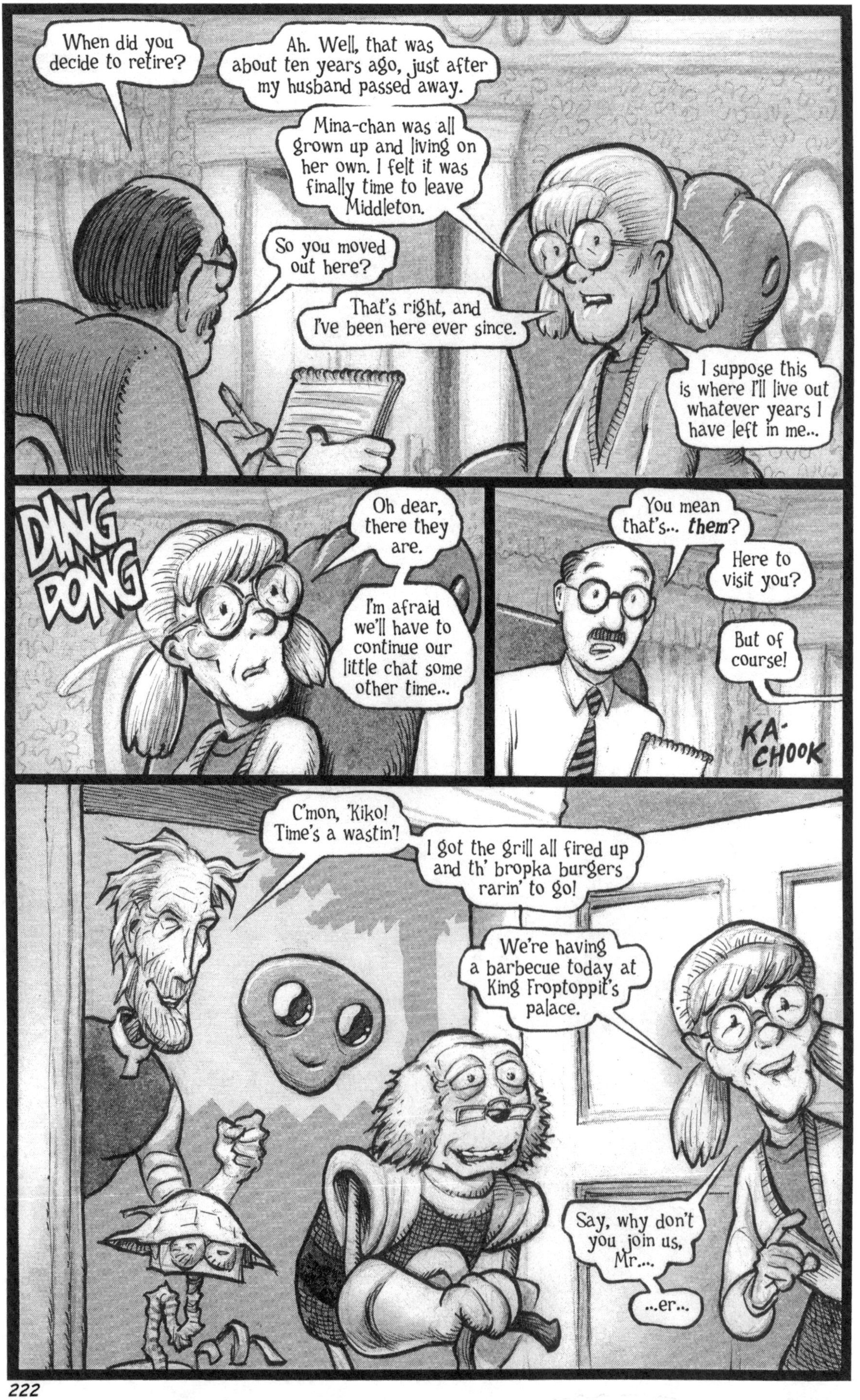

When did you decide to retire?
Ah. Well, that was about ten years ago, just after my husband passed away.
Mina-chan was all grown up and living on her own. I felt it was finally time to leave Middleton.
So you moved out here?
That's right, and I've been here ever since.
I suppose this is where I'll live out whatever years I have left in me...
DING DONG
Oh dear, there they are.
I'm afraid we'll have to continue our little chat some other time...
You mean that's... *them*?
Here to visit you?
But of course!
KA-CHOOK
C'mon, 'Kiko! Time's a wastin'!
I got the grill all fired up and th' bropka burgers rarin' to go!
We're having a barbecue today at King Froptoppit's palace.
Say, why don't you join us, Mr....
...er...

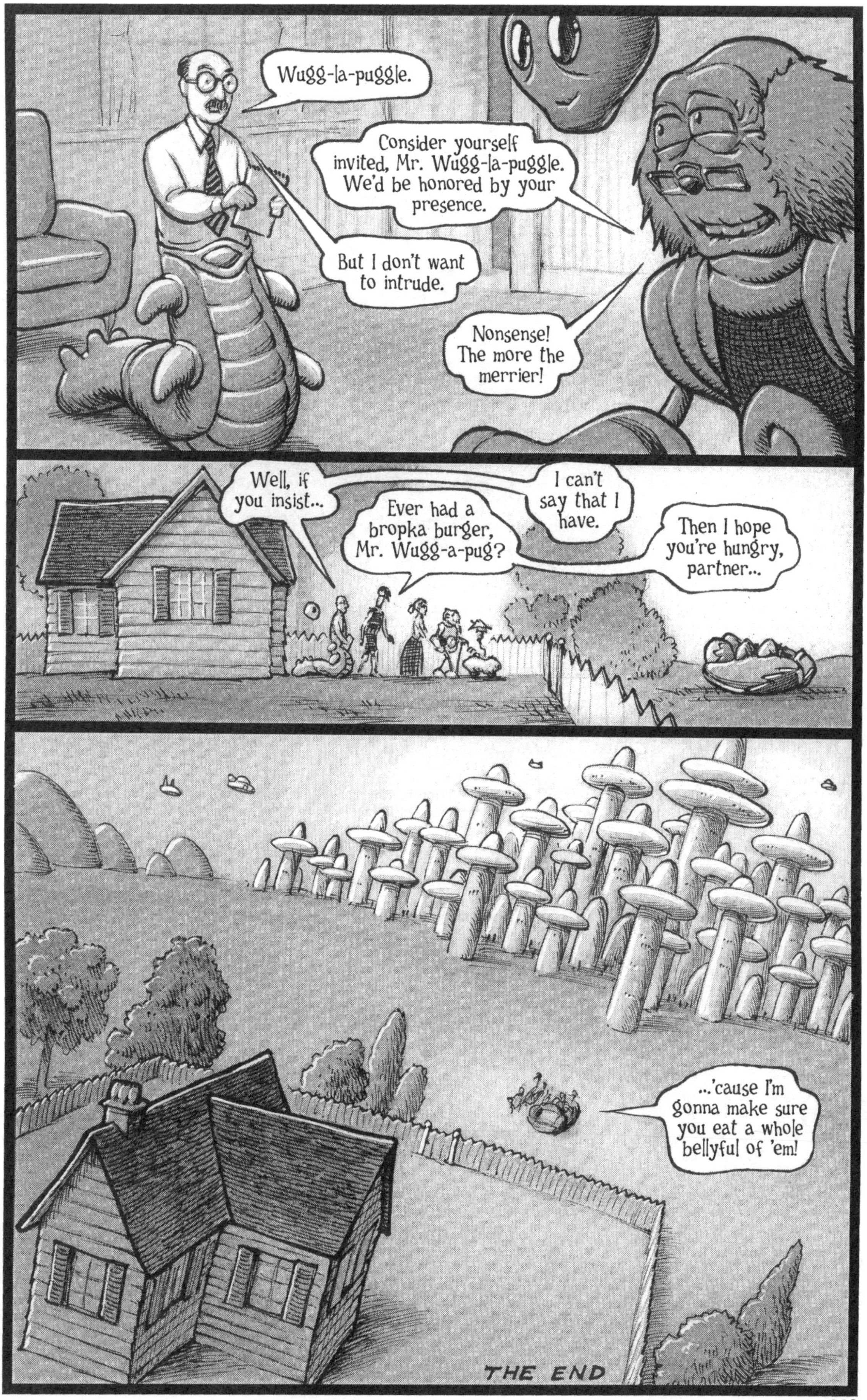
Wugg-la-puggle.
Consider yourself invited, Mr. Wugg-la-puggle. We'd be honored by your presence.
But I don't want to intrude.
Nonsense! The more the merrier!
Well, if you insist...
I can't say that I have.
Ever had a bropka burger, Mr. Wugg-a-pug?
Then I hope you're hungry, partner...
...'cause I'm gonna make sure you eat a whole bellyful of 'em!
THE END

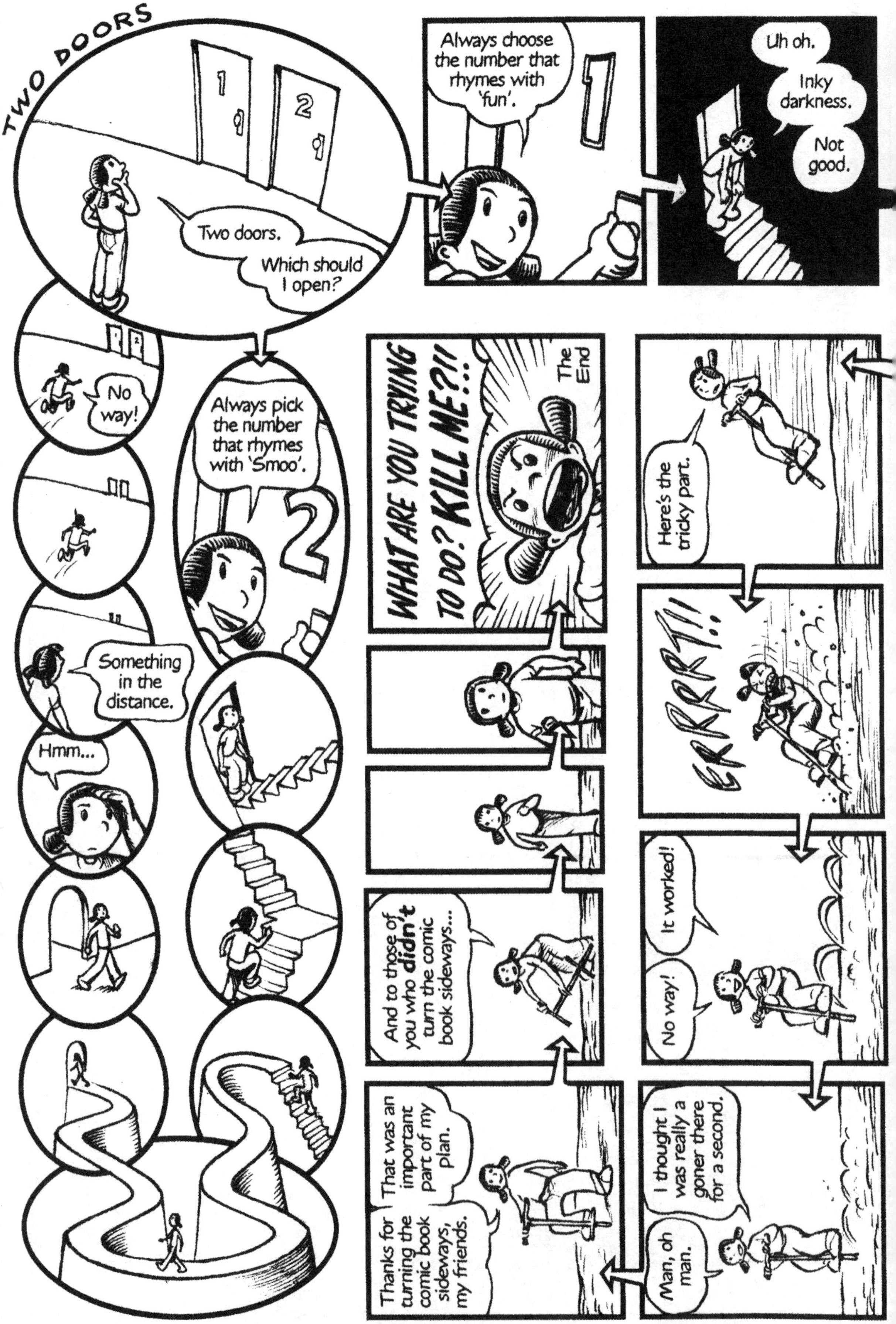
TWO DOORS
Two doors.
Which should I open?
Always choose the number that rhymes with 'fun'.
Uh oh.
Inky darkness.
Not good.
Here's the tricky part.
ERRRRT!!
No way!
It worked!
Man, oh man.
I thought I was really a goner there for a second.
Thanks for turning the comic book sideways, my friends.
That was an important part of my plan.
And to those of you who **didn't** turn the comic book sideways...
WHAT ARE YOU TRYING TO DO? KILL ME?!!
The End
Always pick the number that rhymes with 'Smoo'.
No way!
Something in the distance.
Hmm...

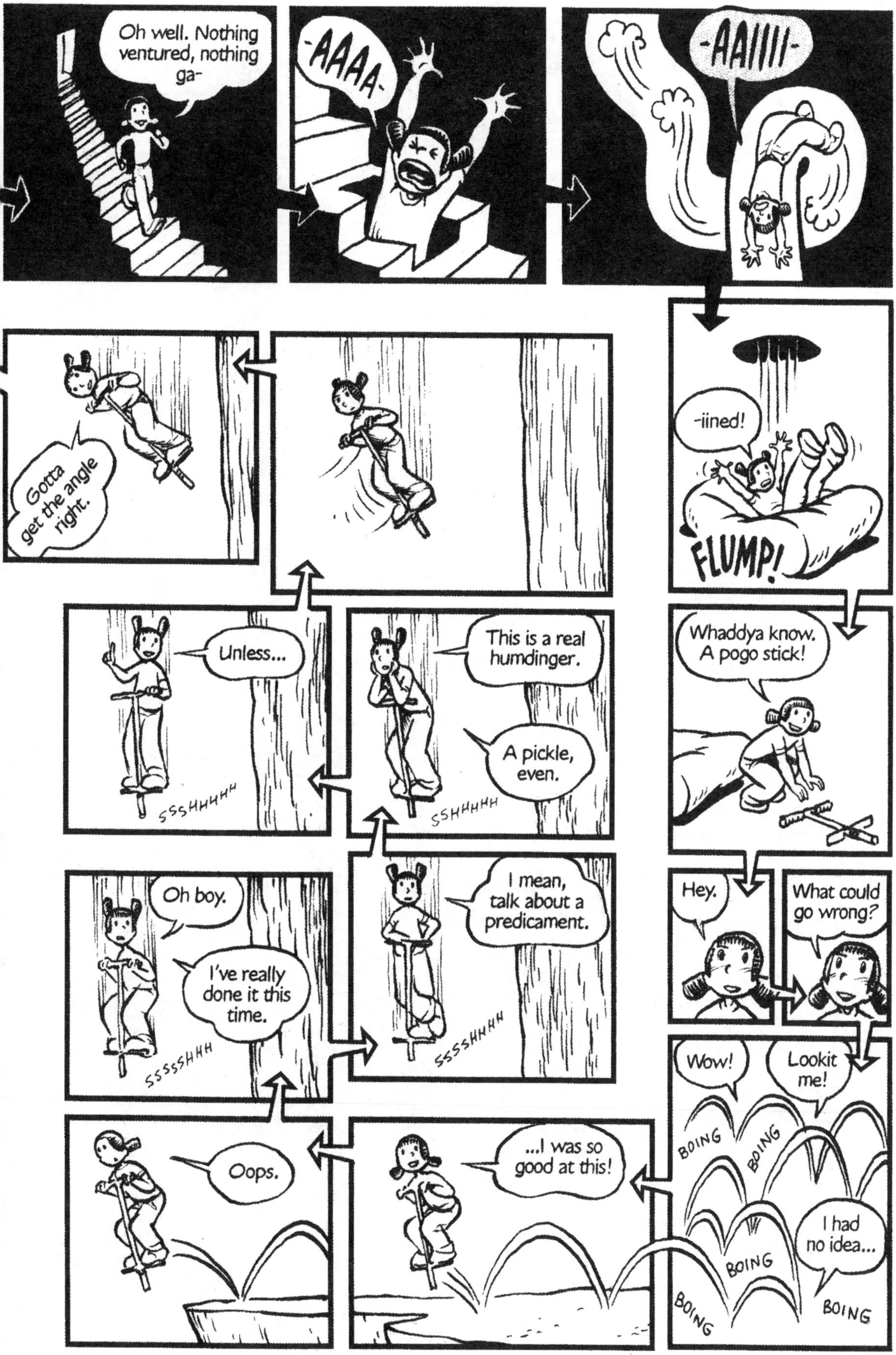
Oh well. Nothing ventured, nothing ga-
-AAAA-
-AAIIII-
-iined!
FLUMP!
Whaddya know. A pogo stick!
Hey.
What could go wrong?
Wow!
Lookit me!
BOING
BOING
BOING
BOING
BOING
I had no idea...
...I was so good at this!
Oops.
Oh boy.
I've really done it this time.
SSSSSHHH
I mean, talk about a predicament.
SSSSHHHHH
This is a real humdinger.
A pickle, even.
SSHHHHH
Unless...
SSSHHHHH
Gotta get the angle right.

Beeba's 'Bot

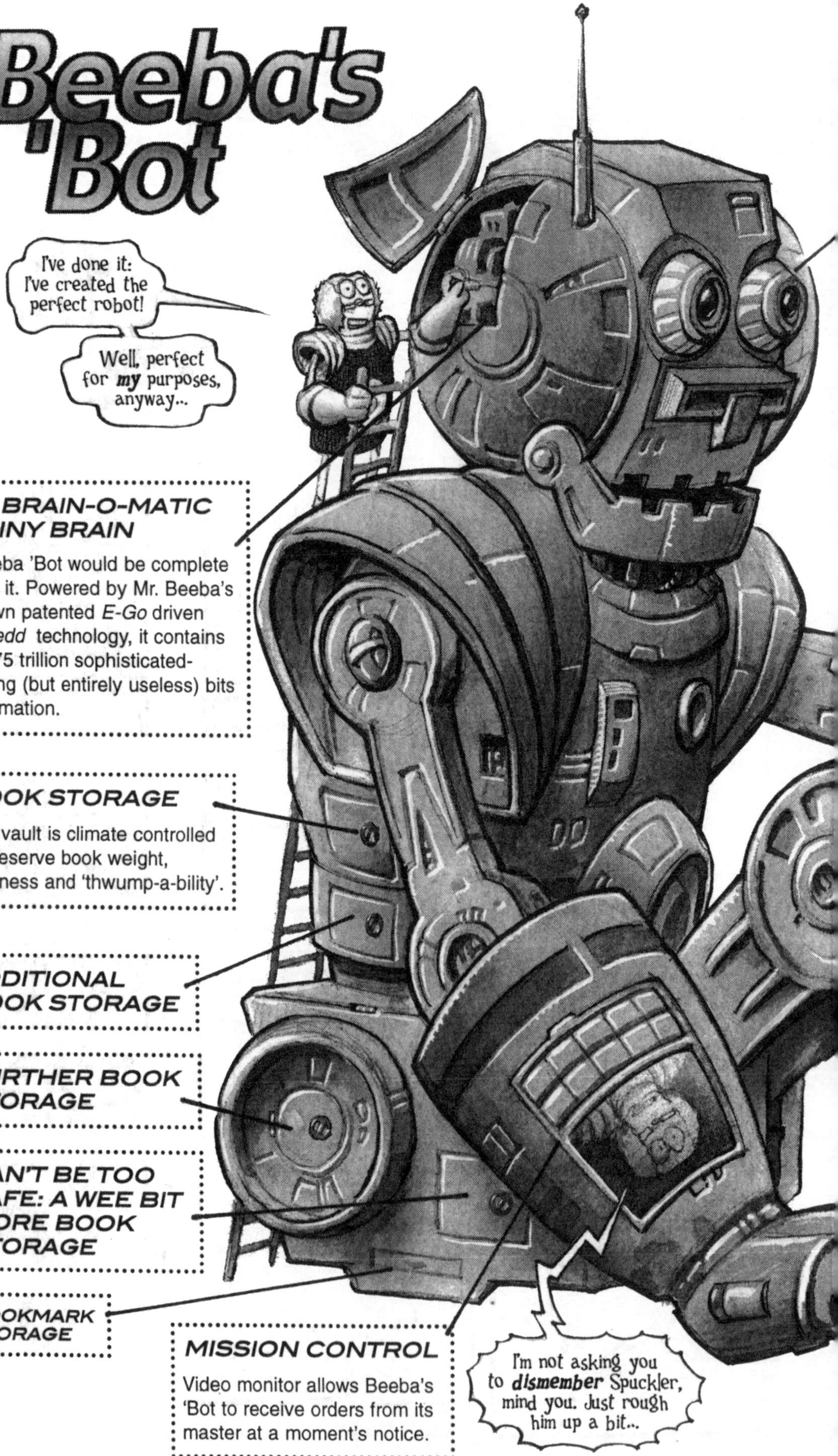
I've done it: I've created the perfect robot!
Well, perfect for ***my*** purposes, anyway...
I'm not asking you to ***dismember*** Spuckler, mind you. Just rough him up a bit...

THE BRAIN-O-MATIC BRAINY BRAIN

No Beeba 'Bot would be complete without it. Powered by Mr. Beeba's very own patented *E-Go* driven *Egg-Hedd* technology, it contains over 175 trillion sophisticated-sounding (but entirely useless) bits of information.

BOOK STORAGE

This vault is climate controlled to preserve book weight, thickness and 'thwump-a-bility'.

ADDITIONAL BOOK STORAGE

FURTHER BOOK STORAGE

CAN'T BE TOO SAFE: A WEE BIT MORE BOOK STORAGE

BOOKMARK STORAGE

MISSION CONTROL

Video monitor allows Beeba's 'Bot to receive orders from its master at a moment's notice.

NITPICK-A-VISION

State-of-the-art optical receptors allow Beeba's 'Bot to scan massive texts at lightning speeds in order to ferret out any and all dangling participles.

THE BROPKA SEARCH-AND-DESTROY-ALATOR

The universe's only weaponry system designed exclusively to hunt down and promptly vaporize all rancid meat and bropka-derived food products. Its accuracy is over 99.98%. *

* Provided the Thrumple engine is in good working order.

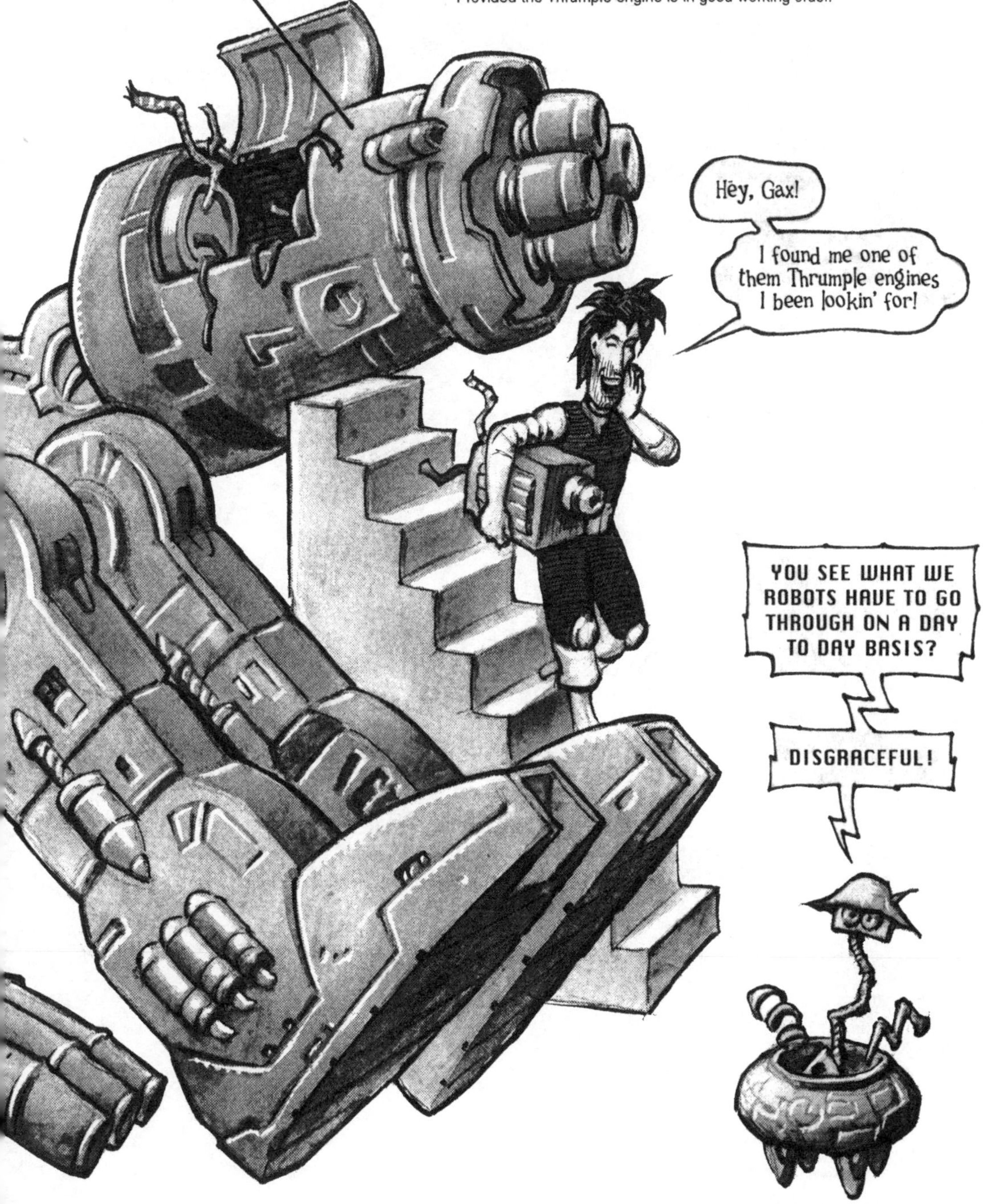

Hey, Gax!
I found me one of them Thrumple engines I been lookin' for!
YOU SEE WHAT WE ROBOTS HAVE TO GO THROUGH ON A DAY TO DAY BASIS?
DISGRACEFUL!

Here's what critics are saying about Markayo Crillazaki's latest animated masterpiece....

My Neighbor *Akiko's* Spirited Delivery Service

"Once in a generation a film comes along that redefines what a movie ought to be: a living, breathing, work of art that sweeps audiences away to a land of wonder and enchantment, leaving them wishing to begin the journey again as soon as the credits roll. *My Neighbor Akiko's Spirited Delivery Service* is not such a film."

~Time Magazine

"A $5.75 box of Raisinets comes off as a shrewd investment by comparison."

~Newsweek

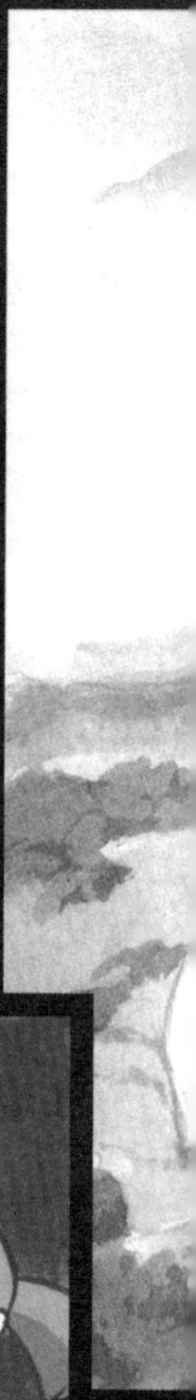

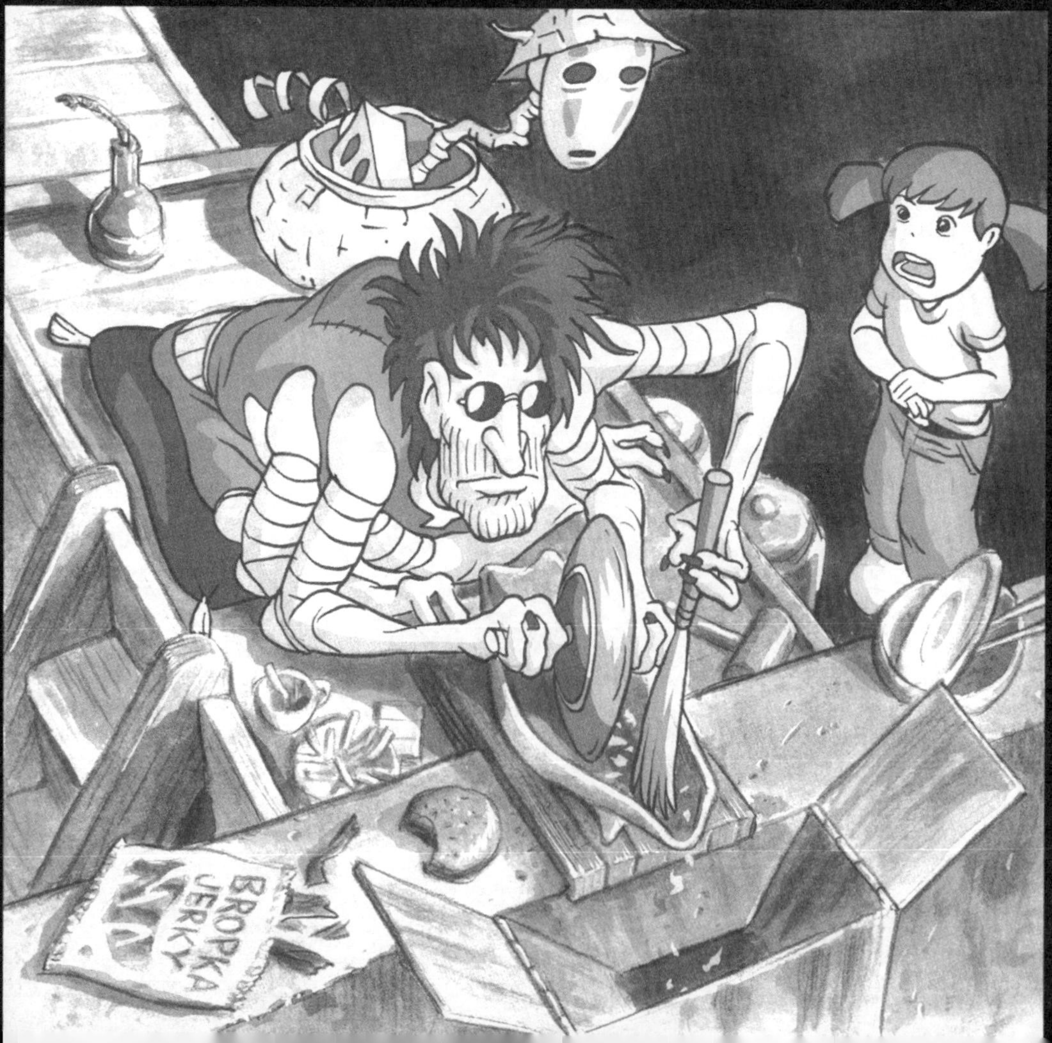
BROPKA JERKY

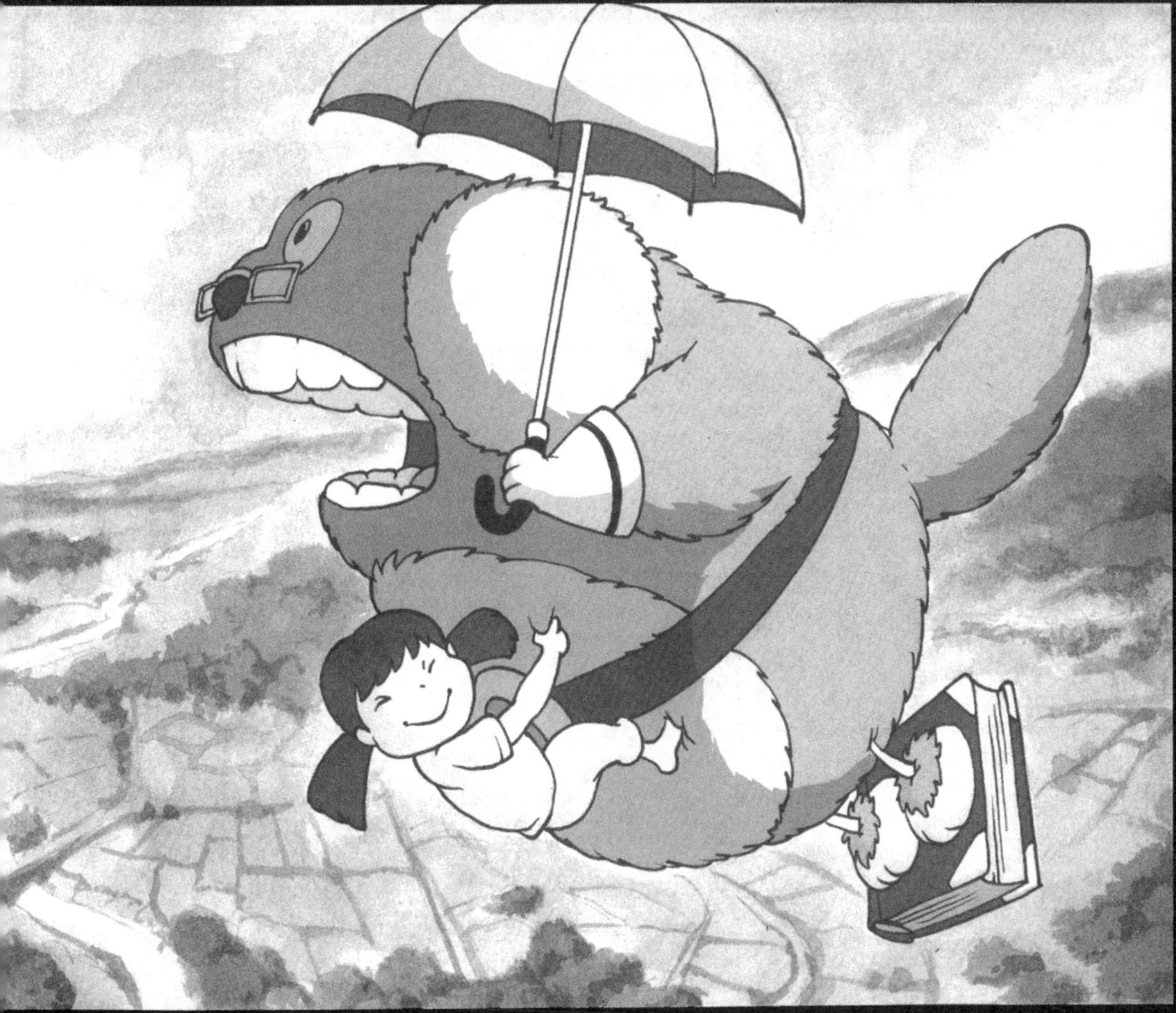

"Two thumbs down.
Way down."

~Ebert & Roeper

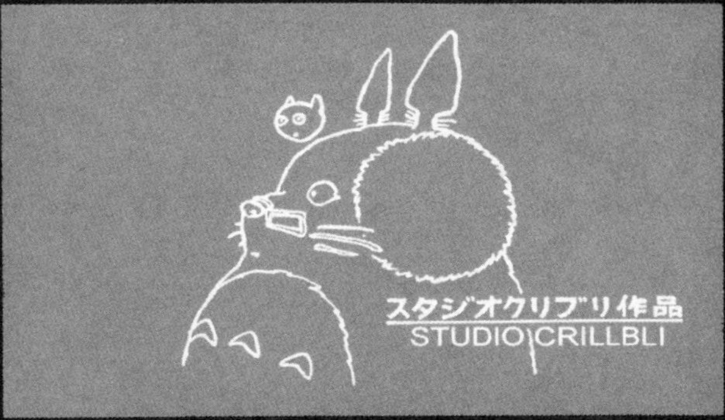
スタジオクリブリ作品
STUDIO CRILLBLI

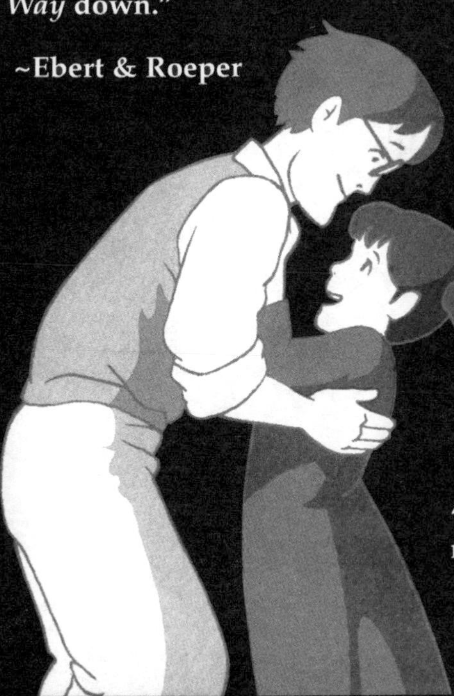

"We don't normally review movies, but this one is so bad it is our duty to spread the word."

~National Geographic

"I really wish he'd stop ripping off all my movies."

~Hayao Miyazaki

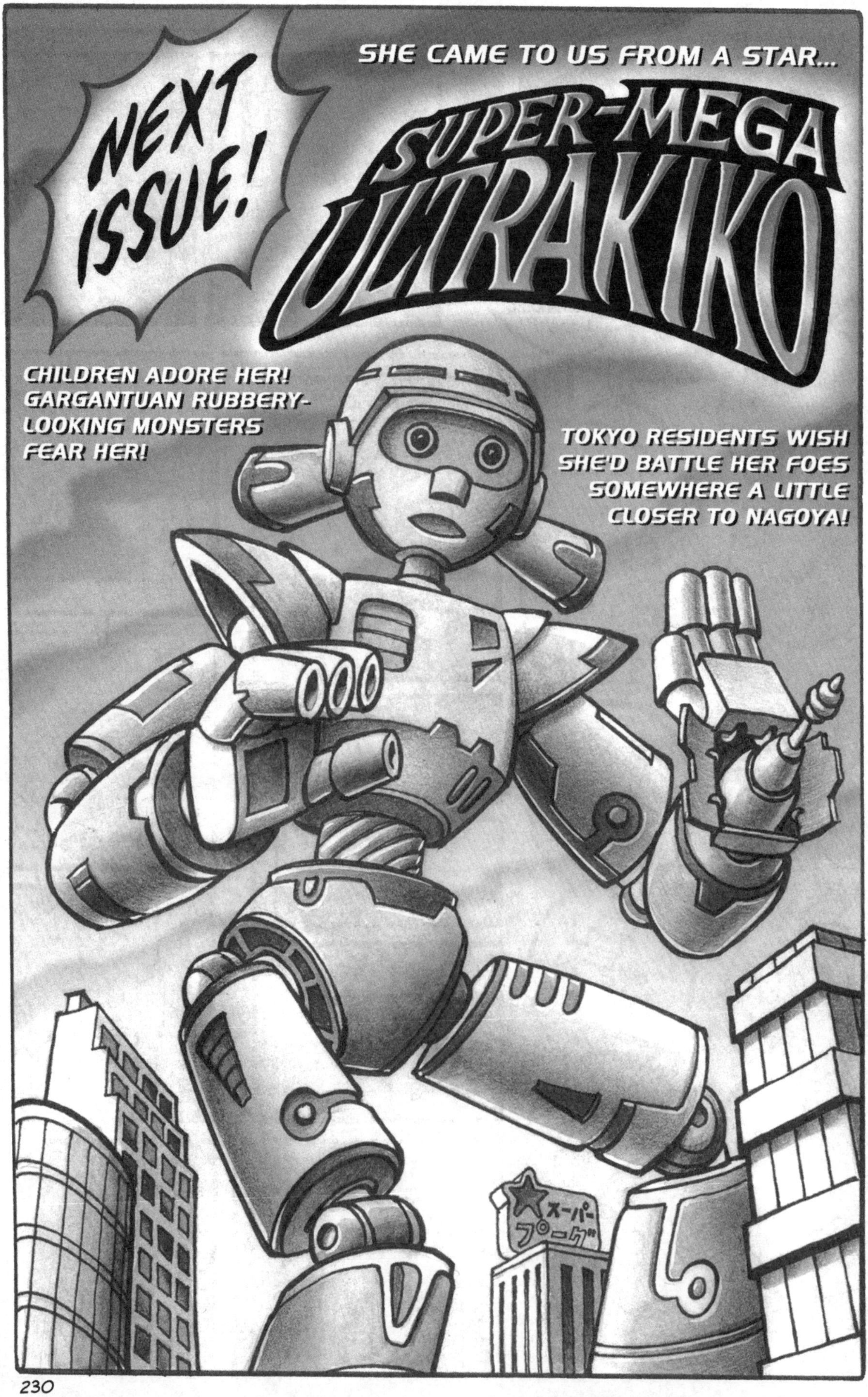
NEXT ISSUE!
SHE CAME TO US FROM A STAR...
SUPER-MEGA ULTRAKIKO
CHILDREN ADORE HER! GARGANTUAN RUBBERY-LOOKING MONSTERS FEAR HER!
TOKYO RESIDENTS WISH SHE'D BATTLE HER FOES SOMEWHERE A LITTLE CLOSER TO NAGOYA!
スーパー

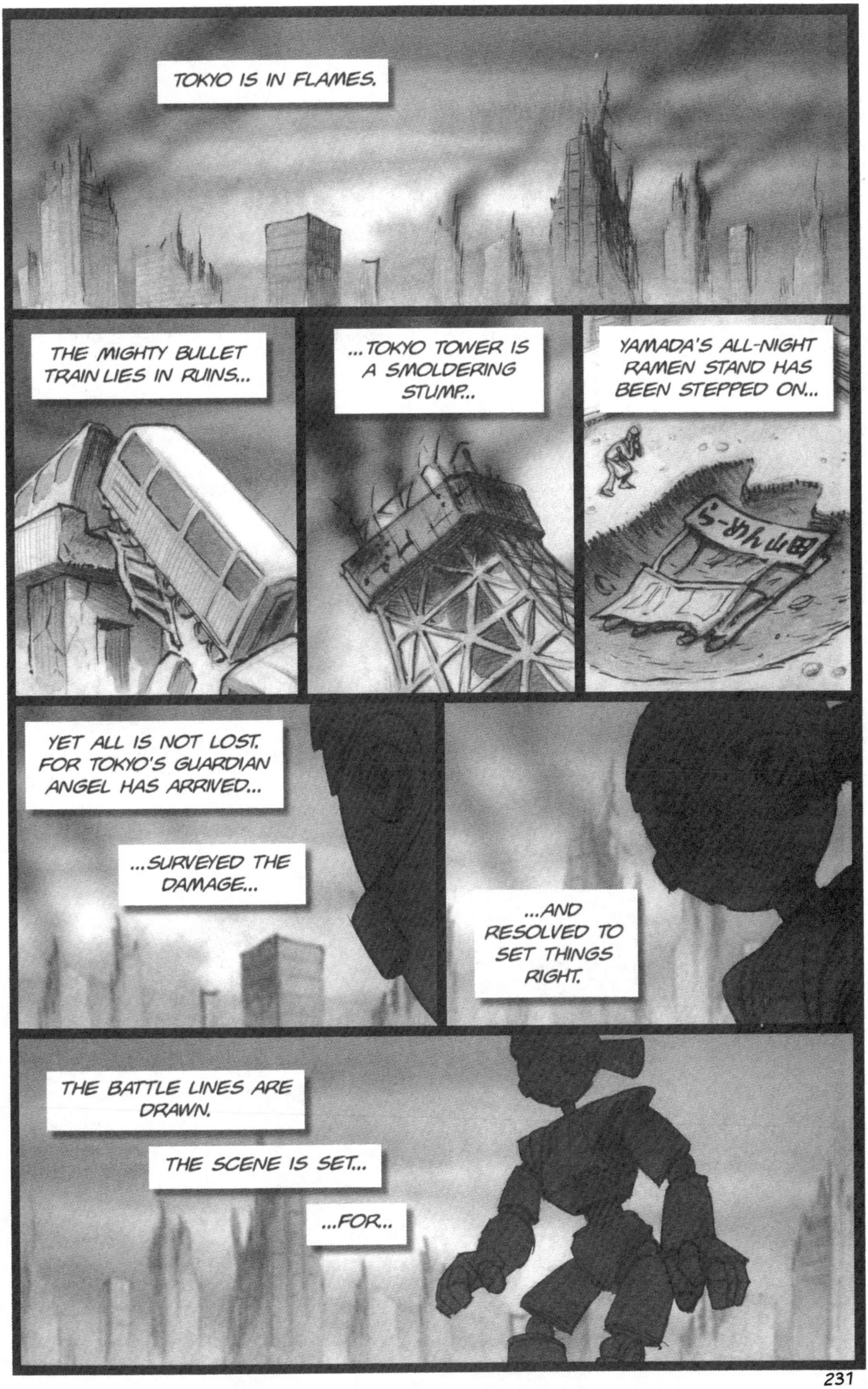
TOKYO IS IN FLAMES.
THE MIGHTY BULLET TRAIN LIES IN RUINS...
...TOKYO TOWER IS A SMOLDERING STUMP...
YAMADA'S ALL-NIGHT RAMEN STAND HAS BEEN STEPPED ON...
YET ALL IS NOT LOST. FOR TOKYO'S GUARDIAN ANGEL HAS ARRIVED...
...SURVEYED THE DAMAGE...
...AND RESOLVED TO SET THINGS RIGHT.
THE BATTLE LINES ARE DRAWN.
THE SCENE IS SET...
...FOR...

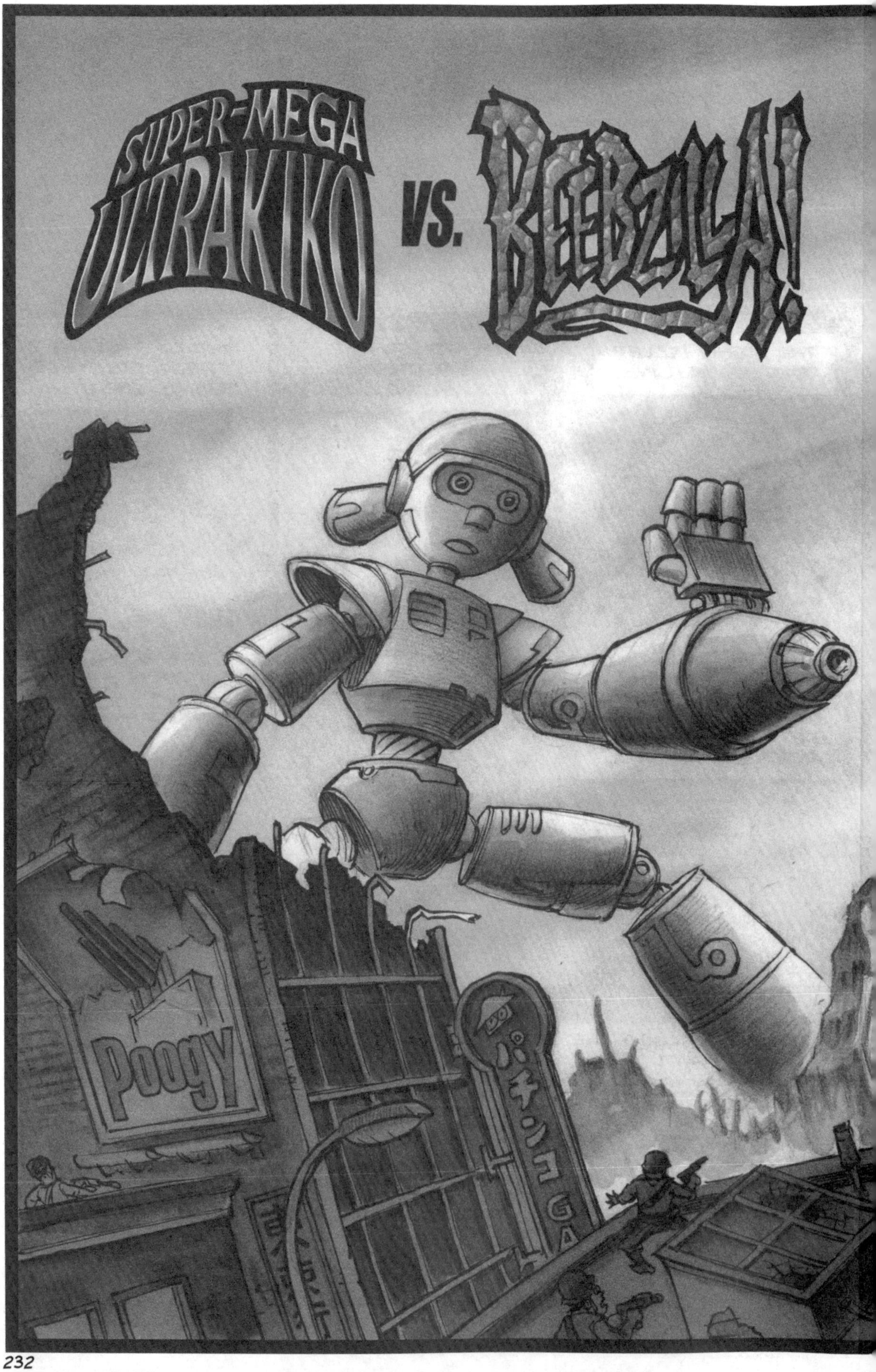
SUPER-MEGA ULTRAKIKO
VS.
BLEEBZILLA!
Poogy
パチンコ

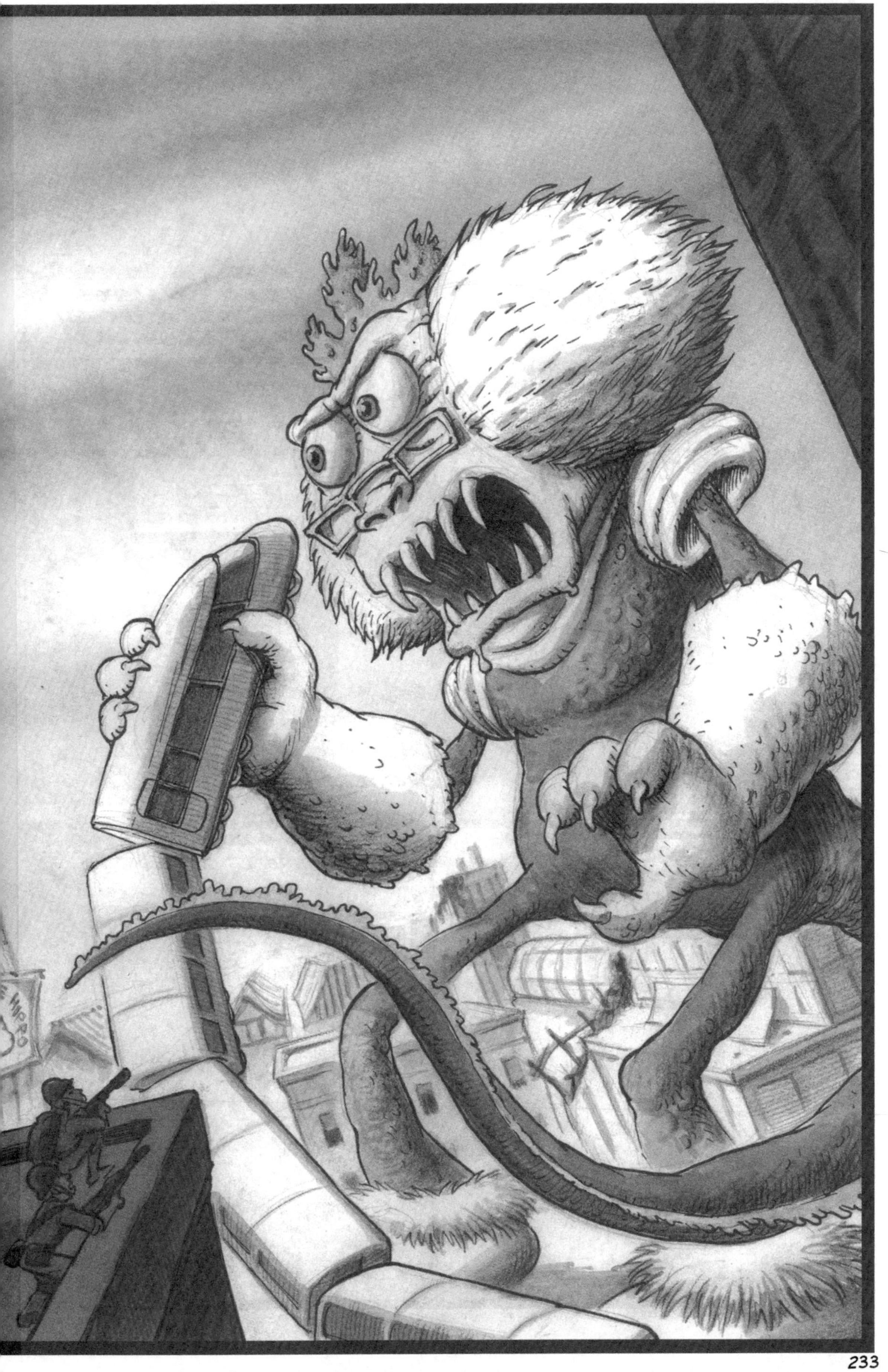

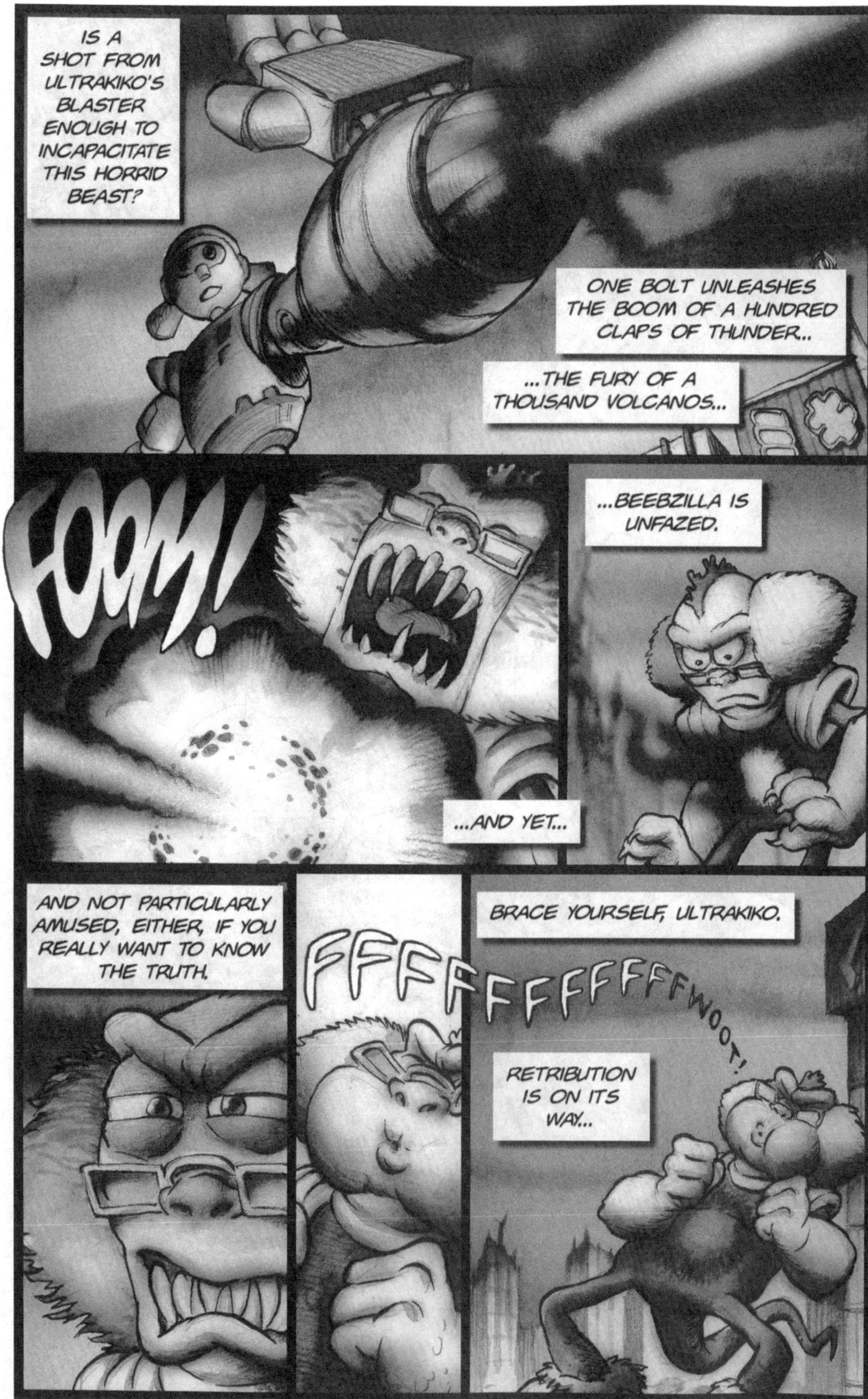
IS A SHOT FROM ULTRAKIKO'S BLASTER ENOUGH TO INCAPACITATE THIS HORRID BEAST?
ONE BOLT UNLEASHES THE BOOM OF A HUNDRED CLAPS OF THUNDER..
...THE FURY OF A THOUSAND VOLCANOS...
FOOM!
...AND YET...
...BEEBZILLA IS UNFAZED.
AND NOT PARTICULARLY AMUSED, EITHER, IF YOU REALLY WANT TO KNOW THE TRUTH.
FFFFFFFFFFFFFFWOOT!
BRACE YOURSELF, ULTRAKIKO.
RETRIBUTION IS ON ITS WAY...

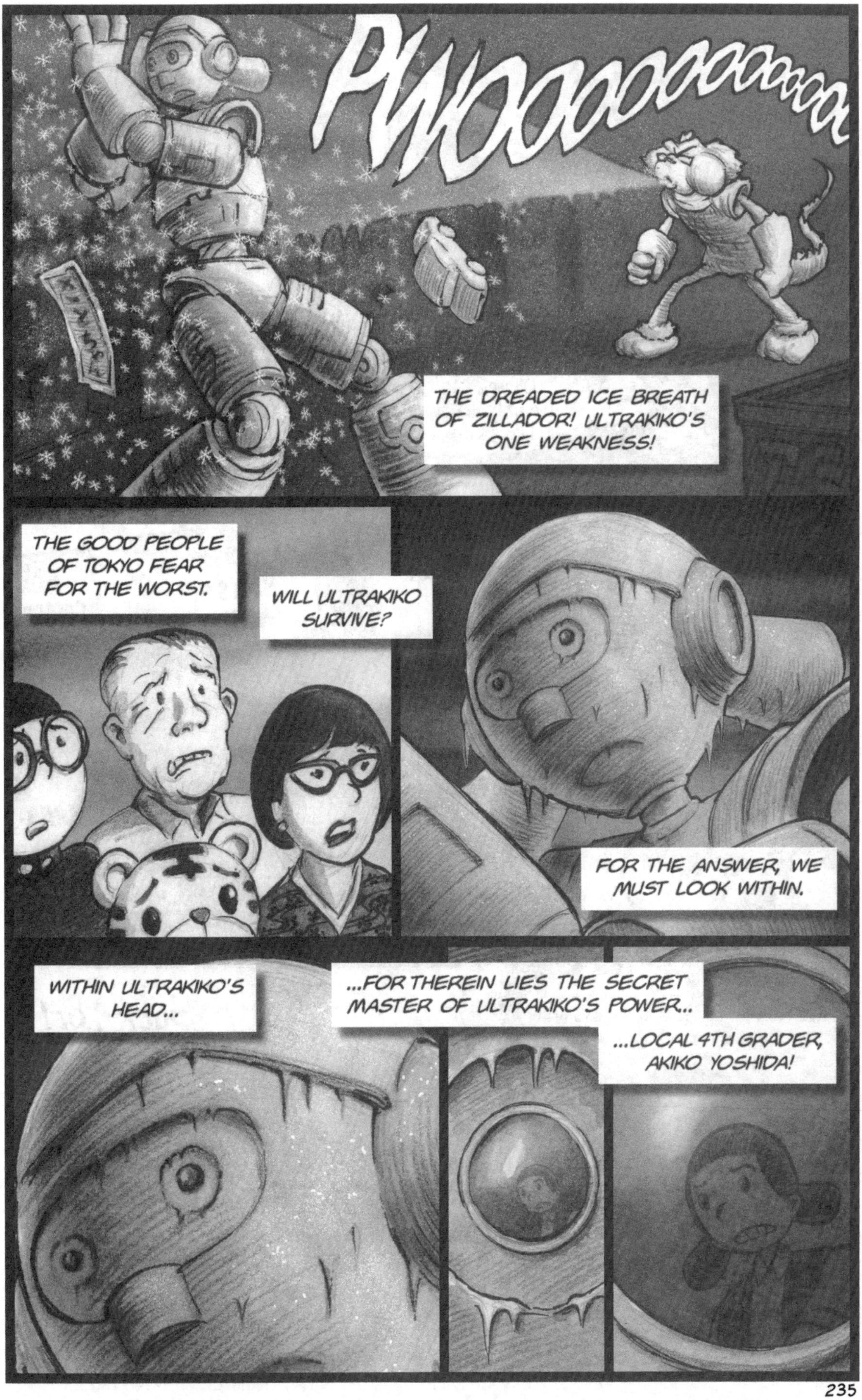
PWOOOOOOOOOOO
THE DREADED ICE BREATH OF ZILLADOR! ULTRAKIKO'S ONE WEAKNESS!
THE GOOD PEOPLE OF TOKYO FEAR FOR THE WORST.
WILL ULTRAKIKO SURVIVE?
FOR THE ANSWER, WE MUST LOOK WITHIN.
WITHIN ULTRAKIKO'S HEAD...
...FOR THEREIN LIES THE SECRET MASTER OF ULTRAKIKO'S POWER...
...LOCAL 4TH GRADER, AKIKO YOSHIDA!

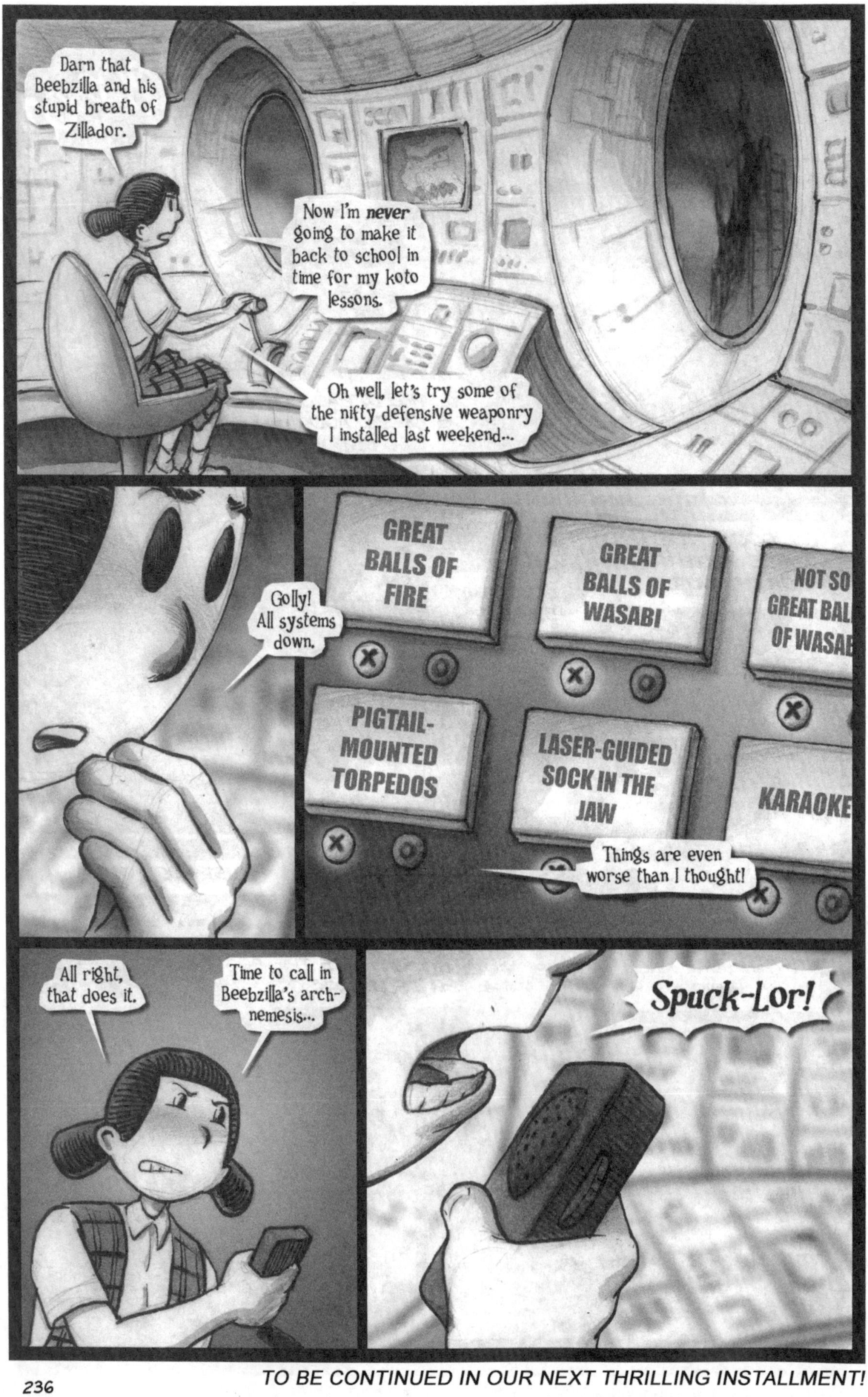
Darn that Beebzilla and his stupid breath of Zillador.
Now I'm ***never*** going to make it back to school in time for my koto lessons.
Oh well, let's try some of the nifty defensive weaponry I installed last weekend...
Golly! All systems down.
GREAT BALLS OF FIRE
GREAT BALLS OF WASABI
PIGTAIL-MOUNTED TORPEDOS
LASER-GUIDED SOCK IN THE JAW
KARAOKE
Things are even worse than I thought!
All right, that does it.
Time to call in Beebzilla's arch-nemesis...
Spuck-Lor!

TO BE CONTINUED IN OUR NEXT THRILLING INSTALLMENT!

'Kiko & Beebs in "The Portrait"

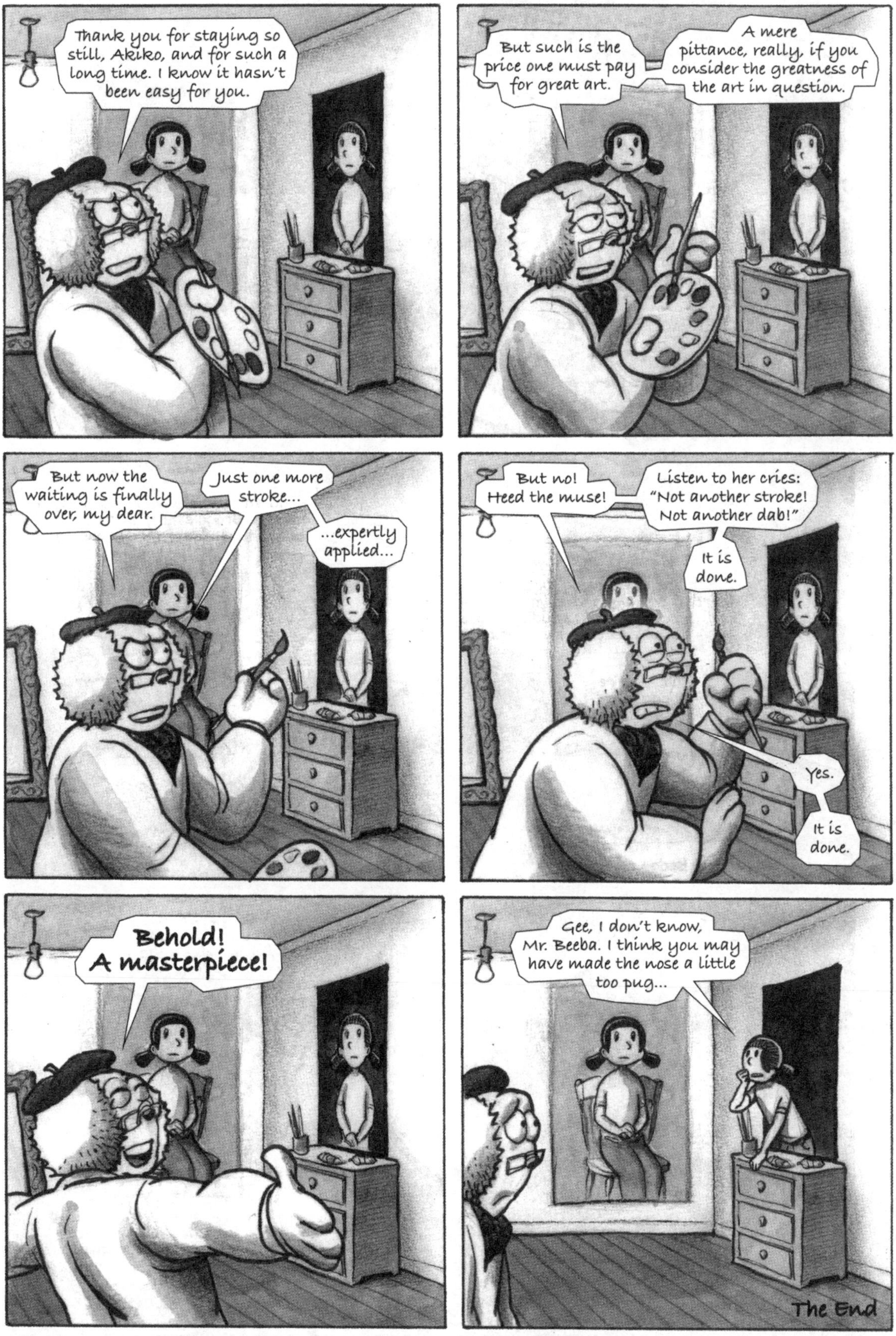

Thank you for staying so still, Akiko, and for such a long time. I know it hasn't been easy for you.
But such is the price one must pay for great art.
A mere pittance, really, if you consider the greatness of the art in question.
But now the waiting is finally over, my dear.
Just one more stroke...
...expertly applied...
But no! Heed the muse!
Listen to her cries: "Not another stroke! Not another dab!"
It is done.
Yes.
It is done.
Behold! A masterpiece!
Gee, I don't know, Mr. Beeba. I think you may have made the nose a little too pug...
The End

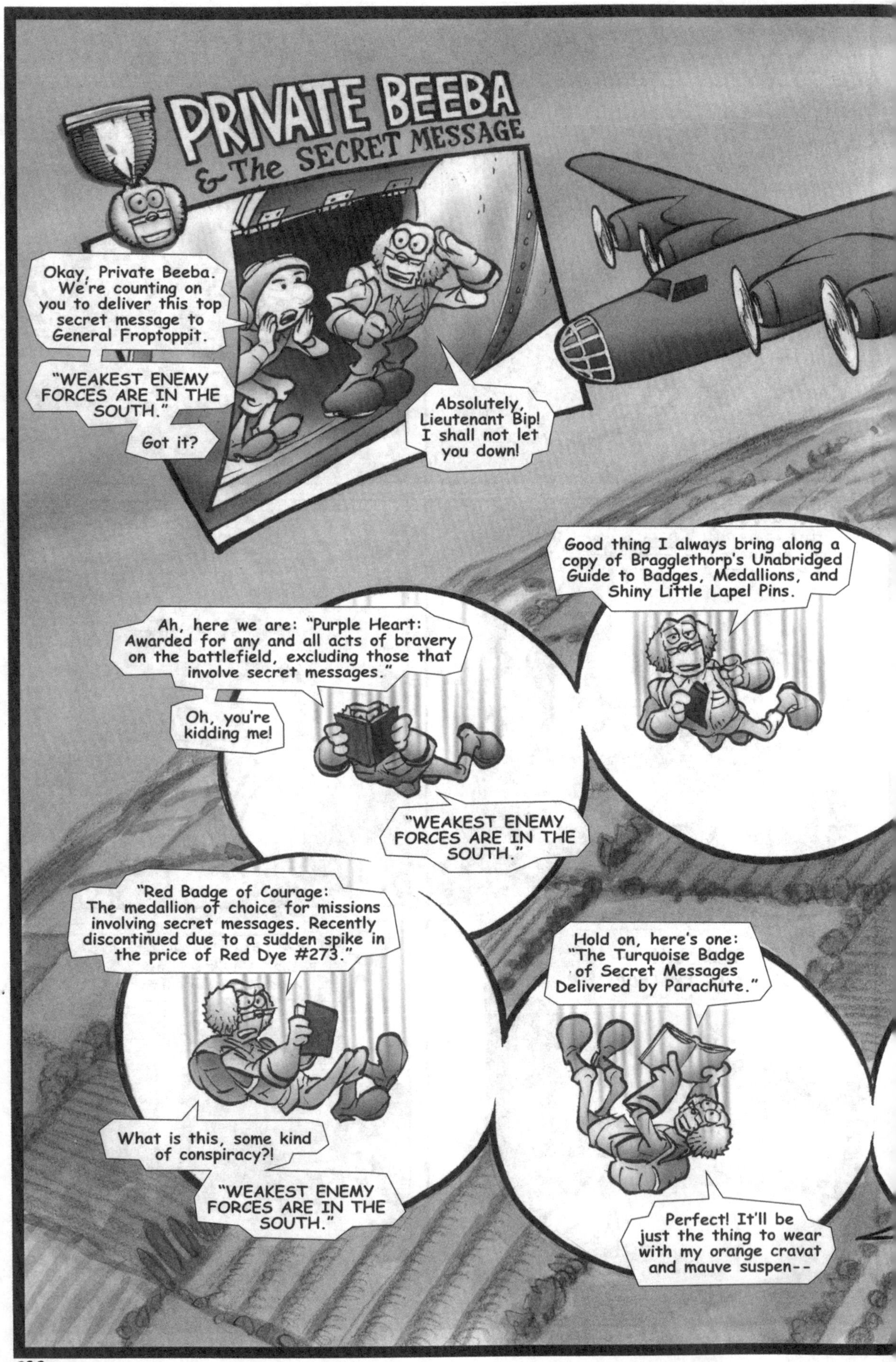
PRIVATE BEEBA
& The SECRET MESSAGE
Okay, Private Beeba. We're counting on you to deliver this top secret message to General Froptoppit.
"WEAKEST ENEMY FORCES ARE IN THE SOUTH."
Got it?
Absolutely, Lieutenant Bip! I shall not let you down!
Good thing I always bring along a copy of Bragglethorp's Unabridged Guide to Badges, Medallions, and Shiny Little Lapel Pins.
Ah, here we are: "Purple Heart: Awarded for any and all acts of bravery on the battlefield, excluding those that involve secret messages."
Oh, you're kidding me!
"WEAKEST ENEMY FORCES ARE IN THE SOUTH."
"Red Badge of Courage: The medallion of choice for missions involving secret messages. Recently discontinued due to a sudden spike in the price of Red Dye #273."
What is this, some kind of conspiracy?!
"WEAKEST ENEMY FORCES ARE IN THE SOUTH."
Hold on, here's one: "The Turquoise Badge of Secret Messages Delivered by Parachute."
Perfect! It'll be just the thing to wear with my orange cravat and mauve suspen--

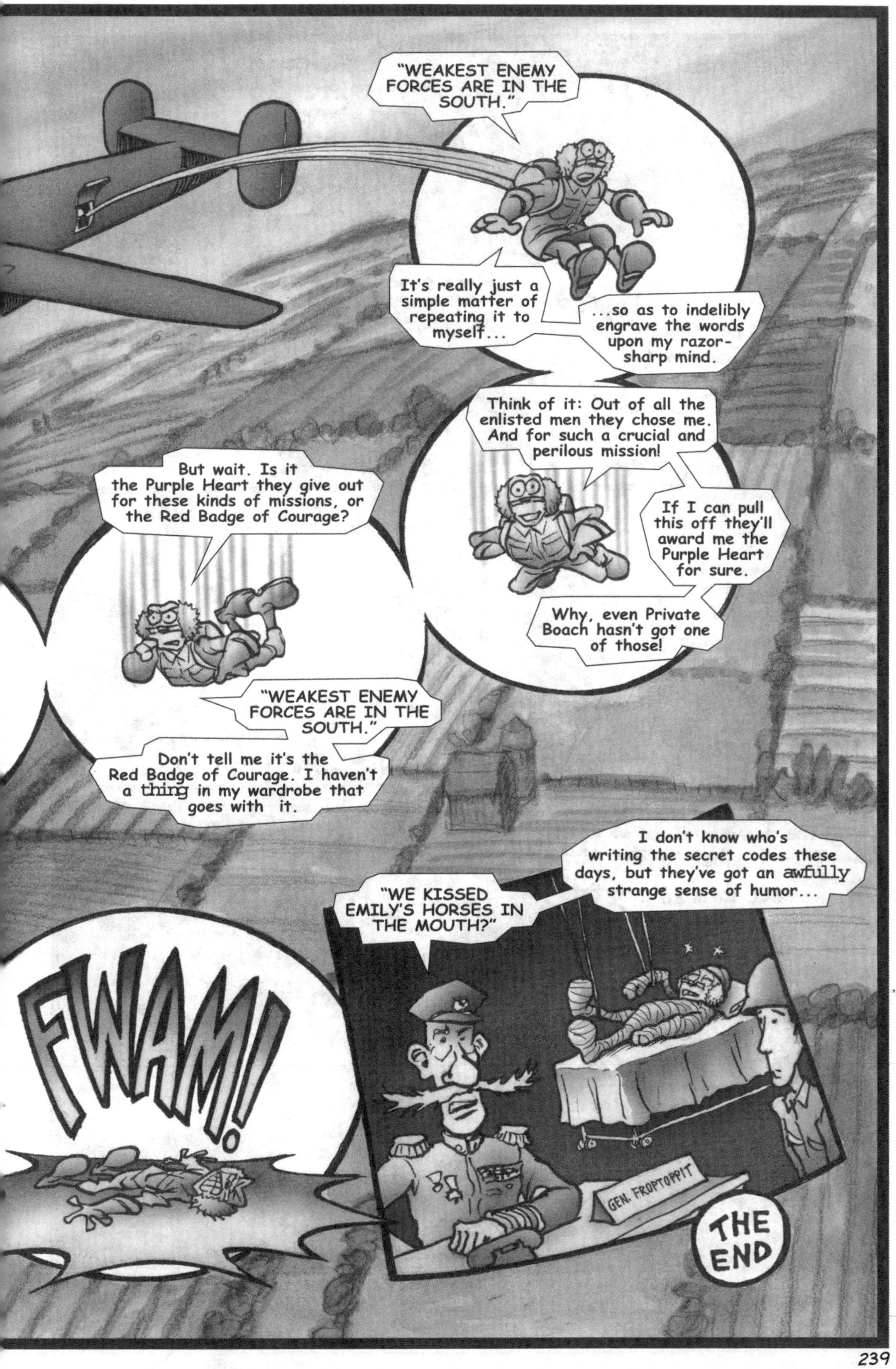
"WEAKEST ENEMY FORCES ARE IN THE SOUTH."
It's really just a simple matter of repeating it to myself...
...so as to indelibly engrave the words upon my razor-sharp mind.
Think of it: Out of all the enlisted men they chose me. And for such a crucial and perilous mission!
If I can pull this off they'll award me the Purple Heart for sure.
Why, even Private Boach hasn't got one of those!
But wait. Is it the Purple Heart they give out for these kinds of missions, or the Red Badge of Courage?
"WEAKEST ENEMY FORCES ARE IN THE SOUTH."
Don't tell me it's the Red Badge of Courage. I haven't a thing in my wardrobe that goes with it.
FWAM!
"WE KISSED EMILY'S HORSES IN THE MOUTH?"
I don't know who's writing the secret codes these days, but they've got an awfully strange sense of humor...
GEN. FROPTOPPIT
THE END

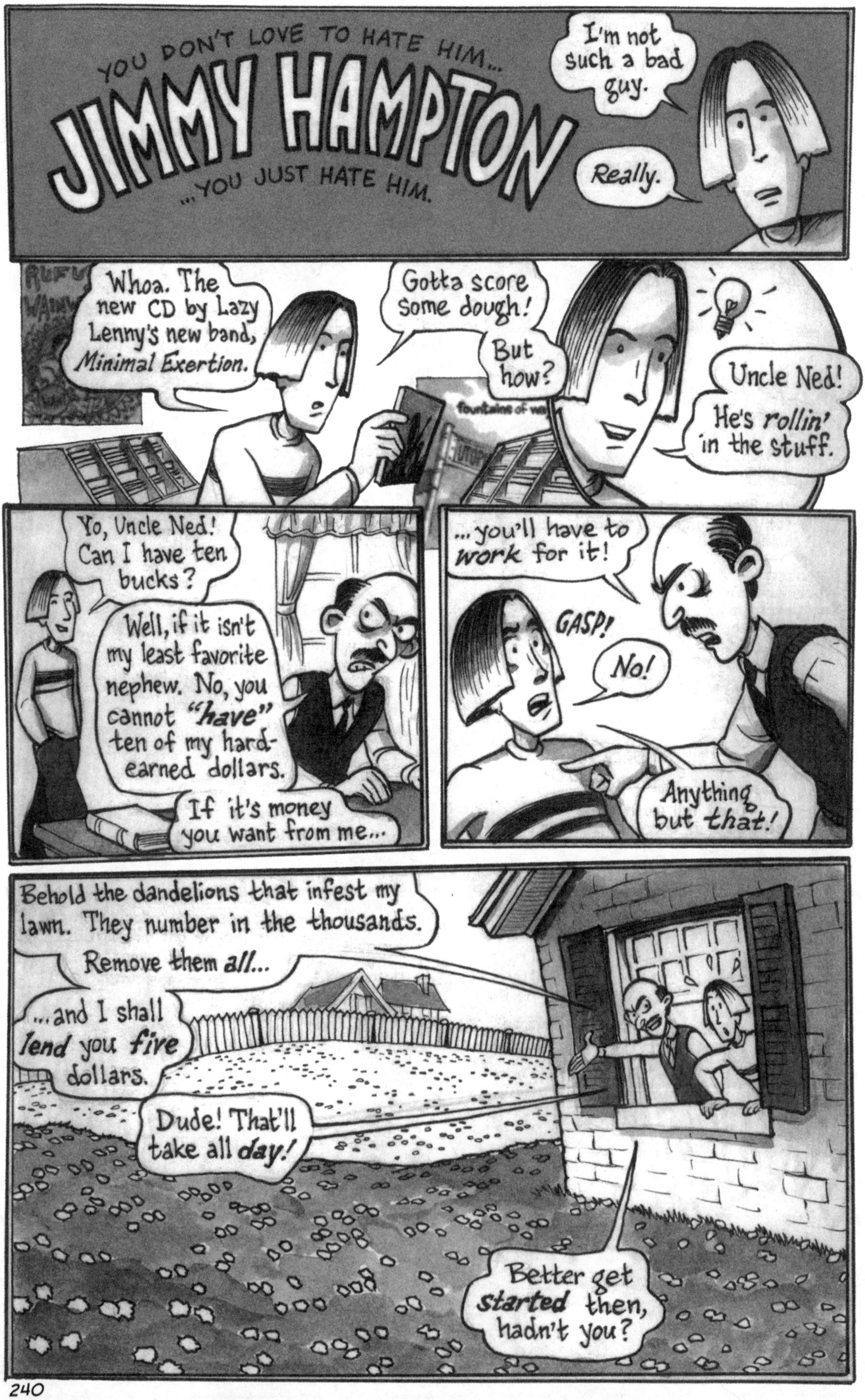
YOU DON'T LOVE TO HATE HIM...
JIMMY HAMPTON
...YOU JUST HATE HIM.
I'm not such a bad guy.
Really.
Whoa. The new CD by Lazy Lenny's new band, Minimal Exertion.
Gotta score some dough!
But how?
Uncle Ned!
He's rollin' in the stuff.
Yo, Uncle Ned! Can I have ten bucks?
Well, if it isn't my least favorite nephew. No, you cannot "have" ten of my hard-earned dollars.
If it's money you want from me...
...you'll have to work for it!
GASP!
No!
Anything but that!
Behold the dandelions that infest my lawn. They number in the thousands.
Remove them all...
...and I shall lend you five dollars.
Dude! That'll take all day!
Better get started then, hadn't you?

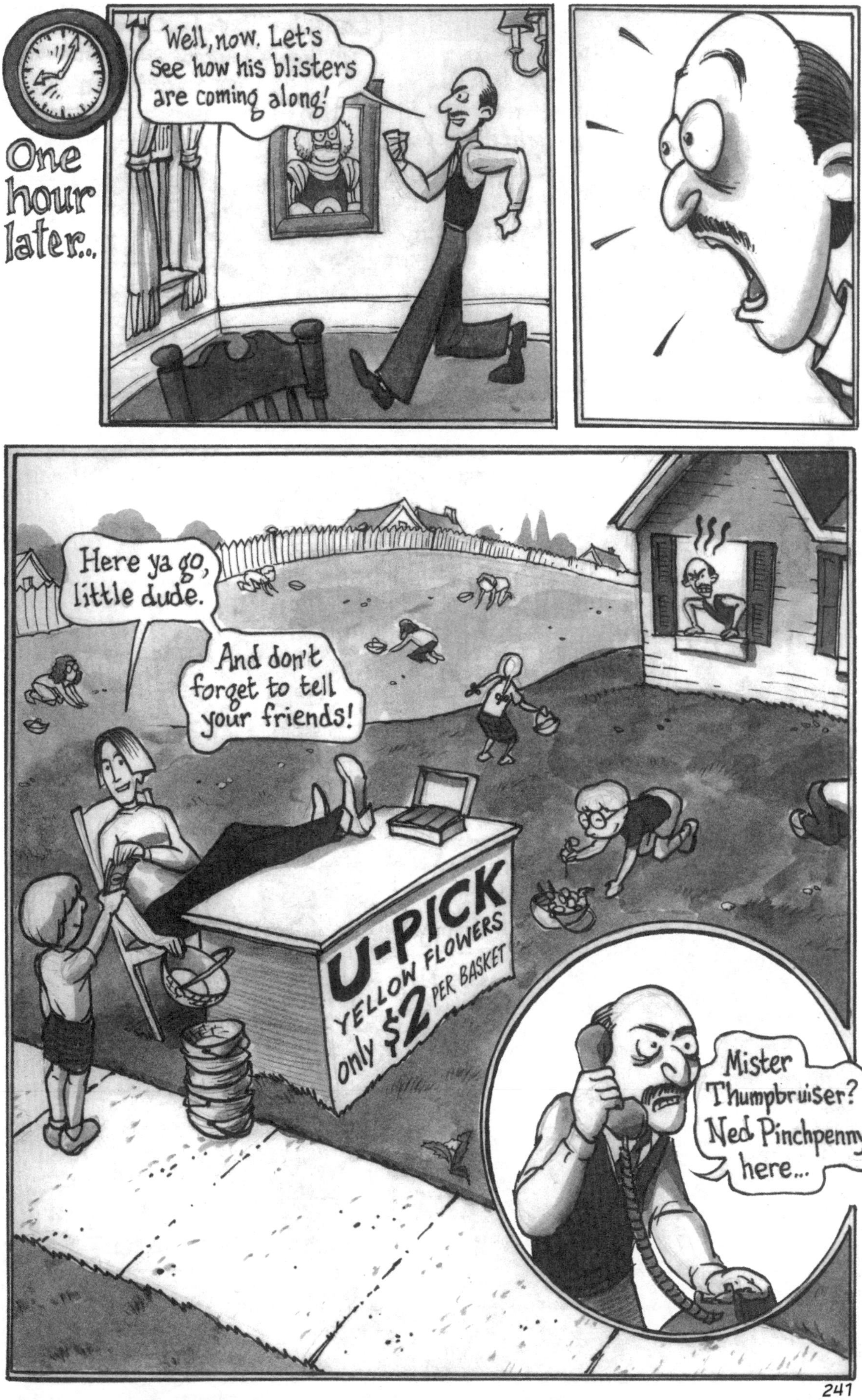
One hour later...
Well, now. Let's see how his blisters are coming along!
Here ya go, little dude.
And don't forget to tell your friends!
U-PICK YELLOW FLOWERS only $2 PER BASKET
Mister Thumpbruiser? Ned Pinchpenny here...

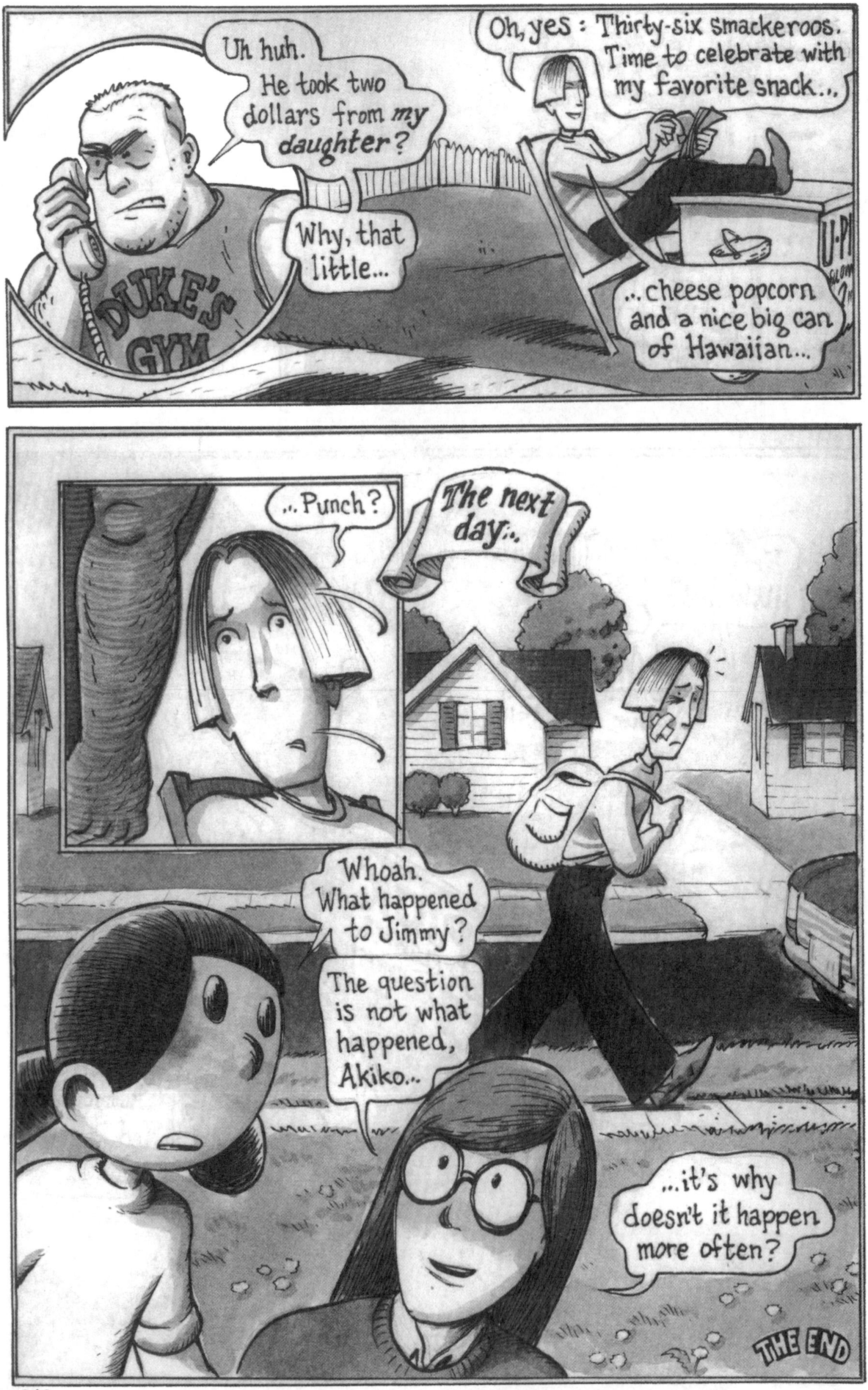
Uh huh.
He took two dollars from my daughter?
Why, that little...
Oh, yes: Thirty-six smackeroos. Time to celebrate with my favorite snack...
...cheese popcorn and a nice big can of Hawaiian...
DUKE'S GYM
...Punch?
The next day...
Whoah. What happened to Jimmy?
The question is not what happened, Akiko...
...it's why doesn't it happen more often?
THE END

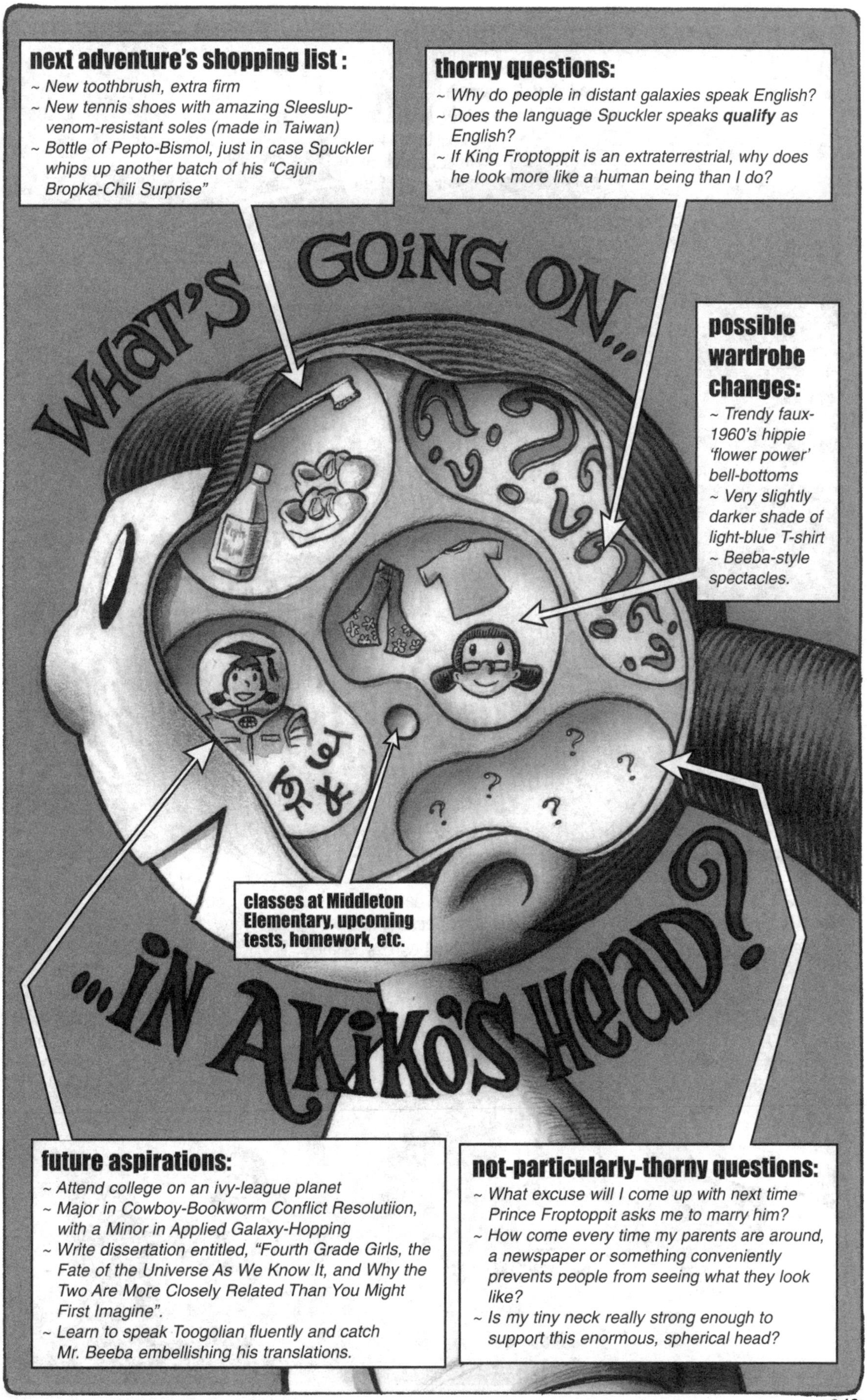

next adventure's shopping list :
~ New toothbrush, extra firm
~ New tennis shoes with amazing Sleeslup-venom-resistant soles (made in Taiwan)
~ Bottle of Pepto-Bismol, just in case Spuckler whips up another batch of his "Cajun Bropka-Chili Surprise"
thorny questions:
~ Why do people in distant galaxies speak English?
~ Does the language Spuckler speaks **qualify** as English?
~ If King Froptoppit is an extraterrestrial, why does he look more like a human being than I do?
WHAT'S GOING ON...
possible wardrobe changes:
~ Trendy faux-1960's hippie 'flower power' bell-bottoms
~ Very slightly darker shade of light-blue T-shirt
~ Beeba-style spectacles.
classes at Middleton Elementary, upcoming tests, homework, etc.
...IN AKIKO'S HEAD?
future aspirations:
~ Attend college on an ivy-league planet
~ Major in Cowboy-Bookworm Conflict Resolutiion, with a Minor in Applied Galaxy-Hopping
~ Write dissertation entitled, "Fourth Grade Girls, the Fate of the Universe As We Know It, and Why the Two Are More Closely Related Than You Might First Imagine".
~ Learn to speak Toogolian fluently and catch Mr. Beeba embellishing his translations.
not-particularly-thorny questions:
~ What excuse will I come up with next time Prince Froptoppit asks me to marry him?
~ How come every time my parents are around, a newspaper or something conveniently prevents people from seeing what they look like?
~ Is my tiny neck really strong enough to support this enormous, spherical head?

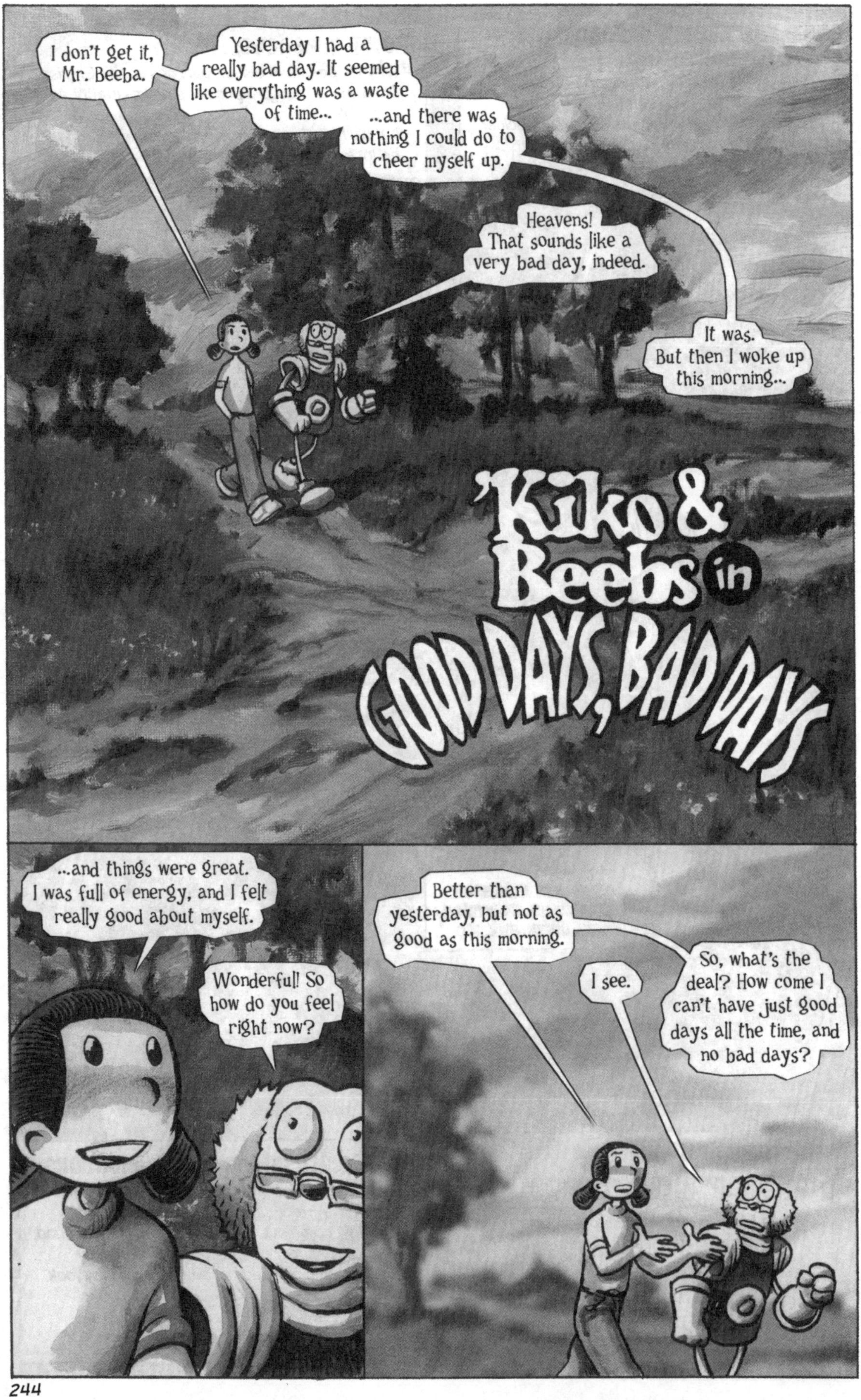
I don't get it, Mr. Beeba.
Yesterday I had a really bad day. It seemed like everything was a waste of time...
...and there was nothing I could do to cheer myself up.
Heavens! That sounds like a very bad day, indeed.
It was. But then I woke up this morning...
'Kiko & Beebs in
GOOD DAYS, BAD DAYS
...and things were great. I was full of energy, and I felt really good about myself.
Wonderful! So how do you feel right now?
Better than yesterday, but not as good as this morning.
I see.
So, what's the deal? How come I can't have just good days all the time, and no bad days?

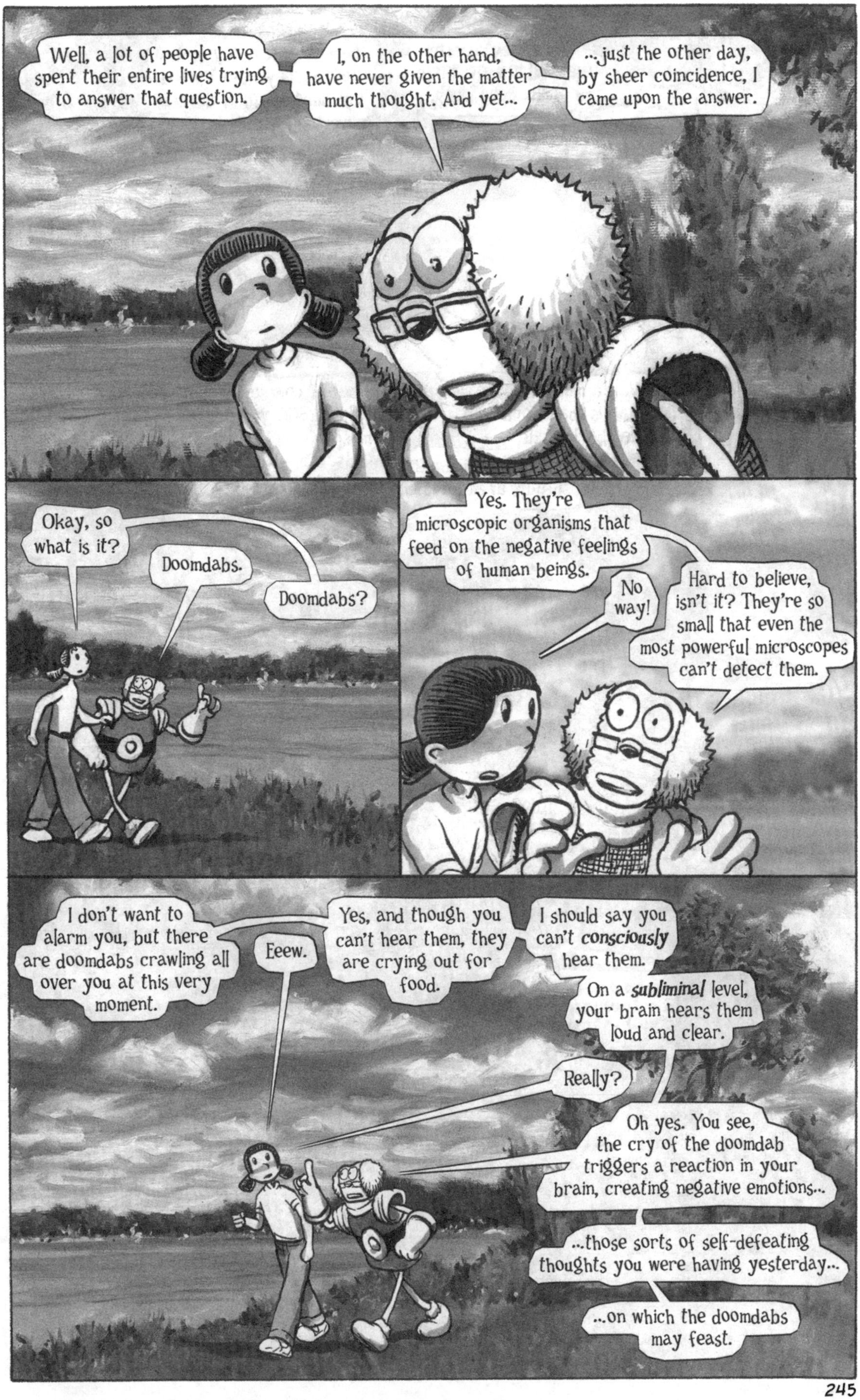
Well, a lot of people have spent their entire lives trying to answer that question.
I, on the other hand, have never given the matter much thought. And yet...
...just the other day, by sheer coincidence, I came upon the answer.
Okay, so what is it?
Doomdabs.
Doomdabs?
Yes. They're microscopic organisms that feed on the negative feelings of human beings.
No way!
Hard to believe, isn't it? They're so small that even the most powerful microscopes can't detect them.
I don't want to alarm you, but there are doomdabs crawling all over you at this very moment.
Eeew.
Yes, and though you can't hear them, they are crying out for food.
I should say you can't *consciously* hear them.
On a *subliminal* level, your brain hears them loud and clear.
Really?
Oh yes. You see, the cry of the doomdab triggers a reaction in your brain, creating negative emotions...
...those sorts of self-defeating thoughts you were having yesterday...
...on which the doomdabs may feast.

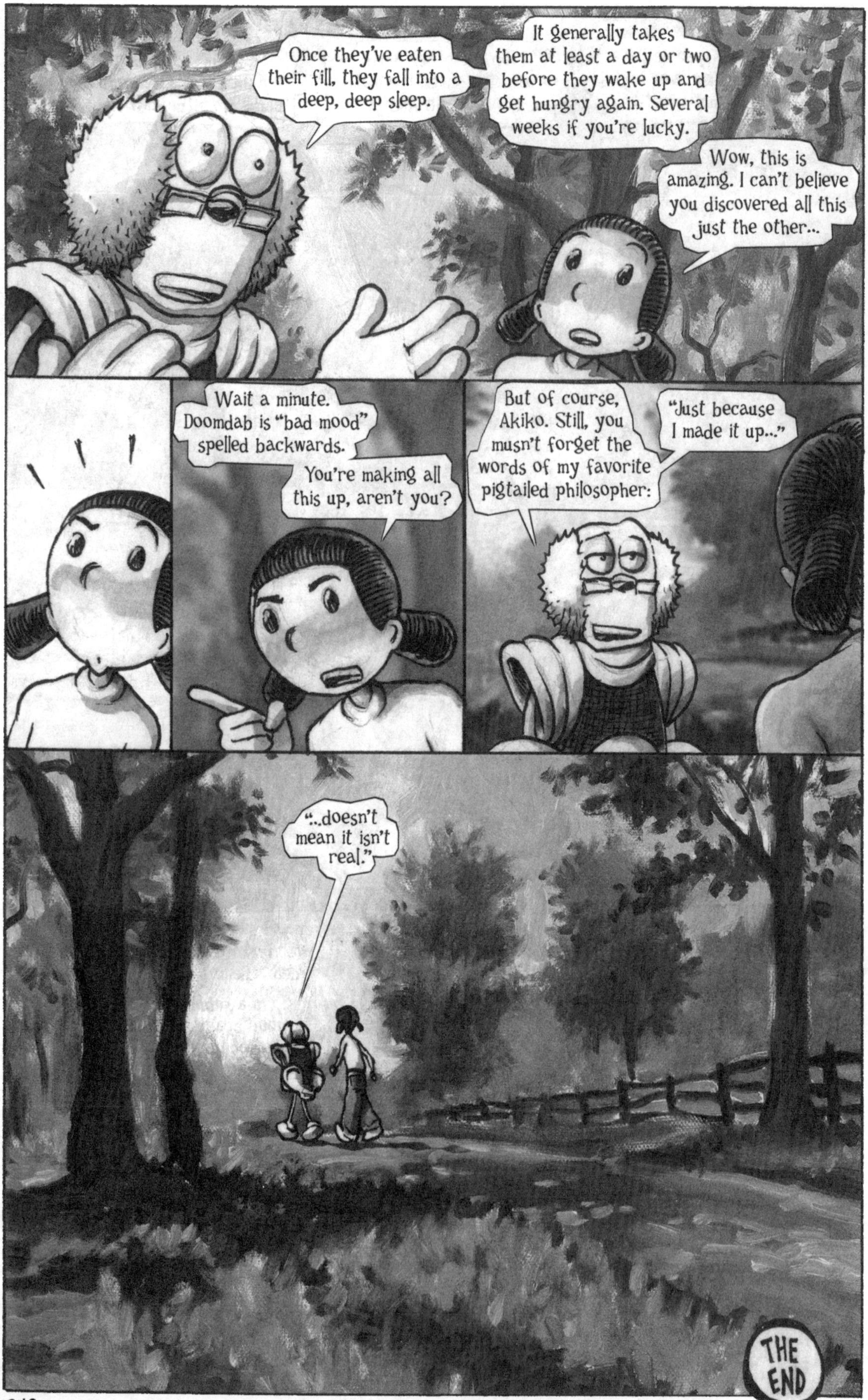
Once they've eaten their fill, they fall into a deep, deep sleep.
It generally takes them at least a day or two before they wake up and get hungry again. Several weeks if you're lucky.
Wow, this is amazing. I can't believe you discovered all this just the other...
Wait a minute. Doomdab is "bad mood" spelled backwards.
You're making all this up, aren't you?
But of course, Akiko. Still, you musn't forget the words of my favorite pigtailed philosopher:
"Just because I made it up..."
"..doesn't mean it isn't real."
THE END

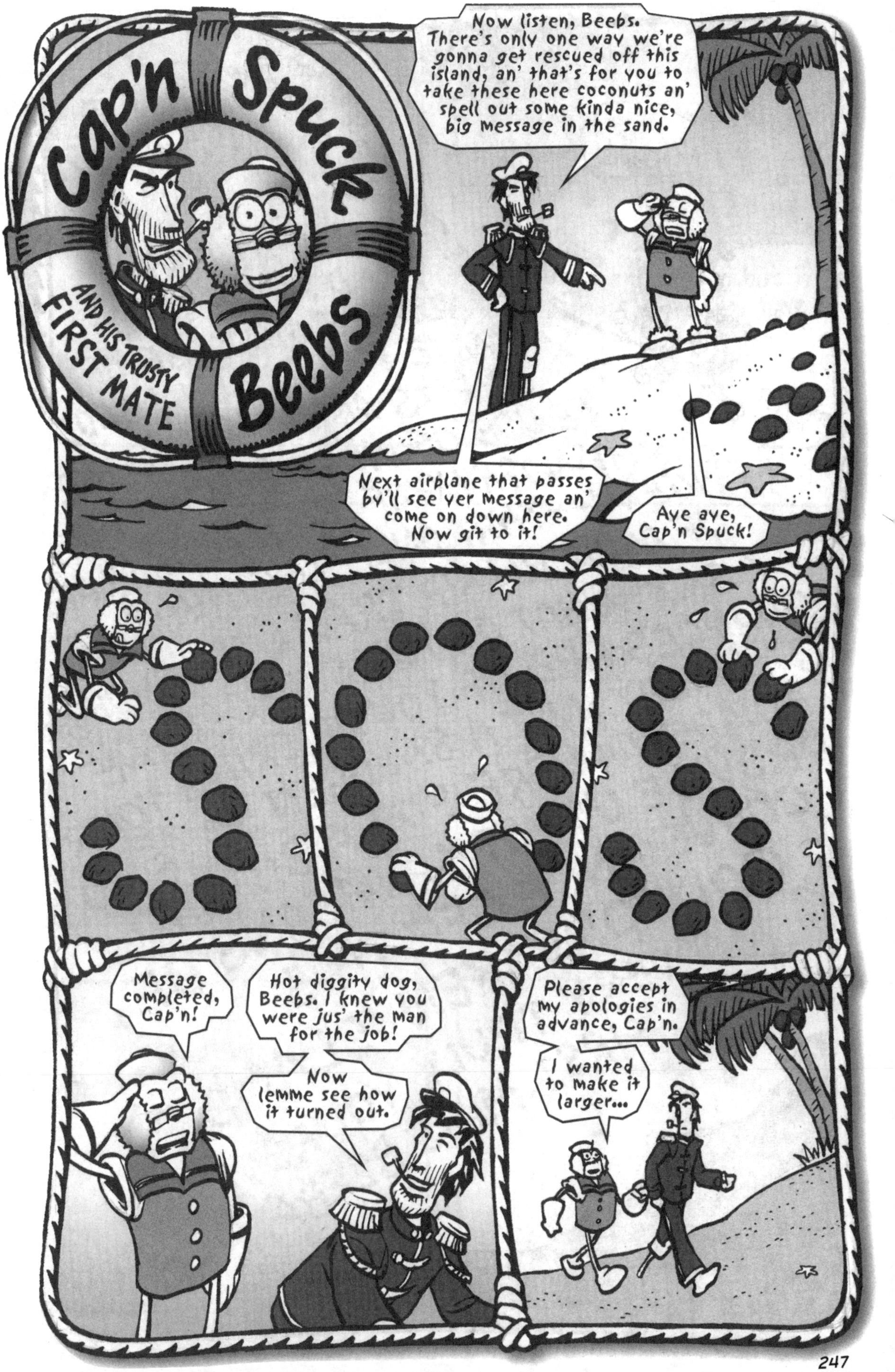
Cap'n Spuck
AND HIS TRUSTY FIRST MATE
Beebs
Now listen, Beebs. There's only one way we're gonna get rescued off this island, an' that's for you to take these here coconuts an' spell out some kinda nice, big message in the sand.
Next airplane that passes by'll see yer message an' come on down here. Now git to it!
Aye aye, Cap'n Spuck!
Message completed, Cap'n!
Hot diggity dog, Beebs. I knew you were jus' the man for the job!
Now lemme see how it turned out.
Please accept my apologies in advance, Cap'n.
I wanted to make it larger...

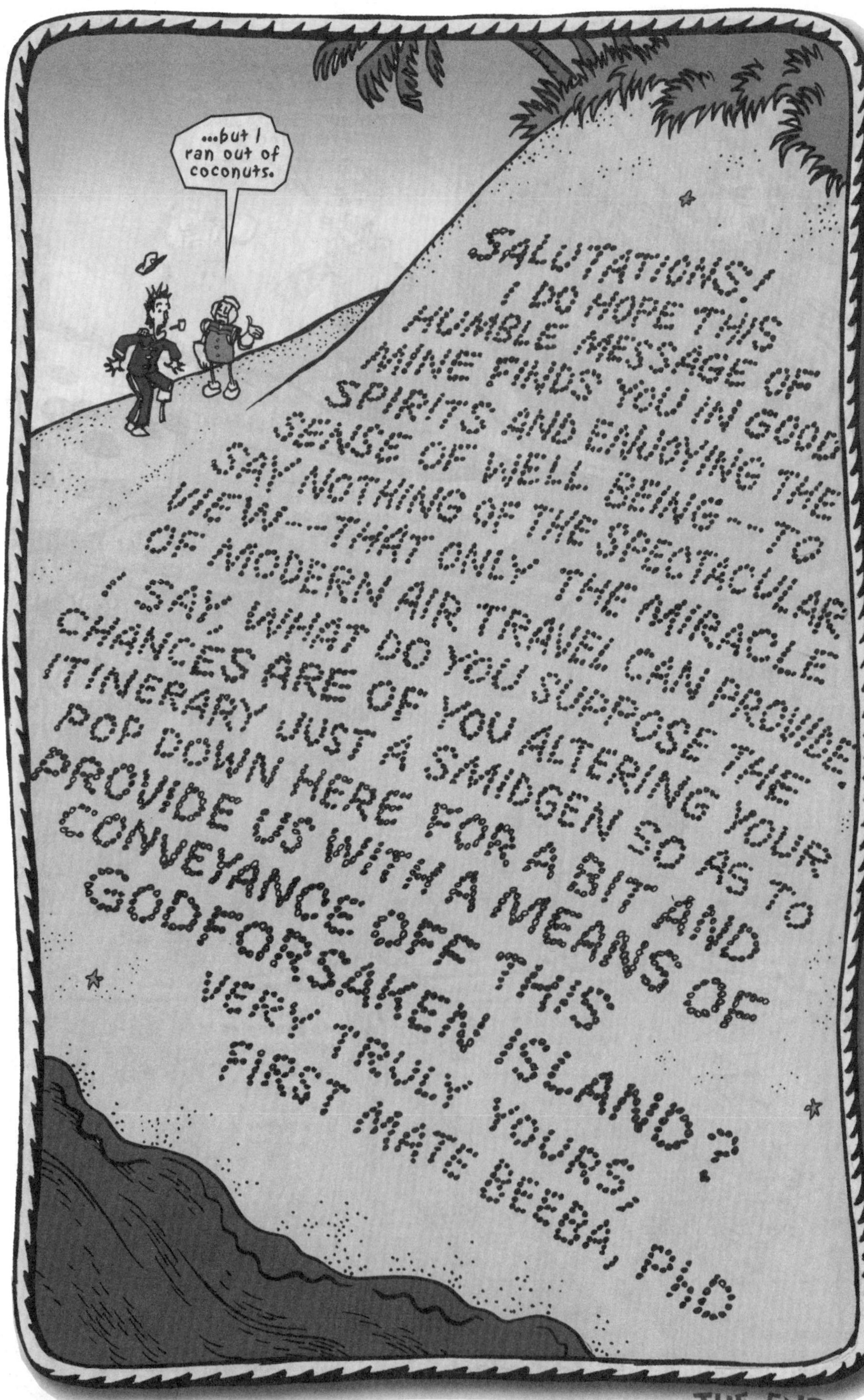
...but I ran out of coconuts.
SALUTATIONS! I DO HOPE THIS HUMBLE MESSAGE OF MINE FINDS YOU IN GOOD SPIRITS AND ENJOYING THE SENSE OF WELL BEING---TO SAY NOTHING OF THE SPECTACULAR VIEW---THAT ONLY THE MIRACLE OF MODERN AIR TRAVEL CAN PROVIDE. I SAY, WHAT DO YOU SUPPOSE THE CHANCES ARE OF YOU ALTERING YOUR ITINERARY JUST A SMIDGEN SO AS TO POP DOWN HERE FOR A BIT AND PROVIDE US WITH A MEANS OF CONVEYANCE OFF THIS GODFORSAKEN ISLAND?
VERY TRULY YOURS,
FIRST MATE BEEBA, PHD
THE END

24 WAYS TO DRAW AKIKO

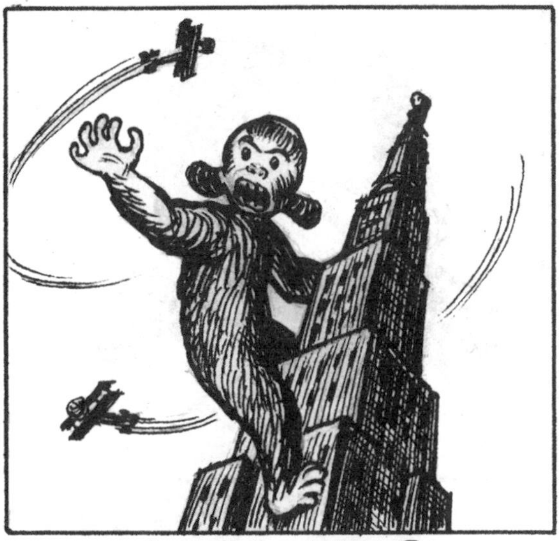

'KIKO KONG

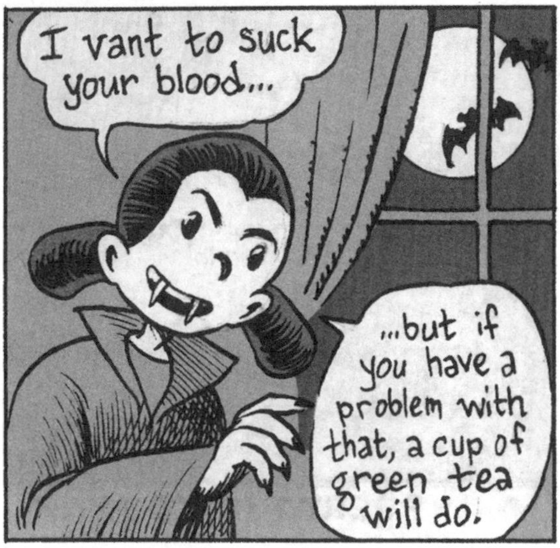
I vant to suck your blood...
...but if you have a problem with that, a cup of green tea will do.

COUNT AKIKULA

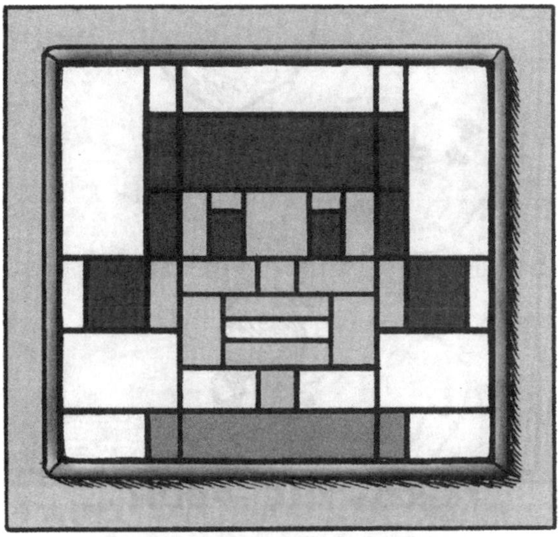

MONDRIAN 'KIKO

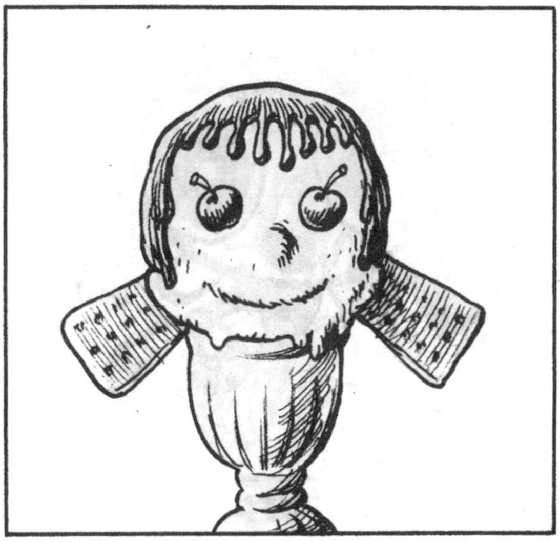

'KIKO SUNDAE

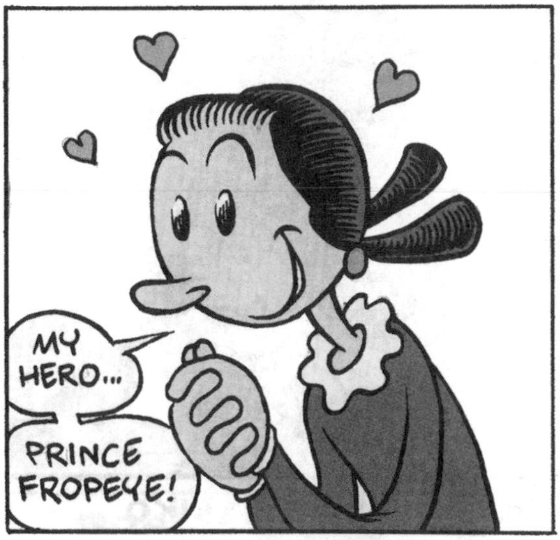
MY HERO...
PRINCE FROPEYE!

OLIVE 'KIKO

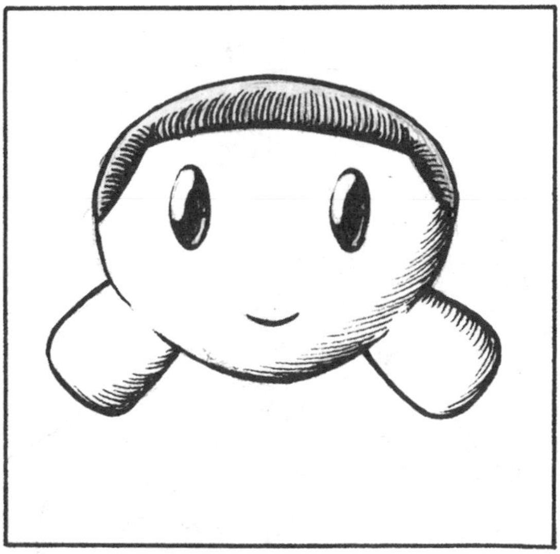

POOGIKO

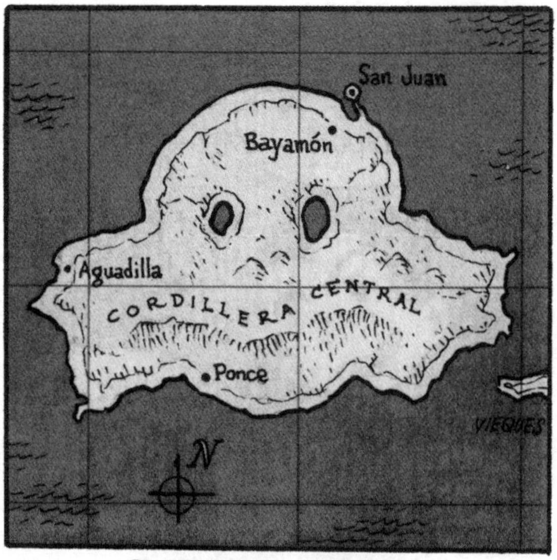
San Juan
Bayamón
Aguadilla
CORDILLERA CENTRAL
Ponce
VIEQUES
N

PUERTO 'KIKO

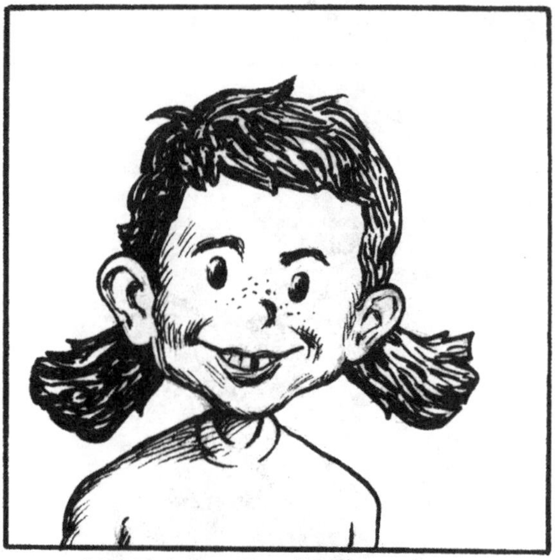

AKIKO E. NEUMAN

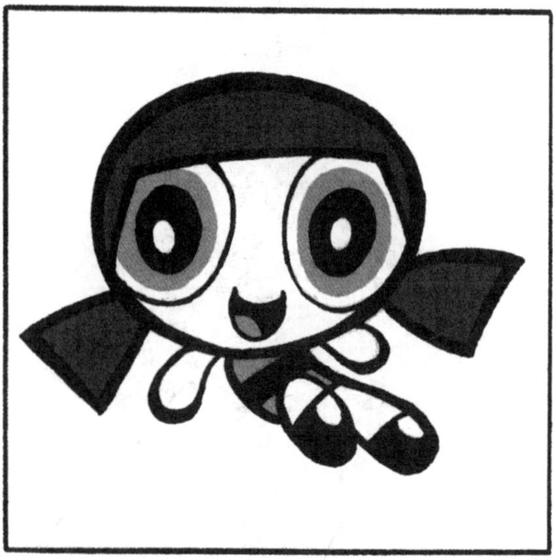

POWER PUFF 'KIKO

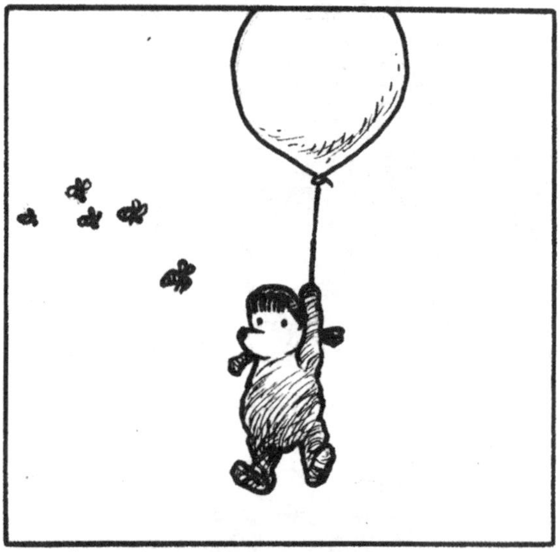

'KIKO-THE-POOH

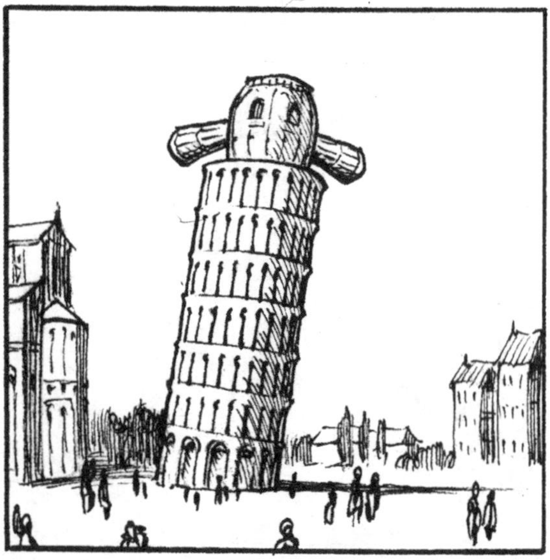

THE LEANING TOWER OF 'KIKO

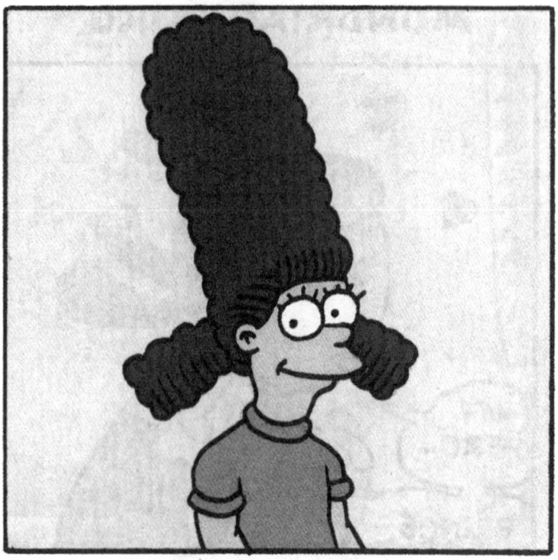

MARGE 'KIKO

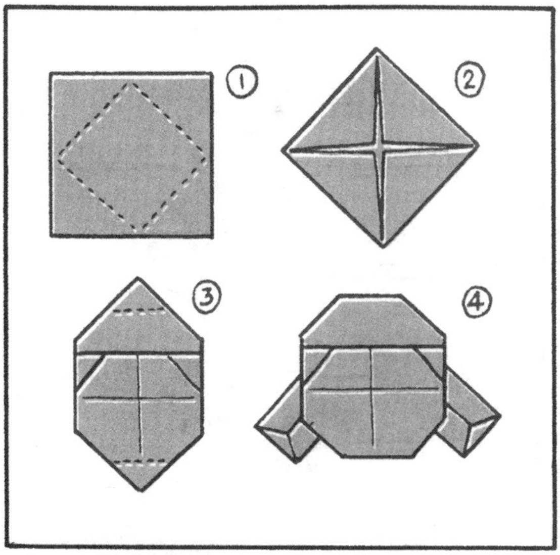
1
2
3
4

ORIGAMI 'KIKO

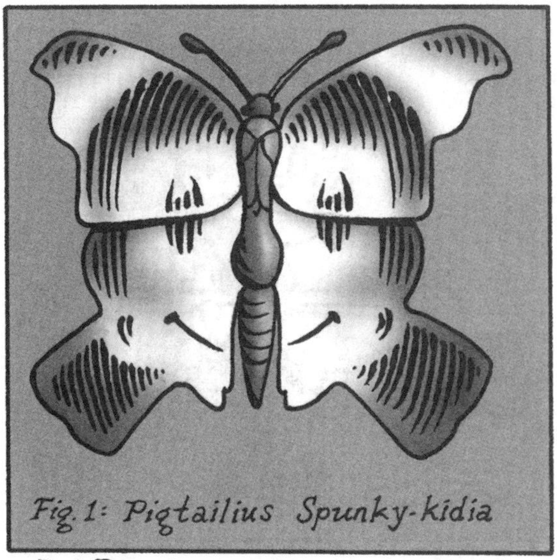
Fig. 1: Pigtailius Spunky-kidia

RARE BUTTERFLY 'KIKO

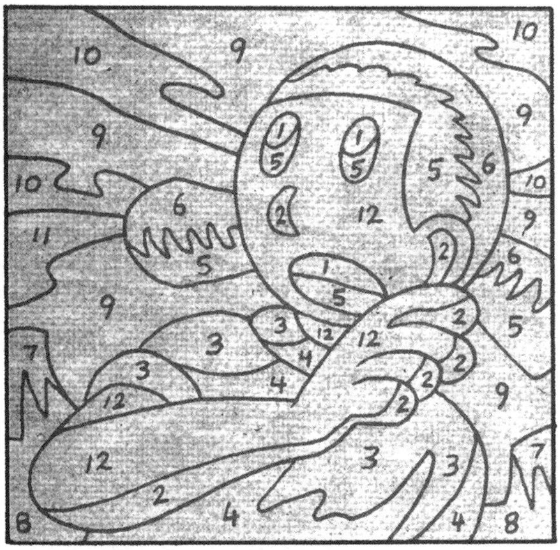

PAINT-BY-NUMBERS 'KIKO

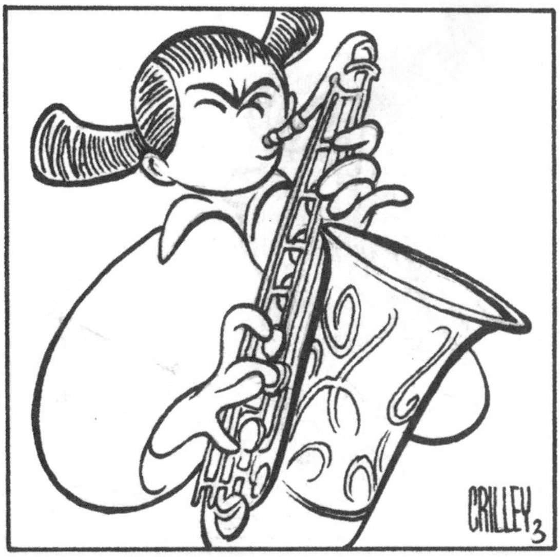
CRILLEY3

HIRSCHFELD 'KIKO

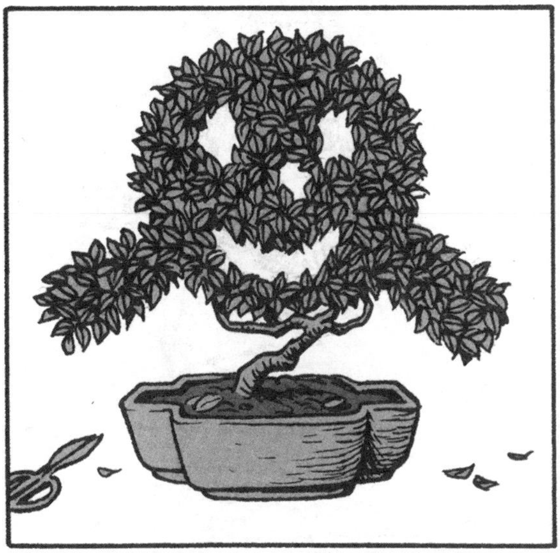

BONSAI 'KIKO

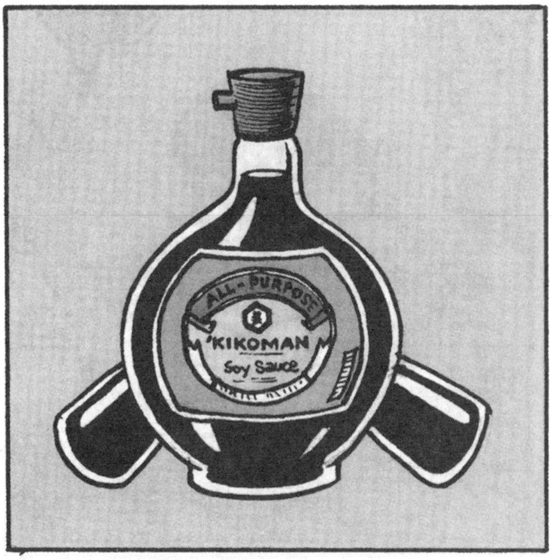
ALL-PURPOSE
'KIKOMAN
Soy Sauce

'KIKOMAN

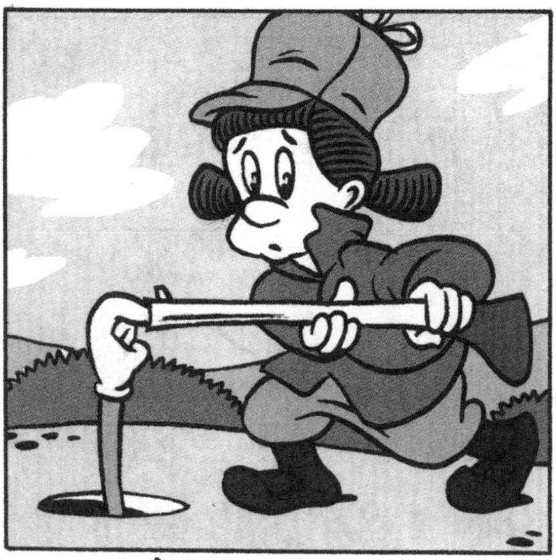

'KIKO FUDD

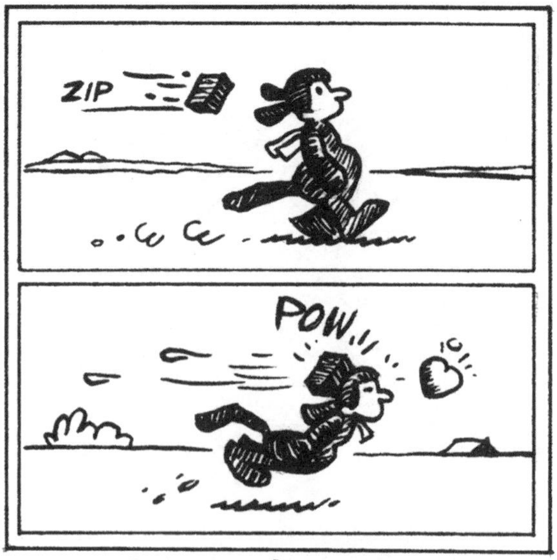
ZIP
POW

KRAZY 'KIKO

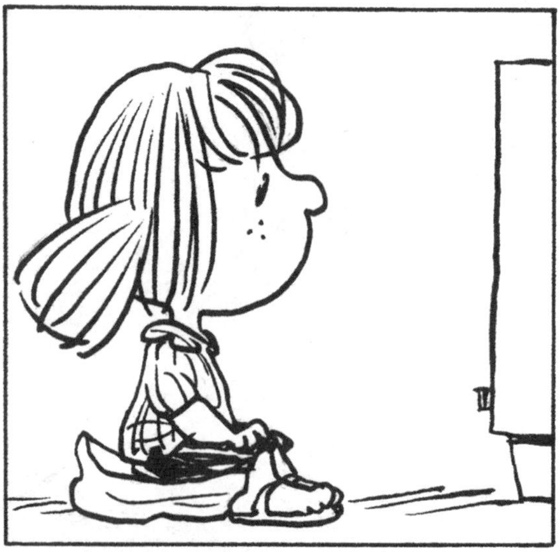

'KIKOMINT PATTY

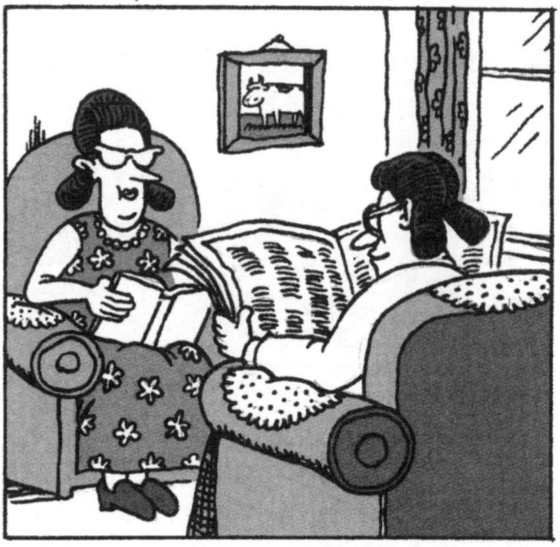

THE 'KIKO SIDE

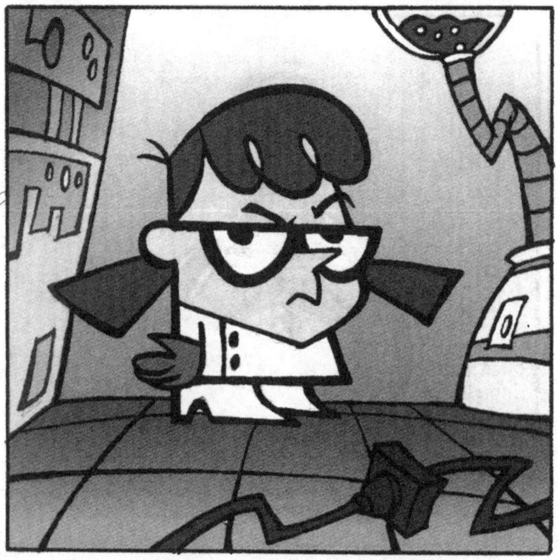

'KIKO'S LABORATORY

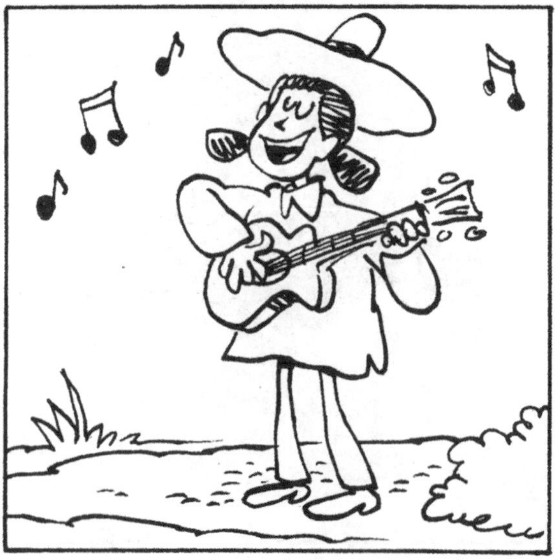

KIKIO ARAGONES

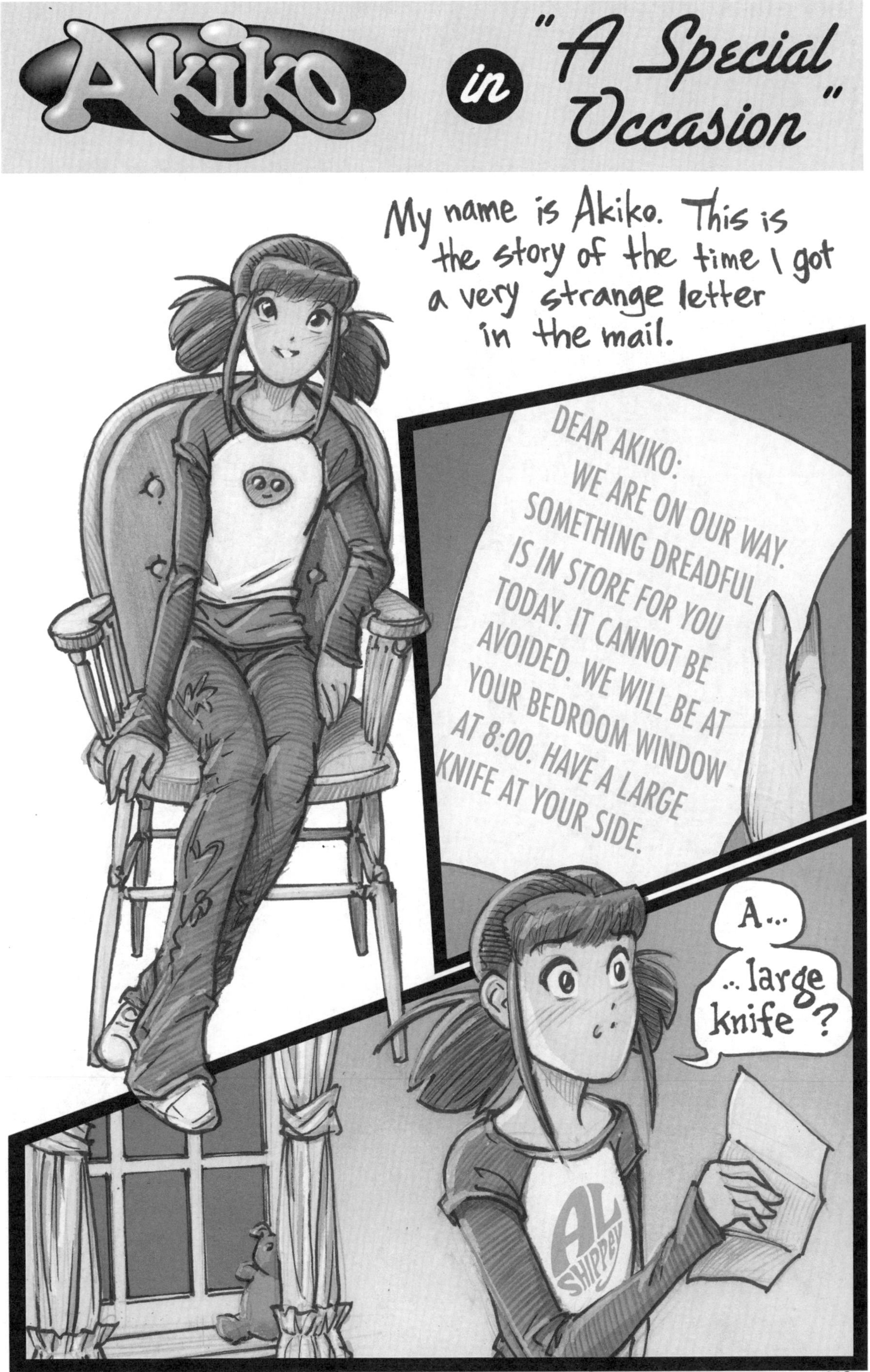
Akiko in "A Special Occasion"
My name is Akiko. This is the story of the time I got a very strange letter in the mail.
DEAR AKIKO:
WE ARE ON OUR WAY. SOMETHING DREADFUL IS IN STORE FOR YOU TODAY. IT CANNOT BE AVOIDED. WE WILL BE AT YOUR BEDROOM WINDOW AT 8:00. HAVE A LARGE KNIFE AT YOUR SIDE.
A... ...large knife?
AL SHIPPEY

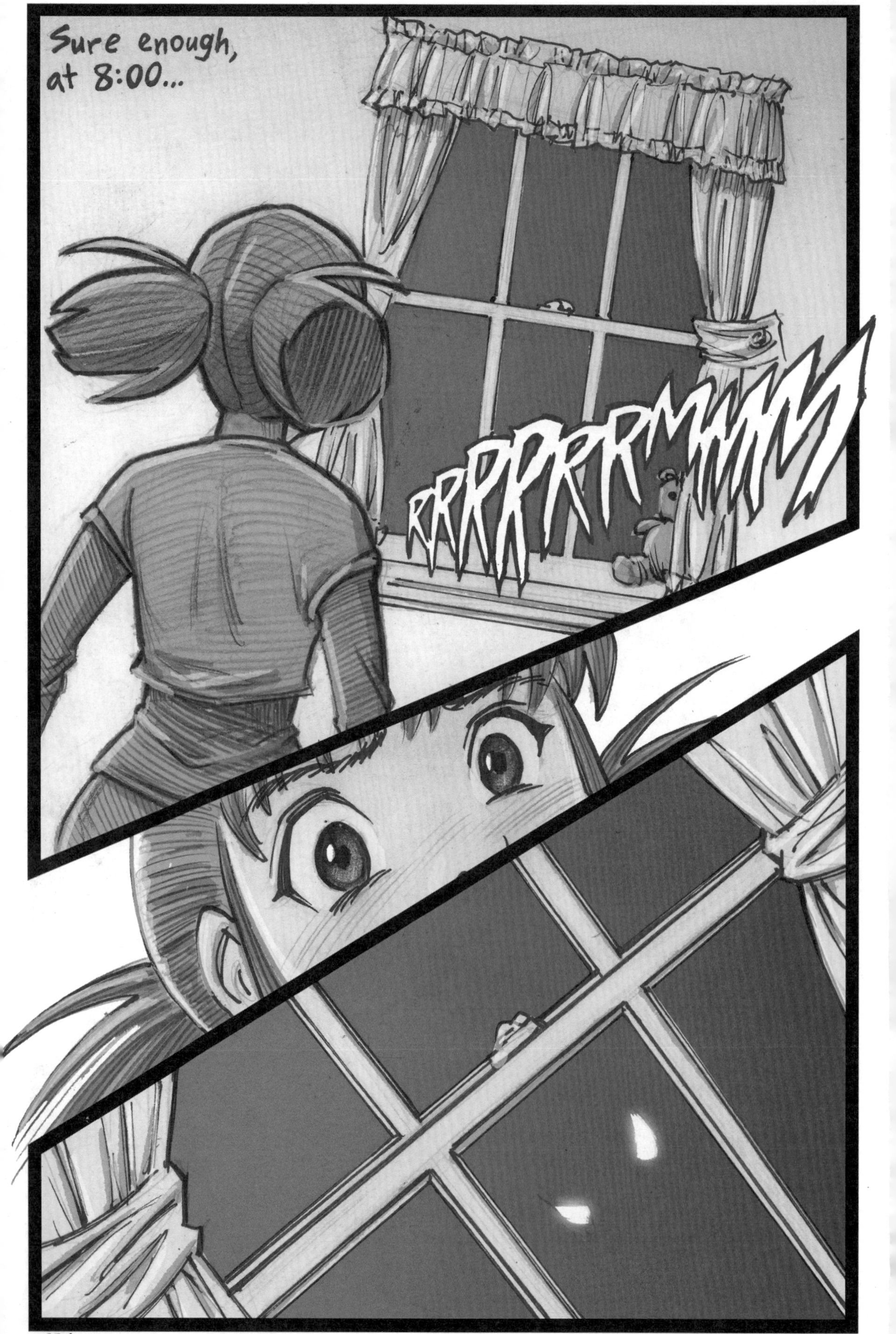
Sure enough, at 8:00...
RRRRRRRMMMM

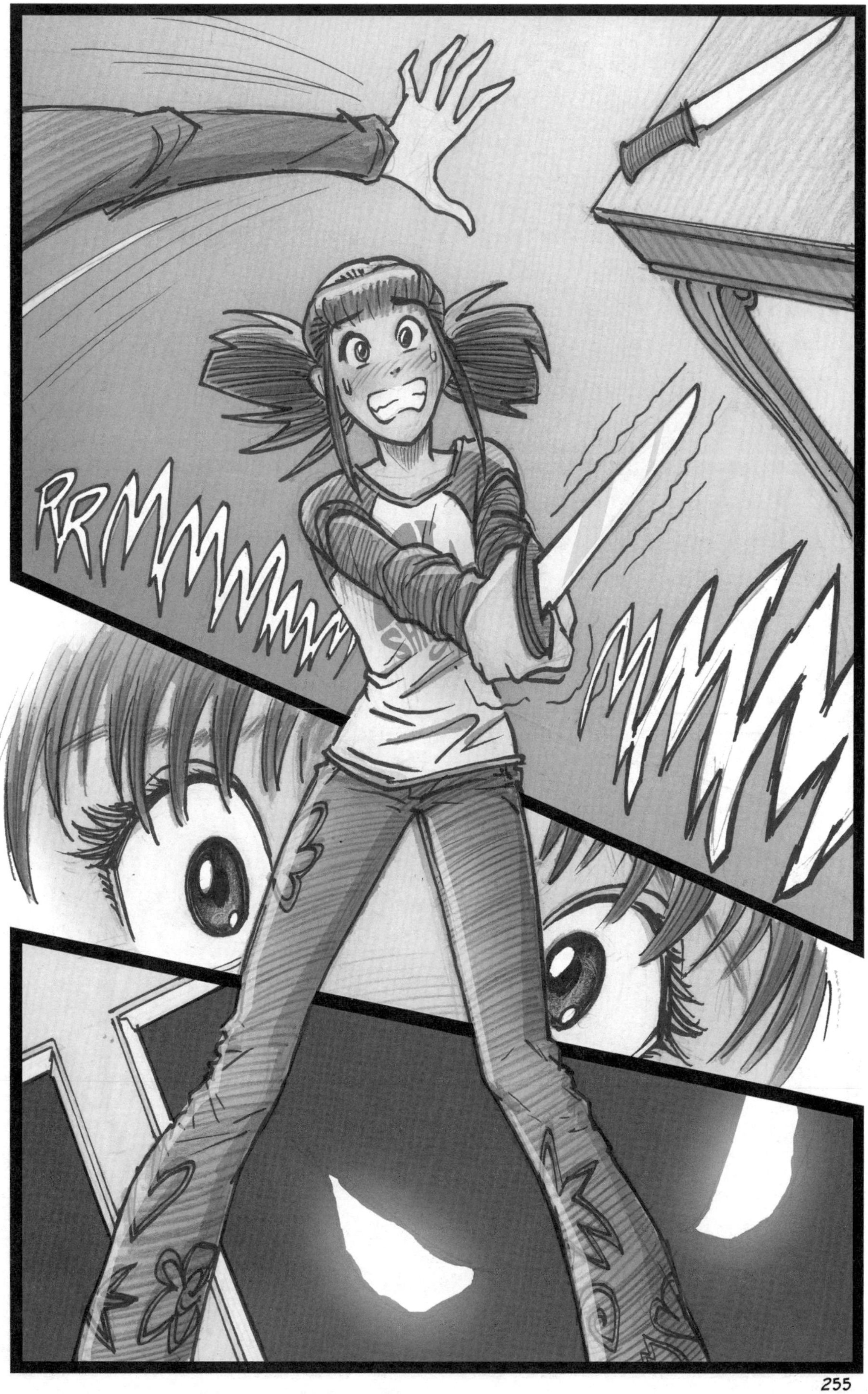
RRMMMMMMM
MMMM

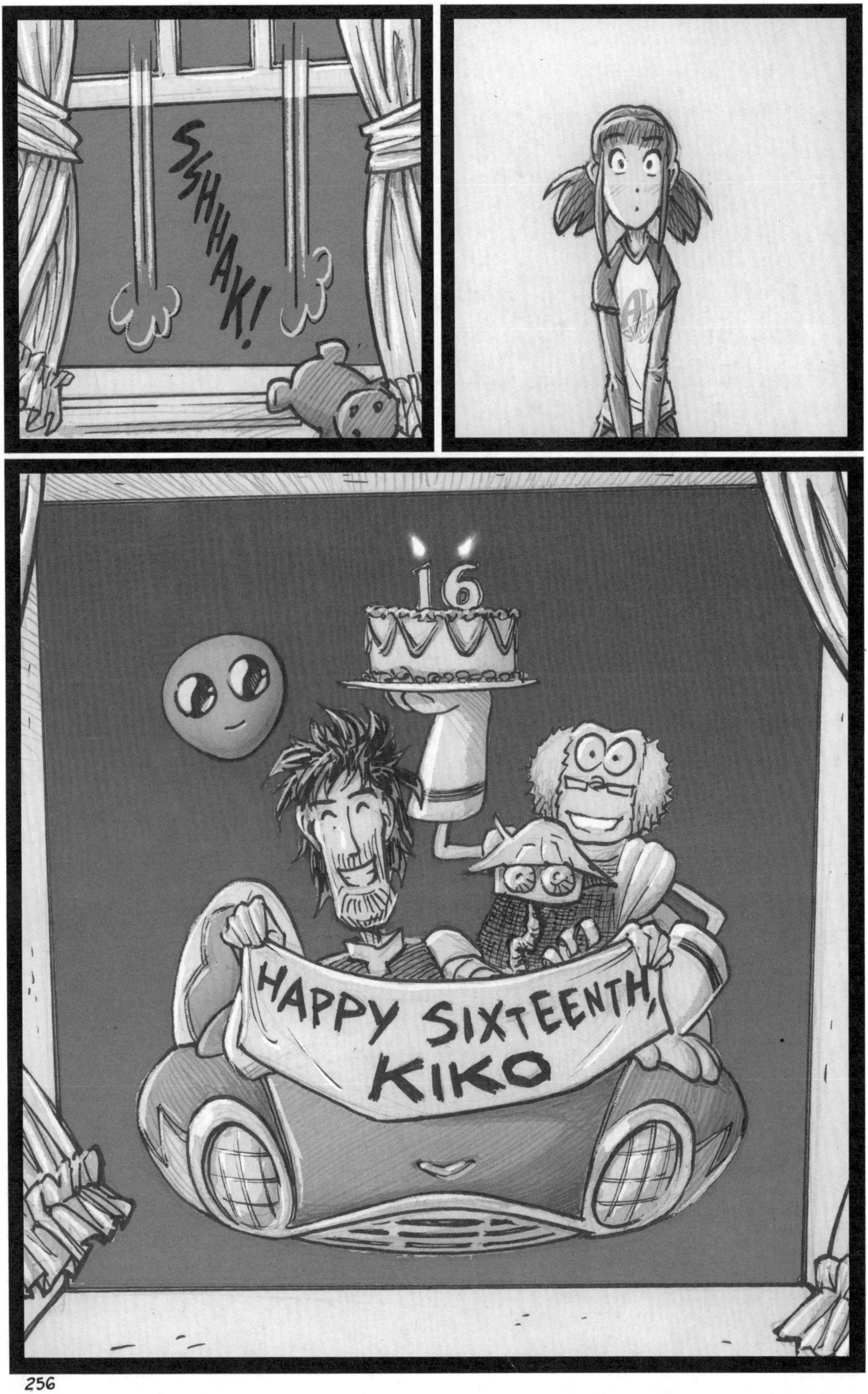
SSHHAK!
AL SHARPER
16
HAPPY SIXTEENTH, KIKO

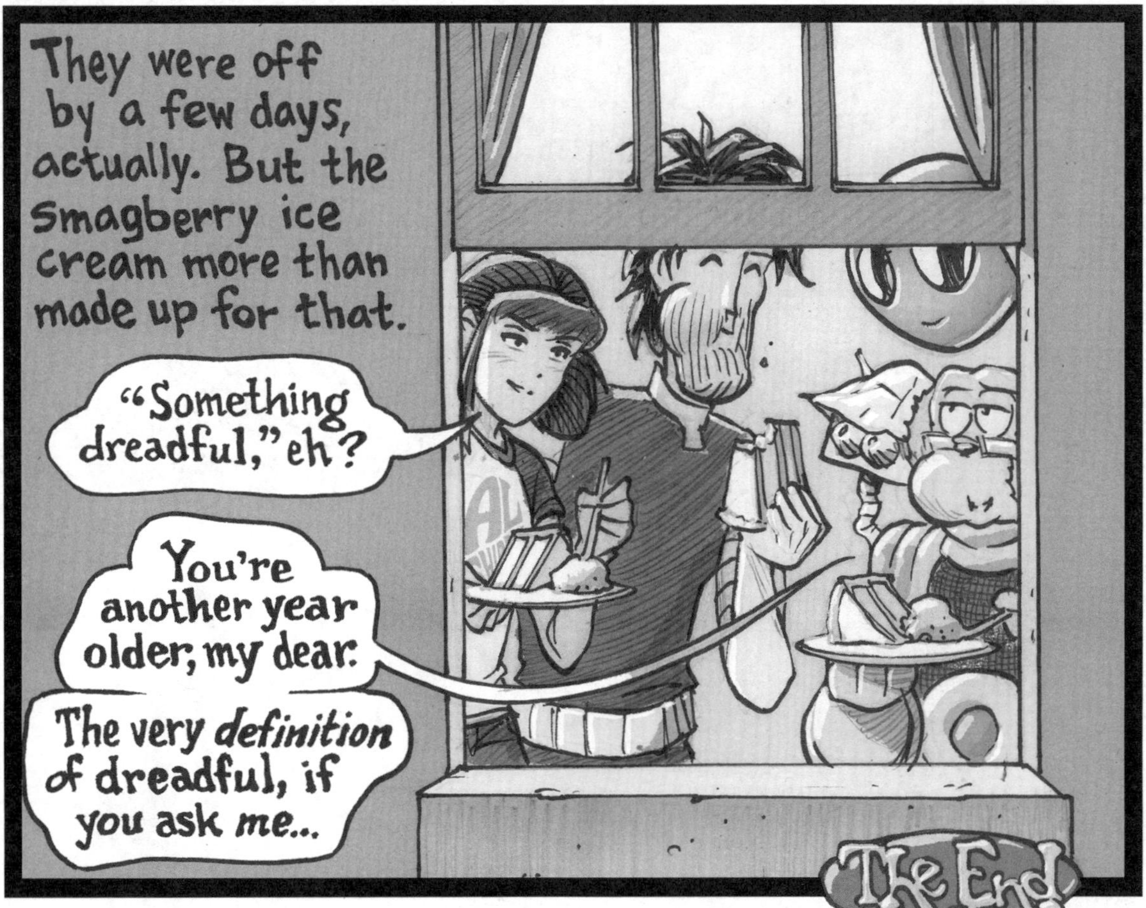
They were off by a few days, actually. But the Smagberry ice cream more than made up for that.
"Something dreadful," eh?
You're another year older, my dear.
The very *definition* of dreadful, if you ask *me*...
The End

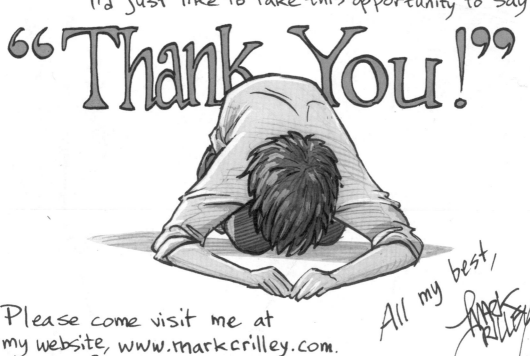

To anyone who ever bought one of my books:
I'd just like to take this opportunity to say,

"Thank You!"

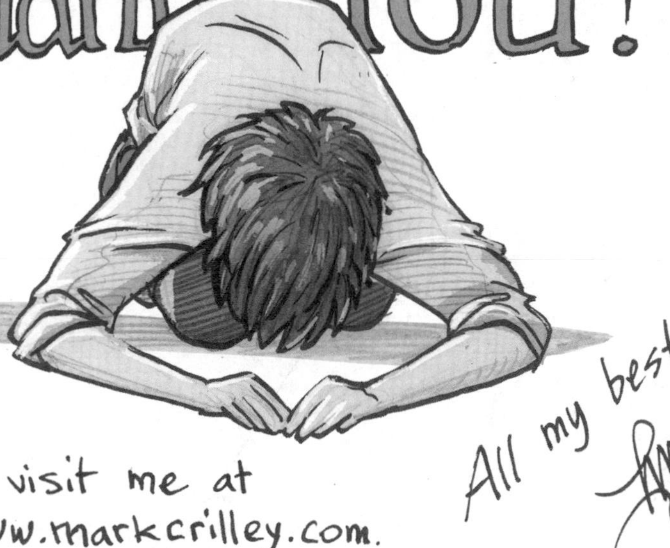

All my best,
Mark Crilley
2007

Please come visit me at my website, www.markcrilley.com. I'd love for you to see what I'm up to these days!

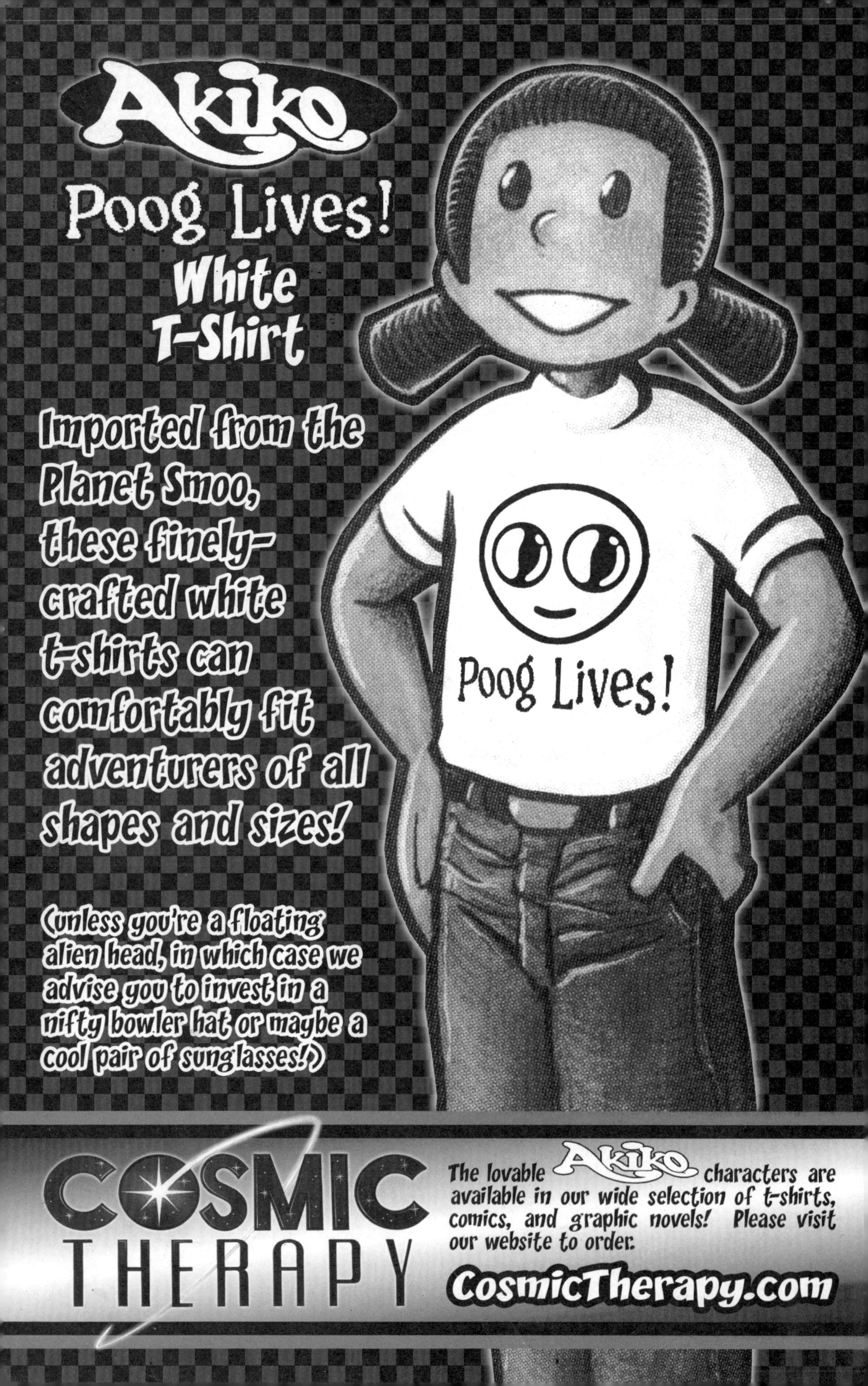
Akiko
Poog Lives!
White T-Shirt
Imported from the Planet Smoo, these finely-crafted white t-shirts can comfortably fit adventurers of all shapes and sizes!
(unless you're a floating alien head, in which case we advise you to invest in a nifty bowler hat or maybe a cool pair of sunglasses!)
Poog Lives!
COSMIC THERAPY
The lovable Akiko characters are available in our wide selection of t-shirts, comics, and graphic novels! Please visit our website to order.
CosmicTherapy.com